W9-AXS-901

Modern
Times

Cover design by Vito Fiorenza

MAINSTREAMS OF CIVILIZATION

VOLUME I: ANCIENT CIVILIZATIONS
PREHISTORY TO THE FALL OF ROME
Carlton J. H. Hayes and James H. Hanscom

VOLUME II: MEDIEVAL AND EARLY MODERN TIMES
THE AGE OF JUSTINIAN TO THE EIGHTEENTH CENTURY
Carlton J. H. Hayes and Frederick F. Clark

VOLUME III: MODERN TIMES
THE FRENCH REVOLUTION TO THE PRESENT
Carlton J. H. Hayes, Margareta Faissler, and Judith Walsh

THE FRENCH REVOLUTION TO THE PRESENT

Modern Times

CARLTON J. H. HAYES
MARGARETA FAISSLER
JUDITH WALSH

MACMILLAN PUBLISHING CO., INC.
NEW YORK
COLLIER MACMILLAN PUBLISHERS
LONDON

THE AUTHORS

Carlton J. H. Hayes

Late Seth Low Professor of History, Columbia University

Margareta Faissler

*Former Chairman, Department of History, Roland Park Country School,
Baltimore, Maryland*

Judith Walsh

*Assistant Professor, Department of History, Essex County College,
Newark, New Jersey*

Copyright © 1983 Macmillan Publishing Co., Inc.

All rights reserved. No part of this book may be reproduced
or transmitted in any form or by any means, electronic or mechanical,
including photocopying, or by any information storage or retrieval
system, without permission in writing from the Publisher.
Earlier edition copyright © 1969 Macmillan Publishing Co., Inc.

MACMILLAN PUBLISHING CO., INC.
866 THIRD AVENUE, NEW YORK, N.Y. 10022
COLLIER MACMILLAN CANADA, INC.

Printed in the United States of America
ISBN 0-02-185600-1

Contents

MAPS:

USING DOCUMENTS AS EVIDENCE:

Prologue

The fascination of the study of history is its concern with people—people who have actually lived. Some have been leaders whose decisions have influenced the futures of their own countries and of the world. Countless others have been the unremembered people whose hopes, fears, beliefs, and accomplishments have, taken together, constituted the most important force of the past. Indeed, history is the record of the whole human past. No one can become acquainted with even a small part of it without understanding all people, including himself, just a little better than before. But the huge number of past events, each unique in itself and never to be exactly repeated, presents the historian with an overwhelming difficulty. Unless he can bring his knowledge of past times, places, events, institutions, and persons into some sort of order, his learning is too disorganized to have value.

Yet although each historical event is indeed unique, even the beginning student soon discovers that when he considers closely related events together, he begins to discern long-term trends and developments. These trends and lines of development have a fascination of their own, for they outline the routes and stages by which the present grew out of the past and by which the people of the past unconsciously created the world of today.

Each student of history, young or old, experienced or just beginning, must select for himself those trends or themes of history that seem to him most worthy of his attention, most likely to provide him with deeper understanding. In every period of the past there are, however, some developments that almost everyone agrees are important. Any historian surveying the past two centuries would take into account, for example, the increasing importance of science and technology; the increase in number and size of cities, which changed profoundly the circumstances of daily living; the altering relations between governments and peoples; and the increasingly close relations among various parts of the world. A tabulation of impor-

EUROPE

ATLANTIC OCEAN

North Sea

Baltic Sea

Mediterranean Sea

Black Sea

Aegean Sea

Ionian Sea

Adriatic Sea

Tyrrhenian Sea

Lake Ladoga

Gulf of Finland

Gulf of Bothnia

Kattegat

Skagerrak

Irish Sea

English Channel

Strait of Dover

Bay of Biscay

Strait of Gibraltar

Sea of Azov

Bosporus

Dardanelles

Volga River

Don River

Dnieper River

Dniester R.

Niemen R.

Vistula River

Oder River

Elbe River

Danube River

Rhine R.

Seine R.

Loire R.

Thames

Rhone R.

Po R.

Tiber R.

Ebro R.

Douro R.

Tagus River

Guadalquivir R.

CAUCASUS MTS.

CARPATHIAN MTS.

TRANSYLVANIAN ALPS

BALKAN MTS.

RHODOPE MTS.

PINDUS MTS.

DINARIC ALPS

ALPS

APENNINES

VOSGES MTS.

PYRENEES

CANTABRIAN MTS.

CENTRAL SIERRAS

HUNGARIAN PLAIN

Asia Minor

AFRICA

tant developments in Europe and in the world since 1789 would include, among other trends, the following:

SCIENTIFIC AND TECHNOLOGICAL ADVANCE

The rapid advance of both science and technology has been perhaps the most striking characteristic of recent centuries. Science has opened to men many previously unknown secrets of nature and the universe, as in nuclear physics and radio astronomy. Inventions, often made possible by new discoveries in science, have followed each other in dizzying succession. For just one example, the rapid transportation of 1789 was by horse-drawn vehicles; today men seriously discuss visiting the planets in space ships. So steady has been the advance in science and technology that people everywhere take for granted man's ever-increasing power over nature and his ever-deepening understanding of himself and of the universe.

ECONOMIC AND SOCIAL CHANGE

Because of the invention of new machines and processes, workers on farms and in factories are producing more than ever before, and their products can be far more widely distributed. It is possible to feed and clothe a much larger world population, to concentrate many more people in cities, and to enable a larger proportion of the people in the industrial countries to enjoy some comfort and leisure. In the course of these changes the predominant social classes of earlier times, landed nobility and peasantry, have in the more advanced countries been replaced in importance by business and professional people and by factory and office workers.

POLITICAL REVOLUTION

Such profound social changes have inevitably been accompanied by revolutionary changes in government. Hereditary autocratic monarchy, the usual European government of 1789, has given way in some places to increasingly democratic governments. In other places it has been replaced by totalitarian dictatorships that exert far greater control over the lives of their citizens than the autocratic monarchs would have dreamed possible.

NATIONALISM

Since 1789 the great emotional power of modern nationalism—an intense patriotic devotion of citizens to their own countries and their fear and distrust of rival countries—has become more than ever a force in the world. In the modern world, nationalism has some of the same kind of importance that religious faith had in medieval Europe.

INTERDEPENDENCE OF NATIONS

The diverse areas of the world have been drawn together and made interdependent as never before in history. World trade not only has increased but also has become a more vital part of the economic life of all countries. Travel to distant regions has become a common experience. European imperialism, now rapidly declining, has made various parts of the earth known to each other, although sympathetic understanding between the peoples involved has all too often been sadly lacking. So closely interrelated are the various areas of the earth today that men of all nations have become to some extent citizens of the world, although they may neither comprehend nor welcome this status.

◌ ◌ ◌

So many, so important, and so profound have these changes been that it is possible to look upon the last two centuries as a time of continuous revolution. Different kinds of change have been especially marked in different periods, but each of these important trends has had significant development throughout these two centuries.

PART 1

Revolutionary Europe

1789 to the 1840's

There are no well-defined beginning-points in history, for important developments generally come about gradually from roots deep in the past. Only occasionally does some single event seem to the people of the time and to later historians an especially fitting symbol of a significant change in human affairs. One such milestone was the beginning of the French Revolution in 1789. During the course of a few years, the French people overthrew the centuries-old absolute government of their king; broke from their established church; dispensed with their titled nobility; lightened the burdens of their peasants; and attempted to establish a society of "liberty, equality, and fraternity." Although many of these steps almost at once proved too advanced for the times, they made impossible a return to the old France of the years before 1789. The ideas that had animated the French Revolution refused to die; and in the following decades they spread over Europe and the world, inspiring not only other revolutions but also more peaceful and gradual kinds of change. Liberals sympathetic to the revolutionary ideas argued and sometimes fought with conservatives who preferred the pre-1789 world. In the leading countries of western Europe, it was clear by the 1840's that the liberals had gained the upper hand.

# 1

The
Old
Regime

To understand revolutionary Europe of the years between 1789 and the 1840's, one must first know something of the society that the revolutions replaced. Latter-day admirers of the French Revolution, looking back upon it as one of the thrilling episodes of human history and the source of much good for the world, have called the pre-revolutionary period in France and Europe the "Old Regime." The words seem to emphasize the age-old, almost medieval characteristics of the late eighteenth century and to suggest that growth and needed change could not occur under the circumstances of the time. A close look at Europe on the eve of the French Revolution reveals a society with many traditional ways of living, working, and governing; but it also reveals new developments that in time would inevitably change profoundly the seemingly unchanging world of the Old Regime. Only by noting the conflict between the old and the new in the late eighteenth century can one understand the coming of the French Revolution and the other revolutionary movements that were encouraged by the French example.

ᕭ TRADITIONAL ASPECTS OF SOCIETY IN THE OLD REGIME

The Old Regime was a predominantly agricultural society with governments headed by kings, with established (officially recognized) churches, and with sharp divisions between the classes of society. The symbols of power were the king's scepter, the bishop's miter, and the noble's sword.

THE PEOPLE UNDER THE OLD REGIME

In the eighteenth century every person was born into a social class where he usually remained for his lifetime, bringing up his children to obey its customs. Classes were set apart from each other not only by birth but also by dress, by manners, and often by laws prescribing special duties or privileges for one class or another. Some especially able or fortunate individuals managed to rise above the station of their birth, but such persons were rare.

The Peasantry. At least nine tenths of the people of Europe were peasant farmers. From France to Russia the plowland was still divided into narrow, unfenced strips. These strips were parceled out to individual peasants, to the landlord, and to the church; but they were farmed in great fields. All the peasants of an estate or a village worked together to farm their own lands and those of lord and church, each peasant contributing whatever he owned—his ox, his wagon, his plow—as well as his own skill and labor. At harvest time the products of the lord's strips and of those of the church went into the barns owned by each. The peasant gathered the grain from his own scattered strips for his winter living. Although some peasant families lived comfortably, many had barely enough land to keep alive.

The knowledge and skill required for this kind of life were passed on from father to son and from mother to daughter. Few peasants could read. Few knew much of the world outside their own cluster of village cottages, the surrounding fields and woodlands, and the neighboring market town. The landlord or his representative directed the farming activities. Where the peasants were still serfs bound to the land—as they were almost everywhere in eastern and east-central Europe—the landlord had fairly complete jurisdiction over them. In France and western Germany, where serfdom had largely disappeared, the peasants still made special payments to the landlord, to the church, and to the government. Everywhere they also had the special duties, not required of other classes, to labor on the roads

An eighteenth-century satirical drawing showing the peasant in his typical dress and wooden shoes, bearing on his back the clergyman (left) and the noble in their elegant costumes. The artist is making bitter comment on the fact that the peasants must pay taxes and other dues to support the church, the nobles, and the government, while the clergy and nobles are free from many of the most burdensome taxes.

and to perform military service. It was, of course, unthinkable that peasants should have any voice in government. Their simple dress, their rough manners, and their imperfect use of the national language seemed to indicate to their social superiors that the peasants were by nature inferior. They were looked down upon by all other classes for their ignorance, their superstition, and their supposed laziness and stupidity.

In comparison with twentieth-century conditions, this life of incessant labor, little comfort, few privileges, and many dangers seems cramped and miserable indeed; but the eighteenth-century peasant was accustomed to his world and knew nothing different. His complaints, although they were many, were not concerned with the class system itself, but with such immediate needs as more firewood, more and better acres to farm, and the right to pasture more animals in the woodland. He did not expect to rise above the station of his ancestors.

Shopkeepers and Laborers of the Towns. In every country there were lower "middle-class" people, neither noble nor wealthy but not farmers. This class, which was larger in western than in eastern Europe, lived in rural villages or more often in the growing towns. Some were craftsmen working in small shops either alone or with a few employees to turn out cloth, pots and pans, hats, horseshoes, or similar products. Others were small merchants who sold food and other necessities, each specializing in a single kind of merchandise. The poorer townspeople were constantly preoccupied with the high cost of bread (the staple food of the poor), with any rise in prices, and with the possibility of unemployment. The more fortunate worried less about these basic matters and managed to enjoy some of the comforts available in that day.

Wealthy Bourgeoisie. At the summit of the non-noble group were well-to-do townsmen—the upper "middle-class" or "bourgeoisie." This class was especially numerous in western Europe; it included the most vigorous, aggressive, and competent people: great financiers, wealthy merchants, important lawyers and government officials. All could secure comforts unknown to less fortunate people. They could afford the best of educations, they could travel, they could mingle in the society of the great and become friends of leaders in all walks of life. Some were wealthy enough to live like great nobles, sometimes marrying into noble families and acquiring landed estates. Others secured government positions conferring noble status upon them.

An afternoon in the home of an eighteenth-century French noble. Bewigged gentlemen and elegantly dressed ladies converse and play games in the pleasant atmosphere of a costly, tasteful, lavishly furnished drawing room.

The legal status of the bourgeoisie, however, was the same as that of the poorest peasants and town laborers; they were simply commoners. Above them in the social scale was the privileged class of nobles.

The Nobility. The superior position of the aristocracy in eighteenth-century society is scarcely to be comprehended today. The aristocrats believed that their noble birth so far set them apart from other people that it was possible to speak with seriousness of "noble blood." They would have regarded with shocked horror the idea that all men are created equal.

Outwardly all nobles were marked off from commoners in a number of ways. Each of them inherited a title and the right to display the insignia of his family—its coat of arms—on his carriage and over the door of his house. The wealth of most nobles was in inherited land. Some were heirs to great landed estates handed down from father to eldest son. Others had more modest wealth, and some were no better off than the more prosperous peasants. The great nobles surrounded the kings and were everywhere regarded as the leaders of society, but even the poorest aristocrat claimed superiority to all non-nobles.

THE CHURCH AND THE OLD REGIME

A second medieval characteristic of the late eighteenth century was the close relationship between established church and government. England had its Church of England, Scotland its Presbyterian Church of Scotland. In Denmark-Norway, Sweden, and northern Germany, the established churches were Lutheran. In the Catholic countries—France, Spain, Portugal, and Austria, for example—the rulers usually appointed the bishops. In Russia the Orthodox Church was controlled by the government. The higher clergy of the established churches usually enjoyed positions of special importance. They controlled the extensive tax-free lands and other wealth of the church; dominated education; supervised poor relief; and regulated marriage, burial, and often inheritance. Bishops and abbots ranked even above great nobles. Because of the position they enjoyed, the clergy naturally approved of the government and society of the Old Regime.

But in spite of the great influence of organized religion in the eighteenth century, there were signs that the hold of churches over the people was weakening. The Catholic rulers, often personally indifferent to religion, forced the papacy to suppress the energetic religious order of the Jesuits, of whose power and influence they were jealous. In all western countries the writings of the time were full of attacks on the various state churches, their teachings and practices, and their power.

GOVERNMENT OF THE OLD REGIME

A third remnant of the late Middle Ages was hereditary monarchy. In the eighteenth century the vast majority of people everywhere accepted it as the natural and best form of government. Indeed, it was almost the only one the continent of Europe knew in 1789. (The exceptions were Poland, where the king was elected, and a few small republics like the Dutch Netherlands and Switzerland.) Even the radical writers of the time, who criticized the church, the nobility, and much else connected with the Old Regime, did not suggest getting rid of kings.

Late eighteenth-century kingdoms were absolutisms. The kings ruled through officials they themselves had appointed. They no longer summoned the "estates" (parliaments) with whom medieval kings had shared their author-ity. In comparison with medieval governments, the governments of the eighteenth century were strong and efficient, with able ministers, councils, and bodies of civil servants. The monarchs could make their authority felt in all parts of their kingdoms.

Thus the government, religion, and social structure of the Old Regime retained several important characteristics of the medieval order. Toward the end of the eighteenth century, however, the forces threatening the continu-ance of the Old Regime were multiplying and growing stronger.

◌ NEW FORCES CHALLENGING THE OLD REGIME

By the late eighteenth century the Old Regime was being undermined by economic change; by the intellectual movement called the Enlightenment; and—inspired by British and American examples—by enthusiasm for govern-mental systems that allowed more individual freedom.

ECONOMIC CHANGE

Although economic life had developed slowly in the centuries before 1789, that growth, with its important if limited consequences, affected farming, transportation, and manufacturing. By rotating crops—planting soil-building clover for a year, turnips for cattle fodder the next year, and grain for human consumption the year after that—farmers could abandon the wasteful practice of leaving each field idle every third year to recover its fertility. They could also keep a larger number of cattle alive over the winter. Canals and improved roads made easier the transportation of the increased agricultural product to the towns, which could thus grow larger and more numerous. By 1789 both Paris and London had more than half a million inhabitants, and in all Europe there were perhaps fifty towns of 50,000 or more. When more people lived closer together, the system of manufacturing called the "putting-out system" or the "domestic system" flourished. This was an early form of capitalism: a wealthy merchant would furnish flax, wool, or other raw material to his workers, who made the finished products in their own homes. In a few places revolutionary experiments in manufacturing were being tried: a few machines for spinning were being operated by water power, sometimes in factories where many workers could be brought together under one roof.

The most notable economic change of the eighteenth century was the expansion of world commerce. There were European colonies in the Americas, Africa, Asia, and the East Indies. (See map, page 14.) For more than two centuries the wealth of these overseas areas had been pouring into Spain, Portugal, the Dutch Netherlands, Great Britain, and France—gold and silver from Peru and Mexico, sugar from the West Indies, fabrics and tea from India, spices from the East Indies. This expanding trade, coupled with the more gradual improvements in farming and manufacturing, made many homes more comfortable, brought more varied diets to many tables, and generally raised the standards of living not only of the wealthy but also of many more modest families. Trade also created the great merchant fortunes whose owners were the leading members of the bourgeoisie and were sometimes able to intermarry with the aristocracy. These able men of great wealth were beginning to resent the exalted position that nobles enjoyed simply by accident of birth. Bourgeois unrest was further encouraged by the general intellectual atmosphere of the time, and especially by the Enlightenment.

THE ENLIGHTENMENT

The "Enlightenment" was a lively literary movement of the eighteenth century. It centered in France, where its leading members were a group of writers called *philosophes*. They were not philosophers in the usual meaning of the word, but rather persons interested in reforming government and society.

The *philosophes* and their contemporaries in other countries borrowed the fundamentals of their thinking from the ideas about the universe set forth by Sir Isaac Newton (1642-1727), the great English scientist and

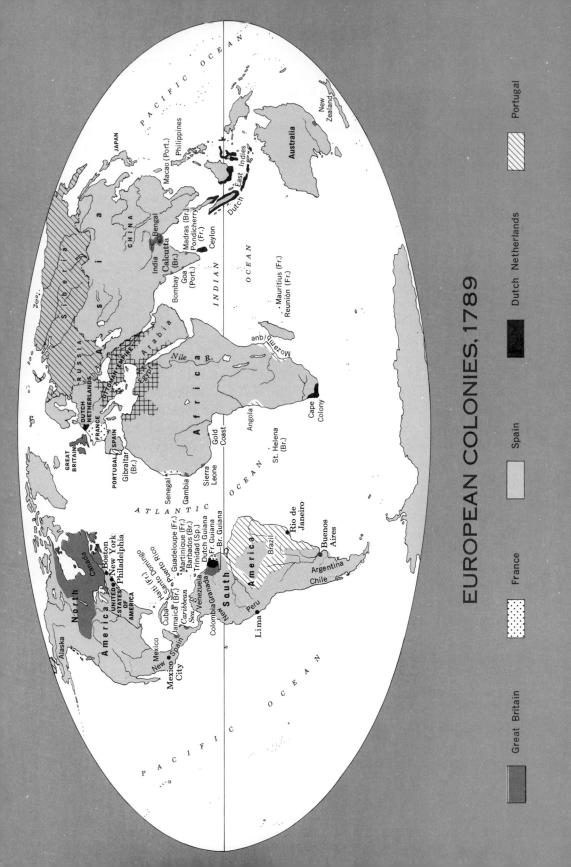

EUROPEAN COLONIES, 1789

Great Britain

France

Spain

Dutch Netherlands

Portugal

mathematician. It was Newton who formulated the laws of motion, including celestial mechanics relating to the motion of heavenly bodies. He showed that all motion on earth or in the solar system followed the same natural laws, that every body—a tiny particle or the sun itself—attracted every other body with a force proportional to the product of the masses of the two, and inversely proportional to the square of the distance between them. It was this "universal gravitation," Newton made clear, that held the planets in their orbits and prevented them from flying off at tangents into outer space.

Both the mathematical calculations that brought Newton to his conclusions, and his tremendously influential book, the *Principia*, were far beyond the understanding of the ordinary person or even of most of the *philosophes*. Watered-down versions were nevertheless widely read. As a result, the *philosophes* came to regard the universe as a great machine, created by God but left to operate according to fixed laws that men themselves can discover, as Newton had, by the use of their powers of observation and reason. The *philosophe* writer Voltaire claimed to have learned from Newton's stepniece that the great scientist had been inspired to make his studies of motion by observing an apple falling from a tree. With such a persuasive example of the power of seeing and reasoning before them, eighteenth-century intellectuals believed they could ultimately solve the most difficult problems of science and life simply by the fullest use of their own powers of mind.

From the search for the physical laws of nature it was but a step to the concept that man and society were also governed by natural law. It therefore seemed logical that men could use reason to formulate their own laws and organize their governments in such a way as to bring them into harmony with natural law. It became fashionable in intellectual circles to question all institutions—the government, the church, social customs—in order to correct what was not in harmony with reason or nature. This emphasis on the power of human reason gave the period the names "Age of Enlightenment" and "Age of Reason."

The French writers Voltaire and Rousseau were the most prominent *philosophes*. Voltaire (1694-1778) was a poet, historian, playwright, pamphleteer—the first man, in fact, to make a fortune from authorship. Although sickly, fearful, and overly eager not to be thought unduly different from other middle-class people, Voltaire was one of the great personalities of his age. His charm, his ironic wit, his "malicious good sense," and the extraordinary vigor with which he attacked outmoded social customs and defended those who had been wronged, gave him a foremost place where social, literary, and political leaders gathered. It was not surprising that he spent a time in the Bastille prison and in exile in England, where he became familiar with the work of Newton. For three years he was the guest of King Frederick the Great of Prussia. In his last years his home was close to the Swiss border, so that he could seek refuge in Switzerland if necessary. To the end of his days he argued in all his writings for freedom of thought and particularly for tolerance in matters of religion. He especially denounced what he considered the superstition and cruel intolerance of the Catholic Church of his day.

Jean Jacques Rousseau (1712-1778) was a maladjusted man, unconventional and irresponsible (he put his own children in an orphanage, for example). He was, nevertheless, a great writer. His criticisms of society were based on his belief that all men have a right to equality with all others, and that all have the right to be respected citizens of the country in which they live. He praised the common man and all the natural things of life so eloquently that even Queen Marie Antoinette, wife of Louis XVI of France, played at being a milkmaid in a "cottage" in the gardens of the palace of Versailles. His influence tended especially to cast doubt on the sharply divided system of classes of the Old Regime.

The achievement of writers like Voltaire and Rousseau was to put into words what many other people thought but were unable to express. The *philosophes* deprived the institutions of the Old Regime of some of the sanctity of tradition and readied many people for change, even for revolutionary change.

CONSTITUTIONAL DEVELOPMENTS IN GREAT BRITAIN AND AMERICA

When continental Europeans began to criticize the weaknesses of their own society, many of them turned for examples of freer peoples to Great Britain (England and Scotland, united in 1707) and to America. Revolutions had already taken place in England in 1688 and in America in 1775-1783.

Great Britain. In 1688 the English people had driven King James II from the throne and replaced him with William III and his wife Mary II as joint sovereigns. Parliament required the new sovereigns to accept a Bill of Rights, which considerably limited royal authority.

After 1688 the British government developed features that were unique in the Europe of that day. The king was still head of the state, but only Parliament, with its hereditary House of Lords and its elected House of Commons, had the power to levy taxes and pass laws. Although only a small percent of Englishmen had the privilege of voting, this partly-elected government was far more representative of the popular will than were the absolute monarchies of the continent. Moreover, the British enjoyed civil liberties unknown to the rest of Europe, including freedom from arbitrary arrest or long imprisonment without trial, the right to speak and write with some freedom, and the right of Nonconformists (Protestants not members of the established Church of England) to worship in public. Regulation of commerce was also less rigid in Great Britain than on the continent. Foreigners often argued that the freedom enjoyed by the British had been responsible for the size and wealth of their colonial empire and for the victories won by the British armed forces in the wars of the eighteenth century. The French *philosophes* particularly enjoyed pointing out the excellence of British government and society.

The United States. The political experiment that began in the United States in 1783, when the Revolution ended, was even more radical than what the British had tried. Even before the Revolution the thirteen British colonies had enjoyed a degree of self-government not known even in Great Britain. Each colony had its elected legislature, in some colonies elected by almost all the free men of the colony. The civil liberties enjoyed by the British at home were extended to the colonies. After the Revolution each colony became a state, electing its governor but keeping most of the other features of colonial government. At first the states were bound together in a loose confederation, but in 1788 they adopted the stronger Constitution that is still in effect. The framers of that document were much influenced by the ideas of the *philosophes,* with which they were all familiar.

The American Constitution was radical indeed in those days of the Old Regime. There were no official social classes and no titles of nobility. The law treated all citizens alike. There was no national established church. In the place of a king there was an elected President. The House of Representatives was elected directly by the people, the Senate by the state legislatures. Authority of government was divided among President, Congress, and the courts. Civil liberties were guaranteed.

The American experiment was too radical and too untried to have as much influence on European thinking as did the British example, although many French leaders were influenced by their acquaintance with Benjamin Franklin and Thomas Jefferson, who were the American ministers to France during and just after the American Revolution. It was the piling up, one

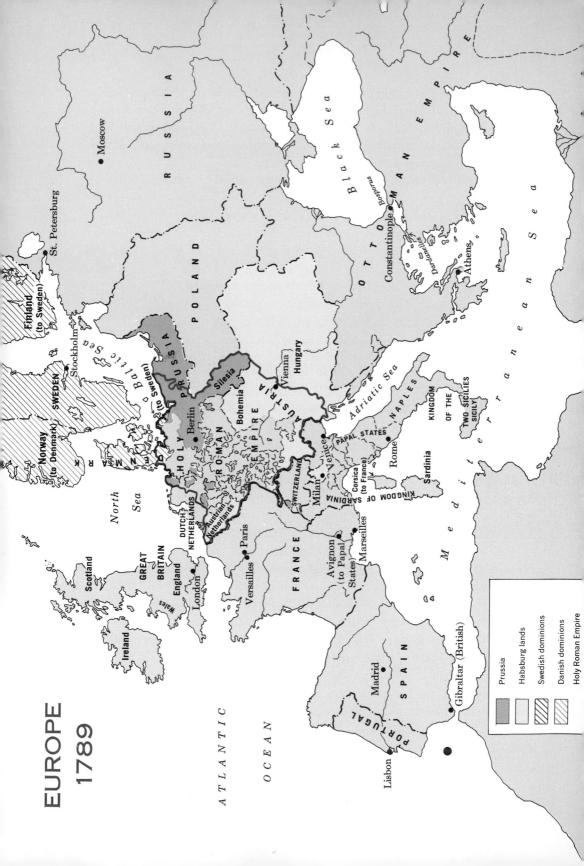

EUROPE
1789

RUSSIA

Moscow

St. Petersburg

Finland
(to Sweden)

Stockholm

SWEDEN

Norway
(to Denmark)

DENMARK

Baltic Sea

POLAND

PRUSSIA

(to Sweden)

Berlin

Silesia

Bohemia

HOLY
ROMAN
EMPIRE

AUSTRIA

Vienna

Hungary

Black
Sea

Bosporus

Constantinople

OTTOMAN EMPIRE

Dardanelles

Athens

North
Sea

Scotland

GREAT
BRITAIN

England

Wales

London

Ireland

ATLANTIC

OCEAN

DUTCH
NETHERLANDS

Austrian
Netherlands

Versailles

Paris

FRANCE

Avignon
(to Papal
States)

Marseilles

SWITZERLAND

Milan

Venice

PAPAL STATES

Rome

Corsica
(to France)

KINGDOM OF SARDINIA

Sardinia

Adriatic Sea

NAPLES

KINGDOM
OF THE
TWO SICILIES

SICILY

Mediterranean Sea

Madrid

SPAIN

PORTUGAL

Lisbon

Gibraltar (British)

Legend:

- Prussia
- Habsburg lands
- Swedish dominions
- Danish dominions
- Holy Roman Empire

atop the other, of the ideas imported from Britain and America, the arguments of the *philosophes*, and the restlessness of middle-class business and professional people that was weakening the Old Regime in Europe and preparing France for its own revolution.

☊   INTERNATIONAL RELATIONS

The Old Regime cannot be adequately understood without some knowledge of relations among the many European states. There were some twenty independent governments, not counting the smallest ones or the virtually independent members of the Holy Roman Empire. Of them, Spain, Portugal, and the Dutch Netherlands still possessed extensive overseas empires, but they no longer exerted an important influence in European affairs. Sweden, still the master of Finland and of a bit of northern Germany; Denmark, still ruling Norway; and the Ottoman Empire, whose lands extended far into southeastern Europe, all looked more powerful on the map than they actually were. The sprawling kingdom of Poland was so weak that it had already lost its borderlands to its three neighbors, Russia, Prussia, and Austria. The strongest countries of Europe (called "powers" or "great powers") were at the western and eastern edges of the continent—Great Britain and France in the west, and Austria, Prussia, and Russia in the east. Central Europe was a mass of small states almost or altogether independent.

THE WESTERN EUROPEAN POWERS: GREAT BRITAIN AND FRANCE

Great Britain and France were the only powers with significant influence both in Europe and overseas. Britain had no continental territory except for the fortress of Gibraltar at the southern tip of Spain, but it was a powerful factor in continental affairs. Its mighty navy, which patrolled the Mediterranean to assure the safety of British commerce with the Middle East, made Great Britain the greatest single Mediterranean power. British policy for the continent was the maintenance of the "balance of power"—that is, preventing any single great power of the continent or any likely alliance of powers from becoming strong enough to dominate all Europe. Any power dominating the whole continent would, of course, be able to invade Great Britain itself. The British were also always concerned lest the Netherlands coast opposite England fall under the control of a single powerful country. Britain had fought a number of wars to prevent that situation from arising.

Unlike Britain, France was primarily a land power, although it maintained a fairly powerful fleet. The great concern of its Bourbon kings was the east and northeast border of their country, for all along the other side of that frontier stretched the lands controlled by the Habsburg archdukes of Austria, who ruled the southern Netherlands (today's Belgium) and were emperors of the Holy Roman Empire. The wars of the past century had with one exception found France and Austria on opposite sides.

France and Britain were also rivals, having waged five wars between 1689 and 1783. In North America and India the struggle between them had been bitter. In the Seven Years War, which ended in 1763, the British had halted French expansion in India and had driven the French from Canada, where the French-Canadian settlers came under British rule. Although France later supported the American colonists in their successful Revolution, it did not recover its lost empire.

THE LANDS OF CENTRAL EUROPE

Central Europe was weak and divided in a way that today seems inconceivable. Neither Italy nor Germany was united into a single country. In Italy there were a dozen principalities, kingdoms, and republics. The peninsula had long been a bone of contention among Spain, Austria, and France. In 1789 Milan in the north was an Austrian possession, and the kingdoms of Naples and Sicily (or "the Two Sicilies") in the south were ruled by a Bourbon relative of the king of Spain. In the middle of the peninsula the pope ruled in full sovereignty over the States of the Church (the Papal States).

In Germany there were more than three hundred independent states, some microscopically small, each with its own absolute ruler—a bishop, a knight, the officials of a city, or a powerful king or archduke as in Prussia and Austria. Most of Germany was included in the Holy Roman Empire, whose emperor was elected for life by nine of the most important princes. The vote almost always fell to the Habsburg archduke of Austria, who was also king of Hungary and king of Bohemia. Although the prestige surrounding the emperor gave value to the office, any real power the emperor possessed came from his hereditary lands; his influence over the hundreds of little German states was insignificant. The failure of Germany to attain the kind of national union long since achieved in many other European countries was partly caused by rivalry between two especially powerful German states: Prussia, ruled by the Hohenzollern family, and Austria, ruled by the

Habsburgs. Neither would permit the other to dominate all Germany. In the past Austria had been much the stronger, but wars between the two in the eighteenth century had resulted in Austria's ceding the large and rich province of Silesia to Prussia, which made them more nearly equal in power. Nevertheless, Austria still enjoyed far more prestige than Prussia.

THE GIANT IN THE EAST: RUSSIA

The European country occupying most space on the map in 1789 was Russia, for its pioneers moving eastward had long since crossed Siberia and reached the Pacific. (See map, page 14.) But the Russians lacked outlets to the sea. They had, it is true, secured ports on the Baltic Sea, but these ports were too inconveniently far from the ocean. They had also recently acquired a coast on the Black Sea. The exit from the Black Sea into the Mediterranean through the straits of the Bosporus and Dardanelles was, however, controlled by the Ottoman Empire. It was natural that Russia should therefore seek some sort of control over the Ottoman Empire—a policy bound to be opposed by such Mediterranean powers as France and Britain.

∽ ∽ ∽

In 1789 the Old Regime seemed relatively stable; no evidence has been produced to indicate that all Europe was inevitably headed toward political revolution. There were, of course, dissatisfied people—wealthy bourgeoisie envying the nobles their special place in society, poor workingmen wanting more work and cheaper bread, peasants desiring more land and an end to their labors on the roads. The *philosophes* had condemned intolerance and injustice, some had demanded political equality, and all had urged that church and government examine their practices in the light of reason to eliminate anything merely superstitious or traditional. None of these dissatisfactions or suggestions for change was in itself, however, an adequate basis for real revolution—not even with the addition of a bad harvest in 1788 and a disastrously cold winter following it. The revolution of 1789 occurred in France, and it is to circumstances in France that one must turn for a fuller explanation.

A NOTE TO THE STUDENT:

The study of history may already delight you, or it may seem to you to be a jumble of dull and nearly unrelated facts. You can find the fullest enjoyment in it only if you understand that history is a story—a continuing story, in which each chapter develops from what has gone before. If you have been using the earlier books of the *Mainstreams of Civilization* series, you know that the story becomes clear when you have mastered the facts that go to make it up and are familiar with the principal themes of European and world history, which this volume will carry forward to the present time. If, on the other hand, you are beginning your study of history with this volume, you will have to pay even greater attention to mastering the facts, so that you can discover how facts are related to each other and how together they form the themes and plot of the historical story.

The questions and activities at the end of each chapter are designed to help you master and understand the important developments discussed in the chapter. They may be used in many ways, for example: Try using these aids to study in this way:

- Read the list of persons, places, and terms *before* you read the chapter. After reading the chapter, go over the list again, making brief notes in your notebook that identify each person or group of persons. Identify and locate each place, and define or identify each term. There may be other unfamiliar names or terms in the chapter, but those listed are most valuable to you. Terms that reappear throughout the book are defined in the Glossary, pages 525-527; use it frequently to fix these definitions in your mind.

- After you have read the chapter, answer the review questions under "To Master the Text." Writing the answers in your notebook (organizing your information under the headings in the chapter) will give you a convenient aid to review.

- Draw or trace the maps suggested under "To Master the Map," and fill in the places listed. Answer any questions asked about the maps.

- Broaden your understanding of the facts in this chapter by answering the questions under "To Interpret the Facts."

- Relate this chapter to what you have learned elsewhere by answering the questions under "To Put This Chapter into a Larger Setting." This last group also suggests activities that you may enjoy undertaking with other students.

Persons, Places, and Terms

Master this long list of persons, places, and terms with great care, since most will appear frequently in this book.

Sir Isaac Newton	Prussia	West Indies
Voltaire	Austria	Peru
Rousseau	Hungary	Mexico
Marie Antoinette	Bohemia	
Louis XVI	Switzerland	Old Regime
Bourbon family	Italy	peasantry
Habsburg family	States of the Church	serfdom
Hohenzollern family	Milan	bourgeoisie
	Naples	aristocracy
Great Britain	Sicily	established church
England	Poland	hereditary monarchy
Scotland	Russia	absolutism
Dutch Netherlands	Siberia	estates
Austrian Netherlands	Baltic Sea	putting-out system
France	Black Sea	standard of living
Portugal	Ottoman Empire	Enlightenment
Spain	Bosporus	*philosophes*
Gibraltar	Dardanelles	natural law
Sweden	Mediterranean Sea	Parliament
Norway	Middle East	House of Lords
Denmark	East Indies	House of Commons
Holy Roman Empire	India	civil liberties

To Master the Text

1. Under the Old Regime, what were the special privileges, opportunities, duties, and hardships of the peasantry? The poorer townspeople? The wealthy bourgeoisie? The nobility?
2. What methods of farming were used under the Old Regime? How was the making of goods carried on? How were goods sold?
3. What special privileges did established churches usually enjoy? To what extent could their clergy influence the governments? To what extent was the church likely to be influenced by the government?
4. In what ways were the rulers of the Old Regime more powerful than medieval kings?
5. How did changed economic conditions in the late eighteenth century affect the peasants? The workingmen? The wealthy merchants? For what classes and in what ways was the standard of living being improved?
6. What specific characteristics of the Old Regime did the *philosophes* attack? On what concepts did the *philosophes* base their attacks?

7. How had the power of the English king been limited in 1688? What civil liberties did the English people enjoy after 1688?

8. To what extent and in what ways did the British colonists in America exert more control over their colonial governments than Englishmen at home could exert over the English government? What control did Americans have over their government after the adoption of the Constitution? How did American society differ from European?

9. In what ways and for what reasons were France and Great Britain the greatest powers in western Europe in the late eighteenth century? What were the basic foreign policies of each?

10. What was the political condition in the eighteenth century of Italy? Of Germany? Within Germany, how important was the Holy Roman Empire? Austria? Prussia?

11. What lands were controlled by the Russians in the latter part of the eighteenth century? In what directions did the Russians wish to expand?

To Master the Map

1. From studying the sizes and locations of European colonies on the map on page 14, in what order of strength and importance would you put the world empires of the late eighteenth century? For what reasons?

2. On a blank map of Europe, locate and label all the European places in the list on page 23. Color or shade the areas controlled by the Habsburgs, by the Ottoman Empire, and by Russia, making particularly clear how Russia was cut off from water communication with the rest of Europe.

To Interpret the Facts

1. What seem to you to have been the aspects of the Old Regime most difficult to change and most likely to be long-lasting? Why does each of these aspects of eighteenth-century society seem to you to be fundamental to the life of the time?

2. What varied explanations can you find to suggest why thinkers like the French *philosophes* were more common in France and Great Britain than in the rest of Europe?

3. In what specific ways did changes in commerce and manufacturing threaten to alter western European life in the late eighteenth century?

To Put This Chapter into a Larger Setting

1. In what ways did absolute monarchy and the division of society into classes suit the argicultural life of the eighteenth century better than present-day America with its factories and cities?

2. What facts presented in this chapter help you better understand today's relations between Russia and the West?

2

The French Revolution: Reform of the Monarchy

1789-1792

The French Revolution began with the assembling in 1789 of the Estates-General, the long-forgotten three-house parliament that had not met for 175 years. From that beginning, events rushed on until French government and society had been altered in a revolutionary way. Europe and the wider world were also affected to such an extent that the results of the revolution are still apparent today.

Fundamentally the revolution stemmed from the conflict—present in some degree all over Europe—between forces supporting the Old Regime and those promoting change. Within France a series of events sharpened that discord and brought it to the exploding point. The first of those events was a prolonged quarrel between the king and the nobles.

◠ THE TAX CRISIS

The problem between king and nobles can be simply stated: the French government was bankrupt, the nobles refused to assume their full share of the tax burden, and Louis XVI was not the man to force the nobles to do what they were determined not to do.

BANKRUPTCY OF THE GOVERNMENT

The financial plight of the French government grew largely out of the cost of the numerous wars of the previous century—most recently the American Revolution (1775-1783), to which the French had contributed both financial aid and outright military assistance. By 1789 the government not only was unable to repay its debts, but could not even meet the interest payments on them without borrowing more money. Finally it found itself unable even to borrow the money it needed. France was a rich country, but its government was bankrupt.

The financial plight of the government reflected a deeper problem: the need for far-reaching constitutional reform. Earlier French kings had granted special privileges to newly acquired provinces, to the church, and to the nobles in order to win their support; these privileges no longer had any purpose. Governmental bureaus and ministries that had once been adequate no longer performed efficiently under the changed conditions of the eighteenth century. The greatest need was tax reform, for nobles and other privileged groups with landed wealth did not pay the more burdensome taxes. This tax exemption of the nobles began in the Middle Ages, when as armed knights they had constituted the only military force able to protect the kingdom. At that time the lesser people, who had neither the money for expensive armor nor the time to learn to use it, made their contribution by paying tax money into the treasury, while the nobles gave their whole lives and wealth to the service of the king. In the eighteenth century, however, the nobles made no such essential contribution to the nation, although their lands remained free of many taxes. Likewise the clergy paid no taxes except what they voted voluntarily.

THE ATTITUDE OF THE NOBLES

A movement to modernize the French government had been afoot since before 1774, when Louis XVI had ascended the throne. But to become law, such proposals required the assent of the highest law court of the land, the *parlément* of Paris, which was composed entirely of nobles. By refusing to register a new law, the *parlément* could prevent it from being enforced. The *parlément* had used its power to stave off any reforms that threatened to deprive the "privileged orders" (clergy and nobles) of their special advantages. When the king had tried to punish the *parlément*, the nobles as a class had refused to co-operate with the government in any way and appeared to be preparing for open revolt. They argued that new taxes could legally be levied only by the Estates-General, which had last met in 1614. The Estates-General was organized into houses representing the three "estates" or classes of the realm: the First Estate (clergy), the Second Estate (nobles), and the Third Estate (commoners). Since voting would be by house, the clergy and nobles could expect to have a two-to-one majority.

The attitude of the nobles, inconceivable in the twentieth century, to them seemed right and just; for their whole lives had been ordered by the belief that aristocrats had a native superiority to all commoners. (See page 11.) Moreover, nobles of the late eighteenth century were accustomed to holding all the highest offices in the realm, both religious and political, and to believing that only they could properly perform the duties involved. Earlier kings had employed commoners in important government posts, but in the eighteenth century that practice had largely been abandoned. The nobles would not voluntarily accept constitutional changes that did not preserve their claim to the places of highest honor in political and ecclesiastical affairs.

LOUIS XVI

A more able king might have forced the nobles to accept constitutional reforms, but Louis XVI was not that man. Although he was personally a good man, he was neither particularly intelligent nor strong of will. His chief interests were hunting, tinkering with machines, and copious eating and drinking. He did not even enjoy the parties and balls that occupied the time of his court. His marriage to the frivolous Marie Antoinette, sister of the Holy Roman Emperor and archduke of Austria, Joseph II, did not endear him to the French people, who had been taught to regard Austria as an enemy. Louis sincerely desired to please everyone, but he was too slow of wit and too weak-willed to select a wise policy and keep to it. He finally decided to summon the Estates-General only because he had no other choice.

∽   THE BOURGEOISIE AND THE MAKING OF THE NATIONAL ASSEMBLY

Although the decision to summon the Estates-General was taken under pressure from the nobles, it was the bourgeoisie who profited from it. The meeting of the Estates that began in May, 1789, eventually adopted the program favored by the bourgeoisie.

PREPARATIONS FOR THE ESTATES-GENERAL

Between the time the king called the Estates-General and the election of delegates, educated and reform-minded members of the Third Estate enjoyed an unaccustomed and exhilarating activity. For the first time in living memory they had a legitimate opportunity to engage in politics. They held planning meetings in Paris, wrote letters to friends in other areas, and composed model pamphlets to be imitated by anyone who desired to respond to the king's request for suggestions about the organization of the Estates-General. The most stirring pamphlet was by a member of the upper clergy, the Abbé Sieyès. Six staccato sentences from it served enthusiastic propagandists as a statement of their own fundamental beliefs: "What is the Third Estate? Everything. What has it been until now? Nothing. What does it ask? To be something."

The bourgeois leaders demanded the "doubling of the Third"; that is, giving the Third Estate as many members in the Estates-General as the other two estates combined. They intended to argue for having the Estates meet in a single house where each member would cast one vote. The commoners, if joined by a few allies from the other estates, would then have a majority. An assembly of aristocrats called by the king agreed to "doubling the Third," expecting that voting would be by house with the First and Second Estates outvoting the Third.

The elections themselves were an educational experience for all. The electoral system, planned according to estates, was complicated indeed; but a surprisingly large proportion of male Frenchmen were permitted to take some part in the choice of delegates. There were no private voting booths. The voters gathered in assemblies according to classes. The lower classes usually voted by voice. Each assembly was asked to prepare a list of the grievances the Estates-General should try to remedy. Not surprisingly, the best informed and most experienced speakers took the lead in arguing for candidates and for the content of the list of grievances. These accomplished orators often were lawyers. In consequence the delegates of the Third Estate, even when elected by rural areas, were lawyers or other important and educated bourgeois. No peasants were elected. Among the clergy the vast majority of delegates were parish priests, many of them bitterly hostile to the bishops and sympathetic to the ideas of the Third Estate. The nobles elected their more conservative members.

The election assemblies were excellent schools of politics, where ideas were exchanged and clarified and the programs of the various estates were

The opening session of the Estates-General, May 5, 1789, with the king presiding, the First and Second Estates at the sides, and the Third Estate at the rear. Left, the styles of dress of the clergy (top), the nobility (center), and the commoners.

threshed out. By the time the Estates-General met, millions of French people not previously concerned with political questions had acquired some understanding of the great public issues confronting their country.

THE OPENING OF THE ESTATES-GENERAL

On May 4, 1789, the Estates-General assembled in the shadow of the king's great palace of Versailles eleven miles from Paris. The members joined with the king and court in a procession through the streets and to the church, where Mass was said. The traditional etiquette of the old Estates-General was preserved, the members of the Third Estate garbed in black marching first, followed by the nobles in their gorgeous robes, then by the parish priests in black, and finally by the bishops and cardinals in their colorful attire. The next day the opening session took place. Following court etiquette, the king sat down and put on his hat, and the nobles did likewise. Wearing a hat in the king's presence was a privilege limited, by tradition, to the nobility; but in a quick symbolic gesture the members of the Third donned their hats, too. The startled king then took his hat off, and all followed his example.

This unexpected by-play was a fitting prologue to the ill-prepared early days of the session. The king and his advisers had not decided what program should be discussed or whether the Estates-General should vote by house or head. The Third Estate was determined that the three houses should meet together and vote by head. For the moment the delegates convened in three houses; but the Third, by refusing to organize itself for business, prevented anything from being accomplished until it could have its way. For a month this inactivity continued, while delegates and the already aroused people of France became more restive and more ready to act with vigor—or even with defiance.

THE CREATION OF THE NATIONAL ASSEMBLY

By the beginning of June the Third Estate was ready for action. The members had developed a spirit of fellowship, had found their natural leaders, and had learned what reforms the bourgeoisie could be counted on to support. Among the leaders was the Abbé Sieyès, a clergyman but elected by the Third Estate. Born a commoner, he had risen far in the church, but had been unable to become a bishop. This frustration had developed in him the bitterest feelings toward the nobles. He was neither an outstanding speaker nor writer nor a man of action, but rather a theorist, interested in constitutional law and forms of government. His famous pamphlet had given the deputies a sense of their mission. In the meetings of the Third Estate he continued to argue that the Third was the true representative of the nation with sovereign power to act for the nation. Under his prodding and that of other leaders, the program of the Third came to include demands for a written constitution providing for an elected legislature; equal treatment of all Frenchmen by the law; converting the tithe (payments in grain to the church) into money to be given to the parish priests and the poor; and ridding peasants of their medieval feudal obligations to landlords. Such a program could be made into law only if the Estates-General were reorganized into a single house with the Third and its friends in a majority.

Before June was over, the Third Estate had won its great victory. After trying in vain to persuade the other estates to sit in a single house, the Third, at Sieyès's suggestion, declared itself (and a few priests who had come over from the First Estate) to be the "National Assembly," the representatives of the French nation. This bold action aroused the members to a new pitch of excitement. On June 20 their meeting hall was closed in preparation for a session to be presided over by the king. Suspecting that the government was about to act against them, they moved their meeting to an indoor tennis court. There they took a solemn oath to "meet in any place that circumstances may require, until the constitution of the kingdom shall be laid and established on secure foundations." This "Oath of the Tennis Court" was the true beginning of the French Revolution; for there the king was defied for the first time, and a course of action that clearly intended to limit the royal power was announced.

Two days later most of the First Estate and a handful of nobles joined the National Assembly. The vacillating king first ordered its members to return to their houses; but when the Third refused, he gave in and reluctantly commanded the clergy and nobles to join the National Assembly.

☌ THE POPULAR REVOLUTION

The Third Estate had succeeded in creating the National Assembly. But the future of that body was far from secure: it was strongly opposed by the majority of the upper clergy and of the nobles, and by the king as well. Indeed the king, now the ally of the nobles, began to assemble troops with the almost certain intention of disbanding the National Assembly by force. He was prevented from acting only by the peasants and the people of Paris.

CAUSES OF POPULAR UNREST

In the winter of 1788-1789 there had been great unrest among the poorer people. A bad harvest in 1788 meant that bread, the basic food of the poor, would be scarce and dear. By July, 1789, grain prices were the highest since 1715. At the same time a general slowing down of business put thousands out of work in the towns. In despair, many townspeople wandered in the countryside searching for food. Mobs attacked peasants' grain supplies. People from the rural areas, on the other hand, flocked to the cities, especially to Paris, seeking work and bread and finding neither. To these desperate people the National Assembly was the only hope. A rumor that the aristocrats planned to overthrow the Assembly aroused them to a high pitch of excitement.

THE STORMING OF THE BASTILLE, JULY 14, 1789

In Paris rumors of an expected attack on the city gates by "the enemy" or "the brigands" (bandits) were circulated. In a panic of fear everyone sought some sort of weapon to protect himself. Owners of small businesses, sometimes even aided by the wealthy, encouraged their workmen to demonstrate in the streets. Mobs surrounded places where weapons were reported kept. Since it seemed essential that to defend itself the city must be strongly governed, a truly revolutionary proposal was put forward that the electors who had chosen the Paris delegates to the National Assembly should now set up a bourgeois government for the city. Such a government, the "Commune," was in existence by July 13. One of its first acts was to establish a "National Guard," a bourgeois armed force to protect the city from outside attack and to defend private property from the Paris mob.

On July 14 the event occurred that, more than any other, has symbolized the French Revolution—the storming of the Bastille. The Bastille was a medieval fortress orginally built to keep the city in order, but in later times used as a prison for persons whose families had managed to keep them out of the ordinary jails. A crowd surrounded the Bastille hoping to secure weapons and demanding the removal of some cannon the governor of the prison had placed facing outward. The crowd got out of hand; the governor of the prison handled the situation unwisely; fighting began; and soon the prison was in the hands of the mob. The governor of the prison was murdered, as was also the mayor of Paris. Their heads were mounted on pikes and paraded through the city.

The taking of the Bastille saved the National Assembly from destruction at the hands of the king. Louis did not want to use troops against the people, and in any case he did not have soldiers enough to subdue Paris and other cities where disorders were bound to take place. He realized that he must either accept the new situation in Paris or flee from France. Yielding to necessity, he went to Paris on July 17 to prove that he accepted the Commune and the National Guard. The Marquis de Lafayette, called the "hero of two worlds" for his participation in the American Revolution and his friendliness to the bourgeois cause in France, was made commander of the National Guard. It was Lafayette who gave revolutionary France a new flag by combining the white of the Bourbons with the red and blue of Paris to make the "tricolor," as the French call it.

THE NIGHT SESSION OF AUGUST 4

In late July, 1789, serious unrest called the "Great Fear" broke out in rural areas with the frequently heard cry, "The brigands are coming!" The frightened peasants believed, mistakenly, that bandits were being sent by the nobles. Driven by fear and anger, the peasants attacked many manor houses, often hoping to destroy the records of dues and services owed to the lord.

News of these disorders alarmed both noble and bourgeois landowning delegates in the National Assembly. On the evening of August 4, when few deputies were expected to be present, a group of members presented a drastic solution to the problem. Liberal nobles offered to surrender many of the rights they still exercised over the peasants, so that the remnants of medieval feudalism would largely disappear. The clergy agreed to abandon the tithe. Indeed as one excited deputy after another rose to renounce some privilege of the upper classes, the Old Regime vanished. The writing into law of these resolutions of the "Night Session of August 4" was accomplished within a few weeks. Two years later the remaining money payments to the lords were also abandoned, and the French peasant could become an altogether free landowner.

THE OCTOBER DAYS, 1789

August and September, 1789, were more peaceful than July had been, but new tensions were building. Within the National Assembly there were bitter disputes over the amount of authority to be left to the king by the new constitution. Among the nobles, those altogether opposed to what had been going on in France, including the king's two brothers, left the country (*émigrés*, they were called) to take up residence in the courts of nearby princes and to plot the restoration of the Old Regime in France. At Versailles the queen urged her husband either to join the *émigrés* abroad or to use troops to disband the Assembly. In Paris the people were growing more restless. The excellent harvest of 1789 was not yet threshed and ready for breadmaking. The departure of the nobles had created new problems by taking employment away from servants and the makers of luxury goods.

In this tense situation any sort of incident could start trouble. A rumor circulated in Paris that at a banquet in Versailles, newly arrived soldiers had treated the tricolor with disrespect. Immediately, on October 5, a mob of some six or seven thousand persons, the majority of them women, set forth in the rain from Paris with the cry, "To Versailles!" Although Lafayette and twenty thousand National Guardsmen soon followed them, the ill-clad, weary, disorderly women gained entrance to the elegant apartment of the queen.

The king finally yielded to the demands of the women and under their escort journeyed with his family to Paris. The National Assembly soon also moved to the capital. The "March of the Women" had all along been favored by members of the National Assembly as a means of putting pres-

The March of the Women to Versailles, October, 1789. The women (and men dressed as women) are armed with clubs, pitchforks, and similar weapons, and drag along a cannon.

sure on the king. He justified those hopes by approving certain decrees of the Assembly over which he had been hesitating and by ordering grain for Paris. Thereafter for many months the Assembly was able to go about its work without serious opposition.

☙ THE CONSTITUTION OF 1791

Before it disbanded two years later, in September, 1791, the National Assembly accomplished much. It wrote its famous statement of constitutional principles, "The Declaration of the Rights of Man and of the Citizen"; reorganized the church; put into law the economic decisions of the Night Session of August 4; and finally completed the Constitution of 1791.

THE DECLARATION OF THE RIGHTS OF MAN AND OF THE CITIZEN

The Declaration of the Rights of Man and of the Citizen, adopted before work on the constitution was seriously begun, was a stirring statement of the principles upon which the National Assembly proposed to erect the new government. The Declaration reflected the ideas of the *philosophes*. It declared that the authority of a government is derived from the people; that all citizens should be equal before the law; that all should have the right to influence the making of the law; and that the purpose of government should be the preservation of the natural rights of men to "liberty, property, security, and resistance to oppression." Freedom of thought and religion should be guaranteed to all.

The Declaration was circulated in cheap printed form all over France and in translation to the rest of the world. It still ranks as one of the great documents of modern times. Its principles, however, were only partially put into practice in the National Assembly's reorganization of the church, the economy, and the government.

THE CIVIL CONSTITUTION OF THE CLERGY

In endeavoring to solve the financial problems of France, the National Assembly attempted to alter the character of the Catholic Church in France and to make it virtually an arm of the government. Since many people had taken advantage of the general confusion to pay no taxes at all, the French government was worse off financially after the election of the National Assembly than it had been before. The Assembly, many of whose members were influenced by the *philosophes*, tended to be highly critical of the church. It decided to seize the church lands and to use them to help pay the government's debts. Having deprived the church of its income, the Assembly agreed to pay the clergy and to support such traditional church activities as education and the care of the poor. Hereafter priests and bishops, like members of the Assembly, were to be elected by the whole body of voters, whether Catholic or not.

The pope immediately denounced this new order of things, which was quite out of keeping with fundamental doctrines of the Catholic faith. In reply, the Assembly adopted the "Civil Constitution of the Clergy," putting into more emphatic form the new ecclesiastical legislation. All clergy were required to take an oath to support the provisions of the Civil Constitution. Many of the clergy took the oath; they came to be known as "juring" clergy, from the Latin word for taking an oath. "Nonjurors" could not legally perform their duties inside the country, although many continued to do so.

The Civil Constitution of the Clergy had momentous results, for it divided the country religiously into two hostile groups. It was also a turning point for Louis XVI. His religious scruples, added to his naturally aristocratic attitudes, now made him a real enemy of the revolution as he had not previously been. In June, 1791, he attempted to flee from Paris to join the *émigrés* across the border. He and the queen, disguised as a valet and a governess, traveled in a coach, accompanied by his sister, his two children and their governess, and three loyal servants. A Swedish nobleman devoted to the queen acted as coachman. Almost at his destination, the king was recognized and stopped. The royal family was escorted back to Paris by a committee sent from the National Assembly.

ECONOMIC LAWS

When the economic decisions of the Assembly were written into law, they proved helpful to the well-to-do bourgeoisie and peasants, but disappointing to poorer peasants and workingmen. In keeping with the theories of the *philosophes*, the Assembly frowned upon any device limiting the freedom of economic life. Workingmen were forbidden to coerce their employers by organizing unions of any sort or by going on strike. Well-to-do landowners were now declared free to put hedges around their own lands, with the result that their poorer neighbors lost pasture lands. (Previously their animals could run on all the fields of the village after harvest time.) The sale of the confiscated church lands pleased well-to-do peasants and bourgeois landowners, but not the poor and landless persons who had no money to invest. Thus the revolution was beginning to disappoint the lowest classes in towns and in rural areas.

THE CONSTITUTION IN ACTION

The Constitution itself, as it was finally written in September, 1791, failed to put into practice all the idealism of the Declaration of the Rights of Man and of the Citizen. The old absolute government of the king was replaced by a "limited" or "constitutional" monarchy. An elected one-house legislature was henceforth to make the laws, levy taxes, and spend the public moneys. The king, acting through his ministers, was to execute the laws. An independent system of courts would treat all citizens equally without regard

1788	AUGUST: Louis XVI summons the Estates-General
1789	MAY: Meeting of the Estates-General in Versailles JUNE 17: The Third Estate declares itself the National Assembly JUNE 20: Oath of the Tennis Court JUNE 22: Many clergy and some nobles join the National Assembly JUNE 27: Louis XVI orders seating in one house JULY 13: Paris Revolutionary Commune sets up the National Guard JULY 14: Storming of the Bastille JULY 17: Louis XVI, in Paris, accepts the revolution LATE JULY: The Great Fear AUGUST 4-5: Night Session of August 4 AUGUST 26: Publication of the Declaration of the Rights of Man OCTOBER 5-6: March of the Women to Versailles OCTOBER 6: Return of Louis XVI to Paris
1790	JULY 12: Adoption of the Civil Constitution of the Clergy
1791	JUNE 21-25: Flight and arrest of the king and queen SEPTEMBER 14: Louis XVI accepts the Constitution of 1791 SEPTEMBER 30: National Assembly disbands

to rank. But all citizens were not alike in political influence, for some were to be "active" and some were "passive" citizens. The active citizens, those who paid a certain amount of taxes, could participate in the election of the legislature; the others, although they had equal protection of the laws, could not vote.

The Legislative Assembly provided for in the Constitution convened in October, 1791. Since the members of the retiring National Assembly had excluded themselves from it, the Legislative was an inexperienced body. It represented a much divided people because some Frenchmen still opposed all the recent changes, some wanted to halt the Revolution where it was, and others were eager to press on toward a more extreme remaking of French society and perhaps the establishment of a republic. Popular debate on the burning questions of the time was encouraged by political clubs, the most famous of them the Jacobin Club of Paris with its more than 1000 branches over the country. Divisions among the French people were reflected in the many factions into which the Legislative Assembly was divided. In its sessions, factions with similar views tended to sit together: the conservatives at the right side of the hall, the moderates in the center, and the radicals at the left. (We still use "Right" and "Left" to designate conservatives and radicals.) Leadership in the Legislative was furnished by a radical faction, mostly members of Jacobin Clubs, called the Girondins (from the *département* of the Gironde whence many of them came). But the Girondins could accomplish little, for they were in a minority in the Legislative and had no important party of followers in the country at large.

⌒ ⌒ ⌒

By the time the Legislative was in operation it was clear that the Old Regime had been destroyed forever; legal class distinctions, royal absolutism, and the privileged position of the Catholic Church were gone. All this had been accomplished with little bloodshed or disorder. But lack of unity in the Legislative and among the French people boded ill for the future.

Persons, Places, and Terms

Abbé Sieyès	constitution	Declaration of the
Marquis de Lafayette	constitutional law	Rights of Man and
	sovereign power	of the Citizen
Paris	legislature	Civil Constitution of
Versailles	tithe	the Clergy
	National Assembly	nonjuring clergy
Parlément of Paris	the Bastille	limited monarchy
Estates-General	Jacobin Clubs	constitutional
First Estate	Girondins	monarchy
Second Estate	National Guard	active citizens
Third Estate	Night Session of	passive citizens
revolution	August 4	Legislative Assembly
ministry	*émigrés*	the left
privileged orders	Constitution of 1791	the right

To Master the Text

1. Why were French nobles exempt from many taxes? What was the Estates-General? What estates were represented in it? When had it last met? What did the French government expect it to accomplish?

2. What plan of organization for the Estates-General was the goal of the bourgeois members? Why? Trace the developments that led to the achievement of this goal.

3. What conditions in France in the summer of 1789 caused unrest among the poorer peasants? Among the working people of Paris? What circumstances led to the storming of the Bastille? What events resulted from or were influenced by the storming of the Bastille?

4. What was the "Great Fear"? What effect did it have on the National Assembly?

5. What conditions caused the March of the Women to Versailles? Why did this event please some members of the National Assembly? What were its results?

6. Why did the National Assembly write the Declaration of the Rights of Man and of the Citizen? What specific rights were listed as belonging to all French citizens? What were the practical effects of the Declaration?

7. What were the provisions of the Civil Constitution of the Clergy? How was it related to the bankruptcy of the government? How did it divide the French people against each other? How did the king show his attitude toward it?

8. How did the Constitution of 1791 limit the king? What rights did it grant all citizens? What special powers to active citizens?

9. What further changes did some Frenchmen want to make? Why?

To Interpret the Facts

1. To what extent was the Abbé Sieyès's description of the Third Estate as "nothing" accurate at the beginning of 1789? By 1792, had the Third Estate become "something," as Sieyès declared it wanted to be? Had it become "everything"? Or had it reached neither goal?

2. In what ways did the Constitution of 1791 put into practice the ideals stated in the Declaration of the Rights of Man and of the Citizen? In what ways did it fail to put those ideals into practice? From what you know of conditions in France about 1790, do you think the ordinary French people were ready for more privileges and duties than were granted them by the Constitution of 1791?

To Put This Chapter into a Larger Setting

1. Putting together what you know about the English Revolution of 1688, the American Revolution of 1775-1783, and the events of 1789-1791 in France, what seem to be the characteristics common to revolutions?

2. Read and compare the American Declaration of Independence and the French Declaration of the Rights of Man and of the Citizen. Explain the similarities and differences in the two documents by comparing conditions in colonial America in the 1770's with those in France in the 1780's.

3

The French Revolution: The First French Republic

Between 1789-1802 the French Revolution passed through three stages. In the first, 1789-1792, France was at peace abroad and, except for local rioting, also at home. A constitutional monarchy was created, favoring the bourgeoisie. In the second stage, 1792-1794, there was war abroad and civil war at home. A strongly centralized radical republic was created favoring the workingmen and peasants. In the third stage, 1794-1802, there was peace at home but war abroad. The republic, now controlled by the wealthier bourgeoisie, lacked popularity and strength. Eventually a popular general, Napoleon Bonaparte, seized power and made plans to keep it for his lifetime.

The second, most radical and violent period of the revolution began in August, 1792, with the fall of the constitutional monarchy.

THE FALL OF THE CONSTITUTIONAL MONARCHY, 1792

Until the early months of 1792, the French Revolution had taken its course without interference from abroad. Thereafter unrest at home was coupled with foreign war. With these combined pressures the newborn constitutional monarchy could not cope.

EUROPE AND THE FRENCH REVOLUTION, 1789-1791

A combination of circumstances had at first prevented other European countries from involving themselves with the French Revolution. Of course, the absolute rulers heading most governments opposed the changes in France. In many countries, however, there were revolutionary movements sympathetic to the French, establishing revolutionary clubs and agitating for change. On the other hand, less adventurous citizens, and later some of the early enthusiasts for revolution, agreed with the British statesman Edmund Burke, whose *Reflections on the French Revolution* appeared in 1790. Burke pointed out that so sharp a break with the past as had occurred in France wastefully destroyed the results of centuries of invaluable human thought and experience. These differences of public opinion discouraged the rulers from intervening in French affairs.

More important was the involvement of Austria and Russia in events in eastern Europe. Since 1787 both countries had been at war with the Ottoman Empire—the latest of a series of wars that had given each of them extensive once-Turkish territories. In 1792 they made peace with the Turks, but only in order to turn their attention to another of their neighbors, the kingdom of Poland.

Poland was one of the largest countries of Europe and one of the weakest. The king, often a foreigner, was elected for life by the diet (parliament) of Polish nobles, to whom he had to make promises that inevitably weakened his authority. In the diet any single member could veto any measure, sometimes with civil war as a consequence. Such weaknesses of government explain the First Polish Partition of 1772, when Austria, Prussia, and Russia took large slices of Polish territory. (See map, page 42.)

To strengthen their country and prevent further partition, the Poles elected their famous "Four Year Diet" in 1788. Patterning themselves on the French National Assembly and hoping to win the support of the bourgeoisie, the nobles gave up many of their special privileges and arranged to reform the diet and strengthen the power of the king. In 1791 they put a new constitution into effect.

But these reforms only encouraged Russia and Prussia to take more Polish territory before it was too late. The Second Partition occurred in January, 1793 (see map, page 43), leaving a diminished Poland too weak to maintain its independence for long. While these events were taking place in eastern Europe, the Russian, Prussian, and Austrian monarchs could pay only divided attention to France.

THE PARTITIONS
OF POLAND

THE OUTBREAK OF WAR, APRIL, 1792

Although France had so obviously profited from peace abroad while the constitutional monarchy was being established, Frenchmen who held the most opposed views began to see advantages in a foreign war. The king dreamed that the victorious armies of the absolute monarchs would invade France and restore him to his full power. Moderates like Lafayette pictured the French nation as responding to wartime demands and rallying loyally to the support of the constitutional monarchy. In the Legislative Assembly the Girondins, convinced that the king was a traitor to his country, believed that only war could fully reveal his treachery and pave the way for further reform. In April, 1792, France declared war on Austria. Soon thereafter Prussia allied with Austria against France.

THE END OF ROYAL GOVERNMENT, AUGUST 10, 1792

The war began with defeats for the French armies. Tensions mounted rapidly among the people, especially in Paris. It was a time of hardship, with renewed food shortages and a rapid rise in prices. People from the *départements* (the eighty-three sections of France that the National Assembly had substituted for the old provinces) were pouring into Paris. Some came to celebrate the anniversary of the taking of the Bastille; others were

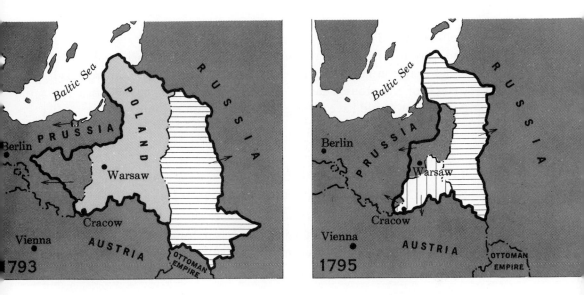

soldiers on the way to the front (including a group from Marseilles singing their war song against tyranny, "the Marseillaise," today the French national anthem). The more radical Jacobins, busy with secret plans for rising up against the government and establishing a republic, made many converts among these new arrivals. Rumors, not altogether unfounded, accused the king of being in communication with the Austrians and furnished a basis for the plea that the monarchy must give way to a republic.

On August 10, 1792, the Parisians awoke to find themselves under the authority of a new revolutionary commune that had been established during the night by the Jacobin leaders. A crowd of workingmen and others then stormed into the royal palace and took the king and his family prisoners. Since the Constitution of 1791 could not function without a king, a new constitutional convention had to be elected to establish a republican government. This "Convention," as it was called, was to govern France and write a new constitution. The constitutional monarchy was dead.

Between August 10 and the first meeting of the Convention in September, 1792, France scarcely had a government at all. Something of the disorder, fear, and hysteria of that time was revealed in the "September Massacres." Some of the soldiers in Paris declared that they could not go to the battlefield leaving behind them "traitors" in the prisons—that is, nobles and nonjuring clergy. Mobs of people began going from prison to prison, holding "trials" on the spot and sending to execution all whom these self-established "courts" judged to be enemies of the state. Over a thousand perished in this way, including ordinary criminals and many nobles and clergy in no way guilty of treason. This terrible event revealed the strength of the aroused people of Paris and made it obvious that the next government would have to take their wishes into account.

⌒ THE RADICAL REPUBLIC, SEPTEMBER, 1792, TO JULY, 1794

The National Convention met on September 20, 1792, and promptly declared France a republic. Although its members had ideas far more radical than those of the National Assembly of 1789, even they could not foresee the extreme lengths to which circumstances would soon drive them.

THE FIRST MONTHS OF THE CONVENTION

The first months of the Convention's history were encouraging. On the very day the Convention first met, French armies achieved a slight victory. Thereafter they not only kept the enemy from French soil, but managed to conquer considerable areas around the borders of France. French soldiers were often welcomed by revolutionary groups in the regions they occupied. But it was not so much the skill of the French armies as the preoccupation of Austria and Prussia with Poland (above, page 41) and their habitual rivalry in Germany (see page 20) that accounted for these French victories.

In spite of these successes abroad, divisions within the Convention soon began to be troublesome. The Girondins (see page 38), most of them representing the *départements*, had been the radical members of the Legislative Assembly; but in the Convention they were the conservative members, arguing for a decentralized government with a good deal of independence for the *départements*. The Girondins feared the Paris mob, and they would not consent to the creation of a strong war government lest the Parisians control it. A more radical group of Jacobins, called "the Mountain" because its seats were high in the meeting hall, became increasingly impatient with the hesitant policies of the Girondins. The Montagnards (Mountain men) were as good bourgeois as were the Girondins;

The execution of Louis XVI, January 21, 1793. The guillotine is set up in the Place de la Revolution (now the Place de la Concorde) in Paris. The executioner is displaying the king's severed head to the soldiers and the crowd of spectators.

but they were more willing to use the support of the Parisians, which was to be gained by laws remedying the problems of city dwellers. With the Parisians behind them, these Jacobins hoped to establish a strongly centralized national government. The most important leader of the Mountain was Maximilien Robespierre, an earnest young lawyer whose solemn and fanatical speeches had the ring of religious conviction. He was a follower of Rousseau, convinced of the goodness of man and of the excellence of any government based on the "general will." This neat and carefully dressed young man led the opposition to the Girondins.

The rivalry between Girondin and Mountain was clearly evident by January, 1793, when the Montagnards decided to try the long-imprisoned Louis XVI for treason. In spite of Girondin disapproval, after one hundred continuous hours of voting a narrow majority declared "Citizen Louis Capet" guilty of treason and sentenced him to death. He died bravely on the guillotine, a well-meaning and not unpatriotic man never meant to be king of a troubled country.

The execution of the king horrified many not only in France but also abroad, where rulers were shocked and frightened. The British prime minister, William Pitt, the Younger (son of the great William Pitt, Earl of Chatham) was engaged in a series of reforms and desired to remain at peace. But he had been seriously alarmed when the French armies, following the traditional French policy of extending the boundaries outward, occupied the Austrian Netherlands (Belgium) in November, 1792. It had long been British policy to prevent this area's falling under the control of a strong hostile power. (See page 19.) The British were further alarmed when, late in 1792, the Convention adopted "propaganda decrees" offering to assist "all peoples who might wish to recover their liberty"—proposing, in other words, to carry French revolutionary ideas into other countries. To the British the execution of Louis XVI was the last straw. War broke out between France and Britain in February, 1793. Pitt began organizing and subsidizing those countries that were already enemies of France—Austria, Prussia, the Dutch Netherlands, Spain, and Sardinia—who with Britain comprised the "First Coalition."

For a time the coalition was victorious, recovering all the areas previously conquered by France and again exposing the French borders to invasion. To meet this danger the Convention was compelled to make further revolutionary changes within France.

THE CRISIS OF 1793, SPRING AND SUMMER

The months from February to June, 1793, were desperate ones in France. Whatever steps the Convention took to increase the military strength of the country or to alleviate economic distress led only to further division among the French people. An emergency draft law was passed. Armed rebellion immediately flared up in the western part of the country, where royalist demands for the restoration of a king were strong and where there were many nonjuring priests.

In Paris the greatest difficulty was the scarcity and high price of food and other items, especially of fats, soap, and coffee, which had all but disappeared from the markets. Workingmen were demanding bread and work. Although the members of the Convention accepted the economic theory of the *philosophes* that government should leave business alone, Robespierre finally persuaded his followers that something must be done for the Paris *sans-culottes* (the working people, so called because they wore long trousers instead of the upper-class knee breeches or *culottes*). Simply to avoid an uprising in the city, he brought about the adoption of a price-control law for grain.

But Robespierre's law did not have the desired effect. The people of Paris had been too long dissatisfied with the leadership in the Convention, where Girondins still held important posts. On May 31 and again on June 2 mobs surrounded the Convention's place of meeting. In fright, the Convention arrested thirty of its own members, including the Girondin leaders, ordering them to remain in their homes until they could be tried. Some of them managed to escape to the *départements*, where they stirred up so many new insurrections that there was soon civil war in half of France. Within the Convention the departure of the Girondins left Robespierre and his radical Jacobin followers in control.

To meet the desperate threat posed by foreign and civil war, the Jacobins developed a new concept of patriotism and of the responsibilities of the citizen—a concept that has been important in the world ever since. Until this time the French people had looked upon the revolution primarily as a means toward a better life for the individual Frenchman, especially for the bourgeoisie. Now they learned that freedom and equality must be paid for by the performance of duties from which no citizen could be exempt. If revolutionary France were to repel its enemies, it must have a strongly centralized government and citizens prepared to serve their country.

The Jacobins therefore established a vigorous administration which affected every Frenchman. They organized a "Committee of Public Safety" within the Convention and gave it dictatorial powers. They sent "representatives on mission" to all parts of France and to accompany the army, with orders to encourage citizens and soldiers and to check disloyalty and revolt. To please the *sans-culottes*, they rationed food, fixed maximum prices to be charged for other necessities, and regulated wages. To please the poorer folk of the countryside they made it easier for peasants to purchase land and even gave outright to the poor peasants some of the land confiscated from suspected or known enemies of the state. To symbolize that equality of all men in which Robespierre, the devoted follower of Rousseau, so deeply believed, they abolished titles of nobility and required that all persons, even the imprisoned queen, should be addressed as "citizen" or "citizeness." They found time for even less immediately urgent reforms, such as improving education, granting rights to women, introducing the metric system of weights and measures, and freeing slaves in the French colonies.

For this effective government with its interest in the welfare of the less fortunate classes, the French people had to sacrifice much personal freedom.

A general draft law required all citizens to put themselves and their posses-sions at the service of the state. Young men had to join the armed forces, talented scientists had to work for the government, others had to man the factories, and all had to pay income taxes. France thus became the first example in modern history of a whole nation in arms—of a nation acting under the tremendous emotional impetus of modern nationalism. National-ism had been developing in western Europe for centuries, gradually strengthening in the people of each country the sense of belonging to their nation and deepening in them their devotion to that nation. National feel-ing had played its part in many wars since late medieval times. But never before had so much been demanded of so large a portion of the citizens of a country as was now required of loyal Frenchmen. It was a great upwell-ing of the French people that made tolerable the harsh Jacobin regime and fired the soldiers of the republic with the pride and confidence necessary to suppress civil war and to repel foreign invasion.

The sacrifices demanded of the French people soon proved justified, at least by their military results. In late 1793 there were 650,000 men in the armed forces. Since the officers of the king's army, almost all nobles, had emigrated in large numbers, a whole new corps of officers came into being. These men were chosen for ability alone, and they remained in command only so long as they won victories. They worked out revolutionary new concepts of warfare. But it took time to put these improvements into effect. Until the results began to be felt, the Convention employed as a means of protecting itself against its enemies within France a ruthless and brutal weapon, the "Terror."

THE TERROR, SEPTEMBER, 1793, TO JULY, 1794

The Terror, first adopted as a policy in the late summer of 1793, was intended to hunt out and destroy the internal enemies of the government; to force people to co-operate with the demanding policies of the Jacobins; and to stamp out the costly rebellions in the *départements* so that all France could unite against the foreign enemy. The method of the Terror was to search out persons in any way suspected of treason or enmity to the state and to bring them to trial before one of the ruthless "revolutionary tribunals" set up all over France. Those tried were all too frequently con-victed, and thousands were beheaded by the guillotine. Among the victims was the long-imprisoned Marie Antoinette, the "Widow Capet," as she was then called, who was taken to the place of execution in an open cart like any other convicted French citizen.

The immediate purpose of the Terror was achieved. Civil war was ended; and after 1793 the enemies of France won no significant successes while the French again conquered Belgium and the Rhineland (the German land west of the Rhine). But the fear that the Terror inspired made the Jacobins detested all over France. Other Jacobin policies were also widely opposed, especially those concerned with religion. Many of the Jacobin leaders were fanatically anti-Christian. One of the early acts of the Convention had been the adoption of a revolutionary calendar designating the convening date of the Convention as the beginning of the "Year I of the French Republic." The new calendar abolished not only saints' days but Sundays as well, substituting a day of rest in every ten. Antireligious parades were held, a "Festival of Liberty" took place in Notre Dame Cathedral in Paris, and in November, 1793, all Paris churches were closed. Robespierre opposed this discrediting of supernatural religion, vainly trying to substitute for it a religion of the Supreme Being with its own ceremonials.

The Terror could not go on forever. In the end it destroyed itself. Bitter differences of opinion among the members of the Convention led to the use of the guillotine by the dominant majority to rid itself of its most dangerous opponents within the Convention. This process continued until it seemed to many persons that Robespierre himself must go if there was ever to be an end to the Terror. He was finally brought to trial, condemned, and executed on July 28, 1794, or 9 Thermidor, as the date was called in the revolutionary calendar. His death ushered in a period called the "Thermidorian Reaction," which was characterized by the end of the Terror and the abandonment of the most extreme policies of the Convention, including its religious policies.

Thus the French Revolution had followed full cycle the traditional course of most revolutions. It had begun gradually with the removal of conditions generally believed to be undesirable. Some people had wanted to stop there; others were determined to make still further changes. As the revolution moved toward the left, there remained behind more and more enemies bitterly opposed to its increasingly radical policies. By 1794 it was this group of enemies who succeeded in preventing further change and began to take France back in the direction of—but not as far as—the Old Regime.

⌒ THE CONSERVATIVE REPUBLIC, JULY, 1794, TO DECEMBER, 1802

In the months immediately after the death of Robespierre, both the internal situation and the position of France in Europe improved. The laws on which the Terror had been based were repealed, prisoners were released, the Jacobin Clubs were closed, and the churches were reopened. The Convention wrote a new constitution for a government called the "Directory"—a fairly conservative republic. At the same time Pitt's coalition (see page 46) collapsed, leaving France at war with only Britain and Austria. The Third Partition of Poland in 1795, by which Austria, Prussia, and Russia divided among themselves all that remained of Poland (see map, page 43), helped France by occupying the attention of the participating powers.

FRENCH MILITARY TRIUMPHS, 1796-1802

After 1795 the French had still to fight Austria and Britain. Unable to defeat Britain at sea, they decided to attack Austria and in 1796 prepared to launch a great drive through southern Germany to the Austrian capital, Vienna. To keep part of the Austrian forces occupied elsewhere, a young

General Napoleon Bonaparte as he looked in 1803, when he was first consul.

general named Napoleon Bonaparte was sent to northern Italy. Acting with the speed and brilliance always characteristic of him, Bonaparte made the Italian phase of the war the important one. He forced Austria to make a peace most advantageous to France.

The Directors, more afraid of Bonaparte's growing popularity in France than grateful for his achievements, encouraged him to undertake another project outside the country. In 1798 he went to Egypt, where he hoped to injure British commerce and perhaps later move toward India. He was successful on land, but his navy was destroyed by the British Admiral Lord Nelson in the Battle of the Nile, leaving Bonaparte bottled up in Egypt. A Second Coalition was quickly organized by Britain, Austria, and Russia. Bonaparte escaped from Egypt and commanded another brilliant campaign against the Austrians in Italy. The coalition soon collapsed, and in 1802 peace was made between France and all of her enemies.

For the first time since 1792, Europe was free of war. France was left with full possession of Belgium and the German territory west of the Rhine, both of which it had annexed, and with a ring of satellites (supposedly independent states, but in reality controlled by France), called "sister republics," in Italy, Switzerland, and the Dutch Netherlands.

THE SEARCH FOR A STABLE GOVERNMENT

These triumphs of the battlefield were not, unfortunately, matched by equal success with the problems of government. The constitution of 1795 continued the republic. To avoid any resemblance to a monarchy, the five-man executive, the Directory, was purposely made weak. In other ways the constitution was an effort to stabilize the most useful changes in the French government made since 1789. There were property qualifications for voters and age qualifications for members of the two-house legislature and for the directors. Various safeguards were included to protect private property and to avoid the intimidation of the government by the people.

On paper the constitution seemed wise and effective. In practice, however, the government under the Directory was dishonest and incompetent. It remained in power only by interfering illegally with elections. Finally in December, 1799, a group of impatient leaders (including the Abbé Sieyès of earlier fame) determined to bring about a *coup d'état* (a brief, bloodless revolution) to replace the Directory by some popular general whom they could control. The only available general was Bonaparte. The *coup d'état* succeeded; a three-man executive called the "Consulate" was established, and

THE FRENCH REVOLUTION, 1791-1803

	IN FRANCE	THE WARS	OUTSIDE FRANCE
1791	Limited monarchy begins		
1792	AUG. 10: Louis XVI suspended: end of the limited monarchy SEPT. 2-6: September Massacres SEPT. 20: The Convention meets NOV.: First Propaganda Decree	APRIL: France declares war on Austria NOV.: French armies in Belgium	
1793	JAN.: Louis XVI executed MARCH: Beginning of civil war MAY-JUNE: Girondins expelled from the Convention SEPT.: Beginning of the Terror	FEB.: France declares war on Great Britain MARCH: French lose previously conquered border areas	JAN.: Second Partition of Poland MARCH: Pitt organizes the First Coalition
1794	JULY: Robespierre executed; end of the Terror	JUNE: French armies again victorious in Belgium	
1795	OCT.: Convention closes NOV.: Government by the Directory begins	SPRING: Collapse of the First Coalition	NOV.: Third Partition of Poland
1796-1797		Bonaparte's first campaign in Italy	
1798		SUMMER: Bonaparte in Egypt	DEC.: The Second Coalition organized
1799	DEC.: Bonaparte's **coup d'état**; the Consulate established		
1801	JULY: Concordat with the papacy	SPRING: Collapse of the Second Coalition	
1802	AUG.: Napoleon becomes consul for life	MARCH: Peace with all enemies	
1803		MAY: War renewed between France and Britain	

Bonaparte became the head of the state with the title "first consul." But the conspirators who hoped to control the first consul had chosen the wrong man; for Bonaparte would not tolerate dictation, or even interference, from others. Although he was originally to have a ten-year term, in 1802 a plebiscite (a formal vote of the French people) granted him the office for life. Thus the government of France was again in the hands of a single powerful head of state, who was king in all but name.

୭ ୭ ୭

Although France had taken something of a step backward toward the Old Regime in permitting Bonaparte to become the lifelong head of state, much remained of the changes made since 1789. French people had become accustomed to equality before the law, to elected legislatures, to a state without an official church, and to the absence from the country of a large part of the hereditary aristocracy. Yet the people were still divided between those who preferred the Old Regime (or at least many of its characteristics) and those who considered the recent revolutionary changes better for France. How the future would answer the great social and political questions that had agitated France and much of the western world in the late eighteenth century would depend to a great degree upon General Bonaparte.

Persons, Places, and Terms

Napoleon Bonaparte	Nile River	propaganda decrees
Edmund Burke	Rhine River	coalition
Catherine II		*sans-culottes*
Maximilien	radical	nationalism
Robespierre	diet	the Terror
William Pitt, the	*département*	civil war
Younger	the "Marseillaise"	satellite
	the Convention	sister republic
Avignon	September Massacres	the Directory
Sardinia	republic	*coup d'état*
Vienna	the Mountain	the Consulate
Egypt	Montagnards	plebiscite

To Master the Text

1. What kept foreign rulers from interfering in France before 1792?
2. What particular weaknesses of the Polish government enabled Russia, Austria, and Prussia to seize some of its territory in 1772? What steps

did the Poles take to overcome their weakness? How successful were
they? Why? How did events in Poland influence the French war?

3. Which groups or individuals inside and outside France desired war
between France and Austria in April, 1792? Why, in each case?

4. By what train of events did the outbreak of war lead to suspending
Louis XVI from his throne? Why did the September Massacres take
place? Why did France have to establish a new government after the
suspension of the king? What was that new government?

5. What areas were conquered by the French armies in the first months of
the Convention government? How do you explain those victories?

6. What were the differences between the Mountain and the Girondins in
the Convention? How did this rivalry affect the fate of Louis XVI?

7. What caused France and Great Britain to go to war with each other?
How did William Pitt keep his coalition of allies together? What losses
did the French suffer after the foreign wars became more widespread?

8. What was the fate of the Girondins in 1793? What were the consequences for France as a whole?

9. In what ways did the Jacobin government of 1793 try to please the
people? What did it demand of them? What dangers did it confront at
home and abroad? How did French nationalism of this time differ from
earlier nationalism? How did its strength influence the war?

10. What was the Terror? Why was it adopted? What were its results?
How was it finally brought to an end? Which laws passed during the
Terror were kept afterward? Which were soon repealed?

11. In what areas were French armies victorious before 1795? Under
Napoleon Bonaparte, 1795-1802?

12. What happened to Poland, 1793-1795?

13. What kind of government was set up in France in 1795? What event
provided General Bonaparte the opportunity to form another government in 1799?

To Interpret the Facts

1. Under what four governments did Frenchmen live, 1791-1802? What
were the most important reasons for the establishment of each? What
was the most important accomplishment of each? The greatest weakness?

2. What new ideas about government and the organization of society grew
out of the events in France, 1789-1802?

To Put This Chapter into a Larger Setting

1. In what ways did events in Poland parallel those in France, 1788-1793?
How do you explain why the Poles failed to strengthen their country,
while the French were successful against enemies at home and abroad?

2. Read about and report on Maximilien Robespierre.

The Era
of
Napoleon

1802-1815

In 1802 when General Bonaparte became consul for life, he began to sign his name simply "Napoleon," in the manner of kings. For the next ten years his power over France appeared to be ever greater, the dominating position of France in Europe ever more secure. The period is still called the "Era of Napoleon." Yet Napoleon's reorganization of France was largely a moderating and stabilizing of changes that the revolution had made. The armies he led in his many wars had been organized by the revolutionary governments; the enemies he fought had already warred against the Bourbon kings of France. When he was finally sent into exile in 1815, France and Europe were indeed different from what they would have been had he not lived; but his ultimate effect on the course of history was here and there to give it a new twist without altering its general direction.

○ THE RISE OF NAPOLEON BONAPARTE

When Bonaparte became first consul in 1799, he was only thirty years old. He had made his reputation in his Italian campaign of 1796-1797 against Austria and in his Egyptian expedition of 1798. (See page 51.) When he returned to France in 1798, French armies had already made progress against the Second Coalition. After the *coup d'état* of 1799 he conducted his second successful campaign against Austria in Italy. In 1802 he made peace with all enemies, leaving to France the Austrian Netherlands (Belgium), the German lands west of the Rhine, and control of sister republics in the Dutch Netherlands, Switzerland, and Italy.

Bonaparte was a strange man to have become master of France, for he was not really a Frenchman at all. He was born of an Italian family on the island of Corsica just after France had acquired the island. Until the Bonaparte family quarreled with other Corsican patriots and fled to France, he had agitated for the independence of his homeland. He was educated in French military schools. A taciturn, withdrawn young man, he already exhibited extraordinary energy, powers of memory, and capacity for long-sustained hard work. He was short—only five feet two inches tall—and slender, with olive complexion, sharply chiseled features, and a large head topped by straight black hair. The most striking aspect of his appearance was the penetrating gaze from his gray, deep-set eyes, not easily forgotten by one who had met him. A resentful older general forced to serve under Bonaparte said after meeting his commander, "This little runt of a general frightened me. It is impossible to understand how he made me feel that he was the master from the moment he looked at me." In his maturity Bonaparte proved to be a shrewd judge of men, always eager to learn from those who knew more than he did. He could inspire confidence, respect, and and devotion in others. His self-confidence was boundless, his belief in his fate almost superstitious, his ambition limitless.

During the revolution Bonaparte had been outwardly sympathetic to the Jacobins, but his experience with the Paris mobs convinced him of the danger they posed to the country. Yet he always claimed to be the true heir of the revolution. As head of state he was, however, less interested in revolutionary theory than in practical methods of government; he borrowed ideas from the revolution, but he employed them for his own purposes.

☙   BONAPARTE'S REORGANIZATION OF FRANCE, 1799-1804

Bonaparte's first concern as head of state was the reorganization of the government and the reform of the country. Immediately after the *coup d'état* of 1799 he plunged into the writing of a new constitution.

THE CONSTITUTION OF THE YEAR VIII

The "Constitution of the Year VIII" (1799), which established the Consulate, was drafted by Sieyès and adroitly altered by Bonaparte. To avoid the incessant disorders of the previous decade and to satisfy his own ambition and drive for power, Bonaparte vested in himself as first consul the real authority of both central and local governments. Believing that a government was stronger if the people could be convinced that it represented them, he retained the appearance of democracy. From among a group of "notables" elected by universal manhood suffrage, the government chose the members of the legislative bodies and all public officials. The legislature had very little power; but it is to be noted that Bonaparte submitted not only his original constitution but later revisions of it to a plebiscite, and that the voters in each case voted an overwhelming "Yes." In the *départements* appointed officials collected taxes and kept order, thus preventing a return either of the bankruptcy of the royal and republican periods or of mob violence. Bonaparte had established a government with much of the authoritativeness of the royal governments of the Old Regime. Even so, he called himself a "child of the revolution"; and part of his justification was the appearance of republicanism in the constitution.

In 1804 he made a significant change in the constitution by adopting the title "Emperor of the French." An overwhelming vote of the French people approved this change. Thus began what is now called the "First Empire," which lasted until 1814. Always the showman, Napoleon arranged a spectacular coronation in the Cathedral of Notre Dame in Paris. Pope Pius VII journeyed all the way from Rome to consecrate Napoleon, but the emperor himself placed the crowns on his own head and on the head of his wife, who became the Empress Josephine.

THE REFORM OF FRANCE

Once in power Napoleon interested himself in all aspects of French life. He built roads and other public works, began a system of public schools, and established a national bank. He abandoned the more extreme revolutionary social practices by bringing titles into use again (even encouraging the return of some *émigré* nobles) and by maintaining a formal court, although without the elaborate etiquette of the Old Regime. He continued the revolutionary practice of choosing officials on the basis of merit.

The Concordat of 1801. In 1801 Bonaparte brought to an end the long-standing religious conflict that had grown out of the adoption of the Civil

Constitution of the Clergy. (See page 35.) With Pope Pius VII he concluded a concordat (a treaty with the papacy) advantageous to both church and state. Although Catholicism was not made the sole religion in France, it was formally recognized as the faith of most of the French people. Public worship, including processions in the streets, was permitted; seminaries were reopened; and the pope received a long-lost power to remove French bishops (although Napoleon continued to appoint them). The state continued to pay the salaries of priests and of Protestant ministers as well. Since the signing of the concordat indicated that the papacy recognized the permanent loss of the tithe and of the church lands that had been confiscated, the new owners of the land were henceforth more loyal supporters of Napoleon.

The Napoleonic Codes of Law. The other especially significant Napoleonic reform was a codification of all French law. The writing of a new code of laws had begun early in the revolution, but it was Napoleon who pushed the project to completion and who gave the code its name. He often appeared in person to urge the lawyers to hurry on with their mighty task.

The *Code Napoléon* took into account some of the most important and useful of the revolutionary changes. The laws now recognized each person as legally an individual instead of as a mere member of a class. All persons were equal before the law and were entitled to the same privileges. Private property was safeguarded. Elaborate provisions were made for its inheritance, especially for equality of inheritance among all the heirs of a deceased person. (Long thereafter this provision kept France a land of small farms.) There was to be religious toleration. The growth of business was encouraged by the development of a body of law concerning contracts, leases, debts, and similar commercial matters. In keeping with eighteenth century ideas about individual freedom, labor unions were banned. Civil marriage (marriage outside the church) was recognized, and divorce was permitted; but the male head of the family retained a strong control over the other members of his household. In general these laws favored especially the bourgeoisie and the landowning peasants.

When the reforms were complete, France was more peaceful at home than it had been for many years. There were, to be sure, limitations on personal freedom—press censorship, the use of spies, the imprisonment of extremists—but there was also a comfortable certainty about the operation of government and law. For the time being the people were fairly well satisfied.

Napoleon's coronation as emperor: a sketch by the painter Jacques Louis David. Napoleon, wearing coronation robes and a golden laurel wreath (in imitation of the emperors of ancient Rome), is himself placing the crown on his head, a break with the tradition of sovereigns being crowned by a dignitary of the church. Pope Pius VII looks on.

⌂ NAPOLEON'S WARS, 1803-1807

The name Napoleon recalls to mind great battles won, mighty countries humbled, and the near establishment of a union of all Europe under the supreme leadership of Napoleonic France. This picture is accurate; but today, after more than a century and a half, the battles and the short-lived international agreements seem relatively unimportant. Of greater moment are the national interests that caused France and its enemies to fight each other and the effect of the wars on the countries involved. Especially to be noted is the rapid growth of strong national feeling—nationalism—which increased in France in consequence of its victories, and in the nations opposing it because of their ever-mounting hatred of the French domination of Europe.

ISSUES AT STAKE IN THE WARS

When Europe was restored to peace in 1802, the wars were popularly believed to be over for good. Rich young Englishmen set forth on the usual young man's tour of the continent. British merchants dispatched their cargoes to ports long closed. Napoleon, however, was collecting ships in his ports on the English Channel as if he were about to invade Britain. But at the end of 1803, before any invasion could be attempted, Britain and France went to war again over some of their old subjects of dispute. Later, but not all at the same time, the Austrians, Russians, and Prussians also fought Napoleon. Each power had its own special reasons for fighting.

Great Britain. Except for the few months of peace in 1802-1803, Britain was at war with France from 1793 to 1814. No British ministry could permit the country to remain long at peace while France controlled the Austrian and Dutch Netherlands, those very coastal regions from which the British were determined to exclude all strong powers. (See page 20.) The French were equally determined to retain these areas so long desired by all French monarchs. (See page 21.) The French also threatened British routes to India. By controlling the Dutch Netherlands, Napoleon indirectly controlled the Dutch colony of Cape Town in South Africa, the key to Britain's all-water route to India. From Italy he threatened the route through the Mediterranean. Finally, the prime minister, William Pitt, saw that unless Napoleon was crushed he would one day master the entire European continent. Thereafter he could easily invade the British Isles. Pitt was willing, therefore, to pay large subsidies to secure the alliance of continental powers.

Austria, Prussia, and Russia. The situation of Austria was more complicated than that of Britain. Like Britain, Austria had been much injured by France. A lasting Austro-French peace was not possible until Austria recovered the Austrian Netherlands and Milan and until the German princes with lands west of the Rhine recovered them from France. But Austria feared Prussia and Russia as well. Since 1795 Prussia (with Napoleon's permission) had controlled northern Germany, threatening Austrian leadership in the Holy Roman Empire. To the Austrians this was an intolerable situation. Austria's fear of Russia was based on rivalry in the Adriatic Sea and the Balkan Peninsula. Ever since Catherine the Great had secured a Black Sea coast for Russia, the Russians had tried to push into the Mediterranean region, which Austria had long sought to dominate.

Russia and Prussia returned the suspicions that Austria harbored toward them. But like Austria, they were also hostile to France. Rulers of both countries were afraid of Napoleon's aggressiveness. Tsar Alexander I of Russia would inevitably oppose any French effort to push into the eastern

Mediterranean, perhaps by way of the Balkan Peninsula. Thus both governments watched Austria, but also turned a wary eye toward France.

France. Napoleon, for his part, realized that he could not secure permanent peace for his expanded empire without first decisively defeating both
Britain and Austria. Austria was the lesser problem because he could
meet its forces on land. There he could rely on his own military genius; on
the excellent army he had inherited from the revolution; and on his devoted
soldiers, inspired by patriotism and by their pride in the freedom now
enjoyed by Frenchmen. But Britain, with its two-to-one naval superiority
over France, posed an insoluble problem. The British could not defeat the
French on land, but they could always hire continental allies to fight for
them; and meanwhile they controlled the seas.

NAPOLEON'S VICTORIES OVER
THE CONTINENTAL POWERS, 1805-1807

The war between France and Britain that began anew in 1803 developed
into a series of four wars. (1) The first, involving only France and Britain,
culminated in the decisive naval battle of Trafalgar (1805) off the coast of
Spain, where the renowned British admiral, Lord Nelson, lost his life and
France lost its navy. Thereafter Napoleon had no hope of making war on
the sea. (2) In 1805 Pitt organized his Third Coalition, the last he lived to
see, joined by both Austria and Russia. Prussia remained neutral, relying on
the friendship of France, which had kept Prussia in control of northern
Germany since 1795. Before the end of the year Napoleon defeated the
Austrian and Russian armies and deprived Austria of still more territory. (3)
Suddenly in 1806 the patience of Frederick William III of Prussia was
exhausted, and quite unaided he attacked France. Within a month Napoleon
and his army were in the Prussian capital, Berlin. (4) In the first months of
1807 Napoleon again defeated the Russians, with whom he had not yet
made peace. He thus became for all practical purposes the master of the
continent.

Napoleon used his strong position to make an ally of Tsar Alexander I.
In 1807 they met at Tilsit on the Niemen River, where a raft was built so
that they could talk together in a neutral spot midway between their two
armies. Uninvited at first, Frederick William III of Prussia remained miser-
ably on the bank of the river, seated on his horse. The two rulers planned
to divide Europe between them. Alexander accepted Napoleon's dominance
of central Europe, believing that Napoleon would aid him in the Balkans.

◌ THE CONTINENTAL SYSTEM

In spite of his triumphs Napoleon was not secure, for the British remained undefeated. Unable to attack Britain with armed force, he determined to destroy its business, which was the life blood of Britain. He ordered all the continental European ports under his control closed to British imports. As he was allied with Russia and directly controlled the coasts of Italy, Belgium, the Dutch Netherlands, and Germany, he expected to be able to destroy Britain's commerce and therefore its manufacturing and its banking. He also expected that the blockade would aid French manufacturers, who, free from British competition, would have all the markets of the continent to themselves. Napoleon named this anti-British blockade policy the "Continental System."

The Continental System succeeded to some extent: in spite of a lively smuggling trade, British merchants found it difficult to reach their former continental markets. But they soon found new markets in the non-European world. Napoleon probably suffered more than did the British. Serious shortages began to appear in France, and in the conquered continental lands the disruption of the accustomed commerce gave rise to much anti-French feeling. The blockade was an especially severe strain on Napoleon's alliance with Russia. Meanwhile, the British retaliated against the Continental System by taking measures to prevent neutral nations from trading with the continent. Although their efforts provoked the War of 1812 with the United States, that conflict diverted little of their attention from their wars in Europe.

The Continental System soon brought Napoleon back to the battlefield, for he had to fight a series of wars to enforce it. In 1807 he attempted to close the most serious gap in the system by sending an army into Portugal, Britain's staunch ally, whose king fled to Portuguese Brazil. Later he deposed the king of Spain and put his own brother Joseph on the Spanish throne. He did not, however, succeed in closing the Spanish and Portuguese ports. The Spanish people made war against Joseph, receiving aid from a British force under the Duke of Wellington; peace was not restored until the fall of Napoleon. Then in 1809 Austria revolted against Napoleon and he had to wage yet another war (his fourth) against it. Austria was quickly defeated, and its territory was reduced still further. Thereafter, although leaks in the Continental System were numerous, Napoleon used an interval of quiet to attend to his extended empire.

∩ NAPOLEON'S REORGANIZATION OF EUROPE

Napoleon's most lasting work, aside from his reorganization of France, was his remaking of Europe. His purpose was primarily to strengthen the military position of France.

THE REORGANIZATION OF GERMANY AND ITALY

For the future of Europe, the most important of Napoleon's changes were made in Germany and Italy.

In Germany he tried to construct a group of friendly states allied with him for his inevitable conflicts with Austria and Prussia. He suppressed almost all of the smallest states, giving their lands to those that were somewhat larger. He took particular care to destroy the states ruled by bishops, for they had usually allied with Austria. Then he created the "Confederation of the Rhine," his chief German satellite, which originally had sixteen members and then later included most of the German states except Austria and Prussia. Since the members of the Confederation withdrew from the Holy Roman Empire and allied themselves with France, the thousand-year-old Empire collapsed. Unable to resist Napoleon's changes, Emperor Francis announced that the Holy Roman Empire had ceased to exist and that his hereditary lands would henceforth be known as the Austrian Empire.

Napoleon also created the "Kingdom of Italy," including all of north Italy except the extensive areas annexed to France. When Pope Pius VII refused to enforce the Continental System, Napoleon deposed him, forced him to take the long journey to France when he was almost dying, and kept him prisoner until the end of the war in the Chateau of Fontainebleau near Paris. The Papal States were annexed to France. In 1811, when Napoleon's son was born, he was given the title "King of Rome," and Napoleon himself became king of Italy. Both Italians and Germans, now more united than ever before, began to develop a feeling of national unity.

THE EXTENT AND ADMINISTRATION OF NAPOLEON'S EMPIRE

The map on page 65 shows the boundaries of Napoleon's empire in 1810 at its greatest extent. The Netherlands, much of the coast of Germany, and the parts of Italy annexed to France were divided into *départements* and governed as part of France. Spain, the Confederation of the Rhine, the

Grand Duchy of Warsaw (a part of Poland), and the remainder of Italy were French satellites, many of them ruled by members of the Bonaparte family and all closely supervised by Napoleon. In the rest of the continent, Denmark, Austria, and Prussia were French allies, willing or not. As for Russia, Tsar Alexander had decided to end his alliance with Napoleon, but had not yet taken any definitive action against him.

POPULAR FEELING IN THE NAPOLEONIC EMPIRE

The permanence of Napoleon's empire depended to a great extent upon the loyalty of the rank and file of the subject peoples. For a time Napoleon enjoyed a good deal of popular support in spite of the harshness with which he suppressed freedom of speech and the press, enforced the Continental System, and compelled the use of the Napoleonic Codes whether or not they were suited to existing society. Some middle-class people in the conquered countries were already familiar with the teachings of the *philosophes* (see pages 13-14) and therefore appreciated some of Napoleon's goals.

The real threat to the permanence of the Napoleonic empire was the vital force of nationalism, which was aroused in the people of the subject countries by their dislike of foreign rulers and their eagerness and determination to be rid of them. The Spanish people, previously very little united, developed a vehement loyalty to Spain out of their desperate struggle against Napoleon. In Austria a period of reform and increased national spirit preceded the war of 1809.

It was in Prussia, however, that national feeling had the most important results. Although a French army of occupation remained in Prussia, the Prussian government retained control of domestic affairs. Immediately after the Peace of Tilsit of 1807, King Frederick William III called in new advisers who virtually remade his country. They abolished serfdom, although leaving the landlords in control of their vast estates and permitting them to exercise some of their former legal jurisdiction over the now freed peasants. They gave some self-government to towns and cities. They particularly concerned themselves with the army, which Napoleon had strictly limited in size. In order to provide an adequate military force, they invented the practice, widely used today, of rotating men in service. Thus many were trained and available for war, even though at any given moment the numbers in active service did not exceed Napoleon's limits. Perhaps most important of all, a group of inspiring writers stirred the patriotic feelings of the people and aroused them against the French.

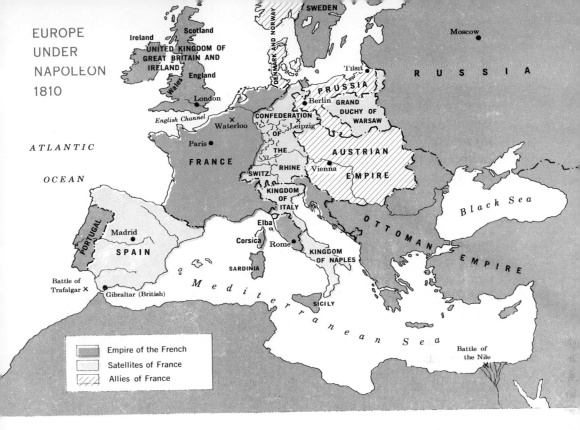

EUROPE
UNDER
NAPOLEON
1810

Empire of the French
Satellites of France
Allies of France

THE COLLAPSE OF NAPOLEON'S EMPIRE, 1812-1815

In 1812 Napoleon's empire was fatally shaken by military defeat. But even before this critical event took place, there were growing signs that his hold over his extensive domains was weakening. He himself was older and less flexible in his thinking than he had once been. His armies were filled with non-French soldiers from various parts of the empire. With the passage of time the subject peoples were becoming increasingly restive. Most important of all, the kings and statesmen of Europe were by now fully aware that unless each was to be defeated separately, all must join together in a firm alliance against Napoleon.

THE RUSSIAN CAMPAIGN, 1812

The military defeat that began Napoleon's downfall was inflicted upon him in 1812 by Russian soldiers and the Russian weather. He himself made the dangerous decision to invade Russia. He wished to punish Alexander I, who had opened Russian ports to British commerce. Believing that a short summer war would bring Alexander to terms, Napoleon moved into Russia

with a force of 600,000 men and with supplies for only three weeks. No
decisive battle was fought; the Russians simply retreated before him, destroying everything as they went. When Napoleon reached Moscow, a fire
virtually destroyed the city. He remained in the neighborhood of Moscow
for several weeks without having an opportunity to fight a Russian army.
Finally, at the beginning of an unusually early, severe winter, he began to
retreat. Intense cold, starvation, and the attacks of the Russians reduced the
French army to 100,000 men by the time it emerged from Russia.

THE WAR OF LIBERATION, 1813-1814

After this crushing disaster Napoleon hastened back to France in a sleigh
over frozen roads to raise another army. He could not, of course, replace
his seasoned troops nor his own earlier vigor. Only the lack of unity among
his opponents gave him time to prepare to meet them. Austria, fearing
Russia, delayed in joining an alliance with the other powers. All the continental powers distrusted Britain, but in the end they accepted its alliance
in order to secure British subsidies. Finally, in 1813, Britian, Russia, Austria,
and Prussia joined for the first time in one great alliance. In a decisive battle at Leipzig, in central Germany, they defeated Napoleon.

From Leipzig Napoleon retreated across Germany into France and on to
Paris, with the allies at his heels and his satellites collapsing behind him. At
last he accepted the terms of the victors, yielding his throne to Louis XVI's
brother, the Count of Provence, who became Louis XVIII. (Louis XVI's
son, Louis XVII, had died.) Napoleon was exiled to the little Italian island
of Elba, which he was to be allowed to rule as "emperor."

THE HUNDRED DAYS

In 1814 the statesmen of Europe gathered in Vienna to restore peace; but
they were not yet finished with Napoleon, who was encouraged by tales of
disagreement in Vienna and of unrest in France to try to return to power.
Escaping from Elba, he landed in France on March 1, 1815. Within weeks
he had organized a new army and led it into Belgium, hoping to defeat the
allies separately before they could unite against him. But at Waterloo on
June 18 the allies again defeated him, ending Napoleon's brief return from
exile (called, not quite accurately, the "Hundred Days"). This time the
allies took no chances: they exiled him to the remote South Atlantic island
of St. Helena, where he remained a prisoner until his death in 1821.

THE NAPOLEONIC ERA, 1803-1815

	IN FRANCE	NAPOLEON'S WARS	OUTSIDE FRANCE
1803		MAY: War with France renewed by Britain	
1804	MARCH: Civil code becomes law MAY: Empire established DEC.: Napoleon crowned		
1805		MAY: Napoleon crowned king of Italy OCT.: Trafalgar DEC.: Third Coalition destroyed	JULY: Pitt organizes the Third Coalition
1806		JULY: Confederation of the Rhine established OCT.: War with Prussia NOV.: Continental System begun	JAN.: Death of Pitt AUG.: Holy Roman Empire dissolved
1807		JAN.-JUNE: War with Russia JULY: Tilsit treaties OCT.: French invade Portugal	OCT.: Nationalist reforms begun in Prussia
1808		DEC.: Napoleon in Spain	JUNE: Joseph Bonaparte king of Spain
1809		APRIL: Revolt in Austria MAY: Papal States annexed OCT.: Austrian revolt suppressed	
1810		JULY: Dutch Netherlands annexed DEC.: Northern Germany annexed	DEC.: Russia admits British goods
1812		JUNE: Invasion of Russia OCT.: Retreat from Moscow	JUNE: U.S.-British War of 1812 begins
1813		OCT.: Battle of Leipzig	JUNE: Alliance of Britain, Prussia, Russia, and Austria
1814	APRIL: Abdication of Napoleon MAY: Louis XVIII king	MARCH: Allies in Paris	MAY: Napoleon in Elba SEPT.: Congress of Vienna meets
1815	MARCH: Return of Napoleon	JUNE: Waterloo	OCT.: Napoleon on St. Helena

ᴑ ᴑ ᴑ

The fall of Napoleon was the end of an era. Since 1789 France and many other parts of Europe had been breaking the ties with the Old Regime and experimenting with governmental and social change. But those monarchs and statesmen who had united to bring about the defeat of Napoleon were no longer interested in radical change. They had fought not only to drive France back within her borders but also to secure for Europe a period of quiet and stability. It is not surprising that their efforts inaugurated a period of conservative reaction.

Persons, Places, and Terms

Pius VII	Belgium	Era of Napoleon
Lord Nelson	Austrian Empire	First Consul
Frederick William III	Confederation of	universal manhood
Alexander I	the Rhine	suffrage
Duke of Wellington	Kingdom of Italy	First Empire
Louis XVIII	Rome	concordat
	Grand Duchy of	*Code Napoléon*
Corsica	Warsaw	civil marriage
Adriatic Sea	Moscow	Continental System
Balkan Peninsula	Leipzig	blockade
Trafalgar	Elba	neutral
Berlin	Waterloo	War of 1812
Tilsit	St. Helena	

To Master the Text

1. What personal qualities and early experiences helped prepare Napoleon Bonaparte for his career? What aspects of his life and early experience seemed ill-suited as a background for what he later did?
2. Which aspects of Napoleon's Constitution of the Year VIII helped make it acceptable to the people? Which made the new government stronger than its predecessor? To what extent was it democratic? To what extent did it borrow ideas from the earlier revolutionary governments?
3. Which of Napoleon's reforms made France a better place in which to live? How did the Concordat of 1801 alter the position of the Catholic Church in France? What changes made by earlier revolutionary governments were preserved in Napoleon's law codes?
4. After 1802 what factors prevented Great Britain from remaining at peace with France? What made France an enemy of Britain? Why were Austria and Russia enemies of France? Why were these two countries

suspicious of each other? What grounds of hostility were there between Austria and Prussia?

5. How did the battle of Trafalgar change the military position of France? By what stages did Napoleon bring central Europe under his control between 1806 and 1807?

6. What was the Continental System? What did Napoleon hope to accomplish by it? Did it fulfill his hopes? How did it affect France? What alliances or wars did Napoleon enter into in order to support the Continental System?

7. Why did Napoleon remake the maps of Germany and Italy? What territories in each region were annexed to France? Why were they annexed? Was Napoleon's government popular in the areas under his control?

8. By 1808 how had national feeling against France been exhibited in Spain? In Prussia? In Austria?

9. What were the results of Napoleon's invasion of Russia? Of the battle at Leipzig? Of his return from Elba?

To Master the Map

Study the map of Europe under Napoleon (page 65) to find those particularly sensitive areas that one or another of the European governments would not willingly leave in French hands. Could Napoleon have given up these same places without also abandoning his other conquests?

To Interpret the Facts

1. It has been argued that except for some one fatal error, Napoleon might have succeeded in making permanent his conquests and reorganizations in Europe. With another student, hold a debate before the class, arguing both sides of these propositions: (1) Had Napoleon not invaded Spain, he might have kept his empire. (2) Had Napoleon not invaded Russia, he might have kept his empire.

2. What specific facts show that French nationalism was an important factor in the great success of Napoleon? That nationalism in other countries was largely responsible for his final defeat?

3. In what ways did British naval superiority influence the course of the Napoleonic Wars?

4. What permanent changes did Napoleon make in France? In Europe?

To Put This Chapter into a Larger Setting

1. To what extent did Napoleon's reorganization of France indicate that he was, as he claimed to be, a "child of the French Revolution"? To what extent would his policies have pleased the *philosophes?* The Jacobins? Which of his policies would either group have disapproved?

2. In your mind, which man contributed more of permanent benefit to France and to Europe, Robespierre or Napoleon? Why?

5

The Conservative Restoration

The European statesmen of the allied countries to whose lot it fell to make peace in 1815 had acquired most of their political experience in wartime, for Europe had been almost continuously at war since 1792. All these men sincerely desired to create lasting peace. All tended to take for granted that the costly wars had been the direct outcome of the French Revolution—of "Jacobinism," as they said. All were prone to remember the French Revolution as a time of continual and fruitless disorder, caused, many of them believed, by the lessened authority of church and nobility and by too much freedom for workingmen and peasants. With such thoughts in mind, they naturally saw as their first duty the establishment of safeguards against further outbreaks of "Jacobinism." The years after 1815 were therefore a time of conservative reaction; any hint of popular revolt in any country received the immediate and alarmed attention of governments in all countries.

☊ THE CONSERVATIVES

Conservatives of any period of history believe, as did Edmund Burke in 1790 (see page 41), that change should come slowly so that the good

already achieved will not be lost in the search for something better. At
various times different kinds of people tend to be the conservatives. In the
early days of the French Revolution, it had been the nobles and upper
clergy who resisted the revolutionary changes; but by 1815 many of the
bourgeoisie also looked back upon the revolution with disapproval and
regret. They had forgotten the idealism of liberty, equality, and fraternity;
they remembered only the disruption of orderly society by undisciplined
mobs. At the other end of the social scale, the peasants also tended to be
conservative after 1815, if only because lack of education and of wide
experience made them cling to what was familiar.

Conservatives of 1815 tended to accept the leadership of men of rank or
wealth. They encouraged the government to censor the press, to inspect
schools, to limit the right of public meeting; for only thus, they believed,
could the spread of "dangerous" ideas be prevented. They were glad to
put education in the hands of the clergy. In brief, they favored a society
that had more in common with the Old Regime than with the French
revolutionary governments.

METTERNICH OF AUSTRIA

Prince Klemens von Metternich, the Austrian foreign minister, had contributed much to the defeat of Napoleon and was the best-known conservative statesman of the day. So powerful and long-lived was he that the
decades after 1815 are often called the "Age of Metternich."

Metternich was ideally suited to play a conspicuous part in the conservative years. As a young man he had seen the destructive side of revolution,
for Napoleon's soldiers had seized his family estates. His adult life had been
spent among aristocrats in the service of the Austrian emperor, close to the
affairs of state but far removed from any knowledge of the lower classes.
He was handsome and extraordinarily well schooled in the social graces of
high society. His admirers claim that his ability to persuade others to compromise opposing views permitted him to create a spirit of unity never
before known in Europe. His critics insist that he was conservative to that
absurd degree called "reactionary," unable and unwilling to recognize and
make provision for the new circumstances of the time. Undoubtedly he had
a most extravagant admiration for himself. In his old age he was heard to
remark, "Error has never approached my mind."

To avoid further turmoil, he wished to restore the balance among the
great powers and to re-establish the former balance among classes within

the various countries. His policy was particularly suited to the needs of Austria, whose responsibilities extended from Germany to Italy to the Danube valley. Only in a peaceful Europe could Austria preserve stability and prosperity in those diverse regions.

ALEXANDER I OF RUSSIA

The other most talked-of personality among the statesmen of the day was the handsome, charming tsar of Russia, Alexander I (tsar 1801-1825). His temperament and his background tended to make him unpredictable. He inherited the pride and autocratic attitudes of his Romanov ancestors; but under the supervision of his grandmother, Catherine II, he had also learned to know the writings of the *philosophes*. Sometimes he conversed like a liberal. Had he lived in western Europe and associated with British or French leaders, his ideas might not have seemed unusual; but to his fellow sovereigns of eastern Europe, one of his favorite topics, the importance of constitutions, sounded dangerously "Jacobin." At the time of the defeat of Napoleon he became deeply interested in religion.

Klemens von Metternich, Austrian foreign minister and leading statesman of Europe in the years after 1815.

OTHER CONSERVATIVE STATESMEN

Other European leaders shared Metternich's conservatism. In Britain there were the aristocratic foreign minister, Lord Castlereagh, and the ultraconservative Duke of Wellington, who had forced Napoleon from Spain and decisively defeated him at Waterloo. Frederick William III, admirer of Tsar Alexander, controlled Prussian policy. In France the most important statesman was Talleyrand, who had managed to serve several French governments since 1789. Though he shared many conservative views, his principal goal was to restore France's leadership in Europe, for he was above all a French patriot.

To an unusual degree the leading statesmen of the day knew and understood each other. Together they had followed Napoleon's retreating armies across Europe after the battle of Leipzig, often spending the night in the same convenient inn. They were well prepared to co-operate with each other for the welfare of Europe.

∽ THE CONGRESS OF VIENNA

The longest-lasting accomplishment of the years 1815-1823 was the drafting of the treaties of peace. The first of these was agreed to in Paris at the time of Napoleon's abdication, but the really troublesome questions were deferred to a congress sitting in Vienna from September, 1814, to June, 1815. The Congress of Vienna was attended by delegates from all nations involved on either side of the Napoleonic wars. At first all major decisions were made by the representatives of Britain, Prussia, Austria, and Russia; in the later months of the Congress, Talleyrand of France participated as an equal. Discussions were carried on with hitherto unknown directness and informality. For delegates from less important countries, the Congress was lively and amusing. Having no work to do, they dined and danced in an atmosphere of elegance that only Vienna could then provide.

The work of the Congress was important for what was accomplished— and also for two topics that were carefully avoided: nationalism and popular participation in government. The negotiators feared both, and they believed that both could be eliminated by a wise reorganization of Europe. As a blow to nationalism, Italy was again broken up into a number of independent states. The thirty-eight remaining German states were but loosely bound together in a "Germanic Confederation" with a diet sitting at

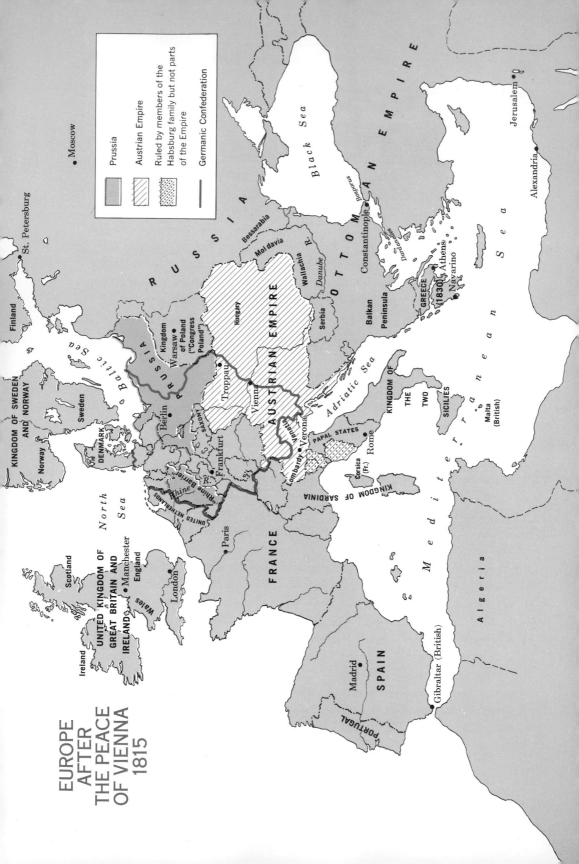

EUROPE
AFTER
THE PEACE
OF VIENNA
1815

Prussia

Austrian Empire

Ruled by members of the
Habsburg family but not parts
of the Empire

Germanic Confederation

Moscow

St. Petersburg

Finland

RUSSIA

Bessarabia

Moldavia

Wallachia

Danube R.

Black Sea

OTTOMAN EMPIRE

Constantinople

Bosporus

Dardanelles

GREECE

(1830) Athens

Navarino

Jerusalem

Alexandria

KINGDOM OF SWEDEN AND NORWAY

Norway

Sweden

Baltic Sea

DENMARK

P R U S S I A

Kingdom of Poland ("Congress Poland")

Warsaw

Hungary

AUSTRIAN EMPIRE

Serbia

Balkan Peninsula

Mediterranean Sea

Berlin

SAXONY

Troppau

Vienna

Frankfurt

R.

Rhine Barrier

Venetia

Verona

Lombardy

Adriatic Sea

KINGDOM OF THE TWO SICILIES

Malta (British)

North Sea

Scotland

UNITED KINGDOM OF GREAT BRITAIN AND IRELAND

Manchester

England

Wales

London

Ireland

UNITED NETHERLANDS

Paris

F R A N C E

PAPAL STATES

Rome

Corsica (fr.)

KINGDOM OF SARDINIA

Algeria

Madrid

S P A I N

PORTUGAL

Gibraltar (British)

Frankfurt. The diet was to represent the ruling princes and be presided over by the Austrian delegate. Metternich opposed a strongly united Germany, not only because he disliked and feared nationalism, but also because Austria had too many non-German subjects to be a suitable leader of a purely German state.

THE RESTORATION OF LEGITIMATE RULERS

One of the principles on which the Congress based its work was that of "legitimacy," a convenient word suggested by Talleyrand. It carried the idea that the Congress was justified in restoring whatever had been part of the "public law" of the Old Regime—hereditary or "legitimate" monarchs, for example. One legitimate monarch was already on his throne before the Congress assembled: Louis XVIII of France, brother of Louis XVI, who had been brought to Paris with the victorious allies when they defeated Napoleon. Louis granted a "Constitutional Charter" so phrased as to suggest that he held his power directly from God. But the Charter left all lands that had been confiscated from nobles and church in the possession of those who acquired them during the revolution; it guaranteed liberties for individuals; and it established a two-house legislature, the upper house hereditary and the lower house elected by the wealthier citizens.

The rulers were also restored in the Dutch Netherlands, Spain, Portugal, the Papal States, the kingdoms of Naples and Sicily (now united as the kingdom of the Two Sicilies), and elsewhere. In Germany, however, the reduction of the more than three hundred states to thirty-eight meant that many petty princes did not recover their thrones. The Holy Roman Empire, which had been dissolved in 1806, was not revived. The Habsburg ruler continued to use the title emperor of Austria.

THE BALANCE OF POWER

The second principle employed by the Congress was the recognition of a balance of power among the nations of Europe so that no one of them could again threaten to control the whole continent. All the victorious allies feared that France might again disturb the peace of Europe, and all except Prussia also feared the expansionist tendencies of huge and populous Russia. The territorial changes made by the Congress were largely directed against France or were intended to prevent Russia or any other power from dominating Europe.

To guarantee the good behavior of France, the Congress strengthened the countries around its borders. Belgium (the former Austrian Netherlands) was given to the Dutch Netherlands, the "Rhine Barrier" (land on both sides of the Rhine River) went to Prussia, and the port of Genoa to the king of Sardinia. Switzerland was to be neutral. The borders of France were to be those of 1790.

As a step toward a stable balance of power, the peacemakers attempted to keep the relative strength of the victorious countries about as it had been before the war. If one of them gave up a piece of territory, efforts were made to give some other territory as compensation. Russia had acquired Finland and Bessarabia during the war and managed to keep them. As compensation for the loss of Finland, Sweden received Norway, formerly the possession of Napoleon's ally Denmark. Austria was compensated for the loss of the Austrian Netherlands to the Dutch by acquiring Lombardy and Venetia in northern Italy. Britain, with no interest in continental land, instead received conveniently placed islands and ports of call all over the world.

Remaking the map brought about the one dangerous disagreement at Vienna. Alexander I of Russia was determined to annex all of Poland, and Frederick William III of Prussia wanted to take the German kingdom of Saxony. Castlereagh and Metternich resolved to block so great an enlargement of either country and to prevent the extension of Russia into central Europe. War actually threatened. But Castlereagh and Metternich secured the support of Talleyrand, who naturally welcomed so excellent an opportunity for France to exercise influence again in an important European crisis. Outnumbered three to two, Russia and Prussia gave way. Russia annexed only those areas of Poland that Austria and Prussia had gained in the Third Partition of 1795. (See map, page 43.) To this "Congress Poland," as it was called, Alexander, in one of his liberal moods, granted a constitution. Prussia annexed only a part of Saxony.

The hope of the peacemakers that these arrangements would keep Europe stable and at peace were not entirely fulfilled. Yet no war involving all Europe broke out for a century—not until 1914.

⌒ THE CONCERT OF EUROPE

Hopes for lasting peace were increased by the adoption of a plan for "concerted" action among the great powers to prevent minor international disputes from growing into major ones. Calling themselves the "Concert of Europe," Russia, Prussia, Austria, Britain, and later France made definite arrangements to "concert" (co-operate) to keep Europe free of war. For a few years the Concert of Europe gave some promise of success.

THE PROMISING YEARS, 1815-1819

One of the foundations of the Concert was the "Quadruple Alliance" of Austria, Britain, Russia, and Prussia, established by a treaty that Castlereagh and Metternich promoted. Its purpose was to prevent France from again threatening the European balance of power. The four powers agreed to call another congress whenever France seemed to threaten the peace. This arrangement was to last for twenty years.

A less practical basis of the Concert was the "Holy Alliance," established under a treaty drawn up by Tsar Alexander and signed first by the rulers of Prussia and Austria and later by almost all European monarchs. It was Alexander's belief that peace would reign in Europe if the rulers would consciously perform their duties in a Christian manner, treating their subjects as their children and their fellow rulers as their brothers. Lacking any detailed plan for action, this vague treaty had little meaning even for those who signed it. But Alexander believed that he had committed all rulers to help suppress revolution whenever it threatened to spread from one country to another.

At first it seemed that the Concert might go far toward preserving peace. A congress of the Quadruple Alliance in 1818 arranged for the withdrawal of allied occupation troops from France and admitted France to the Concert. Since all governments were for the moment in the hands of conservatives, all put special emphasis on the discovery and suppression of radicalism and of anything that seemed in any remote way likely to lead to riot or rebellion. Repressive measures were adopted everywhere. In Britain the writ of *habeas corpus* (the legal document that prevents persons from being held in jail indefinitely without trial) was suspended. Public meetings and freedom of the press were curtailed. Similar action was taken in France.

Metternich did the most thorough job of hunting out troublemakers. He was alarmed in 1817 when German student organizations celebrating the beginning of Lutheranism imitated Luther's burning of the pope's document against him by burning a wig, a policeman's pigtail, and a corporal's stick—symbols of the Old Regime. When soon thereafter an unbalanced German student assassinated a secret Russian agent, Metternich took action. In 1819 he persuaded the member states of the Germanic Confederation to ban student organizations, to censor the press, and to secure the dismissal of university professors who seemed unduly critical of the government. Similar restrictions were soon in operation in Italy, which was largely controlled by Austria.

THE CONCERT AND THE REVOLUTIONS OF 1820

In 1820 the Concert met its first real test. In January of that year revolt broke out in Spain. The folly of King Ferdinand VII had brought on this trouble. When he was restored to the throne by the victorious allies in 1814, he made no effort to improve conditions in his country nor to conciliate the Spanish colonies in the Americas, which were then in revolt against their mother country. (Chapter 6.) Troops he was preparing to send to America, angered by his careless preparations for feeding and housing them, began the revolt of 1820, and were soon joined by dissatisfied elements in other parts of the country. The king became a virtual prisoner of the rebels and had to promise to restore the impractical Constitution of 1812, a poorly thought-out imitation of the French Constitution of 1791. The rebels abolished the tithe and seized church property.

Here was the very kind of rebellion the continental monarchs were determined to prevent. They were not, however, able to concert together to suppress it. Alexander immediately offered to send his army, the only one in Europe on a war footing, to the aid of Ferdinand. To go from Russia to Spain the troops would, of course, have to pass through Austrian and French territory. Both Metternich and Louis XVIII were far more alarmed by such a prospect than by the fate of Ferdinand. They found excuses, and no action was taken.

Almost immediately a similar problem arose in the kingdom of the Two Sicilies, where the restored monarchy of Ferdinand I was generally hated. Because the press was censored and public meetings prohibited, secret societies sprang up to advocate freedom. The most important of these was the "Order of the Carbonari," which was active in France and Italy. It took its name from a semi-secret organization of charcoal burners (*carbonari*) of the Napoleonic period. In Italy after 1815 it advocated popular participation in government, freeing the state from too much control by the church, and an independent, united Italy. It made secret plans for uprisings against the conservative governments. In July, 1820, the Carbonari brought about a successful revolt against the king of the Two Sicilies.

This time Metternich was determined to take action, for a successful revolt in southern Italy would inevitably spread to other parts of the peninsula and would very likely threaten Austrian control of the whole area. He encouraged the calling of another European congress, which met at Troppau on the Austrian-Prussian border, to onsider the case of the Two Sicilies. Metternich received permission to send troops to southern Italy, where the revolt promptly collapsed.

A more important result of the Congress of Troppau was the division of the Concert of Europe into two parts. Prussia, Austria, and Russia drew closer together. In the course of a famous tea party, Alexander is reported to have confessed to Metternich that he no longer cherished any liberal ideas at all. The representatives of the three powers signed a document in which they declared their intention of intervening in any country from which revolution threatened to spread to other countries. This doctrine of intervention by great powers in the internal affairs of another country was so frightening to the French and British governments that they would not participate in the congress.

In 1822 another meeting of all the powers was attempted at Verona. One of the principal topics was the situation in Spain, where Ferdinand VII was still under the control of the revolutionaries. By this time the government of France had become more conservative than in 1820; and French ministers, eager to put their country in a position of European leadership, asked permission of the congress to send troops into Spain to free the king. In spite of angry opposition from Britain, permission was granted. In 1823 French troops moved into Spain, and soon the king was free to re-establish his autocracy. The European Concert was, however, really dead. It was obvious that it could not again have the co-operation of Britain, and there was no certainty that France would support it except where French interests were involved. The expression "Concert of Europe" was used throughout the nineteenth century, but it no longer represented any real attempt of the great powers to act together in important matters. The expression "Holy Alliance" was also sometimes still used, but only as a quite unofficial designation for Austria, Russia, and Prussia.

ᴖ ᴖ ᴖ

The period of conservative reaction after 1815 was useful in that it provided an opportunity for recovery from the long years of war. The conservative attitudes of the governments in power reflected the desires of a great part of their peoples. The conservatives did not, however, reverse all that had happened in Europe since 1789. The reforms achieved in France during the revolution, consolidated by Napoleon and carried by his armies into many parts of Europe, still remained in many places and were not forgotten in the others. By 1823 conservatism in western Europe had begun to wear itself out. Thereafter a new movement for change—liberalism—challenged the conservatism of the immediate postwar years.

Persons, Places, and Terms

Klemens von
  Metternich
the Romanovs
Lord Castlereagh
Talleyrand

Germanic
  Confederation
Rhine Barrier
Genoa
Switzerland

Bessarabia
Lombardy
Venetia
Kingdom of
  the Two Sicilies
Saxony
Troppau
Verona

conservatism
balance of power

legitimacy
Constitutional Charter
  of France
Concert of Europe
Quadruple Alliance
Holy Alliance
writ of *habeas corpus*
Spanish Constitution
  of 1812
Carbonari

To Master the Text

1. What ideas were accepted by the majority of conservatives in 1815? What experiences made Metternich a conservative? To what extent was Alexander I a conservative?
2. Representatives of what countries made the major decisions at the Congress of Vienna? What country did Talleyrand represent? What part was he expected to play?
3. What two especially important topics were avoided at Vienna?
4. Why were Germany and Italy again divided into many small states? To what extent was Napoleon's reorganization retained in Germany? What organization replaced the Holy Roman Empire?
5. What was the meaning of Talleyrand's word "legitimacy"? To what countries were legitimate monarchs restored in 1815? Where were rulers not restored? To what extent did the Constitutional Charter of 1814 fail to restore all aspects of the Old Regime in France?
6. What does "balance of power" mean? What provisions of the treaties of Vienna were intended to prevent France's again becoming too powerful? What territories changed hands at Vienna primarily in order to compensate a country for the loss of other territory?
7. What did Alexander I and Frederick William III hope to do with Poland and Saxony? What countries objected? How was this problem solved? In what ways was Talleyrand's part in the settlement important?

8. What was the purpose of the Quadruple Alliance of 1814? Of the Holy Alliance? What future action did each provide for? By what measures did the various governments try to prevent the spread of revolutionary ideas after 1815?

9. What caused revolutions in Spain and the kingdom of the Two Sicilies in 1820? Why did the members of the Concert fail to act in Spain? Why did they later act in Italy? What statement of principle did the powers of eastern Europe make in regard to revolutionary uprisings in other countries? What principles did Great Britain follow? Why and in what way did France intervene in Spain?

10. Why was it said that by 1823 the Concert of Europe was dead?

To Master the Map

Compare the maps of Europe in 1789 (page 18) and 1815 (page 74). What changes in the European balance of power are apparent?

To Interpret the Facts

1. On what principles did the Congress of Vienna base its decisions? On what grounds could those principles be justified in 1814? What facts known in 1814-1815 might have indicated to the peacemakers that times were changing too rapidly for the kind of system they established?

2. What reasons are there for naming the years after 1814 the Age of Metternich? What developments make this name somewhat unsuitable?

3. Did Alexander I's Holy Alliance have any prospect of success at the time of its establishment? In later years, to what extent was the Holy Alliance a basis for the policies of some rulers?

4. In 1814 it appeared to the people of Europe that France had been soundly defeated. What evidence can you find from the succeeding years to prove that the statesmen of other countries still feared France? What facts relating to the years 1815-1822 seemed to justify those fears?

To Put This Chapter into a Larger Setting

1. Hold an imaginary session of the Congress of Vienna in which members of the class impersonate important members—Metternich, Castlereagh, Alexander I, Talleyrand, and others. Each student should study the policies of the country he is to represent and of the man he will impersonate. After the session, discuss the accuracy of the presentations.

2. To what extent did Russian policy in the late eighteenth and early nineteenth centuries justify the fears that statesmen of other countries had of Russia in 1815?

3. List the important coalitions and alliances that came into existence between 1793 and 1815. Which best suited its purpose? Which held together best? Which accomplished the greatest part of its purpose?

6

Europe
and
the World

1789-1825

During the exciting decades of the French Revolution and of the wars and peacemaking that followed, European statesmen attended largely to the affairs of their own continent. But in those same years, significant developments were taking place outside Europe: the British Empire continued to grow as British world trade expanded tremendously, and a series of wars for independence freed most of the Latin-American colonies of Spain from their mother country. Both of these developments were connected with events in Europe; both in turn were important factors in subsequent European international relations, especially as liberalism was beginning to challenge the hold of conservatism on the policies of many statesmen.

∩ THE GROWTH OF THE
BRITISH EMPIRE, 1789-1825

It has often been said that "the British Empire was established in a fit of absence of mind." Of no time was this statement more true than during the years between 1789 and 1825. The loss of the thirteen North American colonies in 1783 had led many Englishmen to believe that all colonies would seek their independence as soon as they were able to fend for themselves. Thus the mother country could gain no continuing advantage from the expense of establishing and protecting them. This pessimistic attitude and the need to concentrate on events in France and Europe prevented making any systematic plans for the further growth of the empire after the 1780's.

Nevertheless the empire grew—in America, in Asia, in Africa, and in the oceanic islands. In each area some special circumstances contributed to British expansion. Everywhere the growth of British commerce was a stimulating factor. Even during the war years the British had plenty of goods to export. By 1815 they were sending abroad three times as much as in 1788. The war itself and the demands of the armed forces made it worthwhile for businessmen to buy expensive but more efficient machines, especially for the textile and metal industries. Raw materials were plentiful, as British blockades prevented foreign shippers from seeking continental European markets. With these advantages British industry could manufacture the best and cheapest goods in the world in sufficient quantities to fill the foreign as well as the domestic demand. Since British naval superiority kept the sea lanes of the world open to British merchant vessels and closed them to ships of enemy nations, old and new markets were readily available. Where British ships could go, laden with British goods, the British were bound to be interested in colonization.

THE BRITISH IN INDIA

The most important areas added to the empire between 1789 and 1825 were in India. Military operations during the Napoleonic Wars gave the British secure control of the whole Indian peninsula for the first time.

British India in the Late Eighteenth Century. By the end of the eighteenth century the British had been involved in India for almost two hundred years. On the last day of the sixteenth century the British East India Company, a private trading company, had received a charter granting it the monopoly of British trade in India. Like its only important rival, a French company, the British East India Company established trading posts in India (called "factories" in those days) where business could be carried on and where teas, spices, cotton and silk cloth, and other products of the East could be assembled for shipment.

When the first Europeans arrived, India had a fairly unified government under the Mughals (Moguls), Muslim conquerors who ruled from Delhi. By the late eighteenth century, however, the Mughal regime was almost powerless and India had become a chaos of virtually independent states whose princes were frequently at war among themselves. The companies began to fortify their posts and to train Indian soldiers ("sepoys"). In time the Europeans became involved in Indian politics. When the trade of a company's factory was threatened by rivalry between two native princes, the company often supported by armed force that prince most likely to be favorable to its commercial interests. When wars occurred in Europe (the War of the Austrian Succession, 1740-1748, and the Seven Years War, 1756-1763), there was serious fighting in India as well; the British with their sepoys and Indian allies warred against the French and their sepoys and allies. The Treaty of Paris of 1763, which ended the Seven Years War, altered the situation in India by preventing the French from further interference in Indian politics but leaving the British free to go on as before. Since at the same time the British East India Company acquired from a native ruler the rich province of Bengal in northeastern India, the British position in India was greatly strengthened.

Thus by 1763 the British were no longer mere traders in India. They were also the governors of the great cities of Madras, Bombay, and Calcutta, where their factories were, and of the province of Bengal. These segments of India were, it is to be noted, owned and governed not by the British government but by the British East India Company—a private trading company. Soon, however, so many complaints came from India describing the dishonesty, cruelty, and greed of company employees that the British government was forced to take a hand in Indian affairs. In 1784 Parliament set up a secretary of state to supervise the governmental and military activities of the company. This dual control of company and British government was to continue in India for three quarters of a century.

India during the Napoleonic Wars. The next great step in British-Indian relations was taken during the Napoleonic Wars, in the course of which a firm basis was laid for British control of all of India. Again a French-British war was indirectly and in a minor way fought on Indian soil.

In 1798, Napoleon began his campaign in Egypt (see page 51), apparently looking upon that land as a stepping stone to India. He encouraged Indian princes to adopt the ideas of the French Revolution and to prepare to expel the British. Tipu, the ruler of the southern Indian state of Mysore, was especially receptive to French suggestions. He was already an archenemy of the British, who in previous wars had seized some Mysore territory. To prove his devotion to France, Tipu had joined the Jacobin Club and called himself "Citizen Tipu."

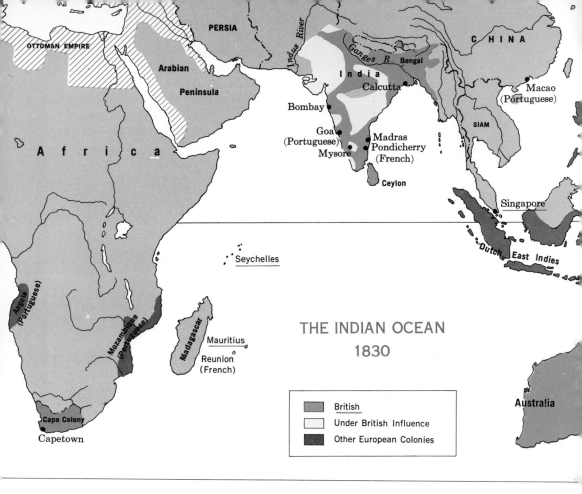

THE INDIAN OCEAN
1830

British

Under British Influence

Other European Colonies

In 1798 there arrived in India a new British governor general, Lord Wellesley, a brilliant and ambitious man, who had as his subordinate his younger brother Arthur, later to be Duke of Wellington. Noting the renewed French activity in India, Wellesley concluded that the British must take drastic action: they must either defeat their most determined enemies among the Indian princes or withdraw from the peninsula altogether. He began an energetic campaign of diplomacy and war not only against hostile princes but also against those who were too inefficient to keep order in their own realms. Under his pressure some princes voluntarily became vassals of the company; others, defeated in battle, lost their lands to the company or to its Indian allies. Tipu was killed during the fighting, and his lands were divided among his enemies.

The British government and the company directors, frightened by Wellesley's aggressiveness, recalled the governor general before his work was completed. But later successors continued his conquests, so that by 1825 Britain dominated all of India but the states along the northern border. Most of the princes who had not actually been conquered were persuaded to accept British garrisons and to follow the advice of British emissaries— "residents"—living in their courts.

The Sea Route to India. Political control of India naturally increased British-Indian trade and magnified the economic importance of India to Britain. It was, therefore, more than ever essential that the water routes between the two countries be kept open. In those days of wooden sailing vessels, the long journey around Africa required way stations where ships could stow away fresh food to prevent the ravages of the dreaded disease scurvy. At the Congress of Vienna, therefore, Castlereagh secured a number of ports of call, important among them the former Dutch Cape Colony at the southern end of Africa and the island of Mauritius in the Indian Ocean. The large tea-producing island of Ceylon off the tip of India, a convenient way station on the India-China route, also went to Britain. In 1819, to facilitate still further the trade between India and China, Britain took over the island of Singapore and later erected a great fortress there.

BRITISH EXPANSION IN OTHER AREAS

In less dramatic ways the British expanded their empire to other parts of the earth. Canada, a British possession since 1763, gained many thousands of English speaking settlers—American "Loyalists" or "Tories" who had remained loyal to the king during the Revolution and who were ill-treated in the United States. Their settlements in New Brunswick and Ontario established a British culture that has ever since flourished alongside the original French life of the colony. In 1788 the first British settlers arrived in Australia. They were convicts with their guards, for after the American Revolution minor British criminals could no longer be sent to the United States. Free British colonists followed soon on the heels of the convicts and by 1840 were numerous enough to prevent the sending of more convicts to Australia. In 1840 the British government also extended its authority over New Zealand.

Had the beginnings of these settlements been made in peacetime, they would have been disputed by the French and the Dutch. It was only because of the Napoleonic Wars that the British Empire could expand so rapidly in so many parts of the world.

◌ REVOLUTIONS IN LATIN AMERICA

While Britain was using the opportunities offered by the Napoleonic Wars to build up its commerce and its empire, revolution had spread to the Latin-American colonies of Spain, Portugal, and France.

The most important revolts were those in the Spanish colonies, beginning after 1808. Although interrupted by the Peace of Vienna and the restoration of the king of Spain to his throne, revolution continued until by 1825 all the Spanish colonies in the Western Hemisphere except Cuba and Puerto Rico were free. (See map, page 419.) This breach between Spain and most of its American colonies can be explained in part—but only in part—by the character of colonial society and by the previous relations between colonies and mother country.

SPAIN AND ITS COLONIES IN THE LATE EIGHTEENTH CENTURY

By the late eighteenth century the Spanish colonies in the Americas had achieved a remarkable development. In comparison with the United States of that day, they were populous, urban, and wealthy. The population of the single Spanish colony of Mexico was greater than that of the whole United States. Mexico City was larger than New York or Philadelphia. Two thirds of the world supply of silver came from the mines of Mexico alone.

In contrast to the United States, Spanish-American society was aristocratic and class-ridden. In the most privileged position were the "Creoles," families of pure Spanish descent who lived in luxury on the income from their gold and silver mines, their sugar plantations, and their cattle ranches. Legally, although not always in actual fact, the ownership of all land was restricted to white persons. In the numerous towns the Creoles lived as would wealthy people in Spain. Their elegant, many-roomed houses built around series of patios permitted their women to live in the seclusion approved for Spanish women of the upper classes. Servants, horses, carriages were numerous; costly furniture, tapestries, and table services were often imported from Spain.

Below the Creoles were a numerous class of "mestizos" of mixed Spanish and Indian ancestry. Some of these, artisans in the towns or overseers on plantations or in mines, occasionally rose to positions of moderate importance. Along the Caribbean coast and in a social position similar to the mestizos were people of mixed Indian and Negro or white and Negro ancestry. At the bottom of the social scale were the Indians and the Negroes, free or slave. These toiled in the fields or the mines, in conditions of near or actual slavery, living in one- or two-room huts with dirt floors and furnished with the barest necessities.

The laws prescribed many differences between classes. Only white men could attend the universities and secure the education necessary for the professions. Even differences in dress were required by law. Indian and Negro women, for example, could not dress as did women of the upper classes and were forbidden to wear gold, pearls, or silk.

The government of the Spanish colonies was autocratic. There was almost no opportunity for even Creoles to hold public office or to vote for the officials. All important officials were sent from Spain to govern autocratically in the name of the king. There was much jealousy between the "peninsular Spaniards," as the officials were called, and the Creoles. The peninsulars looked down upon the Creoles, and the Creoles resented the superiority of the peninsulars. Since the Spanish government considered the colonies to exist for the enrichment of Spain, economic life was as closely controlled as possible. The government collected a certain percentage of the yield of the rich gold and silver mines, which were legally the property of the Spanish crown. To make sure that it received its share of colonial wealth, the government also closely regulated the trade of the colonies.

The Catholic Church in the colonies was not only the chief cultural agent but also practically an arm of the government. Most education was either directly provided by the church or closely supervised by it. Many people when they died willed the church their property, the income from which was used for schools, hospitals, and charitable work. The church also exerted control over the kinds of books that might be circulated and thus over the ideas being discussed in the colonies. The government, in its turn, controlled the church through the collection of church taxes and through the appointment of bishops and other clergy. Peninsulars were likely to hold the most important church offices.

THE BEGINNING OF THE REVOLUTIONARY MOVEMENT

It was not easy for a revolutionary movement to make a beginning in Spanish America. Contact with the outside world was so carefully restricted by government and church; geographical isolation among the colonies and from other countries was so great; and the desire of many wealthy Creoles, the natural leaders of society, to keep things as they were was so strong, that any revolutionary interest would naturally be restricted to relatively few people. In the late eighteenth century, nevertheless, the ideas of the French *philosophes* (see pages 13-14) became known in Spanish America, partly because the government lightened trade restrictions somewhat and partly because rich Creoles were finding it easier to travel abroad, where they made firsthand acquaintance with European intellectual life. Interest in revolution was at first limited to a few people, mostly of the Creole class; but these few began to prepare themselves to lead possible revolts.

Equally important were events in Europe. Spain, after 1795 an ally of France, lost its fleet in the battle of Trafalgar in 1805. (See page 61.) Thereafter Spain could neither control nor defend its colonies, which were thus left to fend for themselves. When a British fleet attacked Buenos Aires in 1806 and 1807, the inhabitants organized and defended themselves with such success that the British withdrew. Spanish government was never restored in that area, although the formal independence of Argentina came some years later and a unified government much later still. After 1808, when Napoleon put his brother on the Spanish throne and the Spanish people rose in revolt against him (see page 62), royal officials in many other parts of Spanish America were overthrown and were replaced by committees of Creoles. The rebels were not, however, agreed among themselves as to whether they were seeking local self-government under the general authority of the Spanish king, or whether they wanted independence and republican government. Moreover, they represented a minority of the Creole class, many of whom opposed change. Thus even in the present countries of Venezuela and Colombia, where revolutionary movements were strongest, the restoration of Ferdinand VII to the Spanish throne in 1815 and the arrival of troops from Spain temporarily ended the revolts.

FULL-SCALE REVOLT, 1816-1824

Rebel leaders, some with more than a decade of revolutionary experience, were not ready to abandon their cause, especially when it appeared that King Ferdinand's government was to be no more liberal than before the French wars. In 1817, therefore, revolution broke out again in full force in almost all parts of Spanish America. The revolts that largely determined the outcome of the revolutionary movement took place in three areas—in modern Venezuela and Colombia; in Chile; and in Ecuador and Peru. In those areas the paramount heroes were José de San Martín and, even more important, Simón Bolívar, often called the George Washington of Latin America.

The first to win uninterrupted success was San Martín. He was the son of a Spanish army officer who had been stationed in present-day Paraguay.

The young San Martín also became an officer of the Spanish army, but he remembered the land of his birth with affection. In 1812 he returned to South America to serve in the Buenos Aires revolutionary movement. Like many others, he believed that one part of South America could not be permanently free unless the rest was also independent of Spain. Acting on this belief, he conceived the plan of freeing Chile from Spain and then moving northward to defeat the royalist forces in Peru. Without advertising his purpose, San Martín secured the governorship of a province on the east side of the Andes Mountains, where he began assembling and training troops and pack animals and collecting supplies, some of them made by the women of the province. When after three years his plans were worked out to the last detail, he performed the extraordinary feat of leading his army safely over the more than 12,000-foot Uspallata Pass into Chile, dragging portable bridges and countless other necessities with him. Within a year (1818) he had freed Chile from the royalist troops.

San Martín's ultimate purpose proved too much for his army alone. He and his army sailed to Peru; and Lima, the capital, received him with enthusiasm. But the royalist troops were well entrenched above the city; San Martín had to secure help before he could meet them.

The man who brought the necessary help was Bolívar. Since 1810 he had been a leader of revolutionary forces in present-day Venezuela and Colombia. At first he suffered many reverses and was forced to go into exile in the West Indies. Beginning in 1816, however, his efforts met with such success that by 1819 he had freed Venezuela and been elected its president. Then he led his troops over the high Andean passes in a march not unlike that of San Martín, defeating the startled Spanish in a battle that ultimately freed the whole northern part of the continent. In 1821, he was elected president of Greater Colombia (present-day Colombia, Venezuela, Panama, and Ecuador). In 1822 he appeared in Peru.

Bolívar was well suited to lead the liberation of a continent and to symbolize Spanish-American independence to the world. He was a born leader, handsome, charming, resourceful, ambitious, and capable of arousing devotion and determination in others. As the son of a wealthy Venezuelan Creole family, he had been brought up in a life of ease. He had been educated in Europe, where he met exiled Latin-American revolutionaries and became acquainted with radical European thought. On his family's estates in Venezuela he had learned to know cowboys. This was the man who met with San Martín in 1822 to discuss co-operation in the struggle for Peruvian freedom.

Simón Bolívar, Venezuelan revolutionary leader and most famous of the liberators of Latin America.

Nobody knows what passed between them, but the upshot of their talk was that San Martín put his soldiers under the command of Bolívar and left the country. Bolívar, for his part, completed the emancipation of the rest of Spanish South America by 1824.

A year or two earlier Mexico and Central America had won their independence. Thus with the exception of Canada, Alaska, the Guianas, British Honduras, and some West Indian islands, the Western Hemisphere was politically independent of Europe. (See map, page 419.)

THE INDEPENDENCE OF BRAZIL

In 1822 Brazil became independent of Portugal. When Napoleon's armies had invaded Portugal in 1807, the royal family had come to Brazil, which thus became the center of the Portuguese empire. Even during the residence of the king, however, a movement for Brazilian independence developed. In 1821 when the king returned to Portugal, leaving his son Pedro to rule Brazil, the independence movement grew. In 1822 Pedro declared the separation of Brazil from Portugal and assumed the title of Emperor Pedro I of Brazil. Thus Brazil gained by easy, peaceful means the status for which the Spanish colonies had to fight so long.

☊ THE MONROE DOCTRINE

The independence of Latin America and the wartime expansion of British commerce had an unexpected influence on the foreign policy of the United States, for those two developments helped to bring about the original statement of the Monroe Doctrine.

Both the United States and Great Britain approved the independence of the Spanish colonies. British trade with Spanish America had increased almost beyond belief since the beginning of the Napoleonic Wars. There were, however, some indications that Spain might attempt to recover the colonies. To be sure, the king was in poor position to take action, for it was the mutiny of soldiers about to be sent to the Americas that precipitated the revolution of 1820 in Spain. (See page 78.) Since 1820 the king had been so much under the control of revolutionary factions at home that he could take no initiative in America. The Prussian, Austrian, and Russian governments had expressed sympathy for Spain, but without strong navies they were powerless. But when French troops invaded Spain in 1823 and restored the king, it seemed possible that France might assist Spain in the New World. Both Britain and the United States wanted to prevent such a step. The British foreign secretary suggested that the two countries make a joint warning; but the American Secretary of State, John Quincy Adams, was always suspicious of Britain and refused any joint action. The British government then strongly warned France against helping Spain regain her colonies. In Washington, Adams encouraged President James Monroe to state what came to be called the "Monroe Doctrine."

In December, 1823, Monroe included in his annual State of the Union message to Congress certain principles that have ever since gone by his name. He warned the European powers against any interference in the Western Hemisphere, declaring that ". . . we should consider any attempt on their part to extend their system to any portion of this hemisphere as dangerous to our peace and safety." He gave assurance that the United States did not intend to intervene in the affairs of Europe or to interfere with existing European colonies in the New World; but he added that the United States would oppose any further European colonization on its side of the Atlantic.

The Monroe Doctrine has become one of the principal policies of the United States. Its formulation so early in American national life lent it an authority that has increased each time it has been restated as a basic policy in American foreign affairs. In 1823, however, it was received abroad with mixed feelings. Even the British foreign minister was irritated because the United States had acted alone. Metternich said that the whole declaration was "indecent."

ᴑ　ᴑ　ᴑ

By 1823 conservatism was no longer the most important force in Europe, although conservative governments were still in control. The new liberalism that was to characterize the next decades in western Europe could not but be encouraged by the economic development of Britain, already a country with liberal tendencies, and by the freeing of most of Latin America. Even before the Latin-American revolutions came to a successful end, the liberal forces in Europe began to win triumphs of their own.

Persons, Places, and Terms

Tipu	Mysore	Colombia
Lord Wellesley	Cape Colony	Chile
José de San Martín	Mauritius	Ecuador
Simón Bolívar	Indian Ocean	Andes Mountains
Pedro I	Ceylon	Lima
John Quincy Adams	Singapore	Brazil
James Monroe	China	
	Canada	British East
India	Australia	India Company
Delhi	New Zealand	Mughals
Bengal	Mexico City	sepoy
Madras	Caribbean Sea	bond servant
Bombay	Buenos Aires	Creole
Calcutta	Venezuela	mestizo
		Monroe Doctrine

To Master the Text

1. At the beginning of the nineteenth century, why had people in Britain lost interest in colonies? What encouraged British commerce at this time? What connection was there between the growth of commerce and further growth of the British Empire?
2. When did British trade in India first become important? How was it organized? How was India governed at the time? How did the British become involved in Indian governmental affairs? By what stages did they come to govern parts of India? When and why did the British government begin to supervise the activities of the British East India Company?

3. How did the Napoleonic Wars affect India? What did Lord Wellesley accomplish? What were the later results of his work? Why did the British East India Company send residents to live in the courts of many Indian princes?

4. How and where did Britain secure stopping places on the route to India and beyond? How was the population of Canada increased at the end of the eighteenth century? How did British settlements begin in Australia?

5. How did the people of the Spanish colonies in America differ among themselves in wealth, in social position, and in privileges? What similarities were there between Creole life and that of wealthy people in Spain?

6. What control did the Spanish government have over the colonies? Over the Catholic Church in the colonies?

7. What encouragement was given to revolution in Latin America by the spread of revolutionary ideas from Europe and North America? By the destruction of the Spanish fleet at the battle of Trafalgar? By the British attack on Buenos Aires, 1806-1807? By Napoleon's attack on Spain?

8. What experiences helped make San Martín a successful revolutionary leader? What did he accomplish? What kind of man and from what kind of background was Bolívar? What obstacles did he meet as a revolutionary leader? How much did he accomplish before he met San Martín? How much afterwards?

9. How did Brazil achieve independence?

10. What principles of American foreign policy did President Monroe state in his famous message to Congress? What was he attempting to prevent?

To Master the Map

Trace or draw a map of the world showing the areas into which British people moved or which Great Britain or the British East India Company conquered, 1789-1815. On the same map locate and name the regions of Latin America freed by San Martín; those freed by Bolívar; and Brazil.

To Interpret the Facts

1. Canada, Australia, New Zealand, Cape Colony, and India all later developed into important parts of the British Empire. How did their beginnings differ? If you had been alive in 1825, which would have seemed to you most promising? Which the least promising?

2. What proof can you find in this chapter that the Napoleonic Wars were to an extent world wars?

To Put This Chapter into a Larger Setting

1. In what ways was Great Britain the leading power in the world in 1825?

2. In what ways can Bolívar rightfully be compared with George Washington? How did he differ?

Liberalism
and
Nationalism
1821 to the 1840's

By the 1820's the almost universal fear of immediate war and revolution that had gripped Europe after 1815 had abated. People again began to discuss the need for increased popular participation in government and for greater freedom for individuals. At this time anyone advocating such reforms was called a "liberal." Liberals were found in all European countries, usually among people with a certain amount of education and leisure. In such countries as Great Britain, France, and Belgium, where the Industrial Revolution was making great strides in these years (Chapter 8), businessmen were usually liberals.

Conditions of the time encouraged liberalism. The advantages won by the middle class in France and in the countries influenced by France during the French Revolution made it easier to secure further liberal reforms. Statesmen coming to power in western Europe in the mid-1820's were of the first generation to take somewhat for granted the ideals of liberty, equality, and fraternity. They were accustomed to a greater degree of equality among classes than had existed in 1789, to greater liberty for individuals, and to the "fraternity" among citizens that resulted from the rise of national feeling. In spite of the strength of the liberal movement, however, many thoughtful, patriotic people—probably a majority of people everywhere—remained conservatives, accepting things as they had been. The liberals, therefore, had to struggle for their program, sometimes by armed force—a struggle frequently complicated in one way or another by rising nationalism.

◌ NINETEENTH-CENTURY LIBERALISM

The liberals of the early nineteenth century inherited many ideas from the eighteenth-century Enlightenment and from the American and French Revolutions. Liberal programs differed somewhat from one country to another; but liberals everywhere were critics and reformers of existing governments and societies. They placed their emphasis on the individual man instead of on such organized groups as social classes, established churches, or guilds. They were convinced that the individual person, free from the pressures and restrictions of class, church, and occupational group, making his own choices and acting in his own best interest, inevitably made the greatest possible contribution to society.

Liberals believed that governments should follow a *laissez-faire* (let-alone) policy toward their citizens, carefully protecting such civil rights of individuals as those of life, liberty, and property. To limit the autocratic powers of monarchs, liberals favored written constitutions and legislatures elected by property holders. Since liberals tended to emphasize the worldly rather than the spiritual side of life, they did not argue for established churches.

In the industrially advanced countries of western Europe, liberals accepted the economic views of a group of British writers called "classical economists." The classical economists believed they had discovered natural "economic laws" that kept economic life in good order, with prices low and the quality of goods high. A manufacturer, mine owner, or farmer who charged too high prices or produced bad goods would, so they argued, soon see his customers going elsewhere. He would have to mend his ways if he were not to be forced out of business.

One famous classical economist was the English clergyman Thomas Malthus, author of *An Essay on the Principle of Population* (1798). He held that the population was increasing faster than the food supply and that the future of the impoverished workingman was therefore gloomier than his present situation. Later economists, continuing this line of thought, argued that it was useless for employers to try to improve the lot of their workers. Better-paid workers would simply marry earlier, have more children, and thus increase the number of workingmen competing for jobs. These ironbound "economic laws" seemed always to prove that business should be let alone and that the individual industrialist should be allowed to run his affairs for his own profit. It began to seem that governments would be wise to repeal the whole body of mercantilist regulations concerning commerce, manufacturing, and labor.

It is obvious that liberal thinking would have greatest appeal to middle-class business and professional men, people often frustrated by restrictions remaining from the Old Regime. Businessmen felt themselves injured by tariffs arranged especially for the benefit of agriculture; wealthy non-nobles resented the social superiority of the aristocracy; educated middle-class people in all walks of life objected to the press censorship that prevented them from freely expressing their ideas. On the other hand, neither nobles nor the majority of the peasants were drawn toward liberalism. The Old Regime against which the liberals were protesting had especially favored the nobles. The peasants for their part could find few advantages for themselves in the liberal program, which made no provision for extending to the lower classes such privileges as the right to vote.

♙ LIBERALISM AND NATIONALISM IN ACTION

The 1820's and the 1830's provided no such historical spectacle as the French Revolution of 1789. But many less exciting events took place, proving the growing strength of liberalism in conflict with the still-powerful conservatism, and also demonstrating the increasing power of nationalism. The first of these events was the Greek War for Independence.

THE GREEK WAR FOR INDEPENDENCE, 1821-1830

The Greek War for Independence illustrates the interplay of liberalism and nationalism in European affairs. It was the first success in the long struggle of the Christian Balkan peoples for independence from the Muslim Ottoman Empire.

Liberal Greek nationalism was the direct cause of the outbreak of the war. The Greeks were the most modern of the Balkan peoples. Some of them had served the Turks as government officials; others had bought ships and amassed fortunes by carrying Austrian and Russian commerce in the Mediterranean and Black Seas. These wealthy Greeks, inspired by liberal ideas and by the love of their country, established schools where young Greeks became familiar with their ancient culture. Greeks who had been in France during the revolution returned to acquaint their kinsmen with the revolutionary ideals. A nationalist secret society similar to the Italian Carbonari (see page 78) was organized to encourage revolution.

Revolt began in 1821. Because of the universal respect for classical Greek culture, events in Greece attracted intense interest all over the western world. Even in the far-off United States, balls were held to raise money for Greek independence. The English poet Byron became a martyr by dying of a fever when he went to serve as a volunteer in the Greek army. To all liberals the Greek people seemed as much entitled to national freedom as was an individual to personal freedom.

At first the rebels were successful. Then the sultan summoned his vassal the governor of Egypt, whose troops ruthlessly suppressed the revolt and sold thousands of Greeks into slavery. The great powers, especially Russia, considered intervening. The Orthodox Russians deeply resented the hanging by the Turks of the Orthodox patriarch of Constantinople, still garbed in his ecclesiastical vestments, on Easter Sunday. The Russian government for its part longed to secure control of Constantinople and the Straits (the Bosporus and Dardanelles) in order to be able to send warships freely into and out of the Black Sea and to stop the annoying Turkish practice of delaying Russian merchant vessels. Alexander I hesitated to aid the rebels, however, fearing that the British and French would suspect his motives and oppose him—and also fearing Metternich, who maintained that the Greeks were simply lawless rebels like those recently suppressed in Spain and the Two Sicilies. (See pages 78-79.) In any case the death of Alexander in 1825 and subsequent trouble in Russia postponed action by the Russians.

The trouble in Russia was itself caused by liberalism. Alexander was to have been succeeded by his second brother, Nicholas, since the one next in age, the mentally unbalanced Constantine, had agreed to renounce the crown. In December, 1825, however, the unexpected "Decembrist Revolt" broke out. A group of aristocratic Russian army officers, familiar with liberal ideas through their experiences in western Europe during the campaigns against Napoleon, attempted to put Constantine on the throne, as it was thought that Constantine had indicated a liking for constitutions. The rebel leaders favored an elected legislature and a free press. Since Constantine loyally kept his word and refused the throne, the revolt promptly collapsed, leaving Nicholas I as tsar; but it had become clear that liberal ideas could make their way even into ultraconservative Russia.

In 1827 Russia, Britain, and France, foreseeing the total destruction of Greece, finally moved to support the Greeks against the Turks. At the Battle of Navarino, allied forces met and destroyed the Turkish fleet. Although Britain and France then withdrew, Russia pressed the attack until in 1829 the Turks promised to free Greece and to give local self-government to others of their Christian subjects, to the Serbs and to the Romanians of Wallachia and Moldavia. The powers acting together then established a constitutional monarchy for Greece. (See boundary on map, page 74.) The Greeks were the first of a long line of subject peoples to gain freedom from foreign rule.

THE "JULY REVOLUTION" OF 1830 IN FRANCE

Just after the independence of Greece was assured, a series of liberal revolts broke out in western and central Europe. The first was the "July Revolution" of 1830 in France, a decisive struggle between the liberals who wanted to preserve the Charter of 1814 (see page 75) and the conservatives who hoped to restore much of the influence enjoyed by nobles and clergy before 1789.

Charles X (king 1824-1830) determined to undo what he considered to be the intolerable injury done the nobles and clergy during the French Revolution. To lessen the influence of the middle class, he limited the right to vote. He extended the influence of the clergy over education, and he used public money to pay the nobles who had lost their lands when they were *émigrés* after 1789. Since these payments to the nobles meant reducing interest on government bonds owned by middle-class investors, there was increased bitterness between classes. In an attempt to regain popular favor, Charles sent aid to Greece in 1827, and in 1830 he began the French conquest of North Africa by dispatching a military expedition to Algeria.

Finally Charles thought that he could safely attack the Charter of 1814 and alter it to reduce still further the influence of the middle class in the government. Believing that circumstances were favorable, he dissolved a parliament that had not yet met, issued decrees further limiting the right to vote and controlling the press; and called for a new election, expecting a conservative parliament to be elected.

Street fighting in Paris during the Revolution of 1830. Rebels protect themselves behind their barricade of paving stones, boards, barrels, and wagon wheels, while government troops charge up the narrow street to attack them.

The reaction of the people was prompt and unmistakable. Liberal businessmen of Paris closed their shops and encouraged their workers to set up barricades in the narrow, crooked streets, from behind which they could fire on the king's troops. There was, however, little fighting, for within three days Charles X fled to England.

But what kind of government should replace him—another king, or, as the elderly Lafayette suggested, a republic? Most Frenchmen preferred a monarchy, especially because the king would be the popular Louis Philippe, Duke of Orleans. His background and personality recommended him. Those who valued legitimacy (see page 75) liked his family ties with the Bourbons; liberals remembered that his father had participated in the revolution. He had already taken pains to win approval from all factions and classes. At the critical moment he and Lafayette appeared together on the balcony of the Paris city hall enfolded in a great tricolor, the flag of the revolution. When they embraced each other the crowd below shouted enthusiastically. Two days later Louis Philippe was proclaimed king.

Louis Philippe, the "citizen king," takes the oath of allegiance to the Constitutional Charter after the Revolution of 1830. Because he was brought to the throne by the "July Revolution," Louis Philippe's regime has come to be called the "July Monarchy."

A slight liberalizing of the government resulted from the revolution. Property qualifications were reduced enough to double the number of voters, although they were still a small percentage of the male population. Press censorship was abolished. It was made evident that the king ruled by the will of the French people and not by the will of God. To symbolize these changes, the tricolor replaced the white flag of the Bourbons. Louis Philippe indicated his willingness to be the "Bourgeois Monarch," as he was called, by mingling freely with the people. The government of France remained under the control of the wealthy middle class.

THE BELGIAN REVOLUTION OF 1830

In the next month, August, 1830, the Belgian people revolted and established their national independence. Subjected by the Congress of Vienna to the Dutch king, the Belgians had from the first resented their connection with the Dutch Netherlands. They objected to having to use Dutch law and language, and they protested against Dutch censorship of their press.

As Catholics they were embittered by the sending of Protestant Dutch inspectors to their schools. Even the stimulation of their industry, which resulted from the union with the agricultural and commercial Dutch, did not reconcile them to Dutch rule.

For a time it looked as if Austria, Russia, and Prussia would intervene to suppress the Belgian revolt, but all three were soon threatened by revolution nearer home. Aided by France and Britain, Belgium became a separate country with a liberal monarchy, a written constitution, and a two-house legislature with the lowest voting qualifications in Europe. In 1839 all the great powers signed an agreement that guaranteed Belgian neutrality.

UNSUCCESSFUL REVOLTS, 1830-1831

No other revolts of 1830-1831 were successful. Metternich's opposition guaranteed the failure of those in Germany and Italy. A revolt in "Congress Poland" was ruthlessly suppressed by Tsar Nicholas I. Polish leaders who were unable to escape to France were exiled to Siberia. All vestiges of Polish nationality were outlawed—the constitution, the use of the Polish language, Polish universities. Poles had to act as if they were Russians. But in private they passed on to their children the Polish language and culture against the hoped-for day of Polish independence and reunion.

REFORM IN GREAT BRITAIN, 1828-1832

Although the British were spared armed revolt between 1815 and the 1840's, they experienced near-revolutionary governmental changes made by Parliament. By 1815 Britain was ripe for change. Although the rest of Europe still looked upon the government of the island as a shining example of liberalism, British citizens had in some ways less voice in their government than did the citizens of the more advanced continental countries. For example, only members of the established Church of England could hold office, including seats in Parliament. The laws against Dissenters (Methodists, Baptists, Presbyterians, and others) were not strictly enforced, but for Catholics there was no relaxation. This arrangement was particularly unjust to Catholic Ireland, whose government had been forcibly joined to that of Great Britain in 1801. The Irish people were represented only by a few elected members in the British Parliament. These had to be Anglican, although only a small Irish minority belonged to the Church of England.

Another feature of the British government needing reform was the method of representation in the House of Commons. Two members were elected from each shire (county) and two from each of a number of towns that many years before had been given the right to send members to Parliament. As there had been no redistribution of seats in Parliament for more than a century, the fast-growing industrial towns where many of the wealthy middle class lived had no representation. Old towns were still represented, although many had lost population and one had even sunk into the sea. Members representing these decaying towns were so often appointed by the local nobility that the House of Commons was to a considerable extent controlled by the aristocracy.

In the late 1820's an irrepressible movement for reform struck Great Britain. Although the more conservative Tory party was in office, many of its members were young men of liberal outlook. In 1828 without difficulty they removed the religious restriction against officeholding for Dissenters— a relatively uncontroversial step, as many Dissenters were wealthy and powerful. The repeal of the laws against Catholics—far more difficult—was largely the work of an Irish lawyer, Daniel O'Connell. A powerful speaker and a magnetic personality with an overriding hatred of all things English, O'Connell organized the Irish peasants under their priests into the Catholic Association, a mass movement supported by penny-a-month dues called "Catholic Rent." In 1829 O'Connell was elected to Parliament, but as a Catholic he was of course debarred from taking his seat. Fearing an Irish rebellion if O'Connell was not seated, Parliament repealed most laws against Catholics in both Great Britain and Ireland. Yet the universities at Oxford and Cambridge were still closed to all but Anglicans, so that young people of other branches of Christianity (and also Jews) were prevented from securing the best preparation for political life.

In 1831, when the more liberal Whig party was in power, what is now called the "First Reform Bill" was introduced in the House of Commons. This bill would transfer seats from the decayed towns to those with expanding industrial populations. The vote for town representatives would be given to every man in the town owning or occupying a house of a certain fairly high rental value. In 1832 the House of Commons passed the bill, but the House of Lords rejected it. As the people as a whole, including the workingmen, were loudly for the bill, Britain seemed on the brink of civil war. For two days rioters controlled the city of Bristol; Nottingham Castle was burned because its owner had the right to appoint members to the

House of Commons; and there were serious disorders in other places. Finally the king agreed to add enough liberal noblemen to the House of Lords so that the bill could pass. Rather than permit their social position to be cheapened by the creation of many new aristocrats, enough Lords remained away at voting time so that the measure passed. Thereafter the middle class controlled the House of Commons and entered into a partnership with the nobles, who still controlled the House of Lords.

THE LIBERAL PROGRAM OF LEGISLATION

Once liberal ministers were in power, they busied themselves with repealing old laws regulating business and commerce rather than with passing new legislation. Their belief in *laissez faire* made them want to limit the activities of government as far as possible. The most important example of this attitude was the 1846 repeal of the British "Corn Laws," which were import duties on all grain (called "corn" in England). Manufacturers had long wanted to repeal the grain duties so that their costs for labor would not be so high; but the Lords, all of them landowners, refused to pass such a bill, as it would let cheap grain into the country and thus lower the sale price of their grain. A terrible famine in Ireland in the 1840's, resulting from the potato blight, finally forced the repeal in order that grain might be imported to keep the starving Irish peasants alive. After the Corn Laws were gone, the British began to remove other import duties until Britain had almost none left.

Other countries followed this example by lowering their tariffs to some extent. In general, however, except for the abolition of slavery in the British colonies (1833) and for laws to improve education in Britain and France, the liberals were more concerned with removing the useless or harmful laws suited to a no-longer-existing society than in making new ones.

◌ CRITICS OF THE LIBERALS

Many thoughtful, informed, and idealistic people were highly critical of the liberal program. Conservatives held that the liberals were taking society too far too fast. Other critics were convinced that the program of the liberals would not produce the best life for all classes, but rather would enrich the businessmen at the expense of all others. The English clergyman Charles Kingsley put it this way: "All systems of society which favor the accumulation of capital in a few hands, which oust the masses from the soil which their forefathers possessed of old, which reduce them to the level of serfs and day-laborers, living on wages and on alms, which crush them down with debt, or in any wise degrade or enslave them, or deny them a permanent stake in the Commonwealth, are contrary to the kingdom of God which Jesus proclaimed." Since the critics of the liberals were not agreed among themselves as to remedies, a number of different alternatives to liberalism were proposed.

EFFORTS TO IMPROVE THE LOT OF THE WORKERS

Some reformers, among them some of the nobles, concentrated on securing laws to protect the workers. The nobility's outlook was generally conservative; but some among them were readier than were the liberal factory owners to attend to the needs of oppressed working people. For example, between 1833 and 1847 the Earl of Shaftesbury persuaded Parliament to limit hours for women and older children in factories to ten a day, to prohibit their employment in mines, and to prevent small children from working in textile mills.

The march of the Chartists to Parliament, London, 1848. The Chartists and the crowd of their followers, who have just left a Chartist rally, are carrying banners publicizing their six-point demand for reform of the British government.

Workers themselves began agitating for political rights, hoping to secure laws in their own favor. In 1838 a group of workingmen drew up a "People's Charter" (harking back to the Great Charter, or Magna Carta, of 1215) demanding, among other things, universal manhood suffrage, abolition of property qualifications for members of Parliament, and payment of salaries to members. Hundreds of thousands of signatures were collected to petitions to Parliament. On one occasion there was a procession two miles long carrying on poles a petition alleged to have more than 3,000,000 signatures. It had to be cut into pieces to be brought into the House of Commons. There a Whig member, the historian Thomas Babington Macaulay, expressed the view commonly held by members of the House with regard to votes for workingmen: "Universal suffrage would be fatal to all purposes for which government exists. . . . Civilization rests on the security of property. . . ." With such ideas often repeated in Parliament, it is not surprising that the Chartists, divided among themselves, had no immediate success.

SOCIALIST PLANS FOR REORGANIZING SOCIETY

Some critics of the liberals believed that it was the fundamental organization of society that brought misery to the poorest workers, and that only change from the bottom up could remove the evils under which working people lived. These "socialists" believed that the way to reform society was to abolish individual ownership of land, factories, and other means of producing goods and replace it by common ownership of these basic assets by all the people. Socialists of that day were called "Utopian" by their enemies because of their supposed dreamy idealism. They believed in the establishment of small communities in which people would live and work together, managing together whatever business they were engaged in. One Utopian Socialist, the Frenchman Louis Blanc, urged the government to set up "social workshops" to turn out goods under the direction of the workers themselves. Others wrote about or even experimented with communities of workers. For the moment the Utopians had little practical effect, but they stirred up discussion that influenced later thinkers.

RELIGIOUS OPPONENTS OF LIBERALISM

Among various religious groups there were persons who shared the socialist view that if factory owners would not improve the lot of their workers, laws should be passed to prevent the wealth of the country from finding its way so largely into the pockets of the employers. Clergymen in various countries headed movements that worked among the poor. In France Frédéric Ozanam, leader of a movement known as Social Catholicism, organized a world-wide charitable organization, the Society of St. Vincent de Paul. In England the Anglican clergyman Charles Kingsley, the best-known of the Christian Socialists, argued against the virtual enslavement of wage earners whose income could not possibly provide a decent living.

๑ ๑ ๑

The argument between the liberals and their opponents was by no means settled by the late 1840's. The liberals had succeeded in making room in governments of western Europe for middle-class people—sometimes for a middle-class majority. They had swept away much legislation suited to an earlier agricultural society but harmful to a country rapidly developing its industry (or even to a nineteenth-century agricultural country). In some places the liberals had supported the nationalist aspirations of peoples (in Greece, for example). But the opponents of the liberals were making strong points with their argument that the liberals, for all their idealism, were providing only for the middle class.

Persons, Places, and Terms

Thomas Malthus	Dardanelles	Decembrist Revolt
Lord Byron	Black Sea	July Revolution
Nicholas I	Navarino	Dissenters
Charles X	Serbia	Tory party
Louis Philippe	Wallachia	First Reform Bill
Daniel O'Connell	Moldavia	Whig party
Earl of Shaftesbury		Corn Laws
Louis Blanc	liberalism	free trade
Frédéric Ozanam	Industrial Revolution	People's Charter
Charles Kingsley	classical economists	socialists
	laissez faire	Utopian socialists
Greece	civil rights	Society of St. Vincent
Bosporus	economic laws	de Paul

To Master the Text

1. In the 1820's and later, what class of people was most likely to be liberal? In what ways, according to the liberals, could the individual best serve society? In what ways could governments best serve individuals? What theory of economics did the liberals tend to support? What

was the theory put forth by Thomas Malthus? What laws did liberals advocate repealing? What classes were most likely *not* to be liberals?

2. What factors stimulated the Greeks to revolt against the Turks in 1821? Why was there so much sympathy, the world over, for the Greeks?

3. Why did the Russians consider going to the aid of the Greeks? Before 1827, what factors kept them from doing so?

4. To what extent was the Decembrist Revolt related to the ideas and events of the French Revolution? What was the outcome of the revolt?

5. What countries finally aided Greece? Why? What was the outcome of the Greek war?

6. What train of events brought about the French Revolution of 1830? How did the new government differ from the previous one?

7. What were the reasons for, and outcome of, the Revolution of 1830 in Belgium? Where were there unsuccessful outbreaks in that year?

8. By the 1820's in Great Britain, what requirements for holding office and what provisions for representation in Parliament were no longer suited to the times? What caused limitations on office-holding to be lessened? What did the Reform Bill of 1832 provide? What two classes thereafter controlled the British government?

9. How did the repeal of the British Corn Laws illustrate liberalism in action? Who favored the repeal? Who opposed it? Why was repeal finally a necessity?

10. Among the critics of the liberals, what kinds of reform were desired by the followers of the Earl of Shaftesbury? By the Chartists? By religious reformers? By Utopian socialists?

To Interpret the Facts

1. In what ways were French and British history parallel during the years covered by this chapter? In what ways did the two countries follow quite different courses?

2. Which dissatisfied peoples or groups discussed in this chapter wanted independence from another country? A change of ruler? The extension of the right to vote? Less government interference with business? Greater financial security for the poorer citizens? Which demands seem to have been least well satisfied, and which best satisfied?

To Put This Chapter into a Larger Setting

1. Debate this proposition: The revolutions described in this chapter were continuations of the French Revolution rather than movements arising only from local conditions.

2. Which of the reforms demanded in the early nineteenth century are today so much a part of our lives that we take them quite for granted? Which demands have been forgotten?

Looking Back to 1789

Between 1789 and the 1840's the Old Regime disappeared in France. A constitution; an elected legislature; equality of all citizens before the law and in such matters as taxation; the limitation of the influence of the Catholic clergy—all these, by the 1840's the order of the day, had been unknown to the Old Regime. In Britain, Belgium, and to a lesser extent in some states of western Germany, comparable changes had taken place. In Britain the wealthy middle class had entered into partnership with the nobles as the dominant political power; in France the middle class had taken over from the nobles and the clergy. Liberal ideas had influenced all parts of the continent, even Russia and the Ottoman Empire. Could Sieyès, Lafayette, and Robespierre have returned to earth in the mid-1840's, they might well have taken satisfaction in the results of the Age of Revolution to which they had given the impetus.

But times were changing in other fields besides politics. Industrial development, growth of cities, improvement in transportation, and many other factors were transforming the traditional ways of living, and thus were creating problems that earlier liberals had not taken into account. Nationalism was injecting an unknown force into international relations. The 1840's did not mark as definite a turning point in human history as did 1789, but by the late 1840's the course of history was actually taking a new direction.

Some Questions to Answer

1. Revolutions come about because some people are dissatisfied. Try to determine to what extent the years between 1789 and the 1840's removed the dissatisfactions of (1) the French peasants, (2) the French workers in the towns, and (3) the French bourgeoisie, by answering the following questions: In 1789, what were the chief dissatisfactions of each group? In each case, which of these dissatisfactions had been removed or lessened by the 1840's? Was the total effect of these changes great enough to deserve the name "revolution"?
2. To what extent did British farmers, workers, and middle class experience the same changes in their circumstances as the similar classes in France?

3. In what countries were there important changes in the power, the wealth, and the independence of the established churches during this period? In each case state the precise change.

4. In what countries, at what times, and to what extent did the people secure increased control over their government? By the 1840's, how much control over the government was enjoyed by the nobles in France? In Great Britain? By the middle class in each country? By the peasants in each country? By the town workers in each country?

5. Make a table similar to that on page 67, but with seven columns. Label the columns *France, Great Britain, Belgium, Italy, Germany, Poland,* and *Russia.* On the left side of the table, write the following dates: 1789, 1790-1800, 1800-1810, 1810-1820, 1820-1830, 1830-1840, the 1840's. On the table, enter all the events discussed in Part I that go by the name "revolution." Is there any definition of the word "revolution" that applies to all these events?

6. Taking into account your answers to Questions 1-5, do you believe the five decades covered by Part I of this book are properly named an age of revolution? In answering this question, how have you defined the word "revolution"?

7. To what extent were relations between Europe and other parts of the world revolutionized during this period?

8. Although there has been no extended discussion in Part I of such matters as the ways of living and working, nor of the arts, nor of religion, nor of science, what sense of development and change in these realms have you gained?

9. What conditions in the Europe of the 1840's seem to you to have been most likely to produce further revolutionary change in Europe?

Using Documents as Evidence

The beginning of the French Revolution marked a significant change in human history. A whole series of many events led to the revolution. Among them was Louis XVI's calling a meeting of the Estates-General because France was nearly bankrupt and the nobles would not accept increased taxes. The Estates-General soon gave way to a National Assembly dominated by commoners. The Assembly prepared a "Declaration of the Rights of Man and the Citizen," published on August 26, 1789. A part of it follows.

DECLARATION OF THE RIGHTS
OF MAN AND THE CITIZEN

The representatives of the French people, organized as a national assembly, believing that the ignorance, neglect, or contempt of the rights of man are the sole causes of public calamities and of the corruption of governments, have determined to set forth in a solemn declaration the natural, inalienable, and sacred rights of man, in order that this declaration, being constantly before all the members of the social body, shall remind them continually of their rights and duties. . . .

Article I. Men are born and remain free and equal in rights. Social distinctions can only be founded upon the general good.

2. The aim of all political association is the preservation of the natural and imprescriptible [inalienable] rights of man. These rights are liberty, property, security, and resistance to oppression.

3. The principle of all sovereignty resides essentially in the nation. No body nor individual may exercise any authority that does not proceed directly from the nation.

4. Liberty consists in being able to do everything that injures no one else; hence the exercise of the natural rights of each man has no limits except those that assure to the other members of the society the enjoyment of the same rights. These limits can only be determined by law.

5. Law can only prohibit such actions as are hurtful to society. Nothing may be prevented that is not forbidden by law, and no one may be forced to do anything not provided for by law.

6. Law is the expression of the general will. Every citizen has a right to participate personally or through his representative in its formation. It must be the same for all, whether it protects or punishes. . . .

7. No person shall be accused, arrested, or imprisoned except in the cases and according to the forms prescribed by law. . . .

8. The law shall provide for such punishments only as are strictly and obviously necessary, and no one shall suffer punishment except it be legally inflicted in virtue of a law passed and promulgated [publicized] before the commission of the offense.

9. As all persons are held innocent until they shall have been declared guilty, if arrest shall be deemed indispensable, all severity not essential to the securing of the prisoner's person shall be severely repressed by law.

10. No one shall be disquieted on account of his . . . religious views. . . .

11. The free communication of ideas and opinions is one of the most precious of the rights of man. Every citizen may, accordingly, speak, write, and print with freedom, being responsible, however, for such abuses of this freedom as shall be defined by law.

16. A society in which the observance of the law is not assured nor the separation of powers defined has no constitution at all.

17. Property being an inviolable and sacred right, no one shall be deprived thereof except where public necessity, legally determined, shall clearly demand it, and then only on condition that the owner shall have been previously and equitably indemnified.

It is difficult to read the Declaration of the Rights of Man . . . without being aware of phrases that sound much like those in the American Declaration of Independence (1776), and the U.S. Constitution (1788) and its Bill of Rights (1791). All these documents are *primary* sources, or original sources of history. (Descriptions of them by historians are called *secondary* sources.) Locate these American documents in your classroom or school library, and then answer the following questions.

Which articles in the French Declaration most strongly resemble the Declaration of Independence? Which articles most resemble those in the Constitution? Those in the Bill of Rights? Which of the four documents being compared directly describes the structure of government to be established?

ᘛ ᘛ ᘛ

Maximilien Robespierre was the leading figure in the radical-dominated revolutionary government of France from 1792 to 1794. The Reign of Terror, which he launched in 1793, was intended to destroy enemies of the new French government and to unify France. Thousands of Frenchmen went to the guillotine. The following speech contains part of Robespierre's defense of the Reign of Terror before he himself was sentenced to death.

ROBESPIERRE DEFENDS THE REIGN OF TERROR

It has been said that terror is the instrument of a despotic government. Does yours then resemble despotism? Yes, as the sword which glitters in the hand of a hero of liberty resembles that with which the satellites of tyranny are armed! The government of a revolution is the despotism of liberty against tyranny. Is force, then, only made to protect crime? Is it not also made to strike those haughty heads which the lightning has doomed? Nature has imposed upon every being the law of self-preservation. Crime massacres innocence in order to reign, and innocence struggles with all its force in the hands of crime. Let tyranny but reign one day, and on the morrow there would not remain a single patriot. Until when will the fury of tyranny continue to be called justice, and the justice of the people, barbarity and rebellion? How tender they are to oppressors, how inexorable [unmoving] to the oppressed! Nevertheless, it is necessary that one or the other should succumb. "Indulgence for the Royalist!" exclaimed certain people. Pardon for wretches! No! Pardon for innocence, pardon for the weak, pardon for the unhappy, pardon for humanity!

One of the oldest of all sources of conflict arises from attempts to change a society and, at the same time, to unite it in dealing with external enemies. France during the Reign of Terror was at war, and a whole new army had to be organized and supported by its citizens. The nobles who had been its leaders had fled. How did Robespierre justify the terror? Can you recall other examples in history of revolutionary attempts to change or unify a society?

PART 2

Meeting of the Frankfurt Parliament, 1848, in St. Paul's Cathedral

Nationalist Europe

1840's to the 1870's

Between the 1840's and the 1870's political change continued, sometimes with violent revolution, but in a new setting. The growth of factories and the other economic changes, together known as the Industrial Revolution, were progressing at an ever-accelerating rate, touching at least indirectly the lives of people the world over. Scientific advance was altering profoundly man's view of nature and of himself.

Nationalism was the overriding political force of the time. Under its influence the Italian and German peoples, so long divided among weak, warring princes, secured single powerful governments able to take significant or even decisive parts in international affairs. At the same time, nationalist movements among the suppressed Slavic and Hungarian peoples of the Austrian Empire threatened the very existence of Habsburg rule. In Russia, where a suspicious government prevented the free exchange of ideas and the spread of information about the rest of the world, nationalism and the demand for liberal reform often appeared in the form of conspiracy.

In these changing circumstances of the mid-nineteenth century, ideas of what constituted reform also changed. Not all the demands of the earlier liberal reformers seemed worth struggling for. New needs became apparent. In the turmoil of these years, it was not easy to adjust the organization of society and government to each newly arising situation. Men of the time could recognize new needs, but many adjustments had to wait until the quieter years after 1870.

 8

The
Industrial
Revolution

1830-1870

In the years 1830 to 1870 the Industrial Revolution came of age in western Europe. Progress was greatest in Britain and Belgium, with steady if slower industrial growth in France and important beginnings elsewhere. With more factories came improved transportation and communication, more efficient methods of agriculture, more numerous large cities, and a transformed society. These developments taken together are called the "Industrial Revolution." The name is not a perfect one—the changes were not restricted to industry, and they occurred gradually rather than with revolutionary speed—but the term has been used too long to be abandoned.

During this period Great Britain's industrial leadership was undisputed. The British had adequate deposits of coal and iron, access by sea to the markets of the world, and capital—the saved-up wealth used in business to create new wealth—amassed in earlier trading ventures. Moreover, their island had been spared invasion during the Napoleonic Wars at the same time that increased wartime demands for textiles and metal products had stimulated the use of machines in factories. When the wars ended in 1815, Britain was already well in advance of its nearest industrial rival, France. With this head start the British maintained their industrial and commercial leadership of the world until well after 1870.

◌ COTTON, COAL, AND IRON

Cotton cloth, coal, and iron were the first industries to receive the full impact of the Industrial Revolution. In each case, growth was based on important developments that had already taken place in the eighteenth century.

COTTON CLOTH

In the last decades of the eighteenth century several successful cotton-spinning machines had been invented, some of them run by water power. Many of these power driven machines, too heavy and expensive for cottage use, were housed in factories near the streams that furnished the water power. The cotton industry was stimulated during the Napoleonic period by a drop in the price of the raw materials, for in 1793 the American Eli Whitney invented the cotton gin, which eliminated the once tedious task of separating the cotton seeds and fibers by hand. As cotton cloth became cheaper it grew in demand, and more manufacturers bought machines. By 1830 almost all cotton spinning in Britain was carried on by power machines in factories.

Power weaving developed more slowly. The first successful power loom for making cotton cloth was invented in 1785, but years elapsed before it was perfected and yet more years before there were power looms in quantity. Until about 1830 hand weavers were in such demand in England that immigration of Irish and Scottish weavers was encouraged. By the 1830's enough factories were equipped for power weaving so that many men who had once made a good living as weavers were out of work.

No other textile industry had the extraordinary growth of British cotton. Even in Britain the wool, silk, and linen industries continued for decades in the time-honored ways of working, which were sometimes established by law. Not until about 1870 was all British textile manufacture mechanized. In other countries the example of the British cotton industry was followed only slowly. The British Parliament forbade the export of information about the new machines or the emigration of skilled workers. France, the home of handmade luxury items, was not suited to machine methods in any case; and French peasants, often small landowners, were not interested in moving to factory towns. Although textile machinery was in use in France and also in western Germany by 1870, in both areas the greater part of the production was still by hand.

COAL AND IRON

Like cotton, the coal and iron industries had already made great strides before 1830. In Britain, by the end of the eighteenth century, three important innovations had been adopted: (1) the use of coke (coal from which impurities have been removed) in the blast furnaces where iron ore was smelted to extract the iron; (2) "puddling," a method of stirring the molten metal to remove impurities and thus produce more usable iron; and (3) passing white-hot iron bars between rollers to remove other impurities. These improvements made it possible to produce fifteen tons of superior smelted iron in the time previously required to produce one ton of iron of poorer quality. The British iron industry became the most modern in the world, and Britain produced as much coal and iron as the rest of the world put together.

Britain was also the first important producer of coal. There was increasing need for fuel for steam engines; and the early disappearance of British forests (from which had come the charcoal for smelting iron ore) created a demand for coking coal. Since British coal fields lay close to the sea, coal could be easily transported by water. Steam engines to pump water from the mines made possible deeper shafts and longer horizontal galleries. Along these galleries, with agonizing labor, women and girls dragged baskets of coal to the shafts. By 1800, however, it had become the practice to lay down metal plates (later replaced by rails) over which ponies could drag wagonloads of coal to the shaft to be lifted to the surface by steam engines. A verse of the time indicates the reaction of miners to this simple improvement:

> God bless the man wi' peace and plenty
> That first invented metal plates.
> Draw out his days to five times twenty
> Then slide him through the heavenly gates.

A further improvement was the invention in 1815 by the British chemist Sir Humphry Davy of the miner's safety lamp, which greatly reduced the danger of explosions in mines.

The development in Britain and elsewhere of coal mining and the improvement in methods of iron extracting and refining made the decades 1830-1870 truly an Iron Age—the first time in the world's history when a metal became really plentiful. British iron production was seven times as great in 1870 as it had been in 1830 and coal production more than four times as great. Booming iron-manufacturing cities had sprung up in the neighborhood of ore deposits. Iron manufacturers became the industrial giants of the day, wielding important influence in various aspects of national life. Iron was put to new uses, especially in heavy parts for the new fast-moving machines where wood and leather were not sturdy enough. Even in Britain, however, making small iron products like nails and horseshoes remained a small-scale industry.

What amounted to a second revolution in metals began in the 1850's, when the old, expensive method of making steel (iron with less than one per cent of carbon) gave way to the new, less costly Bessemer process. In the late 1860's the open-hearth process of making steel, the one most commonly used today, was invented. By 1870 the price of British steel had been cut in half, and six times as much of it was manufactured as in the 1850's. These revolutionary techniques made the period after 1870 an Age of Steel.

In time other countries revolutionized their metal industries. France was held back by limited supplies of usable iron and coking coal; even after the middle of the century, small smelters using charcoal dotted the regions where iron was available. But Belgian metal industries, after a time, aided by British

A glass factory in Pantin, France, 1862. This factory is typical of those that sprang up in several parts of Europe in the nineteenth century. While different in many respects from modern factories, it is even more unlike the small workshops of individual craftsmen, which until the Industrial Revolution had been the rule everywhere.

money and engineers, grew so rapidly that Belgium soon became the most urban and densely populated part of the continent. In the 1860's the Germans began such rapid expansion that by 1870 the German states surpassed Belgium in coal production and France in iron.

Coal, iron, and cotton are simply the prime examples of industrial development before 1870. Great improvements were also made in printing, and there were the beginnings of canning, of photography, and of the use of electricity and petroleum, to cite but a few examples. During this period, however, none of these rivaled coal, iron, and cotton, and only in these three prime fields were there large-scale businesses or anything like complete mechanization.

THE USE OF POWER AND
THE DEVELOPMENT OF ENGINEERING

The very essence of the Industrial Revolution was the development of new sources of power. Between 1830 and 1870, water wheels were rapidly being replaced by steam engines, which did not have to depend on running streams.

The steam engine was one of the most important developments of the Industrial Revolution. The idea of operating machinery by using steam, with its power to expand, was not new: steam engines had pumped water from mines in the eighteenth century. But James Watt, a Scottish instrument-maker, was the real creator of the modern steam engine. In the 1760's, when he was employed to repair a model of an older steam engine, he became interested in steam power. Later he designed a new engine that used steam far more efficiently than had the older types. He went into business, and by 1800 Watt and his partners had placed almost 500 engines in operation in mines, potteries, textile factories, and flour mills. The steam engine surpassed all previously-known sources of power in amount of energy produced, and it could be used almost anywhere.

The slowness with which the steam engine and machines of all types replaced hand methods before 1830 is explained in part by the lack of machine tools to make the new machines and the lack of engineers who knew how to design either the machine tools or the machines themselves. The first steam engines, for example, were unbelievably inefficient: their cylinders varied in diameter by as much as three eighths of an inch, so that steam escaped around the pistons. Only as mechanical engineers mastered the art of designing and building machines could the Industrial Revolution make rapid progress.

RAILROADS AND STEAMBOATS

The steady progress of industrialization was closely linked to better means of carrying goods. Without improved transportation, heavy raw materials could not have been hauled to factories, finished products to market, or food to the workers in the cities. At the same time, it was industrialization that made it possible to build railroads and steamboats.

Before 1830 there had been progress in transportation. Eighteenth-century Scottish engineers had developed much-improved road-building techniques. These methods were used in Britain to build thousands of miles of roads, over which freight could be hauled in wheeled vehicles rather than, as formerly, on the backs of pack-train mules. The London-Edinburgh stage-coach journey, once a fourteen-day trip, could by 1850 be made in forty-eight hours. In Napoleonic France, Belgium, the Dutch Netherlands, and parts of Italy the same pattern was followed; but in the German states, separated as they were politically and in some areas also by forests or low mountains, the great period of road-building did not start until after the beginning of the railroad age. There was also a fever of canal building, especially in western Europe and the United States.

The first practical application of steam power to transportation was the river steamboat, made commercially successful by the American Robert Fulton in 1807, when his boat the *Clermont* made the New York to Albany run in thirty-two hours. The speed of the steamboat and its ability to go upstream without difficulty were its great assets. By mid-century it was a familiar sight on European and American rivers. At sea, however, steam power had little use for a fairly long time. The paddle wheel (not replaced by the screw propeller until about 1850) was a poor device in ocean waters. Nor could the small ships of the day carry enough fuel for long voyages. Only in 1838 did a steamship manage to make an all-steam Atlantic crossing. Not until the 1890's were a majority of the ships at sea steamers.

The climax of the development of faster and cheaper steam transportation came with the railroad, the early history of which falls entirely within this period. Engineers had long experimented with rails over which to haul heavy freight, especially in mines, and also with the adaptation of the steam engine to locomotion on land. The first really successful combination of the two was George Stephenson's *Rocket*, which in 1830 sped over the Liverpool-Manchester line in England at the rate of thirty-one miles an hour. Immediately there began an epidemic of building short rail lines to connect places between which heavy freight was carried—or, as in Germany, to connect rivers. The first American line was laid down in 1830, the first in France in 1832, and the first in Germany in 1835. The general public was not altogether pleased. It was said that trains would terrify horses, frighten cows out of giving milk, cause soldiers to be unable to fight, and give lung trouble to passengers riding through tunnels. But the need for the railroad prevailed over fears.

By the middle of the nineteenth century the many short, scattered railroad lines began to be united into larger systems. Bessemer and open-hearth steel made possible steel rails and steel locomotives. A constant succession of inventions increased the efficiency of operation and the comfort and safety of travelers. More and more tracks were laid down—after 1860, even in backward Russia. By 1870 the British railroad system was virtually complete, and the systems of the other western countries were well on the way to their final form.

One invention of great service to the railroads, the electric telegraph, which allowed communication between moving trains and railroad officials, had many other uses in an increasingly industrial and mobile society. In 1844 Samuel F. B. Morse climaxed years of experiment by sending the famous message, "What hath God wrought," from Baltimore to Washington. By 1846 Britain had its first telegraph company, and in 1866 the Atlantic Cable, laid under the ocean, carried messages between Britain and America.

☊   NEW DEVELOPMENTS IN AGRICULTURE

Another accompaniment to industrialization, equally as important as improved transportation, was the increased productivity of agriculture, without which the fast-growing population could not have been fed nor the hungry machines supplied with raw materials.

A number of developments enabled European farmers to fulfill the new demands put upon them. New crops were widely produced during this period—notably sugar beets, which freed Europeans from their dependence on imported cane sugar, and the American white potato, once believed to be poisonous but now second to wheat among foodstuffs consumed in northern Europe. More and better wool was also produced after the importation of Spanish merino sheep into the northern countries. Greatly improved treatment of the soil was made possible by the work of chemists. The productivity of each farm worker was increased with the invention of machines pulled by animals for cutting grain (the reaper), for planting seeds, and for cultivating the planted fields. Threshing machines powered by steam also began to appear. More land could be put into cultivation after clay pipes began to be used as tile to drain marshy areas.

Although knowledge of these improved methods was available all over Europe, it was employed more extensively in some countries than others. English farmers were ready for it. Centuries before, English landlords had begun putting hedges around the common fields (previously used by all villagers) and forcing the small holders to exchange their lands so that the holdings of each tenant were consolidated in one place. The landlords had thereby already built up large estates, often of thousands of acres, which they rented out in separate farms to energetic farmers. British landlords, and often the tenants also, had capital to make the needed improvements. In consequence, English agriculture was the model for all Europe in the decades just before 1870. But agriculture did not keep pace with population in Britain. By 1850, although about half of the people were still on the land, wheat and meat were being imported in increasingly large quantities.

In a large part of the continent, systems of landholding prevented the immediate adoption of new farming methods. Until the railroads opened wider markets and there was promise of greater profits, village-type agriculture, often by farmer-owners, was the usual rule in France and western Germany. After the building of the railroads there was some change from the medieval open-field farming and some bringing together of all the holdings of single farmers—with such unequal results, especially in Germany, that the smallest holders often lost their farms altogether. Making great fields out of small ones came about slowly, however, and even today it is still possible to see German peasants cultivating their tiny strips, cutting the grain with sickles in the age-old manner, while nearby farmers with large holdings may be using the most advanced machinery. In contrast to western Germany, most of the land in the part of Prussia east of the Elbe River was in large estates owned by landlords called *Junkers*, who had the education and the capital to employ the new methods with excellent results.

◌ CHANGES IN WAYS OF LIVING

Changes in industrial production, transportation, and agriculture inevitably produced changes in ways of living. By 1870 so much had been altered in Britain and Belgium, and to some extent also in France and in parts of

A bad aspect of the Industrial Revolution: a shut-down factory in the industrial center of Manchester, England, in 1847. While the workers gather in a protest meeting (right), their worried families discuss the hardships that unemployment will undoubtedly bring.

Germany, that a man of the eighteenth century would scarcely have recognized the land he once had known.

The population of Europe was larger than it had ever been before, and it was increasing rapidly. Various influences were helping to keep more people alive. Better and more plentiful food made people more vigorous, while cheaper clothes from the textile factories and cheaper dishes from English pottery works made for greater cleanliness. Increased medical knowledge had also begun to lessen the ravages of some diseases.

Perhaps the most immediately apparent result of industrialization was the increased number and size of the cities that grew up around the factories, the mines, and the ports. Britain and Belgium had the greatest number of cities as well as the largest and most rapidly growing ones. Each of the industrial cities contained many factories ringed by the cramped and unsanitary houses of the workers. At dawn and at dusk, or in the winter darkness, workers—often women and, in the early industrial days, small children, who would accept low wages and had nimble fingers—could be seen hurrying to or from the factories. Paved streets, supplies of good water, and sewage systems were unknown. There were, of course, elegant neighborhoods where the factory owners and other business and professional people lived, but even those lacked many of the comforts of a modern city.

Two new classes of society were replacing those that had dominated the Old Regime. In the industrial cities the most numerous was that of the factory workers—"labor," as it would generally be called today, or the "working class," the "proletariat," or "proletarians." Not so numerous but far more influential was the other new class of the factory owners and managers and the lawyers, engineers, bankers, and other technically trained professional people whose services were required by businessmen. Today this class is called simply "business," "capital," "capitalists," or (omitting the enormously rich businessmen) "the middle class" or "the bourgeoisie."

In the mid-nineteenth century the middle-class businessman was likely to be in full charge of his own business. He was the "capitalist," owner of at least a considerable part of the capital required to build and operate his enterprise. Thrifty, hard-working, decisive, he took his own risks and saved his profits to expand his plant.

The factory workers, whose labor was essential to industry, enjoyed few advantages. Many of these people had left the farms of their ancestors, sometimes because the enclosure of the common lands by hedges and the redistribution of the medieval strips of land had taken their means of livelihood. In the city they were among strangers in an unknown environment. Before the adoption of laws to regulate factory hours, fourteen-hour days or longer were not unusual. Little attention was paid to the safety and comfort of the workers. The work was monotonous, as the workers simply kept the machines running and lacked any sense of creativity. There was the lurking fear of unemployment, for whenever the factory shut down for any purpose, wages of all workers stopped. In time, partly as the result of the organization of labor unions, the lot of the workers was improved, but most of the changes for the better came after 1870.

ᴏ NEW DEVELOPMENTS IN FINANCE

In all industrial countries there was a search for new ways of financing businesses that required great amounts of capital. Earlier businesses with more than one owner were partnerships. When a partnership went bankrupt and only one partner had the means to pay its debts, he had to pay all of them, even if he were utterly ruined in consequence. Small investors, therefore, could not contribute funds to partnerships without risking all of their savings. By mid-century governments were reacting to this problem by passing "limited liability" acts, symbolized in Britain by the abbreviation "Ltd." after the name of a company. In the United States similar legislation permitted partnerships to become "corporations." The corporation itself owns property and pays debts as if it were a single person. A stockholder of a bankrupt corporation loses his shares of stock, but he is not obligated to pay the entire corporate debt even if he is well able to do so. These new arrangements made it possible for businesses to grow much larger than formerly.

๑ ๑ ๑

It is not difficult to see why earlier historians used the words "Industrial Revolution" for the great changes that took place in Britain, Belgium, France, and elsewhere, beginning in the eighteenth century and developing rapidly in the years 1830-1870. There was scarcely an aspect of the national life of any of these countries that was not affected by the changes in industry, transportation, and agriculture. But it must also be remembered that the world of 1870 was not the world of today. In 1870, even in Britain and Belgium, a large percentage of the people were still on farms, and in all the other countries of the world many more than half the people were still rural. Even in Britain there was still much cottage industry. The story of the years 1830-1870 is merely one important chapter in the history of industrialization; the further mechanization of industry is still in progress today.

Persons and Terms

Eli Whitney	Industrial Revolution	turnpike
Sir Humphry Davy	capital	proletariat
James Watt	cotton gin	partnership
Robert Fulton	Bessemer process	limited liability act
George Stephenson	open-hearth process	corporation
Samuel F. B. Morse		

To Master the Text

1. List the changes that made up the Industrial Revolution.
2. What factors were responsible for Great Britain's early leadership in the Industrial Revolution? How was the growth of the British cotton industry affected by the cotton gin? By water power? By the rate at which the power loom was developed? When was British cotton manufacturing wholly mechanized? Why was the mechanization of wool and silk so much slower? How did the British government attempt to keep the secrets of machine manufacturing from being known abroad? Why were the French slower than the British to make cloth by machine?

3. What progress in coal mining and iron refining had been made in Britain before 1830? Why were the decades after 1830 "truly an Iron Age"? What inventions turned the Age of Iron into an Age of Steel? Name other countries that followed the British lead in iron and steel production. Which was the most successful? Which the least successful? Why?
4. How did the steam engine further the Industrial Revolution? Why did it come into use so slowly? What did engineers contribute to the Industrial Revolution?
5. List the varieties of mid-nineteenth century improvements in transportation. To what extent was road transportation improved? What was the particular advantage of canals? Of the steamboat? Why did ocean-going steamships replace sailing vessels so slowly? Trace the stages of development of the railroad. In what countries was it important by 1870?
6. What were the new agricultural products of this period, and why was each important? What agricultural improvements were made in methods of farming? What proof is there that in spite of improvements, British agriculture did not keep pace with population growth? What changes were made in the size of farms in Britain? In Germany?
7. How can the rapid growth of population of this era be explained?
8. Describe the early industrial cities. What classes of people lived in them? What kinds of people owned factories? How did the workers live?
9. What is a limited liability act? What was its importance?

To Interpret the Facts

1. To what extent did the development of factory industry depend on coal mining? On the steam engine? On the railroad? On improvements in agriculture? How much progress could industrialization have made without any one of these?
2. In what ways is the expression "Industrial Revolution" a poor one? What term would be more descriptive and more accurate?
3. Describe a factory town of 1870 in such a way as to show both (1) the changes in the town brought about by industrialization and (2) the differences between such a town and an industrial city of today.

To Put This Chapter into a Larger Setting

1. Compare the classes of people in a mid-nineteenth century factory town with those in France in the late eighteenth century. In each case, how many classes were there? How important was each? How were the classes differentiated from each other? In what ways did they depend on each other? In which period were class distinctions sharper?
2. Hold a class debate on this proposition: Between 1830 and 1870, the Industrial Revolution brought progress and a better life to most of the people of Britain, France, and Belgium.

9

Literature,
Art,
Science,
and Religion

The century between 1789 and the 1870's was a time of change not only in government, in the organization of society, and in industry and agriculture, but also in the arts, in science, and in religion. Poems, plays, novels, paintings, and music could not but reflect in some degree the political and economic developments of the time. On the other hand new scientific discoveries profoundly altered men's thoughts about government and society, about religion, and about man himself and his place in the universe.

⌒ THE ROMANTIC MOVEMENT

Just as the eighteenth century is often called the Age of Enlightenment or the Age of Reason (see pages 14-16), the last years of the eighteenth century and first half of the nineteenth can be called the Age of Romanticism. It is true that well into the nineteenth century, government and economics were still strongly influenced by the eighteenth-century emphasis on reason, but art and literature took a new turn. The romantic writers and artists who set the intellectual and artistic tone of the period no longer thought of the world as a great machine operated by the "natural laws" of science and society, which men could discover by employing their powers of reason. The romanticists reveled in the beauties of nature, they emphasized the importance of human emotions and intuitions, and many of them turned back to religion, toward which the *philosophes* had been indifferent. In short, the romanticists took the attitude that many other aspects of human life were as important as or more important than reason.

ROMANTIC LITERATURE

An excellent illustration of romanticism can be found in the lively literary movements well under way in Germany and Britain by 1800. In England there was a famous group of poets including William Wordsworth (1770-1850), Samuel Taylor Coleridge (1772-1834), Percy Bysshe Shelley (1792-1822), John Keats (1795-1821), and George Gordon, Lord Byron (1788-1824), who lost his life in the Greek war for independence. (See page 98.) All of them revolted against the strict rules of form that the earlier "classicists" had followed in imitation of ancient Greek and Roman writers. All protested against the eighteenth-century emphasis on reason. Their poetry reflected a close acquaintance with nature, a probing of those mysteries of life not explained by Newton's laws, and a respect for the emotions of individual men. A few lines from Wordsworth exemplify these tendencies:

> One impulse from a vernal wood
> May teach you more of man,
> Of moral evil and of good,
> Than all the sages can.

> Sweet is the lore which Nature brings;
> Our meddling intellect
> Mis-shapes the beauteous forms of things:—
> We murder to dissect.

A Scottish example of the romantic writer is Sir Walter Scott (1771-1832). A passionate reader of the ballads and romances of semi-legendary British history, he used much of that early material in long narrative poems like *The Lady of the Lake* and in novels like *Ivanhoe*, which recounted the exploits of Robin Hood and Richard the Lion-Hearted. Scott's work brought him world-wide fame; even Tsar Nicholas I of Russia read his novels aloud to the tsarina. Scott's success encouraged writers of other countries to study the legends of their own people.

In France, where romanticism did not take hold until after the defeat of Napoleon, Victor Hugo (1802-1885) is the best example of a romantic writer. In his preface to his play *Cromwell*, published in 1827, he declared that he was freeing the French theater from the "swaddling clothes" in which the earlier dramatists had wrapped it. His departures from the accepted standards of playwriting so shocked the classicist literary critics that riotous disturbances broke out between them and Hugo's romantic followers. Nothing persuaded him to abandon his crusade, however, and in such great novels as *The Hunchback of Notre Dame* he continued to display his romanticist tendencies. Hugo was also the best-known French poet of his day.

In Germany Johann Wolfgang von Goethe (1749-1832) was unquestionably the foremost writer of the time, a many-sided and long-lived genius whose influence on German literature was enormous. As a young man his own emotional experiences furnished his themes, especially for the sentimental novel *The Sorrows of Young Werther*, the hero of which, like the author himself, had a disappointment in love. All Europe grieved over the suicide of the fictional Werther—even Napoleon, who confessed that he wept as he read. Although Goethe did not remain a sentimental romanticist, his greatest work, the dramatic poem *Faust*, a philosophical work based on an old legend of an elderly scholar who sold his soul to the devil in payment for a period of renewed youth, showed many romantic attitudes. Goethe's close friend Friedrich Schiller (1759-1805), usually considered first among German dramatists, wrote stirring plays such as *William Tell*, distinguished by high ideals of personal freedom. Outstanding among the purely romantic German writers was the lyric poet Heinrich Heine (1797-1856), whose "Die Lorelei" is perhaps the best-known of German songs.

In Russia the outstanding poet of the time, and indeed in all the history of Russian literature, was Alexander Pushkin (1799-1837), a nobleman and great-grandson of Hannibal, an African slave whom Peter the Great had brought to Russia and elevated to the gentry. Pushkin was interested in the Decembrist rising, although not able to be a participant, and was for a time an ardent admirer of Byron's poetry. Like a good romanticist he glorified the natural beauty of Russia's newly acquired provinces of the Crimea and the Caucasus. His *Boris Godunov*, a tragedy based on the life of a tsar, introduced the Shakespearian type of historical drama to Russia. Pushkin's most famous work, the verse novel *Eugene Onegin*, is considered by many Russians to be the greatest work in their language.

ROMANTIC PAINTING AND MUSIC

Romantic literature was paralleled by romantic painting and music and by a Gothic revival in architecture. Eighteenth-century painting, like the literature of the time, had followed the classical rules, even to the extent of painting the portraits of living persons garbed in Roman togas. By the first years of the nineteenth century, however, a romantic revolution had been started by the British painters John Constable (1776-1837) and J. M. W. Turner (1775-1851), who specialized in painting natural scenes. Turner's truly awe-inspiring canvases represented raging storms, battles at sea, the grandeur of nature. In 1824 Constable exhibited in Paris a simple country scene called "The Haywain," a work just the opposite of Turner's, showing the quiet beauty and approachability of nature. This work encouraged French painters to rebel against classicism. Eugene Delacroix (1799-1863) became the most significant of French romantic painters. He emphasized color and movement and loved to portray exciting dramatic actions from the past in such a way as to share the emotional intensity of the situation with the beholder.

In music there were similar revolutionary innovations. Just as Paris was the painter's capital of Europe in the early nineteenth century, Germany was the musical center. There was a revival of social singing of the old German folk tunes. This kind of music, and his own genius for the creation of rare beauty out of sheer sound, inspired Franz Schubert (1797-1828) to write more than six hundred songs (Lieder in German) to be sung with piano accompaniment. Some were musical settings of poems by Goethe and Schiller. All are full of feeling and imagination. Ludwig van Beethoven (1770-1827), the greatest genius among the German composers of the day, displayed romantic tendencies in some of his works. Toward the end of the romantic period Richard Wagner (1813-1883) began to compose romantic music dramas based on legends of medieval Germany. Felix Mendelssohn (1809-1847) and Robert Schumann (1810-1856) were other important German romantic composers.

In France the most characteristically romantic composer was Hector Berlioz (1803-1869), who studied the variety and power of the orchestra as a means of conveying his romantic ideas. One of his compositions called for 465 instruments. Frédéric Chopin (1810-1849), a native of Poland but a resident of Paris his entire adult life, composed numerous romantic works for the piano.

In other artistic fields the Romantic Movement was less important. There was no true romantic style in architecture, although there was a great

"Salisbury Cathedral," a painting by John Constable, illustrates two important aspects of the Romantic Movement: enjoyment of the quiet beauty of nature, and renewed interest in the Middle Ages and their Gothic style of architecture.

interest in the study of medieval building. Some of the important structures of the past, such as the Cathedral of Notre Dame in Paris, were restored to their original form, and new buildings were erected in Gothic style, such as the largely rebuilt Houses of Parliament in England.

HISTORY IN THE ROMANTIC PERIOD

The study of history received much impetus from the romanticists. Their love of the past caused them to delve into old records. The publication just at this time of many volumes of the original documents of medieval history furnished them with much rich material. Since historians could now achieve an accuracy of fact never before possible, it was at this time that the modern scientific study of history began.

In every country there was also a new, intense interest in the legends, folklore, ancient literature, and folk music of the past. Old languages, long since unused, were revived; it sometimes became a patriotic duty to master them. This particular kind of study of the national past was especially important in divided countries like Germany and Poland or among any peoples subject to the rule of an alien state, as the Greeks had been before

1829. Among such peoples the study of history and language stirred up a loyalty to the nation and a strong sense of national unity. One interesting illustration of this kind of romantic nationalism was the publication in Germany by the brothers Jakob and Wilhelm Grimm, learned specialists in language and grammar, of the medieval German legends that are now known as *Grimms' Fairy Tales.*

THE DECLINE OF ROMANTICISM

The great period of the Romantic Movement was over by the middle of the nineteenth century. It was succeeded in literature and painting by an increased emphasis on realism. The novels of Charles Dickens (1812-1870), for example, exhibited many of the qualities of romanticism, but they also illustrated the evil conditions of English slums. Hugo's great novel *Les Miserables* is more realistic and less romantic than his earlier work. Nevertheless, the Romantic Movement remains important even today, not only for the works of art and history that it inspired but also for the influence that it still has on today's art and thought.

◌ ADVANCES IN SCIENCE

The mid-nineteenth century was a time of rapid scientific advance. Earlier scientists had collected and classified great bodies of data, from which the men of this age could draw important conclusions and set up new theories. New connections were found among the various fields of science. Especially important advances were made in the physical sciences and biology.

ASTRONOMY, CHEMISTRY, AND PHYSICS

In the fields of astronomy, chemistry, and physics, scientists were investigating both the far reaches of the universe and the smallest particles of matter. In these fields much new data was accumulated and important new theories were set forth.

It was the astronomers, using contemporary advances in mathematics, who explored nature on the grand scale, showing how in our solar system the movements of the planets, of our moon, and of the moons of Jupiter were all in accord with predictions based on Newton's theories. (See page 15.) Two astronomers, working independently, one in Paris and the other in Cambridge, England (1845), assumed that what appeared as small dis-agreements with Newton's theories were due to the omission of something in their calculations. To explain this disagreement they postulated (assumed) the existence of a previously unknown planet and roughly calculated what its orbit must be if Newton's laws were valid. In 1846 a German astronomer actually found the planet Neptune in almost the exact position calculated by his two fellow scientists. To all educated people, whether scientists or not, it now appeared that Newton's laws of motion accurately described the solar system, which could be expected to remain essentially unchanged for billions of years to come. Later scientific developments, however, have in some ways challenged the finality of Newton's theories.

Chemists and physicists were meantime investigating the minute composi-tion of matter. They founded their work on the advances made by the Frenchman Antoine Lavoisier (1743-1794), who had been guillotined dur-ing the French Revolution for acting as one of the hated royal tax collec-tors. As a result of his studies, old mistaken ideas, especially about the nature of combustion, were abandoned. Chemistry began to be based on careful measurements, which produced more exact results than had before been possible. The Englishman John Dalton (1766-1844) for the first time made a clear statement of the theory that all matter is composed of atoms and that the atoms of each chemical element (basic substance) have a definite weight. Other chemists later discovered that when the elements were listed in order of increasing atomic weight, a wider than usual difference of weight between atoms of any two neighboring elements revealed the exist-ence of some hitherto unknown element, a search for which could then be instituted. Still further understanding of the nature of matter was achieved by scientists who created in their laboratories substances that previously had only been obtainable from animals and plants. A new relationship between inorganic and living things was thus established.

Physicists interested themselves in studies of heat and energy and of the way in which heat can be converted into mechanical energy—studies neces-sitated by the development of the steam engine. They also learned a great deal about the nature of electricity, which before the nineteenth century had been little more than a scientific curiosity. By 1800 the Italian Count Alessandro Volta (1745-1827) had developed a kind of battery. From the battery it was possible, as the Frenchman André Ampère (1775-1836) sug-gested, to develop the telegraph systems of Sir Charles Wheatstone (1802-1875) in England and Samuel F. B. Morse (1791-1872) in America. Before the middle of the century Michael Faraday (1791-1867) in England had discovered the principle of the dynamo. A Scotsman, James Clerk Maxwell (1831-1879) was able to put Faraday's principles and those of other physicists into mathematical equations which, along with Newton's laws, were basic to all later work in physics and formed a major part of what has come to be called "classical physics."

DISCOVERIES AND THEORIES IN BIOLOGY

Nineteenth-century biologists, for their part, were making excellent use of the recently improved microscope to study the foundations of living matter (organisms). It became known that both plants and animals are compounded of tiny cells that are the building blocks of all organisms. Practical use was made of this knowledge by Louis Pasteur (1822-1895) in France, who discovered that some diseases of plants and animals are caused by bacteria—minute plants. Under the microscope he differentiated "good" and "bad" yeasts, which are either helpful or harmful in making beer, and "good" and "bad" ferments for making wine. He also discovered how bacteria can be killed by heat, as in the method of pasteurizing milk, and that farm animals and chickens can be protected against certain diseases by vaccination. Joseph Lister (1827-1912), an English surgeon, studied chemical methods of destroying bacteria. His work helped prevent the death of surgical patients from infections.

The most lively achievement of biology was, without doubt, the theory of the process of evolution set forth by Charles Darwin (1809-1882) in *The Origin of Species*, published in England in 1859. The book caused so violent a reaction that people can still argue about it today.

Evolution (the idea that plants and animals have, over countless years, developed or evolved from simpler forms of life) had long been discussed. For example, the Frenchman Jean Baptiste Lamarck (1744-1829) had tried to explain how evolution might take place. According to his theory, organisms acquire characteristics useful in their particular environment and lose those no longer useful, passing on the changes to later generations. Giraffes, he argued, by stretching their necks to reach for higher leaves in the trees, were able after innumerable generations to hand down longer and longer necks to their offspring; while moles, having no use for eyes, lost them. This theory of "the inheritance of acquired characteristics," although not accepted today, served to encourage the search for other explanations.

Darwin based his theory of evolution and its processes on the discoveries of thinkers in other fields and on his own experiences. Geologists, finding fossils of less developed forms of life embedded in older rocks, were declaring that the earth was older than the Bible indicated and that it and all plants and animals had developed to their present forms instead of having been created at a single time. The economist Malthus (see page 96) had pointed out that there must naturally be a struggle for survival, since all organisms, including man, tend to multiply faster than their food supply. Darwin made a five-year journey along the South American coast and in the South Seas on the surveying ship *Beagle*, developing his talent for observing, classifying, and explaining scientific data. Correspondence with Alfred Russel Wallace (1823-1913), a younger naturalist with similar ideas, convinced him that he should publish the theory he had long been maturing.

Darwin's argument ran in this way: Since more individuals of any species are born than can find food enough to survive, there is a "struggle for existence." Among the offspring of a pair of parents there are always differences, such as those in size and strength. It is natural that the weakest and least healthy will perish so that (in Darwin's words) there is "the survival of the fittest." The survivors will pass on to their children those slightly more advantageous qualities that kept them alive. By this process of "natural selection" and over the course of countless generations, a species will gradually evolve into another, more highly developed species. Darwin did not believe that men were descended from apes, but he was convinced that all animals—and human beings as well—had gradually evolved from much simpler forms of life.

Scientists were well prepared for Darwin's ideas. But to many others—those who believed literally in the story of the Creation in six ordinary days and in the population of the earth by the people and animals from Noah's ark—Darwin's arguments were shocking indeed. Nevertheless the theory of evolution, considerably modified and refined by later biologists, has long been generally accepted. The majority of educated and sincerely religious people have learned to harmonize not only evolution but also even more challenging scientific theories with their religious convictions.

⌒   DEVELOPMENTS IN RELIGION

The mid-nineteenth century was not favorable to organized religion. Country folk seeking work in the cities scarcely knew how to find a church where they would be welcome. City people could find activities and interests other than churchgoing to occupy their Sundays. But there were also some evidences of deepening religious interest. The Church of England, following the example of the Methodists, put greater emphasis on preaching. Other Anglicans put a new emphasis on the sacraments (baptism, penance, and the Eucharist, for example) and on the traditional liturgies, the outward expressions of the sacraments. Some leaders of this group, notably John Henry Newman, eventually joined the Catholic Church, and Newman became a cardinal. But others remained to foster within the Church of England this "Oxford" or "Anglo-Catholic" movement.

The first six decades of the nineteenth century were not encouraging to the papacy. For centuries rulers of important Catholic countries had appointed the bishops; the antireligious influences of the French Revolution had seemed to threaten papal influences still further. But other factors tended to increase papal power, including the patience and dignity of Pope Pius VII under Napoleon's harsh treatment, the romanticists' interest in religion, and the power given the popes by Napoleon's Concordat to approve the appointment of bishops and to remove those already in office. Thereafter French priests looked to the papacy for support against bishops, and bishops had to take into account the wishes of the popes.

The strengthened position of the papacy was revealed to the world during the pontificate of Pius IX (1846-1878). In 1864 he published the *Syllabus of Errors,* declaring it to be an error to deny the divine origin of the church, or to deny that there exists a spiritual side of life, or to declare that the state is the most important institution in the world, or that other churches have as much hold on truth as has the Catholic Church. In 1870 the First Vatican Council declared that the pope is infallible when he speaks officially (*ex cathedra*) on the beliefs of the church or morals.

These pronouncements aroused a storm of protest. Devout Protestants naturally believed them both extravagant and meaningless, as did the increasing numbers of people without religious affiliation. Non-Catholic statesmen feared that the papacy looked forward to re-establishing its medieval claims to superiority over secular governments. Liberals looked upon the *Syllabus* as opposing many necessary reforms. But time was to prove that the spiritual leadership of the papacy in the Catholic Church was being strengthened.

ᴖ ᴖ ᴖ

It was in the environment created by the Industrial Revolution, by the advance of science, by romantic art and literature, and by the changing influence of religion, that the political development of Europe continued after the mid-1840's.

Persons and Terms

William Wordsworth
Samuel Taylor
   Coleridge
Percy Bysshe Shelley
John Keats
George Gordon,
   Lord Byron
Sir Walter Scott
Victor Hugo
Johann Wolfgang
   von Goethe
Friedrich Schiller
Heinrich Heine
Alexander Pushkin
John Constable
J. M. W. Turner
Eugene Delacroix
Franz Schubert
Ludwig van
   Beethoven
Richard Wagner

Felix Mendelssohn
Robert Schumann
Hector Berlioz
Frédéric Chopin
Jakob and Wilhelm
   Grimm
Charles Dickens
Antoine Lavoisier
John Dalton
Alessandro Volta
André Ampère
Sir Charles
   Wheatstone
Michael Faraday
James Clerk Maxwell
Louis Pasteur
Joseph Lister
Charles Darwin
Jean Baptiste Lamarck
Alfred Russel Wallace
John Henry Newman

romanticism
atoms
elements
dynamo
classical physics
organisms
cells
bacteria
pasteurize
antisepsis
evolution
The Origin of Species
acquired
   characteristics
survival of the fittest
natural selection
Oxford (Anglo-
   Catholic) Movement
Syllabus of Errors
ex cathedra
infallible

To Master the Text

1. When did the romantic movement reach its height? How did the ideas of the romanticists differ from those of the eighteenth-century Enlightenment?

2. What ideas did British romantic writers have in common? What forms of literature did they write? Why did legends of the past appeal to them?

3. Which works of Hugo identified him as a romanticist? What works of Goethe, Schiller, Heine, and Pushkin contained romantic elements?

4. What romantic characteristics were present in the painting of the time? Who were among the important romantic painters? Identify the important romantic composers, and describe special characteristics of their music.

5. How did the romanticists regard history? How does architecture of the time reflect their attitude? How was the romantic attitude toward history related to nationalism?

6. By the mid-nineteenth century what new movement was replacing romanticism?

7. How had previous developments prepared the way for scientific advance in the mid-nineteenth century? What was the significance of the discovery of the planet Neptune? Did its discovery support Newton's

theories or weaken them? What was the importance of the work of Lavoisier? Of Dalton? What was known about electricity by the mid-nineteenth century? To what practical use was it being put? What is "classical physics"?

8. Describe the practical results of the work of Pasteur and Lister. On what biological knowledge were those results based?

9. What is the theory of evolution? What ideas about evolution were accepted by some scientists before the time of Darwin? What were Lamarck's theories? Describe Darwin's theory, mentioning the "struggle for existence," the "survival of the fittest," and "natural selection."

10. How did conditions of the mid-nineteenth century bring about changed attitudes toward religion among many people?

11. List the ways in which the authority of the papacy over the Catholic Church was increased after 1800. What was the purpose of the *Syllabus of Errors?* According to the First Vatican Council, when are papal pronouncements to be held infallible by Catholics? What was the attitude of non-Catholics to the doctrine of Papal Infallibility and to the *Syllabus?*

To Interpret the Facts

1. List the characteristics of romantic writing in what seems to you to be the order of their importance. For each characteristic, mention as many authors as you can in whose work it appears. Make similar lists of the characteristics of romantic painting and of romantic music. On the basis of these lists, write your own personal definition of romanticism.

2. Would you expect to find romantic literature and art developing in a period of rapid scientific advance? Why? Were the two movements entirely separate in the mid-nineteenth century, or were there any scientific aspects of the romantic movement or romantic aspects of developments in science?

3. In what ways did religion and romanticism strengthen and encourage each other during this period?

4. Between 1830 and 1870, which of the sciences discussed seem to you to have made the greatest practical contributions to the welfare of human beings? Which advanced most as a science?

To Put This Chapter into a Larger Setting

1. In class, read romantic poems, show prints of romantic paintings and sculpture, and play records of romantic music. Point out in what ways each is an example of romanticism. When possible, compare with eighteenth-century examples, pointing out the differences.

2. What explanations can you offer for the decline of interest in the ideas of the eighteenth-century Enlightenment and for the widespread influence of romanticism?

 **10**

The
Revolutions
of 1848

The year 1848 was a year of revolutions. All over Europe demands for liberal reform and for national unity or independence caused barricades to be thrown across streets, thrones to totter, and constitutions to pour from the printing presses. Even before the end of the year, however, reaction set in. By 1850 most of the revolutionary changes had disappeared. To many people of the day it seemed that, after all, nothing of real importance had occurred. To the historian, however, the events of the year have a long-term importance and furnish besides a fascinating object lesson through which to study the influence upon each other of the great forces of the time—romanticism, industrialism, socialism, and especially liberalism and nationalism.

◔ THE FRENCH REVOLUTION OF 1848

In each country where revolutions occurred, almost accidental circumstances seemed to give rise to the disturbances. The real causes must be sought in long-developing discontent among one or another class of people. A February revolt in France helped precipitate uprisings in other capitals.

THE BACKGROUND OF THE REVOLUTION IN FRANCE

By 1848 the Orleanist regime, in power since 1830, not only had lasted an unusually long time but also had kept the country in peace at home and abroad. Louis Philippe's ministers included some of the foremost men of the country. Business prosperity had been encouraged, and France had remained at the front of European intellectual and artistic life.

But many Frenchmen were dissatisfied. Workers listened to the Utopian Socialists, especially to Louis Blanc's talk about the "right to work." (See page 106.) Middle-class persons not wealthy enough to vote demanded a wider franchise and the right to join the National Guard. "Legitimists" agitated for putting the grandson of Charles X on the throne. "Bonapartists," who hoped to replace Louis Philippe with a man of their family, encouraged the growth of the "Napoleonic legend," which pictured Napoleon I as having been devoted to the interests of "the little man." The removal of Napoleon's body from St. Helena to a splendid tomb in Paris increased popular enthusiasm for Bonapartism. Almost everyone hated Louis Philippe's chief minister, the able but tactless François Guizot, who was heard to declare that France was truly a land of equality, since everyone was equally free to try to grow rich and secure the vote. Nor was there any popular enthusiasm for the king, who was often (because of his appearance) called the "crowned pear."

Depression all over Europe in the 1840's, brought on in part by bad harvests, of which the Irish potato famine (see page 104) was only one example, helped stir up discontent. Liberals and radicals increased their agitation, holding public banquets, since ordinary meetings were illegal. It was

King Louis Philippe of France: an unflattering cartoon of his day, emphasizing his likeness to a pear and indicating his unpopularity among the French people.

such a banquet—one that in the end was not even held—that brought on the French Revolution of 1848. On the morning of February 22, 1848, France was a monarchy; by the morning of February 25 the Second French Republic had been unofficially proclaimed. The people of Paris made this revolution.

THE COURSE OF THE REVOLUTION IN FRANCE, FEBRUARY TO APRIL, 1848

Fearful that a banquet scheduled for February 22 in Paris would lead to serious disorder, the French government forbade the holding of it. Although those who had planned to attend accepted the cancellation with relative calm, the working class districts were angrily aroused. In anticipation of fighting, paving stones were pried from the streets and piled into barricades, atop which were thrown wagons, trees, and anything else at hand. To restore quiet, the king immediately dismissed the unpopular Guizot, but the workers were not satisfied. Crowds gathered, and troops were called out. On February 23 shots were accidentally fired, and then more shots, until about fifty people had been killed. At night the corpses, piled into a wagon drawn by a white horse and lighted by a torch, were paraded around the city. By the morning of February 24 the people were uncontrollable. The king refused to order an armed attack on the city. The National Guard would support him only if he would promise far-reaching reforms of which he disapproved. In desperation he abdicated and fled to England. As soon as he had left his palace, the mob rushed in, some to eat the lunch prepared for royalty, others to try sitting on the throne or to help smash the royal china.

By February 24 a provisional government was in existence, including the romantic poet and liberal Alphonse de Lamartine and the socialist Louis Blanc. The presence of a man known simply as Albert the Workingman indicated that for the first time in French history there were to be working people in the government. These men refused the extremist demand that they adopt the red socialist revolutionary flag, but they were forced by the excited Parisians to set up a republic.

One step was taken toward socialism. To aid the many Paris unemployed, Louis Blanc's plan for National Workshops was put into limited practice. Far from being the co-operative factories advocated by Blanc, however, these workshops were merely groups of workers on public relief, paid a tiny wage by the government to labor in the parks and similar places.

The "Terrible June Days," Paris, 1848. Rioting employees of the disbanded National Workshops defend themselves from government troops by erecting a street barricade. The street fighting was the bloodiest that had ever been experienced in Europe.

Quite naturally the unemployed from other parts of France flocked to the capital in hopes of joining the workshops. As the cost mounted, peasants and less wealthy townspeople of the *départements* complained of paying taxes to support the near-idle of Paris.

THE ESTABLISHMENT OF THE NEW GOVERNMENT, APRIL TO DECEMBER, 1848

Meantime steps were being taken to establish a permanent government. In April, 1848, on Easter Sunday, all the men of France were permitted to vote for members of a constitutional convention called the National Assembly. Since in this election the conservative-minded peasants and townspeople were in a great majority, the members of the National Assembly proved to be far less radical than the people of Paris. Although they were willing to make France a republic, they were not ready to establish socialism.

The Assembly soon decided to close down the National Workshops. The immediate reaction of the Paris people was another uprising known as "The Terrible June Days" (June 23-26), when there occurred the fiercest street fighting yet seen in Europe. The regular troops and the bourgeois National

Guard co-operated to defeat the workers. Many of the rebels were put to death; others were sent to prison colonies overseas. The government imposed strict censorship of the press. Thus the great radical experiment of 1848 had failed, and France prepared to turn back toward a more traditional and conservative government.

The National Assembly spent the next months writing the constitution of the Second French Republic. When it was completed, this document introduced full political democracy in France for the first time. All male citizens could vote for members of the legislature and for the president, who was to have a single four-year term. The president could choose his own ministers, and thus the way was open for conflict between the legislature and the president.

In December, 1848, elections were held. By that time the French people had moved far from socialism or any other kind of radicalism. An overwhelming majority of the votes went to Prince Louis Napoleon Bonaparte, nephew of the great Napoleon and heir to the "Napoleonic legend." A monarchist was now to be president of the Second French Republic.

FROM REPUBLIC TO EMPIRE, 1848 TO 1852

Events were soon to prove that France was not yet ready for even a conservative republican government. If Louis Napoleon had been a real republican, events might have taken a different course. He was, however, determined to remain head of the state for life; and that he could do only if he persuaded the French people to restore a monarchy.

For four years he strove to secure popular support for his government. To please the Catholics, he removed restrictions on Catholic schools and sent French troops to restore the pope to Rome after a revolutionary uprising there. He won the approval of the bourgeoisie by preserving order, so that property was secure. He pleased the workingmen of Paris by limiting child labor there and by reducing the working day to twelve hours. By journeying over the country to attend local celebrations, he made himself familiar and well-liked in all parts of France.

In December, 1851, when Louis Napoleon believed that his position was strong, he seized dictatorial power by a nearly bloodless *coup d'état* and had his action confirmed by a plebiscite. He wrote a constitution similar to the one his uncle had drafted for the Consulate, outwardly democratic but concentrating all real power in his own hands. In December, 1852, a second plebiscite recognized him as Napoleon III, Emperor of the French. (Napoleon II, son of Napoleon I, had died and had never ruled.) The new government was known as the Second French Empire.

Thus the French Revolution of 1848, which had begun as a movement led by liberals and radicals, ended conservatively. A similar cycle of events marked each of the other revolutions of the year.

◠ UPRISINGS IN GERMANY

Although it was the revolution in France that set in motion the revolutions in Germany, both the aims and the course of the German revolutions were determined by conditions within the German lands.

CONDITIONS IN THE GERMAN LANDS

Germany was less advanced industrially than France. There were fewer factories and cities, fewer roads and canals. A larger percentage of the people were peasants and cottage workers. Politically, Germany was a group of thirty-eight almost independent states loosely joined in the Germanic Confederation, established by the Congress of Vienna in 1815. Austria was the dominant power in the confederation; its delegate presided over the Confederation diet at Frankfurt.

There were, nevertheless, some signs of change within Germany. Most important was the creation of the *Zollverein* (the German word for *customs union*). Before the formation of the *Zollverein*, goods passing from one small German state to another—even if only in transit to still another state—had to pay duty. A German economist of the time described the results:

> Thirty-eight customs and toll boundaries in Germany paralyze communication within and result in approximately the same effect as if every limb of the human body was tied up so as to prevent the flow of blood from one to the other. In order to carry on business between Hamburg and Austria or between Berlin and Switzerland, one must traverse 10 states, master 10 customs and toll systems and pay transit duty 10 times.

Since Prussian lands were scattered over various parts of Germany, the Prussian government attempted to ease the difficulties of commerce within its own lands by abolishing all internal duties and putting a single moderate tariff around all parts of the kingdom. Other states, especially those surrounded by Prussian territory, soon saw the advantage of joining the

Zollverein. By 1834 most of the German states (except Austria) were members, and most of Germany was thus one free-trade common market. Since by the 1840's telegraph wires were being strung between German cities and railroads were being built, not only did commerce increase but also a sense of German unity unavoidably began to develop.

There was also the beginning of a liberal movement in Germany, both among bankers and merchants, whose business activities were hampered by outmoded governmental regulation, and among professors and students in the German universities, who saw the need for freedom of press, speech, and teaching. These German liberals confronted difficulties not faced by French reformers. The Germans had neither the French experience with violent revolution nor the British experience with the gradual development of free government. Moreover, German liberals were always confused as to which they should seek first, liberalism or national unity. They had, however, thought and agitated enough to be ready to seize the opportunities for action offered by the revolutionary year 1848.

REVOLUTION IN THE SMALLER GERMAN STATES

The French revolution of February, 1848, ended the hesitation of the German liberals. There were demonstrations in those states in southern and western Germany that had been influenced by France in the Napoleonic period. Carl Schurz, then a young student at Bonn and later as an exile a distinguished citizen of the United States, wrote in his *Reminiscenses*, "The word democracy was on all tongues and many thought it a matter of course that, if the princes should try to withhold from the people the rights and liberties demanded, force would take the place of mere petition." Many princes, sensing the mood of their peoples and wishing to avoid bloodshed, yielded to such demands as those for freedom of the press and for citizens' militias like the French National Guard. They appointed liberal ministers and made promises to grant constitutions.

REVOLUTION IN PRUSSIA

Frederick William IV of Prussia also wanted to avoid bloodshed, but he did not make positive concessions soon enough. He was not the sort of man who could deal successfully with explosive situations. Full of conflicting, impractical ideas, he wanted to be a divine-right ruler, loved by his people and looked upon as their father. He was not, however, willing to make the liberal reforms that alone could satisfy his subjects.

As soon as Prussians heard of the February Revolution in France, demands for reform poured in from all parts of the kingdom. Berlin, the capital, seethed with unrest. On March 18 the frightened Frederick William finally acted, promising to grant a constitution and to encourage remaking Germany into a strong national state. Next day a crowd gathered near the palace, presumably to thank the king. The sight of so many people frightened the troops into trying to clear the area. As in Paris, accidental shots led to street fighting so violent that it could not be stopped by the soldiers. The king refused to permit the bombardment of the city. The soldiers were withdrawn from Berlin altogether, leaving Frederick William defenseless against his "dear Berliners." Next day he stood hatless in the palace courtyard while the crowd exhibited to him the bodies of those who had been killed. He agreed to the establishment of a national guard and announced that he would summon a constitutional convention. Then for greater safety he and his family left Berlin.

Like the French, the Prussian revolution soon lost its liberal character. A constitutional convention, elected by universal manhood suffrage, deliberated during the summer of 1848, listening to unending arguments between constitutional monarchists and those few members who preferred a republic. While the convention was arguing, serious disturbances in Berlin, including the seizure of the armory by a mob, so frightened property owners that conservative influences were strengthened. By November, 1848, Frederick William sensed that popular opinion had become opposed to the revolutionary movement to the extent that he could safely suspend the constitutional convention. The regular troops returned to Berlin, followed by the king.

The Berlin revolution had, however, one important consequence: an ultra-conservative constitution, devised by Frederick William himself and completed in 1850. The constitution established a legislature with a partly appointed upper house and a lower house elected by universal manhood suffrage—but in such a way that the wealthier a voter was, the more heavily his vote counted. Prussia was governed under this document until 1918.

∩ REVOLTS IN THE AUSTRIAN EMPIRE

The Austrian Empire was even more seriously threatened by revolution in 1848 than was Prussia. There were no fewer than five different revolutions: in Vienna itself, in Bohemia, in Italy, in the South Slav areas, and in Hungary —all in progress at the same time and all interacting with each other.

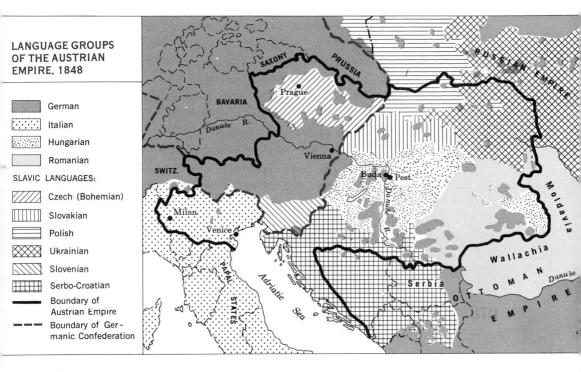

**LANGUAGE GROUPS
OF THE AUSTRIAN
EMPIRE, 1848**

German
Italian
Hungarian
Romanian
SLAVIC LANGUAGES:
Czech (Bohemian)
Slovakian
Polish
Ukrainian
Slovenian
Serbo-Croatian
Boundary of
Austrian Empire
Boundary of Ger-
manic Confederation

THE LANDS OF THE HABSBURG MONARCHY, 1848

The "ramshackle Habsburg empire" had been brought together over the
centuries by means of wars, marriages, and diplomacy. In 1848 it was united
only by the Austrian emperor and by his German-speaking officials. Most
of his subjects were Catholics, and most were agricultural workers.

Ethnically the Habsburg empire can be considered as falling into four
major parts. (See map, above.) To the north were several peoples speaking Slavic languages: Bohemians (Czechs), Slovaks, Poles, and Ruthenians
(Ukrainians), all directly subject to the emperor. South of this band of
Slavic peoples were the German Austrians to the west and the Hungarians
(Magyars), with their many Romanian subjects, to the east. Still farther
south was another band of Slavic peoples, the Serbs, Croats, and Slovenes,
collectively called the South Slavs (Yugoslavs). The westernmost South
Slavs were directly subject to the emperor, and those to the east were sub-
ject to the kingdom of Hungary, of which the emperor was, of course, king.
In northern Italy, Lombardy-Venetia, including the important cities of
Milan and Venice, belonged to the Habsburgs.

The imperial regime was incredibly inefficient, cumbersome, and old-fashioned. The chief policy was to keep all just as it had been. The Emperor Francis (emperor 1792-1835) declared, "I won't have any innovations. Let the laws be justly applied; they are good and adequate." He maintained tight censorship of the press and an elaborate system of spies, who are alleged to have opened the letters even of Metternich. To a group of teachers he said, "I do not need scholars but obedient citizens. Your task is to educate the youth in this sense. Whoever serves me must teach what I command.

The revolution in Vienna, 1848. Angry citizens have posted a placard declaring that Metternich will fall from power within a month and that Austria will soon have a constitutional government.

Those who are unable to do that or wish to bring new ideas can leave or I shall remove them." What teachers and pupils read had to be approved by the government; spies appeared at will in classrooms; students were forbidden to study abroad.

But there were changes in the Habsburg lands. Factories were springing up in Bohemia and Lombardy. Among the educated there was talk of constitutions, parliaments, trials by jury, and national guards. The subject peoples, stimulated by the German romantic movement, began to be conscious of their separate national backgrounds. Among the middle classes there was interest in a rash of dictionary-making and grammar study that was expected to enable each of the subject peoples to use its own language instead of the official German and Latin. Poles, Czechs, and Hungarians, once important nations, each looked toward a new period of national greatness.

REVOLUTION IN VIENNA

A revolt of students and workers broke out in Vienna on March 13, 1848. Emperor Ferdinand (emperor 1835-1848) was immediately forced to dismiss Metternich, the very symbol of despotic government. Ferdinand also granted a free press, a national guard, and a constitutional convention, soon elected by universal manhood suffrage. Shortly he himself fled the capital, but the convention stayed on, wrangling over questions that divided middle-class liberals from the radicals.

Meanwhile the problems of the emperor were multiplied by the outbreak of revolts in Bohemia, Italy, and Hungary and by unrest in all parts of his domains. Fortunately for him, by midsummer, 1848, his loyal generals were able to suppress the Italian and Bohemian risings. When further outbreaks occurred in Vienna in October, the Hungarian rebels sent troops to assist the Viennese. Again Ferdinand's faithful generals put down the uprising, this time aided by contingents of those South Slavs ruled by Hungary, who hated their Hungarian masters. After the October flare-up the Viennese revolt came to an end. The constitutional convention sat on until it finished its work, but the constitution it wrote was ignored.

Only two important consequences came of the Vienna revolts. Serfdom was abolished in all the Austrian lands, and the Emperor Ferdinand was replaced by his young nephew, Francis Joseph. More long-lasting were the results of the Bohemian and Italian revolts and of the independence movement in Hungary.

THE BOHEMIAN REVOLT

The importance of the short-lived Bohemian revolt was the proof it gave of the strength of Czech national feeling. A Czech historian, invited early in 1848 to Frankfurt to help write a German constitution, refused to go, saying, "I am not a German but a Bohemian, belonging to the Slav race. . . . My nation is certainly a small one, but it has always maintained its historic individuality." Hearing of the proposed Austrian constitution, Czech patriots declared that they would not be subject to it and demanded a separate constitution of their own. In June, 1848, in their capital, Prague, they assembled the first Pan-Slav Congress, with representatives of the Slavic peoples of the Habsburg empire, Russia, and the Ottoman Empire. The members had to speak German, for they had no common Slavic tongue.

The Austrian government was frightened by these developments in Bohemia, which threatened the unity of the empire. Student disorders provided an opportunity to use troops to suppress the entire Czech nationalist movement on June 17, 1848. The quick success of the soldiers was due in part to divisions among the Czechs themselves. Czech workers were more angry at their employers and Czech peasants at their landlords than either at the Habsburgs. Moreover, the large group of Germans living in Bohemia opposed Czech self-government, which would subordinate them to the Czech majority.

UPRISINGS IN ITALY

There were revolutions all over Italy in 1848, but only those in the north concerned the Habsburgs. As soon as news came of the flight of Metternich from Vienna, the people of Milan expelled the Austrian troops, Venetia declared a republic, and King Charles Albert of Sardinia made war on Austria. But the Sardinian armies were soon defeated, and Austrian authority was later re-established in Milan and Venetia. Charles Albert abdicated in favor of his son Victor Emmanuel II, who retained a constitution that his father had granted.

HUNGARY AND THE SOUTH SLAVS

It was the revolt in Hungary that caused the greatest difficulty for the Habsburgs. The Hungarians were neither Slavs nor Germans. Their kingdom had been conquered by the Turks and later by the Habsburg rulers, who became hereditary kings of the country. In the nineteenth century, Hungarians developed a romantic nationalism that glorified their own culture. They demanded the use of their vernacular Magyar in place of the official Latin; a separate tariff; and separate governmental institutions. In Lajos Kossuth, a lawyer and journalist, the more extreme Hungarian nationalists found a leader. Kossuth was a romantic and magnetic personality and one of the great popular orators of the century. An impassioned anti-Austrian speech by Kossuth had helped bring about the original Viennese uprising of March 13, 1848.

On March 15, 1848, the Hungarian diet announced a new Hungarian constitution that left Hungary within the empire but gave it almost complete self-government. Confronted with trouble everywhere in his empire, Emperor Ferdinand had no choice but to accept the constitution. The Hungarians were not able, however, to win the support of all their own people, for they were unwilling to yield to the demands of their own subject nationalities, the South Slavs and Romanians. Even when the South Slavs aided Emperor Ferdinand against Hungarian troops in October, 1848, (above, page 149), the Hungarian leaders remained blind to the need to win over their South Slav subjects.

Yet in spite of these divisions within Hungary, the emperor was unable to suppress the Hungarians even after the revolts in Vienna, Bohemia, and Italy had been put down. He withdrew his concessions and sent troops against them, but in the early months of 1849 the Hungarians won the battles. In April they set up an independent republic with Kossuth as president. The new Emperor Francis Joseph then appealed to Russia for aid. Fearful of the spread of revolt to Russia and always eager to maintain autocracy anywhere, Nicholas I sent enough troops to crush the Hungarian republic. Kossuth and other leaders fled, but a terrible punishment was meted out to those who remained. Only the emancipation of Hungarian serfs was left as a permanent result of the Hungarian upheaval. By mid-1849 the Habsburgs were again masters of the entire empire.

ᴑ THE FRANKFURT PARLIAMENT

There still remained a threat to Habsburg leadership in Germany. From the member states of the Germanic Confederation there had been elected members of an all-German National Assembly, which began meeting in Frankfurt in May, 1848, replacing the diet of the Confederation. The members, mostly professors, lawyers, and other intellectuals, managed after much debate to draft the "Fundamental Rights of the German Nation," a document similar to the French "Declaration of the Rights of Man and of the Citizen."

But before further progress could be made, the Frankfurt Parliament was confronted by the problem of Schleswig-Holstein. These were duchies, largely German in population, long ruled by the kings of Denmark. Under the influence of rising Danish nationalism, the king of Denmark attempted to strengthen the ties between his kingdom and the duchies. German nationalists protested. In the name of the Frankfurt Parliament, Prussia made a futile attack on Denmark. Not wishing to see Prussia strengthened in the Baltic, Britain and Russia encouraged the great powers to intervene. In 1852 it was decided that future kings of Denmark should inherit the duchies, but should govern them separately from Denmark.

The problem of the duchies interrupted the work of the Frankfurt Parliament, giving the Habsburgs time to restore order in their own domains and to consider means of recovering their leadership in the Germanic Confederation. The Frankfurt Parliament debated the areas to be included in the new united Germany—especially whether Austria, with its large non-German population, should be included. It was finally decided to exclude Austria, but to keep close relations with it. In March, 1849, the crown of a new liberal German monarchy was offered to Frederick William IV of Prussia. Afraid of Austria and unwilling to accept a crown offered by an elected parliament, the king refused. The parliament soon collapsed.

The Habsburg government was determined that its own leadership in Germany again be clearly recognized. When the king of Prussia attempted to organize a league of German states under his own patronage, the Habsburgs were able to force him to give up his idea. The Germanic Confederation was re-established, and Prussia promised not to form other German leagues. By 1850, the Habsburgs were again secure, not only in their own empire, but also in their traditional leadership of Germany.

⚬ ⚬ ⚬

The immediate results of the revolutions of 1848 were meager. There were new rulers in Austria, France, and Sardinia, and new constitutions in France, Sardinia, and Prussia. The serfs of the Habsburg empire had been freed. Otherwise, Europe seemed little changed after all the months of turmoil. Neither liberalism nor nationalism had made important gains. Nevertheless, to the people of the day—statesmen, intellectuals, clergymen, businessmen, workingmen, peasants—the events of these months had been

THE REVOLUTIONS OF 1848

	FRANCE	GERMANY		AUSTRIAN EMPIRE
		PRUSSIA	FRANKFURT PARLIAMENT	
1848 FEB.	Banquet prohibited Rioting in Paris Louis Philippe flees Republic proclaimed National Workshops established			
MARCH		Rioting in Berlin King Frederick William accepts demands of revolutionaries King flees Berlin	Meeting of commission to prepare for the parliament	Rioting in Vienna Metternich flees Hungarians proclaim self-government Milan expels Austrians Venetian republic established Sardinia declares war on Austria
APRIL	Constitutional convention elected			
MAY		Constitutional convention meets	The parliament meets	
JUNE	National Workshops closed Terrible June Days, June 23 26			Pan-Slav Congress meets Rioting in Prague; Austrian troops suppress riots
JULY				Austria defeats Sardinia
AUG.				Austro-Sardinian Truce
SEPT.				Yugoslavs invade Hungary
OCT				Uprising in Vienna Hungarians invade Austria Order restored in Vienna; Hungarians expelled
NOV.	Republican constitution completed	King returns to Berlin and suspends constitution written by constitutional convention		Francis Joseph becomes emperor
DEC.	Louis Napoleon Bonaparte elected president	King dissolves constitutional convention and issues his own constitution		
1849 MARCH			Frankfurt parliament completes constitution Frederick William of Prussia invited to be emperor of the Germans	Sardinia again makes war on Austria and is again defeated
APRIL			Frederick William refuses to become emperor Frankfurt parliament collapses	Hungarian republic proclaimed
AUG.				Austria, aided by Russia, defeats Hungarians Venice surrenders to Austria

a valuable education. Each group now knew which reforms were possible and what obstacles stood immovably in the way of others. In the years that followed, many of the changes sought in 1848 became realities without violent revolution. Others were abandoned forever.

Persons, Places, and Terms

François Guizot
Alphonse de
  Lamartine
Albert the
  Workingman
Louis Napoleon
  Bonaparte
  (Napoleon III)
Carl Schurz
Francis Joseph
Charles Albert
Victor Emmanuel II

Lajos Kossuth

Frankfurt
Bohemia
Prague
Schleswig
Holstein

Orleanist regime
legitimate
republic
National Workshops

Terrible June Days
democracy
Second Republic
Second Empire
Zollverein
ethnic
vernacular
Czech
Pan-Slav
Fundamental Rights
  of the German
  Nation

To Master the Text

1. In what ways was Louis Philippe's government a good one? By 1848 who was becoming dissatisfied with it? Why? How did the legend of Napoleon increase that dissatisfaction? Why was Guizot unpopular? How were public banquets connected with revolution in France in 1848?

2. How did barricades lead to the fall of the French government? What was the character of the provisional government? Why was the subsequent National Assembly less radical? What caused the "Terrible June Days," and what resulted from them? What kind of government was established in December, 1848? How long did it last? Describe the stages by which it was replaced by another form of government.

3. How did mid-nineteenth century German life differ from life in France? How did the *Zollverein* affect Germany? What other developments were having a similar effect on Germany? What two conflicting goals confronted German liberals?

4. How did the revolutionary movement affect the small German states? Trace the course of the revolution in Prussia. Describe the Prussian constitution of 1850. How much control over the government did it give to the ordinary people?

5. How many revolutions occurred in the Austrian Empire in 1848? How much unity was there in the lands governed by the Habsburgs? What ethnic groups lived within the empire and in what areas? From what weaknesses did the Habsburg government suffer?

6. Trace the course of the 1848 revolt in Vienna. What complications made it particularly difficult to suppress? How was it put down? What consequences did it leave?

7. How did nationalism affect the Bohemian revolt? Why did that revolt particularly alarm the Habsburg government? How did nationalism and divisions between classes figure in the outcome of the revolt?

8. How were the Hungarians related to the other peoples of the Austrian Empire? What brought about the uprising in Hungary? How did the Hungarian revolutionaries treat their South Slav subjects and with what consequences? How was the Hungarian revolt suppressed? What were its consequences?

9. What nationality lived in Schleswig-Holstein? What changes were proposed in its government in 1848? How was the Schleswig-Holstein question resolved? With what results?

10. What was the purpose of the Parliament of Frankfurt? What sorts of people sat in it? What actions did it take? Did it achieve its purpose? Why? By 1850 what relationship existed between Austria and Prussia?

11. Summarize the results of the revolutions of 1848.

To Master the Map

Study the map of the Austrian Empire (page 147), noting carefully where the various nationalities lived in relationship to each other. In what specific ways does the map illustrate the events and developments of the revolutions in the Habsburg lands?

To Interpret the Facts

1. Make separate lists of the demands of the revolutionaries in each center of revolution. From these lists, make a general list showing the changes that all revolutionaries believed desirable.

2. List the instances in which nationalism influenced the course of the revolutions. On the basis of this list, make a general statement concerning the importance of nationalism in the 1848 revolutions.

To Put This Chapter into a Larger Setting

1. By dividing Priscilla Robertson's book *The Revolutions of 1848: A Social History* among several members of the class, prepare a group report to be presented to the class. Each student should summarize the aspects of the chapters he has read that reveal (1) the feelings and actions of the ordinary people in 1848 and (2) the differences between ordinary daily life in 1848 and today.

2. Draw cartoons supposedly made in March, 1848, to show the feelings of the French people toward Guizot; of the Prussians toward Frederick William IV; of the Viennese students toward Metternich; and of the Hungarians toward Austria.

11

The Second Napoleonic Empire

1852-1870

The accession of Prince Louis Napoleon as Napoleon III in 1852 (see page 144) marked the beginning of an era in European history. The revolutions of 1848, although they had few concrete results, left Europe in a new mood that encouraged statesmen to adopt ruthless nationalistic methods and policies. No longer did it seem important to uphold the treaties of 1815. The acceptance of Napoleon III as emperor of France was itself an infringement of the Vienna settlement, for the peacemakers of 1815 had specifically declared that a Bonaparte could not again be permitted to occupy the French throne.

Of the three foremost statesmen of this period—Napoleon III in France, Cavour in Italy, and Bismarck in Germany—Napoleon was the first to come to power. He was the least ruthless and the least successful of the three; his policies played into the hands of the other two, who could not have achieved their own goals without him.

NAPOLEON III AND THE FRENCH PEOPLE

Napoleon III was the first important politician of modern industrializing Europe. He saw the necessity for popular approval of his policies. He realized that any successful government of his day must understand the needs both of bankers and businessmen and of the growing class of factory workers.

NAPOLEON III: THE MAN AND HIS IDEAS

Louis Napoleon had been born a prince, but he had lived the life of a conspirator. His father, King Louis of Holland, was a brother of Napoleon I, who had no legitimate children when Louis Napoleon was born in 1808 and therefore looked upon his nephews as his successors (until the birth of his own son in 1811). The fall of Napoleon I in 1814 made fugitives of many of his relatives, among them young Prince Louis Napoleon, who lived at various times in Germany, Switzerland, England, and the United States. In 1831 the prince participated in a futile uprising in Italy against the papacy; twice he led unsuccessful raids into France to seize the throne. After the second of these raids he served a prison sentence until he managed to escape. During these years his own political ideas matured.

Louis Napoleon's thinking can be summed up in words he uttered after he became president: "The name of Napoleon is in itself a whole program. It means order, authority, religion, popular welfare at home, national dignity abroad." Thus he indicated that he would try to be a genuine successor to his uncle Napoleon I. Although he understood better than had his uncle that his government must command popular support, he put order and obedience before democracy. Not himself religious, he nevertheless determined to remain, as his uncle had not, on good terms with the papacy and with the entire Catholic Church. He took far more apparent interest in the welfare of the individual citizen than had his uncle, and he always maintained that Napoleon I had also cherished the well-being of the individual Frenchman. In foreign relations Napoleon III was determined to re-establish the leading position of France in Europe, but he hoped to use peaceful means. He was genuinely interested in the rights of small nations and hoped to make France their champion.

In spite of his little beard and his waxed mustache, Louis Napoleon was not an impressive man. Queen Victoria of England, with whom he exchanged visits and who was charmed by his personality, wrote of him: "He is extremely short; but with a head and bust which ought to belong to a much taller man." Perhaps because of his long life as a conspirator and prisoner he had the habit of such absentmindedness and remoteness that he often seemed scarcely to be present on public occasions. Queen Victoria

Napoleon III. Note those qualities of his appearance often commented upon in his day: his large head, his waxed mustaches and little beard, the expressionless look of his eyes.

said he was "quiet, amiable, and easy to get on with." Another observer, who noted his friendly, good-natured smile, also spoke of a "sort of immobility of features and the almost extinct look in his eyes" and of his habit of sitting "quietly with his head on one side." Often he seemed indolent and indecisive. But none of these qualities could detract from the political good sense that was his strength.

Because no royal family of Europe would provide him a bride, he married a beautiful Spanish lady, a deeply devout Catholic. Queen Victoria described her as a "most graceful and pleasing" woman. The Emperor Napoleon and Empress Eugénie created a brilliant court that outshone those of St. Petersburg and Vienna. The Emperor, "civil and amiable" and "so full of tact," was the gracious host whose numerous delighted guests helped spread throughout Europe his reputation for charm.

THE ECONOMIC POLICIES OF NAPOLEON III

Shortly before he became emperor, Napoleon made a clear statement of his economic policies:

> We have immense uncultivated districts to bring under cultivation, roads to open, harbors to construct, rivers to render navigable, canals to finish, and our network of railways to bring to completion. . . . This is what I understand by the Empire. . . . These are

the conquests which I contemplate, and all of you who surround me, who like myself, wish the good of our common fatherland, are my soldiers.

The times were favorable to his hopes. Gold, discovered in California in 1848 and shortly thereafter in Australia, increased the money supply of the world. The resulting mild inflation raised wages as well as prices in many countries and encouraged a general feeling of optimism. The difficult beginnings of the construction of French railroads and factories and of the growth of industrial cities were already over, so that Napoleon had good foundations on which to build.

Like all countries in the process of becoming industrialized, France needed great amounts of capital. The bigger businesses of the day required more money than could be supplied by single persons or by families, no matter how wealthy. With the enthusiastic encouragement and co-opera- tion of the emperor, many new ways were found to provide this capital. Under Napoleon III France in 1863 adopted a limited liability law, enab- ling small investors to invest in large businesses without danger of losing more than the money they had paid for their shares of stock. (See page 124.) With the larger number of investors, stock exchanges became import- ant. Another device for gathering together the savings of many prosperous but not rich people was the "investment bank," the most famous of which, the *Crédit Mobilier*, sold its shares to individuals and invested the money in railroads, harbor facilities, gas works, and the like. A land bank was established to secure funds for improving agriculture.

One of Napoleon's favorite policies was lowering tariffs by means of trade treaties with Britain, the German *Zollverein*, and others. He argued that French iron mills could in consequence buy cheaper pig iron and French textile mills cheaper yarn, while French producers of wine and luxury goods would be better able to sell their wares abroad. He partic- ularly desired a brisk trade with Britain, whose political alliance he was seeking. This tariff policy was not entirely popular with the French people, for influx into France of cheap foreign goods proved harmful to certain manufacturers.

In general, however, France prospered under Napoleon's government. In 1848 there had been about 2,000 miles of railroad; by 1870 there were some 11,000 miles. The fifty-five small railway companies of the late 1840's were by 1870 consolidated into sixteen large ones, all united in a great sys- tem centered on Paris. Locomotives and railway cars were built in quantity, terminals were constructed, iron rails replaced those made of wood. At sea, iron ships were replacing wooden ones. A French company dug the Suez Canal and opened it to world commerce in 1869. In such ways as these, France, encouraged by its emperor, kept abreast of the industrial world.

Napoleon also interested himself in the problems of labor and agriculture, although with less enthusiasm than he bestowed on industry and transportation. The growth of industry offered opportunities for employment. In Paris Napoleon provided work by remaking the whole city, widening and straightening the little medieval streets previously so convenient for barricades, erecting handsome public buildings like the Opéra and the spacious railway stations, and providing such public services as an improved sewer system. By 1864 he was willing to permit labor unions a limited right to strike. To encourage agriculture he saw that swamps were drained, that agricultural societies were established and model farms set up. In such activities, as in his encouragement of banking and his remodeling of Paris, he used public money for the public good and thus gained for himself the reputation of being a "socialist Caesar."

NAPOLEON III'S GOVERNMENT

Napoleon was able to influence these many aspects of French life in part because of his firm hold on the government. Until 1860 his regime was deservedly called the "despotic empire." It is true that the legislature provided for in the constitution of 1852 was elected by universal manhood suffrage, but the elections were far from free. An official list of candidates was provided, for whom all government workers were forced to vote. Obstacles were put in the way of nonofficial candidates: they could not hold political meetings and were required to use a special kind of paper for their campaign posters. The legislature itself could only vote, with very little discussion, on matters presented to it by the emperor's council of state. Debates in the legislature were not published, and few political views contrary to the government could appear in the tightly censored press. The emperor carried on the real business of government with little interference or criticism from any source. Nonetheless the general satisfaction with his accomplishments was such that for the first decade of his reign he did not encounter serious opposition.

Beginning with 1860, however, those who felt themselves injured by one or another of his policies grew more restless. Probably motivated in part by a genuine desire to grant more liberty to his subjects, Napoleon began to allow a degree of popular participation in the government, so that the last ten years of his reign are called the "liberal empire." But by the mid-1860's the successful days of the empire were over. Napoleon was an increasingly old and sick man, his colonial and foreign policies were beginning to backfire, and the French people found themselves facing serious foreign dangers.

☾ NAPOLEON'S COLONIAL POLICY

One of the achievements of Napoleon's reign was the extension and development of the French colonial empire. He concerned himself actively with Algeria, visiting it twice and becoming intensely interested in the people and their culture. Meantime his generals and officials were extending the influence of France elsewhere, building the port of Dakar, important for the prosperity of French Senegal in West Africa, and creating the naval base of Obok on the Gulf of Aden at the south end of the Red Sea. French troops joined with British to force the Chinese government to sign the Treaty of Peking (1860), which opened Chinese ports to European commerce and permitted Europeans to go into the interior of China to trade. To open southeastern China to French trade, French troops landed in Saigon in modern South Vietnam. Their avowed purpose was to avenge the death of French missionaries, but they remained to lay the basis for the French colony of Indochina, up the rivers of which traders could journey toward the interior of China. Other French expeditions occupied islands in the far Pacific, the most important of which was New Caledonia.

The most extensive of Napoleon's colonial ventures ended in defeat and tragedy. In 1861, the first year of the American Civil War, a French-British-Spanish expedition went into Mexico to overthrow the newly established government of Benito Juarez, which had repudiated the debts of its predecessor and was taking strong measures against the Catholic Church and its properties. When their demands had been satisfied, the British and Spanish withdrew; but Napoleon went ahead with plans to transform Mexico into a French satellite with the Austrian Archduke Maxmilian as emperor. Besides hoping to build a new French empire, Napoleon apparently believed that his Mexican policy would satisfy French Catholics, whom he had offended in other ways, and would help French businessmen. Maximilian was unpopular with the Mexicans, however, and had to be supported by French troops. Moreover, when the American Civil War was over, the American government protested that his presence in Mexico was an infringement of the Monroe Doctrine. Not wishing trouble with the United States, Napoleon withdrew his soldiers. The Mexicans executed the unfortunate Maximilian. Juarez returned to power, resumed his attack on the Catholic Church, and canceled all the contracts recently made with the French businessmen. The Mexican affair simply increased the dissatisfaction of Catholics and business people with Napoleon's government.

⟳ NAPOLEON'S FOREIGN POLICY

When Prince Louis Napoleon became president of the Second French Republic, and later when he became emperor, European international relations were as much affected as were French politics. Other governments, noting the importance of the Bonaparte name in the French elections of 1848, feared that his policies would parallel those of his warlike uncle. Although Napoleon protested that "the Empire means peace," his two great ambitions—to restore France to the position of leadership it had enjoyed under the first Napoleon and to aid in the freeing of subject nationalities— both contained within themselves the seeds of war. Thus his rise to power opened a period of restlessness in European international relations that contrasted with the time between 1815 and 1848, when there had been no wars among the European great powers. The first significant episode in this period of restlessness was the Crimean War. Napoleon had only a small part in provoking it, but he took an active part in the war itself and used it to further his own purposes.

THE CRIMEAN WAR, 1853-1856

The Crimean War was related to some of the great problems of nineteenth-century Europe, but its immediate cause was a series of incidents so trivial that it almost seemed to come about by accident.

Origins of the War. History and the map explain the origins of the war. By the nineteenth century the Ottoman Empire, once the terror of Europe, was in its second century of decline. It had long since lost Hungary to the Austrian Habsburgs and the north coast of the Black Sea to Russia. In 1830 Greece had won its independence. By the 1840's it was being referred to as the "sick man of Europe"; and the great powers, anticipating its complete collapse, became rivals for its territory.

THE CRIMEAN
WAR
1853-1856

Russia, because of its geographical position, was the country most interested in the fate of the Ottoman Empire. The Straits (the Bosporus and the Dardanelles), controlled by the Ottoman Turks, were the only route from the ports of southern Russia to the Mediterranean. Ottoman officials often delayed Russian merchant ships; and since international agreements closed the Straits to all but Ottoman warships, the Russians could not send their Black Sea fleet to protect their Mediterranean commerce. Thus Russia was eager to open the Straits to its navy; but at the same time it hoped to keep them closed to other navies, so that other powers could not invade the Black Sea. Naturally other powers opposed such an arrangement, which would permit Russia to attack Mediterranean commerce; to threaten an important British route to India; and to strengthen its influence in the Balkan Peninsula, the neighbor of Austria.

By the 1840's Tsar Nicholas I was convinced that the collapse of the Ottoman Empire was near and that he must act soon if Russian ends were to be achieved. He expected support from Francis Joseph of Austria, to whose aid he had gone in 1849 at the time of the Hungarian revolt. (See page 151.) He also interpreted some vague words of the British government as a promise of collaboration.

In the late 1840's Nicholas saw an opportunity to establish a kind of Russian protectorate over Turkey. President Louis Napoleon Bonaparte, seeking ways of pleasing the French Catholic peasants on whose support he depended, demanded that the Ottoman sultan put certain places in Palestine connected with the life of Jesus under Catholic control. These Holy Places, although formerly in Catholic charge, had been controlled for some time by Orthodox monks. Nicholas, hoping by doing so to increase his influence within the Ottoman Empire, urged the sultan to refuse. The Holy Places controversy was soon settled by a compromise suggested by the British ambassador in Constantinople. But Nicholas, still seeking to gain an advantage from the controversy, made an outright demand that he be considered protector of all Ottoman subjects of the Orthodox faith—the vast majority in the European part of the Ottoman lands. The British ambassador persuaded the sultan to refuse this demand. In reply, Nicholas sent Russian troops into the Ottoman principalities of Moldavia and Wallachia (modern Romania). The sultan promptly declared war on Russia.

The Course of the War. No other power supported Russia. The Austrians did not want Russian troops to remain in the Romanian principalities, which bordered on Hungary. In Britain anti-Russian feeling grew so intense that when the Russian navy destroyed an Ottoman squadron in the Black Sea— an ordinary act of war—British newspapers referred to the event as the "massacre of Sinope." Tension heightened until Britain declared war on Russia in March, 1854. Napoleon III did likewise, hoping to cement an alliance with Britain and to secure glory for his regime. Austria remained neutral.

The war itself was an inglorious affair, centering about the Russian fortress of Sevastopol in the Crimea—whence the name of the war—which finally fell to an allied siege in September, 1855. The years of peace before the war had seriously weakened the allied armies and disrupted many of their services. The number of sick and wounded soldiers in the hospitals organized by the famous nurse Florence Nightingale actually posed a greater problem than did the enemy on the battlefield. Diplomacy was often more

A British military hospital in the Crimea during the Crimean War. The total inadequacy of the care is starkly clear: some of the wounded have no beds, and the body of one who has died has not been taken away. The efforts of Florence Nightingale to relieve such conditions were to lead to major reforms in military hospital procedures.

important than the fighting. During the entire course of the war, allied diplomats struggled to bring Austria into their alliance and at the same time to arrive at some basis for peace with Russia. The Austrians secured the withdrawal of the Russians from the principalities, but did not join in the fighting. A new and unexpected ally appeared, however, when Sardinia sent troops to fight beside the British, French, and Turks. Nicholas I died in 1855, and after the fall of Sevastopol his successor, Alexander II, was willing to yield to the demands of the allies and make peace.

The Peace of Paris, 1856. The peace conference to conclude the war was held in Paris in the spring of 1856. This congress was in some ways the pinnacle of Napoleon III's reign. Not only did he preside over a great international conclave, but during the course of it his son, the prince imperial, was born, and thus the continuity of his dynasty seemed assured. He could well believe that he was on the way to restoring French leadership in Europe.

The terms of peace were a serious reverse for Russia. There was to be no Russian protectorate over the Ottoman Empire, and the Ottoman Empire was for the first time to be considered a great power, a member of the

Concert of Europe. The Russians could no longer intervene in the Romanian principalities. Since the Black Sea was to be neutralized, they could not keep warships in it nor fortify the coast. The mouths of the Danube were surrendered by Russia to the Ottoman Empire.

The long-range consequences of the Crimean War did not enhance the likelihood of continued European peace. Defeated Russia was now added to France as a country desiring to upset existing treaty arrangements.

NAPOLEON AND THE SUPPRESSED NATIONALITIES

Almost as soon as the Crimean War and the Paris congress were successfully concluded, Napoleon III embarked upon a second phase of his foreign policy. He dreamed of reorganizing Europe on the basis of the right of all nationalities to be governed as they wished, so that the continent would be a kind of federation of satisfied nations.

Romania. At the Congress of Paris in 1856, Napoleon had encouraged granting semi-independence to the two Romanian principalities, Wallachia and Moldavia, the latter of which controlled the mouths of the Danube. In 1858 at his urging the two principalities were permitted to elect their own parliaments and also a prince for each. The peoples of the two provinces, descendants of ancient Roman settlers and speaking a language derived from Latin, were eager to become united. They elected the same prince. Napoleon persuaded the powers to permit this infringement to the original arrangement. In 1866 Romania became a self-governing principality with a constitution patterned on that of Belgium and with a German prince, Charles of Hohenzollern-Sigmaringen, as ruler under the overlordship of the sultan.

Italy. In January, 1858, as Napoleon and Eugénie were entering the Opera, shots were fired at them by conspirators led by the Italian Felice Orsini. The royal pair were not harmed, although others were injured and several killed. Orsini was tried and condemned to death, but before his execution a letter of his was read in court appealing to Napoleon to secure the independence of the Italian people. Napoleon was much shaken by this episode. His sympathy for Italian national aspirations was deepened. Within a year he had yielded to the pleas of the Italian statesman Camillo Cavour to go to war with Austria in behalf of the Italian kingdom of Sardinia. The story of the Italian war belongs to the history of Italy (Chapter 12), but indirectly it brought France the only European territories acquired by Napoleon III: Nice and Savoy, annexed in 1860.

Germany. In the middle 1860's the most important international event was the transformation of the northern part of the Germanic Confederation into the more closely united North German Confederation. (Chapter 13.) Napoleon could not be entirely sympathetic with this particular nationalist development, although he would not have opposed the movement if he could somehow have strengthened France by acquiring territories along her German border. In 1870, however, the Franco-Prussian War broke out; and before the year was over Napoleon had been taken prisoner, his armies had been defeated, and his regime destroyed; he himself followed many other royal exiles to England. Thus the force of nationalism—German nationalism —destroyed the power of the champion of nationalities, Napoleon III.

ᴏ ᴏ ᴏ

The reign of Napoleon III strengthened France economically and as a colonial power, but failed to make it again the leading country on the continent. Indeed, Napoleon's policies opened the way to two other adventurers, Cavour and Bismarck, whose careers, even more eventful than his own, helped reduce the relative importance of France in Europe.

Persons, Places, and Terms

Eugénie	Obok	Sinope
Benito Juarez	Gulf of Aden	Crimea
Maximilian	Indochina	Sevastopol
Florence Nightingale	New Caledonia	Danube River
Alexander II	Constantinople	
Felice Orsini	Balkan Peninsula	investment bank
	Romanian	Ottoman Turks
Senegal	Principalities	Holy Places

To Master the Text

1. What was the background of Napoleon III? How was he related to Napoleon I? Explain the five points of his program. How did his personality affect others?
2. How did Napoleon describe the goals of his economic plans for France? What economic factors helped his program at the beginning of his reign? Summarize his economic policies. What were their effects on industry? On transportation? On labor? On agriculture? On the city of Paris? On Napoleon's popularity?

3. How did Napoleon attempt to preserve the appearance of democracy? How did he control the elections? The legislature? How popular was his government before 1860? After 1860? What changes did he make in the government after 1860?

4. Where were French colonies enlarged or new ones established during Napoleon's reign? What did he attempt in Mexico? With what results?

5. What was the condition of the Ottoman Empire in the late 1840's? What did Russia seek in the Ottoman Empire? Why? What governments opposed the Russian goal? Why, in each case?

6. What were the Holy Places? Who started the controversy over them? What demands did he make, and for what reason? Who came in on the other side of the controversy? With what demands? Why? How was the controversy ended? What further developments led to war? Who entered the war, and for what reasons?

7. Why is the military side of the war described as "inglorious"? What part in the war was played by Austria? By Sardinia? By Florence Nightingale? By Alexander II? What were the provisions of the Peace of Paris? How did they affect Russian interests?

8. What was Napoleon's attitude toward suppressed nationalities? What developments did he encourage in this regard?

To Interpret the Facts

1. What is meant by the term "socialist Caesar," often used to describe Napoleon III? Did he deserve to be called a Caesar? Was he a socialist in the manner of Louis Blanc? To what extent was he a socialist in the sense of wishing to use public funds for the welfare of all the people?

2. List all the important international disputes and rivalries that contributed to the outbreak of the Crimean War. Explain in what way each helped bring about the war.

3. How accurate did Napoleon III prove to have been when he declared that his empire "meant peace"? What wars or other military activity grew out of his policies?

To Put This Chapter into a Larger Setting

1. Even today, historians differ in their interpretations of the character and policies of Napoleon III. With this in mind, read (or divide among several students) Albert Guérard's biography. (See book list, page 214.) In your report, point out the ways in which Guérard's interpretation of Napoleon differs from that of this chapter.

2. Do you believe that if Napoleon's dream of reorganizing Europe according to nationalities had been fully carried out, a more peaceful Europe would have resulted? State specific reasons for your answer, taking into account your knowledge of the present-day world.

12

The Unification of Italy

1859-1871

The spirit of restless nationalism that characterized European international relations after the revolutions of 1848 made Italy a united nation. In 1859 the Italian peninsula was divided into a number of separate states; in 1871 almost all Italians were living under the government of an Italian king with his capital in Rome. Thinking of their ancient glory in the days of imperial Rome, the Italians called their movement for independence and unity the *Risorgimento* (revival).

♫ ITALY IN THE 1840'S

In the 1840's there were seven important Italian states, each entirely independent of the others. From south to north, they were the kingdom of the Two Sicilies (Naples and Sicily); the States of the Church, ruled by the pope; the duchies of Tuscany, Modena, and Parma; the kingdom of Lombardy and Venetia, a part of the Austrian empire; and the kingdom of Sardinia, comprising the island of Sardinia and the mainland areas of Savoy and Piedmont (and called at various times by the names of all three parts).

The rugged character of the Italian landscape had hindered Italian unity. More important, since the collapse of the Roman Empire in the fifth century A.D., the peninsula had been a prey to many kinds of foreign interference. These factors and the poverty of the land prevented the building up of a political power strong enough to dominate the peninsula. Italy lacked most of the resources necessary for modern industry. After the age of discovery it was too far from the Atlantic Ocean to participate easily in world trade. To be sure, the Lombard plain in the north had good agricultural land with an adequate supply of water, but the south of Italy was less fortunate. It suffered from worn-out soil, drought, malaria, and earthquakes. Its forests had long since been used up. The people were too poor and the government too indifferent to provide adequate transportation or improved methods of farming.

Under these circumstances it is not surprising that the Italian people remained divided, loyal to their separate states, with little sense that they were all Italians. Each region had its own dialect, not understood elsewhere, and its own laws, weights and measures, and coinage. Customs barriers discouraged trade between the separate states.

Italian society retained many characteristics of the Old Regime. All states were despotically ruled. The clergy and nobility controlled the wealth and the political power. The middle class, mostly made up of professional people, was small, although in the northern part of the peninsula businessmen had organized some large industries. Peasants were the vast majority of the population, most of them poor, ignorant, and uninformed about the world outside their own villages. Thus the Italy of the 1840's seemed far from ready for national unification. Forces of unity were, nevertheless already at work.

◌ THE GROWTH OF NATIONAL FEELING

The first half of the nineteenth century was the seedtime of the Italian *Risorgimento*. Napoleon I's efficient government of the peninsula had contrasted sharply with the political and economic backwardness of the Italian states under their hereditary rulers. When those rulers were restored in 1815 by the Congress of Vienna, they abandoned the enlightened policies of Napoleon. It was then that such secret revolutionary societies as the Carbonari (see page 78) were organized. Although revolts led by the

Carbonari in 1820 and the early 1830's were failures, the society influenced some leaders who later became important in the unification movement, and it set an example for later revolutionary organizations. Of individuals who encouraged the unification movement in the first half of the nineteenth century, three were especially important: Mazzini, Gioberti, and Pope Pius IX.

MAZZINI, PATRIOT AND REVOLUTIONIST

Giuseppe Mazzini (1805-1872) was the thinker and dreamer who encouraged and inspired others to work and struggle toward the ideal of Italian unity. He was not a practical man, but he profoundly influenced other men who were better suited than he to achieve concrete results. He dreamed of a democratic Italian republic that would express the general will of all the people and guide them to work co-operatively for the common good. Such a government could, he believed, be established by an uprising of the common people of Italy. He was convinced that a democratically united Italy would inspire the people of other countries to follow its example.

In his young manhood Mazzini was an active conspirator, an agitator, and a member of the Carbonari. After 1831 he was forced to leave Italy, and most of his remaining life was spent in England. From his exile he organized revolutionary societies, the best-known called "Young Italy"; he founded newspapers; he wrote pamphlets and thousands of letters that were smuggled into Italy. With his encouragement, groups of his followers in Italy led small-scale uprisings, usually hopeless from the start, with the purpose of weakening the existing governments and of keeping revolutionary zeal alive.

Although no lasting practical results came from Mazzini's efforts, he aroused enthusiasm and devotion in the hearts of many Italians, and he taught some valuable lessons to those leaders who later unified the Italian people.

GIOBERTI AND POPE PIUS IX

Moderate intellectuals, fearful of Mazzini's use of violent methods, hoped to bring about reform more peacefully. They encouraged practical reform in agriculture, banking, and education, especially in northern Italy. They were sympathetic to the arguments of the priest Vincenzo Gioberti (1801-1852), who suggested a Catholic basis for Italian unification with the pope as head of a confederation of the existing states. In 1846 the newly elected Pope Pius IX, far more liberal than his immediate predecessor, made such a plan seem possible by bringing about some long overdue reforms in the

States of the Church. He pardoned political prisoners, lessened censorship, permitted some popular representation in government, and organized a national guard. It seemed that such a pope might well preside over a confederation of Italian states.

THE REVOLUTIONS OF 1848 IN ITALY

The revolutionary year 1848 saw revolutions in all parts of Italy. For a time unity seemed almost achieved, only to be lost again.

The Revolution of the Moderates. Before the revolutions of 1848 occurred in Paris, Berlin, or Vienna, Sicily had declared its independence of the kingdom of the Two Sicilies, and the frightened rulers of Tuscany, Sardinia, the States of the Church, and the Two Sicilies had been forced to grant mildly liberal constitutions. As soon as the March revolt occurred in Vienna (see page 149), Lombardy and Venetia expelled their Austrian garrisons, and in Venetia Daniele Manin brought about the establishment of a republic.

King Charles Albert of Sardinia immediately seized the leadership of the movement for Italian independence from Austria. He was an indecisive man, unsuited to so difficult a struggle; but he believed that he would lose prestige, even endanger his kingdom, unless he acted. Educated people of all Italy acclaimed him a hero. Even from the Two Sicilies and the States of the Church volunteers flocked to his armies. As long as Austrian forces were busy in other parts of the Habsburg domains, his well-trained troops were successful; but in July, 1848, he was decisively defeated. Next year he attacked again, only to be defeated in two weeks. He abdicated in favor of his son Victor Emmanuel II, who preserved the constitution his father had granted.

It was by this time clear that the mass of the Italian people were indifferent to the effort to drive Austria from Italy and that middle class liberals were too few. Nor did the other Italian rulers long support Charles Albert. The king of the Two Sicilies withdrew his soldiers after he discovered that his own throne was really not in danger. Pope Pius IX also withdrew from the war because he realized that he could not take sides between two Catholic countries, Austria and Sardinia. Thus the hopes of the moderate liberals for independence from Austria and possibly for an Italian federation under papal leadership ended in failure.

The Democrats. But there were radical leaders, especially Mazzini, who had other dreams for Italy. Events in Rome soon played into their hands.

Pius IX, finding his control over his territories shaken when he withdrew from the Austro-Sardinian War, fled to the kingdom of the Two Sicilies in November, 1848. At once a three-man board headed by Mazzini established a republic in the papal city. The pope sought the aid of the Catholic rulers. The first to respond was Napoleon III, always eager for the support of French Catholics. He landed troops in Italy, April, 1849.

Then occurred a heroic struggle between the French forces and the supporters of Mazzini's radical government. The republicans were led by Giuseppe Garibaldi (1807-1882), one of Italy's heroes, a great military leader and the most romantic figure of the *Risorgimento*. As a young man under the influence of Mazzini he had taken a solemn oath, to which he adhered to the end of his life, to fight to make Italy a united nation. Expelled from Sardinia, he spent thirteen adventurous years in Latin America, leading guerrilla troops in the local wars and developing remarkable skill in such irregular warfare. He was a man of nobility and simplicity, caring nothing for his own advancement and devoted only to the cause he served. The intense loyalty of his troops—his "Red Shirts"—was inspired in part by their trust in his honesty, in part by his impressive appearance and his personal magnetism, and in part by their belief in his invincibility. He was a restless, undisciplined, untutored man, better suited to irregular warfare than to the political activity of building up the Roman Republic which he served with such devotion. With his hastily-trained, ill-equipped troops, Garibaldi made a heroic stand against the French army, holding off defeat for two months, only yielding the city of Rome to the enemy in early July, 1849. After the republic collapsed and the pope was restored, Garibaldi led a famous retreat across Italy to the Adriatic. His faithful wife Anita, whom he had married in Brazil, accompanied him, only to die of exhaustion just as the journey ended. Utterly disheartened, he again became an exile.

The remaining Italian republic was Venice, still holding out against the Austrians under the leadership of Manin. Here more than in most other parts of the peninsula there was some real popular support for the revolutionary government. Manin himself was a competent leader. But an Austrian siege, begun in May, 1849, reduced the city to starvation. Cholera broke out, and no help came from the outside. In August Venice yielded to the Austrians. A month earlier the king of the Two Sicilies had recovered control of the island of Sicily. The revolutions of 1848 in Italy were over.

As in other regions of Europe, the results of the year of revolutions seemed at the time to be largely negative. Sardinia had a new king and a constitution, to be sure; but the other constitutions of 1848 had been withdrawn, and both republicanism and papal leadership—previously the hope of so many reformers—had been proven impractical. It was clear that Italians alone could not drive Austrian influence from the peninsula; help from outside was required. Within a decade that help was found.

◠ THE ESTABLISHMENT OF THE KINGDOM OF ITALY

In the 1850's Italy found two new leaders, King Victor Emmanuel II of Sardinia and his chief minister Count Camillo Cavour. Emperor Napoleon III of France proved willing to furnish the aid required to expel the Austrians. Garibaldi, republican though he was, lent his genius to the task of unifying Italy on nonrepublican lines. The work of these four men, often so different in their objectives, created the modern kingdom of Italy.

SARDINIA AND CAVOUR, 1850-1859

The Sardinian constitution of 1848 gave more power to King Victor Emmanuel than was available to most constitutional monarchs. It was he who appointed and removed the ministers. He could issue proclamations with the force of law. He appointed the senate and called and dismissed the parliament. To this constitutional authority he added the force of his own personality. In body he was small and unimpressive, in mind he was superstitious and without a good education. Nevertheless his bluff, soldierly manners, his vigor, and his common sense made him popular with his people. Perhaps the best proof of his natural shrewdness was his appointment of Cavour, whom he personally disliked, as his most important minister.

Cavour entered the Sardinian cabinet in 1850 and became prime minister in 1852. He was not a popular figure like the king, but he was well prepared by a variety of experience to assume a position of political leadership. His family was a noble one with wide and varied connections. He had successfully managed his father's estates and shrewdly invested his own money in newly established banking and shipping concerns, learning to know the ups and downs of business life. He traveled much abroad, becoming familiar with the operation of the British government, which he greatly admired. He was acquainted with the writings of the British classical economists (see page 96), whose ideas seemed to him sound ones for Sardinia. He also

Two heroes of the Risorgimento: the inspiring, romantic military leader, Giuseppe Garibaldi (left), and the creative statesman, Count Camillo Cavour (right).

wrote articles (in either Italian or French, for he was bilingual) on his favorite topics of agricultural, industrial, or commercial development. He helped found a newspaper, *Il Risorgimento*, in which he could express his own moderately liberal political views.

In office Cavour bent his energy and his talent toward strengthening Sardinia economically and, if possible, territorially. He built railways, established shipping companies, secured the passage of a limited liability law to encourage the growth of bigger businesses, improved agriculture, and removed tariffs that hampered the freedom of trade. Under his management Sardinia became an increasingly commercial and industrial state. Hoping to bring his country favorably to the attention of other nations that might in the future prove useful allies, he took it into the Crimean War on the side of Britain and France. (See page 165.) In short, he prepared Sardinia for whatever opportunities might present themselves, hoping especially for a chance to expel Austria from northern Italy.

THE UNIFICATION OF NORTHERN ITALY

Cavour's great opportunity came in 1859. Everything required for the success of the independence-unification movement in northern Italy seemed suddenly to be present. The most important factor was the willingness of Emperor Napoleon III to assist Sardinia against Austria.

The Plombières Meeting. In July, 1858, Cavour and Napoleon held a day-long secret meeting at Plombières in northeastern France, where Napoleon was vacationing and where he invited Cavour to visit him. Part of their talk took place during a carriage drive in the Vosges Mountains with the two quite alone, Napoleon himself driving the horses and a single servant following them. It was agreed that if Cavour could bring about an Austro-Sardinian war in such a way that Austria would appear to be the aggressor, Napoleon would attempt to keep the other countries neutral and would aid Sardinia. Sardinia would annex Lombardy, Venetia, Parma, Modena, and part of the Papal States. The enlarged Sardinia would become a part of an Italian federation under the presidency of the pope. As a reward for his help, Sardinia would cede to Napoleon the French-speaking lands of Nice and Savoy. Victor Emmanuel's fifteen-year-old daughter would marry Napoleon's dissipated and aged cousin, thus proving that the Bonapartes were welcomed into the old reigning families of Europe.

The purposes of Cavour were clear. After the Austro-Sardinian war of 1848-1849, sentiment for unification had become so strong in Italy that it was possible that the movement to expel Austria from the peninsula would be taken over by the followers of Mazzini if Cavour himself did not lead it. To keep matters in his own hands, he sought the aid of Napoleon. To Napoleon, the plans of Sardinia offered an opportunity to strike a blow against Austria, with the goal of destroying the arrangements made at the Congress of Vienna of 1815 and restoring French leadership in Europe. Moreover, Napoleon claimed to be interested in the independence of nationalities—and especially of Italy, where in 1831 he himself had participated in a Carbonari uprising.

The War with Austria, 1859. Ten months elapsed before the Austro-Sardinian war broke out—nervous and anxious months for the two plotting statesmen. Napoleon seemed full of enthusiasm at one moment and at the next ready to abandon the whole scheme. The attempt on his life by the Italian revolutionary Orsini in January, 1858, (see page 166), had seemed to persuade him that Italy must be reorganized if the danger of disorder there was to be eliminated. Orsini's defense at his trial had led to pro-Italian feeling in France. Still Napoleon hesitated. It was Emperor Francis Joseph of Austria who brought matters to a crisis. Angered by the attitude of the Sardinian government, he took steps leading directly to war. Napoleon honored his agreement and sent troops to support Sardinia.

French troops and artillery pass through Turin, the capital of the kingdom of Sardinia, on their way to fight for the liberation of northern Italy from Austria, 1859.

The fighting lasted from April to July, 1859, with the French-Sardinian armies winning important victories. But suddenly Napoleon withdrew from the war and negotiated an armistice with Francis Joseph. According to the terms, Sardinia might annex Lombardy; Venetia would remain Austrian; and all Italy would become a confederation under the pope.

Napoleon had strong reasons for withdrawing from the war. He was sickened by the horrors of the battlefield. The French people from the beginning did not approve of the war, especially ardent Catholics, who were afraid it would endanger papal control of the States of the Church. Perhaps most important, the Prussian army was mobilizing along the Rhine, and Napoleon was worried lest Prussia enter the war on the Austrian side. Cavour, for his part, was so angered when he heard of the armistice that he went quite out of control of himself. Rather than agree to such a settlement, he resigned his office; the king, with his earthy common sense, accepted the terms because no others seemed possible.

The Union of the Italian Duchies. The cessation of war did not have the effects expected by Napoleon and Francis Joseph. During the war Tuscany, Parma, Modena, and the northern States of the Church had driven out their rulers and now refused to take them back again. Assemblies in the duchies voted for annexation to Sardinia. In January, 1860, after an uneasy period,

THE UNIFICATION
OF ITALY

Kingdom of Sardinia, 1859	
Kingdom of Italy, 1861	
Added to Italy, 1866	
Added to Italy, 1870	

Cavour returned to office and again bargained with Napoleon. They agreed that if favorable plebiscites were held in the duchies, all four would be annexed to Sardinia, while Nice and Savoy would finally go to France. Thus France acquired some strengthening of her southeastern border in return for permitting Sardinia to grow larger than had been planned at Plombières. French Catholics were not satisfied, for the policy of Napoleon had resulted in the loss to the pope of his northern provinces.

GARIBALDI AND SOUTHERN ITALY

The next step in Italian unification was taken by Garibaldi, returned from exile and now willing to work toward a united Italy, even though it would be a monarchy under the king of Sardinia rather than the republic of his dreams. He gathered a thousand red-shirted followers and in May, 1860, transported them in two battered steamers to Sicily. Disorders had already occurred there, and Garibaldi's magnetic presence and a few successful military encounters brought thousands of volunteers to his side. By the middle of July he was in full control of the island. In August he crossed to the mainland, where the appearance of his Red Shirts so terrified the regular troops that they yielded without fighting.

Although Garibaldi claimed to be furthering the unification of Italy, his achievements did not altogether please the Sardinian government. Victor Emmanuel apparently gave him some secret encouragement; but Cavour had no confidence in him, fearing that he would create a Mazzinian republic in the south of Italy or that he would attack the pope in Rome, as he had in 1849. (Above, page 173.) To prevent Garibaldi from taking either of these steps, Cavour seized the initiative. Securing the consent of Napoleon III, he threw Sardinian troops into the eastern part of the States of the Church while Garibaldi was still involved in the Kingdom of Naples. After they had defeated the papal forces, the Sardinian troops completed the conquest of the Kingdom of Naples. By October, 1860, the fighting was all but over. Plebiscites were held in Naples, Sicily, and in the papal areas of the Marches and Umbria. All voted overwhelmingly for annexation to Sardinia. Garibaldi gave over his conquests and returned to the home he had made for himself on an island north of Sardinia. Except for Venetia, which still belonged to Austria, and the remaining States of the Church, all Italy was now ruled by Victor Emmanuel, who was declared king of Italy. This was the culmination of Cavour's shrewd, patient, unrelenting, and sometimes ruthless work; for he died in 1861, before the last steps in achieving a fully united Italy had been taken.

☉ FINAL UNIFICATION

The remaining two stages of Italian unification do not belong solely to the history of Italy. In 1866 Venetia became part of the kingdom of Italy as a result of a war between Austria and Prussia. In return for a Prussian promise to secure Venetia for them, the Italians became Prussia's allies. Even though the Italian forces were defeated in the fighting, the Prussian promise was fulfilled.

But Rome, to all Italians the rightful capital of their country, remained a papal possession. The view was widely held in Catholic circles that unless the papacy had political control over some area of land, the popes would have difficulty maintaining their world-wide spiritual authority. During the 1860's papal control of Rome was protected by French troops sent originally in 1849. (See page 143.) Twice (1862 and 1867) Garibaldi led volunteers against Rome, and twice he was defeated. But in 1870 Napoleon III, then at war with Prussia, was at last forced to withdraw his Roman garrison. Italian troops immediately entered the city, and Victor Emmanuel made it his capital. Pope Pius IX shut himself inside the Vatican as a voluntary prisoner, refusing the money payment offered him in return for his territory. The quarrel between Italy and the papacy was not resolved until 1929.

☺ ☺ ☺

The unification of Italy was important not only to the Italian people but also to all Europe. No longer could the other powers fish in the troubled waters of Italian interstate politics. Italy had a greatly increased political importance of its own. Moreover, Italian unification inspired other disunited peoples to follow its example—first of all, Germany.

Persons, Places, and Terms

Giuseppe Mazzini	Tuscany	the Two Sicilies
Vincenzo Gioberti	Modena	Plombières
Pius IX	Parma	Nice
Daniele Manin	Savoy	
Giuseppe Garibaldi	Piedmont	*Risorgimento*
Victor Emmanuel II	Kingdom of Sardinia	Young Italy
Camillo Cavour	Sardinia (island)	Red Shirts

To Master the Text

1. How was Italy divided in the 1840's? What factors contributed to its division? What characteristics of the Old Regime did it retain? How did southern Italy differ from northern Italy?

2. In the growth of Italian national feeling up to 1848, what part was played by Napoleon I? By Mazzini? By Gioberti? By Pius IX? Who among the Italian people supported each?

3. What revolutionary changes took place in Italy in early 1848? Why did Charles Albert fight Austria? What support did he receive from the rest of Italy? How successful was he? Why? Was the 1848 movement in Italy a liberal one? Was it nationalist?

4. What train of events drove Pius IX from Rome in November, 1848? What government replaced his? What was the background and character of Garibaldi? Who defeated him in 1848 and for what purpose? What happened to the radical revolutionary movement in Venice? In the kingdom of the Two Sicilies? What were the permanent results of the revolutions of 1848 in Italy?

5. Characterize Victor Emmanuel II. How much authority did he have under the Sardinian constitution? How did he strengthen Sardinia?
6. What hopes and plans were in the minds of Cavour and Napoleon III when they met at Plombières? List the steps leading from Plombières to the Austro-Sardinian war of 1859. Why was the war terminated before its planned conclusion? What were the terms of peace?
7. How were the Italian duchies united with Sardinia? What part did the Italian people play in this development? What was Cavour's part?
8. Trace the course of Garibaldi's activities in 1861. How did Victor Emmanuel view his exploits? How did Cavour? How did Cavour prevent Garibaldi from making his own arrangements for southern Italy? What new title was given to Victor Emmanuel?
9. How was Venetia secured for Italy? How was Rome secured? How did Pius IX react to his loss of Rome?

To Master the Map

1. Make your own map-history of the unification of Italy by drawing a series of freehand maps so constructed as to tell the whole story with nothing but brief captions to explain their meaning.
2. Study the Mediterranean on the map on page 74. What countries would the unification of Italy be likely to affect? In what ways?

To Interpret the Facts

1. Write brief (two- or three-sentence) characterizations of Mazzini, Victor Emmanuel II, Cavour, Garibaldi, and Napoleon III, describing each man's personality and indicating his part in the unification of Italy.
2. To what extent was the unification of Italy an international struggle?
3. How do you explain Napoleon's willingness to use armed force to oppose Italian revolutionaries who had expelled Pius IX from Rome, when in the same year he had already used armed force to aid other Italian revolutionaries in their war against Austria?
4. Compare Napoleon III, Cavour, and Victor Emmanuel as statesmen, taking into consideration their personalities and early experiences, their objectives, their ideals, their methods, and the good or bad fortune that seemed to be the lot of each.

To Put This Chapter into a Larger Setting

1. What problems for Italy, for Europe, and for the world grew out of or were left over from the course of Italian unification?
2. Does Napoleon III's policy in Italy seem to you to have been wise from the point of view of France? Why?
3. Could Italy have been united in the mid-nineteenth century without the aid of Napoleon III? Support your answer with specific evidence.

13

The Making of the German Empire

1862-1871

The most significant achievement of mid-nineteenth-century nationalism, even more important than the unification of Italy, was the transformation of the many small German states into the German Empire under the Hohenzollern rulers of Prussia. For centuries the powerful and progressive neighbors of Germany—notably France—had worked to keep the Germans divided. Then suddenly in the decade of the 1860's favorable conditions occurring simultaneously inside and outside Germany enabled King William I of Prussia, his chief minister Otto von Bismarck, and his general Helmuth von Moltke to bring together some three dozen separate German states (but not including Austria) into a single unit.

☊ THE GERMANS IN 1862

In the early 1860's the thirty-eight states of the Germanic Confederation and the other German-speaking areas of Prussia and the Habsburg empire seemed to indicate that Germany might well remain divided politically for a long time to come. Nevertheless, forces of change were making significant progress in many areas of Germany.

DIVISION AND UNITY WITHIN GERMANY

Loyalty of the people to the ruling families so long in power in the separate states was probably the greatest impediment to German unification. Another was the bitter rivalry beween Austria and Prussia. Either of these great states might have absorbed their smaller neighbors as Sardinia had absorbed the rest of Italy, but neither would permit the other to take the lead in unification. The strength of this jealousy was amply proved by the feud between Austria and Prussia in 1849 and 1850. (See page 154.) Then there was the religious division of Germany between the Protestant north and the Catholic south. Finally, there was no really effective leadership capable of forcing unification on the unwilling rulers. Many of the liberals of 1848 were in exile, and others who might have led a national movement were in the employ of the individual German states.

But Germany was not standing still economically. The German people were being drawn together by improved roads, telegraph lines, canals, and railroads. The *Zollverein* (see page 144) expanded, encouraging the loyalty of its members by paying them larger sums from the common tariff than they had previously received from their individual tolls. Coal mining and iron manufacturing were encouraged by the increased ease with which heavy goods could be carried from place to place (often from state to state) and by the demand for iron for building railroads. The Prussian Rhineland and Silesia were the most important centers of the iron industry; textile manufacturing flourished in Saxony. Numbers of German businessmen came to look upon enlarged economic opportunities as more important than the preservation of the small independent German states. Thus the accelerating industrial development of Germany was laying the foundations for political unity.

PRUSSIA, WILLIAM I, AND BISMARCK

At the death of King Frederick William IV in 1861 his brother, who was already regent, became King William I. In 1862 William appointed Otto von Bismarck his minister-president. Although neither William nor Bismarck could look so far into the future, the history of German unification began when Bismarck took office.

In 1861 Prussia remained a conservative, authoritarian state. The *Zollverein* had, to be sure, been organized by Prussia. Prussian population had increased from 11,000,000 to 18,000,000 since 1815; Prussia had secured a

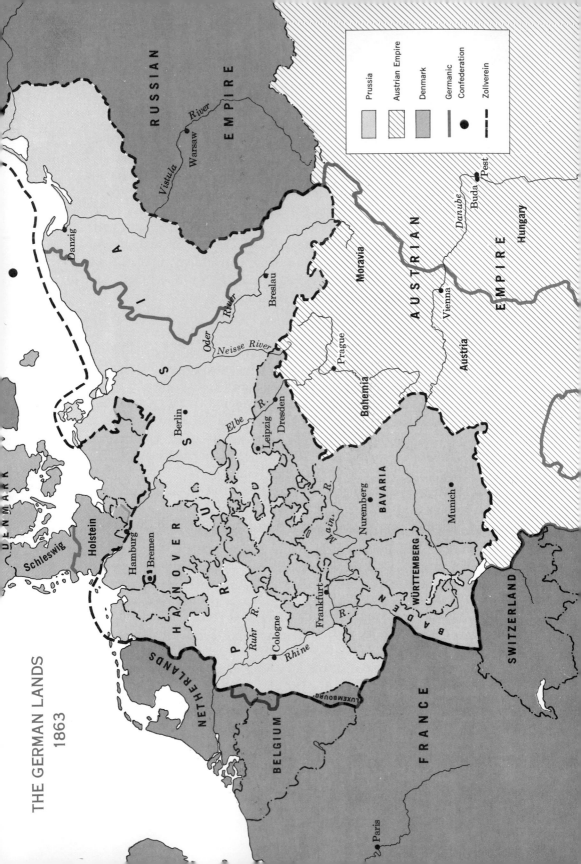

THE GERMAN LANDS
1863

Legend:
Prussia
Austrian Empire
Denmark
Germanic Confederation
Zollverein

RUSSIAN EMPIRE

Vistula River
Warsaw
Danzig

Oder River
Breslau
Neisse River

Danube
Buda
Pest
Hungary

AUSTRIAN EMPIRE

Moravia
Prague
Bohemia
Vienna
Austria

Berlin
Elbe R.
Leipzig
Dresden

P R U S S I A

Nuremberg
BAVARIA
Munich

WÜRTEMBERG
B A D E N

DENMARK
Schleswig
Holstein
Hamburg
Bremen

H A N O V E R

Main R.
Frankfurt
Cologne
Ruhr R.
Rhine

NETHERLANDS
LUXEMBOURG
BELGIUM

SWITZERLAND

F R A N C E

Paris

large share of recent German industrial advance, and had acquired a constitution. (See page 146.) But the constitution not only gave special weight to
the votes of the wealthy; it also left full control of the ministers in the
hands of the king. It was not a liberal document. Moreover, the structure of
Prussian society remained thoroughly aristocratic. Serfdom had been abolished in Prussian lands only at the beginning of the century. (See page 64.)
Landlords in the easternmost parts of the kingdom still in some cases acted
as judges over the peasants on their lands. Peasants could not yet freely
migrate to the towns in search of work. Not surprisingly the owners of
Prussian factories took a more authoritarian attitude toward their workers
than was the custom in the older industrial countries.

William I was well fitted to rule over an energetic people accustomed to
accepting the directions of a strong government. He was above all else a
soldier, with a soldier's loyalty, courage, devotion to duty, and love of the
army. He was not an intellectual, but he had sober common sense—a welcome change from the romantic instability of his brother. (See page 145.)
The poor showing of the Prussian army when it was mobilized in 1859
during the Austro-Sardinian war (see page 177) had frightened him. The
militia had to be called out because there were not enough regular troops.
The army did not have space to train the growing number of young men
who were eligible for service. Recruits were sent home after two years
instead of being kept to the full legal three-year limit. Since 1813 no new
weapons had been put into use. William sought funds for reform, asking
parliament for amounts adequate for full three-year training. He wanted to
call up a larger number of young men, to develop new weapons, and to
provide everything necessary for doubling the size of the army. To William's chagrin, the parliament refused to grant funds. The quarrel between
the king and parliament soon developed into a full-scale national crisis.

The reasons for parliamentary opposition were several. The lower house
was controlled by the middle class, which was largely opposed to the power
of the military officer class and was eager to keep the budget as low as
possible. As the deputies resisted the king, they saw the chance of using
the thorny army question as a means of forcing the king to grant powers
to the ministers similar to those enjoyed by British ministries. Thoroughly
opposed to having ministers responsible to the parliament instead of to him,
the king was in despair; he contemplated abdicating the throne. Instead he
was persuaded to appoint as minister-president Otto von Bismarck.

In 1862 Bismarck was forty-seven years old. A *Junker* (see page 122), he
prided himself on the rugged character of his class. A tall, powerful figure,

Otto von Bismarck in 1863, at the end of his first year as chief minister of the king of Prussia, as he was about to take the first steps leading to the Prussian unification of Germany.

he liked to be portrayed with his large dogs; but his voice did not match his stature, for it was high and thin. He was a person of strong emotions, quick to anger, weeping easily, finding deep enjoyment in music, devoted to any cause he served. Toward all with whom he worked he felt a need to dominate, although with King William he secured his own way only by respectful persuasion. Even though he was often difficult to get along with, he could also be charming—a quality he used with effectiveness in his public life. His wife was a pious woman, a devout Lutheran, utterly devoted to him, wrapped up in domestic matters, and glad not to take any part in public affairs. Before he took office his experience of life had been rich. He had had the usual upper-class university education, had traveled widely, read voraciously, made friends with aristocratic and important people from many parts of Europe, and spent successful years managing his family estates.

Bismarck was completely devoted to Prussia. He wished to maintain the conservative character of Prussian government and society and to strengthen and expand the country in whatever way might prove possible. Earlier he had been Prussian representative to the diet of the Germanic Confederation and Prussian ambassador to Russia and France. His deepest interest was always in foreign affairs, for the management of which he had genius. But in spite of his skill he was a nervous worrier, at any one time fearful of Prussia's being threatened from several directions at once. He would develop plans for every possible danger or opportunity, so that he had a ready plan of action for whatever circumstances might arise.

When Bismarck confronted the first problem of his ministry, the question of the army budget and the liberals in parliament, he could find no solution. So he decided simply to pay no attention to parliament. Officials collected the new taxes and called up the recruits as if no parliament existed. Only Bismarck's iron nerve permitted him to withstand the storm of criticism aroused by his unconstitutional policy. But his plan succeeded; the army reform, under General von Moltke, went forward without hindrance.

☖ THE AUSTRO-PRUSSIAN CONFLICT

It was natural that Bismarck, with his devotion to Prussia, should concern himself deeply with relations between Prussia and Austria. Prussian economic and territorial advance had again and again been obstructed by Austria. As Prussian representative at the diet of the Germanic Confederation, Bismarck himself had often been exasperated by the condescending ways of the Austrian president of the diet. According to a famous story, Bismarck refused to abide by the long-standing custom that permitted only the Austrian delegate to smoke. At his first session Bismarck pulled out a cigar and lit it. As minister-president, although he studied every aspect of European international relations to discover steps to be taken to strengthen Prussia or to ward off dangers, he continued to pay greatest attention to Austria. His first important action was taken in alliance with Austria.

THE SCHLESWIG-HOLSTEIN QUESTION, 1863-1864

The first serious international problem of Bismarck's ministry was a revival of the Schleswig-Holstein question, which had caused so much trouble for the Frankfurt Parliament in 1848. (See page 152.) The situation remained about the same as in 1848: the king of Denmark, influenced by Danish nationalism, was drawing the duchies closer to Denmark; the nationalist-thinking members of the Germanic Confederation protested that the king was infringing old treaties providing for the perpetual union of the duchies with each other and their separation from Denmark—treaties that had been reaffirmed by the great powers in 1852. At the end of 1863 a new king of Denmark, Christian IX, signed a constitution that made Schleswig practically a part of Denmark and almost completely separated it from Holstein. German protest was immediate and loud. The Germanic Confederation put forward the hereditary claims of a German noble, the duke of Augustenburg, to the thrones of the duchies, arguing that Christian IX, who inherited his Danish throne through a female line, could not rightly rule the duchies, where the succession was through male lines only.

Bismarck had to deal somehow with this crisis. It is not possible to reconstruct his train of thought; he acted secretly, for the policy he adopted displeased both Austria and the Confederation. Apparently he determined to sever the duchies from Denmark and at the same time to prevent Augustenburg from acquiring them, since in Augustenburg's possession and as members of the Confederation they would be likely to support Austria against Prussia. He hoped to leave open the possibility of Prussian annexation of the duchies at some time in the future. Toward this end he guided, directed, and forced events.

One of Bismarck's greatest diplomatic successes was the signing with Prussia's rival, Austria, of an agreement (January, 1864) for joint action apart from the Confederation to force Denmark to give up its plans for Schleswig and to abide by the 1852 decisions of the powers. The Austrian alliance strengthened Bismarck against the German nationalist sentiment of the Confederation and permitted him to deal with the Danish question from the point of view of Prussia. In February, 1864, the armies of Austria and Prussia, following the terms of the alliance, made a quickly successful invasion of Denmark. The results of the Prussian army reforms were obvious to all. The Prussian railroad system, carefully planned with military needs in mind, permitted unexpectedly rapid movement of troops. One of Bismarck's problems was now the conscience of William I, for the king was at first convinced that Prussia was following an immoral course. This time, as on many later occasions, Bismarck finally persuaded William that what Prussia was doing was morally right. In October, 1864, the war ended with the surrender of the duchies to the joint ownership of Austria and Prussia.

THE GERMAN CIVIL WAR, 1866

The common ownership of the duchies by Austria and Prussia gave rise to endless disputes between the two powers and finally to war.

Growing Austro-Prussian Hostility, 1864-1866. For the twenty months after the peace with Denmark, Austria and Prussia both tried to strengthen themselves at home and abroad. Hard-pressed by financial troubles, Francis Joseph tried to placate his restless Hungarian subjects by offering them more self-government within the empire. Unfortunately the negotiations dragged on and were of little use. Meantime friendly foreign statesmen advised the emperor to remove one of his many problems by selling Venetia to Italy, thus securing needed funds and lessening by one the number of his enemies. Francis Joseph's pride did not, however, permit him to abandon a part of his hereditary lands without receiving compensation somewhere else.

Bismarck used the interval to win friends for Prussia in anticipation of probable war with Austria. He struggled to persuade the king to put the interests of Prussia ahead of those of Germany (for William liked to think of himself as a German prince as well as king of Prussia). Bismarck visited Napoleon III (October, 1865) to learn what policy France would follow in the event of an Austro-Prussian war. Although nothing definite was agreed upon during the visit, Bismarck came away convinced that Napoleon would not oppose Prussian territorial expansion provided France secured some territory in the Rhineland at the same time. Napoleon for his part expected a prolonged German war that would enable him to work out a desirable French policy while the war was going on. He did not, therefore, press Bismarck to make definite commitments. With French neutrality assured, Bismarck negotiated an alliance treaty with Italy (April, 1866) providing that Italy would support Prussia in a war against Austria and would receive Venetia in return. Finally, to gain the support of German liberals everywhere, Bismarck suggested to the diet of the Confederation the establishment of an all-German parliament to be elected by universal manhood suffrage. Meantime incidents between Austria and Prussia—often instigated by Bismarck— had the effect of persuading William I that Austria was really the enemy and that it was morally right for Prussia to annex the duchies. In June war finally broke out between the two German states.

The Military Aspects of the War. So rapidly did the Prussians move, once the fighting began, that the whole conflict has gone down in history as the "Seven Weeks War." Many of the smaller German states allied with Austria, but these were defeated one by one before they could bring their troops together. For the Austrians there were two fronts: in Italy, where they were soon victorious, and in Bohemia, where they engaged the Prussians. The network of Prussian railroads conveyed troops to Bohemia with unprecedented speed while the Austrians struggled with the single rail line northward from Vienna. The tireless, brilliant work of the Prussian chief of staff Moltke had supplied the Prussian army with its new "needle gun," which fired more rapidly and farther than the outmoded Austrian weapons, and with a plan of battle that permitted the Prussians to surprise and outfight the Austrians at the decisive battle of Königgrätz (known also as Sadowa), which brought the war to a conclusion.

The Peace of Prague, August, 1866. For Bismarck making peace proved difficult. King William and the Prussian generals agreed on the desirability of further fighting to secure large annexations of territory. Bismarck was altogether opposed to prolonging the war, partly because he feared the intervention of other powers and partly because, foreseeing the need to preserve the friendship of Austria, he was eager to end the war with a minimum of bitterness. By securing the consent of Napoleon III to the creation of a North German Confederation in the place of the old Germanic Confederation, he won over the king and the generals to accepting the mild Peace of Prague, August, 1866. Austria ceded Venetia to Italy and agreed to end the Germanic Confederation, to permit the establishment of the North German Confederation, and to pay a small indemnity. Thereafter Bismarck was free to reorganize North Germany as he thought best. The four south German states (Württemberg, Bavaria, Baden, and Hesse-Darmstadt) officially ranged among the enemies of Prussia during the war, lost no territory, but each signed a treaty of alliance with Prussia putting its army under Prussian command in the event of foreign war.

◌ CONSTITUTIONAL REORGANIZATION OF THE GERMAN LANDS

The Seven Weeks War proved that the union of all Germans under one government was impossible. The war destroyed the Germanic Confederation, through which Austria had maintained its leadership in Germany. The fact that Austria and Prussia were both German was no longer fundamentally important; hereafter each was first and foremost simply a great power. Each had to find as many friends as possible among its neighbors. Bismarck set about organizing the North German Confederation. Francis

Joseph, twice defeated by a western great power within seven years, turned east and began to improve his relations with his Hungarian subjects.

THE AUSTRO-HUNGARIAN COMPROMISE OF 1867

In 1867 Francis Joseph was ready to yield to the long-sought demands of the Hungarians. By good fortune a skillful and devoted Hungarian leader, Ferencz Deák, was willing to meet him halfway; for unlike Kossuth in 1848 (see page 151), Deák believed it best for Hungary not to seek independence, but to remain associated with Austria.

According to the "Compromise of 1867," the Austrian Empire was to be divided into two parts, together called "Austria-Hungary" or the "Dual Monarchy." For home affairs each half would have its own legislature and officials, but foreign, military, and financial affairs would be handled jointly. In each half the Slavs were a majority, but the German and Hungarian minorities controlled the two parliaments. Francis Joseph was king in Hungary and emperor in Austria. The Hungarians, pleased with the compromise, became more loyal to Francis Joseph; but the Slavs' dissatisfaction with Habsburg rule was naturally increased.

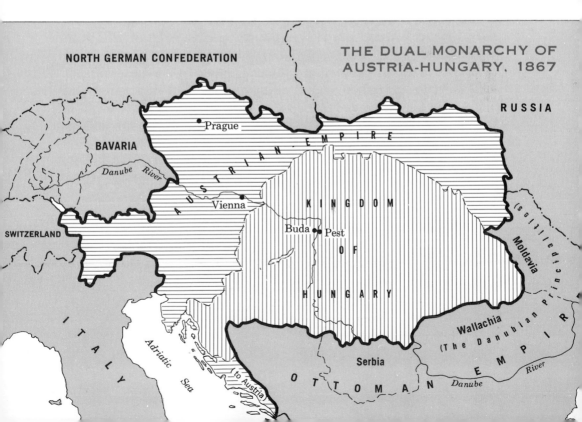

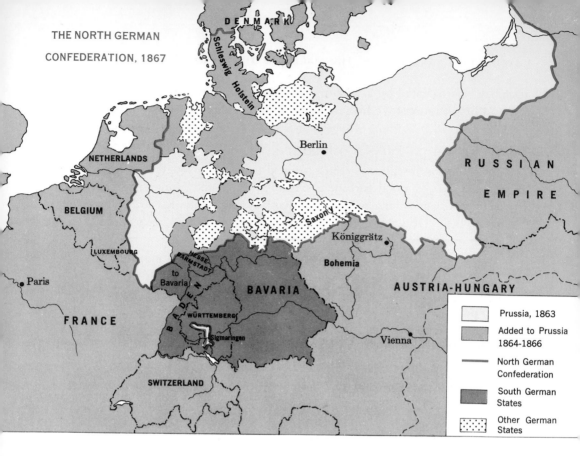

THE NORTH GERMAN
CONFEDERATION, 1867

Legend:
- Prussia, 1863
- Added to Prussia 1864-1866
- North German Confederation
- South German States
- Other German States

BISMARCK'S NORTH GERMAN CONFEDERATION

Bismarck's reorganization of north Germany began with the annexation to Prussia of Schleswig-Holstein and the states between the Prussian Rhineland and the older Prussian territories in eastern Germany. The enlarged Prussia and the twenty-one remaining independent states north of the Main River were made into the North German Confederation, much more tightly knit and stronger than the old Germanic Confederation and obviously to be dominated by Prussia. Thus had Bismarck proved the truth of something he had said in one of his first speeches to the members of the Prussian parliament—that "the great questions of the time" would be solved not by parliaments, but in a military way "by blood and iron." The Prussian parliament now passed a resolution forgiving Bismarck for having collected taxes illegally since 1862. (Above, page 187.)

The constitution of the North German Confederation was skillfully arranged to preserve Prussian dominance, Bismarck's own power, and the control of the Confederation by the conservatives. The king of Prussia was always to be president of the Confederation. The chancellor, appointed by and responsible to the president, was the only minister mentioned specifically in the constitution. Bismarck, of course, expected to occupy the chancellorship. The upper house of the legislature, the *Bundesrat*, would consist of ambassadors from the member states and would be presided over by the chancellor. The lower house, the *Reichstag*, was to be elected by universal manhood suffrage, for Bismarck believed that the lower classes were less liberal-minded than the middle class and would elect members more to his liking. The *Reichstag* could only discuss and vote on questions submitted to it by the *Bundesrat*.

Until 1867, when the North German Confederation was complete, Bismarck had always been more of a Prussian than a German. From this time on, however, as he tried to draw the southern German states closer to the Confederation, he himself acquired a more German outlook. He also came to believe that only war with France could complete his plans for unification.

☾ THE GERMAN-FRENCH CONFLICT

Like Bismarck, Napoleon III learned from the Austro-Prussian War to evaluate the position of Germany in a new light. For centuries the French had looked upon Austria as the enemy, but after 1867 Napoleon realized that the greater danger came from Prussia. He saw that unless he could find some way of adding to French territory and population to match the recent Prussian gains, France could no longer enjoy a dominant position in Europe.

THE DIPLOMATIC DUEL BETWEEN NAPOLEON III AND BISMARCK

During the years immediately after 1866, Napoleon sought some "compensation" in the way of territory to be added to France to make the balance of power between France and the North German Confederation what it had been before the Seven Weeks War. He made a number of specific suggestions: (1) that Prussia cede the Rhineland to France; (2) that Napoleon be allowed to buy Luxembourg from the king of the Dutch Netherlands; or (3) that he annex Belgium. Objections to each of these proposals came from the other powers. The German people became increasingly anti-French, and the southern German states leaned more and more toward the North German Confederation for protection against France. The result of Napoleon's efforts was simply to frighten other countries.

More important was the struggle between France and the North German Confederation over the question of a new ruler for Spain. In 1868 a revolution in Spain drove the queen from the throne. Spanish leaders desired as their king Prince Leopold von Hohenzollern-Sigmaringen, a distant cousin of William I and a Catholic. King William, whose consent was required, hesitated to permit the young prince to accept the throne for fear other countries would object. Bismarck, on the other hand, wished the prince to take the throne. He realized that war with France might ensue, but he believed that only a French war would bring the southern German states decisively to the side of the North German Confederation. Prince Leopold accepted the invitation with the grudging consent of King William. Such a storm of French protest then arose that Leopold's father withdrew his son's candidacy.

The withdrawal did not, however, bring the crisis to an end. The ministers of Napoleon III were looking for some resounding diplomatic triumph to restore the emperor's waning popularity with the French people. (See page 160.) The question of the Spanish throne seemed to offer an opportunity. The French ambassador to Berlin was sent to call on King William, then vacationing at the resort of Ems, to get him to apologize to Napoleon and to promise in writing that Leopold's candidacy for the Spanish throne would never again be renewed. William refused to give such a promise for the long future. Here the matter might have rested but for Bismarck. William telegraphed him an account of the conversation with the ambassador. Bismarck edited and shortened this "Ems Telegram" and published it in the newspapers. Readers gained the quite inaccurate impression that William had been abrupt and discourteous to the ambassador. The French people were outraged. On July 19, 1870, the French government, already thinking of war as a means of saving the Bonaparte dynasty, formally declared it.

THE FRANCO-PRUSSIAN WAR, 1870-1871

When the fighting began there were hard-fought battles and German casualties were high, but the struggle went steadily in favor of the Germans. The army reforms and the excellent German transport system again proved their worth. The south-German states immediately joined Prussia. The French, for their part, were ill-prepared; their plans were poor, and their troops could not be brought together quickly. In September Napoleon III and 100,000 troops were surrounded at Sedan and forced to surrender. The government of the Second Empire collapsed and was replaced by a republic headed by Léon Gambetta. Paris was besieged. Gambetta escaped in a balloon to arouse the provinces to further resistance. Within Paris conditions became desperate. No food or fuel could be brought in; supplies of all kinds ran short. The people resorted to eating the animals in the zoo or even rats and to cutting down the trees in the parks for firewood. In January, 1871, Paris surrendered and the fighting came to an end.

CONSEQUENCES OF THE WAR

The war had many consequences. It enabled the Italians to take over Rome as their capital, for French troops had been called home to participate in the fighting. (See pages 179-180.) It also enabled the Russians to put warships in the Black Sea, in defiance of the treaty of Paris of 1856 (see pages 165-166), for no power was willing or able to stop them. The treaty of Frankfurt between France and Germany required France to pay a large indemnity; to accept an army of occupation; and to cede Alsace-Lorraine, a region rich in iron deposits and with a flourishing textile industry.

Most important was the proclamation in Louis XIV's Hall of Mirrors at Versailles of the German Empire, which included the southern German states and the North German Confederation. William I now became German Emperor (in German, *Kaiser Wilhelm I*). Not all Germans were sub-

The proclamation of the German Empire in the Hall of Mirrors at Versailles, January 18, 1871. On the dais stands William I, king of Prussia and now to be German emperor as well. Near the dais are Bismarck (in the white coat) and General von Moltke (in front of Bismarck, facing the emperor).

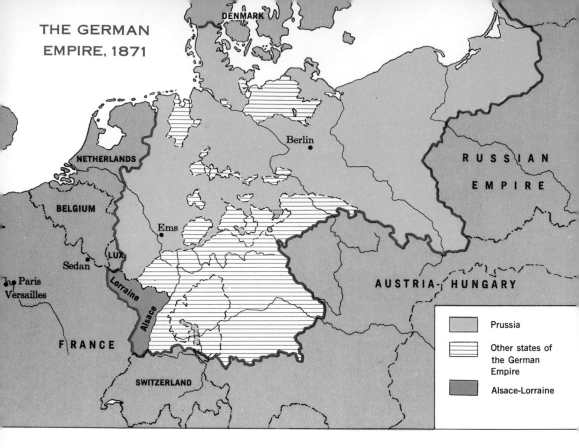

THE GERMAN
EMPIRE, 1871

DENMARK

Berlin

NETHERLANDS

RUSSIAN

EMPIRE

BELGIUM

Ems

LUX.

Sedan

Lorraine

Paris
Versailles

AUSTRIA-HUNGARY

Alsace

FRANCE

SWITZERLAND

	Prussia
	Other states of the German Empire
	Alsace-Lorraine

ject to the new empire, for Austria and other lands inhabited by Germans
were not included. Nevertheless, for the first time in modern history most
Germans were under a single government that was as close-knit and powerful as the Germanic Confederation had been divided and weak. The previous balance of power in Europe was destroyed. For the next decades the
new German Empire would unquestionably be the strongest state on the
continent.

ᗯ ᗯ ᗯ

Thus was concluded the remaking of the map of Europe begun when
Napoleon III assisted Sardinia against Austria. Napoleon III, Cavour, and
Bismarck had furnished examples of the new kind of statesmanship produced by the age of science and industry. Abroad they were arch-national-
ists. At home they courted popular favor by attending to the problems of
banking, transportation, agricultural advance, and the like. They controlled
military might of a kind never before available. Their example had an
important influence on their successors.

Persons, Places, and Terms

William I	Rhineland	Compromise of 1867
Otto von Bismarck	Königgrätz	Dual Monarchy
Helmuth von Moltke	Württemberg	Austria-Hungary
Christian IX	Bavaria	North German
Duke of	Baden	Confederation
Augustenburg	Hesse-Darmstadt	*Bundesrat*
Ferencz Déak	Main River	*Reichstag*
Leopold von	Luxembourg	territorial
Hohenzollern-	Ems	compensation
Sigmaringen	Sedan	Ems Telegram
Léon Gambetta		

To Master the Text

1. In the early 1860's, what forces held back German unification? What economic forces were at the same time making Germany more of a unit?

2. In what ways was Prussia advanced economically? In what ways was it a markedly authoritarian state? Was William I suited to be the ruler of such a state? What alerted William I to the need for army reform? What specific reforms were needed?

3. What did the Prussian parliament hope to achieve by opposing William's reforms? Why did the king appoint Otto von Bismarck his minister-president? Describe Bismarck's character, personality, and background. What was Bismarck's attitude toward Prussia and toward Prussia's future? How did he secure the money for the army reforms?

4. What action, taken by whom, revived the question of Schleswig-Holstein? What was the reaction of the Germanic Confederation?

5. What possible solutions to the Schleswig-Holstein problem did Bismarck apparently hope to avoid? For what reasons? Why did he prefer to act in alliance with Austria? What action did Prussia and Austria take? With what consequences?

6. How did Francis Joseph try to prepare for a possible war with Prussia? How successful was he? Why? As part of his preparation for such a war, how did Bismarck secure the neutrality of Napoleon III? The alliance of Italy? The support of German liberals? The consent of King William? What was the outcome of the Austro-Prussian War? How can that result be accounted for? What were Bismarck's arguments against a prolonged war or severe terms of peace? What changes of territory and what other changes resulted from the war?

7. What were the provisions of the Compromise of 1867? Who benefited by it? Who did not?

8. What states made up the North German Confederation? What were the general purposes of its constitution? The specific provisions? What

aspect of Bismarck's thinking changed after the establishment of the North German Confederation?

9. Why did Napoleon III seek territorial compensation for France? Where did he try to find it? With what results? Trace the steps by which the quarrel over the Spanish throne led to war. To what extent and by what means did Bismarck affect this train of events?

10. Trace the course of the Franco-Prussian War. As a result of the war, what changes were brought about in France? In Germany? What effects did these developments have on other countries? On the European balance of power?

To Master the Map

1. By drawing a series of small freehand maps and writing meaningful captions under them, tell the story of German unification.

2. Compare the maps of Prussia in 1863 and of the German Empire in 1871. How might the German Empire be expected to be stronger than the Prussia of 1863 in world commerce? As an influence in western Europe? As a military power (on both land and sea)?

To Interpret the Facts

1. In your opinion, to what extent did Bismarck follow a step-by-step plan toward German unification, and to what extent did he simply make good use of the opportunities that presented themselves? What facts lead you to your conclusion?

2. Imagine that you are Napoleon III in exile in England in 1871. Giving many details to prove your point, try to convince an Englishman how difficult it was for you to deal with Bismarck, how ruthless and unreliable he was, and how his promises could never be trusted.

3. What specific actions indicate that until 1867 Bismarck was interested primarily in the welfare of Prussia, but that after 1867 he became interested in Germany as a whole?

4. In your opinion, how much did the creation of the German Empire owe to Bismarck's genius, and how much to circumstances outside Germany over which he had little control? Support your opinion with specific evidence.

To Put This Chapter into a Larger Setting

1. With another student, recreate the 1865 conversation between Napoleon III and Bismarck as you think it might have been.

2. Debate this proposition: Napoleon III was less ruthless than Cavour or Bismarck.

3. To what extent and in what way did the unification of Germany destroy the previous balance of power in Europe?

14

Nineteenth
Century
Russia

"The name Russia at once calls to mind the notion of vastness. It is a land of long broad rivers, of deep dark forests, of sultry heat and extreme cold, of limitless plains. From central Russia the flat land spreads out towards the four points of the compass. Far to the north are the Arctic ices, far to the south the great mountain ranges and the closed sea. To the east the land rolls on, barely broken by the low-lying Urals, until it reaches the Pacific, separated at its northern corner by only . . . [fifty-six] miles from America. To the west it rolls into Europe and meets no important physical barrier. . . ."*

Although by the nineteenth century this vast country was so much a part of Europe that it shared the general history of the European peoples, many influences of its geography and of its past kept it apart from western Europe. The effect of the new forces of the nineteenth century was not the same in Russia as in western and central Europe.

* Hugh Seton-Watson, *The Decline of Imperial Russia, 1855-1914* (New York: Praeger, 1952), p. 1.

☉ RUSSIAN SOCIETY

Russian society at the beginning of the nineteenth century was in many ways like that of the early Middle Ages in France and England. Class distinctions were sharp, most peasants were serfs, the middle class was an unimportant part of the population, and the lives of the overwhelming majority of Russians centered in one way or another on agriculture.

THE NOBLES AND THE SERFS

By the middle of the nineteenth century the population of Russia had risen to nearly 70,000,000, of whom only about 250,000 were noble landlords owning serfs. The greatest lords counted their serfs by the hundreds or even the thousands, but more than half the nobles were poor, owning fewer than a dozen serfs apiece. The nobles collected taxes from their serfs, recruited young serfs for the army, and usually, for want of better employment, served as government officials and army officers.

Serfs constituted more than three fourths of the Russian population. About half the serfs—"state serfs"—were owned by the government, the rest by the landowners. Russian landlords, unlike the medieval nobles of France and England, could sell their serfs, mortgage them, rent them out to other employers, or send them into exile in Siberia. In Russia the serf was bound to his owner instead of being bound to the land as the western European serf had been.

Most serfs were farmers, although some made money payments to their lords in place of working in the fields. For most of them the agricultural village with its peasant officials (the "mir," or "world") was all they knew. Some of the village land was cultivated for the benefit of the noble or the government under the direction of the landlord or of a government official. The rest was farmed for the benefit of the serfs themselves, the council of the mir regulating the rotation of crops, the time of planting, and the periodic redistribution of land to care for the increase or decrease in the size of families. The serfs' lands were thus treated as common property. The mir cared for any helpless aged, very young, or sick serfs. Such co-operative control of its own affairs by the mir, a special characteristic of Russian serfdom, helped make the serfs conscious of the importance of membership in a social group.

Using the labor of state serfs, government factories made military supplies. Noblemen also sometimes set up factories on their own estates using their own serfs for labor. Persons of noble status were permitted by law to increase their labor forces by buying whole villages, since serfs constituted the only supply of labor in Russia. In the heavy forest region stretching across northern Russia, where the land is poor and the winter darkness long, serfs often earned the money payments due their lords by making, in their own cottages, cloth and small objects to sell to merchants. The fact that Russian manufacturing long relied so exclusively on unfree labor helped make the course of Russian industrialization very different from that of the West.

One notable aspect of noble-serf relations was the wide gap that separated the two classes. This existed in part because the intermediate middle class was so very small. The greatest nobles with their sumptuous houses in St. Petersburg and Moscow and with the cosmopolitan manners that their freedom to travel abroad permitted them to acquire were, of course, farthest removed from the serfs; but even lesser nobles who could maintain houses only in Moscow, or the most numerous group who lived only on their own estates, had at least the outward ways of European high society. It became fashionable for nobles to imitate the French—to wear French clothes, adopt French manners, read French books, and even to teach the children French as a first language and Russian only later. Thus the nobles became as French as they could while the serfs remained Russian, and the distance between the two classes became the greater, even to the point where it was difficult for them to understand each other's language.

TOWNS AND THE MIDDLE CLASS

The sleepy, stagnant towns of Russia little resembled the thriving, fast-growing western European industrial cities with their alert, competitive businessmen. In the early nineteenth century a mere five per cent of the Russian people were town dwellers, and of these only a small part were middle-class professional and business people. In the summertime some towns became more populous because serfs, hard-pressed to earn the dues owed to their lords, secured permission to leave their farming to their wives and daughters and (like migrating birds, it has been said) went to seek employment in the factories.

THE POSITION OF THE ORTHODOX CHURCH

Religiously, the Russian people belonged to the Eastern or Orthodox branch of Christianity, which in the eleventh century had separated from the western Christian church headed by the papacy. Except for the denial of the headship of the pope, the doctrines of Orthodox Christianity have remained largely the same as those of the Roman Catholic Church. The liturgy has much in common with that of western Catholicism except that it is more ceremonious, invariably sung, and that instead of statues, the use of which is forbidden, sacred pictures (icons) are hung on a great screen separating the sanctuary with its altar from the body of the church. There is no single head of the Orthodox Church to perform the functions that in Roman Catholicism belong to the pope.

The clergy of the Russian Orthodox Church were either "black clergy" —monks who could not marry—or "secular clergy"—priests who could be married. Bishops came only from the black clergy. The secular clergy was almost a hereditary class. It had less esteem in Russian society than did the priesthood in western Catholic countries. The Holy Synod, which headed the Russian church, had much less influence than the chief procurator, a government official who was by no means necessarily a religious man. The revenues of the church came in considerable part from the government. In return, the government expected the clergy to inform their parishioners of the content of official proclamations and to co-operate with the police in hunting down and reporting persons possibly dangerous to the state.

All the subjects of the tsar were not, however, Orthodox. The Poles were Roman Catholics, the Finns and their neighbors Protestants, the Turks and Iranians Muslims, and a few people in the Asiatic provinces Buddhists. Many Jews lived in the Russian lands, especially in or near the Polish regions.

The official church suffered under so many handicaps and weaknesses that it was apparent that in spite of the piety of many individual Russians, leadership in Russian society would have to come from outside any religious group. It did, in fact, come from the small body of educated people who were beginning to take an important part in mid-nineteenth century Russia.

THE RUSSIAN INTELLIGENTSIA

In the first decades of the nineteenth century the gradual improvement of education and the increasing need for professional people produced a small group of intellectuals with training and attitudes similar to those of the educated upper classes in the western countries. In Russian history these people are known as "the intelligentsia." Some were nobles, but not all of them. Although the intelligentsia were in so many ways like western intellectuals, their position in Russia was unlike what it would have been in the West, for they were cut off from the two most important segments of

Russian society. They were not peasants, so they knew almost nothing of peasant life and could not hope to establish any contact with the great bulk of people. On the other hand, they were also cut off from the government officials, because they were critical of the Russian government and more ready to reform it than serve in it. Since the intelligentsia were thus set apart from practical contact with the problems of the time, their discussions and arguments had something of the unreal quality of classroom debates. But what they thought and said was important; they laid the foundations for later revolutionary ideas that had much practical consequence.

The intelligentsia were divided into two groups called "Westernizers" and "Slavophiles." Both groups were loyal Russians and both agreed that the time had come to make serious reforms in Russia. They disagreed when they tried to explain how Russia's problems had originated and what should be done to remove them.

The Westernizers claimed that Russia was a truly European nation that had had the bad fortune to have been Christianized and civilized from Byzantium instead of from Rome and to have experienced two centuries of Mongol occupation of southern Russia. Peter the Great (tsar 1682-1725) had set the right course for Russia, so the Westernizers believed, when he tried to make the country more similar to the West. It was the duty of nineteenth-century Russians to follow in the way Peter had marked out.

The very word *Slavophile* (admirer of Slavic culture) was adopted to show that persons in this group believed that Orthodox Christianity was preferable to what they conceived to be the narrowly legalistic Roman Catholicism, that the simple Russian peasant in his co-operative mir had more to contribute to the world than the money-making western bourgeoisie, and that Peter the Great had made a serious error when he tried to turn Russia away from being itself.

Although there was much debate among the intelligentsia, until the middle of the century they did not act. They frightened the government, nevertheless. Much of the activity of the secret police was devoted to watching them and limiting their activities. The higher schools and universities were also regulated and watched closely, and higher education came to be limited mostly to the sons of the nobles. The ferment of ideas continued, nevertheless. Exiled members of the intelligentsia managed to smuggle their writings back into Russia. More and more people were being educated in the Russian universities. A movement had been started that could not be stopped.

THE NATIONALITIES OF RUSSIA

All other aspects of Russian life were complicated by the fact that Russia was scarcely more of a single nation than was the Habsburg empire. The Russians, or "Great Russians," who occupied the central part of European Russia and who were the most numerous single group, were a minority of the population. Centuries of conquest and of the movement of explorers and settlers in Siberia had not only pushed the Russian boundaries east to the Pacific and west into Europe, but had also brought Finns, Poles, Lithuanians, Ukrainians, and many Asiatic peoples under Russian rule. Only the Great Russians spoke standard Russian, for the Ukrainians and the other peoples spoke their own languages. The government constantly vacillated between trying to make true Russians out of all these peoples and trying to make loyal subjects out of them by letting them alone. The question of the nationalities remained, therefore, a central problem of Russian life.

◠ THE RUSSIAN GOVERNMENT

The government of nineteenth-century Russia was an autocracy. There were, of course, ministers appointed by the tsars, and an army of officials served under the ministers; but it was only the tsar who could co-ordinate the activities of the various governmental agencies. No civil rights were guaranteed to the people. The tsar was not subject to the law; he was the maker of the laws, any of which he could alter at will.

There were two tsars in the first half of the nineteenth century, the brothers Alexander I (tsar 1801-1825; see page 72) and Nicholas I (tsar 1825-1855). Nicholas was a steadier man than his brother and lacked his interest in reform. He had been taught by a French *émigré* who had no love of the French Revolution nor of the Enlightenment preceding it, and who encouraged Nicholas's leanings toward autocracy. Nicholas traveled in western Europe after the Peace of Vienna, coming home at the end of his journey with intensified dislike of limited monarchy as he had seen it in action and with a deepened determination to preserve tsarist despotism. Since it had not originally been planned that he would succeed Alexander I, he had been given no experience in the work of government, but had rather been associated with the army, which he loved. He remained for life a soldier at heart, never so happy as when he was deciding some military matter, whether it was the choice of a uniform or of an expensive piece of heavy artillery.

Two brothers who ruled Russia for half a century: Alexander I (left), an autocrat who toyed with liberalism, and Nicholas I (right), who believed that liberal policies would destroy the true greatness of Russia.

Nicholas made much use of his Private Imperial Chancery—the ministers directly under his control. This chancery was divided into five separate sections, of which the infamous "Third Section" was the secret police. The Third Section hunted out heretical or subversive religious groups, kept watch over foreigners, and arrested and exiled a great many possible or actual enemies of the state and countless literary persons. One of these was the novelist Ivan Turgenev, who was detained in a police station for writing a death notice of the writer Nikolai Gogol. The novelist Feodor Dostoevski was one of a group of young socialists sentenced to death "to frighten them," then released at the scaffold to an exile at hard labor. The Third Section could on its own authority order "administrative arrest" and "administrative exile," often to Siberia. Banishment to Siberia was reasonably comfortable, since the exiles could take their families with them and engage in their ordinary occupations; but imprisonment within Russia was a grim matter. The thoroughness and severity of the Third Section too often succeeded in frightening into silence those very leaders of whom Russia had most need. Unfortunately the secret police were only the most obvious manifestation of the generally oppressive atmosphere characterizing the whole reign of Nicholas I.

◯ THE REFORMS OF ALEXANDER II

In spite of Russia's despotic government, the middle reign of the century, that of Alexander II (tsar 1855-1881), included a notable period of reform. Alexander was as conservative as his predecessors; but the defeat of Russia in the Crimean War (1853-1856) at the hands of France, Britain, and Turkey (see pages 162-166) was a warning to him and to other Russians that changes had to be made. It was clear that the more economically advanced and politically free nations could wield a force in international relations that the larger and more populous Russia could not match. Since Alexander II came to the throne just at the end of the war, he was swept along by the general desire to strengthen Russia by reforming her. The condition of the serfs, whose performance as soldiers had been wanting, was first to demand his attention. He decided that they must be freed.

THE EMANCIPATION OF THE SERFS

The decision to free the serfs did not come about solely because of the defeat in the Crimean War. Serf revolts had become increasingly and alarmingly frequent. At the same time the economic value of serfdom was being questioned, especially by noble wheat farmers of southern Russia engaged in a growing export trade, who were finding free labor—such as there was of it—more efficient.

Immediately after the Crimean War Alexander II began to prepare the nobles to accept emancipation. He set in motion a nation-wide discussion of possible methods. Never before had educated Russians talked so freely about a public problem. Committees were formed to sift the various proposals and to draft suggestions. Finally the whole matter was submitted to high state councils attended by the tsar. In 1861 the archbishop of Moscow wrote the imperial decree of emancipation.

All serfs were to be personally free. Each peasant family was to acquire ownership of some land, but they were to be required to pay for it. For the time being the government advanced the purchase price to the lords and, in return, the serfs were to make annual payments to the government for half a century thereafter. Since the mirs took the responsibility for the payments to be made by their peasants, the peasants themselves were still bound to their villages almost as effectively as they had been as serfs.

In spite of these limitations, it was a considerable achievement to free roughly 22,500,000 serfs in so short a time and without any kind of disorder or use of force. But carrying out the emancipation edict was a long and painful ordeal. The serfs had always looked upon the land that they farmed for their own use as belonging to them, and they were bitterly resentful when they were called upon to pay for it. In many areas the price of the land was set above the usual sale price in order to compensate the lords not only for the land but also for the services the serfs no longer had to perform. The amount of land given a serf was not always adequate. Fortunately when the state freed its serfs in 1863, it gave somewhat more generous terms. Whatever the difficulties, however, serfdom had to be destroyed before Russia could become a modern industrialized nation.

The emancipation of a group of Russian serfs, 1861. The serf being granted his freedom is prostrate on the ground, kissing the shoe of his landlord—a ritual that betrays the underlying Oriental nature of many Russian customs. Note also the contrast between the European style of clothing of the nobility (observing the ceremony from the porch of the manor house) and the quite different traditional attire of the Russian peasants.

OTHER REFORMS

The emancipation of 1861 was followed by a series of reforms, some made necessary by the emancipation itself.

The Zemstvos. Government service previously performed by the nobles had now to be put into the hands of others. Assemblies called "zemstvos" were established in all counties and provinces of Russia. Lords, townsmen, and peasants, each voting in their own groups, elected the members, although many peasants were too timid to vote. The zemstvos controlled the roads, sanitation, education, poor relief, and the like. For the first time ordinary Russians had a limited opportunity to take part in public affairs.

The Courts. The courts were also reformed to provide equality before the law, trial by jury, and judges holding office for life. The effect of this reform was, however, limited by the many special courts still in existence and by frequent interference by the tsar in the operation of justice. One of the results of the judicial reforms was the development of the profession of lawyer, of great importance in Russia in later years.

Education. Education was also becoming more widely available. Women had more opportunities for schooling, sometimes even being admitted to the universities. But after a time there was further restriction on schools, especially a strict limitation of science teaching, for the study of science had come to be connected in the minds of officials with radicalism.

For any country these reforms, made so quickly, would have been a notable achievement; for Russia they marked a decisive stage in the development of the nation. Then in 1863 there was a revolt in Poland, and in 1866 an attempt was made on the life of Alexander II. Always a conservative at heart, the tsar would thereafter permit no further reform. Since the intelligentsia remained profoundly dissatisfied with conditions in Russia, it is not surprising that revolutionary movements of various kinds marked the later years of the reign of Alexander II.

⌒   POLITICAL MOVEMENTS

The period after 1866 was a time of conflict between those forces of reform let loose early in the reign of Alexander II and the essentially conservative tsar and aristocracy. After the first years of his reign, Alexander appointed ultraconservative ministers whose first concern was to keep Russian young people from coming into contact with what were thought to be dangerous ideas. All student activities in the universities were forbidden, and professors were forced to make reports to the government about what their students seemed to be thinking. The young intelligentsia were angered. Both informal and organized reform movements sprang up among them.

One unorganized and relatively unimportant development was a tendency on the part of young people to follow a doctrine called by the word "nihilism" (from the Latin word meaning "nothing"). The term was introduced by Turgenev in his novel *Fathers and Sons*, published in 1862. Bazarov, a character in the novel, was a model nihilist: he could accept no idea at all from the older generation without the most critical examination of it. The nihilists believed that the individual must be freed from the traditional responsibilities placed upon him by family, church, and government, so that he could develop his own powers to the fullest. Most studies were thought by the nihilists to be useless, except for science, which was admired partly because it was not religious and partly because its teaching was discouraged by the government.

Another development was the "go-to-the-people" movement. Groups of young intellectuals went to live in the villages to teach the peasants how to improve their own conditions, somewhat as young American members of the Peace Corps have gone to live and work along with the people of today's underdeveloped lands. In preparation for this work young Russian intellectuals learned trades or professions useful in the villages. Young women became nurses, for example, and worked with the zemstvos to improve community health. All these young people hoped for a new society, not unlike that envisioned by the Utopian Socialists (see page 106), in which the mirs would be active, productive socialist units. In this way they hoped to improve the downtrodden lowest class without Russia's having to go through the Industrial Revolution with its bad as well as its good consequences. Along with other like-thinking reformers, they called themselves "Narodniks" (from *narod*, meaning "people"). They achieved little immediate success, for the village people did not respond enthusiastically to their work.

The government soon applied severely repressive measures to stop the Narodniks. In reply, a few of the most extreme Narodniks tried to attack the government through terrorism, hoping that by assassinating some leading persons they would frighten the officials into abandoning the policy of repression. They killed a number of high-ranking officials, and in 1881 murdered Alexander II. Their purpose was not achieved, however, for they simply frightened the next tsar, Alexander III, into adopting still more thorough measures against revolutionary activity.

ᴑ ᴑ ᴑ

At first glance it may seem that the history of nineteenth-century Russia had little in common with that of the other powerful countries of Europe. There is, however, the common factor of nationalism shared by all. Russian nationalism simply followed a different course from nationalism in the West. Unable to reform their country by open discussion and the making of laws, Russian patriots resorted to illegal and sometimes terrorist methods. Their fundamental purpose was no less nationalist for the fact that it was not carried out in partnership with their government or that for the time being it failed.

Persons, Places, and Terms

Nicholas I	state serfs	Slavophiles
Ivan Turgenev	mir	Great Russians
Nikolai Gogol	Orthodox Church	Third Section
Feodor Dostoevski	icons	zemstvos
Alexander II	black clergy	nihilism
Alexander III	secular clergy	"go-to-the-people"
	Holy Synod	movement
Siberia	intelligentsia	Narodniks
Ukraine	Westernizers	terrorism

To Master the Text

1. What percentage of early nineteenth century Russians were serfs? Who owned the serfs? What powers did the owners have? Describe the mir and the part that it played in the life of the serf. What other work did serfs do beside farming?
2. What percentage of the Russian population was the nobility? How did nobles differ from serfs? What divisions were there among the nobles?
3. Describe a Russian town of the mid-nineteenth century. How important were towns in Russia? Why?
4. To what branch of Christianity did the majority of Russians belong? How was it like and how was it unlike Catholicism in beliefs, liturgy, and church government? What was its relationship to the government? What other religious groups were there in Russia?
5. Who were the intelligentsia? From what classes did they come? What was their position in Russia? How did Westernizers and Slavophiles differ from each other? On what matters did they agree?
6. What non-Russian peoples lived within the borders of Russia? How were they treated?

7. How much power did the organization of the Russian government give to the tsar? How were the education and background of Nicholas I related to Russian autocracy? What was the Third Section? What were its duties? What effect did its activities have on the intellectual life of Russia?

8. By the time of Alexander II, what circumstances were encouraging emancipation of serfs? Trace the steps by which the decree of emancipation was prepared. In what way did the serfs remain bound to the government? To their villages? What problems developed as the emancipation edict was put into operation? What was done about the state serfs?

9. What were the zemstvos? How much authority did they have? To what extent were the courts improved? How much were educational opportunities widened?

10. List and describe the various ways in which young Russians attempted to extend the movement for reform.

To Interpret the Facts

1. What forces held back industrialization and reform in Russia? What reforms seem to you to have been most needed? Why?

2. In what ways was Russian life affected by events and developments outside Russia in this period?

3. Reread the concluding paragraph of this chapter, and cite specific facts that support it. Are there any exceptions to this general statement?

4. By 1881 was Russia a better place than it had been in 1815 for the nobles? For the townspeople? For the intelligentsia? For the peasants? Prove your point in each case.

To Put This Chapter into a Larger Setting

1. With two groups of classmates hold an imaginary conversation, one group representing and arguing for the ideas of the Westernizers and the other group for the ideas of the Slavophiles.

2. In other books find descriptions of Russian climate zones, forests, types of soil, river transportation, and other natural features. Explain how these influenced Russian history.

3. Report on the life of Alexander II.

4. Write and produce an informal play representing two simultaneous conversations going on in a single neighborhood in Russia in about 1865. On one part of the "stage" have three nobles discussing in specific detail the changes in their lives brought about by the emancipation of the serfs. On another part have a group of serfs discussing their disappointment in the results of emancipation. Alternate the conversations so that the two groups appear to be answering each other.

Looking Back to the 1840's

The years from the 1840's to 1871 were marked in Europe by much tension and warfare, beginning with the revolutions of 1848 and including the Crimean War and the wars of Italian and German unification. Nationalism was a factor in these struggles as never before in history. So great had the power of nationalism grown to be that all European and world affairs were bound to be strongly influenced by it for years to come. On the other hand, the simultaneous development of industry and transportation was drawing nations ever closer to each other and making them more interdependent. Like nationalism, industrialism bade fair to develop further and to affect more profoundly the lives of an ever-increasing number of people. To the problems it raised within the various industrialized countries, few solutions had yet been worked out; much waited to be done.

Some Questions to Answer

1. To make clear to what extent nationalism was the dominant theme of European history from 1848 to 1871, make a six-column table. Label the columns *Great Britain, France, Prussia, Austrian Empire, Russia,* and *Other.* At the left write the following dates: 1848-1849, the 1850's, the 1860's, the 1870's. Fill in the table by placing in the proper box each event or development that was strongly tinged with nationalism.
2. Although many revolutionary changes occurred quietly and without violence, revolution remained an important theme of European history after 1848. Determine the extent of revolutionary change during these years by answering the following questions: In what countries were new governments established? In what countries and in what ways was popular control of governments increased? In what ways did governments assume wider responsibilities for the welfare of their citizens? Were these changes rapid and important enough to be called revolutionary? Which of these changes were related to nationalism? Was nationalism itself revolutionary?
3. Although (1) industrial, (2) artistic, (3) intellectual, and (4) religious developments are treated in this book in separate chapters, all were

constantly interrelated with political history. Take each of the four separately and search for interrelations between it on the one hand and the political histories of the separate countries and the relations among countries on the other. Look particularly for interrelations with nationalism.

4. List those nations that achieved national governments of their own, 1848-1871. Make another list of peoples who in 1871 still lived under the governments of foreign nations but who had become acutely aware of their own national identity. How important do these lists lead you to expect nationalism to be after 1871?

5. Besides nationalism, what tensions seem to you to have been building up between the 1840's and 1871 that might prove troublesome in the succeeding decades? (Consider conflicts and rivalries between pairs of countries; conflicts between economic or social groups within specific countries; and conflicts in any one country between those wishing to experiment with new ways and those desiring to preserve the old ways.)

6. Is it accurate to say that between the 1840's and the 1870's, statesmen were more ruthlessly determined than their predecessors to advance their own countries and less willing to consider the interests of Europe as a whole?

7. During this period how did the continent of Europe become somewhat more of a unit than it had been before?

8. By 1871, what improvements had the Industrial Revolution made in the lives of ordinary individuals? What hardship had it caused?

Using Documents as Evidence

Giuseppe Mazzini (1805–1872) was a nationalist whose ideas and patriotic fervor helped lead the way to the unification of Italy in the nineteenth century. After centuries of fragmentation and domination by many other nations, Italy was finally unified in 1871. Two of Mazzini's most important writings follow.

GENERAL INSTRUCTIONS FOR
THE MEMBERS OF YOUNG ITALY

Section I. Young Italy is a brotherhood of Italians who believe in a law of Progress and Duty, and are convinced that Italy is destined to become one nation. [They are] convinced also that she possesses sufficient strength within herself to become one, and that the ill success of her former efforts is to be attributed not to the weaknesses but to the misdirection of the revolutionary elements within her, that the secret of force lies in constancy and unity of effort. They join this association in the firm intent of consecrating both thought and action to the great aim of reconstituting Italy as one independent sovereign nation of free men and equals....

Section 3. . . . The aim of the association is revolution; but its labors will be essentially educational. . . . By preaching exclusively that which it believes to be truth, the association performs a work of duty, not of usurpation. . . .

Section 4. The means by which Young Italy proposes to reach its aim are education and insurrection, to be adopted simultaneously. . . . Education must ever be directed to teach by example, word, and pen the necessity of insurrection. Insurrection, whenever it can be realised, must be so conducted as to render it a means of national education.

TO THE YOUNG MEN OF ITALY

Love your country. Your country is the land where your parents sleep, where is spoken that language in which the chosen of your heart, blushing, whispered the first word of love; it is the home that God has given you. . . . It is your name, your glory, your sign among the people. Give to it your thoughts, your counsels, your blood. Raise it up, great and beautiful as it was foretold by our great men, and see that you leave it . . . unprofaned by dismemberment. Let it be one. . . . You are twenty-five millions of men, envy of the nations of Europe. An immense future is before you; you lift your eyes to the loveliest heaven, and around you smiles the loveliest land in Europe; you are encircled by the Alps and the sea, boundaries traced out by the finger of God for a people of giants. You are bound to be such, or nothing. . . .

On the basis of these documents, what hypothesis could you form about the underlying causes of the unification of Italy? What beliefs did Mazzini set forth regarding the idea of equality? How did Mazzini believe that unification was to be achieved, that is, what methods did he advocate? What kinds of feelings did Mazzini appeal to in addressing the young men of Italy?

PART 3

Europe and the World

The 1870's to the 1910's

In the forty years after 1871 there were no wars between the European great powers, but these were not years of easy peace. In every industrial country rapid economic and social change created tensions for which remedies had to be sought, often in vain. In spite of the absence of war, each great power feared the possibility of attack from abroad. Elaborate plans for defense were made, alliances were arranged, and fear of war intensified every international dispute. A safety valve was sometimes found in the renewed interest in colonization that engaged the attention of the British, French, Germans, and Russians, as well as of the Japanese and the Americans. International crises could sometimes be resolved by colonial bargains among the empire-building nations; but at other times, colonial rivalries actually increased tensions among the powers. By the 1910's all the European powers had joined one or the other of two great armed alliances. Also by that time Africa was partitioned among European countries, and Asia was largely under European influence. The European countries were more closely interrelated than ever before, and European domination of the world had reached its greatest limits.

15
Industrial Society

1870-1914

Fundamental to all other late nineteenth-century developments was industrial expansion. After 1870 large-scale industry grew by leaps and bounds in Britain and Belgium and more gradually in France. It spread with amazing rapidity to many other parts of Europe, to North America, and even to the Far East. For the first time in history there came to be regions of considerable size in both Europe and America where industry was as important as or more important than agriculture. A new kind of society came into being in which people lived, worked, and spent their leisure time in ways never before possible. Art, literature, science, and religion—the ideas in men's minds—were profoundly affected. But the first and most obvious of these changes was industrial growth.

☾ INDUSTRIAL GROWTH

Steel and steam were the backbone of industrial growth from 1870 to 1914; but before the end of the period chemicals, oil, and electricity, expanding with the aid of scientific discoveries, were laying the foundations for new giant industries.

STEEL, RAILROADS, AND STEAMSHIPS

Steel and fast steam-powered transportation dominated the forty years after 1870 much as cotton, coal, and iron—still flourishing after 1870—had dominated the immediately preceding period.

Steel. World production and use of steel grew almost beyond belief— from 703,000 metric tons in 1870 to 58,656,000 metric tons in 1910. What with steel rails many times longer-lasting than those of iron, steel boilers capable of withstanding high pressures, steel locomotives, and steel steamships, steel was transforming the whole system of transportation. The expanding food-preserving industry used quantities of sheet steel for its "tin" cans. Especially in the United States, tall buildings—the first authentic skyscrapers—were built with riveted steel frames capable of bearing the whole weight of the building. There were steel typewriters, steel farm machines, steel sewing machines, steel bridges—in some cases altogether new devices not feasible without inexpensive steel. For special purposes other metals were added to the molten steel to produce alloys with such qualities as hardness, pliability, or resistance to rusting.

So profitable a business could not be monopolized by one or two countries. By 1900 the United States and Germany had overtaken Great Britain, and by the outbreak of the First World War in 1914 Germany produced in a year 24,000,000 tons of steel, the United States 31,000,000 tons, and Great Britain only 8,000,000.

Steam Transportation. Meantime the railroad systems of the United States and Europe were essentially completed. In the United States the first transcontinental line was ready for use in 1869, running westward from Chicago to San Francisco and opening to settlers the region between the Mississippi River and the Rocky Mountains. Soon the whole country was drawn together by a web of railroads. In Germany the railroad was also of special importance because the central position of the country permitted freight to be shipped to neighbors to the east, south, and west. Russia also began railroad building, largely under the leadership of Sergei Witte, once a railway stationmaster and by 1892 the minister of finance. Costs were paid by the government, partly from foreign loans, so that although Russia had more rail mileage than Germany by 1914, one third of the national debt had to be charged to railroads. Witte's most spectacular achievement was the construction (1892-1906) of the Trans-Siberian Railroad across the Russian Asiatic region of Siberia to the Pacific. Russian pioneers could then more easily move into Siberia—5,000,000 of them within ten years—sending back such necessities as grain and butter.

"The Old St. Lazare Station, Paris," by Claude Monet, 1877. The painting not only is an excellent example of the French Impressionist style, but also is evidence of the impact on all aspects of life—including the subject matter of the fine arts—of continuing rapid industrialization and the resulting changes in the character of cities.

Ocean steamships were also multiplying, for not only were they faster and more reliable than sailing vessels, but they had become increasingly spacious and economical. In 1883 half the tonnage of British merchant vessels was in steamships, and by 1893 the steam tonnage of the world was larger than that of all seagoing sailing ships.

ELECTRICITY, PETROLEUM, AND CHEMICALS

Meantime inventors, using the findings of science, were developing new sources of power and important new products. Among these were new uses of electricity, new chemical products, and the gasoline engine.

Electricity. Although the principle of generating electricity by the use of the dynamo had long been known, until the 1890's electric power was too expensive to be used for much except street lighting. Thereafter various improvements cheapened production. One of these, important in such mountainous but coal-poor countries as northern Italy, was the use of waterpower—"white coal," as it was called—to turn electric generators. Gradually electricity was used to light houses, convey telephone messages, and drive streetcars. Wireless telegraphy sent its first message across the English Channel in 1899, and within a decade ships were being equipped to send and receive wireless messages.

The Gasoline Engine. By the 1890's the internal combustion engine, run by gasoline and used today in automobiles and airplanes, was well enough developed to make automobiles practical, although before 1914 they were mostly the toys of the well-to-do. By 1910 three quarters of them were manufactured in the United States, and Henry Ford had already begun his effort to produce a car cheap enough to fit the budgets of ordinary families. The airplane was first successfully flown in the United States in 1903 and across the English Channel in 1909. Its development was slow at first, for in 1914 only forty-nine aircraft were built in the United States; but the groundwork was laid for an expanding industry.

Chemicals. Scientific advances in chemistry led to the manufacture of hitherto unknown products from the most unlikely materials. In both chemistry and electricity the Germans took the lead. From coal, for example, they extracted dyes more cheaply and in greater quantity and variety than had ever been procurable from plants and animals. By 1913 they were making 88 per cent of the world's dyes. In many countries celluloid, rayon, photographic film, and cheap paper were being manufactured from wood pulp. The list of these synthetics—often better, more plentiful, or cheaper than natural products—was long and growing, making the quantity of useful things so much greater than ever before that many more people could possess them.

THE ORGANIZATION OF INDUSTRY

New ways of financing had also to be developed because of the vast amount of capital required to build great steel mills, shipyards, and railroad lines, and also because of the long period of time required (especially for railroads) before any profit could be realized from the investment. Even the device of the corporation (see page 124) was now inadequate. Supercorporations, variously called "trusts," "holding companies," or "cartels," brought together the necessary huge sums of money. Sometimes a single company, like John D. Rockefeller's Standard Oil Company, bought out its competitors or forced them out of business altogether. Sometimes a company would buy other companies whose products it needed. The German steel and armament manufacturer Krupp, for example, bought coal mines in Germany, iron mines in Spain, ore boats, and a shipyard. Lever, the English soap manufacturer, had factories in many countries and plantations in Africa and Australia. Such organizations were enormous and powerful, controlling the lives of thousands of workers and their families, setting the prices of goods and services needed by many people, influencing the whole economic life of a nation, and sometimes exerting undue influence on governments. In the United States antitrust laws were passed to break up such huge organizations as Standard Oil.

INDUSTRIAL EUROPE AND THE WORLD

The influence of large-scale industry was felt over the world, in agricultural areas as well as in cities. Increased movement of populations and changes in world trade were among the most obvious of these world-wide results.

Emigration from Europe. The populations of Europe and the world continued to multiply (see page 123) and to move about. No longer was it so likely that a man would live out his life in the neighborhood of his birth. It is estimated that of every seven persons added to the western European population only one stayed on the land. Of the other six, one left Europe altogether, and five went to the growing cities. Of the 60,000,000 who are thought to have left Europe between 1815 and 1914, about half went to the United States, others to the British colonies and Latin America, and 5,000,000 to Siberia, all hoping for more prosperous lives in a new land.

World Trade. Goods also moved more easily over the world. Total world trade increased six times between 1880 and 1913. Manufactures went overseas from Europe, while agricultural and tropical products—wool, wheat, rubber, ivory—went to Europe in return. The industrial countries also exchanged manufactured products among themselves. At first the export of industrial products brought more money into Europe than was needed to pay for agricultural products imported from overseas. Much of this excess money was invested by European capitalists in such ventures as the railroads of North and South America, which were partly built with British and French money. In the twentieth century Europe began spending more money overseas than was being brought in by selling industrial products; but profits from the investments abroad helped pay the difference, and thus Europeans were able to maintain their high standard of living.

INDUSTRIAL CITIES

Migration of country people into the ever-growing cities continued at such a rate that by 1914 there were in the world fourteen cities with more than a million inhabitants: London, Paris, Berlin, Vienna, St. Petersburg, Moscow, New York, Chicago, Philadelphia, Buenos Aires, Rio de Janeiro, Tokyo, Osaka, and Calcutta. The city became the characteristic feature of the industrial world, and the factory and office worker replaced the peasant as the typical kind of person.

Although cities still contained dreadful slums, they also began to secure public services like gas and electricity, water and sewage systems, and paved streets. Newspapers, museums, and lecture halls as well as the expanding public school systems offered new educational opportunities to old and young. For the first time in history working people had a considerable share of such comforts as cheaper and better food, clothing, furniture, and books. But in the cities the neighborliness of rural life was lacking; neighbors were often strangers to each other, and only the police and charitable organizations were expected to care for persons in need.

☻ MARXIAN SOCIALISM

To radical thinkers of the time, the uneven distribution of wealth and the poverty of the slums proved that industrial society was basically so evil that it could be improved only by a revolutionary reorganization. Many programs of revolution were suggested, but the "scientific socialism" of Karl Marx and Friedrich Engels overshadowed all others.

MARX AND ENGELS

Karl Marx (1818-1883) was a Rhineland German. After taking his university degree in law in 1842, he became editor of a liberal newspaper, interesting himself deeply in the social questions of the day and becoming increasingly radical. When his paper was banned, he moved first to Paris and then to Brussels, each of which he was asked to leave. He then settled for life in London, where he spent his days working in the library of the British Museum on his three-volume book *Das Kapital* ("Capital"), in which he set forth his theories. He was a solitary, uncongenial man with few friends

Karl Marx, the formulator of the principles of communism or, as he also called it, "scientific socialism."

outside his devoted family. Marx had no direct experience with the industrial life about which he wrote; but his lifelong friend and collaborator, Friedrich Engels (1820-1895), was the son of a wealthy Rhineland manufacturer and the manager of a family factory in England. Engels collaborated with Marx in working out the theories of communism, supplied his firsthand knowledge of the industrial world, and gave Marx much-needed financial assistance.

THE THEORIES OF MARXIAN COMMUNISM

The first statement of their theories made by Marx and Engels was in their pamphlet *The Manifesto of the Communist League* (usually referred to as *The Communist Manifesto*), published just before the outbreak of the revolutions of 1848. They used the word "communist" to distinguish their "scientific socialism" from what they called "Utopian" socialism (see page 106), which they judged to be impractical; but they also often called themselves "socialists" to indicate that they believed that the wealth of society should be owned by and used for the benefit of society as a whole.

The argument of the *Manifesto* may be summarized in this way: The fundamental motive for all human actions is an economic one—the desire to gain wealth. In every past epoch of history a few fortunate people have had control of the greater part of the available wealth. The less fortunate classes have naturally been in conflict with the single ruling class. After a time economic changes have enabled some new class to become powerful enough to replace the former ruling class, as the industrial bourgeoisie replaced the feudal nobles. In industrial society there are only two classes of any consequence: the bourgeois factory owners and the proletariat (the factory workers). Two characteristics of industrial society are particularly important. The first of these arises from the facts—or, rather, what the *Manifesto* claimed to be facts—that the worker by his labor puts the whole value into any manufactured product, while the factory owner pockets the profits and pays the worker only so much as is required to keep him alive. Thus the workers are cheated out of the rightful reward of their labor. According to the *Manifesto*, this situation will not continue forever because of the second important characteristic of industrial society: the tendency for the richest factory owners to become even richer and to buy out or force out of business their less rich competitors. As all the wealth thus comes into the hands of a very few men and as the growth of the factory system brings into existence a larger and larger proletariat, the day will come when the desperate proletarians will rise in revolution, destroy the bourgeoisie, and seize the factories. They will then establish a "dictatorship of the proletariat," destroy all bourgeois institutions, and create a classless "communist" society in which all will work together for the common good and each will have the goods and services he needs. Marx and Engels believed that the communist revolution was inevitable at some future time; but they encouraged the workers to try to hasten it by working closely with Marxian revolutionary groups.

In 1864 Marx attempted to bring radical workers from all countries into a single organization called the "First International Workingmen's Association." After a few years, opposition from governments and disputes among the members brought about its collapse. The "Second International," organized in 1889, lasted until the First World War. It, too, was plagued by differences among its members. Some obeyed Marx's precept to avoid all co-operation with ordinary political parties. Others, called "revisionists," renounced the belief that violent revolution was necessary and formed regular political parties seeking the adoption of laws favorable to working people.

∩   NEW DEVELOPMENTS IN SCIENCE

Closely connected with late nineteenth century industrial growth was the continuing advance of science; for "pure science"—that is, science studied simply for the purpose of increasing knowledge, without expectation of immediate usefulness—laid the basis for many technological changes.

PHYSICS AND CHEMISTRY

Until 1895, the "classical physics" of Newton and Clerk Maxwell (see pages 132-134) gave scientists the comfortable feeling of understanding the basic character of the universe. Then came a number of startling discoveries showing that in spite of their rapidly increasing *control* over nature, men were still far from a complete *understanding* of nature.

First came the accidental discovery of X rays in 1895 by the German physicist Wilhelm Roentgen (1845-1923). There followed a search for substances giving out similar rays. In 1900 a Polish woman living in France, Marie Curie, working with her husband, extracted from uranium-bearing earth a remarkably radioactive element (one sending out rays), which they named radium. Further experimentation revealed that radioactivity in an element is accompanied by the production of new elements, a change due to the explosion of an occasional atom of the original element. Thus the old idea that the elements were unchangeable had to be abandoned.

The concept of the atom had now also to be changed. Since the time of Dalton, the atom had been regarded as the indivisible, indestructible unit of matter, in its movements obeying Newton's law of motion. The discovery of radioactivity proved that the atom was not indestructible. The work of J. J. Thomson, Ernest Rutherford, and others showed that the atom had a structure, that it was made of electrically charged particles arranged in a pattern similar to that of the solar system. A problem arose, however, for it was impossible to use the laws of classical physics to explain such an atomic structure. It was necessary to work out profound modifications of those laws. The German physicist Max Planck (1858-1947), studying the radiation of heat, assumed that energy is emitted in small bursts—indivisible "quanta"—rather than in a continuous stream, as classical mechanics had assumed. The Danish physicist Niels Bohr (1885-1962) applied this "quantum theory" to the study of the atom. Another modification was the theory of relativity developed by Albert Einstein (1879-1955). The understanding of Einstein's theory, which deals with the motions of bodies at extremely high velocities, demands the treating of time as a fourth dimension along with length, breadth, and thickness. By the end of this period physicists realized that Newtonian-Maxwellian mechanics applied only to objects between the size of bacteria and the size of the earth and to velocities much less than that of light. Outside this range new theories were needed.

BIOLOGY AND PSYCHOLOGY

From the publication in 1859 of Darwin's best-known work, *The Origin of Species* (see pages 134-136), biology aroused intense interest among non-scientists. Not only did a religious controversy ensue, but there also came to be an entirely unscientific use of Darwin's ideas called "Social Darwinism." Successful businessmen who had achieved their success by ruthless methods argued that they had "survived" in the fierce competition of business because they were the "fittest." Similarly, white peoples who had succeeded in subjecting colored colonial peoples claimed that white men were the "fittest" of the human race. Darwin himself would have been shocked by this misuse of his scientific work, but Social Darwinism had a considerable popularity.

Meantime biologists were seeking to discover by what means and by what stages the process of evolution takes place. By raising peas in his monastery garden, Gregor Mendel (1822-1884), an Augustinian monk, abbot of an Austrian monastery, gathered data about the inheritance by generations of plants of such characteristics as tallness and shortness. Other biologists, going beyond his work, developed the theory that evolution sometimes takes place by sudden spurts instead of gradually over very long periods of time, as Darwin had believed. These studies of heredity enabled breeders of animals and of new strains of plants to make progress with their work.

Psychology also made advances before 1914. In 1875 the German physiologist and psychologist Wilhelm Wundt (1832-1920) established the first laboratory for experimental psychology. Later scientists applied his experimental methods to the study of such aspects of human personality as the senses, the emotions, and the processes of learning.

The most controversial figure among psychologists was the Viennese Sigmund Freud, the founder of psychoanalysis. Work with mentally ill patients convinced him that much human behavior is not altogether controlled by conscious reason, but rather by unconscious or partly conscious sides of man's nature. He traced much mental illness to childhood experiences. His method of treatment, involving the recall by his patients of their reactions to events of their childhoods, has not only served as a basis for the work of psychiatrists but has also thrown light on the development of individual personalities and of the cultures of the whole human race.

ᅀ ART AND LITERATURE

While scientists were developing their important and profitable theories, artists and writers were abandoning some of their old forms and methods in favor of new ones somewhat influenced by the advance of industrialism.

The literature of the day tended to be realistic, depicting the dirt, the toil, and the poverty of the new city life. There was no unified movement to replace romanticism, however. Some of the realistic novels of George Eliot were written in this period, as were those of the Englishman Thomas Hardy, the American Henry James, and the Frenchman Emile Zola. In Russia Leo Tolstoy wrote *War and Peace*, a novel of the time of the Napoleonic invasions, picturing a many-sided and very real Russia with unsurpassed fullness and vividness. Other writers pointed out weaknesses in the society of the time, as in the clever plays of the British socialist George Bernard Shaw.

Painting had no cause to strive for exact realism because the camera had been perfected for that purpose. Instead the most important group of painters, the French "impressionists," strove to fill their pictures with the light, color, and movement that the observer sees in his first quick impression of a scene. Edouard Manet (1832-1883), Claude Monet (1840-1926), and Auguste Renoir (1841-1919) were leaders of this group. Later came the "postimpressionists" like the Dutch Vincent van Gogh (1853-1890), with his bright, thick colors, and the French Paul Cézanne (1839-1906), who tried to unite the strengths of the impressionist painters with those of the more classical past—to use light and color but to give his paintings a clearly defined form.

Music remained generally romantic, as in that of Richard Wagner (1813-1883), Johannes Brahms (1833-1897), and Gustav Mahler (1860-1911) in Germany and Austria, Giuseppe Verdi (1813-1901) in Italy, and Peter Tchaikovsky (1840-1893) in Russia. There was a marked tendency toward music that reflected strong national feeling, as in Wagner's operas based on medieval German legends. The folk music of their own people was used by such composers as Antonin Dvořák (1841-1904), a Czech; Edvard Grieg (1843-1907), a Norwegian; and Modeste Moussorgsky (1835-1881), a Russian.

Architecture followed no well-marked line during the first years after 1870, for it was fashionable both in homes and public buildings to imitate the outward appearance of the building styles of any past time or place from Greek to Renaissance. Before 1914, however, "functionalism" or "modernism" developed buildings especially suited to their purposes and to the materials from which they were constructed. Simple straight lines and undisguised use of such materials as concrete characterized not only sky-scrapers and factories but often expensive homes as well.

◌ DEVELOPMENTS IN RELIGION

It was not surprising in a scientific, industrial, realistic age that many people should turn away from organized religion. The years 1870 to 1914 could not be called a particularly religious period, but there were interest-ing developments among both Protestant and Catholic Christians and among Jews.

Protestants reacted to the new scientific theories in a number of ways. Some of them, called "fundamentalists," rejected those theories not in harmony with a literal interpretation of the Bible and clung to what they believed to be the fundamentals of the Christian religion. Others, called "modernists," became less concerned with the precise points of religious doctrine and turned rather to trying to put into active practice the moral teachings of Christianity. They made their churches centers for community reform, worked among impoverished people, and performed other services intended to lessen the evils of industrial and urban life.

Catholics had the same trouble with the new scientific theories as did Protestants. The attitude of Pope Leo XIII (pope 1878-1903) was, how-ever, instrumental in preventing a great conflict between religion and science. This scholarly pope encouraged Catholics to follow the teaching of the medieval scholar St. Thomas Aquinas, who argued that there could be no fundamental conflict between science and religion.

Leo XIII also took the attitude that men could remain good Catholics and at the same time take active roles in the new democratic industrial society. He urged that the church continue to play an important part in education. He encouraged the formation of Catholic political parties and urged French Catholics to co-operate with the Third French Republic. He hoped for a Catholic movement to combat Marxian communism while also opposing the mistreatment of workers and seeking a wider distribution of private property. He set forth his ideas in his encyclical (letter) to Catholics *Rerum Novarum* ("Of Modern Things"). The next pope, Pius X (pope 1903-1914) followed a somewhat different line, trying especially to combat modernism as a force weakening Catholic doctrine.

Jews were also divided in their reactions to the thinking of the time. "Orthodox" Jews clung literally to the words of the old writings and maintained the ancient social and religious customs. "Reform" Jews abandoned the strictest social practices and emphasized the moral aspects of Judaism.

One striking aspect of the religious life of these decades was the increase in missionary activity. Catholics, long active in such work, continued it so successfully that by 1900 there were almost 6,000,000 Catholics in Asia and Africa. Protestants entered the field with much increased vigor. By 1910 there were more than 4,000,000 Protestant Christians in Asia and Africa. Both groups sent as missionaries persons trained as doctors, as teachers, or in other ways that made them able to improve the lives of the people among whom they lived.

ᴕ ᴕ ᴕ

This was the industrial society of the years 1870-1914. It was a time of rapid change in material things such as manufacturing, transportation, cities, homes, and science. Art and religion suffered somewhat because of the emphasis on the material aspects of life, but even in these realms significant developments were taking place. It was against the background of this industrial society that the political growth of individual countries took place and that the relations among those countries and between Europe and the rest of the world were worked out.

Persons, Places, and Terms

Sergei Witte	Friedrich Engels	Ernest Rutherford
Henry Ford	Wilhelm Roentgen	Max Planck
John D. Rockefeller	Marie Curie	Niels Bohr
Karl Marx	J. J. Thomson	Albert Einstein

Gregor Mendel	Pius X	bourgeoisie
Wilhelm Wundt		proletariat
Sigmund Freud	Ruhr Valley	dictatorship of the
George Eliot	Mississippi River	proletariat
Thomas Hardy	Rocky Mountains	First International
Henry James	Trans-Siberian	Workingmen's
Emile Zola	Railroad	Association
Leo Tolstoy	Rio de Janeiro	Second International
George Bernard Shaw	Tokyo	revisionist socialists
Edouard Manet	Osaka	pure science
Claude Monet	Calcutta	applied science
Auguste Renoir		radioactivity
Vincent van Gogh	alloy	radium
Paul Cézanne	dynamo	quantum theory
Richard Wagner	internal combustion	relativity
Johannes Brahms	engine	Social Darwinism
Giuseppe Verdi	trust	impressionism
Gustav Mahler	holding company	postimpressionism
Peter Tchaikovsky	cartel	functional
Antonin Dvořák	antitrust laws	architecture
Edvard Grieg	scientific socialism	*Rerum Novarum*
Modeste Moussorgsky	communism	Orthodox Jews
Leo XIII	*Communist Manifesto*	Reform Jews

To Master the Text

1. How rapid and widespread was industrialization, 1870-1910? What industries were the backbone of this expansion? What new industries became important before 1914?
2. How important was steel during this period? What was the order of importance of the steel producing countries in 1914?
3. What was the importance of railroads in the United States? In Russia? In Germany? To what extent did steam navigation develop at this time?
4. To what extent had electricity developed by 1914? Automobiles? Airplanes? List the new products of the chemists.
5. Describe the new kinds of business organization. What advantages did they give businessmen?
6. Where did the growing populations of Europe find new homes during this period?
7. What goods were exported from Europe to less industrialized regions? What goods were sent back to Europe in return? Which trade was more profitable at first? Which later? In the later period what helped the Europeans pay for imports?
8. Why was the peasant no longer the typical European? How were cities being improved? Was it easy for country people to adjust to city life?

9. Why were theories about reorganizing society put forward at this time? How did the personal experiences of Karl Marx and Friedrich Engels prepare them for the kind of work they did? What did they mean by "socialism," "scientific socialism," and "communism"? Outline the argument of the *Communist Manifesto*. In what ways did revisionist socialists differ from Marx and Engels?

10. What scientific findings caused the abandoning of the idea that chemical elements were unchangeable? What new ideas were embodied in the quantum theory? In the theory of relativity?

11. What use did the Social Darwinists make use of Darwin's ideas? How were Darwin's theories altered by later biologists? With what results?

12. What were the developments in psychology during this period?

13. How was realism in literature related to industrial expansion? Name some outstanding realistic writings and their authors. What were the characteristics of impressionist painting? Of postimpressionism? Name artists from each school. Name important composers of the time. What kind of music did each write? What are the characteristics of functional architecture?

14. How do religious fundamentalists differ from religious modernists? How did Leo XIII suggest that the religious problems arising from the new science be solved? What part did he believe that Catholics should play in the modern world? In what document did he state his ideas? What is the difference between Orthodox and Reform Jews?

To Interpret the Facts

1. Compare the development by 1914 of each category mentioned under the heading "Industrial Growth" with developments since 1914 that you are familiar with. What conclusions do you reach regarding industrial development after the period discussed in this chapter?

2. The development of giant organizations (big business and big unions, for example) is characteristic of the modern world. How was the tendency to bigness evident in this period?

To Put This Chapter into a Larger Setting

1. Which of the prophesies made by Marx and Engels have been proved inaccurate? Why might the arguments of Marx nevertheless appeal to impoverished peoples? Why do those arguments have less appeal to prosperous peoples or to those who have opportunities for advancement?

2. How did the industrial development of 1870-1914 compare with that before 1830? With that between 1830 and 1870?

3. Prepare a report on one of the literary or artistic developments of the period or on a specific writer, painter, or composer. Supplement your report with excerpts from writing, reproductions of paintings, or recordings of music.

Great Britain
and
France

1867-1914

By the last third of the nineteenth century the effects of rapid industrial growth were transforming not only the lives of individuals but also the activities of governments. Governments were having to pay heed to the demands of powerful big businesses and also sometimes to the demands of labor unions and of labor parties. The laissez-faire ideas of the classical economists (see page 96) were no longer so generally accepted as they had been in the earlier part of the century. There was a growing feeling that governments had an obligation to encourage business and to give aid to the less fortunate classes of people.

These general tendencies affected the countries of Europe in different ways. In Russia the Industrial Revolution had begun, but the tsars remained firmly convinced that most demands for political and social change were evidences of disloyalty. In Germany, Italy, and Austria-Hungary, where there was more industrialization and where there was some popular voice in government, changes could more easily be made to meet the new conditions of the time. France and Great Britain were (except for Germany) the most fully industrialized of the great powers and their governments were also the most democratic and reform-minded. The domestic histories of the leading European countries reveal these differences in economic development and political outlook.

◠   GREAT BRITAIN

In Great Britain more than in any other large European nation, the political problems of the day were related to industrialization and to social changes resulting from industrial growth. In addition, Britain had the age-old question of Ireland.

In the 1870's Great Britain was still the "workshop of the world," as its businessmen liked to boast, and also the world's leading trading nation, the world's banker, the greatest naval power, and the possessor of a larger colonial empire and greater prestige than any other nation on earth. British bankers made loans to the less developed countries for building railroads and other expensive installations; British ships carried the goods of foreign nations; and the superior manufactures of British producers went to all parts of the earth.

In the 1830's the earlier stages of industrialization had helped produce near-revolutionary changes in the British government (see pages 102-104) but by the 1860's the country was again ripe for reform. In the towns the right to vote was still restricted to men occupying houses of a fairly high rental value. Only gradually were a few working people becoming prosperous enough to meet this test. Seats in Parliament were not yet distributed to the towns strictly according to population. As working people acquired better wages and more education, they began to organize unions (called in Britain "trade unions") and to agitate for the extension of the right to vote. They hoped to elect to Parliament men interested in the problems of labor. They were opposed by businessmen and others who argued that the country as a whole could only be well governed by property-holders. Out of arguments like these there grew a series of laws that occupied the attention of Parliament until the outbreak of war in 1914.

THE REFORMS OF GLADSTONE AND DISRAELI 1867-1885

The years 1867-1885 were the midpoint of the Victorian Age, named for Britain's popular, long-lived Queen Victoria, who reigned from 1837 to 1901. Political life was dominated by two rival statesmen, William Ewart Gladstone and Benjamin Disraeli.

Gladstone was the leader of the Liberal party, the successor to the old Whig party. A gifted man of impressive appearance, he had from the first enjoyed success in life. The son of a wealthy merchant of Liverpool, he was an outstandingly brilliant student at Oxford. His devotion to the Church of England was so deep that he considered going into the priesthood; but instead at the age of twenty-four he entered Parliament, where he remained for over sixty years. Throughout those decades he was one of the greatest of orators, famous for his command of facts and especially of figures. His deep moral convictions helped give an air of righteousness to any cause he supported. The Liberal party that Gladstone led was dominated by businessmen and townspeople. Many of its members clung to the earlier liberal *laissez-faire* ideas, but the party as a whole claimed to stand for reform.

Benjamin Disraeli, leader of the Conservative party (formerly the Tories), was a man as unlike Gladstone as could be imagined. His enemies called him un-English; for although he was an Anglican in religion, his ancestors were Venetian Jews who had come to England in the mid-eighteenth century. He began his career as an eccentric sort of person, writing daring novels, going about in unusual clothes. When he entered Parliament as a young man, his vanity and affectations made him seem ridiculous—a striking contrast to the more conventional Gladstone. Before long, however, his agile mind, his shrewdness in debate, his capacity for leadership, and his personal charm made him the leader of the Conservative party. He was proud to belong to that party, for it was the party of the aristocracy (of which he was an enthusiastic admirer) as well as of the farmers and the dwellers in small towns. Disraeli saw that the Conservatives had a better chance than did the Liberals to be the party of all Englishmen. The Liberal party was too much restricted to business people, unwilling to consider the needs of the workingmen. But the Conservatives, so Disraeli believed, could develop programs pleasing to aristocrats and workingmen alike. Disraeli was also an enthusiastic promoter of the British Empire and was able to arouse British patriotism by his vigorous foreign policy.

The Reform Bill of 1867. The first important law of this period was the Reform Bill of 1867. This carried further the work of the First Reform Bill of 1832. (See page 103.) It transferred more seats in Parliament to the growing towns, and in those towns the law established almost universal manhood suffrage. In 1868 an election held under the terms of the new act gave the Liberals a majority in the House of Commons and made Gladstone prime minister.

The Reform Ministry of Gladstone, 1868-1874. As prime minister Gladstone followed the policies to be expected of a businessman with a leaning toward *laissez faire* and a passion for moral right. He instituted the secret ballot so that the new workingmen voters would not be forced to vote as their employers directed. For the first time he made trade unions altogether legal, but without a guarantee of the right to strike. Where there were as

William Ewart Gladstone (left) and Benjamin Disraeli (right), later Earl of Beacons-field, leaders of the British Liberal and Conservative parties. Gladstone, here addressing the House of Commons on the Irish question, was noted for the fervor with which he fought for causes that he considered righteous; Disraeli, or "Dizzy," as he was called, was famous in his youth for the pains he took to be conspicuously different in dress and manner from the ordinary run of Englishmen.

yet no schools, he provided elementary education, to be supported jointly by government and parents. But school attendance was not yet compulsory. He admitted non-Anglican students to Oxford and Cambridge. He reformed the courts and the army. He began the selection of government employees on the basis of competitive examinations.

Each of these reforms made enemies among conservative-minded people, who accused Gladstone of rushing toward the destruction of the whole British political and social system. Workingmen, on the other hand, complained that Gladstone made too few reforms that helped them. In the election of 1874 Disraeli saw his opportunity. He pledged the Conservative party to maintain the traditional principles of British government and at the same time to become the party of "Tory Democracy," devoted to the interests of the working people. The Conservatives won the election of 1874 and Disraeli became prime minister.

Disraeli's Ministry, 1874-1880. In office, Disraeli secured the passage of a number of acts to improve the conditions of working people. A Public Health Act provided such necessary modern improvements as sewers, and an Artisans Dwelling Act permitted town governments to clear slums and build better workers' houses. A Factory Act brought up to date all the laws limiting the labor of children and women and prescribing proper factory conditions. Trade unions were permitted to picket factories during strikes, and employers were prevented from bringing in strikebreaker workers to keep the plants going.

The Reform Bills of 1884-1885. Disraeli's ministry was followed in 1880 by a second Gladstone ministry, which secured the passage of the Third Reform Bill of 1884. This bill enfranchised most of the agricultural workers. By 1885, then, most British men could vote; but the British had not yet achieved the universal manhood suffrage enjoyed by white males in the United States since the 1830's, by Frenchmen since 1848, and by Germans since 1867. The country was now divided into districts of equal population, from each of which a representative was elected to the House of Commons.

THE END OF LAISSEZ FAIRE

By the early twentieth century new questions came to the fore. Both the evils arising from industrialism and the enfranchising of new classes of voters put pressure on the government to move further and further away from laissez faire and to assume more responsibility for welfare of the individual citizen. In the 1870's many towns adopted what was called "gas and water socialism" by establishing publicly-owned organizations for sewers, gas, water, and slum clearance.

The Rise of the Labor Party. In 1906 the Labor party was formed by bringing together a number of organizations interested in social reform. Some of these organizations were inspired by the philosophy of Karl Marx, but more were interested only in gradual progress toward socialism, which they believed would remove the most urgent problems of the time. In the election of 1906, twenty-nine Labor candidates were elected to the House of Commons. They remained a separate group, but co-operated with the Liberals, who won a large majority.

The Welfare Program. The new Liberal ministry of 1906 embarked immediately upon a program of vigorous social reform. A Workman's Compensation Act made employers liable for injuries suffered by their employees at work. State employment bureaus were established to assist unemployed workers. In some businesses where workers had been grossly underpaid, minimum wage levels were set. Laws were also passed to promote the general health of the nation and to aid dependent children and impoverished old people. An old-age pension was granted to all people over seventy who had an annual income of less than a certain set amount. A National Insurance Act provided against sickness and unemployment. Britain was fast becoming something of a "welfare state" whose citizens could look to the government for aid when they could not supply their own basic necessities.

The Reform of the House of Lords, 1911. The reform program was expensive. Finding money to pay for it led to an important constitutional change. The finance minister, a dynamic Welshman named David Lloyd George, determined that the wealthy must pay a larger percentage of the taxes than formerly. Taxes were proposed on inheritances and on any land that was not farmed or that had increased in value not because of improvements but simply because land was scarce. These taxes would be particularly burdensome to the great nobles, who owned large estates passed down from generation to generation. It was clear that hereditary fortunes would soon disappear if these taxes were adopted. The budget passed the Commons, but was defeated in the House of Lords. A new and greater issue now confronted the country.

The right of the House of Lords to reject bills passed by the democratically elected House of Commons had long been in question. This new action of the Lords brought to a head the whole problem of the usefulness in a democratic country of a hereditary legislative house. The Liberal ministry was determined to settle the matter by limiting the control of the Lords over lawmaking. This could be done only by persuading the king, George V, to agree to create enough new noblemen to make a majority favorable to the bill in the Lords. As in 1832 (see page 103), the Lords yielded to this threat; enough of them remained at home to permit the passage of the Parliament Act of 1911. This law prevented the Lords from defeating a bill passed three times by the Commons or from holding up a money bill for more than a month. It was also arranged that members of the Commons would be paid, so that persons without wealth could sit in Parliament.

IRELAND: A CONTINUING PROBLEM

Aside from social and constitutional problems, the most urgent matter confronting the British government in the last part of the nineteenth century was Ireland. The Irish island was too far away and too different to be simply absorbed into Great Britain, but it was too near to be treated as a foreign country. It had been conquered by Britain centuries earlier. Its lands were largely owned by British nobles and farmed by Irish peasants. There were no laws preventing the landlords from putting the peasants off the land without even so much as paying them for the improvements they had made. The Church of England was the established church in Ireland in spite of the fact that except in the northern counties almost all Irish were Catholics. The Union of 1801, which had forcibly merged the Irish government with the British, had never pleased the Irish, for so few Irish members could sit in Parliament that they could not secure laws favorable to their country. It had taken the famine of the 1840's to bring about even so urgent a law as the repeal of the import duties on grain. (See page 104.)

Many Irish sought a way out of their difficulties by emigrating, mostly to the United States. Between 1840 and 1900 Ireland lost almost half its population. In the late 1850's a secret organization, the Fenian Society, with members in Ireland and America, pledged to win Irish independence by force of arms. During the 1860's one Fenian outrage after another concentrated British and world attention on Irish problems.

Gladstone became the champion of Irish reform, trying in each of his four ministries to pass laws to alleviate distress in Ireland. He "disestablished" the Church of England in Ireland, so that the Catholic Irish no longer had to pay taxes to support it. He made it more difficult for landlords to put their tenants off the land, and he required them to pay evicted tenants for improvements they had made. But the Irish wanted a parliament of their own—"home rule," they called it. He introduced a home-rule bill, but his own followers rejected it. In 1892, when he was for the last time prime minister at the age of eighty-three, he tried again. This time the bill passed the Commons, but was defeated in the Lords.

In 1914, after the reform of the House of Lords, a home-rule bill actually became law. The Protestants of northern Ireland opposed it violently, however, fearing that they would be at the mercy of the Catholic majority. The First World War prevented the law from being put into effect.

ᴑ THE THIRD FRENCH REPUBLIC

January, 1871, saw the beginning of a new chapter in French history. In that month Paris surrendered to the besieging German armies and the Franco-Prussian War was over. In May a National Assembly accepted the humiliating Treaty of Frankfurt. (See page 195.) By that time Paris was again in revolt. In protest against the policies of the National Assembly, a new Paris government called the "Commune" managed to defend the city against troops sent by the Assembly and at the same time attempted the kind of reforms that Robespierre's Jacobins (see page 47) would have approved. But when peace with Germany had been concluded, the troops of the National Assembly quickly suppressed the Commune in spite of fierce resistance.

THE ESTABLISHMENT OF THE THIRD REPUBLIC, 1871-1876

The question of what kind of government France was to have had now to be answered, but it proved a difficult one. At first it seemed certain that the monarchist majority in the National Assembly would set up a king. But there were two candidates for the throne: the Count of Paris, grandson of Louis Philippe, and the Count of Chambord, grandson of Charles X. Since the Count of Chambord had no children and was the elder of the two, it was decided that he should reign until his death and be succeeded by the Count of Paris. The Count of Chambord soon made that arrangement impossible by resolving to abandon the tricolor and to use instead the white flag of the Bourbons—a symbol of his intention to rule in the manner of his Bourbon ancestors of the days of the Old Regime. Unwilling to return to absolute monarchy, the French leaders continued the temporary government, at the moment headed by the monarchist General MacMahon.

This unsettled government could not be permanently satisfactory, especially since more and more French people were becoming republicans. No formal constitution was ever drawn up, but in 1875 a number of new laws established the basis for the government of the Third French Republic. A two-house legislature was provided for, the Chamber of Deputies to be elected by universal manhood suffrage and the Senate to be elected indirectly. A president was to be chosen by the two houses every seven years, while the real government was to be in the hands of a ministry responsible to the legislature. The first chambers elected under these laws took their seats in 1876 with a republican majority. Soon the tricolor was again the official flag and the "Marseillaise" (see page 43) the national anthem.

THE TESTING OF THE REPUBLIC

Although the majority of the French people supported the republic, many remained monarchists, still eager for a king. It is not surprising that the new government's strength was tested by a series of severe crises. Most important were the "Sixteenth of May," the Boulanger affair, and the Dreyfus affair.

The first crisis, called in France "the Sixteenth of May," was one last proof that a monarchy could not be reestablished. It occurred because President MacMahon, always a monarchist, became convinced that the republic was ruining France and must be brought to an end. On May 16, 1877, he replaced the republican ministry by royalists and dissolved the Chamber of Deputies in order to hold new elections. He toured the country speaking in favor of monarchist candidates. But Gambetta, the opposition leader, was a far more effective campaigner. By his oratory and his obvious devotion to the people, he stirred them to vote republican. The new chamber, like the old, had a majority of republicans. MacMahon was forced to appoint another republican ministry. This episode not only proved that France would continue to be a republic; it also revealed that the prime minister, not the president, was the real head of the government, in the same way that the prime minister, not the queen, was head of the British government.

The second test of the republic, the Boulanger affair of 1889, presented the threat of a military dictatorship like that of the first Napoleon. People were becoming critical of the government, which seemed to pay no attention to national problems. Instead of leading the nation, political parties spent their time quarreling among themselves. Many Frenchmen began to believe that only a strong military man who would lead the country in a war of revenge against Germany could unite the nation and solve its problems. The minister of War, General Georges Boulanger, seemed just such a man. Strikingly handsome, he had red hair and a blond beard and rode about Paris on a splendid black horse. Believed to be a republican, Boulanger rallied to his side those republicans eager for the war of revenge. But the "man on horseback" also had a following of "clericals" (persons wanting to strengthen Catholicism) who thought the republic too anti-Catholic. At the same time, Bonapartists and other monarchists admired him. People of such unlike views could unite behind Boulanger because he said so little and gave no indication what his program might be. By keeping still he gained the reputation of being a strong, silent man, ready to solve all problems and to satisfy everyone. But he had no real plans, nor was he really a person of courage and leadership capacity. When the ministers finally ordered his arrest, instead of putting himself at the head of his followers, he fled to Belgium, where he later committed suicide.

The final test of the republic was the most complicated, the most serious, and the most prolonged. It drew together all the enemies of the republic. It rose out of a fairly minor and purely personal matter. In 1894 Captain

Alfred Dreyfus, a Jew, was convicted of selling military secrets to the Germans. He was sent to life imprisonment on Devil's Island, a French prison off the coast of French Guiana in South America. But soon facts came to light suggesting that the guilty person was another army officer. The case began to arouse national excitement and somehow became the focal point of all the political, class, or religious hatreds of the day. Republicans generally took the attitude that Dreyfus was innocent. Monarchists, many Catholics, and most army officers declared that he was guilty. Another group convinced of his guilt was the growing number of French "anti-Semites" (those hostile to Jews, so called because Jews, like many other Middle-Eastern peoples, originally spoke a Semitic language). The case for Dreyfus was taken up with vigor by a number of writers, especially by the novelist Émile Zola, whose writings further aroused the French people. The evidence for Dreyfus's innocence grew ever stronger. In spite of the powerful opposition he finally was pardoned, but only years later was he tried in a civil court and acquitted.

The Dreyfus affair strengthened the republic by lessening the influence of various groups most vigorously opposed to it. The monarchists were greatly weakened; monarchist officers were weeded out of the army. The antagonism of many republicans toward the Catholic Church was deepened. The republic had proved its strength by surviving so much turmoil, and its supporters were prepared to see that all danger of attacks from its enemies was removed.

THE CHARACTER OF FRANCE UNDER THE THIRD REPUBLIC

Although industrial development was slower in France than in England, the considerable economic improvement that took place in the last years of the nineteenth century led to renewed demand for social reform. Since the mood for reform that grew out of the Dreyfus affair strengthened the hands of reform-minded ministers, important changes were made.

Anticlericalism. The question of the proper place of the Catholic Church in French life went back, of course, to the Old Regime. Anticlericalism—opposition to the privileged position of the clergy—had been a factor in the French Revolution of 1789 and in the Revolution of 1830. On the other hand, Napoleon III, in his desire to strengthen his regime, had sought Catholic support by giving the clergy increased control over education. After 1870 the tendency was again reversed, for republicans leaned toward anticlericalism. Before 1900 laws had reduced the number of nuns and teaching brothers in the schools and had in other ways limited the influence of religious orders over education. Civil marriage (marriage by a government official) was made compulsory, although a couple could in addition have a religious ceremony. After the Dreyfus affair, hostility against the clergy was so much intensified that most religious orders were expelled from France. More drastic was the Separation Law of 1905, which canceled Napoleon's I's Concordat of 1801 (see page 57) and separated church and state altogether, leaving the choice of bishops to the church and terminating the practice by which the government had paid the salaries of the clergy.

The Economic Improvement of the Country. Although French industrialization progressed only gradually, it received much encouragement from the republican government. With government support railway mileage was doubled and canals, rivers, and harbors were improved. Unlike the British, the French began to protect their farmers from competition from foreign agricultural products by raising tariffs on wheat, meat, and sugar. In consequence, a larger proportion of farmers remained on the land than was the case in Britain. The French economy was thus better balanced than that of Britain, for more of the necessary raw materials and foodstuffs were produced in France, and more of the products of French factories were bought by the French people themselves.

The Rise of Socialism. As French factory workers became more numerous they, like British workers, sought ways to improve their own conditions. Laws limited hours of work, reduced the working week to six days, and provided some old age pensions and some compensation for workers injured in the course of employment. But the small scale of French businesses, the slower growth of French industrial cities, and the continuance of much rural and small-town life resulted in less support than in Britain for social legislation. In the 1880's, partly to lessen Catholic Church influence, the government established a system of free elementary schools and made attendance compulsory. Trade unions were made legal, but continued to be opposed by employers and government.

Meantime Marxist socialism had taken a stronger hold in France than it had in Britain. There were socialist members of the French parliament from the 1880's onward. For a time they co-operated with the other radical parties, but in 1905 they established a party of their own. Similarly, trade unions became more radical in France than in Britain. They planned to use the nation-wide strike as their weapon. These more extreme movements did not, however, have important practical influence before 1914.

ᖉ ᖉ ᖉ

Although the French and British people reacted in different ways to late-nineteenth-century economic and political conditions, it is clear that there were important factors common to the changing societies of the two countries—factors also apparent in other democratic and industrialized countries of Europe and America. Opportunities for popular participation in government were widened, church and state were less intertwined, and governments tended to assume greater responsibility for the welfare of their citizens. Some but not all of these factors also affected the less democratic countries of central Europe.

Persons and Terms

Victoria	Tory democracy	budget
William Ewart	picket	Parliament Act
Gladstone	strikebreaker	of 1911
Benjamin Disraeli	gas and water	Fenian Society
David Lloyd George	socialism	home rule
General MacMahon	Labor party	Paris Commune
Georges Boulanger	Workmen's	Third French
Alfred Dreyfus	Compensation Act	Republic
	minimum wage	Sixteenth of May
trade union	National Insurance	anti-Semitism
Liberal party	Act	anticlericalism
Conservative party	welfare state	Separation Law

To Master the Text

1. Were the industrialized countries more or less willing than the unindustrialized to assume responsibility for the welfare of individual citizens? Would the classical economists have advised that governments take such responsibility? Why?
2. In what ways was Great Britain the leading nation of the world in 1871? By what methods did Britain pay for what it imported?
3. Describe the backgrounds and personalities of Gladstone and Disraeli. Of which party was each the leader? How did the two parties differ in membership? In principles? What was Disraeli's attitude toward his party? What were the provisions of the second reform bill?
4. List the reform measures adopted by Gladstone's ministry of 1867-1874. What were the Conservative arguments against each reform? What was the workers' attitude toward Gladstone's reforms? What laws favoring workers were passed by Disraeli's government, 1874-1880? What were the terms of Gladstone's reform bills of 1884 and 1885?

5. What pressures encouraged government interest in the welfare of individuals? Why was the Labor party organized? What important social-welfare legislation was passed before 1914? What is a "welfare state"?
6. How did Lloyd George propose to pay for the welfare legislation? Who opposed his plan? Why? What change in the British constitution resulted from this controversy?
7. List and explain the three most serious grievances of the Irish people against the British government. What happened to the Irish population in the late nineteenth century? Why? Describe the Fenian Society and its methods. What reform laws did Gladstone secure for Ireland? What reform did he fail to secure? Through what train of events did he fail?
8. What troubles beset France in the autumn of 1870? Why did the French government abandon the defense of Paris? What were the terms of the Treaty of Frankfurt? Why did the French government accept them? Why did the Parisians revolt?
9. By what process was the Third Republic established? How was the legislature chosen? The president? What powers did each have?
10. Why was the Third Republic threatened? Trace the events of the Sixteenth of May crisis. What was the result of the crisis? What groups brought on the Boulanger crisis? With what results? Trace the course of events of the Dreyfus affair. What were its consequences?
11. To make clear the character of France under the Third Republic:
    (a) Explain anticlericalism and list the laws passed under its influence;
    (b) list economic improvements of this period, and explain in what ways the French economy was well balanced; (c) list welfare laws; and
    (d) explain the importance of Marxian socialism in France.

To Interpret the Facts

1. Which country, Britain or France, seems to you to have been more democratic before 1914? Why? In which country would you rather have lived? Why?
2. State as fully as you can the contribution made by each, purposefully or accidentally, to the welfare of his country: Gladstone, Disraeli, Lloyd George, MacMahon, Boulanger, Dreyfus, Zola.

To Put This Chapter into a Larger Setting

1. List the laws passed in any one country, 1789-1914, that can be considered welfare legislation. What does this list make clear?
2. Compare Lloyd George and his program with Franklin D. Roosevelt and his New Deal. How were the two programs similar? How different?
3. Report on Cecil Woodham-Smith, *The Great Hunger: Ireland, 1845-1849.*

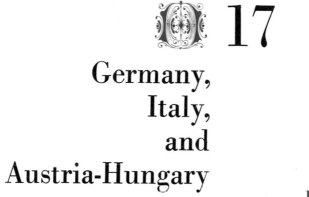

17

Germany, Italy, and Austria-Hungary

1871-1914

The countries of central Europe—Germany, Italy, and Austria-Hungary—all experienced some of the effects of industrialization between the 1870's and the 1910's. All had to cope with demands for increased popular participation in government, and in quite unlike ways all felt the effects of intensified nationalism. Like France, each began this forty-year period with a new government.

☊ THE GERMAN EMPIRE

The determining factors in German history during this period were unification and the swift advance of industrialization. In these forty years German industry overtook and in some ways surpassed British. In iron and steel, and especially in chemicals and in electricity, Germany took the lead. Railroads, canals, and shipping lines expanded in proportion to manufacturing. Population grew. In 1870, when France still had Alsace-Lorraine, the French population was greater than the German. By 1915, in spite of large German emigration to the Americas, Germany had almost 68,000,000 people and France only about 40,000,000. German towns multiplied and expanded; 60 per cent of the people were town-dwellers by 1910. As early as the 1890's Germany had to import food, for in spite of the higher yields resulting from the use of chemical fertilizers, German farmers could not feed the expanding population.

THE GOVERNMENT OF THE GERMAN EMPIRE

The government of the German Empire was established in 1871 before the explosive growth of German industry had begun. Bismarck drafted the framework of the imperial constitution, simply expanding the constitution of the North German Confederation (see page 192) to suit the increased dignity of the empire and to include the newly annexed territories. He kept the two-house parliament with the *Reichstag* elected by the vote of all male citizens, and he arranged that the chancellor—Bismarck himself—should still be responsible only to the emperor. The empire continued to be a confederation, for the member states retained their former rulers, some of them kings. Each state controlled its own police, educational system, and—most important—the levying of direct taxes, as well as other internal matters. The imperial government controlled foreign and military affairs and such activities of general concern as the postal service. Its revenues came from the member states or from customs duties.

It is obvious that there was little real democracy in this government in spite of the election of the *Reichstag* by universal manhood suffrage. One must remember that it was Prussia with its conservative, authoritarian society (see pages 183-184) that had created the German Empire. Moreover, it was Bismarck with his high-handed ways who headed William I's government—not only of Prussia, but also of the German Empire during the first twenty years of its existence. These two facts help explain why Germany was by the 1910's the only highly industrialized western country without genuine democracy.

But in spite of his great influence, Bismarck soon discovered that he must have the support of a strong party in the *Reichstag*. Although that body could not itself initiate a program of legislation, it could interfere with Bismarck's plans by refusing to pass his laws or to grant the money he needed. He had, therefore, to ally himself with the party most sympathetic to his program of the moment, and had to support the laws particularly desired by that party. For some ten years he allied himself with the National Liberal party and in partnership with them waged war against the Catholic Church.

THE KULTURKAMPF

Bismarck's ten-year attack on the Catholic Church (from the early 1870's to the early 1880's) goes by the name of the *Kulturkampf* (German for "battle for civilization"). It can be explained in part by the attitude of the National Liberal party, Bismarck's allies, and in part by Bismarck's genuine fear of German Catholics.

The National Liberals were the big businessmen and upper officials. They approved of Bismarck's early policies. He was striving to unite the member states of the empire more closely by creating as many institutions as possible for the empire as a whole—courts and a body of law, a banking system, coinage, a unified railroad system. Many Germans, loyal to their individual states or fearing the power of a strongly centralized government, opposed this program; but the National Liberals, as individuals, often stood to profit from the breaking down of barriers between the states. Like many liberals in other countries, members of this party were inclined to be indifferent to religion or even to be anticlerical, opposing church control of such matters as education and marriage. Many National Liberals welcomed a lessening of the authority of religious bodies. They also believed that the imperial government should take a laissez-faire attitude toward business and let it manage its own affairs. For the time being Bismarck was willing to let business alone.

Bismarck's fear of Catholics was related to both the internal situation of the German Empire and to its foreign affairs. Prussia had originally been a Protestant country, but its wars of conquest had brought it large numbers of unwilling Catholic citizens—Poles from the eighteenth-century partitions, Rhinelanders in the area annexed in 1815, and finally south Germans and people of Alsace-Lorraine, annexed to the empire in 1871. Bismarck doubted the loyalty of all these peoples, especially of the Poles. The Catholics had formed a party of their own, the Center party, which grew steadily, as Bismarck noted with alarm. He was also convinced, erroneously, that there was likelihood of the formation in Europe of an anti-German coalition to include the pope and both France and Austria, the Catholic powers so recently defeated by Prussia. He believed that many Germans shared his fears. Many Germans, including most liberals and even some Catholics, had opposed the promulgation of the doctrine of papal infallibility by the Vatican Council in 1870. (See page 137.) Bismarck believed there would be popular support for an attack on the Catholic Church, a policy that he hoped would remove one of his most dangerous political opponents.

The *Kulturkampf* consisted of a series of laws against Catholics, most of them passed by the parliament of Prussia where Lutherans were the major religious group, but some passed by the imperial parliament and applied to the whole empire. The purpose of the laws was to take education and marriage out of the hands of the clergy and to put the Catholic Church under the close supervision of the government. The Jesuits were expelled from Germany, and other teaching orders were suppressed. Civil marriage was required. The education of Catholic priests was put under the supervision of the government.

The *Kulturkampf* failed to weaken the Catholic influence in Germany, nor did it destroy the Center party. Instead, it aroused vehement opposition to Bismarck. Pope Pius IX condemned the new laws; the Catholic clergy in Germany went to prison or exile rather than accept them; the Center party grew in numbers. By 1877 no Catholic bishop in all Germany was at his post, and hundreds of priests were also in prison or in exile. Even Protestants took alarm, fearing that the government would broaden its attack to include their churches.

Partly sensing the failure of his policy, partly for other reasons, Bismarck began to shift his course. In 1878 Pope Pius IX died and was succeeded by the liberal-minded Leo XIII, whose attitudes and policy made it easier for Bismarck to withdraw from his extreme position. Gradually a number of the anti-Catholic laws were repealed and German Catholics could again practice their religion. Catholic schools were re-established with some government supervision. By the mid-1880's the *Kulturkampf* was over.

BISMARCK AND THE SOCIALISTS

As early as 1878 Bismarck had begun to draw away from the National Liberals, who were demanding that the ministers be responsible to the parliament, as in France and Britain. Such a plan was intolerable to a man of Bismarck's character. Meantime the Conservative party, its great landlords of eastern Germany injured by cheap grain from abroad and its industrialists seeking ways to keep foreign manufactured goods out of Germany, wanted higher tariffs. Bismarck, too, was beginning to favor tariffs, believing that if they were not too high they would bring money to the imperial government and thereby make it less dependent on the states. Gradually separating himself from the National Liberals, he began to build a coalition of Conservatives and some individual members of the Center and National Liberal parties.

At the time that he acquired new friends, Bismarck also found a new enemy—socialism. The rise of cities with their multitude of unfamiliar problems had encouraged the growth of socialism in Germany. In 1875 the movement was given great impetus when previously separate socialist groups met at the town of Gotha to adopt a workable socialist program. Although the Gotha socialists accepted the teachings of Marx as basic, they abandoned Marx's belief that workers could only secure their rights by violent revolution. Within a few years German socialism became openly "revisionist" (see page 224), putting faith in laws favorable to workers rather than in revolution. A Social Democratic party was organized. Bismarck feared this movement as he had the Catholics. When in 1878 two attempts were made to assassinate Emperor William I, Bismarck hinted (inaccurately) that the socialists were somehow responsible. Drawing his political allies closely around him, he began a fierce attack on the Social Democratic party.

Bismarck's attack was two-pronged. He tried to prevent people from being socialists by making party membership difficult. He outlawed the party, prohibited its publications and meetings, and encouraged the police to use particularly stringent methods to enforce the anti-socialist laws. At the same time he tried to make socialism less appealing to workingmen by demonstrating that the government would do more for them than the Social Democratic party could do. Beginning in the early 1880's he persuaded the *Reichstag* to adopt a program of social insurance against sickness, accident, and old age. The costs were to be paid jointly by the workers and employers, with some help from the government. British workers did not gain similar protection until 1911 (see pages 236-237) and Americans not until 1935. Neither of Bismarck's efforts had the results he desired, however, for even during the period of his most bitter attack on them, the Social Democrats increased in number.

GERMANY AFTER BISMARCK, 1890-1914

In 1890 Bismarck's three decades as chief minister came to an abrupt end. Emperor William I died in 1888; and his son and successor, Frederick III, died three months later. Emperor William II, an ill-prepared, impetuous young man, lacking in tact and in an understanding of the feelings of others, became the next ruler. He was determined to take the guidance of German policy into his own hands. Soon he quarreled with Bismarck and dismissed him. Thereafter Germany followed a less clearly defined policy than Bismarck had charted.

"Dropping the Pilot," a cartoon by Sir John Tenniel from the British magazine *Punch,* commenting on the dismissal of Bismarck by Emperor William II in 1890. Bismarck, the pilot who has guided the German ship of state through difficult waters, is being put ashore by the young, self-confident emperor, who will now take full charge.

As in all industrial countries, there was unrest among the working people. William II secured the reversal of Bismarck's laws against the socialists. He also encouraged new legislation forbidding child labor, limiting hours of work for women and young people, and requiring safety measures in factories. But William II was no more successful than Bismarck had been in winning the genuine good will of labor. The Social Democrats increased in number and in their demands until they became the largest single party in the *Reichstag.*

Abroad, William II's government followed two policies not before characteristic of Germany. The first was the decision to build up a colonial empire in Africa and the Pacific islands and to gain a foothold in China. Interest in colonies had gained some headway in Germany in Bismarck's day, and he had finally given it support. Patriotic Germans liked to argue, as did leaders in other western countries of the day, that a great power was characterized in part by its overseas holdings—that an overseas empire was proof of greatness. Most of the valuable colonial areas had already been taken over by other countries, but the Germans were able to secure fairly extensive if less valuable areas during the latter years of Bismarck and the first years of William II. These gave the Germans a feeling of power, especially at the time when they had achieved so much greater unity than they had ever known before.

The second new policy was the decision to build a navy strong enough to be able to challenge the mighty British fleet in time of war. The navy was thought to be necessary to protect German overseas trade with the colonies and elsewhere, but it was also another indication of the growing German strength and a source of pride to the German people.

The growth both of the colonies and of the fleet brought Germany into many conflicts with the other western powers, and particularly with Britain. These difficulties were aggravated by William II's conduct of the German government. The lack of firm leadership permitted the various branches of the armed forces and of the government to act without consulting each other, so that German policy was often changeable and contradictory. William II was prone to make blustering speeches, to use unrestrained language, and to irritate other countries without cause and perhaps without meaning to do so.

But Germany under William II was undoubtedly a vigorous, progressive nation. A visitor to the country would have noted the thriving industry, the prosperous and energetic people, the handsome cities, the theaters and symphony orchestras, the universities. It was a land of material, intellectual, and artistic achievement. In government, however, it remained what Bismarck had made it: in the early twentieth century it was still governed under the constitution he had written for the North German Confederation in 1867.

⌒ THE KINGDOM OF ITALY

Although Italy achieved national unity almost simultaneously with Germany, its history after unification was quite different. Italy had no such rapid industrialization as did Germany. The old geographical features remained a hindrance—lack of raw materials, especially coal and iron, and the mountains impeding railroad building, for two examples. The poverty of the land and of the people also still remained, as did the feeling of separateness of the various regions. (See pages 169-170.) Organized banditry, as practiced by the Mafia and similar organizations, still plagued the southern part of the peninsula and the island of Sicily. The one resource Italy had was people, for the Italian population was growing more rapidly than any other in Europe. Finding few opportunities at home, millions of

Italians emigrated to the Americas, sometimes half a million in a single year. Some returned, bringing their savings with them, but many were lost to Italy forever.

In spite of economic backwardness and political inexperience, Italy attempted to establish a constitutional monarchy along British lines. There was a two-house legislature with the upper house partly hereditary and partly appointed and the lower house elected by the small number of male voters with the required amount of education and property. The ministers were responsible to the legislature. Unfortunately it proved impossible to develop a stable party system. The political leaders were inexperienced. Ministers often had no policies other than keeping themselves in office. The result was misgovernment, disorder, and sometimes near-dictatorship. Only toward the end of this period, as opportunities for education increased and more men acquired political experience, did political life become healthier. In 1912 universal manhood suffrage was adopted.

Relations between church and state were especially difficult in Italy because of the presence of the pope in the country. Pope Pius IX steadfastly refused to accept the loss of the city of Rome. The Italian government offered to guarantee the pope's safety and his sovereignty as ruler of the Vatican and promised him an annual money payment in the place of his lost revenues. All this the pope refused, shutting himself into the Vatican and declaring that he was a prisoner. Neither he nor his three immediate successors ever left the papal residences. He forbade Italian Catholics to act as government officials, and he attempted to secure the aid of foreign governments to recover the papal lands. Many Catholics followed his instructions; but others, alienated from the papacy, became anticlericals, determined to reduce the power of the church over the lives of the people. After 1903 the state-church antagonism was lessened by Pope Pius X's decision to encourage Italian Catholics to participate in political life.

In spite of the difficulties, the Italian people advanced slowly toward economic and social betterment. Railroads were built to connect the parts of the country, harbors were improved, a public school system was begun, trade unions and collective bargaining were legalized, and factory acts were passed. By 1900 silk and cotton goods were being exported. Genoa became more important than Marseilles as a Mediterranean port. Italian pride was satisfied by the acquisition of colonies in North Africa.

But in spite of this progress, Italy, which was called a great power, was scarcely in the class of Britain, France, and Germany.

Francis Joseph, emperor of Austria and king of Hungary, whose bearing suggests something of his devotion to duty and his lack of imagination.

AUSTRIA-HUNGARY

The third important central-European state, Austria-Hungary, was like no other in Europe. Not only had it become a double state by the Compromise of 1867 (see map, page 191), but its many regions still lacked those ties of language and national feeling that, in the modern world, have operated increasingly to weld nations into indivisible units.

GOVERNMENT IN THE DUAL MONARCHY

Taking the Habsburg realm as a whole, the dual government established in 1867 worked fairly well. Francis Joseph lived on as emperor of Austria and king of Hungary until 1916. Assisted by his ministers of war, finance, and foreign affairs, he ran the dual government in his plodding, unimaginative, conscientious way. Now that the intense dissatisfaction of the Hungarians had been removed, the Habsburg rule was not threatened by immediate collapse. Neither the Germans nor the Hungarians alone could have wielded as much influence in Europe as they exerted together, nor could commerce have flourished so well without the extensive free market of the combined Habsburg lands. Most affairs of government were, however, carried on quite separately in German Vienna and Hungarian Budapest.

Austria's government was the more liberal of the two. It gave some voice to the Slavic peoples and, by a complicated system of indirect voting, provided for the lower house of the parliament to be composed of property owners and educated persons. Liberal attitudes were encouraged by the growth of industry, especially in Bohemia and around Vienna. Bohemia became famous for the Skoda armament works, rival of the German Krupps, and for lace, porcelain, and glassware exported to all parts of the world. Laws were passed establishing civil marriage and a freer press, encouraging industry, and establishing free compulsory elementary schools removed from religious control. Finally in 1907 the emperor granted universal manhood suffrage. Later social insurance laws were adopted. In Vienna publicly owned gas, electricity, and water companies were established, and bridges, streets, and parks were improved. Milk was supplied free to school children of poor families.

Hungary was less like the West. The elected lower house of the legislature was chosen by a strictly limited number of voters. The Magyars, determined to rule their lands without consulation with their subject peoples, gave no representation to the Slavs. Indeed they did all in their power to force everyone in the Hungarian half of the empire to use the Magyar language—the only language in the army or the post office, for example. By 1900 the Magyars again began to demand independence from Austria, acting on the belief that Hungary had grown strong enough to be an independent nation.

THE NATIONALITY PROBLEM

The unique problem of Austria-Hungary was, of course, the inclusion within its borders of so many different nationalities with their hostilities toward each other. (See pages 147-151.) Part of the difficulty stemmed from the fact that the Habsburg government—whether under the influence of Metternich, as it had been to 1848, or of Francis Joseph, as it was thereafter until 1916—could imagine no solution to the nationality problem except that of carefully keeping things exactly as they were, lest one slight change should fatally jar the whole shaky structure of the empire. But fear of change was not the only obstacle to reform. The various peoples of the empire were difficult to manage. In 1871, for one example, Francis Joseph yielded to the demands of the Bohemians for self-government by promising to be crowned as king in Prague, their capital. He intended to make Bohemia a third self-governing part of his realm along with Austria and Hungary. But his plan soon was abandoned because of the vehement protests of the German inhabitants of Bohemia, who feared being governed by the Slavic Czech majority. This hatred for each other of the various national groups could be illustrated by many other examples. Thus when the government yielded to one group, it inevitably stirred the bitter resentment of another.

The demands of the subject peoples varied. The Bohemians wanted nothing more than self-government within the empire. The Hungarians demanded the right to secede. The Italians, Serbs, and Romanians wanted to join the independent nations already established by their kinsmen. Of all the subject peoples, the Poles were the least restless for they were better treated than their kinsmen, the Poles of Germany and Russia.

Austro-Hungarian problems were not well understood in the rest of Europe, but Austria-Hungary was a powder keg of discontent that might easily explode to set the world on fire.

☌ ☌ ☌

Central Europe was closer in spirit to the Old Regime than was western Europe, but it was also somewhat affected by the influences of industrialism, liberalism, and socialism. The three central countries followed in the footsteps of their western neighbors, but sometimes slowly and not far.

Persons and Terms

William II	National Liberal party	German Social
	Center party	Democratic party
chancellor	Conservative party	Social insurance
Kulturkampf	Gotha socialists	Magyars

To Master the Text

1. What facts illustrate the rapid economic growth of Germany between 1871 and 1914?
2. What were the governmental powers of the German emperor? The imperial government? The state governments? Was his state government or the imperial government more important to the individual German? How much democracy was there in the imperial government? Why did Bismarck need the support of a strong political party?
3. What does *Kulturkampf* mean? To Bismarck, what was the struggle about? What party supported him? Why? What laws carried out the *Kulturkampf?* How did Catholics react to them? How did other religious groups react? What was the eventual outcome of the *Kulturkampf?*
4. Why did Bismarck's attitude toward the National Liberals change? With whom did he ally? Why? What other groups joined his coalition?

5. What terms were used to describe the moderate German socialists of the 1880's? What political activities did they engage in? Why did Bismarck fear them? How did he restrain them? What laws did he pass for the benefit of workers? Why? Did these laws achieve Bismarck's basic goal? What policies did William II follow toward the Socialists?

6. How did Bismarck fall from office? What new policies were introduced by William II? Did the German people support these policies? Why? How did statesmen of other countries view them?

7. What were the special problems of Italy? Its economic difficulties? Its difficulty in operating its government? When did all Italian men secure the vote?

8. What circumstances gave rise to conflict between the kingdom of Italy and the papacy? What policies were followed by the popes immediately after 1871? After 1903?

9. How much economic advance was there in Italy before 1914?

10. How was authority divided between the Austrian and Hungarian governments on the one hand and the central government of Austria-Hungary on the other? How much democracy was there in each half? How did the Hungarian government try to keep the Magyars in full control?

11. What problem was posed for the Austro-Hungarian government by the many nationalities within its borders?

To Interpret the Facts

1. Taking into account only his conduct of home affairs after 1871, do you believe that the Germans of 1914 should have looked back upon Bismarck as a great and successful chancellor, or the opposite? Why?

2. For each of the three governments discussed in this chapter, make a list of problems confronting it, 1870-1914. From each list choose the one most difficult problem, and prove why it was the most difficult.

3. In what ways were the histories of these three countries similar?

To Put This Chapter into a Larger Setting

1. Write a German newspaper editorial of early 1914 explaining to the public how great has been German economic development since 1871 and to what extent German unification has been responsible.

2. Compare the government of the German Empire after 1871 with that of Great Britain after 1911, considering such matters as the degree to which the people could control governmental activities, the powers of the head of the state, and the powers of the chief minister.

3. At this point in your study does it seem that nationalism or industrialism was having the greater effect on governments and on the lives of ordinary people? On what facts do you base your opinion?

 18

Russia
and the
Balkan
Peninsula

In the 1880's eastern and southeastern Europe—Russia, the independent Balkan countries, and what remained of the European part of the .Ottoman Empire—were still peasant lands. In Russia, to be sure, industrialism was beginning to make a noticeable advance; but the Balkan states had as yet almost no experience with steam and steel. Such changes as had recently occurred in eastern Europe had made for unrest. In Russia revolutionary movements already at work (see pages 208-209) were encouraged by the advance of industry. Balkan nationalism was not stilled but rather was intensified by the independence of Greece in 1830 and the grant of autonomy to Serbia and Romania in 1856.

☊ RUSSIA

In Russia the hopeful mood created by the emancipation of serfs and other reforms (see pages 206-208) had already been destroyed in the 1870's by the stern repressive measures of the last years of Alexander II and by the failure of such Narodnik efforts as the "go-to-the-people" movement. (See page 209.) The assassination of Alexander by terrorists in 1881 ushered in another period of reaction and repression, which lasted until 1905.

THE RUSSIAN EMPIRE 1914

Russian Empire 1815
Annexed 1815-1905
Trans-Siberian Railroad

THE PERIOD OF REACTION, 1881-1905

The official policy of repression was based on the belief that the unrest and wave of assassinations of the 1870's had resulted from the reforms of Alexander II. It was hoped that firmer control of all aspects of the lives of the people would put an end to conflict and disorder. This hope was doomed to disappointment, however, for during the years when the policy of repression was at its height, economic changes were creating new problems that only encouraged the development of new revolutionary parties.

Aspects of the Repression Policy. The stern policy to which the government adhered until 1905 was in part a natural consequence of the education, outlook, and personal characters of Alexander III (tsar 1881-1894) and Nicholas II (tsar 1894-1917). Both were conscientiously devoted to the traditional Russian ideals of "autocracy, Orthodoxy, and nationalism." Personally Alexander III was stalwart in character, sincere, and devoted to duty. "His tall and massive figure was the last impressive symbol of Russian autocracy." He was respected even by those who most disagreed with him. In policy he was thoroughly reactionary, for he believed that the government of his grandfather, Nicholas I, embodied all that was best for Russia.

Alexander's son and successor, Nicholas II, shared his father's reactionary and autocratic ideals and brought to his task equal conscientiousness and much charm. He was, however, a weak man, always under the influence of others, especially of his German-born wife, whose stubborn determination to carry through any policy she favored was unfortunately not combined with sound judgment.

After the assassination of Alexander II, the government whittled away many of the powers that he had granted to the zemstvos. By a thorough program of thought control, it attempted to prevent the spread of ideas that it considered dangerous. After three warnings, any newspaper had to submit all subsequent issues to the censor in advance. Public libraries and reading rooms, especially those frequented by poorer people, could not open until they had received government permission. Any of their books might be removed by the officials on the ground that the content did "not correspond to the level of intellectual development and understanding of

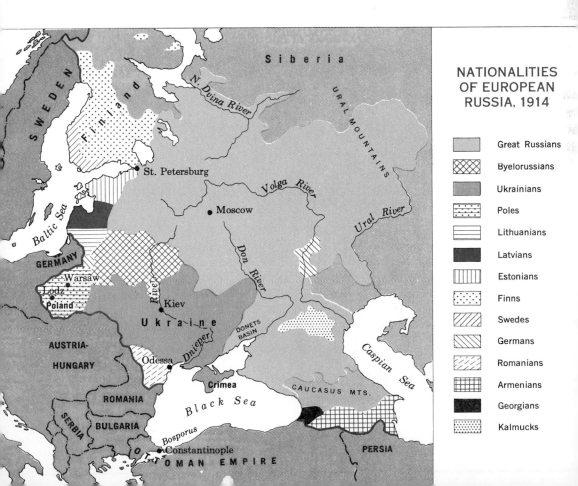

NATIONALITIES
OF EUROPEAN
RUSSIA, 1914

Great Russians

Byelorussians

Ukrainians

Poles

Lithuanians

Latvians

Estonians

Finns

Swedes

Germans

Romanians

Armenians

Georgians

Kalmucks

the simple people." Universities were put directly under government-appointed officials. Such elementary education as existed was directed toward making school children satisfied with the place in society to which they had been born. As late as 1894 only 21 per cent of the Russian people could read.

The ideal of "nationalism" promoted by both Alexander III and Nicholas II meant the "Russification" of all non-Russian peoples living within the empire—including, for example, the Germans in Latvia, Lithuania, and elsewhere; the Poles; the Armenians living along the borders of Turkey; and even the Finns, who had been promised special liberties. These peoples were now forced to use the Russian language. Their native schools were closed, Orthodox missionaries were encouraged to convert them, and difficulties were put in the way of non-Orthodox churches. Many of these policies were in direct contradiction to rights once solemnly guaranteed the subject peoples. The worst suffering was experienced by the Jews. They were subject to terrible pogroms—beatings and lootings by their non-Jewish neighbors—which the government could have prevented, but which instead it encouraged. Many newly adopted limitations were placed on the freedom of movement of Jews, on their education, and on the kind of occupations they could enter.

Economic Development. The policy of repression was doomed to failure from the beginning, partly because new revolutionary forces were being brought into existence by changing economic conditions that were often promoted by the government itself.

Most obvious was the gathering momentum of the Industrial Revolution. Expansion of the Russian railroads in the 1870's had given the initial push to large-scale industry. Demand for rails and locomotives stimulated mining and the iron and steel industries. During the 1880's pig-iron production expanded more rapidly in Russia than anywhere else in the world. The railroads, carrying coal to iron ore and ore to coal, facilitated the making of iron and steel. The industry soon concentrated in the Donets Basin in southern Russia, where today 60 per cent of Russian coal is produced. The textile industry also expanded, as did oil production in the Caspian Sea region.

The Russian Industrial Revolution enjoyed several special advantages. It made use of the scientific and technical knowledge long and painfully built up in the West. New industries were largely financed by the Russian government, which was primarily interested in modernizing and building up its

Building the Trans-Siberian Railroad, 1893. The difficulty of the task, which took almost fifteen years to complete, was increased by a lack of construction equipment; the builders were forced to depend on men and horses to do even the heaviest work.

armed forces. For military purposes the government encouraged railroads (including the Trans-Siberian; see page 218) and heavy industries like iron and steel, but paid relatively little attention to those consumer goods that were currently making the home lives of western Europeans more comfortable. Extensive government assistance enabled Russian manufacturers to build large plants concentrated in a few places—the Donets Basin and the regions around Moscow, St. Petersburg, and Lodz in Russian Poland. Thus the industrialization of Russia, though late in coming and limited in comparison with the West, was rapid and large-scale.

The great majority of the Russian people were still peasants living on the land. Changes in agriculture were creating new dissatisfactions. The peasants complained that they had too little land and that payments to the government begun at the time of emancipation were too heavy. With the rapid growth of peasant population, land allotted to each family became ever less adequate. Since the mir, which was the legal owner of the land and was responsible for the payments to the government, continued the group-farming of the old three-field system, the adoption of efficient modern agricultural methods was impossible. In any case most peasants were too poor to buy the improved tools or the commercial fertilizer that would have made it unnecessary to leave each field idle one year out of three. Russian farmers therefore produced few bushels per acre in comparison with western farm-ers. There were recurring food shortages, including a terrible famine in 1891-1892. Moreover, the peasants, like the town laborers, were required to bear too large a share of the taxes.

A small percentage of the peasants managed to become fairly prosperous. These "kulaks," as they were called, bought or rented many extra acres, kept horses and cattle in considerable numbers, and hired the poorer peasants to work for them. A good example of a kulak was the father of the Com-munist leader Leon Trotsky. Trotsky's father could not read; yet he man-aged to operate 640 acres of land (a square mile), hiring much extra help at harvest time and employing all year a stable boy, a mechanic, a shepherd, and three household servants. Such peasants could add to the staple rye-bread diet of the poorer folk both wheat bread and meat. That a few were so much better off than the many did not help solve the peasant problem; instead it caused jealousy among the peasants and created a class of able but dissatisfied men determined to secure the right of participation in public affairs.

New Revolutionary Movements. Although the government's repressive policies kept movements for reform from operating in the open and sent many of the leaders to prison or into exile, the political groups later to de-termine Russia's future came into being between 1895 and 1905. It is con-venient to call these groups "parties," but they did not take responsibility for the day-to-day political life of Russia as do political parties in the United States today. There were few offices to be filled by election, and in any case most of the leaders were in exile, arguing with each other and writing papers, pamphlets, and books to be smuggled into Russia.

Most popular was the Social Revolutionary party (the "S.R.'s"), organ-ized in Switzerland by Russians sympathetic to the Narodnik ideas of the 1870's. (See page 209.) The particular emphasis of the S.R.'s was on "land socialism." They held that individuals had no right to own land, which indeed should not be owned at all. Rather, land should be controlled by the officials of the local government and parceled out to the peasants on the basis of "labor ownership," giving to each what he had the means to culti-vate. This doctrine naturally appealed especially to the poorer peasants, whom the party made an effort to reach through pamphlets with special appeal to the peasant outlook. Among the S.R.'s were many teachers in the small towns and the rural areas, and students with a variety of backgrounds. Since a second principle for which the S.R.'s fought was equality between the Russian and non-Russian inhabitants of the empire, the party easily gained members among the non-Russian nationalities. Although terrorism was not a party principle, a small group of the Social Revolutionary extremists continued the terrorist activities of the earlier Narodniks, assassinating a number of important persons. Obviously the S.R.'s were not a closely unified party and could thus accommodate more different kinds of people than could their rivals, the Social Democrats (the "S.D's").

The Social Democratic party was Marxist. Its founders had adapted to Russia the ideas of Marx, originally intended for industrial countries like Britain and Germany. Many Social Democrats believed that Russia must be industrialized before a socialist revolution could take place. After industrialization would come the overthrow of the tsar and a period of bourgeois democratic government. Only then, they believed, could the proletariat—the workers—bring about a revolution to create a communist state.

One of the early theorists of the Social Democratic party was Vladimir Ilyich Ulyanov, who adopted the name Lenin. He differed from some of the other leaders in regard to two principles: (1) He believed that the bourgeois stage of government could be short-lived and that the communist revolution could be expected without a prolonged wait; also (2) he held that the party should not operate democratically, but rather should be dominated by a small, highly disciplined, trained, and experienced group of revolutionary leaders, who would make all important decisions. This small nucleus would operate in secret and would become a conspiratorial party within a party. At a party meeting in London in 1903 Lenin's group, momentarily in a majority, secured the general adoption of his two principles. His followers were thereafter called "Bolsheviks" (adapted from the Russian word for "majority"). The minority of that time, the "Mensheviks," held views more like those of the revisionist socialists in western Europe. Most of the time the Mensheviks were the majority of the S.D.'s, although their name indicated that they were a minority.

Nonrevolutionary reform groups also appeared at this time, most notably the Constitutional Democrats, called "Kadets" from the initials of their party name in Russian. They hoped to secure constitutional liberties and some participation in government, at least for the educated people. Most of them were professional people, liberal nobles, and others with ideals similar to those held by the upper middle classes in the West. Although the Kadets did not use the secret, violent methods of the revolutionary parties, they did not win any support from the tsar's government.

The unrest to which these parties bore witness was also affecting the non-Russian peoples within the empire. There was little or no connection between one of these nationalist movements and another, but all alike were becoming more and more resentful of the relentless government policy of Russification. Some individuals among them joined the S.D.'s, and greater numbers joined the S.R.'s. Some committed acts of terrorism. All were eager to enjoy the liberties previously promised them by the tsars. They added their bitterness to the general restlessness that brought about the Revolution of 1905.

THE REVOLUTION OF 1905 AND ITS AFTERMATH

In the first years of the twentieth century, restless Russia was overwhelmed by a new deluge of troubles. Between 1899 and 1903 there was an industrial depression, particularly severe in the iron and oil industries, putting many people out of work. Before business was altogether back to normal, the tsar's government declared war on Japan (1904). Peasants had to be drafted into the army, thus reducing farm production and bringing about food shortages. As if these troubles were not enough, an unbroken succession of Russian defeats was reported from the battle front—a most humiliating circumstance, for Russia was a great country, and to Russians and other Europeans of the time, the Japanese were merely a backward Oriental people.

The Revolution. This situation furnished an excellent opportunity for the reform and revolutionary parties. The liberal groups, unable to hold public meetings, resorted to political banquets like those held in France before the Revolution of 1848. The extremist wing of the Social Revolutionaries increased its program of terror, killing two governors of provinces and three of the tsar's ministers. The Social Democrats stirred up the factory workers to strike.

An important consequence of all this activity was "Bloody Sunday," in January, 1905. A number of strikes were in progress in St. Petersburg at the time. Many of the unemployed workers joined a protest march to the tsar's palace to lay their grievances before him. The police tried to halt the procession and then fired into it, killing or wounding hundreds of the marchers. This terrible event led inevitably to others. Terrorists killed the tsar's uncle. Peasant revolts broke out in many places. From the fighting fronts the news continued uninterruptedly bad. The crew of the battleship *Potemkin* mutinied. A new wave of strikes affected the industrial centers, the railroads, the universities. In October, 1905, workers of St. Petersburg established the first "Soviet [council] of Workers' Deputies," which demanded the right to have an elected city government.

The hesitant tsar was now persuaded to act. In the so-called "October Manifesto" he promised freedom of press, speech, and meeting, and the calling of a "Duma," or parliament. Although the Manifesto provided that the Duma should be elected by a wide suffrage, the general tone of the document was not in the least democratic. It described the tsar as the "supreme autocratic power" and noted that "acceptance of his authority is dictated not alone by fear and conscience but also by God Himself." Nevertheless many liberal reformers were satisfied with the Manifesto and transferred their support to the tsar. The police then felt strong enough to disband the St. Petersburg Soviet.

The Fate of the Reform Movement. The movement for reform had limited success but some important indirect consequences. The tsar fought with his first two Dumas and dissolved them at once. He accepted a third only after he had reduced its power to do much more than debate. But in other ways Russian life was becoming freer and more comfortable. In spite of censorship, more and better newspapers appeared, including the Marxist daily *Pravda* ("Truth") in St. Petersburg. A law of 1908 for universal education enabled more people to read. Public discussion was freer. Economic life was also quickened. From 1905 to 1914 coal mining doubled, pig-iron production expanded markedly, and such food items as butter and sugar became more readily available. From 1906 to 1912 the use of paper almost doubled. Most important of all, the peasants were excused from their remaining money payments to the government and therefore from their obligation to remain with their mirs. They could now consolidate their strips of land by selling or exchanging them and so were able to use better farming methods. Grain production immediately increased.

Thus Russia entered the First World War in 1914 still a backward country, but stronger economically and in general morale than before 1905.

☉ THE BALKAN PENINSULA

The Balkan Peninsula was akin to Russia in two ways: its people were largely Slavs, and their religion was largely Orthodox. But in other ways it was like no other part of Europe. It was a backward, illiterate, misgoverned region. Yet it was of interest to all the great powers of Europe;

for the Ottoman Empire, to which most of the peninsula belonged, controlled the straits leading from the Black Sea to the Mediterranean as well as the routes to India by way of the Red Sea and the Persian Gulf.

The confusion of peoples, languages, and religions in the Balkan lands resulted from invasions in ancient and medieval times. There were Albanians on the Adriatic coast, Romanians north of the Danube, Bulgarians on the Black Sea, Serbs in the western part of the peninsula, and Greeks at the southern tip and in the Aegean islands. All used their own languages. The Ottoman Turks who had conquered the region in the fourteenth and fifteenth centuries were Muslims. In general, the subject peoples retained their old customs, little disturbed by their Turkish conquerors, although some individuals did become Muslims.

Economically the Balkan Peninsula kept to its medieval ways. Most of the inhabitants were either herdsmen or farmers using primitive methods with poor results. Much of the peninsula is mountainous, and in many regions the population was sparse. In some of the more remote and wilder mountain areas the people lived in half-settled clans, feuding with each other and paying scant regard to the sultan's government. Although there was some export of cotton, tobacco, and other agricultural products, the peninsula was in general cut off from the developing commercial and industrial life of western Europe.

As rulers of their extensive empire, the Turks had at first been efficient and not oppressive masters. But by the nineteenth century, Ottoman government had become so incompetent that the real power of the state lay in the hands of the local officials. These were all too often inefficient, brutal, and subject to bribery.

The Balkan peoples, like other Europeans of the time, began to take a romantic pride in their own histories. Looking back on whatever period of its past had been the greatest, each longed for a restoration of the conditions of that day. By the early 1870's Balkan nationalism had already helped win independence for Greece (see pages 97-99) and self-government for Romania and Serbia. (See pages 99, 166.) Montenegro, a small, mountainous country in the western part of the peninsula, had never been subdued by the Turks, although the Turks refused to recognize it as independent. The Greeks, Romanians, and Serbs all plotted to free their many kinsmen still living under Turkish rule in the provinces of Bosnia, Macedonia, and Thrace. In the 1870's only the Bulgarians remained relatively untouched by the contemporary spirit of nationalism. They were an especially submerged people, long subjected to the Greek Orthodox Church, whose priests had labored to destroy every trace of ancient Bulgar culture. So backward was Bulgaria that as late as 1877 there was only one printing press in the country. But Bulgarian books were printed abroad; and in 1870 the Bulgarian national church was revived. It soon became the center of a nationalist movement that within the decade led to Bulgarian self-government. (Chapter 19.)

Although the Balkan countries still remained among the most backward areas of the European continent, economic progress had taken place by the early twentieth century. A few railroads were built. Oil was found in Romania and wells were drilled. But the division of the peninsula into so many small, jealous states was a stubborn obstacle to economic development. In addition, the poverty of the area prevented the spread of education or any extensive popular participation in government, even though most of the countries had constitutions and parliaments.

Persons, Places, and Terms

Alexander III	Bosnia	terrorism
Nicholas II	Montenegro	Bolsheviks
Vladimir Ilyich Lenin	Macedonia	Mensheviks
	Thrace	Constitutional Democrats (Kadets)
Donets Basin		
Caspian Sea	pogrom	Bloody Sunday
Albania	Social Revolutionaries	Soviet of Workers'
Aegean Sea	(S.R.'s)	Deputies
Bulgaria	Social Democrats	October Manifesto
Serbia	(S.D.'s)	Duma

To Master the Text

1. How did Russian home policies change after 1881? Why? How were the personalities of Alexander III and Nicholas II suited to such policies? List the measures taken to prevent the spread of ideas believed to be dangerous. What measures were adopted regarding the non-Russian subjects of the tsar? How were the Jews treated?
2. What industries were developing in Russia during this period? Where? What factors contributed to Russian industrial advance?
3. List the complaints of the Russian peasants. What prevented the introduction of modern farming methods? What was a kulak?

4. What program was advocated by the Social Revolutionaries? Describe their idea of "labor ownership." What kind of people were likely to become S.R.'s? To what extent was the party involved in terrorism?
5. Describe the basic ideas of the Social Democrats. In what two important ways did Lenin differ from many of their other leaders? How did his followers acquire the name Bolsheviks? Who were the Mensheviks? What were their beliefs?
6. What were the principles of the Kadets? Who belonged to the party?
7. How did the non-Russian peoples of the empire add to unrest?
8. What train of events led to the revolution of 1905? How did the parties contribute to the general unrest? What happened on Bloody Sunday? What violent outbreaks followed that day? What was the Soviet of Workers' Deputies?
9. Describe the October Manifesto. What groups did it satisfy? Did it have practical results?
10. What new freedoms did the Russians enjoy after 1905? How was Russian economic life improved?
11. What kinship was there between the Russian people and the peoples of the Balkan Peninsula? Why did the geographical location of the peninsula make it a place of interest to the European powers? How many different peoples inhabited the peninsula? How had the region been affected by Turkish conquest? How did the Balkan peoples earn their livings? What kind of rulers were the Turks?
12. Why did the rise of nationalism cause hostility among the Balkan peoples? How many independent Balkan countries were there by 1870? What had been the fate of the Bulgarians up to that time?
13. List the reasons for the lack of economic progress in the peninsula.

To Interpret the Facts

1. Head three columns with the words "autocracy," "Orthodoxy," and "nationalism." Under each heading, list those policies of the Russian government that particularly related to each.
2. Make a list of the most urgent problems confronting Russia in about 1900. How would each of these problems have been handled by the S.R.'s? The Bolshevik S.D.'s? The Menshevik S.D.'s? The Kadets?

To Put This Chapter into a Larger Setting

1. To what extent did the Russian Industrial Revolution follow a pattern similar to that followed earlier by Great Britain and France? In what ways was the Russian experience different? Why was it different?
2. What differences were there between political parties in western Europe and those in Russia? What western European parties shared views with one or another of the Russian parties?

19

International Relations

1871-1907

The great powers of Europe—Britain, France, Germany, Austria-Hungary, Russia, and Italy—and the lesser countries along the northern and southern edges of the continent, shared the fundamentals of European civilization in spite of differences in government and in economic and military strength. All were neighbors, and the policy of one was bound to affect all others. With the greater ease of travel, the increase of trade, the spread of education and, above all, the growing might of armed forces, both peaceful and warlike international relations took on increasing importance. More than ever before, governments had to devote time, attention, and national wealth to maintaining favorable foreign policies. Ministers had to prepare for war while using every means of diplomacy to keep the peace. During the four decades after 1871 there were no great wars; but since fear of war led to the development of two great systems of alliances, the danger was greatly increased that any war would engulf all Europe.

◯ THE AGE OF BISMARCK, 1871-1890

The years just after 1871 had a certain experimental character as far as international relations were concerned. Europe had to adjust to several new or nearly-new governments: the German Empire, the fully united Italy, the reorganized Austria-Hungary, and the French Third Republic. Of these, only Germany was fortunate enough to have a master statesman to direct its foreign policy. Bismarck's long experience, his insight into the problems of international relations, his tireless genius for diplomacy, and his large degree of control over Germany's internal affairs gave him a place of unrivaled authority in the councils of Europe. Modern students, able to look back on his work through the memory of two world wars, argue over the wisdom of his policies; but in any case his extraordinary influence on international relations makes it natural for the period 1871-1890 to be called the "Age of Bismarck."

THE ARMS RACE

After 1871 Bismarck was no longer the promoter of wars. He believed that Prussia could preserve her recent gains only if Europe remained at peace. Nevertheless he had to work in an atmosphere of militarism, for all the great powers were building up their armed forces in imitation of the pattern already established by Prussia. Among the major nations only Britain made no move to create an army of the German type, relying instead on its fleet.

The new continental armies no longer depended on professional soldiers. Almost all the young men of the nation were liable for a period of one, two, or more years of training. All then returned to civilian life and to membership in the reserves. Thus most of the manpower of the nation was trained for war. New weapons and explosives were developed so rapidly that any one of them scarcely saw two decades of service before it was replaced by something more powerful. Strategic railroads were built, and minutely detailed plans were worked out for their use in wartime. Following the example of Prussia, each nation maintained a general staff—a group of officers engaged in creating plans to meet any conceivable military emergency. The necessarily secret character of staff work encouraged spies and informers who must be carefully guarded against.

These powerful armed forces were symbols of national pride. They were also burdensomely expensive. Moreover, they tended to influence the making of foreign policy, for important political decisions were sometimes made by high military officers, who alone were fully informed about military plans. Thus European international relations were conducted in an atmosphere of increasingly intense military rivalry.

BISMARCK'S EFFORT TO ISOLATE FRANCE, 1871-1878

In spite of the military reforms pressed forward in other countries, Germany remained the strongest power on the continent. But Germany was not secure. German armies could hope to defeat those of any other single power, but not of a combination of powers. Bismarck's nightmare was the "war on two fronts," which he feared France might begin in order to recover Alsace-Lorraine. Although France could not win such a war single-handed, there were two other great powers along Germany's borders —Austria-Hungary and Russia—either of which might well join France for its own advantage. The ultimate goal of Bismarck's policy was thus simple: to prevent the war on two fronts by keeping Germany in close relations with any power likely to ally with France. Britain he did not fear, for it avoided continental alliances. Italy was weak. Only Austria-Hungary and Russia required careful watching.

The Three Emperors' League. In 1872 a series of visits exchanged by Alexander II of Russia, Francis Joseph of Austria-Hungary, and William I of Germany resulted in the establishment of an informal alliance known as the "Three Emperors' League." Although nothing was put into writing, vague promises convinced Bismarck that the alliance was adequate to his needs. But in 1875 the weakness of the League was clearly revealed. By this time France had fairly well recovered from the Franco-Prussian War. A flood of rumors in the press hinted that a new French-German war was in the making. Far from offering to support Germany, the Russian government hastened to join Britain in warning Bismarck against attacking France. Bismarck sensed that the Three Emperors' League might well fall apart in the event of actual war. Since he did not intend to attack France in any case, the war scare of 1875 blew over; but trouble in the Balkan Peninsula soon destroyed the League of the Three Emperors.

The Near East Crisis, 1875-1878. The Balkan troubles began in 1875 in the Turkish provinces of Bosnia and Herzegovina (see map, page 275), where the Christian peasants, encouraged by their Serbian kinsmen and driven to desperation by bad harvests and unemployment, revolted against the Turks. Largely because of the rapid development of Balkan nationalisms and the dishonesty and inefficiency of Turkish officials, the revolt spread to Bulgaria in 1876, and Serbia and Montenegro also went to war against the sultan. Before the end of the year the Turks had defeated the Serbs and had suppressed the Bulgarian rebellion with such ferocity that all Europe was shocked by reports of the "Bulgarian atrocities."

As hope for the hard-pressed Balkan rebels began to disappear, the Russian government was under increasing pressure from its own people to go to war against the sultan. A noisy group of Russians known as "Pan-Slavs" were especially eager to fight. They emphasized the fact that most of the Balkan peoples, like the Russian themselves, were Slavs and also Orthodox Christians; and they insisted that Russia had an obligation to protect these kinsmen.

The Russian government was not averse to fighting the Turks if only Austria-Hungary could in the meantime be restrained from attacking Russia. The tsar had at least to make sure that he had the support of Germany. He inquired of Bismarck what course Germany would follow in the event of an Austro-Russian war over the Balkans. This was an embarrassing question for Bismarck. If he promised to aid Russia, he would lose his alliance with Austria-Hungary; if he refused, he would lose the alliance with Russia. In either case he would destroy the Three Emperors' League. Moreover, it was all too likely that the ally he lost would seek the friendship of France. He replied to the tsar simply that Germany would not permit either Austria-Hungary or Russia to be destroyed. Although no Austro-Russian war broke out, the Three Emperors' League was dead, because the disappointed tsar had lost faith in Bismarck. In April, 1877, Russia, acting alone, declared war on the Ottoman Empire. Austria-Hungary did not attack Russia.

The Russo-Turkish War lasted a little less than a year. Although the Turks resisted with unexpected stubbornness and skill, they were defeated. In March, 1878, the two countries signed a peace treaty at San Stefano, near Constantinople. The most important sections of the treaty made Bulgaria independent and extended its borders not only far to the westward but also southward to the Aegean Sea. Russian troops were to occupy Bulgaria for two years. Since Bulgaria would have ports on both the Black and Aegean Seas, Russia would to an extent be able to by-pass the Straits during the two-year occupation by making use of Bulgarian harbors in the Aegean.

Although not participants in the war, Great Britain and Austria-Hungary protested vehemently against the treaty, which would strengthen Russia in the Mediterranean and the Balkans. Since Bulgaria would presumably be a satellite of Russia, Austria resented the westward extension of that country. Britain objected to the nearness of Bulgaria (and thus indirectly of Russia) to Constantinople and to the Aegean Sea. In protest, the British sent their fleet to anchor off Constantinople. All over Britain people were singing a catchy new song:

> We don't want to fight
> But, by jingo! if we do
> We've got the ships, we've got the men,
> We've got the money too!

Finally the Russians agreed to submit the treaty to a conference of all the powers.

In 1878 a congress of the powers met in Berlin, the capital of the new Germany. Bismarck was president of the congress—an indication of the leading position both of Germany and of her chancellor. The greatest statesmen of the day attended, and the Congress of Berlin was only less brilliant than the Congress of Vienna. A Treaty of Berlin was substituted for the Treaty of San Stefano. The large Bulgaria was divided into three parts. Macedonia and the Aegean coast were returned to the sultan; the middle region, called Eastern Rumelia, became semi-independent under a Christian prince; and that part of Bulgaria north of the Balkan mountains became fully self-governing, with its own prince. Montenegro was recognized as independent, and Serbia and Romania were freed from the last vestiges of Turkish control. In an arrangement destined to cause trouble in the future, Bosnia and Herzegovina, still officially part of the Ottoman Empire, were handed over to Austria-Hungary to be governed. These provisions, so different from those made at San Stefano, lessened the influence the Russians had hoped to obtain in the Balkans and strengthened Austrian influence there.

Some non-Balkan matters were also settled at Berlin, secretly among the statesmen attending. The most important of these were promises to Britain that other nations would not object to British occupation of Cyprus, an island in the eastern Mediterranean, and to France that a French protectorate could be established in Tunisia in North Africa.

In spite of all Bismarck's efforts, the Balkan crisis brought to an end the harmony he had hoped to preserve between Austria-Hungary and Russia. He was president of the congress, claiming to have no interest in its decisions but simply to be acting as an "honest broker" in order to see that all other members of the group received a fair deal. It is not surprising, however, that the Russians believed that they had been unfairly treated, since they had been forced to yield to the demands of the Austrians, who had not entered the war at all. Bismarck realized that he could no longer persuade the Russians and Austrians to work together in co-operation with Germany.

BISMARCK'S NEW SYSTEM OF ALLIANCES, 1879-1890

Unable to depend any longer on the Three Emperors' League, Bismarck looked about for some other way of lessening the chance that a coalition of powers would be organized to attack Germany. It appeared that he could secure the alliance of either Austria-Hungary or Russia, but not of both. He chose to rely on Austria-Hungary, for there were more points in common between the two nations, and Austria seemed more likely to be a docile partner than did Russia.

The Austro-German Alliance of 1879. In 1879 the German and Austro-Hungarian governments entered into a formal alliance by which each was required to defend the territory of the other against an attack from Russia or from any other power supported by Russia. Previous alliances among great powers had generally been made for limited periods and at times when war actually threatened. The Austro-German alliance set a wholly new pattern. It was entered into in peacetime to last for five years with the possibility of renewal. Its terms were kept secret.

Triple Alliance, 1882. The new alignment soon became the Triple Alliance, for in 1882 Italy joined it. The Italians wanted German support in case France should ally with the pope to help him recover Rome. Germany and Italy promised to support each other against a French attack. The Italians were also concerned about the fact that the French, making use of a secret British-German promise given them at the Congress of Berlin, had established a protectorate over Tunis in 1881. Because Tunis was so near Italy and was inhabited by many Italian businessmen, the Italian government had long expected to take it over. Now the Italians hoped instead that the Germans would help them elsewhere in North Africa.

Russo-German Relations, 1881-1890. The dilemma that Bismarck found himself in at the Congress of Berlin, which forced him to choose between Austria-Hungary and Russia as allies, soon vanished. Once Russian officials had recovered from their irritation at him, they became convinced that a Russo-German alliance was necessary for Russian safety. At Russian suggestion the Three Emperors' League was revived in 1881. So secret was

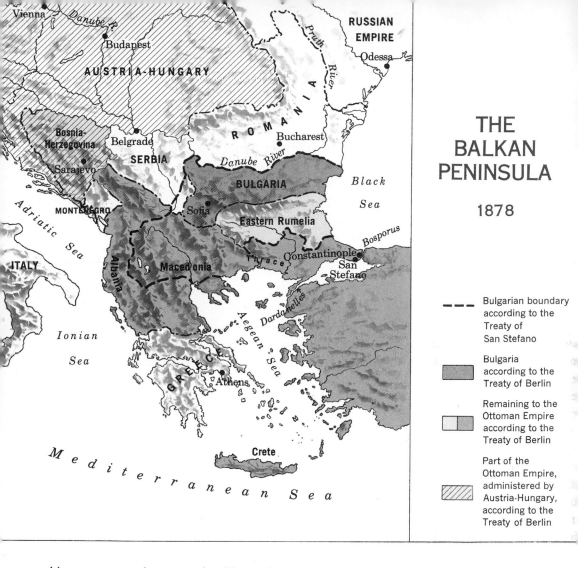

THE
BALKAN
PENINSULA

1878

- - - Bulgarian boundary
according to the
Treaty of
San Stefano

Bulgaria
according to the
Treaty of Berlin

Remaining to the
Ottoman Empire
according to the
Treaty of Berlin

Part of the
Ottoman Empire,
administered by
Austria-Hungary,
according to the
Treaty of Berlin

this agreement—drawn up by Bismarck in his own handwriting—that it was not known of abroad until 1918.

In 1886 German-Russian relations were put under a renewed strain arising out of a situation in Bulgaria. The ruler of that country, a relative of the tsar who had been placed on the throne with Russian support, proved quite unwilling to consider his country a Russian satellite. The Russians removed him, but they could not force the Bulgarian people to accept another prince chosen by Russia. Bismarck foresaw with alarm the possibility of a Russian attack on Bulgaria, likely to be followed by an Austro-Hungarian attack on Russia. Since this was the time of General Boulanger's popularity in France (see page 240), he also feared a simultaneous French attack on Germany.

Bismarck's policy was to prevent war if possible but at the same time to strengthen Germany in case war proved unavoidable. To frighten France, he forced the German parliament to increase the size of the army, and he renewed the Triple Alliance. To hold Russia back from attacking Bulgaria he encouraged Britain, Austria-Hungary, and Italy to make a "Mediterranean Agreement" opposing any change in the Mediterranean, Adriatic, Aegean, or Black Sea areas. Thus a Russian attack on Bulgaria would very likely be followed by an attack on Russia from the Mediterranean Agreement countries. Then in 1887 Bismarck substituted for the Three Emperors' League an extraordinarily secret "Reinsurance Treaty" between Germany and Russia. Although this seemed possibly contrary to Germany's obligations to Austria-Hungary in the Triple Alliance treaty, Bismarck believed he could, with skill, avoid any difficulties. His ability to maintain special relationships with Austria-Hungary and Russia, both at the same time, was a proof not only of his ruthlessness but also of his genius.

The Fall of Bismarck, 1890. Within three years of concluding the Reinsurance Treaty, Bismarck was out of office. (See page 249.) It was not long thereafter that a close relationship between Russia and France, which he had spent twenty years trying to prevent, became a reality. The basic flaw in Bismarck's system of alliances was that it could only be operated by a statesman of his extraordinary skill; in lesser hands it became dangerous.

☾ CREATION OF THE TRIPLE ENTENTE

The fall of Bismarck was the signal for great alterations in European international relations. Countries that were old friends became enemies and vice versa. The first of these developments was the signing of a military alliance between France and Russia.

THE RUSSO-FRENCH ALLIANCE, 1894

Although the fall of Bismarck was the occasion for the drawing together of France and Russia, it was not the only cause. Bismarck himself had forced Russia to enter into closer financial relations with France; for in 1887, during the Bulgarian crisis, he had prevented the Russians from borrowing money in Germany, and thus left them no alternative but to seek funds in

France. In 1890, after the fall of Bismarck, Emperor William II refused to renew the Reinsurance Treaty with Russia in spite of the earnest desire of the Russians to continue it. His motives are not clear; perhaps he believed that Bismarck's system of alliance was dangerously complicated. Perhaps the people newly in charge of Germany's foreign policy were simply eager to initiate a policy that was not Bismarck's.

In 1891 the French and Russian governments took the first steps toward closer relations with each other, although the tsar was reluctant to enter into definite commitments with republican France. In 1894 a military alliance came into effect between the two countries. According to its terms France and Russia would come to each other's assistance if Germany should attack either of them. The alliance was to remain in force as long as did the Triple Alliance. Thus for the first time the continent of Europe was divided into two armed camps permanently ranged against each other. Great Britain still remained, by its own choice, outside the two groups. During the next years the crucial factor in international relations was the relationship of Britain to the two alliances.

GREAT BRITAIN AND THE ALLIANCES, 1894-1904

Although until after 1900 the British government remained officially skeptical of the value of continental allies, there were many important British statesmen who believed that Britain would be more secure if it had an ally. Efforts were made on both British and German sides to bring Britain into the Triple Alliance. The long history of British-German friendship and the numerous sharp colonial disputes in various parts of the world between Britain on the one hand and Russia and France on the other tended to draw Britain toward Germany and away from France and Russia.

But forces were at work preventing a British-German alliance and paving the way for an understanding between Britain and France. With the passage of time colonial rivalries between France and Britain lessened, while those between Germany and Britain grew more severe. The rapid industrial development of Germany meant that British salesmen trying to find markets in various parts of the world frequently encountered Germans whose products were at least as good and as inexpensive as those produced in Britain. In 1898 a new source of difference arose between the two countries when the Germans began to build their great navy, intended eventually to be perhaps two thirds the size of the British. Since the very life of Great Britain depended upon its ability to bring food and raw materials to its islands in wartime, it could not permit any rival to threaten its control of the sea. In Germany there was little understanding of the British attitude toward these forces driving Germany and Britain apart. On the other hand there were important persons on both sides of the English Channel who believed that it was with France that Britain could make the most useful alliance.

THE ENTENTE CORDIALE, 1904

By 1904 concern over the growth of the German navy and growing realization of the usefulness of allies finally led British statesmen to negotiate a series of agreements that settled the most serious difficulties with France. These agreements, taken together, are called the "Entente Cordiale" (French for "friendly understanding"). Most important were a French promise not to protest the continued British occupation of Egypt, begun in 1882, and a British promise not to protest steps that France proposed taking to divide Morocco with Spain. These agreements did not amount to a formal alliance, but they marked the beginning of a period of growing British-French friendship.

In the next year, 1905, an occasion arose to test Anglo-French co-operation: the First Moroccan Crisis. By that time it had become apparent to all that France intended to make Morocco a protectorate, thereby limiting commercial opportunities for other countries. The German government, alarmed by the very existence of the Entente Cordiale, determined to use the situation in Morocco to destroy the British-French understanding. The British had, of course, given their consent to what the French were doing in Morocco, as the Italians had earlier; but the Germans had not been consulted. The Germans now determined to protest, believing that the British would fail to support their French friends.

In the end, however, the Entente Cordiale proved strong enough to resist the German attack on it. In 1906 the Germans were able to force the calling of an international conference at Algeciras in Spain to discuss the whole Moroccan question; but at the conference Britain and France stood strongly together. Immediately thereafter British and French army officers began to discuss plans for collaboration between the military forces of the two countries in the event of war. Thus the Germans, instead of destroying the Entente, encouraged it to become something akin to an alliance.

EUROPEAN
ALLIANCES
1872-1914

Three Emperors
League, 1872-1878
1881-1887

Triple Alliance
1882

Triple Entente
1907

GREAT
BRITAIN

RUSSIA

GERMANY

FRANCE

AUSTRIA-HUNGARY

ITALY

(Br.)

THE TRIPLE ENTENTE, 1907

In the year after the Algeciras Conference, Britain and Russia, both already allies of France but in dispute with each other in various parts of the world, settled their differences and thus made the Entente a triangular affair. France was, of course, eager for this friendship between its two allies. The Russians sought good relations with Britain. After their defeat in the war with Japan (1905), they began at once to consider the possibility of further expanding their interests in the Balkans. They needed European allies to protect them against Germany and Austria-Hungrary. In 1907 a series of agreements were made between Britain and Russia similar to those of 1904 between Britain and France. Tibet and Afghanistan had both been places of rivalry between the two countries. Both powers now agreed to make no move to secure control of Tibet, and to leave Afghanistan within the sphere of British influence. In Persia, a country that both powers wished to control, it was agreed that Russia might establish almost a protectorate over the northern part of the country and Britain over the southern part. The central part was to be free of both powers. Once these arrangements were completed, such cordial relations existed among Russia, Britain, and France that the three were spoken of as the "Triple Entente."

Thus all Bismarck's efforts, begun in 1871, to make Germany the center of a system of alliances to preserve the peace of Europe had resulted not only in the Triple Alliance, but also, indirectly, in the Triple Entente—the purpose of which was to protect France, Russia, and Britain against the Triple Alliance. The purpose of both groups was defense against aggressors and the maintenance of peace. The expanding armies and navies were also looked upon by many people of the time as a step toward peace. But none of these diplomatic or military efforts brought peace and security to the peoples of Europe. The danger of world war was never removed. To some it seemed that peace might be better secured by other means than by preparing for war.

⌒ THE PEACE MOVEMENT

While the greatest armies and navies that had ever been known were being built, idealistic men and women in many countries were trying to promote the idea that the peace that all men longed for could best be achieved by reducing armaments and developing nonmilitary ways of settling international disputes. The peace movement was not a new one. Early in the nineteenth century peace societies had appeared in the United States, France, Switzerland, and Britain. Settling international disputes by arbitration—that is, by submitting the question in dispute to a third country or to several neutral statesmen—had become fairly common. The earliest important example of arbitration, which was arranged between Great Britain and the United States after the American Civil War, settled American claims for damage done by Confederate warships built in British shipyards.

The most elaborate effort after 1871 to further the peace movement was initiated by Tsar Nicholas II, who realized that Russia could not afford to keep abreast of the western nations in the arms race. At his invitation twenty-six nations sent delegates to the First Hague Peace Conference, held in the Netherlands in 1899. It failed to reduce armaments, but it accomplished a number of other things. It drew up agreements concerning such matters as the rights of the Red Cross in wartime, the treatment of war prisoners, and the outlawing of some new practices of warfare thought especially inhumane, such as the use of poison gas. More important, it established a Permanent Court of Arbitration to sit at the Hague in a "Peace Palace" built by the American industrialist Andrew Carnegie. Each of the member nations nominated four persons to the court, and from this group a panel could be chosen to decide any case voluntarily submitted by any nation. A Second Hague Conference met in 1907, called by the tsar at the suggestion of the American President, Theodore Roosevelt. It continued the work of the first conference, but could not agree upon any more far-reaching results.

∽ ∽ ∽

The peace movement was unsuccessful in comparison with the preparations for war, but it kept alive an important idea and the hope that other means than war might be found to settle the world's problems. Meantime the rise of new world powers and an intense struggle among the old and new powers for overseas empires further increased international tensions.

Places and Terms

Eastern Rumelia	war on two fronts	Triple Alliance
Balkan Mountains	Three Emperors'	Reinsurance Treaty
Romania	League	Triple Entente
Bosnia-Herzegovina	Pan-Slavs	Entente Cordiale
Cyprus	Treaty of San Stefano	protectorate
Tunisia	Congress of Berlin	First Hague
Algeciras	Mediterranean	Peace Conference
the Hague	Agreement	

To Master the Text

1. Why did Bismarck desire peace after 1871? What steps did the continental powers take to prepare for war? How did large military establishments alter the character of governments and of international relations?

2. Why was Bismarck wary of France? What was his general plan for keeping France from undertaking a war against Germany? What reliance did he place in the Three Emperors' League? Who were members of it? What event showed him that it was dangerously weak?

3. Why were there revolts in the Balkans in 1876? What countries participated in them? How did they affect the Three Emperors' League?

4. How did the Russo-Turkish War end? What countries signed the Peace of San Stefano? What were its terms? What powers protested? Why?

5. What was the purpose of the Congress of Berlin? What powers were represented? Who presided? Describe the arrangements made at Berlin. In what ways was the Treaty of Berlin unfavorable to Russia? How was Bismarck's system of alliances affected by the congress?

6. When did Bismarck form an alliance with Austria-Hungary? Why? What did each government promise the other? What third country later joined the Austro-German alliance? Why? What was the name of the new alliance? What did its members promise each other?
7. Why was the Three Emperors' League renewed in 1881?
8. For what two reasons was Bismarck alarmed in 1885? What steps did he take between then and 1890? What happened to his policies after 1890?
9. Why, when, and by what steps, did France and Russia become allies? By 1894 which powers were members of permanent alliances?
10. What factors prevented a British-German alliance? What was the Entente Cordiale? When was it made? What promises were made? How did it differ from an alliance? How successful was it?
11. How was the Entente Cordiale strengthened after 1906? What third country was brought into the Entente? How? Thereafter what name was given that group of powers?
12. What was the peace movement? What did it accomplish?

To Master the Map

Study the boundaries of the proposed kingdom of Bulgaria as drawn by the Treaty of San Stefano (see map, page 275), taking into account that according to the treaty Russian armed forces were to have occupied this enlarged Bulgaria for two years. How would the Treaty of San Stefano have strengthened Russian influence in the Mediterranean? How does the map illustrate the reason why other powers objected to this big Bulgaria? Why were the boundaries drawn by the Congress of Berlin more satisfactory to them?

To Interpret the Facts

1. Why was it necessary from Bismarck's point of view for Germany to be allied with both Austria-Hungary and Russia? Why was it so difficult to maintain an alliance with both at the same time? List all the methods by which Bismarck kept both friendly to Germany.
2. How many different factors helped create the Franco-Russian alliance? Did German policy do more to encourage or to discourage the alliance?

To Put This Chapter into a Larger Setting

1. Which of Bismarck's specific policies of the years 1862-1890 can still be adjudged successes? Which cannot? Why? Were his successes largely due to his own skill or to the circumstances in which he did his work?
2. Trace British-French relations since 1789. What problems had made the two countries enemies? What had drawn them together? When? In the light of this review, do you think of the Entente Cordiale as a surprising development or as a natural outgrowth of what had gone before?

 **20**

New World
Powers:
The United States
and Japan

By the end of the nineteenth century, international relations began to be affected by the appearance of two new world powers—the United States and Japan. Neither was yet the equal of the most powerful European nations, but by 1900 each exerted considerable influence on world affairs.

◠ THE UNITED STATES, 1789-1898

The history of the United States in the first century of its national existence was a record of steady growth in territory, in population, and in economic strength. In 1783, at the end of the Revolution, the American people were barely a nation; by 1898, although their foundations were still European, they had developed a national character and had established the institutions that would determine their future at home and in world affairs for decades to come.

THE FIRM ESTABLISHMENT OF THE NATION, 1789-1837

In 1789, when the Constitution was put into operation (see page 17) and President George Washington was sworn into office, the future of the new government was doubtful. The Constitution had been ratified only with difficulty. It was not at all certain that the new government would com-

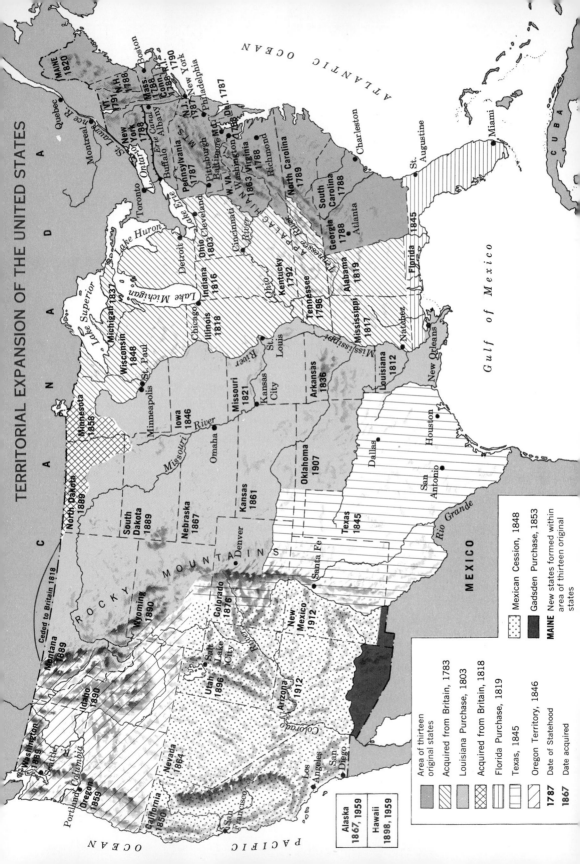

TERRITORIAL EXPANSION OF THE UNITED STATES

CANADA

ATLANTIC OCEAN

CUBA

Gulf of Mexico

MEXICO

PACIFIC OCEAN

Quebec
Montreal
St. Lawrence R.
Toronto
Lake Ontario
Erie Canal
Buffalo
Lake Erie
Boston
New York
Albany
Philadelphia
Baltimore
Washington
Richmond
Charleston
St. Augustine
Miami

MAINE 1820
VT. 1791
N.H. 1788
Mass. 1788
Conn. 1788
R.I. 1790
New York 1788
N.J. 1787
Pennsylvania 1787
Pittsburgh
Md. 1788
Del. 1787
W.VA. 1863
Virginia 1788
North Carolina 1789
South Carolina 1788
Georgia 1788
Atlanta
Florida 1845

Lake Superior
Lake Huron
Lake Michigan
Detroit
Cleveland
Cincinnati
Michigan 1837
Wisconsin 1848
St. Paul
Minneapolis
Chicago
Ohio 1803
Indiana 1816
Illinois 1818
Kentucky 1792
Tennessee 1796
Alabama 1819
Mississippi 1817
Natchez
Louisiana 1812
New Orleans

Minnesota 1858
Iowa 1846
Missouri 1821
Kansas City
St. Louis
Arkansas 1836
Omaha
Missouri River

North Dakota 1889
South Dakota 1889
Nebraska 1867
Kansas 1861
Oklahoma 1907
Texas 1845
Dallas
Houston
San Antonio
Rio Grande

Montana 1889
Wyoming 1890
Colorado 1876
New Mexico 1912
Santa Fe
Denver
ROCKY MOUNTAINS

Washington 1889
Seattle
Idaho 1890
Oregon 1859
Portland
Columbia River
Nevada 1864
Utah 1896
Salt Lake City
Arizona 1912
California 1850
San Francisco
Los Angeles
San Diego
Colorado River

Ceded to Britain 1818

Alaska 1867, 1959 | Hawaii 1898, 1959

Legend

Area of thirteen original states
Acquired from Britain, 1783
Louisiana Purchase, 1803
Acquired from Britain, 1818
Florida Purchase, 1819
Texas, 1845
Oregon Territory, 1846

1787 Date of Statehood
1867 Date acquired

Mexican Cession, 1848
Gadsden Purchase, 1853
MAINE New states formed within area of thirteen original states

mand the loyalty of all the people. The thirteen states, ranged along the Atlantic coast with a total of only four million inhabitants, were separated from each other by inadequate roads and by important economic and social differences. Foreign nations were not overly friendly. Pessimists at home and abroad looked for the quick collapse of the country. Events proved these forebodings to be inaccurate.

Territorial Expansion. The first clear proof of national strength was the acquisition of a vast expanse of new territory. At the end of the Revolution, the British had ceded to the Americans all the land east of the Mississippi River except Florida, which they ceded to Spain and which at that time included all the Gulf of Mexico coast west to Louisiana. Spain also held the territory of Louisiana, which extended from the Mississippi to the Rocky Mountains and controlled the mouth of the Mississippi. The southwestern part of the present United States was also a Spanish possession. In 1800 Napoleon acquired Louisiana from Spain just when the Spanish governor had closed the port of New Orleans to Americans. This was a serious blow to the United States, for frontiersmen living west of the Appalachians could only get their bulk goods (grain, for example) to market by flatboat down the Mississippi to New Orleans, from where it would be shipped overseas or to the east coast aboard ocean-going vessels. In any case Napoleonic France was a frighteningly strong neighbor. The American President, Thomas Jefferson, determined to buy New Orleans. At the same time Napoleon came to the conclusion that Louisiana was of little use to him. In 1803, therefore, to the surprise of Jefferson, he offered to sell the whole of it, including New Orleans. In spite of some doubts as to whether the Constitution gave him the right to do so, Jefferson bought the whole area.

Friction also developed between the United States and Spain over Florida. American criminals were wont to seek refuge there, and Florida Indians frequently raided American settlements. In 1819 these nuisances were brought to an end by the American purchase of the whole of Florida. Together, Florida and Louisiana more than doubled the original area of the United States.

The Westward Movement. As soon as the Revolution was over, settlers began to pour into the region west of the Appalachians. Even before the Revolution, adventurers like Daniel Boone had discovered some of the passes over the mountains. In the three decades after 1790 a fever of road- and canal-building shortened the arduous journey westward. The Ohio River furnished an easy route down which whole families with their household and farm equipment and their animals could float on flatboats. In 1811 the United States government began work on the National Road, which finally reached Illinois in the 1850's. In 1825 the state of New York opened the Erie Canal, which connected Buffalo on Lake Erie with the Hudson River and thus provided an all-water route from the port of New York to the Great Lakes. As early as 1811 steamboats appeared in the western waters, ready to transport people and equipment up the navigable rivers.

The frontiersmen found cheap land, rich soil, and opportunities for advancing themselves in newly formed communities. By 1837 so many had moved westward that the states of Arkansas and Missouri west of the Mississippi had been admitted to the union as well as all those east of the river except Florida and Wisconsin. Even more important was the development of the particularly American kind of society that grew out of frontier life—a society characterized by greater freedom, equality, and opportunity than was to be found in Europe, and also by the roughness and ruggedness that the hardships of the frontier were bound to produce.

Economic Growth. The growing population, augmented each year by immigrants from abroad; the opening of the rich new lands; and the development of industries in the older regions, helped furnish a solid foundation for rapid economic growth. In the Northeast, shipping and manufacturing vied with each other for importance. As early as 1789 Samuel Slater came from England, carrying in his head the plans for British power-spinning machines. The textile mill he built in Rhode Island encouraged the building of similar plants in various parts of New England. These and other mills for the manufacture of such things as small metal products made use of the water power of the New England streams. In the southern states Eli Whitney's cotton gin (see page 116) made slave-tended cotton lands fabulously profitable. Southern planters immediately put new acres into cotton. When their overworked fields began to be less productive, many took their families and their slaves farther west. Meantime farmers of the Midwest (then called the Northwest) began to produce grain and meat in excess of their own needs, to be sent by road, river, or canal to eastern or southern markets.

Extension of Democracy. As the country grew larger and richer, government became more democratic. In colonial times, in spite of some restrictions, the right to vote was widespread, and free citizens were safeguarded against tyrannical actions on the part of the government. (See page 17.) By the 1840's remaining property and religious qualifications for voting had

The Erie Canal locks at Lockport, New York. Canal boats, pulled by mules on the paths at the sides of the canal, were raised or lowered from one water level to another by means of these locks. By providing easy transportation from New York and New England to the Great Lakes region, the Erie Canal helped open vast new areas to settlement.

disappeared in all states. Two strong national parties had come into being, holding conventions to nominate their candidates and running political campaigns to put their men in office. The presidency of Andrew Jackson (President 1829-1837) symbolizes these changes. Jackson came from Tennessee, the first President from west of the Appalachians. He was a popular hero because he had won the greatest battle of the War of 1812 at New Orleans and had led the raid against the Indians in Florida that made the Spanish willing to sell that area. He claimed to represent the interests of the common man, to be the "tribune of the people." After his time all political leaders had to make a conscious appeal to the masses of the voters. At the same time, increasing opportunities for education enabled more and more men to become informed voters and prepared them to take their parts in political life.

Relations With the Outside World. The young United States, although not able to exert decisive influence in world affairs, was already caught up in world events. That fact was obvious during the Napoleonic Wars (1793-1815), when Britain and France attempted to interfere, each to its own advantage, with the flourishing commerce carried on by the United States with both countries. The United States tried in vain to defend the right of the "freedom of the seas" (the right of neutrals to use the high seas without hindrance during wartime). Napoleon cleverly avoided serious trouble with the United States; but the problem of the seas, along with such other factors as the desire of frontiersmen to conquer Florida (then still Spanish) and Canada, led to the War of 1812 with Britain. When in 1814 the fighting in Europe ceased, Britain and the United States also made peace.

The Monroe Doctrine of 1823 (see pages 92-93) is another example of American involvement in world affairs. Although the question agitating the world at the moment—whether Spain should be allowed to recover its rebellious Latin-American colonies—would have been settled as it was without the United States, Monroe's declaration of the separation of the Eastern and Western Hemispheres made an impression. But the most important effects of American participation in the War of 1812 and of Monroe's statement were in America itself, where the American people were helped to realize that they had become a nation with a real, if secondary, part to play in world affairs.

THE THREAT OF SECTIONAL DIVISION, 1837-1865

No sooner had a degree of national unity been achieved, however, than it was threatened by strong sectional differences among the American states. Many of these tensions were in one way or another related to the question of slavery or to the conflict between the slave-based economy of the South and the free-labor and more industrialized economies of the North and West.

The Rise of the Slavery Question. The first Negro slaves had been brought to America in 1619 to furnish labor for Virginia tobacco plantations. Eventually in the colonies north of Maryland slavery was prohibited. Even in the South there was for a time a widespread feeling that all slaves would eventually be freed. But the unexpected boom in cotton planting after the invention of the cotton gin made slave labor so valuable that southerners became too dependent on slavery to give it up. The Ohio River and the 36°30′ parallel of north latitude became the dividing lines between free and slave states (except for Missouri, a slave state). As manufacturing grew in the North and cotton planting expanded in the South, the economic and political needs of the two sections came increasingly into conflict. Northerners, for example, wanted high tariffs to prevent Americans from buying European manufactures, while southerners wanted low tariffs so that they could purchase British goods with the profits from the sale of their cotton in England. Since northern population increased more rapidly than that of the South, the North soon had more representatives in the House of Representatives, although since slave and free states remained equal in number, representation in the Senate (two from each state) was equal.

In the 1830's the question of acquiring the territory west to the Pacific began to be agitated. This expansion, too, became in part a slavery question. Abolitionists (northerners who advocated the total abolition of slavery) opposed any acquisition of lands that might later become slave states. Nevertheless in 1845 the Republic of Texas, recently (1836) independent from Mexico, entered the Union as a slave state. To an extent this addition was balanced in 1846 when the free Oregon territory, previously a joint possession of the United States and Britain, was divided at the forty-ninth parallel and the section to the south of the line became an indisputable possession of the United States. The annexation of Texas led to a war with Mexico (1846-1848), which gave the United States the present southwestern part of the country. The argument as to the future of slavery in this newly acquired area became intense. In 1850 California entered the Union as a free state, but the Abolitionists were unable to prevent slavery from going into the new Southwest (the territories of Utah and New Mexico). In the North, determination hardened to keep the land not yet made into states free from slavery. In the South, on the other hand, people began to realize that there would eventually be more free than slave states and that Congress would thus in the future be fully controlled by northern representatives unsympathetic to the economic life of the South.

The Civil War, 1861-1865. Historians still argue about the fundamental causes for the outbreak of the Civil War. Only the bare facts are agreed upon. In 1860 seven southern states seceded from the Union and established the Confederate States of America, to be joined in 1861 by four more states. Fighting, which soon began between the Confederacy and the Union, developed into a bitter four-year war, probably the bloodiest conflict anywhere in the world between 1815 and 1914. The Confederates had the advantages of fighting on home territory, of defending a popular cause, and of having better officers. But it was the Union armies, with their far greater manpower and backed by more flourishing industry, that finally won the war. Unfortunately the assassination of President Abraham Lincoln just after the end of the war removed the one statesman who might have prevented the continuation of wartime bitterness after the fighting ceased.

Reconstruction, 1865–1877. There followed a period called "Reconstruction," which was even more bitter than the war itself. Southern states were prevented—some of them for a number of years—from being fully restored to the Union. Meantime they were governed by army officers with troops under their command. The slaves were freed without compensation to their owners and with very little help in the adjustment to life as freed men. Plantation owners, unable to re-establish their former way of farming, parceled out their estates to Negro "sharecroppers," who paid rent in a share of their produce. Bitter resentment was aroused in the South, not only by military defeat but even more by the period of military rule and the difficulty of entering into a new relationship with a Negro population unprepared for freedom. This resentment has not yet wholly disappeared.

THE RISE TO GREAT POWER STATUS, 1865-1914

The Civil War ended the threat of political division within the United States. During the next half-century the country experienced a great period of economic expansion.

The most impressive development of the immediate postwar years was the settlement of the Great Plains, the region east of the Rocky Mountains. Although pioneers had crossed this region on their way to the Pacific Coast, they had believed the treeless plains uninhabitable. But with the completion in 1869 of the first transcontinental railroad, running from Chicago to San Francisco; with more than 500,000 immigrants entering the country annually; and with land to be had (under the Homestead Act of 1862) free to anyone who would farm it for five years, there were many reasons for the opening of the plains area. Hunters soon destroyed the buffalo herds that had kept alive the plains Indians. When the Indians could no longer maintain themselves, and had in any event been defeated by armed force, the settlers dared move into the old hunting grounds. The census of 1890 showed that there were enough settlers in all parts of the country so that there could no longer be said to be a frontier anywhere.

By 1890 industry, already stimulated by the Civil War, was becoming even more important to the economy than was agriculture. In 1860 the United States had been fourth in manufacturing among nations of the world. By 1894 it had moved into first place, and twenty years later American industrial production was greater than the combined output of Britain and France. Many factors help explain this magnificent growth, among them the rich American sources of such raw materials as lumber, coal, iron, copper, and oil; the labor force supplied by immigrants and by native Americans who could no longer find opportunities on the frontier; the continent-wide free market protected by fairly high import duties; the availability of capital supplied by Americans or by loans from abroad; and the fact that American machines were new and thus were the latest models (instead of being half worn out, as was much of the British industrial equipment).

There is much in the history of American industrial expansion that parallels that of Britain and Germany. These years were the age of steel and steam in the United States, although by 1914 textiles surpassed iron and steel. Other giant businesses were oil-refining and meat-packing. As in Europe there was a close connection between business and banking. Smaller businesses bought each other out until a few giants remained in the field. To match big business, large labor unions came into being; and in 1886 a super-organization of labor, the American Federation of Labor, the organization of skilled unions, was founded. Cities grew as people came in from the farms hoping for greater opportunities. By 1910 there were fifty cities with 100,000 or more population, and these accounted for more than a fifth of the American population.

The same familiar problems beset American cities as had troubled those of Europe—slums, crime, dirt, overcrowding. There were also the same advantages—better schools, better health services, more amusements. As in Europe the problems of industrial society seemed to some people to demand a socialist approach for their alleviation, but most welfare activity remained on the private or local level. The American government was slow to curb the monopolistic tendencies of big business, but by 1914 steps had been taken to protect the public from too big business.

Obviously an expanding industrial nation with the more than 90,000,000 people who lived in the United States in 1910 would be a world power. By the early twentieth century the United States had joined the company of the great powers of the earth, although not yet in the role of world leader.

⌒ JAPAN TO 1912

Almost simultaneously with the United States, Japan rose to a position of economic and military influence in world affairs. The Japanese experienced a more abrupt Industrial Revolution than did the Americans, and on that basis built up strong armed forces. But otherwise Japan had little in common with the United States, either in culture, in previous history, or in world position.

THE JAPANESE AND THEIR EARLY HISTORY

The Japanese are an Asian people who settled in the fertile valleys of their mountainous islands in the first centuries after Christ. They borrowed much from Chinese civilization. Many of the arts now typically Japanese came first from China—painting on scrolls, the tea ceremony, flower arrangement, landscape gardening. The Japanese language was written with Chinese word symbols. Buddhism also came to Japan from China, but the Japanese made it into an essentially Japanese religion, "Japanizing" it as they had all their borrowings from the Chinese.

Shinto, a native religion, also had great influence on Japanese life. Originally it was simply a feeling of awe in the presence of nature or of a hero; later it added ancestor worship; and in modern times it became the state religion, teaching that the emperor was descended from the sun goddess and was therefore divine. Ancestor worship made the continuity of the family so necessary that to this day a family without a son is likely to adopt one, and family relationships in business are more important than in the West.

Until modern times Japan never had a single centralized government. Great lords, the "daimyo," exercised the real power. There was an emperor and his commander-in-chief, the "shogun"; but first the emperor and then the shogun became mere ceremonial figureheads. Then in 1600 a daimyo of the Tokugawa family gained control of all Japan and made himself shogun.

The Tokugawa shogunate lasted until 1868, always characterized by its determination to keep firm control over the country by shutting Japan off from the outside world and excluding all foreign influences. The many Japanese Christians were killed, reconverted, or forced to go underground; all missionaries were expelled. With the exception of a few Chinese and Dutch, no foreign traders could visit the islands, and Japanese could not go abroad. Thus Japan was sealed off from contact with Europe at the very time when European society was entering one of its greatest periods of change and development.

Within the country the Tokugawa regulated all aspects of life. Social classes were ranged in order according to the theories of the Chinese philosopher Confucius (Kung Fu-tse), but with the difference that in China the most important class was made up of scholars, while in Japan it was composed of the warriors, the "samurai." No class evaded strict governmental supervision. Even the "daimyo," the greatest lords, were carefully watched by one of the world's first secret police forces so that they could not start rebellions.

By thus removing all danger of invasion or revolt, Tokugawa rule gave Japan a stability perhaps experienced by no other important nation in the world of the seventeenth and eighteenth centuries. Kept apart from outside influences and crowded into their narrow land, the people intensified the polite formality in human relationships that still characterizes them, and which enabled them to live together without undue friction. Undisturbed by ideas from abroad, they continued to develop thought and art in ways unique to their own temperament and style of life.

Nevertheless, after two and a half centuries, Tokugawa rule came to an abrupt end.

THE OPENING OF JAPAN, 1853

The appearance of an American war fleet in Japanese waters in 1853 terminated Japanese isolation. Long-developing conditions in both Japan and the West had made possible this event and its consequences.

Internal Changes in Tokugawa Japan. In spite of the tight grip of the Tokugawas on the country, they could not prevent the economic development encouraged by their own regime from bringing about basic changes in the agricultural economy they hoped to preserve. Continued peace and the fact that the whole country was a single free market greatly stimulated commerce. Merchants controlling the national rice market in Osaka became very rich. Some became bankers, lending money to daimyo and samurai. Japan came to have almost as much city life as did the industrializing countries of the West. Tokyo was one of the world's largest cities, with more than a million inhabitants, and Osaka was almost as large. Rich merchants began to dream of the advantages of reopening foreign commerce.

Meantime there was a revolution of ideas. After 1720 foreign books could again be imported (except for those on Christianity). From the Dutch traders in their prison-like station in Nagasaki harbor, a few Japanese learned the Dutch language and studied through Dutch sources such subjects as military science, the handling of metals, and the building of ships. Moreover, the warrior class, now at loose ends, had leisure to read Japanese history, which revealed the one-time importance of the emperor and suggested his restoration to power.

World Interest in Japan. Europeans, especially the British and the Russians, had attempted to open trade with Japan in the late eighteenth century.

The waterfront of the port of Yokohama, with a steam engine of the Yokohama Coastal Line. The railroad was begun in 1870 and opened in 1872. The picture illustrates the power of western influence in Japan.

After the Mexican War (1846-1848), which made the United States a Pacific power, Americans were also eager to open Japanese ports to their ships. They intensified their trade by clipper sailing ship to China, passing always near to Japan. The flourishing American whaling industry brought other Americans into Japanese waters. The United States government sought permission for Americans to stop in Japanese ports for water and also to rescue shipwrecked seamen who were treated according to Japanese law, but in ways that often seemed cruel to westerners. When the Japanese refused these requests, the United States decided on a show of force.

The Perry Expedition, 1853–1854. Commodore Matthew Perry and his "black ships" (as the Japanese called them) dropped anchor in Tokyo Bay in July 1853, bringing presents for the emperor, including a small railway train, and also a letter demanding that Japanese ports be opened to Americans. Almost simultaneously a Russian squadron appeared with a similar demand. But the determination of Commodore Perry resulted in his being the one to force his demands on the Japanese, whose guns could not match those of the American vessels.

The outcome of the Perry expedition was a treaty with the United States opening two Japanese ports to American ships. The Japanese were also forced to agree to some humiliating arrangements, including two which prevented them from raising their tariffs above a certain level and permitted Americans resident in Japan to be tried in courts by their own laws. Treaties with other nations soon followed, patterned closely after that with the United States.

THE MEIJI REFORMS, 1868-1912

Some years after the visit of Perry, the Japanese began to realize that to retain their national independence they would have to make great military, socioeconomic, and political reforms. A number of dedicated, talented young samurai placed themselves at the head of a reform movement. They brought about such important changes that by the beginning of the twentieth century Japan could take its place among the industrialized, militarily strong nations of the world. For the second time the Japanese entered upon a period of conscious borrowing of ideas from abroad.

Governmental Reform. The Japanese government was changed to give it the outward appearance of the western democracies. The shogun was deposed and the young emperor brought from seclusion to head the state. The emperor called the era of his reign "Meiji" (enlightened rule); because he was an able statesman the name proved justified. A constitution gave sovereignty to the emperor but it also provided for a two-house legislature with the lower house elected by about one per cent of the population. The ministers were not, however, responsible to the legislature. Moreover, two kinds of persons, never so powerful in the western world, exerted great influence on the Japanese government. Military leaders on active duty were able to be heard always, as were the "genro"—elder statesmen who had led the revolution from the beginning. Thus Japan was a constitutional monarchy but not a democracy.

Economic Reform. Economic reform was at least as important as was constitutional change. Feudalism was destroyed when the daimyo handed over their estates to the government in return for sums of money. Some of the daimyo invested their money in businesses which in time made them enormously wealthy. But there was not enough private capital in Japan for railroads, shipbuilding, telegraph lines, or factories to produce cloth, paper, or—most important—the materials of war. For these purposes the government made heavy advances of money. Labor was cheap and plentiful, for the population was growing, and the tiny two- or three-acre Japanese farms, even when cultivated as if they were gardens and even when put into that most heavily producing plant, rice, could not support all the children who were born. Many had to seek a livelihood in the city factories. By the twentieth century workers were able to secure schooling, for a system of national schools was established, partly to indoctrinate the young people with love of country. Thus even the three-year compulsory military service did not keep Japan from having an adequate, literate working class.

⌒ ⌒ ⌒

The simultaneous rise of the United States and Japan to the status of world powers was an omen of change in world affairs. The United States, much the larger and more populous, with far richer resources and a more advanced industry, was peopled largely by Europeans, but it could scarcely be considered a European country. Japan was in no way European, except that it had borrowed many ideas from Europe. When these two countries began to share with the European great powers some responsiblity for international relations, the European powers began to lose their monopoly of world leadership. But to the people of the late nineteenth and early twentieth centuries, this development was not apparent.

Persons, Places, and Terms

Samuel Slater	Louisiana Purchase	abolitionists
Andrew Jackson	Ohio River	Confederate States
Abraham Lincoln	Erie Canal	of America
the Tokugawa family	Buffalo	Reconstruction
Kung Fu-tse	Hudson River	sharecroppers
(Confucius)	the Old Northwest	Homestead Act
Matthew Perry	Republic of Texas	American Federation
the Meiji emperor	Oregon Territory	of Labor
	California	Shinto
Mississippi River	Great Plains	shogun
Florida	Edo (Tokyo)	Buddhism
Gulf of Mexico	Nagasaki	daimyo
New Orleans		samurai
Appalachian	westward movement	clipper ship
Mountains	freedom of the seas	genro

To Master the Text

1. Why did the future of the United States under the Constitution seem uncertain in 1789? What were the boundaries of the United States at that time? Who owned the adjacent lands?
2. Why was the closing of the port of New Orleans bound to be an economic danger to the United States? What action of President Jefferson's removed that danger? What was the next important increase in United States territory? When, how, and why was it acquired?
3. What was the "westward movement"? List and describe the important routes used and the areas settled. What advantages did the pioneers find on the frontier? What kind of society grew up on the frontier?
4. In the first half of the nineteenth century what new economic activities

increased the nation's wealth? How did the country become more democratic? Why did President Andrew Jackson seem to be a symbol of the new America of his day?

5. Why did the United States not play a great part in world affairs in the first half of the nineteenth century? What effect did the statement of the Monroe Doctrine have abroad? In the United States?

6. What factors of economics and population tended increasingly to separate North from South before 1860? List the territories acquired by the United States between 1845 and 1848. How did the slavery question become involved with these extensions of territory?

7. Outline the course of the Civil War. What factors contributed to Union victory? What factors made Reconstruction so difficult for southerners?

8. List the factors that helped settle the remaining open areas by 1890. By 1914 what place did the United States occupy among manufacturing nations? What factors explain United States economic growth, 1865-1914? How did American economic development parallel that of Europe? How was it different?

9. How was Japanese civilization influenced by the character of the land? By the nearness of Japan to the Asian mainland? By Shinto ancestor worship? By cultural borrowings from China?

10. What was the basic purpose of the Tokugawa shoguns? List all the methods by which they attempted to achieve that purpose. How and when was the Tokugawa shogunate brought to an end?

11. Describe the Meiji constitution. Was it democratic? Did it grow out of the former Japanese government? How was industrialization financed? What did it accomplish? How did it change the character of Japan?

To Interpret the Facts

1. If you had been alive in 1914 and someone had asked you whether the United States was a great world power, how would you have answered the question? How would you have proved your point?

2. Compare the economic life, the social organization, and the world position of Japan and the United States in 1914.

To Put This Chapter into a Larger Setting

1. How much of the increasing size and wealth of the United States can be attributed to such geographical factors as natural resources, navigable rivers, climate, and the like? How much to the hard work and initiative of the American people? How much to developments and events outside the United States? Prove.

2. Compare the Meiji reforms with what you know of United States political and social development, 1865-1914; with German development, 1871-1914; and with Russian development, 1881-1914.

21

Renewed
Imperialism

1870-1914

The revival of European interest in overseas empires was a striking feature
of the period after 1870. In the previous decades, enthusiasm for acquiring
colonies had died down. The reawakening interest resulted from a number
of circumstances of the 1870's and later. The new empires often grew from
those already existing in 1870 or from quiet colonial expansion that went
on even during the mid-century years of lessened interest. Thus it is necessary to survey the colonial world of the 1870's before trying to understand the renewed scramble for overseas possessions.

☙ THE COLONIAL WORLD OF THE 1870'S

Of the nations that had been involved in the establishment of what are
called the "old colonial empires" founded in the sixteenth and seventeenth
centuries, several still retained in the 1870's some possessions of importance.
The Dutch still had the Netherlands East Indies (now Indonesia); the
Portuguese had Angola and Mozambique along the coasts of Africa and ports
in India and elsewhere; the Spanish had the Philippines, some islands in the
West Indies (Cuba the most important), and posts in Africa. The British

and French had recently made some additions to the remnants of their empires. The Russians continued to expand in Asia.

The colonies making up these empires were of many different sorts. Some, like British colonies in Canada, Australia, and New Zealand, were settled almost entirely by Europeans who took overseas the civilization they had previously known. In others, like British India, many British people spent years of their lives, controlling the political life and often the more prosperous businesses, but were far outnumbered by the native inhabitants, who did most of the work and lived their lives much as they had before they became subject peoples. Still other colonies were mere trading posts, like those established by a number of countries in tropical Africa. Few Europeans came to those posts, although the mother country often had much control of the economic life. All these diverse areas were called "colonies," all the colonies of a European country constituted its "empire," and the effort to secure still other colonies was known as "imperialism" or "colonialism."

Of the several European empires in existence before the 1870's, only the British, French, and Russian require special attention.

THE BRITISH EMPIRE IN THE 1870's

In the 1870's the British Empire, upon which "the sun could never set," was the greatest in the world. In the mid-nineteenth century two notable developments were taking place within it. In a number of areas there was a marked increase in colonial self-government. In India there was rising dissatisfaction among the native population, which the British vainly strove to lessen.

The Development of Self-Government in the Empire. A measure of self-government was not new to British colonies. Since the first meeting of the Virginia House of Burgesses in 1619, many British possessions, especially those settled by immigrants from the British Isles, had had their own legislatures. In the nineteenth century, however, a wholly new concept of colonial self-government was developed, that of the "dominion," a colony that became a virtually independent country while still remaining within the empire.

The first colony to become a dominion was Canada. The initial step was taken after an unsuccessful Canadian rebellion in 1837. A report suggesting ways of lessening discontent was submitted by the governor general, the Earl of Durham. He recommended that Canadians be given the same kind of "responsible ministry" enjoyed by the British. Under such a system, the governor general would have no choice but to appoint the leader of the majority party in the Canadian parliament as prime minister. Thus indirectly the prime minister would be selected by the Canadian people, who had voted his party into power. In spite of opposition in Britain to giving the Canadians so much voice in their own government, Lord Durham's suggestion was soon put into practice.

The next step was the passage in 1867 of the British North America Act, which created the Dominion of Canada, a federation including the colonies of Ontario, Quebec, New Brunswick, Nova Scotia, and Prince Edward Island. This union was in many ways similar to that of the United States. There were democratically elected provincial governments as well as the central dominion government. Although Canada still acknowledged the sovereignty of the British queen, it controlled all its own affairs, even obtaining the right to tax imports from Britain.

Dominion status was later granted to Australia, New Zealand, and South Africa. In each, the separate colonies first gained self-government and later were federated into dominions—Australia in 1900, New Zealand in 1907, and the Union of South Africa in 1910. Toward the end of the nineteenth century it became customary to hold periodic meetings of dominion prime ministers and representatives of the self-governing colonies to discuss with the ministers of Great Britain the many problems of the empire. These "colonial conferences" or "imperial conferences" gained increasing importance with the years.

The British in India. Relations with India, the most prized part of the empire, were always more difficult than with those parts of the empire settled by British people, for few Englishmen could either comprehend or accept a civilization so unlike their own.

Although the British East India Company lost its trade monopoly in India in 1813, it continued, under close supervision of the home government, to rule British India and to control the foreign policies of those hundreds of Indian princes who were its allies. (See page 84.) A number of wars added extensive new territories to the company's holdings and led to the making of so many treaties of alliance that no prince in all India could any longer boast of being wholly independent. In 1857, however, these advances were temporarily halted by a revolt of native troops (sepoys). This "Indian Mutiny" flared up when it was rumored among the troops that a new kind

"New Crowns for Old Ones," a British cartoon of 1876, when Parliament was debating the bill making Queen Victoria empress of India. Disraeli, the sponsor of the bill, is shown as Aladdin, who sought to exchange new lamps for old; here he is handing Victoria the crown of empress in place of that of queen of Great Britain. The cartoonist is obviously hostile to the new title and thinks that the old one was better, as was the old lamp that the original Aladdin was trying to find.

of cartridge, the end of which the soldier must bite off, was greased with either pork fat (considered unclean by Muslims) or beef fat (considered sacred by Hindus). Within a year the mutiny, bitterly fought and bloody, was suppressed. But as a result, the British East India Company was disbanded, and its place in India was taken over by the British government. Later (1877), to give more prestige to British rule, Disraeli, the empire-enthusiastic British prime minister, had Parliament confer on Queen Victoria the title "Empress of India."

The Indian Mutiny was an example of the great difficulty experienced by all British officials and army officers when they tried to establish good relations with the Indian people. Their own attitude was one of the obstacles, for they looked down upon Indian society as clearly inferior to their own. They kept themselves apart from Indians socially and remained ignorant of the great accomplishments of Indian civilization. Another obstacle was the extraordinary diversity of the Indian people. Because many invaders had overrun India over the thousands of years of its history, there were Indians with light skin and others with dark or yellow skin. There were more than a dozen widely used languages and hundreds of dialects. Although the majority of people belonged to one or another branch of Hinduism, there were many Muslims (their descendants today living in Pakistan) as well as several other important religious groups. With such divisions among the Indians, it was impossible for the British to establish any widely accepted policy; for if they pleased one group, they must surely displease others.

Most difficult for the British to understand was the Hindu religion and the way of life it fostered. Englishmen could not read the ancient and beautiful religious poems, legends, and philosophical writings of Hinduism. The many gods, who to the Hindu are different manifestations of a single World Soul, seemed to the English to be mere objects of superstition. Especially difficult for any westerner to understand is the Hindu belief that after death the soul lives on in another body—perhaps in that of an animal or insect, or perhaps in that of a more highly placed Hindu. The station of anyone in that next life is believed to be the result of his keeping or disobeying the Hindu law in his previous lives. He hopes to rise to a higher station in the next life and ultimately to escape from the cycle of rebirths and be absorbed into the World Soul.

Hinduism supplied Indians not only with a religion but also with the pattern for their daily lives. In the villages where most Indians lived, and in their homes where the married sons and their families often lived, religious observances were of daily importance. Hinduism sanctioned the division of the people into castes—originally four, but by the nineteenth century subdivided into many hundreds. For each caste there were rigid requirements of what food might be eaten, with whom one might eat, what work one had to do, whom one might marry, and so on. Caste lines were sharp, far more so than class distinctions of the Old Regime in Europe.

Some of the customs of Indian life seemed to the British so barbarous that they must be abolished. By law the British tried to stop the burning of widows on the funeral pyres of their husbands and the killing of girl babies. These attempts to change traditional ways not only angered many Indians but also created a new problem, for Indian society had no place for single women.

There was also trouble between British and Indians in the economic realm. The British invested much money in India, not only in business enterprises but also in railroads, telegraph lines, hospitals, and especially schools, where English was used and which for the first time gave all educated

British soldiers with Indian prisoners in 1857, at the time of the Indian Mutiny. The difference in appearance between the Indians and the British gives some indication of the difficulties of understanding between the two peoples.

Indians a common language. Nevertheless the Indians complained that much more wealth went from India to Britain than was ever returned. For example, they argued that British machine-made cloth imported free of duty into India could be sold so cheaply in Indian villages that native hand-weavers could no longer make a living. Nor did all Indians look upon the railroad as an unmixed blessing, for Indians traveling away from home had difficulty abiding by their caste laws about eating and other matters.

To counteract Indian restlessness, the British began in the 1860's to put a very few Indians in minor posts in the government. In 1885 the Indian National Congress was organized by leading Indians who hoped that in time India might have dominion government. Under its pressure, more Indians were given government posts; but until the First World War progress in self-government was slow, amounting only to the right of a few Indians to vote for a majority of the members of the provincial legislative councils and for a minority of the governor general's council.

THE FRENCH EMPIRE OF THE 1870's

The only other European overseas empire that grew appreciably between 1815 and 1870 was the French. In 1815 all that remained to France from her one-time empire were sugar islands in the West Indies, posts along the coast of West Africa, and a few other scattered areas.

For the first two-thirds of the century, empire-building was never a first concern of government. Algeria was occupied almost accidentally in 1830 (see page 99) and once occupied was gradually subdued. Napoleon III, more openly interested in colonies, established French posts in Indochina and on the Pacific islands. (See page 161.) But there was no master plan and no national policy behind these colonial adventures.

RUSSIAN EXPANSION

The Russians had been building an empire, but of a quite different sort in that most of it was not separated from Russia by water. The Russian people had pushed into lightly populated Siberia and had arrived at the Pacific before the time of Peter the Great (tsar 1682-1725). Their line of settlement was in the latitude of Russia itself, to the north of the areas where the Asian peoples were concentrated. The first push southward was made into Chinese territory along the Pacific coast, where by 1860 Russians had acquired the land along the north bank of the Amur River and south along the seacoast to the present site of Vladivostok, which they built. In the late eighteenth century they had also explored Alaska and established fur posts there, but in 1867 they sold Alaska to the United States. Between 1865 and 1881 they conquered Turkestan in central Asia. This region was tempting because of its hemp, tobacco, silkworms, and gold. Each time a new frontier was established, warfare with the new set of neighbors was likely to ensue until they, too, had been defeated and their territory annexed. The British in India seemed a threat to the Russians, who were always seeking a defensible border against this mighty neighbor.

◌ REVIVAL OF INTEREST IN COLONIES

In the 1870's the European attitude toward colonies changed abruptly as one nation after another seized some non-European part of the earth.

INFLUENCES ENCOURAGING THE NEW IMPERIALISM

The forces stimulating this extraordinary development of empire-building were the familiar ones of the day: nationalism, religious revival, scientific interest, industrialism. Of these, nationalism came first and was most important. The 1870's were years when the peoples of most of the great powers of Europe were stimulated to a heightened degree of nationalism:

the Italians and Germans by the achievement of unity; the French to lessen the pain of defeat at the hands of the Germans; the Russians, similarly, because of their setback at the Congress of Berlin. It became the fashion of the day for prominent persons in these four countries, and also in Britain, to argue that national prestige would be enhanced by the acquisition of more colonies, and that the greatness of a nation could to an extent be measured by the size of its empire. Professors lectured to their classes on such themes, statesmen gave support to such ideas, colonial societies were established, and newspapers set before the public the wisdom of imperialism.

Christian missionaries also helped stimulate an interest in the areas of the world still available as colonies. On a number of occasions the death of a missionary gave one or another of the European governments an excuse to send troops into an area to take it over. Moreover, some missionaries, quite naturally persuaded of the superiority of the culture in which they themselves had been reared, urged their country to take over the land in which they were working—for its own good. At the very least, missionaries sent home news of the remote places in which they lived and acquainted their fellow citizens with those regions.

The scientific interest of the age also stimulated enthusiasm for imperialism. The interest in science encouraged exploration, and explorers performed some of the same services to empire builders as did the missionaries. Especially important were the theories of Charles Darwin, which seemed to sanction colonialism. The superior military forces of the European countries, so effective against the primitive armies of the peoples of Asia and Africa, seemed to prove a natural superiority on the part of the European peoples. It was easy to use Darwin's theory of the survival of the fittest to argue that the superior Europeans had a duty to rule the less well developed peoples—that, as the British poet Rudyard Kipling wrote, Europeans should "take up the White Man's burden" of governing what Kipling described as childlike and untamed peoples.

Once the rush to seize colonial areas was under way, there were important economic motives to encourage it, most notably the quest for raw materials. Some raw materials were needed in greater amounts than had previously been available, as in the case of cotton—especially when the American Civil War shut off supplies from the American South. Other materials were available only in tropical regions, as was the case with jute, used in Europe for carpets, rope, and burlap bags. There was need for hitherto little-used commodities, not available in Europe, such as rubber for the tires of bicycles, carriages, and later automobiles; or petroleum, used first for lamps and later to power the internal combustion engine. Coffee and tea had become part of the ordinary meals of western Europeans, and neither could be grown in Europe. It was always easier to secure these commodities from an area where the importing nation had a legal means of keeping order and forcing the local people to produce the specific thing wanted. There were other economic advantages to be derived from owning colonies: the citizens of the mother country could the more easily secure the right to open mines, build railroads, and the like, and they could secure monopolies in colonial markets for their own products.

FACTORS FACILITATING COLONIAL EXPANSION

The technological and scientific advances of the day made it possible to open the tropical regions of Asia and Africa to white men. Medicines protected Europeans from the diseases of the jungle. First steamboats and later railroads made it possible to penetrate interior regions and to bring raw materials out to the sea. Improved port facilities could handle the larger ships that were being built. Telegraph lines kept the colonies in touch with the mother country.

The superior military forces of Europe promoted colonizing in two ways. Their superior weapons enabled them to overpower African or Asian armies that were much larger; and military people, interested in establishing naval and other military bases all over the world, were ardent advocates of imperialism. Some of their military bases grew into important colonies.

◌ PARTICIPANTS IN THE NEW IMPERIALISM

Among the participants in the new imperialism were those very nations already well supplied with colonies: France, Britain, and Russia. The Portuguese and Dutch did not try to establish new colonies, but they took greater interest in those they had long held. The opening gesture of the new imperialism in Africa was made in the Congo region by the king of the small but highly industrialized country of Belgium. His example was soon followed by Italy and Germany. Before long the newly developed world powers, Japan (see Chapter 24) and the United States, also entered the race.

It was particularly surprising to find the Americans annexing colonies, since little more than a century earlier they had been unwilling colonists.

UNITED STATES
OVERSEAS POSSESSIONS
1920

Alaska

UNITED STATES
OF AMERICA

Midway

Wake

Philippine
Islands

Guam

Hawaiian
Islands

Puerto
Rico

Virgin
Islands

Panama
Canal Zone
(perpetual lease)

But they had long been interested in the neighboring Caribbean area and had made several attempts to buy Cuba from Spain. Finally the brief Spanish-American War of 1898 resulted in the independence of Cuba and the acquisition by the United States of Puerto Rico in the Caribbean and the Philippine Islands in the Pacific. In the same year Hawaii, greatly influenced by descendants of American missionaries to the islands, became a United States possession at its own request. In 1903 Panama, supported by President Theodore Roosevelt of the United States, revolted from Colombia and leased to the American government a strip of land running from the Atlantic to the Pacific so that the United States might build the Panama Canal. On several occasions in the next two decades American troops were temporarily landed in one or another of the Caribbean countries, including Cuba, where the United States maintained the naval base of Guantanamo. But no further efforts were made to secure American colonies.

It is to be noted that there was no clear logic behind the scramble for colonies. There was simply a frantic rush to divide the areas too weak to defend themselves among the militarily powerful nations. Each imperialist nation tried to seize available territories before they fell into the hands of other countries. Few of those areas were suited to extensive European settlement. Although some of the colonies proved highly advantageous to the mother country, others had little to offer in the way of economic or strategic advantages. But it was so much in the spirit of the times to annex territory that any country able to do so added to its empire. One historian characterized the result as "the most impressive achievement . . . of our age," going on to say of the year 1926, when he was writing:

Every man, woman and child in Great Britain has ten colonial subjects, black, brown and yellow. For every acre in France there are twenty in the French colonies and protectorates. Italy is one-sixth as large as her colonies; Portugal, one twenty-third; Belgium, one eightieth. . . . The nations of western Europe are dwarfs beside their colonial possessions.*

It must also be noted that the imperialist nations often were too ignorant of the areas they were annexing to understand the needs and desires of the people of the area. A country that took over a colony inevitably made changes, which sometimes seriously disrupted the lives of the inhabitants. Such conflicts of culture are not yet clearly understood. Thus it is difficult for any historian brought up in a western culture to do much more than to recount the epic story of late nineteenth century imperialism from a largely European point of view.

Persons, Places, and Terms

Earl of Durham	Quebec	free trade
Rudyard Kipling	New Brunswick	old colonial empires
Theodore Roosevelt	Nova Scotia	dominion
	Prince Edward Island	governor general
Netherlands	Amur River	British North America
East Indies	Vladivostok	Act
Angola	Alaska	sepoy
Mozambique	Turkestan	Indian Mutiny
Philippine Islands	Caribbean Sea	Indian National
Cuba	Hawaii	Congress
Ontario	Panama	

To Master the Text

1. List the different kinds of colonies remaining in European hands in 1870 and give examples of each.
2. Tell the story of the transformation of Canada from colony to dominion. What part of this story could be repeated for what other British colonies? What was a colonial or imperial conference?
3. What changes took place in British-Indian relations 1825-1857? Why did the Indian Mutiny take place? What consequences did it have?
4. How were the Indians divided among themselves? What reasons would British officials and businessmen in India have given for considering

* Parker T. Moon, *Imperialism and World Politics* (New York: Macmillan, 1926). p. 1.

Indians their inferiors? How was Hinduism reflected in Indian ways of living? Why were British efforts to change Indian ways not always acceptable to Indians? In what ways did the British improve Indian education? The Indian economy? In what ways did they harm Indian economic life? To what extent were Indians permitted to participate in government before 1914?

5. What territories did France retain from its former empire? What new French colonies were acquired in the mid-nineteenth century. Where were the Russians expanding in the mid-nineteenth century? Why?

6. When interest in colonial expansion revived in the last quarter of the nineteenth century, to what extent was nationalism responsible? What other factors were also important? How were they important?

7. List the countries participating in the new hunt for colonies. In what part of the world did the United States acquire colonies? Why?

To Master the Map

1. Attach to straight pins little flags of different colors (each color representing a particular European country). Stick the pins on a blank map of the world wherever there were colonies in 1871. As you read the next three chapters, add pins wherever new colonies were established.

2. On the world map study British routes to India and the British way stations. Note also the borderlands of India where the British might come into conflict with other powers. Point out how the map illustrates British policies that you already know of.

To Interpret the Facts

1. How could Englishmen argue that British rule of India was a blessing to the Indian people while at the same time Indian leaders were arguing that the British had injured the Indian economy and interfered with Indian religion and social organization?

2. Among all the suggested causes for the renewed European interest in colonial expansion, which seem to you most important? Why?

3. What European technological achievements help explain the ability of Europeans to conquer and keep possession of so much non-European land?

To Put This Chapter into a Larger Setting

1. From further reading and the study of pictures, describe to the class an Indian street scene, making your description reveal as many aspects of Indian life as possible.

2. Read in a history of the United States about Americans in Hawaii before 1898 and about Theodore Roosevelt's part in the Panama Revolution of 1903. How do these episodes of American imperialist history repeat the general pattern of European imperialism?

22

Imperialism
in North Africa
and
the Middle East

1870-1914

One of the important areas of European imperialist activity was Islamic North Africa and the Middle East. These were the regions conquered by the Arab followers of Muhammad in the seventh century A.D. and later largely subjected by the Ottoman Turks. In the 1870's the Ottoman Empire was overlord of North Africa from Tunisia eastward and ruler of Asia Minor, Syria, Palestine, Mesopotamia, and parts of Arabia. Morocco, Persia, and Afghanistan were independent. Algeria had been conquered by France.

◌ THE ISLAMIC LANDS IN THE 1870'S

So large an area naturally included many different peoples living in a great variety of ways. Some inhabited cities whose histories reached back to ancient times. Many were farmers raising the warm-weather and semi-tropical products favored by the climate. Some were nomadic tribesmen ranging the vast desert areas. The majority were Muslims, but there were many Christians, Jews, and followers of other religions. Many languages were spoken, but Arabic, the language of the Islamic sacred writings, was most widely used.

THE BELIEFS OF ISLAM

As a religion Islam adhered to the teachings of its founder, Muhammad (570?-632), an Arab from Mecca. He became convinced that his religious insights were revelations from God. After his death these were written down in the Koran, the sacred book of the Muslims. His fundamental doctrine was the oneness of God. (*Allah* is the Arabic word for God.) He taught that he himself was the Prophet of God, the last of a line of prophets that included Abraham, Moses, and Jesus. He emphasized a final day of judgment and a blissful eternal life for the righteous. The duties of the Muslim (believer in Islam) were few and simple. They included reciting the Islamic creed, "There is no god but God; Muhammad is the messenger of God"; prayers fives times a day, facing in the direction of Mecca; fasting from dawn to dusk during Ramadan, the ninth month of the Islamic calendar; giving alms to the poor; and making a pilgrimage to Mecca once during a lifetime. Friday was a special day for prayer and sermons in the mosques. Islam furnished detailed rules for personal conduct—the avoidance of certain foods and drink, for example—and for personal relations.

In theory, religion and government were one and the same thing in an Islamic state, for the head of the state was also head of the religion, and all law was directly related to Islamic religious beliefs. Over the centuries the religious emphasis in law and government had broken down somewhat, but it was still stronger than in Christian countries.

RELATIVE ISOLATION OF ISLAMIC LANDS IN THE NINETEENTH CENTURY

In the eighteenth and early nineteenth centuries the Islamic lands had not shared the technological and industrial advances of the western world. At an earlier time it had been the Arabs who transmitted to the relatively less advanced Europeans the learning of the ancient Greeks and Romans, which the Arabs had received from the Byzantines. But with the opening of the world oceans to European commerce in the sixteenth century, the Islamic peoples no longer fronted upon the greatest highroad of sea trade, for much commerce between Europe and the Far East now followed the sea route around Africa instead of passing through the Mediterranean. Thus the Muslims became relatively isolated from Europe just as the Europeans were experiencing their commerical and industrial revolutions and their great age of science. By the late nineteenth century the military superiority of the Europeans was overwhelming.

◠ NORTH AFRICA

The fertile Mediterranean coast of North Africa, with its temperate climate, its subtropical agriculture, and its nearness to Europe, seemed particularly desirable to European empire-builders.

THE FRENCH IN TUNISIA, 1881

French seizure of Tunisia in 1881 is typical of all European imperialism in North Africa. It was the near-bankruptcy of the bey, ruler of Tunisia under Turkish overlordship, that gave the French their opportunity. The bey's extravagance had led him to borrow vast sums, especially in France, at ruinous rates of interest. The French government took the lead in forcing upon him an international commission of financial experts to put his affairs in order. Each of the commissioners immediately set to work to secure for the citizens of his own country the right to build telegraph lines, railways, and port facilities in Tunisia. The commissioner from France soon noted with alarm that the largest share of these profitable opportunities went to Italian firms. The French government resolved to reverse this trend.

As often in imperialist politics, international rivalries in Europe became interrelated with problems in the colonial field. At the Congress of Berlin in 1878 (see page 273), the French government secured from Britain and Germany promises not to oppose French seizure of Tunisia. In 1881, with the excuse that Tunisian raids were being made into Algeria, French troops were sent into Tunisia, and within a few weeks they had occupied the whole country. (See map, page 331.)

The French did not annex Tunisia, but rather established what is called a "protectorate," keeping the bey as head of the state and furnishing him with an adviser (a French "resident general") whose advice, especially in foreign affairs, the bey dared not reject. French troops were stationed in the country. This arrangement was less expensive and less irritating to the Tunisians than taking over the whole government; yet it gave the French enough control of the country so that their businessmen could secure contracts for building roads, railroads, and schools. Tunisian tariffs were imposed on non-French imports, so that Tunisian markets were reserved for French goods.

In Europe, however, French occupation of Tunisia had less favorable results. The Italians, looking upon the country as practically their own because of its nearness to Italy and because many Italians had interests there, were so angered that they joined the Triple Alliance. (See page 276.)

Scots Highlanders at the Sphinx of Gizeh in 1882, sight-seeing after a battle in which British troops defeated the Egyptians. There is symbolism here: the British Empire at its height dominating a country with a civilization thousands of years older than that of Great Britain.

THE BRITISH IN EGYPT AND THE SUDAN

At the very time that the bey of Tunisia was sinking dangerously into debt, his neighbor Ismail Pasha, the khedive of Egypt, a vassal of the sultan, found himself in the same plight. He had spent his money on railroads and schools, on purchasing from the sultan his title of khedive, and in 1869 at the celebration of the opening of the Suez Canal (of which he was a large stockholder) on the construction of a road along which to conduct his distinguished guests to view the pyramids. He had also conquered the part of the Sudan south of Egypt. (The Sudan is a wide desert-grassland area extending east and west to the south of the Sahara and Libyan deserts from the Atlantic coast to Ethiopia.) There was so little limit to his spending for the public good or for his own private amusement that in twelve years he dispensed 500,000,000 dollars, a large part of it borrowed from European bankers. In desperation he sold his Suez shares to the British government, but the bulk of his debt remained.

Then began a series of events ending with the establishment of a British protectorate over Egypt. In 1875 an Egyptian debt commission was established under the combined control of Britain and France. When Ismail would not co-operate with it, the two powers persuaded the sultan to replace him with his more docile son. Measures of economy required of the new ruler stirred up much resentment against foreign rule among the Muslim Egyptians. In 1882, fearing violence, the British and French sent warships into Egyptian waters. Rather than open fire with their guns, the French soon departed; but the British bombarded the city of Alexandria, landed troops, and within weeks were in virtual possession of all Egypt. The British people accepted this expensive policy, for they wanted to protect their investments in Egypt and above all to safeguard the canal, so vital to their commerce with India. A British consul general was sent to reside in Egypt to oversee the activities of the khedive. Thus Egypt, like Tunisia, had become a protectorate.

The British did much good in Egypt. They forced the government to be more honest and less oppressive. They constructed a dam on the Nile at Aswan, which supplied enough additional water so that two crops could be raised annually instead of one. Nevertheless the Egyptians continued to resent British occupation, and in Europe other powers protested. The British government continued to assert that it would withdraw its troops once the country was fully in order; but its concern for the money owed by Egypt to British investors and its intense interest in the Suez Canal caused the occupation to continue.

The course of the occupation did not prove easy or peaceful, especially in the first twenty years. The first serious trouble was a revolt in the Sudan led by a fanatical religious leader called the "Mahdi." Since the khedive had conquered the Egyptian Sudan and had left a line of garrisons in the region, the efforts of the Mahdi to expel all foreigners and establish his own authority in the region were of great concern to the Egyptian government and also to the British consul general. But the British home government was at that moment headed by Gladstone, less interested in the expansion of empire than were many of his contemporaries and always eager to avoid the use of force. After too long a delay he sent troops to escort the Egyptian garrisons from the Sudan, but they were defeated and their commander was murdered. The Sudan was lost to Egypt.

The British government could not, however, long remain indifferent to the fate of a region in which were the headwaters of the Nile, for whoever controlled it could soon starve Egypt. Moreover, the anarchy which prevailed in the region was a constant threat to Egypt. In 1896 Lord Kitchener was placed in charge of an expedition ordered to reconquer the Sudan. By 1898, after a cautious and thoroughly well-planned campaign, he had defeated a new Mahdi and destroyed his forces.

Then occurred a dangerous international crisis, bringing France and Britain to the brink of war. During the years when the Egyptians had withdrawn from the Egyptian Sudan, the French, already expanding into the western part of the Sudan from their colonies in West Africa, decided on a bold stroke. They sent two expeditions, one from the Red Sea and the other from French Gabon on the Atlantic, to meet in the upper Nile area in the southern Egyptian Sudan and lay claim to the area. Their hope was to create a French east-west corridor across Africa. The expedition from the east failed, but that from the west, led by the French explorer Captain Marchand with some two dozen Frenchmen and two hundred Africans, cut its way through swamps and jungles and in 1898, after two years, arrived at Fashoda on the upper Nile. Shortly after Marchand had hoisted the tricolor, Kitchener arrived, fresh from his triumph over the Mahdi, and demanded the withdrawal of the French. Marchand was inclined to stand his ground, but he had no army to oppose Kitchener's, and his home government realized that the only alternative to yielding was an undesired war with Britain. The French gave way. Thereafter the area in dispute was called the Anglo-Egyptian Sudan and was ruled jointly by Britain and Egypt.

THE FRENCH IN MOROCCO

Once Egypt was under British control, the only remaining important independent area of North Africa was Morocco, coveted by the French. France already had control of Algeria and Tunisia, which with Morocco and Libya formed a single geographic unit. Moreover, the French in Algeria were often troubled by raids of Moroccan tribesmen. French businessmen already had investments in Morocco. All these factors led to much talk about the "inevitability" of a French protectorate over Morocco.

But when in 1904 the French took the first steps toward a protectorate by establishing a military police force and a state bank in Morocco and drawing up plans for building various public works, they brought about the First Moroccan Crisis of 1905 and the Algeciras Conference of 1906, called to decide upon the future of Morocco. (See page 278.) The decisions of the conference did not long prevent the French from taking further steps in Morocco, however. Twice in times of disorder they sent in troops. Gradually the German government accepted the inevitability of a French protectorate and began to look about for methods of compensating itself.

It persuaded the French to allow German businessmen to participate in mining, railroad building, and other profitable Moroccan ventures. Then came the Second Moroccan Crisis of 1911. (Chapter 25.) At the end of that, Germany promised no longer to oppose a French protectorate; in return, France gave Germany a large slice of territory in what had become the French Congo.

Beginning with 1912 a French resident took up his abode in the Moroccan capital to advise and assist the sultan. Although French troops had to be used to suppress Moroccan uprisings, French military and civilian personnel performed their duties with such wisdom that the country soon prospered as never before in modern times.

THE ITALIANS IN NORTH AFRICA

The Italians also sought African possessions as a way of reviving the glory of ancient Rome. In the 1880's they established colonies on the two arms of the Horn of Africa: Eritrea, on the Red Sea, and Italian Somaliland, on the Indian Ocean. But in 1896 they were defeated in a war with the kingdom of Ethiopia, and all European empire-building statesmen noted that an African army could win on occasion. In 1911 the Italians seized the arid regions of Tripoli and Cyrenaica (today combined into Libya), which lie between Egypt and Tunisia and were then the only areas of Mediterranean Africa not yet in European hands. After a year of fighting, the Ottoman sultan, who was still overlord of the two areas, abandoned his claim to them; and Italy acquired a large but nearly useless African empire.

⌒ THE MIDDLE EAST

The Middle East (at one time often called the Near East) is the area stretching eastward from Egypt to the borders of India. Its fate in the nineteenth century was different from that of North Africa, for the European powers gained less political control over it than over Africa. The Bagdad Railroad and a series of conflicts between Russia and Great Britain were the most important Middle Eastern questions of the time.

GERMANY AND THE BAGDAD RAILROAD

In the 1890's German firms, encouraged by the German government, began to build railroad lines for the Ottoman government. Once German industrialization was making rapid progress under the strong Hohenzollern monarchy, German bankers and construction firms welcomed opportunities for the kind of economic expansion that had seemed to return such great profits to investors of other countries. Although at first Bismarck had not favored colonial adventures, even he had finally been brought to encourage the development of German colonies in Africa. (Chapter 23.) After the dismissal of Bismarck, William II (emperor 1888-1918), young and impetuous, sought a larger place for Germany in the colonial world. (See page 250.) The already decaying Ottoman Empire seemed to offer particularly tempting opportunities, partly because no other imperialist country was concentrating on it at the moment. Russia was busy in the Far East; Britain, France, and Italy in North Africa. It happened that the Germans already had an important relation with the Ottoman Empire, where a German military mission had for some time been reorganizing the Turkish army. In 1890, and again in 1899, Emperor William II had paid visits to the sultan—an unusual gesture for a western monarch.

In 1888 a group of German businessmen, urgently encouraged by their government, secured from the Ottoman authorities the right to build a railroad beginning directly opposite Constantinople on the Asiatic side of the Bosporus and extending as far as the city of Angora. Ten years later the Ottoman government granted the more important right to build a line to Bagdad. This was the first section of what came to be known as the "Berlin-Bagdad Railroad," although it was later to be continued to the Persian Gulf. (See map, page 318.) The Ottoman government enthusiastically supported the German plan because heretofore there had been no rail connections between Constantinople and the Asiatic parts of the empire. French and British firms, which might have built railroads in Turkey, were not eager to begin their lines at Constantinople because their own national interests would not have been served. Moreover, the Turks believed that, unlike other European powers who had already despoiled the Ottoman Empire, Germany might be trusted to build the railroads without trying, at the same time, to take slices of Turkish territory.

When the Bagdad railroad plan became known abroad, it was treated almost as an international crime. German bankers had hoped to secure financial assistance from bankers of other countries, but neither British nor French businessmen were willing to encourage the Bagdad project. They feared that it would put the Germans in control of the whole economic life of the Ottoman Empire and that the direct rail route from Constantinople to the Persian Gulf would greatly reduce the profits of the shipping

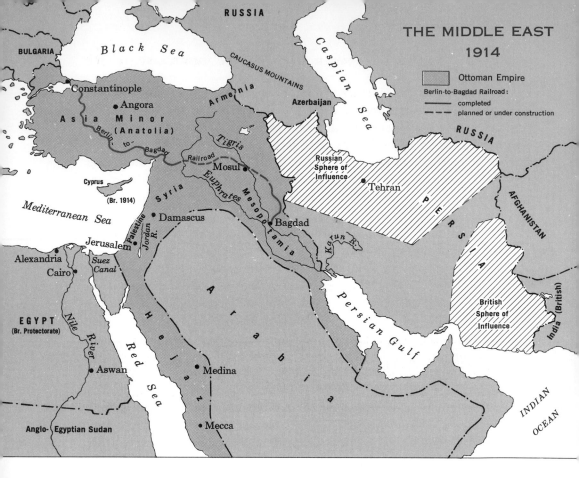

THE MIDDLE EAST
1914

Ottoman Empire
Berlin-to-Bagdad Railroad:
——— completed
- - - planned or under construction

through the Suez Canal. The Russians particularly feared that the railroad venture would give Germany a major political influence in Constantinople. Thus other nations tried to hamper the scheme by refusing to put their money into the Bagdad line.

Since the difficulties of actual construction were greater than had been foreseen, the railroad was far from completed when war broke out in 1914. The slowness of the work allowed for second thoughts on the part of the rival nations. Just before the war, French, British, and Russian governments abandoned their objections to participating in the German project and received in return various concessions. But the war prevented these agreements from being put into operation.

In a number of other ways, western capital and technical knowledge helped develop the resources of the Ottoman Empire. Foreign military and technical advisers served the Turkish government in many capacities. A European debt commission exerted considerable control over Ottoman finances. But until 1914 the Asiatic part of the Ottoman Empire remained virtually intact, and the sultan was never forced to accept from any foreign country a "resident" whose presence and wide-ranging power would have transformed the Ottoman Empire into a protectorate. In 1914 as in the 1880's Germany was the favored European friend, but not the master, of the Turks.

ANGLO-RUSSIAN RIVALRY IN ISLAMIC ASIA

Aside from the Bagdad Railroad, the most important imperialist problem in the Middle East was a long-brewing conflict between Russia and Great Britain. The British had pushed their conquests toward the northern borders of India and the Russians had been driving south into central Asia. (See page 304.) The two countries soon found themselves at odds not only in the Middle Eastern countries of Persia and Afghanistan but also farther east in Tibet.

The most important area of Anglo-Russian rivalry was Persia. Russia was, as always, interested in warm-water ports. Once Russian armies had conquered the area east of the Caspian Sea, formerly a part of Persia, it seemed to the Russian government that it might be possible to conquer the whole of Persia. But the British were already deeply involved in the country. In 1864, when they were connecting India with Europe by telegraph, they had constructed the first telegraph line across Persia. In 1889 a British subject founded the Imperial Bank of Persia, and a British firm started a steamship line to navigate the Karun River into the Persian Gulf. The Russians soon made competing moves, setting up a rival bank and securing a change in the Persian customs duties especially favorable to Russian commerce.

All this Anglo-Russian rivalry was brought to an abrupt end in 1907 by the Anglo-Russian treaties completing the Triple Entente. (See page 279.) Once again the close connection between imperialism and European international relations was clearly demonstrated.

⌒ ⌒ ⌒

Looking back over the history of European imperialism in the Islamic lands, it is apparent that the military weakness of each of these countries left them at the mercy of the technologically more advanced Europeans. The new map of North Africa and the Middle East was drawn not by the inhabitants of the region, but by outsiders whose decisions were made on the basis of their own political and economic needs and their relations with each other. The Islamic peoples often derived the advantages of better order in their countries and the building of schools and of other public works. But their national interests were always subordinated to what the European protecting powers believed to be their own interests or needs. A similar pattern of imperialism can be observed in Africa from the Sahara southward.

Persons, Places, and Terms

Muhammad	Sahara Desert	Angora
Ismail Pasha	Libyan Desert	Persian Gulf
Kitchener	Ethiopia	
Marchand	Alexandria	Islam
	Aswan	Koran
Asia Minor	Gabon	Allah
Syria	Red Sea	Barbary pirates
Palestine	Fashoda	bey
Mesopotamia	Anglo-Egyptian	protectorate
Morocco	Sudan	resident general
Persia	Eritrea	khedive
Afghanistan	Tripoli	consul general
Mecca	Cyrenaica	the Mahdi
Suez Canal	Bagdad	Berlin-to-Bagdad
Sudan	Tigris River	Railroad

To Master the Text

1. What was the dominant religion of North Africa and the Middle East? What was the most widely used language? Summarize the teachings of Islam. What was the relationship between religion and government in the Islamic states? Why were European empire-builders tempted by North Africa?
2. To what extent was fear the real French motive for conquering Tunisia? To what extent was the real motive economic? What other motives did the French have? How did they control the country? Why? How was French seizure of Tunisia regarded by the British government? The German? The Italian?
3. What kind of trouble did the khedive of Egypt get into? How? Why did the British government establish its protectorate over Egypt? How did it establish the protectorate? Did Egypt profit from British occupation? What European powers objected to the occupation? Why? What had been the relationship of the Sudan to Egypt? Why was Lord Kitchener sent to the Sudan? What did he accomplish? What happened at Fashoda and what was the importance of that event?

4. Why did France want to establish a protectorate in Morocco? Who opposed them? By what bargain were the French finally able to set up a protectorate? What African lands did Italy acquire? How?

5. Why were the Germans interested in building a railroad to connect Constantinople with the Tigris River? Why did the Turks favor the Germans as builders? Why did British and French bankers object? How far along was the railroad by 1914? In general, how much economic or military aid did the Turks receive from the European powers up to 1914?

6. In what areas and for what reasons did the British and Russians develop acute rivalry? How and when were these difficulties settled?

To Master the Map

Study the route of the Berlin-to-Bagdad Railroad. What advantages would the railroad give the Turks? The Germans?

To Interpret the Facts

1. In what ways was the Islamic world of the 1870's more backward than Europe? What explanations can you find for that particular kind of backwardness?

2. In general did the establishment of European protectorates in Islamic areas improve the lives of the inhabitants? Does it seem to you that the protectorates were profitable enough to the mother countries to be worth the cost of conquest and of keeping troops in the area? Why?

3. List for each European empire-building country all the different kinds of advantages acquired by that country in the Islamic world. Which country seems to you to have acquired the greatest advantage?

4. How do you explain the fact that the European countries were satisfied with establishing protectorates in the Islamic areas and did not (as they did elsewhere) attempt to establish fully controlled colonies?

To Put This Chapter into a Larger Setting

1. Cite instances after 1870 when the course of European empire-building was influenced by relations in Europe among the imperialist nations. Cite other instances when tensions in Europe were eased by give-and-take in colonial areas.

2. Prepare a report on Islam, noting especially (a) its similarities to and differences from Christianity and Judaism, and (b) the ways in which it influenced the daily lives of the people in Islamic countries.

3. Read further about the building of the Suez Canal and the Berlin-to-Bagdad Railroad. What similarities and what differences can you see in their purposes? In the ways in which they were financed? In the usefulness of each to the world?

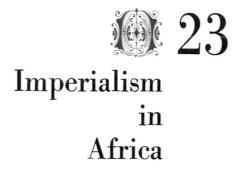

23

Imperialism
in
Africa

1870-1914

Until the 1870's Africa south of the Sahara ("sub-Saharan Africa") was remote from Europe and largely unknown. Then suddenly between 1876 and 1890 European nations divided the whole continent among themselves, leaving very few spots on the map to be labeled independent.

⌒ AFRICA AND EUROPE BEFORE THE 1870'S

Over the centuries, relations between Europe and sub-Saharan Africa had been conditioned by three factors: African geography, the slave trade, and the fact that Africa was so placed that commerce between Europe and the Far East skirted its coasts. In the mid-nineteenth century another factor became important as missionaries and explorers opened the interior of Africa to the knowledge of Europeans.

THE EFFECTS OF AFRICAN GEOGRAPHY

Instead of calling Africa the "Dark Continent," as they often did, Europeans might well have named it the "Inhospitable Continent"; for in a variety of ways nature has contrived to keep outsiders from making their way inland from the coast. Between North Africa and the rest of the continent is the thousand-mile-wide Sahara Desert. All around the continent good harbors are few, and those that exist are often too shallow for big ships. Immediately back of much of the coast is a rim of high land, which prevents easy access to the interior and causes rapids and waterfalls in the rivers as they near the sea.

In the fifteenth century Europeans inched their way along the west coast, seeking the water route to Asia. They discovered the equatorial forests of the Gulf of Guinea and the Congo region, where 150 inches of rain a year create impenetrable jungles. In these hot regions diseases attacked not only people but also the pack animals that might otherwise have been used to transport equipment inland. Thus, although more than half of Africa is neither desert nor rain forest, and large areas (especially in the south and southeast) have an excellent climate, the earliest European visitors did not discover those pleasant regions. Sub-Saharan Africa and Europe were almost entirely isolated from each other.

EARLY EUROPEAN COLONIES IN AFRICA

Until the nineteenth century Europeans and Africans came in contact with each other only in a few struggling trading posts along the African coasts. In 1482 the Portuguese established in present-day Ghana the first permanent European station south of the Sahara. Later they made the beginnings of their present colonies of Angola and Mozambique—stopping-off places where Indies-bound ships could take on fresh food and water or make repairs. South Africa was first occupied by the Dutch, who in the 1650's began stopping at the site of modern Cape Town, not only to take on provisions but also to leave under "postoffice stones" letters to be picked up by the next ship going in the opposite direction. A pleasant climate and good soil encouraged this particular post to grow into a colony. In 1815 at the end of the Napoleonic Wars it passed into the possession of the British. The smaller map on page 331 shows the fringe of European settlements in Africa as they were in the early 1870's.

The lure of the Guinea-coast trading posts was gold, ivory, pepper, and especially Negro slaves. The slave trade was old in Africa. Arabs had long taken slaves from the east coast, and in the Guinea region Africans themselves owned other Africans as slaves. It was from Guinea that European and American ship captains brought slaves to the Americas. In the early nineteenth century, however, led by the British, the western nations began in all their possessions to abolish first the slave trade and then slavery. For some decades British ships patrolled the West African coast to intercept illegal slave ships. This effort to eradicate the slave trade opened up much new knowledge about Africa.

EUROPEAN EXPLORATION IN AFRICA BEFORE 1876

Systematic exploration of West Africa began in the early nineteenth century, encouraged by Protestant missionary societies and by antislavery groups who hoped to discover other resources to substitute for the slave trade. From the Mediterranean, West African, and Guinea coasts, expeditions were sent into the heart of West Africa to discover the character of the land and to persuade the rulers to abandon the slave trade. The hardships encountered by these intrepid explorers are beyond imagination—crossing the Sahara for those from the north, the hazards of the disease-infested equatorial jungles for those from the Guinea coast. Many died on the way, sometimes more than half of a party within a few weeks. Nor would the strong rulers of the interior kingdoms, long established by mixed Negro and Berber peoples, promise to give up their profitable slave trade. So impassable was the belt of tropical forest along the Guinea coast that it took some thirty years and many expeditions to explore the whole length of the Niger, West Africa's longest river. For twenty more years, until the use of quinine to combat malaria was discovered, Europeans could not safely journey up the Niger into the interior.

Exploration of East Africa and of the headwaters of the Nile was also tedious and often dangerous. By all odds the best-known explorer in this region was the Scottish missionary and physician David Livingstone, one of whose motives was opposition to the slave trade. Between 1841 and 1873 Livingstone made three long expeditions, one of which took him from Cape Town northward as far as the sources of the Nile, another west to east across the continent from Angola to Mozambique. Books he wrote and speeches he made during visits in Britain publicized his discoveries: the Zambezi River with its Victoria Falls, named after his queen, and the great lakes of southeastern Africa, not before seen by a European. He captured popular enthusiasm for Africa and aroused further opposition to slavery.

A chance episode in Livingstone's life resulted in further important explorations being made by another man. Livingstone's third journey lasted for five years, during which time he was out of contact with the rest of the world. At the end of the journey he became ill and had to be brought to an

The famous meeting of Henry M. Stanley and David Livingstone, 1871. Stanley and his search party are at the left, Livingstone and the villagers with whom he had been living at the right. After having traveled for months across Africa in search of Livingstone, all Stanley could think of to say was "Dr. Livingstone, I presume?"

African village on the shores of Lake Tanganyika to recuperate. Here he lived in comfort and security, for Africa was his home, and the Africans were his devoted friends.

To the outside world, nevertheless, Livingstone was lost. In 1871 a New York newspaper publisher sent the British-born reporter Henry M. Stanley to find him. Stanley's account of his 236-day journey was a newspaper sensation. Livingstone welcomed him with kindness, and the two were soon friends. They went on a journey of exploration together, by the end of which Stanley had succumbed completely to the fascination of Africa.

In 1874, the year of Livingstone's death, Stanley began a journey of 999 days which took him all the way around Lake Victoria and down the Congo River to the Atlantic Ocean. Tracing the course of the Congo and discovering its usefulness as a roadway through central Africa were Stanley's major achievements. The end of his expedition in 1877 concluded the period of exploration and led directly to the partition of the continent.

⌒ LEOPOLD II AND THE BEGINNING OF THE GREAT COLONY HUNT

While Stanley was still in Africa, the king of the Belgians, Leopold II, began interesting himself in the Dark Continent. Leopold's attempt to gain possession of a large slice of this little-known land set off the "scramble for Africa."

RIVALRY FOR THE CONGO BASIN

When Stanley returned to Europe, Leopold had emissaries on hand to persuade him to return at once to the Congo region. Stanley preferred to give the benefits of his explorations to his native Britain; but since the British government took no interest in his offer, he agreed to serve Leopold. In 1879, with five steamers, he traveled up the Congo River until he reached the rapids. Thereafter he and his party had to cut roads through jungles and make their way over swamps until, at the end of two years, they arrived at the south bank of the river above the rapids. On the north bank, to their extreme displeasure, they beheld the French tricolor. Count de Brazza, a French explorer coming from French Gabon, had established a settlement on the north bank and had made treaties with the African chiefs that put the north bank under French protection. Stanley therefore pushed farther up the river, establishing forts and trading posts on the south bank and making hundreds of treaties with tribal chiefs. The two cities of Brazzaville and Leopoldville directly opposite each other across the Congo are reminders of the rival bravery, determination, and ruthlessness of these two explorers.

INTERNATIONAL ASPECTS OF THE CONGO QUESTION

At this point Britain and Germany took a hand in Congo affairs. To prevent Leopold from monopolizing the whole Congo basin, the British government persuaded Portugal, which owned the colony of Angola just to the south of the Congo and was a close ally of Britain, to claim ownership of the mouth of the river. France, Britain's historic rival in colonial affairs, thereupon sided with Leopold, who promised in return to sell his Congo interests to France in the event of his ever wanting to get rid of them. Bismarck, wishing always to win French good will, also sided with Leopold. To prevent serious friction among the powers, it was decided to hold a conference on African affairs, which met in Berlin at the end of 1884.

The Berlin Conference set the tone for the scramble for Africa. Although slavery was forbidden in the Congo basin, efforts to forbid the sale to

Africans of firearms and alcoholic beverages ended in failure. Leopold was recognized as having sovereign rights over most of the Congo River basin, although both the Congo and the Niger rivers were to be equally open to the trade of all nations. For the rest of Africa, those parts of it not already under European control were considered to be open to seizure by any power. That power could not, however, simply claim the land by staking it out on the map, but must send troops and officials and must inform the other powers that it was occupying the area.

Immediately after the Berlin Conference, Leopold organized his new possession as the Congo Free State. Its government was directed by Leopold himself and had no relationship to the government of Belgium. North of the lower Congo River the French organized a colony, the French Congo. From the Free State, Leopold began to take ivory (elephant tusks) and rubber, which at the time were the known sources of the country's wealth. Elephants had to be killed and rubber vines tapped by unwilling African workers. Leopold never visited his colony and knew nothing of the conditions of tropical life. His officials often used the most brutal means to force unwilling African workers to produce quotas of rubber and ivory assigned to individual villages. In ten years the export of ivory almost doubled, and the export of rubber increased more than a hundredfold. But the stories of the misery of the African people, virtually slaves under Leopold's government, spread to all parts of the civilized world. Finally in 1908 he was compelled to hand it over to Belgium as a colony—thereafter known as the Belgian Congo. (See map, page 331.) The Belgian government tried with some success to see to it that less extreme cruelties were practiced on the natives.

↷ THE RIVALRY OF BRITAIN, FRANCE, AND GERMANY

The making of the Belgian Congo is but one example of the intertwining of European international rivalries with the opening up of Africa. Other such episodes in West, East, and Central Africa caused disputes and conflicts among Britain, France, and Germany.

STAGES IN THE COLONY HUNT

The British, French, and German searches for colonies went through a number of stages. At first each country looked upon this three-way rivalry in sub-Saharan Africa as a minor means of promoting fundamental national policies. Britain's great purpose was to keep control of the route through the Suez Canal to India. To this end the British believed it necessary to prevent others from obtaining concessions in the Nile valley and if at all possible to keep others from the east coast of Africa. France was eager to maintain its strong position in the Mediterranean. French North African possessions were thus so important that the French government tried constantly to extend them to the southward so that no other imperial country could come in behind them. Germany, at first less directly interested in Africa, supported French policy in Africa in order to lessen French interest in a war of revenge against Germany.

Major national policies were, however, soon interfered with by minor circumstances in Africa itself. Adventurous private citizens of all three nations, setting up trading or shipping businesses along the African coasts and rivers, sought the active protection of their home governments. Relations between Europeans and Africans became difficult. To Europeans, all Africans seemed woefully backward because they were illiterate, lacked the scientific and technical knowledge so familiar to Europeans, and were organized into tribes rather than into national states. Moreover, except in the Sudan and along the east coast (where there was a large admixture of Berbers and Arabs), the African people were Negroes, previously known to Europeans only as slaves. It was not long, however, before the "backward" Africans strongly opposed European advance. In the open and well-populated east-west belt of the Sudan, African Islamic leaders had established firm control over extensive areas. Even in the rain forests and deserts, where tribesmen were more thinly scattered and not strongly organized, they were not easy to subdue. It was often necessary for Europeans with a foothold in some African area to wage war for the complete subjugation of the neighboring African people, or else to get out altogether.

Finally as Europe itself advanced industrially and became more nationalistic, the factors encouraging all imperialism (see pages 304-306) became more important in Africa. Once a colony was acquired, no matter how expensive or useless it proved to be, it could not be abandoned.

RIVALRY IN WEST AFRICA

In the 1830's the Guinea coast had been the scene of intense international rivalry for the control of the coastal areas and of the rivers leading into the interior. The struggle for control of the Niger River is a good example, for the Niger could carry commerce to and fro deep into the heart of the great western bulge of the continent. Private British and French companies established trading posts along the lower river and persuaded African tribal leaders to affix their marks to treaties. In the end the British company governed the region as if it were private property. Only in 1900 did the British government take over, making two protectorates in the lower Niger valley.

The upper Niger soon belonged to France, for the French were making an all-out and ultimately successful effort to gain control of the whole interior of the West African bulge. Only in this way could they give full security to their Mediterranean North African holdings by preventing other countries from cutting off Algeria and Tunisia at the south. Since by getting possession of central West Africa the French restricted the British coastal colonies to the neighborhood of the sea, there were inevitably frequent clashes between British and French governors and soldiers. The British yielded to the French in West Africa in order to keep the French out of the Nile valley. Thus the great bulge became almost solidly French.

In 1884 Germany made a surprise entrance into the imperial field. Bismarck had at first claimed to be averse to colonies, but by the 1880's he had either changed his mind or had yielded to the arguments of German enthusiasts who looked upon colonies as one proof of great-power status. In 1884 Bismarck sent one of the greatest German explorers of Africa, Gustav Nachtigal, to sail down the west coast, where he planted the German flag in Togoland, Cameroons, and Southwest Africa. There was friction with the British, but Bismarck took great care not to interfere with places claimed by France. Except for Togoland the German holdings were not valuable, but the new German Empire was at least represented on the map in both West Africa and Southwest Africa.

RIVALRY IN EAST AFRICA

In East Africa the rivalry was largely between Britain and Germany. As in West Africa, the boundaries between colonies in East Africa were fairly well drawn by 1890. Britain was determined to keep control of the headwaters of the Nile. Many people in Great Britain were also eager that an unbroken strip of land running south to north from Cape Colony to Egypt ("Cape-to-Cairo") should belong to Britain, so that a telegraph line and railroad could run from one end of the continent to the other through British territory. But although the British acquired northern East Africa (Kenya and Uganda) and Nyasaland, they could not keep the Germans from taking the southern part of East Africa and breaking into the north-south corridor. The map on the opposite page shows Africa as it was in 1914 after the British had completed their conquest of South Africa.

ᴓ THE BRITISH IN SOUTH AFRICA

Cape Colony at the tip of South Africa—discovered by the Portuguese, first colonized by the Dutch, and acquired by the British in 1815—had a history different from that of any other area south of the Sahara. Relations among the British, the Boers (Dutch settlers—from the Dutch word for "peasant"), and the African peoples were complicated from the beginning. With the discovery of gold and diamonds, they became even more difficult.

SOUTH AFRICA BEFORE 1870

Factors already present before 1870 helped determine later South African history. One of these was the character of the native African peoples. The Dutch came first into contact with the very primitive Bushmen, living today in the Kalahari Desert, and then with the Hottentots, an agricultural-pastoral partly-Negro people. Neither of these impeded European settlement in any important way. After the arrival of the Dutch, militant Negro Bantu peoples from farther north began to move into South Africa to collide first with the Boers and then with the British.

> The Bantu possessed a well-developed tribal system, and had a strong sense of property both in land and cattle. Their large herds were their chief form of wealth. The worth of a bride, for example, was computed in terms of a certain number of cattle, usually from ten to one hundred head. Above all, the Bantu tribes possessed a strong military sense, including a high degree of obedience and fearlessness. The charge of the *impi*, or native regiment, was something much to be dreaded. The emigrant Boers were able to withstand this fearless onslaught only by "laagering" their wagons; that is, by forming them in a compact circle much as the early pioneers of the American prairies defended themselves from Indian attacks.*

By the time the British took over Cape Colony (1815), the Boers had spread along the coast and inland into the higher land. They were a hardy,

---

* Howard Robinson, *The Development of the British Empire* (Boston: Houghton Mifflin, 1922). P. 262.

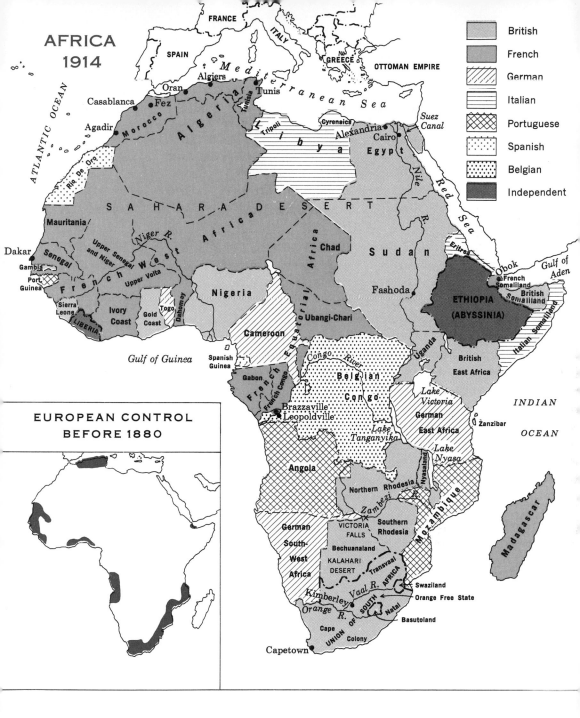

	British
	French
	German
	Italian
	Portuguese
	Spanish
	Belgian
	Independent

AFRICA 1914

FRANCE

ITALY

SPAIN

GREECE

OTTOMAN EMPIRE

Mediterranean Sea

ATLANTIC OCEAN

Casablanca   Fez   Oran   Algiers   Tunis
Agadir   Morocco   Algeria   Tunisia   Tripoli   Cyrenaica   Alexandria   Cairo
Rio de Oro   Suez Canal
Egypt

S A H A R A   D E S E R T

Mauritania   *Niger R.*   French Africa   Chad   Sudan   Eritrea   Obok   *Gulf of Aden*

Dakar   Senegal   French West Africa   Upper Senegal and Niger   Upper Volta   French Somaliland   British Somaliland

Gambia   Port. Guinea   Sierra Leone   LIBERIA   Ivory Coast   Gold Coast   Togo   Dahomey   Nigeria   Fashoda   ETHIOPIA (ABYSSINIA)   Italian Somaliland

Gulf of Guinea   Spanish Guinea   Cameroon   Ubangi-Chari   Uganda   British East Africa

Gabon   French Congo   *Congo River*   Belgian Congo   *Lake Victoria*   Zanzibar

Brazzaville   Leopoldville   German East Africa   *INDIAN OCEAN*

Lake Tanganyika

Angola   *Lake Nyasa*   Nyasaland

Northern Rhodesia   Mozambique

German South-West Africa   *Zambezi*   VICTORIA FALLS   Southern Rhodesia

Bechuanaland   Madagascar

KALAHARI DESERT   Transvaal   Swaziland

Kimberley   *Vaal R.*   UNION OF SOUTH AFRICA   Orange Free State

Orange R.   Natal   Basutoland

Cape Colony

Capetown

Nile R.   *Red Sea*

EUROPEAN CONTROL BEFORE 1880

The larger map shows Africa as it was in 1914, after the European powers had divided it among themselves, leaving only Liberia and Ethiopia independent. Note the contrast with the smaller map, showing areas under European control only thirty years earlier, and with the map on page 500, showing areas under European control in the 1960's.

stubborn people, thrifty, God-fearing, very literal-minded in their interpretation of Christianity. Although they were not notably unkind to the Africans, many of whom they held as slaves, they were convinced that the African peoples were by nature inferior to Europeans.

From the first decades of British rule there was friction between the British and the Boers. In Britain itself the middle third of the nineteenth century was a time of humanitarian and missionary zeal as well as of distrust of colonialism. Dreadful stories sent home by missionaries about alleged inhuman treatment of African slaves by the Boers convinced officials that there was need for restraint and reform in South Africa. In 1833 slavery was abolished all over the British Empire with only limited compensation for the owners. The Boers, already outraged by the missionary reports, were injured economically by the loss of their slaves and by the continued depredations of the Bantu. In small groups similar to those in the United States soon to be traveling westward over the Oregon Trail, they moved northward, first across the Orange River and then across the Vaal, warring with the Bantu and pushing the strong Matabele people into what is now called Rhodesia. Two independent Boer republics were established, the Orange Free State and the Transvaal.

In the succeeding decades, as both Boer and Briton moved farther into Africa, they came into frequent unfriendly contact. Although the Boers had finally abolished slavery, they resented missionary efforts to raise the status of the African peoples. In spite of several attempts, the British did not succeed in taking full control of the two Boer republics.

GOLD, DIAMONDS, AND CECIL RHODES

After 1870 fateful events changed and accelerated South African history. In 1867 diamonds had been discovered near the present town of Kimberley, in a region claimed by the Orange Free State but which the British promptly annexed to Cape Colony. Among the miners was young Cecil Rhodes (1853-1902), son of an English clergyman. Leaving his studies at Oxford to regain his health in South Africa, he had journeyed by oxcart over the high veldt (grassland). He became obsessed with the idea that this beautiful land must one day belong to the most highly developed people of the world— in his mind the British. A many-sided genius, Rhodes soon controlled South African diamond mining, some 90 per cent of the world production. In the Transvaal, where gold was discovered in 1886, he was again enormously successful. His annual income in the 1890's has been estimated at $5,000,000.

In order to promote the Cape-to-Cairo scheme, Rhodes encouraged the British government to annex Bechuanaland, the area between the Boer states and the Zambezi River. He promised to build railroads through the area in return for permission to establish a company to secure treaties with the Matabele chiefs farther north in what is now Rhodesia. Rhodes finally established a British protectorate in present-day Rhodesia, which was named after him and administered by his company until 1920.

THE BOER WAR, 1899-1902

Discovery of the vast mineral wealth of South Africa did not bring peace to the land. The Boers, who had made great sacrifices to find a place in which they could live according to their own ways, were disturbed by an influx of foreign miners into their republics. The Boer governments put every kind of obstacle in the way of the outsiders, but to no avail. Britain sternly supported the demands of British citizens in the Transvaal. In 1899 war broke out between the British and the Boers. The Boer War was bitterly fought, and the British won only by the most strenuous efforts. Having conquered the Boer states, however, the British government made immediate efforts to conciliate them. In 1910 Cape Colony, the Transvaal, the Orange Free State, and Natal (another small British colony east of Cape Colony) were brought together under one dominion government, the Union of South Africa, with all the rights and privileges of the other British dominions.

ʘ ʘ ʘ

On the map the partition of Africa was complete by 1914. Only Ethiopia and the republic of Liberia remained altogether independent. The problems of securing full control of the African peoples and of establishing flourishing economies well-meshed with the economies of the mother countries still remained to be solved. In general it can be said that up to 1914 the African colonies contributed disappointingly little to the wealth of the mother countries. Expensive installations such as railroads, harbor improvements, and roads had to be built before the natural wealth of the colonial regions could be brought to world markets. The Africans themselves, unused to selling for money the products of their forests and plains, seemed to Europeans incredibly lazy. Methods used to force the Africans to work for the purposes and in the manner approved by Europeans aroused strong resentment or violent revolt. Thus the future of colonial Africa was by no means assured by 1914.

Persons, Places, and Terms

David Livingstone
Henry M. Stanley
Leopold II
Count de Brazza
Gustav Nachtigal
Cecil Rhodes

sub-Saharan Africa
Gulf of Guinea
Guinea coast
Congo River
Ghana
Cape Town
Niger River
Zambezi River
Victoria Falls
Lake Tanganyika
Brazzaville

Leopoldville
Congo Free State
 (Belgian Congo)
Togoland
Cameroons
German Southwest
 Africa
Kenya
Uganda
Nyasaland
German East Africa
Kalahari Desert
Orange River
Vaal River
Southern Rhodesia
Orange Free State
Transvaal
Kimberley

Bechuanaland
Union of
 South Africa

"Scramble for
 Africa"
"great African
 Colony Hunt"
Cape-to-Cairo
 railroad
Boer
Bushman
Hottentot
Bantu
Matabele
veldt
Boer War

To Master the Text

1. How had African geography discouraged European exploration? In what places and for what purposes were the first European settlements made in Africa?

2. How did efforts to abolish the slave trade lead to the exploration of West Africa? What new information about Africa was made known by Livingstone and Stanley?

3. How did Leopold II employ Henry M. Stanley? With what results? How did the actions of Britain and Germany bring about the Berlin Conference on Africa? What decisions were reached? What was Leopold's method of getting wealth from the Congo region? Why did the Belgian government eventually take over the colony?

4. What was the basic purpose of Great Britain in sub-Saharan Africa? Of France? Of Germany? How did circumstances in Africa involve the European nations more deeply than they had expected? Trace the Anglo-French struggle in West Africa. Which came out ahead? By what method and in what places did Germany acquire African territories? What was the British dream of "Cape-to-Cairo"? What steps did Britain take toward realizing this dream? What prevented its full realization?

5. What European countries had possessed Cape Colony before 1870? With what Negro peoples had the Europeans come in contact? After 1815 how did the British get on with the Boers in Cape Colony? What was the effect of the abolition of slavery in South Africa?

6. What was the effect on the people of South Africa of the discovery of gold and diamonds? Who was Cecil Rhodes? What was his dream for South Africa? How large a part of it did he accomplish? Why did the Boer War break out? What consequences did it have for South Africa?
7. What countries in Africa remained independent in 1914?

To Master the Map

On a blank map of Africa indicate without names but with different colors the sub-Saharan areas acquired by Great Britain, France, Germany, and Belgium. Indicate also the Portuguese territories. Which African empire was the largest? Which was best placed for commerce with Europe? Choose six colonies that seem to you likely to be valuable to their mother countries, and state your reasons for each choice.

To Interpret the Facts

1. Europeans were almost totally ignorant of sub-Saharan Africa until 1870; twenty years later they had partitioned the continent among themselves. What explains this complete change of circumstances?
2. In how many different and specific ways was the Industrial Revolution involved in the partition of Africa?
3. At what stages in the partition of Africa did European international relations have an important or a decisive influence?
4. Does it seem to you that the acquisition of African colonies was worth the cost in men and money to the European nations? What facts support your judgment?

To Put This Chapter into a Larger Setting

1. In a history of Africa or in biographies of Stanley and Livingstone, read about the achievements of the two men. With another classmate hold an imaginary conversation as if between the two. Let your talk reveal the general European and American ignorance of Africa, the knowledge already gained by Livingstone, his hopes and dreams for Africa, and the growing fascination of the continent for Stanley.
2. Write entries stretching over several years in a diary supposedly kept by Cecil Rhodes. Make the entries reveal the attitude of Rhodes toward (1) South Africa, (2) Great Britain, (3) the Boers, and (4) the Negro peoples. Space the entries over the whole period of Rhodes's life in Africa.
3. Make an African "hall of fame," including the names of all persons, whether African or not, who contributed significantly to African history from the mid-nineteenth century to 1914. Which individual did the most good for the African people? Which the most harm, in your opinion? Support your arguments with facts.

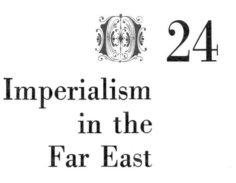

24

Imperialism
in the
Far East

1840-1914

In the Far East, Europeans encountered a situation different from any they had discovered elsewhere. The whole region was influenced by the Chinese Empire, the world's most populous country with the oldest continuous civilization. By the 1840's, Europeans had been in contact with the Far East for three centuries. During that long time there had been little change in Chinese civilization. Thus China in the early nineteenth century retained many of those characteristics that had baffled the first European navigators to reach Far Eastern ports.

CHINA IN THE EARLY NINETEENTH CENTURY

In 1800 China was still looked upon in Europe as a formidable power, although to most Europeans the Chinese people seemed "backward heathens." The Chinese, for their part, thought of all non-Chinese as "barbarians." Differences between Chinese and western ways of working, living, and governing, and between the ideals of East and West—the results of differences in geography, religion, and history—were not understood by either side; but they help explain the course of European imperialism in the Far East.

MAKING A LIVING IN CHINA

Four-fifths of the Chinese made their living by intensive cultivation of tiny plots of land. Since the parts of China with good soil and good climate were densely populated, there was a national average of little more than half an acre for each person to be fed. In the drier and colder northern part of the country, the staple crops were wheat and millet. Rice was the chief food product of the south. Everywhere Chinese farming was characterized by abundance of human labor, scarcity of tools and animal power, and (where at all possible) extensive use of water for irrigation. Houses of bamboo, dried brick, or sometimes stone, always small, built with dirt floors and lacking all conveniences, were clustered in villages.

By nineteenth-century western standards, the peasants were woefully poor. They had, for the most part, to make do with what they themselves could produce after a part had been paid to the tax collector. A fairly large proportion of the peasants owned their land, but many did not. None was a serf in the medieval European sense; all were legally free to buy and sell land and to move from one place to another. In practice, however, their only way of getting enough to eat was to stay on the land and farm it. A bad harvest brought terrible famine and much loss of life.

Most of the people who were not peasant farmers lived in walled cities. Some were craftsmen, for the manufacture of ceramics, silk, and other luxury items had reached a point of rare perfection in China. Good roads and canals made possible a flourishing inland commerce. But neither merchants nor craftsmen developed extensive capitalistic enterprises like those of the West. Landlords and government workers were better off. Since the taking of bribes was common practice among government officials, many of them became wealthy.

THE CHINESE FAMILY

In so large and densely populated a country, order and unity could only be preserved by some very special kind of organization. This was the Chinese family—the fundamental unit of society to an extent scarcely credible to westerners.

The family was composed of its living members, its long-dead ancestors, and its yet unborn descendants, for it was first of all a religious unit. The sixth-century B.C. philosopher Confucius, whose teachings were still fundamental to Chinese thought, had taught that right relationships between father and son, between husband and wife, and between older and younger brother were among the essential bases of a good life. There was also a relationship between the living and the dead, for the dead were venerated by the living, shrines for the dead were maintained in homes, and elaborate family records were kept by those well enough educated to do so. The father, the undisputed head of the family, led the religious observances connected with the ancestors and made sure that the conduct of the family was such as would please them. In the next generation the eldest son (or an adopted son if there was no other) carried on the veneration of the ancestors. Marriage was a family-planned affair, and the bride and groom sometimes did not see each other until the ceremony was over. Wealthy families might maintain large co-operative households with the married sons and their families living in the same courtyard or neighboring courtyards with the parents, but such households were impossible for the poorer people. All families were, however, governed in an authoritarian manner by the oldest male member.

For poor and rich alike the family was an economic unit, each member taking part in the tilling of the family farm or the carrying on of the family business. Even when Chinese went abroad to establish businesses, their enterprises were likely to be under family control. The very young, the ill, and the old were cared for by the family as a whole. Thus all members enjoyed economic security, although the creative and the adventurous could seldom strike out in new ventures of their own.

Many of the functions of government were carried on by the family. If a member was guilty of evil-doing, the whole family was considered responsible and must make amends. Taxes were imposed upon the family rather than upon the individual. Villages were aggregations of families, or sometimes were made up of the members of a single family. Thus there was no important aspect of Chinese life to which the family was not essential.

THE IMPERIAL GOVERNMENT

To an extent the Chinese Empire could be looked upon as an expanded family, administered according to those Confucian principles fundamental to right family living. The Chinese emperor, called the "Son of Heaven," was thought to have the "Mandate of Heaven" to rule his lands. If he practiced the correct moral conduct described by Confucius, heaven would reward him and his people by keeping China free from such natural disasters as floods and famines. The Chinese "Middle Kingdom" was a vast area surrounded by tribute-paying states like Tibet, Annam, Korea, Manchuria, and

Mongolia. The actual administration of government was carried on by various ranks of officials called "mandarins," whom the emperor appointed. This body of government workers—the world's first effective civil service—collected taxes, looked after roads, canals, and irrigation systems, and settled disputes among individuals.

To secure their posts, aspirants to the civil service had to pass exacting written examinations based on Chinese classical literature. Chinese writing had a separate symbol (character) for each individual word and idea. Thousands of characters had to be learned before a student could read the classics of Chinese literature. Many young men labored long years to be ready for the examinations that would lead to wealth and prestige. Any qualified individual might try the examinations, but only the well-to-do people were likely to find the time and means of study. Education was the ladder to success and had tremendous prestige throughout China.

The emperor thought of his "Mandate of Heaven" as extending to the whole earth, so that rulers of neighboring peoples with whom he came in contact were subordinated to the Chinese emperor by Heaven itself. The supreme importance of China was borne out by its power in comparison with that of its neighbors and was reflected in the humble manner of the ambassadors from the tribute-paying states. To the Chinese, all other peoples were barbarians.

Throughout the nineteenth century the emperors of China belonged to the Manchu dynasty, which had ruled the country since 1644, when an invasion of Manchurian Mongolians had taken place. The Manchus had maintained their power by superior military might and by taking over and controlling the age-old system of government under the mandarins.

RELATIONS WITH THE OUTSIDE WORLD

Trade between China and the West was in the hands of western traders whose ships could come only into the port of Macao, taken over in the sixteenth century by the Portuguese, or neighboring Canton, to which went ships of all other nations. Foreign warehouses in Canton were in an area outside the city walls. The merchants themselves were also forced to remain outside the city, taking their recreation only in their gardens, or on holidays in boats on the river. They were permitted to do business only with the *co-hong*, a guild of merchants from whose decisions there could be no appeal.

The Chinese considered Europeans to be "tribute-paying barbarians" like the neighboring vassal states, the only other outsiders with whom the

Chinese were accustomed to doing business. The Europeans were, therefore, required to practice the only kind of conduct considered mannerly in China. This included the kowtow, which in its most extreme form in the presence of the emperor included kneeling three successive times, each time with three prostrations, nose to the floor. All these unfamiliar business and social requirements irritated the westerners, partly because they felt themselves so much superior to the Chinese.

⌒ THE OPENING OF CHINA

From the sixteenth through the eighteenth centuries, this limited right of commerce in China had brought great profits to those who engaged in it. But with the expansion of world trade in the late eighteenth and early nineteenth centuries, western merchants were eager to end the restrictions the Chinese government placed on foreign businessmen. It was Great Britain that forced China to open more of its ports to world trade.

THE OPIUM WAR, 1840-1842

British interest in the China trade increased greatly in the early nineteenth century, for a number of reasons. The extension of British conquests in India and the colonization of Australia and New Zealand brought many more British ships into the Far East. Until 1833 the British East India Company retained its monopoly of British trade with China. During the years before 1833 a triangular trade route, which made the China trade more advantageous than before, was worked out. Opium, produced in India, was taken to China and exchanged for tea, which was then shipped to Great Britain. This system removed one of the most serious drawbacks to British trade with China. Previously the Chinese luxury items bought by western merchants had to be paid for in silver, for the westerners produced nothing the Chinese wanted to accept in return for their exports. Opium was the first item for which the Chinese were willing to barter. After the East India Company lost its China monopoly in 1833, other merchants, including Americans, rushed to participate in the opium trade.

But Chinese officials tried to stop the importation of opium, partly because it was a health hazard and partly because they believed so much of it was being imported that it was draining silver from the country. An energetic Chinese official in Canton seized and destroyed large amounts of British

A naval skirmish in the Opium War between Great Britain and China, 1840-1842. Two British warships are forcing their way through a strait against the ineffective opposition of Chinese shore batteries and a few small boats.

opium that had been illegally imported into China. This action brought on a Chinese-British war.

The Opium War (1840-1842) was the first important armed clash between British military (especially naval) power and the land-based military forces of China. Both at sea and on land the British were the victors. In 1842 the Chinese sued for peace. Brief though the Opium War was, it led to a new relationship between China and the West, gradually spelled out in a series of treaties.

THE UNEQUAL TREATIES

The Treaty of Nanking of 1842, ending the Opium War, ceded the island of Hong Kong as a colony to Britain; opened the ports of Canton, Amoy, Fuchou, Ningpo, and Shanghai to British trade; and, most important of all, arranged that British consuls could reside in these "treaty ports" with the right to negotiate as equals with Chinese officials of similar rank. The British opium destroyed by the Chinese was to be paid for. No longer were British merchants restricted to doing business through the *co-hong*.

France and the United States immediately demanded similar privileges in China. The treaty ports were soon opened to the commerce of all nations.

Chinese tariff rates were arranged only after agreement with the western powers. Christianity was to be tolerated in China, and both Catholic and Protestant missionaries could work in treaty ports. More momentous was the introduction of the principle of "extraterritoriality"—the right of westerners residing in China to be tried according to the laws of their own countries, in courts presided over by their own consuls. Westerners desired this right in order to escape both the Chinese courts, which they did not trust, and the Chinese law, so different from their own.

Westerners were able to impose such humiliating conditions on China partly because the Chinese were in trouble at home. Throughout the nineteenth century the Manchu dynasty was weakening. By mid-century it was faced with a succession of serious revolts. The most disastrous, the Taiping Rebellion, lasted from 1850 to 1865 and took the lives of some 20,000,000 persons. The western powers wanted to preserve the Manchu government and sometimes gave it aid against the rebels.

In 1856 and in 1859-1860, the British and French took advantage of the disturbed times to wage further war against China. In the final peace negotiations the Russians and Americans associated themselves with the victors. It was agreed that western diplomatic representatives of every rank might now reside in Peking, the capital of China, and that they would be treated as equals by Chinese officials. Western ships were permitted to ply the Yangtze River, western citizens could travel inland, Christian missionaries could work everywhere, and eleven more treaty ports were to be opened. The Russians, for their part, were able to move into warmer waters by annexing lands north of the Amur River and east of the Ussuri. (See map, page 258.)

The Chinese deeply resented these "unequal treaties," partly because they gave westerners important rights and privileges not enjoyed by Chinese citizens in western countries. Chinese mandarins especially opposed the rapidly expanding work of Catholic and Protestant missionaries, for Christians were bound to condemn ancestor worship, the very cornerstone of the Chinese family system. Westerners, for their part, resented the restriction of their commerce to treaty ports and the continued Chinese treatment of their officials as inferiors. In their eyes, western military superiority proved the inferiority of Chinese civilization. After 1890 the military power of the West opened a new chapter in Chinese-western relations and threatened to bring about the partition of China.

Under British supervision, Chinese officials weigh gold to be paid to British subjects who had been mistreated in China. Such payments were among the requirements of treaties signed by China with several western powers in 1860. Forced on China by British and French military pressure, the treaties extended the privileges of westerners in Chinese territory and were resentfully called "unequal treaties" by the humiliated Chinese.

◠ THE THREATENED PARTITION OF CHINA

Unexpectedly, it was Japan that revealed to the West the possibility that China might go to pieces altogether. In 1894 war broke out between China and Japan.

THE SINO-JAPANESE WAR, 1894-1895

The opening of Japan by the Americans (see page 293) had occurred within a decade of the opening of China by the British. But the Japanese reacted to western pressures differently from the Chinese. The Japanese adopted many western ways, especially western technology. They built an army and a navy along western lines. The rapid growth of Japanese population necessitated the finding of new markets and sources of raw material. Japanese officials began to look covetously toward Korea, from which rice might be procured. But Korea was a vassal state of China. Rival Chinese-Japanese efforts to control the Korean peninsula brought on the war in 1894. By 1895, with little effort, the Japanese were victorious. Terms of peace made Korea independent and gave Japan a number of nearby islands, including Formosa (Taiwan).

THE FAR EAST, 1914

PACIFIC OCEAN

Tokyo
Osaka
Vladivostok
Korea
Port Arthur (Japanese)
Liaotung Peninsula
Shantung Peninsula
Manchuria
Peking
Yellow R.
Mongolia
Siberia
RUSSIAN EMPIRE
Turkestan
Sinkiang
Tibet
CHINESE EMPIRE
Yangtze River
Kiaochow (German)
Nanking
Shanghai
Ningpo
Formosa
Foochow
Amoy
Canton
Macao (Portuguese)
Hong Kong (British)
Kwangchowan (French)
Philippine Islands
Manila
Borneo
Dutch East Indies
Batavia
Java
Sumatra
Singapore
Malay States
Tonkin
Laos French
Annam
Indochina
Cambodia
Cochin-China
Saigon
SIAM
Bangkok
Mekong
Burma
Rangoon
Bay of Bengal
Bengal
Ganges R.
Calcutta
India
Delhi
Madras
Pondicherry (French)
Ceylon
Mysore
Bombay
Goa (Portuguese)
Karachi
Indus River
AFGHANISTAN
PERSIA
Arabia
Arabian Sea
INDIAN OCEAN

Great Britain
France
Netherlands

Russia
Japan
United States

THE SEARCH FOR CONCESSIONS IN CHINA, 1895-1898

The unexpected defeat of mighty China by little Japan persuaded Europeans that it would be wise to prepare for the total collapse of the Chinese government. Several imperialist powers tried to stake out "spheres of influence" in which only their own citizens could build railroads, open mines, or enjoy the fullest advantages of trade. When a missionary was killed or some other indignity was experienced by a citizen of a western country, that government used the opportunity to demand special rights in the area where the incident had taken place. In such ways Russia gained a special interest in Manchuria, Britain in the Yangtze valley, and France in southeastern China. Germany was granted a long lease on the territory of Kiaochow in the Shantung Peninsula.

The division of China was not, however, really pleasing to either Britain or to the United States, now directly interested in the western Pacific because of the acquisition of the Philippine Islands. (See page 307.) Both tried to persuade the other powers to accept the "open door" in China—that is, to accept the principle that trade in a sphere of influence of any power should be open on equal terms to nationals of all countries. But this policy was not really accepted by the other powers.

THE RUSSO-JAPANESE WAR, 1904-1905

In 1904 the struggle for China led to war between two imperialist powers, Russia and Japan, provoked by the rivalry of the two countries in Korea and Manchuria. In 1902 Japan had secured an alliance with Britain, Russia's colonial rival in many parts of the earth; for the British feared that if the Russians moved southward, they would challenge all Britain's interests in Southeast Asia and India. Supported by British friendship, Japan dared go to war with Russia. In a few months the Russians were defeated on land and sea. Had the war continued, Russian strength might have increased; but with serious troubles at home (see pages 264-265), the Russians dared not let the struggle go on. Peace was made in 1905 at Portsmouth, New Hampshire, under the mediation of President Theodore Roosevelt of the United States. Japan was given a foothold in southern Manchuria and was permitted to dominate Korea (annexed to Japan in 1910). Thus Japan was in a particularly strong position in the Far East when the First World War broke out, but by no means strong enough to bring about the partition of China which the western powers had not accomplished.

CHINESE REFORM EFFORTS

Toward the end of the nineteenth century it became obvious to many leading Chinese that their country would have to be reformed if it was to survive. In 1900, secret societies, among them a group called the "Boxers," staged an uprising intended to expel all foreigners from China. To protect their nationals the western powers immediately suppressed this "Boxer Rebellion" by use of their combined troops. In China a number of other movements with contradictory programs also developed. In 1911 a group headed by Sun Yat-sen overthrew the Manchus and set up a republic. But the Chinese had no experience with such a revolutionary system. When the First World War came in 1914, they had not yet established any sort of workable government. Thus, although the arrival of westerners had finally led to the destruction of much of the old China, it was not clear in 1914 what sort of new China would replace the old.

◯ OTHER AREAS OF THE FAR EAST

To a considerable extent the attitudes and actions of the European powers in China were duplicated in other parts of the Far East—although elsewhere it was easier to annex colonies, since the existing governments were less strong. The foremost colonizing countries in the other parts of the Far East were Britain, France, Spain, and the Netherlands.

Aside from China, the most important regions in the Far East are the Indochina peninsula, the East Indies or Spice Islands (today Indonesia), and the Philippines. In 1800 the Indochina peninsula was divided among Siam (today Thailand), Burma, the Malay States, Cambodia, Laos, and the three states of Tonkin, Annam, and Cochin China, which today form Vietnam. Spain already had possession of the Philippines, and the Dutch owned the East Indies. After the Napoleonic Wars the British established Singapore and began to extend their authority over the Malay States, which they were still organizing and federating in 1914. Their conquest of India led them also to annex Burma. Napoleon III began landing troops in Annam in 1858 with the excuse of avenging the murder of a French missionary. The Second Empire and the Third Republic expanded French control of the Indochina peninsula until France had all of Tonkin, Annam, Laos, Cambodia, and Cochin China. Siam remained independent.

These are tropical lands controlling the passages between the Indian and Pacific Oceans. Most of the inhabitants are still today peasant farmers.

When colonies were established, the mother countries fostered the raising of sugar, rubber, spices, and tea for export in place of purely subsistence farming. Sometimes these changes made hardships for the peasants. The Netherlands government required, for example, that each Indonesian peasant must raise crops for export on one fifth of his land and that he work sixty-six days a year on government plantations.

ᴕ ᴕ ᴕ

In spite of the many interrelations between Europe and the Far East in the nineteenth century and before, eastern Asia remained the area of the earth least dominated by Europe. It did not absorb European civilization as did the Americas and parts of Africa, nor was it as totally under European political control as was Africa after 1914. But by 1914 European influence was vastly greater in the whole Far East than it had been in 1800.

Persons, Places, and Terms

Confucius	Peking	mandarins
Sun Yat-sen	Yangtze River	Son of Heaven
	Amur River	Mandate of Heaven
Tibet	Formosa (Taiwan)	civil service
Annam	Shantung Peninsula	Manchu dynasty
Korea	Indochina	*co-hong*
Manchuria	Netherlands East	kowtow
Mongolia	Indies (Indonesia)	unequal treaties
Macao	Burma	treaty ports
Canton	Siam (Thailand)	consul
Hong Kong	Malay Peninsula	extraterritoriality
Amoy	Cambodia	Taiping Rebellion
Fuchou	Laos	sphere of influence
Ningpo	Tonkin	Boxers
Shanghai	Cochin China	"open door"

To Master the Text

1. Describe the agricultural methods and daily life of the nineteenth-century Chinese farmer. What kinds of people lived in Chinese towns? Were they better off than the farmers? Why? Who constituted a Chinese family? What was its importance?
2. In what way did the Chinese government resemble the Chinese family? What powers did the emperor claim? What were the relations of the Middle Kingdom to the neighboring states? What were the duties of the mandarins? How did they secure their jobs? Who were the Manchus?

How had they secured their power?

3. When, under what circumstances, and with whom could westerners carry on trade in China? Since westerners resented the treatment they received, why did they come to China?

4. Why were British merchants interested in opening more Chinese ports to their trade? Of what advantage to them was the opium trade? Why did Chinese officials oppose the importation of opium? What event brought on the Opium War? Who fought in it? Who won it?

5. What were the "unequal treaties"? What was their importance? What was the Taiping Rebellion? How did it influence Chinese foreign relations? What territory did China lose to European countries before 1900? Why did the mandarins oppose the unequal treaties?

6. Why did the Sino-Japanese War of 1895 suggest to western governments that China might soon fall to pieces? How did the treaty at the end of the war weaken China? What are "spheres of influence"? What powers managed to establish them in China? In what areas?

7. For what purpose did each party enter the Anglo-Japanese alliance of 1902? How did that alliance help make the Russo-Japanese War possible? How did the war alter the balance of power in the Far East?

8. Who were the Boxers? What lesson did their defeat teach Chinese leaders? With what movement was Sun Yat-sen connected?

9. What countries constitute the area generally called Southeast Asia? Why were colonies rather than spheres of influence established in that region? What European countries established colonies? In what areas? What advantages did European mother countries gain from the colonies?

To Interpret the Facts

1. Was the Chinese family a useful institution in the nineteenth century? If you think it useful, do you also believe that it was in any way a hindrance to the development of Chinese civilization?

2. What facts of Chinese life and thought made the Chinese people content to remain isolated from the outside world up to 1840?

3. List the countries that helped open China to foreign trade. What specific purpose of its own did each have? Were any of those purposes helpful to China? Were any harmful?

To Put This Chapter into a Larger Setting

1. Hold a class debate on this proposition: The Chinese, who resisted the coming of foreigners and of foreign ways, were wiser than the Japanese, who accepted foreign ways quickly once they were forced to open their ports to westerners.

2. Read about the teachings of Confucius and also about the influence of Confucianism on Chinese life. Compare this influence with that of Christianity or Judaism in American life.

Looking Back to 1870

The briefest outline of the history of Europe in the world between 1870 and 1914 impresses the student with the swift race of events. During those four decades the Industrial Revolution had spread to new countries and in already industrialized areas had created new and giant industries. Altered economic conditions forced great changes in the political life of the industrial countries and to a lesser extent in other parts of Europe. Meantime the nationalist industrial countries were taking possession of all those parts of the world militarily weak enough to be easily subject to conquest. For the first time the whole world was to a degree Europeanized, either through the inheritance of European culture, as in the Western Hemisphere, Australia, New Zealand, and the Philippines, or through conquest or strong economic pressure, as in Africa and Asia. The world was more unified than ever before. But political, economic, and cultural bonds did not necessarily make for world peace. Already the European nations were divided into two armed camps, the very existence of which threatened to magnify any international incident into an uncontrollable world crisis.

Some Questions to Answer

1. To what extent was Europe already closely related to the wider world in 1871? Up to 1871 had European involvement with the wider world tended to increase steadily, or had Europeans tended at times to withdraw somewhat from outside contacts?
2. List the areas of the world in four columns according to the kind of government each had in 1914: (a) governed by European nations as colonies or protectorates; (b) European sphere of influence; (c) European culture, but not controlled by European governments; and (d) independent of Europe and largely uninfluenced by European culture. What do these lists indicate about the world of 1914?
3. The years 1870-1914 were a time of spectacular industrial growth. During these years, which countries of the world were raised to great power status through industrialization? Were industrialized countries the greatest empire builders, or is there evidence to the contrary?

4. The years 1870-1914 were a time first of increasing political democracy and then of increasing interest in the welfare of the least fortunate classes of people. For each country of the world about which you have adequate knowledge, list steps in the direction of increasing democracy. Put the list in order of the rapidity and completeness with which democracy was adopted. Make a similar list to show which country moved most rapidly toward welfare socialism, which next most rapidly, and so on. Are the countries in the same order in your two lists? Is there any connection between rapid industrialization and increased democracy or increased welfare socialism?

5. List every example you can of long-continued disputes between pairs of nations, 1870-1914. Arrange the disputants in two columns, keeping the Triple Alliance countries in the left-hand column and the Triple Entente countries in the right-hand column. Which disputes do not fit this pattern because both disputants belonged to the same alliance group? How many disputes were related to industrial development? How many to imperialism?

6. Find examples in these chapters of occasions when the colonial world helped prevent European war by furnishing a safety valve for disputing nations, either permitting them to make some colonial bargain to balance the matter in dispute in Europe, or at least turning their attention from Europe to the colonies. Find other examples of times when colonial disputes intensified antagonisms in Europe.

7. Taking into account (a) the benefits and hardships of industrialization, (b) the extension of democracy and of welfare activities, and (c) the drawing together of the whole world by commerce and imperialism, which of the following statements is nearer the truth, and why?

(1) In general, the world over, the world's peoples were living more comfortable and better lives in 1914 than in 1871.

(2) Although the extension of democracy and the opening of many underdeveloped areas to the rest of the world brought benefits to some groups of people, so many other people were harmed that the world was generally less well off in 1914 than in 1871.

Using Documents as Evidence

Rudyard Kipling (1865–1936), the English short-story writer, poet, and novelist was born in British-ruled India. He was one of the most eloquent speakers in the cause of imperialism and colonialism. Kipling was honored by the British government in his lifetime and was buried in Westminster Abbey after a state funeral. A part of one of his most famous poems, written in 1899, follows.

THE WHITE MAN'S BURDEN

The United States and the Philippine Islands

Take up the White Man's burden—
　　Send forth the best ye breed—
Go bind your sons to exile
　　To serve your captives' need;
To wait in heavy harness
　　On fluttered folk and wild—
Your new-caught, sullen peoples,
　　Half devil and half child.

Take up the White Man's burden—
　　In patience to abide,
To veil the threat of terror
　　And check the show of pride;
By open speech and simple,
　　An hundred times made plain.
To seek another's profit,
　　And work another's gain.

Take up the White Man's burden—
　　The savage wars of peace—
Fill full the mouth of Famine
　　And bid the sickness cease;
And when your goal is nearest
　　The end for others sought,
Watch Sloth and heathen Folly
　　Bring all your hope to nought. . . .

Take up the White Man's burden—
　　Ye dare not stoop to less—
Nor call too loud on Freedom
　　To cloak your weariness;
By all ye cry or whisper,
　　By all ye leave or do,
The silent, sullen peoples
　　Shall weigh your Gods and you. . . .

What does Kipling mean by "the White Man's burden"? What are some of the advantages, according to Kipling, that colonial peoples received under European rule? What evidence can you find in the poem to indicate that colonial peoples were opposed to European rule?

William McKinley was the President of the United States during the Spanish-American War in 1898. The war lasted less than four months, yet it demonstrated that the United States had become a world power. In the following account McKinley explains his decision to have the United States acquire the Philippines.

═══════McKINLEY'S DECISION TO ANNEX THE PHILIPPINES ═══════

I have been criticized a good deal about the Philippines but don't deserve it. The truth is I didn't want the Philippines, and when they came to us, as a gift from the gods, I did not know what to do with them. When the Spanish War broke out, Dewey was at Hong Kong, and I ordered him to go to Manila and to capture or destroy the Spanish fleet. And he had to because, if defeated, he had no place to refit on that side of the globe, and if the Dons [Spanish] were victorious, they would likely cross the Pacific and ravage our Oregon and California coasts. And so he had to destroy the Spanish fleet, . . . But that was as far as I thought then.

When next I realized that the Philippines had dropped into our laps, I confess I did not know what to do with them. I sought counsel from all sides—Democrats as well as Republicans—but got little help. I thought first we would take only Manila, then Luzon, then other islands, perhaps, also. I walked the floor of the White House night after night, and . . . I went down on my knees and prayed Almighty God for light and guidance more than one night. And one night late it came to me this way: . . . (1) that we could not give them back to Spain, which would be cowardly and dishonorable; (2) that we could not turn them over to France or Germany—our commercial rivals in the Orient—which would be bad business and discreditable; (3) that we could not leave them to themselves because they were unfit for self-government, and they would soon have anarchy and misrule over there more than Spain's was; and (4) that there was nothing left for us to do but to take them all and to educate the Filipinos and uplift and civilize and Christianize them and, by God's grace, do the very best we could by them, as our fellow men for whom Christ also died. And then I went to bed and went to sleep and slept soundly, and the next morning I sent for the chief engineer of the War Department (our mapmaker), and I told him to put the Philippines on the map of the United States [pointing to a large map on the wall of his office], and there they are, and there they will stay while I am President.

In studying history it is important to be able to detach yourself from today's viewpoints and to see events within a frame of reference based on their own time. It is also important to be able to relate a document to public opinion of that time to see if it was representative of that era and place. The viewpoints of poets and Presidents often reflects those of the society around them. How did President McKinley's views resemble those of Kipling? From what you have read in the text, were Kipling's and McKinley's views representative of most Americans at that time?

PART 4

The World of the Twentieth Century

1914 to the 1980's

When the year 1914 began, the world seemed peaceful. Thoughtful persons could look optimistically toward the future. In the western countries, governments were adjusting their policies to the needs of those groups especially hurt by the Industrial Revolution. Thoughout the world, European leadership was—so it seemed—firmly established. European nations with large empires appeared to be increasingly sensitive to colonial needs and increasingly willing to advance the welfare of the colonial peoples. Given a few decades of relative calm, there was every prospect that many of the world's problems could gradually be reduced.

But decades of calm were not to be. In August, 1914, the First World War broke out. The war caused appalling destruction, and the introduction of tanks and airplanes foreshadowed even greater destructiveness in later wars. Near the end of the war, a Communist revolution established one kind of totalitarian society in Russia. Fascism in Italy and Nazism in Germany soon produced another kind. Then in 1939 came the Second World War with its bombers and, later, its guided missiles and the atomic bomb. After the war a Communist revolution took over China.

After 1945 the world was engulfed in a Cold War between two sets of powers led respectively by the United States and the Soviet Union, with a growing group of neutral nations committed to neither side. The neutrals were for the most part countries that had once belonged to the colonial empires of European powers, for the greater part of the European colonies won their independence in the 1950's and the early 1960's.

Since the 1940's the future of the world has been clouded with uncertainty, partly because of the danger of a Third World War and also because of the rush of scientific discoveries and technological inventions. With the atomic and hydrogen bombs, scientists have provided the means of destroying civilization the world over and of wiping out large parts of the world's population. Meantime other scientists are discovering new ways of keeping an ever larger number of people alive, so that there is a danger of a population explosion that could destroy civilization in another way.

Like the peoples of all past ages, men of today often believe that they confront the gravest problems ever known to humanity.

 25

The Road
to the
First
World War

1907-1914

Between 1907 and 1914 Europe was slipping into the First World War. But the ordinary people of the day did not recognize the danger. Although officials sometimes talked of the "inevitability" of war or planned for some national advantage to be gained from a war if it came, there was a wide-spread comfortable belief that the advance of civilization had made general wars impossible. For a century no war had involved all the great powers at the same time. Although there were acute diplomatic crises in the first years of the twentieth century, all were resolved peaceably without bringing the Triple Alliance and Triple Entente into armed conflict. The early months of 1914 seemed particularly hopeful, for such controversial questions as the Bagdad Railroad were nearing friendly solution.

But historians, with the advantage of hindsight, view the first years of the twentieth century from an angle different from that of the people of the time. The huge collections of government documents and the memoirs of military and political leaders show how tense were many international relations in the years between 1907 and 1914 and help explain the sudden beginning of war in 1914.

⌒ THE ALLIANCES, 1907 AND AFTER

The factor that made the threat of war most dangerous was the existence after 1907 of the Triple Alliance (Germany, Austria-Hungary, and Italy) and the Triple Entente (France, Russia, and Britain). (See pages 274-280.) Once these groups had come into being, each power had to remain loyal to the alliance to which it belonged, lest it be without friends when it dealt with other powers. Consequently, the members of each group tended to draw together and to present a harmoniously united front to the outside world. When a member of one alliance found itself in dispute with a member of the opposite group, the other members of both alliances often became involved; for each power felt that it should support its own ally. Thus matters that actually concerned only two powers were often blown up to continent-wide proportions.

There was also friction within each alliance. The members had been drawn together not so much by common interests as by common fears, and old antagonisms between alliance members still remained. Some of these were serious enough to threaten the breaking up of an alliance—an event that might well disturb all Europe.

It must be noted that the diplomacy of the alliance system was the business of statesmen rather than of their peoples. Officials attempted, of course, to win popular support for their policies; but they made many commitments to other governments without informing their own people. This secrecy was not practiced with evil intent. It was resorted to when a minister of foreign affairs could only secure a favorable bargain for his own country by acting in secret.

CHANGES IN THE TRIPLE ALLIANCE

The Triple Alliance originally had been purely a defensive arrangement, organized by Bismarck to prevent Germany's neighbors from attempting to recover the territories Germany had gained in its wars with Denmark, Austria, and France. (See pages 187-195.) As the time went on, however, the Italians grew eager to expand into North Africa, while the Austrians believed that they must for their own protection take certain aggressive steps in the Balkans. Since the German government dared not offend its allies by opposing these desires, the defensive character of the alliance was somewhat altered.

Another change that came about with time was the lessened loyalty of Italy to the Triple Alliance. The Italians were particularly fearful of a war involving Britain on the opposite side, which would result in a British naval bombardment of Italian coastal cities. The Italians were also rivals of Austria for control of the Adriatic Sea, and they therefore resented any extension of Austrian influence in the Balkan Peninsula. Sometimes they leaned toward friendly relations with France, and at one point they actually made an agreement with France to remain neutral in the event of a Franco-German war. But when the Triple Alliance was renewed for the last time in 1912, the German government believed it could count on Italian support in the event of a major war.

CHANGES IN THE TRIPLE ENTENTE

The Triple Entente was officially not an alliance at all, although it is convenient to use that word in referring to it. The French and Russians had a definite alliance (see page 276); but down to the very outbreak of war in 1914 the British declared that they were not definitely committed to either Russia or France, and that they were free at any time to decide what course of action best suited their needs. British officials felt obliged to retain freedom of action; for they believed that Parliament would refuse to ratify a definite alliance, and that in any case freedom from definite commitments gave strength to their policy.

With France, however, the British entered informally into ever closer relations. As early as 1906 the British foreign minister, informing the prime minister but not other members of the cabinet, permitted the British general staff to develop with French army officers a set of plans for common French-British action in case of war. More important, in 1912 co-operative plans were made for the British and French navies. The British Mediterranean fleet was brought north and stationed in the North Sea, while the French fleet was concentrated in the Mediterranean, where it could protect British shipping as well as French interests. Thereafter if the British refused to support the French in the event of Franco-German war, the north coast of France would be at the mercy of Germany. Since Britain could not safely permit France to be defeated, it was clear to those who knew about the secret military talks that in a general war Britain would almost certainly go to the aid of France.

With Russia, the British began joint military planning only in the last months before the outbreak of war, and no concrete results were achieved. The British were never altogether friendly to the Russians, whose objectives in the Balkans they feared and whose efforts to secure advantages in Persia they opposed. Russia and France, on the other hand, drew closer together.

RELATIONS BETWEEN GERMANY AND BRITAIN

In general the alliances became more tightly knit in 1907-1914, but relations also continued between members of opposite alliances. Although relations between Germany and Britain, the two strongest powers, gradually grew less friendly, the traditional sympathy between the German and British people died slowly. The continued unwillingness of the British to enter into a firm alliance with France or Russia kept alive the expectation among German officials that Britain might yet join the Triple Alliance.

But in spite of the lingering good will between Germany and Britain, much friction developed between the two countries. British and German businessmen tried to sell their products in the same overseas markets. British and German empire-builders were rivals for the same strategic areas in Africa. In the Persian Gulf the British saw their interests threatened by the Bagdad Railroad. (See pages 317-319.) German industrialists and colonial enthusiasts believed that they had as much right as the British to search for markets and for colonies. But in British eyes, the Germans had no right to trespass in areas long before staked out by the British.

The sharpest Anglo-German conflict grew out of the German decision of 1898 to build a navy so large that not even the strongest naval power could risk attacking it without danger. William II was particularly interested in a navy. He was persuaded that German commercial and colonial interests demanded naval protection and that the status of Germany as a great power could not be fully realized without a large navy. To the British, however, a German fleet strong enough to do serious damage to their own navy was a challenge to the very existence of their nation. The British people could not live without imported food and raw materials; consequently, the sea routes had at all times to be kept open to British merchant ships. The British met the German challenge by building more ships, better and more expensive, of new design. The cost to both countries was staggering.

Although these points of friction continued down to 1914, in some ways they became less dangerous. German and British manufacturers learned to live side by side by specializing in different products. Treaties divided colonial areas. The problem of the Bagdad Railroad was smoothed out. But the prime question of the German navy still remained. Moreover, British resentment of Germany was increased by the frequent tactlessness of William II and by his impulsive and warlike speeches. The Germans, for their part, believed themselves to be "encircled," not only by the Entente but also by the barriers put in the way of their colonial expansion; for the other powers, arriving earlier on the scene, had taken the best colonial areas.

An atmosphere favorable to war was inevitably created in Europe by international tensions like these between Britain and Germany, as well as by the universal feeling of insecurity that kept powers loyal (at least in part) to their allies. Between 1907 and 1914 there was a series of severe international crises. Although each of those occurring before 1914 was brought to a peaceful conclusion, each served in some way to increase the danger of major war.

☾ INTERNATIONAL CRISES

Of the three major crises between 1907 and 1914 (the Bosnian crisis, 1908; the Agadir crisis, 1911; and the Balkan Wars, 1912-1913), the first and third were related to the Balkan Peninsula. With the intensifying of Balkan national feeling, that area became the most dangerous in Europe.

THE BOSNIAN CRISIS, 1908

The Bosnian crisis of 1908 resulted from the interplay of several factors: (1) Serbian nationalism, (2) Turkish nationalism, (3) the struggle of the Habsburg government to hold its empire together, and (4) the desire of the Russians to gain the right to send their warships through the straits of the Bosporus and the Dardanelles.

Serbian nationalism was aroused by the decisions of the Congress of Berlin (1878) regarding Serbia and Bosnia-Herzegovina. (See page 273.) At that time Serbia had attained complete independence from the Ottoman Empire. Bosnia-Herzegovina had remained part of the Ottoman Empire but was to be governed by Austria-Hungary. The Serbs immediately began to dream of acting as the magnet around which a large South Slav (Yugoslav) state could be developed, much as Piedmont had been the center for a united Italy. It was therefore natural for them to want to acquire Bosnia-Herzegovina, where many of the people were Serbs. But their relations with Austria remained fairly friendly until 1903, when a revolution brought an anti-Austrian ruler to the throne. Thereafter there was talk in Serbia of trying to detach the South Slav subjects of the Habsburgs in order to unite them with Serbia. Such agitation was naturally alarming to Austro-Hungarian officials.

At the same time evidences of Turkish nationalism became apparent. A group of patriots calling themselves Young Turks agitated for liberal reforms. In 1908 they seized the Ottoman government, revived a constitution that had been adopted in 1876, and prepared to summon a legislative assembly. The Austro-Hungarian government was alarmed lest the Turks demand that the Habsburgs give up control of Bosnia-Herzegovina.

Meantime in Russia new efforts were being made to realize the old dream of sending Russian warships freely through the Straits, with the Turks, as before, preventing ships of war of other nations from navigating the Straits. Russia could thus build warships in the warm waters of the Black Sea and get them out to the Mediterranean and beyond. In wartime the Russian Black Sea fleet could emerge into the Mediterranean or scurry back into the Black Sea to protect itself from a too-powerful enemy. Naturally other nations with interests in the Mediterranean preferred to keep the Russian Black Sea fleet locked up behind the Straits.

In 1908 it occurred to the Russian and Austrian foreign ministers that they might strike a bargain, Russia agreeing to Austria's annexing Bosnia-Herzegovina outright, and Austria agreeing to let Russian warships pass through the Straits. In a secret meeting the two men entered into an agreement, the exact terms of which are still not known. Then the Russian foreign minister toured the capitals of Europe, seeking permission of the other powers to open the Straits to Russian warships. Before he made any real progress, he heard that the Austrians had annexed Bosnia-Herzegovina. He was furious, for once in possession of Bosnia-Herzegovina, the Austrians could no longer be counted on to support his cause. Since he had found no other friends, he had for the time being to give up all thought of opening the Straits.

The Austrian action brought about a serious European crisis. The Serbs were angry because they realized that their chances of acquiring Bosnia-Herzegovina had almost vanished. The Young Turks looked upon the annexation as a theft of Turkish territory. Other powers, less immediately concerned, deplored the fact that Austria had set aside a provision of the Treaty of Berlin without the consent of the other signers. Even the Germans were alarmed lest their friendly relations with the Ottoman Empire and their Bagdad Railroad be endangered by the action of their ally. It was generally feared that the Serbs might attack Austria and that the Russians might then aid the Serbs.

That the crisis did not lead to war was the result of circumstances. Although in the early days of the Triple Alliance Bismarck had declined to support Austria in the Balkans, the German government now made it clear that it would fight in alliance with Austria in an Austro-Russian war growing out of the Bosnian question. The Russians, for their part, came to the conclusion that their country, not yet fully recovered from the war with Japan, was not ready for such a war. Without Russian support the Serbs were not able to fight Austria-Hungary. They made a promise, never kept, to put an end to anti-Austrian propaganda; but there was no war.

The crisis had, nevertheless, important consequences. It inspired the Russians to redouble their efforts to build up military power so that they could have their way in the Balkans. In Serbia it aroused bitter feeling against Austria-Hungary, and at the same time it made the Serbians believe that the Russians would at some later time aid them in an attack on Austria-Hungary. It gave the Austrians confidence that in a future crisis in the Balkans they would have the full support of the Germans. Thus any future trouble in the Balkans bade fair to be more serious than the Bosnian crisis.

THE AGADIR CRISIS, 1911

The next crisis developed in Morocco. It was important because it seemed again to threaten European war and because of its effect on the alliances.

The French had gradually been exerting more influence in Morocco than the decisions of the Algeciras Conference had permitted. (See pp. 278 and 315-316.) Since, however, they secured German consent in advance, no international difficulties seemed likely to arise. Then in 1911, when there was disorder in the Moroccan capital, Fez, the French sent troops to protect French life and property there. The Germans immediately sent a gunboat to Agadir, a Moroccan Atlantic port (where there were no Germans to protect), as a protest against the French occupation of Fez. Other statesmen of Europe were alarmed for fear the Germans were about to make some demand on the French so great that the French would fight rather than accept it. The British government indicated that it would not permit important European questions like that of Morocco to be settled without consultation with Britain. Some preparations for war were made, including further talks between British and French military men.

But the Germans took no extreme step. They agreed to let the French make Morocco into a protectorate in return for the cession to Germany of two strips of territory in French Equatorial Africa along the border of the German Cameroons colony. Thus the Agadir crisis was over, but it left bitter feeling toward Germany and tighter bonds of friendship between France and Britain. Both alliances became more solid. The Germans further irritated the British by stepping up their naval construction.

THE BALKAN WARS, 1912-1913

No sooner was the Agadir crisis over than trouble was again brewing in the Balkans. This time it was the activity of the Balkan people themselves that created the tense situation.

After their disappointment in the Bosnian crisis, the Serbs had increased their nationalist propaganda efforts, founding patriotic societies to inform the people and to train men in the arts of revolutionary guerrilla warfare. Among these organizations was a cloak-and-dagger secret society, the Black Hand, dedicated to terrorism. As the agitators saw it, Serbia's most important enemy was the Ottoman Empire, which still controlled Thrace, Macedonia, and Albania, inhabited largely by Yugoslavs. The second most important was Austria-Hungary, with its Yugoslav subjects and its opposition to Serbian expansion. Russia was the undoubted friend of Serbia.

The Agadir crisis set in motion the train of events in the Balkans. After Agadir the Italians, believing that the French might use their strengthened position in Morocco to acquire the rest of North Africa, made war on the Ottoman Empire to obtain Tripoli and Cyrenaica before France should take them. (See page 316.) The Balkan rulers, in turn, saw the opportunity to attack the Ottoman Empire while the Turks were at war with Italy. With advice from Russia, a Balkan League was organized, consisting of Bulgaria, Serbia, Montenegro, and Greece. In 1912, before the Turkish-Italian war could be concluded, the Balkan League attacked the Ottoman Empire.

This First Balkan War was a triumph for the Balkan states. In short order their armies arrived at the defenses of Constantinople itself. At long last the Turks had been all but driven from Europe. Peace was made in May, 1913, with arrangements for establishing a new kingdom of Albania along the Adriatic coast and for dividing the rest of the conquered territory among the victors. A month later, however, the Second Balkan War broke out, the Balkan states fighting among themselves over the exact boundaries of their new acquisitions. By August, 1913, peace was again restored, but with the Turks back in eastern Thrace.

A special importance of the Balkan Wars was the way in which the European powers collaborated to prevent these localized wars from turning into a world war. Both Austria and Italy were determined to exclude Serbia from the Adriatic coast, while Russia was eager to give Serbia access to the sea. To settle this and other differences, an international conference of the great powers sat for some time in London. There it was decided to create

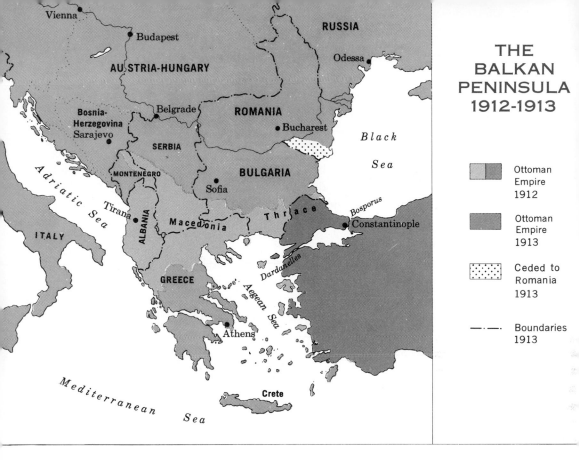

THE
BALKAN
PENINSULA
1912-1913

Ottoman Empire 1912

Ottoman Empire 1913

Ceded to Romania 1913

—·— Boundaries 1913

the new Albania along the Adriatic coast to keep Serbia inland. Although Serbia gained territory to the east of Albania, the Serbs were far from satisfied. Their disappointment was a factor in provoking the Second Balkan War, and it also led to the intensifying of their anti-Austrian propaganda.

It would have been easy for this crisis to have brought about an Austro-Russian war. That such a war did not take place was largely because at the London conference the British and Germans co-operated closely with each other to preserve peace and to prevent their allies, Russia and Austria-Hungary, from taking unwise steps. But the attitudes of Britain and Germany, which kept peace for the moment, may well have contributed to the outbreak of war a year later. Russia was angry at Britain, and Austria-Hungary at Germany, for preventing action in the Balkans. Both Britain and Germany feared that their actions had weakened the relationship with an ally, and each was therefore more ready to support that ally in any future crisis that might develop.

☉ THE OUTBREAK OF WAR

In July, 1914, another crisis developed. Its immediate cause was the assassination on June 28 in Sarajevo, the capital of Bosnia, of the Archduke Francis Ferdinand, heir to the throne of Austria-Hungary. The assassin was a Serbian terrorist who had been trained by a member of the Black Hand. He was a native of Bosnia and thus a subject of Austria-Hungary. The Austrian government had to decide how to react to this deplorable incident.

THE AUSTRIAN ATTACK ON SERBIA

Several factors determined the course followed by Austria. The increasing vigor of Slavic nationalism made more certain every day that a multinational state like Austria-Hungary could continue to exist only under the most favorable circumstances. Austro-Hungarian ministers feared that if Serbian propaganda led to the detachment of the South Slavs from the Habsburg lands, Austria-Hungary would simply fall to pieces. To the Habsburg government, restraint of Serbia was thus a prime policy. At the moment, the military men in power believed that use of force was the best means to this end. Because of German support, offered first in the Bosnian crisis, then in later consultations, and finally offered again immediately after the assassination, the Austrian government was persuaded that July, 1914, was the best time to take decisive action against Serbia.

The Austrians first held an investigation of the assassination. Today it is known that some officials of the Serbian government had much to do with the planning of that deed; but in 1914 the Austrians did not have all the facts. Nevertheless they sent an ultimatum to Serbia demanding that anti-Austrian propaganda cease and that Austrian officials be permitted to help put a stop to it. The Serbs, believing that they would be supported by Russia, refused to accept those parts of the ultimatum that would give Austrian officials the right to interfere in Serbian domestic affairs. On July 28 Austria-Hungary announced that the ultimatum had been rejected and declared war on Serbia.

THE INVOLVEMENT OF THE OTHER POWERS

European statesmen recognized the seriousness of the situation. There were frantic efforts to keep the war limited or to stop it altogether, but it was too late. The very character of the armies of the time, made up as they were both of men under arms and of already trained reserves in civilian life,

The assassination of Archduke Francis Ferdinand of Austria in Sarajevo, Bosnia, June 28, 1914, the event that led directly to the outbreak of the First World War a month later. The goal of the assassin, a Bosnian student named Gavrilo Princip, was the union of Bosnia with Serbia. Princip died in an Austrian prison during the war; but at the war's end his goal was achieved.

stood in the way of peace. Before an army could go into action, a period of "mobilization" had to take place while the reserves joined their units and took possession of the necessary equipment. When one army mobilized, its probable opponent hastened to do likewise; for the first army ready for the battlefield had a great advantage. Army officers had the upper hand in many political decisions, for they alone could say what their troops were capable of doing and could argue for immediate mobilization to be the first in the field. Hence there was pressure on all governments to make the first move toward war.

On July 30, unwilling to permit the destruction of Serbia by Austria-Hungary, which would so greatly increase Austrian influence in the Balkans, Russia began mobilization. The Germans then mobilized, for they were convinced that they must defend their one sure ally, Austria-Hungary, against Russian attack. The next day Germany declared war on Russia.

The Germans were now in a quandary. They were convinced that eventually the French would attack them in order to aid Russia and that Germany would then be confronted by a dreaded "war on two fronts."

They had only one plan of defense against such a war, worked out early in the century by a General von Schlieffen. The basis of the Schlieffen plan was the belief that France would mobilize quickly, but that huge Russia, with its inadequate railroads, could be ready for battle only after a period of several weeks. The plan called for the German armies to invade France immediately in full force, drive France out of the war, and then move eastward for a prolonged struggle with Russia. But this plan required that Germany be at war with France first, whereas it was actually at war with Russia while France was still neutral.

In their quandary the Germans inquired what course France now intended to follow. The French replied that they would act as their interests demanded at the given moment. Convinced that the French would come into the war once the Russian and German armies were fully involved with each other, the Germans declared war on France on August 3.

Until this time the British government still insisted that it was neutral. But the ministers in power were mostly sympathetic to France and some were deeply involved in the secret military plans for co-operation with France. The policy of Britain was, however, soon determined by the Germans.

The Schlieffen plan provided for the invasion of France through Belgium, whose neutrality had been guaranteed in 1839 by all the powers, including Prussia. The reason for this part of the plan was the strength of French fortifications along the French-German border, which the German staff believed to be almost impossible to penetrate. If the Germans were to finish the war with France quickly enough, the German planners believed they must march through Belgium, with or without the permission of the Belgian government.

As soon as German troops entered Belgium, where the Belgians resisted them, the British people were ready to enter the war. The whole world was horrified by the invasion of Belgium. Centuries-old British policy had declared that the Dutch-Belgian coasts must be kept out of the hands of a strong power. More important to the man on the street in Britain was the fact that Germany had made an unprovoked attack on a country whose neutrality had so long been guaranteed both by Britain and Prussia as well as by the other powers. On August 4 Britain declared war on Germany.

Italy, the ally of Germany, did not at this time enter the war. It excused itself by declaring that Germany and Austria-Hungary had provoked the war and that Italy was not obligated by the terms of the alliance to aid them in aggressive war.

໑ ໑ ໑

One can read the history of the outbreak of the First World War in several ways—as an inevitable train of events, as the result of a series of accidents, or as the outcome of the evil-doing of one or more governments. Historians still argue over the responsibility of one or another of the European governments. All that can be said surely is that the great forces of the time helped bring it about—nationalism, economic rivalry, the multiplication of armaments, and the existence of many powerful governments uncontrolled by any international organization.

Persons, Places, and Terms

Francis Ferdinand	Fez	Young Turks
General von Schlieffen	Agadir	Bosnian Crisis
	French Equatorial Africa	Agadir Crisis
North Sea	Sarajevo	Balkan League
		Balkan Wars

To Master the Text

1. How did the existence of the two great alliance systems increase the likelihood of a general European war? What changes were occurring in the Triple Alliance? How did these changes affect the possibility of war? What changes were occurring in the Triple Entente? With what effect on a possible war? Why did Britain not enter into a definite alliance with France? With Russia?

2. About 1900 what policies of Germany were alarming to the British? Why? Why did the Germans follow each of these policies?

3. What was the Bosnian Crisis? What background facts explain Austro-Hungarian actions? Turkish actions? Russian actions? In 1908 why were the Austro-Hungarians especially alarmed for their future? What plan did the Austro-Hungarian and Russian foreign ministers concoct for the future strengthening of their two countries? What train of events spoiled the plan?

4. When Austria-Hungary acted in Bosnia-Herzegovina, what were the reactions of Serbia? Of Russia? Of the Turks? Of Germany? Of other powers? Why was there no general war? What were the results of the crisis?

5. What events constituted the Agadir Crisis? How did French policy help bring it about? How did German policy contribute to it? What changed relations among the powers resulted from the crisis?

6. By what train of events did the Agadir Crisis lead to the First Balkan War? How did the Balkan states prepare for the war? What benefits did they obtain from it? What disappointments did they suffer? With what special hopes had the Serbs joined the war?

7. How did the powers help keep the Balkan Wars from growing into a larger war? How did the efforts of German and British officials to prevent general war in 1912 help bring war about in 1914?

8. What event set off the 1914 crisis? When and where did it occur? How and why did Austria-Hungary react to it? What steps did the Austro-Hungarian government take?

9. Trace the course of events from the Austro-Hungarian ultimatum to the British entry into the First World War, explaining with each step the reason why it was taken. In each case, why did the step seem unavoidable to the officials who decided upon it?

To Master the Map

1. On a blank map of Europe and North Africa, indicate the territories that changed hands between 1907 and 1913.

2. Study the map on page 279. What geographic advantages did the Triple Alliance have for waging war? The Triple Entente? What advantages, if any, had either side gained between 1907 and 1914?

To Interpret the Facts

1. In 1914 what antagonisms existed between Austria-Hungary and Russia? Between Italy and France? Between Germany and France? Between Germany and Great Britain? What part did each of these antagonisms have in bringing about the First World War?

2. Compare the crises of 1907-1913 with those of 1914. Why was the crisis of 1914 not stopped short of war as the others had been?

3. By tracing the policy of each of the great powers separately, 1907-1914, try to explain the conduct of that power in the crisis of 1914.

To Put This Chapter into a Larger Setting

1. Great Britain has been charged by some historians with contributing to the outbreak of the First World War by failing to declare ahead of time that in such a war she would support France and Russia. Why did the British government not make such a declaration? Do you think that such a declaration would have deterred the Germans from supporting the Austro-Hungarians?

2. Support or attack either of the following statements:

 (a) German policy was largely responsible for the First World War.

 (b) French-Russian policy was largely responsible for the war.

26

The
First
World War

1914-1919

The war that began in late July, 1914, is now called the "First World War" (or sometimes "World War I"); until 1939 it was simply "the World War." Neither title is accurate, since earlier wars, such as those against Napoleon, had already been fought on several continents. Nor was the whole world involved in this war. But to the people of the time, this struggle seemed so all-enveloping that nothing less than "world war" could properly describe it. Moreover, when all the peace treaties were finally concluded, victors and vanquished alike entered a world very different from that of July, 1914.

⌒ THE ARMED CONFLICT

The Germans and Austro-Hungarians (the "Central Powers") tried, by striking first, to fight the war on their own terms. They were quickly frustrated on land, and more gradually at sea. But their enemies (called the "Allies") were no more able to achieve a quick, decisive victory. The terrible conflict continued for more than four years, until probably more than 60,000,000 men were brought into the armed forces, some 10,000,000 or more of whom were killed and 20,000,000 wounded.

THE PATTERN OF LAND WARFARE, 1914-1917

On land the Germans tried to follow the Schlieffen plan (see page 366), their only program for a two-front war. On neither front did the fighting develop according to their expectations.

The War in the West. In August, 1914, hoping to drive France from the war before the Russians had completed their mobilization, the Germans sent five armies through Belgium and Luxembourg into France in a great wheeling operation that was expected to take Paris, envelop the French armies, and push them eastward toward Lorraine. The plan was frustrated by the unexpectedly stout resistance of the Belgians, the quick arrival of British forces, the determination and vigor of the French, and the decision of the Germans themselves to send some of their reserves to such other battle areas as East Prussia. In early September, 1914, the Allies were, therefore, able to make a stand against the Germans along the Marne River. Although the Germans had come within sight of Paris, they did not achieve their purpose, but neither were they driven out of France by the Allies.

Both sides now had to settle down to trench warfare along a front soon extending for more than 300 miles from the North Sea to Switzerland. The soldiers dug the trenches, fortified them, and lived in them, combating mud, lice, and rats as well as the enemy in the nearby opposite trenches. At night under the cover of artillery fire they might be sent "over the top" of their own trenches to cut the barbed wire entanglements and capture prisoners from whom to extract information. Major fighting consisted of week- or month-long battles intended to break through some section of the enemy's lines and cut his forces in two. Such battles required tremendous concentrations of men and equipment. In preparation there was incredibly heavy artillery fire. Then came wave upon wave of men advancing from the trenches with fixed bayonets, ready to engage enemy soldiers in single combat. Many of the attackers were cut down by machine-gun fire before they could reach the enemy trenches. To counter the effectiveness of the machine gun, the British developed and made some use of the armored tank; but only toward the end of the war did it have an appreciable effect. The slight gains of territory and terrible loss of life in these protracted battles did not deter the commanders from trying again and again. In 1916, for example, the Germans determined to take the French fortress of Verdun. After ten months they had lost 350,000 men without securing the fortress. Although such battles were undertaken by both sides until the end of the war, in the west neither side succeeded in gaining any decisive advantage.

American troops in a hastily dug and camouflaged trench in France during the First World War. A picture such as this can do little more than hint at the dreadful hardships of the soldiers and the terrible loss of life in and in front of the trenches.

The War in the East. Russian forces were in the field much sooner than the Germans had expected: in August, 1914, they invaded East Prussia. Although the Germans halted this initial Russian drive, they had inadequate support from the Austrians, and they could not afford to move many of their own troops from the western front. But the year 1915 was a turning point on the eastern front. The Germans took charge and interspersed their troops with the Austrians. The Russians, suffering from severe shortages of guns, ammunition, and even food, were pushed far to the east. After 1915, although the Russians continued to fight, they were so weak and war-weary that the Central Powers no longer feared being overrun from the east. But the eastern front took needed German troops from the western trenches.

THE SEARCH FOR ALLIES

From the beginning both sides sought new allies. The Germans, hemmed in by British control of the sea, by the trench line to the west, and by the

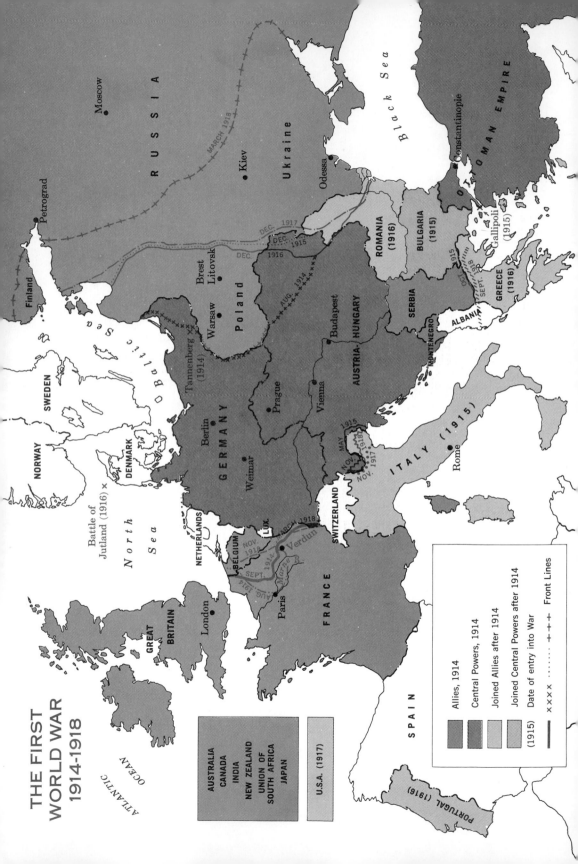

THE FIRST
WORLD WAR
1914-1918

RUSSIA

Moscow

MARCH 1918

Petrograd

Finland

Kiev

Ukraine

Odessa

Black Sea

Constantinople

OTTOMAN EMPIRE

Gallipoli
(1915)

DEC. 1917

DEC. 1915

DEC. 1916

ROMANIA
(1916)

BULGARIA
(1915)

GREECE
(1916)

Brest
Litovsk

AUG. 1914

OCT. 1915

SEPT. 1918

Warsaw

Poland

Budapest

AUSTRIA-
HUNGARY

SERBIA

ALBANIA

MONTENEGRO

SWEDEN

Baltic Sea

Tannenberg
(1914)

Prague

Vienna

1915

MAY 1915

JUNE 1918

NOV. 1917

NOV. 1918

ITALY (1915)

Rome

NORWAY

Berlin

Weimar

GERMANY

Battle of
Jutland (1916) ×

North
Sea

DENMARK

NETHERLANDS

BELGIUM

LUX.

SWITZERLAND

NOV.
1918

MARCH 1918

Verdun

Marne R.

SEPT. 1914

AUG. 1914

Paris

FRANCE

GREAT
BRITAIN

London

ATLANTIC
OCEAN

SPAIN

PORTUGAL
(1916)

AUSTRALIA
CANADA
INDIA
NEW ZEALAND
UNION OF SOUTH AFRICA
JAPAN

U.S.A. (1917)

Allies, 1914

Central Powers, 1914

Joined Allies after 1914

Joined Central Powers after 1914

(1915)   Date of entry into War

×××× ········ +++   Front Lines

Russians to the east, desperately needed a route to the other side of the ring of their enemies. The Ottoman Empire, already drawn toward Germany by the Bagdad Railroad, joined the Central Powers in November, 1914, and Bulgaria joined them in 1915. Japan, the ally of Great Britain, went into the war on the Allied side at the beginning; and in 1915 Italy joined the Allies in return for the promise of Austro-Hungarian and Turkish territory. In 1915, hoping to force the straits so they could send desperately needed supplies to Russia, the Allies made a landing on the Gallipoli Peninsula at the northern edge of the Dardanelles, only to be driven out. In 1916 they brought Romania into their camp, but within a month the Central Powers defeated Romania and thereafter controlled an unobstructed route to the Middle East. Meantime the British moved up the Tigris River toward Bagdad, hoping to open the way to Russia. (See map, page 318.) With the French they pledged themselves to support Arab independence from the Turks, but the two countries also made an agreement with each other for a future division of Arab territory into British and French spheres of influence.

Thus the search for allies was not a definite success for either side. It was the war on the sea that was decisive.

THE WAR ON THE SEA

In spite of the rapid prewar development of the German navy, the Allies had the major share of success at sea. By the beginning of 1915 there were neither German war vessels nor merchant ships on the high seas. Not until May, 1916, did the German battle fleet leave port. Then it encountered the British in the battle of Jutland to the west of the Danish peninsula. Although the German fleet destroyed a number of British ships, it retired to its own harbors at the end of the day and did not emerge again.

The Allies used their naval superiority to establish what was in effect a blockade of the German coasts. In order to prevent the Germans from receiving goods through such neutral countries as the Netherlands and Denmark, Allied war vessels on the high seas stopped and searched neutral cargo ships, seizing as contraband anything that might be useful to the war effort, even though that particular item was not recognized as contraband in international law. This high-handed policy angered neutrals, especially the United States, but it caused increasing shortages in Germany. Control of the seas also permitted the Allies to seize German colonies in Africa with little opposition.

Unable to contest British control of the surface of the sea, the Germans decided to use submarines to sink vessels bringing supplies to France and especially to Britain. In 1915 they declared a war zone, to include the British and French coasts, within which they would sink enemy merchant ships or ships flying neutral flags but suspected of being enemy ships in disguise.

Submarine warfare was a new weapon, and Allied and neutral peoples considered it particularly barbaric. Submarines could not fulfill the requirement of international law that a warship must remove passengers and crew before sinking a vessel. Since a single shot from a gun of a merchant vessel (now often armed) could send a frail submarine to the bottom of the sea, the submarine had to remain submerged when it fired its torpedoes. As soon as the new German policy was put into effect an American vessel was sunk, as were British vessels with Americans aboard—most memorably in May, 1915, the British passenger ship *Lusitania*, on which over a thousand persons lost their lives, including more than one hundred Americans. The United States protest was so bitter that at the end of 1915 the German government agreed to limit its use of submarines—a promise easy to make because at the time Germany had few submarines.

At the beginning of 1917 the Germans, with many new submarines, decided to try again to starve Britain by unlimited submarine warfare. German naval officers estimated that it would take five months to reduce Britain to starvation and drive it from the war. It was clear that the policy might bring the United States into the war, but the navy men believed Germany could win the war before American participation became decisive.

In the first months of the German submarine campaign, the British lost twice as many merchant ships per month as in the immediately preceding period. But in April, 1917, the United States entered the war against Germany, and the German submarine policy was the declared reason. Other factors had, of course, played their part. Many Americans, President Woodrow Wilson among them, admired British and French democracy and had deep sympathy for the Allied cause. News to America from the Central Powers came largely by way of Britain, and therefore had a British slant. American businessmen had advanced the Allies much money, which might be lost if the Germans won the war. There were stories of sabotage promoted by German agents in American factories. The fate of Belgium and France at the hands of the Germans had aroused active American sympathy. But it was the principle of the freedom of the seas and anger at the loss of American lives that were the final factors. The entry of the United States into the war helped turn the tide of victory toward the Allies.

THE COLLAPSE OF THE CENTRAL POWERS, 1917-1918

The year 1917 turned the tide of war sharply in favor of the Allies, although their weariness and lack of spectacular victories prevented them from sensing their advantage. Germany's allies were all near collapse. The Ottoman Empire was battered by the British seizure of Jerusalem and by Allied armies approaching Mosul in Mesopotamia. Bulgaria was suffering from bad harvests; Austria-Hungary was almost ready to fall to pieces. In early 1918, to be sure, the Germans experienced some important successes. In March they signed the Treaty of Brest-Litovsk with the new Communist government of Russia. (Chapter 27.) Russia withdrew from the war and acknowledged the independence of Finland, Estonia, Latvia, Lithuania, Poland, and the Ukraine, leaving them open to German influence. But after a last effort to break the Allied lines to the west, the Germans began to weaken. The Allies, meantime, had the new strength of fresh, well-trained, well-equipped American forces; and for the first time they put their armies under the command of a single chief, the French Marshal Ferdinand Foch. Although German submarines still threatened British food supplies, they did not sink a single American troopship, for the use of great convoys—many ships traveling together under a naval escort—provided adequate protection. After August, 1918, the Germans were in steady retreat on the western front. On October 3 their commander, his armies still on foreign soil, informed his government that it must request an armistice. The Allies required that the Germans withdraw from France and from German territory west of the Rhine. On November 11, 1918, the armistice was granted.

◌ EUROPE IN EARLY 1919

The problems of peacemaking broke upon Europe in late 1918 with the suddenness of the outbreak of war in 1914. Soldiers, statesmen, and ordinary people were all unprepared for peace.

VICTOR AND VANQUISHED AT THE END OF THE WAR

To some extent the war had affected all European peoples alike, even the neutrals. More than any previous conflict, this was a total war. The first disastrous shortages of shells and other war materials were experienced by all the belligerents, and in the later years of the war many of them had suffered shortages of food. Farms and factories had proved to be as important to victory as the conduct of soldiers on the battlefields. All governments were forced to regulate the use of raw materials and to ration food and fuel. Workers were under pressure to labor for long hours and to refrain from strikes. Given the desperate importance of these economic matters to the future of the nation, it was natural that all governments became increasingly dictatorial. Ministers and army officers, even in the democratic countries, acted on their own authority to an extent that would have seemed intolerable in peacetime. Fear of spies and sabotage led to press censorship and to the imprisonment of innocent persons suspected of being enemy agents. Freedom of discussion was limited by lack of information and by the fear of being falsely accused of disloyalty. When to the unaccustomed lack of freedom were added inadequate diets, prolonged hours of work, worry over the fate of loved ones in the trenches and on the warships, it is not surprising that the wartime strain was becoming intolerable.

In the defeated countries there was the serious added difficulty of the collapse of governments. Many Germans had come to the conclusion that they would secure better peace terms by overthrowing the Hohenzollern monarchy. On November 9, 1918, two days before the armistice, Emperor William II abdicated and fled to the Netherlands. In 1919 a convention met at Weimar and wrote a constitution for the new German republic, which as a result often was called the "Weimar Republic." The Austro-Hungarian government collapsed altogether, leaving the various national groups of the Habsburg empire free at last to form separate states. Russia had become a battleground between Communists and conservative Russian forces supported by French, British, and American troops. (Chapter 27.) Since the Allied blockade of the German coast continued, food and other necessities in Germany were scarcer than during the period of actual war.

PREPARATIONS FOR PEACEMAKING

Before the armistice there had been no formal, carefully developed agreement among the victorious nations about the terms of peace, but three factors must be noted as influencing the kind of peace eventually made:

(1) the universal hope for a better world, reflected especially in the idealistic statements of President Woodrow Wilson of the United States; (2) the attitudes of the Allied peoples toward Germany, as expressed in election returns; and (3) earlier wartime agreements among the Allied governments.

With persuasive eloquence the American president declared to the world his program for a better international community. His famous "Fourteen Points," set forth in a message to the United States Congress in January, 1918, outlined the shape of the new world as he saw it and were accepted by the Germans when they agreed to the armistice. Among the Fourteen Points were denunciations of such practices as secret treaties, interference with the freedom of the seas, unduly high tariffs, large armaments, and the establishment of colonies without regard to the wishes of the colonial peoples—practices that Wilson believed likely to lead toward war. He declared for "self-determination of nations"—the right of all peoples to choose the governments under which they would live. Specifically he mentioned the right to self-determination for the Poles and for the subject peoples of the Habsburgs and of the Ottoman Turks. He required the restoration of Belgium and the return to France of Alsace-Lorraine. Lastly he spoke of a league of nations to secure "political independence and territorial integrity to great and small states alike."

Although the other Allied governments accepted President Wilson's program in a general way and with some modifications, and although they subscribed to the use of the Fourteen Points as a basis for the armistice, they were neither willing nor able to put the president's program fully into practice. They were bound in part by the secret promises written into their wartime treaties with each other. They were also restrained by the attitudes of their own peoples. Wartime propaganda of all Allied governments had taught their peoples that the Central Powers had plotted the war and were responsible for the terrible loss of life and the misery of the war years. To the man on the street in every Allied country, it seemed clear that the Germans should be punished and should be forced to pay the whole cost of the war. Assuring their people that Germany would be treated with severity, the governments of Britain and France had won added popular support just before the peace conference. In the United States, on the contrary, the November elections for Congress had given the Republican party a slight majority in both houses, so that Democratic President Wilson could no longer claim to speak so firmly as before in the name of the whole American people.

The peace conference was held in Paris. President Wilson attended in person, believing that only his presence could assure a just and stable peace. The peoples of Europe, quite unaware of his difficult situation in Congress, gave him a hero's welcome that further persuaded him that his program was the hope of ordinary people everywhere. The other dominating figures of the conference were the British prime minister, David Lloyd George, and the French premier, Georges Clemenceau. There were representatives of all the Allied powers, great and small (except Russia, which was already at peace with Germany). Each delegation included large numbers of advisers and experts. The defeated powers were not represented. The fundamental decisions were made by a Council of Ten (consisting of two members each from Britain, France, the United States, Italy, and Japan) or, more often, by Lloyd George, Clemenceau, Wilson, and sometimes the Italian premier, Orlando, meeting privately.

⌒ THE TERMS OF PEACE

There were in all five treaties of peace: the Treaty of Versailles of 1919 with Germany, and later treaties with Austria, Bulgaria, Hungary, and the Ottoman Empire, the last finally concluded in August, 1920.

THE TREATY OF VERSAILLES WITH GERMANY, JUNE, 1919

In the discussions among Wilson, Lloyd George, and Clemenceau, each statesman had a special concern. Wilson was committed to the Fourteen Points, but he was willing to compromise some of them in order to have the Covenant (charter) of the League of Nations included in the treaty. Clemenceau's concern was for the security of France in relation to the more populous Germany. Lloyd George felt bound by his promise to see that the British people were paid for the damage done them by the Germans in the war. The terms of the Peace of Versailles grew out of a series of compromises among the three statesmen.

Germany was deprived of important territory. (See map, page 400.) Alsace-Lorraine was returned to France. A strip of land (the "Polish Corridor") between East Prussia and the rest of Germany was given as a lane to the sea to the newly re-established Poland. The Baltic harbor of the Corridor area, the ancient German city of Danzig, was made a free city under the control of the League of Nations. By plebiscites held later, a rich industrial area of Upper Silesia went to Poland, and part of Schleswig to Denmark. The important coal-producing region of the Saar Valley was given to France for fifteen years in compensation for French mines destroyed by the Germans, and was then to decide for itself whether to be French or German. All Germany's colonies were surrendered and put under the jurisdiction of the League of Nations, to be variously administered as "mandates" (supervised areas) by Japan, France, Britain, or British dominions.

The financial parts of the treaty proved more difficult to agree upon than those relating to territories. The idealism characteristic of so much popular thinking of the time made it seem impossible to require the usual "indemnity"—an outright cash payment—from a defeated power; but it was thought just to demand that the Germans make "reparations" for the damage done to civilians in the Allied countries. Since the Allied leaders could not hit upon any sum that would satisfy their own peoples and still be possible to collect from the Germans, they abandoned for the time being the effort to set the exact amount of reparations. They immediately collected certain payments in materials from the Germans and added to the treaty a statement of the fundamental obligation of the Germans to pay. In the words of the treaty, "The Allied and Associated Governments affirm and Germany accepts the responsibility of Germany and her allies for causing all the loss and damage to which [they] and their nationals have been subjected as a consequence of the war imposed upon them by the aggression of Germany and her allies." This portion of the treaty later came to be known as the "War Guilt Clause."

To protect the world and especially France from future German aggression, the Germans were required to surrender their fleet. They had to promise for the future that they would not manufacture military aircraft or tanks, maintain a large army with short-term enlistments, or include submarines or large ships in their navy. The part of Germany west of the Rhine and a thirty-mile zone to the east of the river were to be free of fortifications or troops. Allied troops were to occupy this "demilitarized" zone until all terms of the treaty had been fulfilled.

The treaty of Versailles was submitted to the Germans for their comment, but their objections to its stern provisions did not result in important changes. They had no choice but to accept it largely as it had been originally written. The document was signed in the Hall of Mirrors of the Palace of Versailles, the same room in which the German Empire had been proclaimed after the defeat of France in 1871. (See page 195.)

THE TREATMENT OF EASTERN EUROPE

Much of the settlement of easten Europe was merely a recognition of already existing circumstances. The newly established countries of Finland, Estonia, Latvia, Lithuania, Poland, and the Ukraine, under German influence by the treaty of Brest-Litovsk, were recognized as independent. Although Russia soon recovered the Ukraine, the other countries remained independent in the two decades following the First World War. With the collapse of the Habsburg monarchy in late 1918, other new governments were established in Hungary, Czechoslovakia (Bohemia, Moravia, and Slovakia, the former northern Slavic subjects of the Habsburgs), and Yugoslavia (a combination of Serbia, Bosnia-Herzegovina, Montenegro, and the South Slav subjects of the Habsburgs). These new governments were recognized by the Allied treaty arrangements. Austria itself was reduced to a part of the strictly German lands of the Habsburgs. It became a republic, and was forbidden to join with Germany. Part of the German-speaking Austrian territory was given to Italy. Romania almost doubled its former size by securing large areas from both Hungary and Russia. The Covenant of the League of Nations was included in all these peace treaties.

TREATMENT OF THE MIDDLE EAST

As for the Ottoman Empire, Constantinople and the Straits were to be put under international control; Asia Minor was to be divided into spheres of influence for the Allies; Syria and Lebanon were to be French mandates; and Palestine, Mesopotamia, and Transjordan would be mandates of Britain. The Arab state of Hejaz was to be independent. A British wartime promise to the Jewish people for the creation of a national home for Jews in Palestine was not recognized in the treaties, but remained a problem for the future.

◠ ◠ ◠

The peace settlement of 1919-1920, built out of idealism, wartime bitterness, careful studies made by hundreds of well-trained experts, compromises among innumerable hopes, needs, and possibilities, was to be the basis for the postwar world. Only the future could show whether the treaties were wise or unwise or whether all the expenditure of blood and wealth between 1914 and 1918 had helped to create a better world. Only after the passing of years could the world know whether Wilson's ringing words had been prophetic—whether the First World War had been "a war to end wars" and whether "the world had been made safe for democracy." Immediately, however, the United States Senate put one stumbling block in the way of the world's hopes by refusing to ratify the Peace of Versailles on the grounds that the Covenant of the League of Nations, included within the treaty, was dangerous to the United States.

Persons, Places, and Terms

Woodrow Wilson	Latvia	freedom of the seas
David Lloyd George	Lithuania	convoy
Georges Clemenceau	Czechoslovakia	armistice
	Yugoslavia	Weimar Republic
Lorraine	Lebanon	Fourteen Points
Marne River	Transjordan	self-determination
Verdun	Hejaz	Treaty of Versailles
Gallipoli		Covenant of the
Polish Corridor	First World War	League of Nations
Danzig	Central Powers	mandate
Upper Silesia	the Allies	indemnity
Saar Valley	contraband	reparations
Estonia	*Lusitania*	War Guilt Clause

To Master the Text

1. To what extent is the name "First World War" suitable?
2. Why was the war in western Europe fought in trenches? Describe that kind of warfare and explain why it was not easy for either side to defeat the other.
3. Discuss the course of the fighting in eastern Europe to 1917.
4. List the countries that voluntarily joined either side or were conquered. Were the Allies or the Central Powers more successful in their efforts to bring other countries into the war?
5. Which side controlled the seas? With what advantage to themselves? Why did the Germans use submarines? Why were neutral peoples so shocked by that policy? Why did the Germans give up submarine warfare in 1916? Why did they resume it in 1917?
6. What events made 1917 a turning point in the war? When and why did the Germans accept an armistice?
7. What is meant by "total war"? How did this war affect the daily lives and work of people in the warring countries? How did it increase government control over individuals?
8. What were the details of the peace program in President Wilson's Fourteen Points? What indication did Wilson have in November, 1918,

that his ideas were not overwhelmingly popular with the American people? Why did he attend the peace conference?

9. What provisions of the Treaty of Versailles were intended to reduce German ability to wage war? What territories were lost by Russia at the end of the war? What happened to the Austro-Hungarian empire? The Ottoman Empire?

To Master the Map

1. On five outline maps of Europe, show the battle fronts of December 1 of each of the years 1914-1917 and of November 11, 1918.
2. Compare the map on page 400 with the one on page 74. What are the most important differences? Which are directly traceable to the First World War? Which to other, earlier developments?

To Interpret the Facts

1. What seems to you to have been the principal reasons for the entrance into the war of Japan? The Ottoman Empire? Italy? The United States? To what extent was the course of the war altered by the addition of each of these countries?
2. Two of the most important policies of Germany in the war were the invasion of France through Belgium and the use of submarines. To what extent does the history of the war indicate that these policies might have succeeded? Why did each fail in the end?
3. To what extent did the settlement of 1919 match President Wilson's dream of a world "safe for democracy"?
4. What other forces beside Wilson's idealism account for the nature of the peace? What was the influence of each?

To Put This Chapter into a Larger Setting

1. Compare the German effort to defeat Great Britain by means of submarines with the effort of Napoleon I to achieve the same result by means of the Continental System. Consider the necessity for each policy, the degree of success it achieved, and the effect on neutral nations. How was each policy suited to the conditions of the time?
2. In what ways and by what events had the collapse of the Austro-Hungarian and Ottoman Empires been foreshadowed before 1914?
3. With two other students hold a peace-conference meeting among Wilson, Clemenceau, and Lloyd George to discuss two or three issues before the conference.
4. Make a series of cartoons supposed to be published in German newspapers in the four successive years of the war and showing the changing German attitude toward the enemies of Germany.

27

The
Establishment
of the
Soviet Union

1917-1939

In the Europe of 1919, no new feature was more important than the Communist government that had been established in Russia two years earlier. From that day to this the existence of a Communist state in eastern Europe and northern Asia has been of greatest importance to the whole world.

THE REVOLUTIONS OF 1917

In Russia, 1917 was a year of revolutions, for the country had three successive governments. When the year began, Tsar Nicholas II was still on his throne; but repeated defeats on the battlefields, where the First World War was still in progress, and serious unrest at home gave solemn warning that the ruling Romanov house was in danger.

THE BACKGROUND OF RUSSIA'S DIFFICULTIES

Unrest in Russia was caused partly by increasing shortage of land. As peasant inheritances were subdivided generation after generation, individual holdings became smaller and smaller. In part, unrest came from the rapidity of recent industrialization. There had been no leadership capable of bringing about needed changes in the lives of peasants and workers.

The war brought Russian difficulties to a head and prepared the way for revolution. It made apparent the inefficiency of the military leaders and the backwardness of Russian industry and transportation. Although Russian troops fought with magnificent courage, they could not overcome woeful shortages of guns and ammunition. Sometimes reserve troops had no rifles until they could take them from their wounded or dead comrades in the front lines. Russian generals were so little abreast of the changes in warfare that they thought of themselves as fighting the kind of war that had defeated Napoleon. The many Russian defeats gradually wore down the morale of the army, until the soldiers were in a mood to support revolution. Civilian morale was undermined by food shortages, caused by drafting peasants into the armies and by lack of transportation that might have brought available stocks of grain to the cities.

The weak and impractical Nicholas II could not cope with these problems. He was much influenced by his wife, who was fanatically determined to preserve the autocratic government at all costs. She in turn was altogether under the influence of Grigori Rasputin, a Siberian "holy man," ignorant and evil, who put her in his power by seeming to improve the health of her diseased only son. In 1915, when the tsar went in person to take command of the troops, the empress and Rasputin ran the government. Able ministers were dismissed or resigned because they could not work with Rasputin. Things reached such a pass by the end of 1916 that a group of the highest nobles assassinated Rasputin. But faith in the tsar's government could not be re-established.

MODERATE REVOLUTION, MARCH TO NOVEMBER, 1917

In March, 1917, revolution finally occurred in Russia without any real plan or leadership. In Petrograd (as St. Petersburg was called after 1914) bread lines had lengthened, and most of the workers in the factories were on strike, demanding food. Nicholas took no action except to order the Duma to go home and to command the city garrison to fire on the strikers if they would not return to work. But the Duma set up a committee to remain in session. The soldiers joined with the workers to establish a "Soviet (council) of Workers' and Soldiers' Deputies" similar to the soviet of 1905. (See page 265.) It was to these two groups that the ordinary people looked for leadership. The Soviet, with its workers and soldier representatives, patrolled the streets, gave food to soldiers who joined the revolutionary movement, and looked after other practical matters. The committee of the Duma sought to provide some sort of machinery of government.

Finally Nicholas was made to realize that he must abdicate. On March 15 he gave up his throne, and a provisional government was set up.

Partly because it was set up under such difficult circumstances, the provisional government was weak from the start. Its best-known member, Alexander Kerenski, was a Social Revolutionary. Its policy was the orderly development of a western-type government offering civil liberties and voting rights to the people. But the peasants and town workers were not interested in liberal reforms; they sought peace, worker participation in the control of the factories, and all the land for the peasants. They listened with ever increasing sympathy to the socialist arguments of the Petrograd Soviet. Other soviets were established in industrial cities, keeping in close touch with the Petrograd Soviet. Although the government gradually grew more liberal, it was never able to win wide popular support.

Events helped prepare the downfall of the Kerenski regime. In April, 1917, German officials aided Lenin, leader of the Bolsheviks (see page 263), to return to Russia from exile in Switzerland. He agitated for socialism, as the Germans had expected. The government alternately attacked the Bolsheviks and called on them for aid. Meantime there was trouble between Kerenski and the chief of the Russian army.

THE COMMUNIST REVOLUTION, NOVEMBER, 1917

By October, 1917, the Kerenski regime, like the tsar's government it replaced, had simply lost control of the country. Any determined, well-organized revolutionary movement could have overthrown it. The Bolsheviks, who in the preceding month had gained control of the Petrograd Soviet, were now strong enough to take over.

Leading Bolsheviks included Lenin and Trotsky. Lenin with his powerful personality, his self-assurance, his clear perception of the way to success, his intolerance of opposition, and his confidence in his own interpretation of Marxism, was the undisputed chief. He was eager to seize power at once without awaiting the preliminary period of bourgeois government foreseen by Marx. His eloquent promises of "peace, bread, and land" were far more appealing to the great mass of Russians than was Kerenski's talk of civil rights and the vote. Lenin made clear that the time for action had come.

Bolshevik troops advance toward the Winter Palace in Petrograd, headquarters of Kerensky's government, November 7, 1917. The capture of the palace a few minutes later climaxed the swift, almost bloodless seizure of the Russian government by the Bolsheviks.

Trotsky was the strategist who worked out the detailed plans for the seizure of the government. Always devoted to revolutionary activity, he had been in and out of prison and exile since he was a very young man. Only a small group of devoted, trained, and experienced revolutionaries worked along with these leaders.

In Petrograd on the night of November 6-7 (October 24-25 by the Russian old-style calendar) the factory militia (called the "Red Guard") of the Soviet, and some regular army units won over by the Bolsheviks, simply seized the strong places in the city, surrounded the palaces where the Kerenski government had its headquarters, and by morning were in control of the city. On the evening of November 7, an "All-Russian Congress of the Soviets" was held, with Lenin as its acknowledged master. The Mensheviks and the more conservative of the Social Revolutionaries walked out of the meeting in protest, but the remaining members established a new government. A "Council of People's Commissars" was elected with Lenin as head and Trotsky as commissar for foreign relations. A "Central Executive Committee" was also elected, with a majority of Bolsheviks and some representatives of the more radical wings of the Social Revolutionaries. Under this leadership the Bolsheviks were able to gain control of other important Russian cities and thus within three weeks to secure a precarious hold on all Russia.

Lenin addressing troops of the Red Army, 1920. Neither the Bolshevik revolution nor the consolidation of Bolshevik power could have been brought about without his unceasing efforts. Leon Trotsky, his principal associate, is standing next to the platform.

⌒ WAR COMMUNISM, 1917-1921

The problems confronting the Bolsheviks seemed far beyond the capacities of a few men, many of whom had spent years of their lives in prison or in exile and none of whom had a following of any size in the country. But among them were truly gifted leaders. All were religiously convinced that Marxism—as they interpreted its doctrines—could establish a good life for the working people. But their personal talents and devotion were weak armor against their enemies within Russia, against the German and Austrian enemies of the First World War (still in progress), and against the developing hostility of the wartime allies of Russia. Only a combination of skill, utmost ruthlessness, and good fortune permitted the new leaders to use four years of foreign and civil war (1917-1921) to establish their authority in Russia, to expel foreign invaders, and to begin the creation of a Communist society.

WAR AT HOME AND ABROAD

In March, 1918, Russia withdrew from the First World War by accepting from Germany the stern Treaty of Brest-Litovsk. (See page 375). The revolutionary Russian governments had already acknowledged the independence of Poland, Finland, Lithuania, Latvia, and Estonia. They had now to give up the Ukraine and to cede areas in the Caucasus region to Turkey. Although the Marxists believed that widespread Communist revolutions would soon alter the whole international situation, this loss of 62,000,000 Russian subjects was bitter medicine to have to swallow. Petrograd was now so uncomfortably near the border that the capital was transferred to Moscow.

But the peace of Brest-Litovsk did not free Russia from European war, for the recent allies now became enemies of a sort. Britain, France, Japan, and the United States sent troops into Russia, hoping to prevent the supplies they had delivered to Russia at such cost from falling into the hands of the Germans. These "Interventionist" armies were not withdrawn from Russia until many months after their governments had made peace with Germany. They occupied areas along all the borders of Russia, especially in the Ukraine, southern Russia, and eastern Siberia.

There were also Russian armies opposing the Bolsheviks, called "White" armies because they opposed the "Red" Communists. The White armies found plenty of support within Russia. Indeed, the vast majority of Russians were unsympathetic to the Bolsheviks, if not bitterly opposed to them. Among active opponents were the non-Russian nationalities, the aristocracy, most army officers, the Orthodox clergy, factory owners, landlords, and such non-Bolshevik revolutionaries as the more conservative members of the Social Revolutionary party. Thus the Bolsheviks were soon confronted by full-scale civil war.

Leon Trotsky organized the Red Army and pressed it on to victory. He assembled a force that eventually numbered 3,000,000 men, including almost 50,000 former tsarist army officers. Like the French revolutionary armies of 1793, units of the Bolshevik forces were accompanied by political officials whose duty it was to make sure of the loyalty of the army officers and to give training in revolutionary theory to the rank and file of the men. The zeal of the officers was encouraged by the knowledge that defeat in battle might result in punishment by death. Trotsky himself "appeared on every front, hectoring, bullying, inspiring men who only months before thought they had thrown away their rifles for the last time. But they fought and fought well, and with their successes came a pride and *élan* that the Whites could not match."* By 1921 the White armies had been destroyed.

* Gordon A. Craig, *Europe since 1815* (New York: Holt, Rinehart, & Winston, 1961). P. 566.

The old leaders of Russian society—nobles, professional men and businessmen, clergy, and even non-Bolshevik radicals—now realized that there was no place for them in the new Russia. Many, including the tsar and his immediate family, were put to death during the civil wars. A million more fled abroad, almost half of them to France and others in large numbers to the Balkan states, Germany, Poland, and China. Thus almost all persons who had occupied stations in Russia above peasants or workers were sacrificed to the Bolshevik revolution—a terrible price for any society to pay.

REMAKING RUSSIAN SOCIETY

The Bolsheviks had no hope of setting up a truly Communist society during the civil wars, but they made a number of changes in order to weaken their enemies or to win the support of one or another class of people. They did away with any institution they could not control. They disbanded a constitutional convention called by Kerenski, for it lacked a Bolshevik majority; they abolished the zemstvos, centers of liberal agitation; and they destroyed the decaying tsarist army. They carried on an antireligious campaign, recognizing only civil marriage, taking education out of the hands of the church, and completely separating church and state. On the other hand, to retain the support of their Marxist followers, they permitted workers' committees to supervise factories. Although Communism opposed all private ownership of land, they permitted peasants to seize the land of large estates, hoping thus to gain peasant support. They abolished all class privileges. They wrote a new constitution providing for an "All-Russian Congress of Soviets" growing out of local worker-peasant soviets, but leaving the real power with the revolutionary leaders. To indicate their devotion to Marxist doctrines, they began to use the name "Communist" for their party.

∿ ECONOMIC PLANS, 1921-1939

With the civil wars over, the Communists were able to pay greater attention to the condition of the country. Although they had won the civil wars and had managed to maintain themselves in power, they could not yet count on the loyalty of the Russian people. Each stage of Communist reorganization offended some new group. They had to rely on the ruthless activity of their secret police, believed by 1922 to have put to death about 50,000 persons. But the great difficulty that dwarfed all others was economic. By 1921 a major famine and a cholera epidemic were in progress, in the end causing the death of some four or five million people. This pitiable situation was in part the result of the civil wars and of a drought in 1920 in the grain-growing basins of the Don and Volga Rivers. In considerable part, however, it had been brought about by Communist economic policies.

In several areas the efforts to organize economic life according to Marxist principles produced disastrous results. The factories, each somewhat under the control of its soviet of workers, and with some disorganized supervision from the government, were turning out only about one fifth as many goods as in 1913. Trade within Russia and with foreign countries was virtually at a standstill. On the farms peasants refused to produce more than enough to feed themselves; for government agents simply seized any surplus, since private buying and selling had been declared illegal. Agricultural production fell to half what it had been in 1913.

THE NEW ECONOMIC POLICY, 1921-1927

At this point one of Lenin's special qualities as a leader asserted itself. Although he was a person of deep conviction, he was flexible enough in his thinking to be willing to adopt new means of reaching his goals. He now determined to permit some slowing down of the drive toward Communism. In 1921 he introduced his "New Economic Policy," or "N.E.P." Although the government retained control of what he called the "commanding heights" of economic life—large factories, the systems of transportation, banking, and foreign trade—it permitted small businesses to be privately owned and allowed the peasants to buy and sell land, to sell surplus crops, and to hire labor. Foreign as well as Russian engineers and scientists were hired at good salaries. Meantime terrorism was lessened and greater freedom of writing and speaking was permitted. Russian economic life recovered, although by the end of 1927 it had only reached the levels of 1913.

In 1922 Lenin suffered the first of a series of strokes, and in 1924 he died. A struggle for leadership ensued between Trotsky and Joseph Stalin. Trotsky was already well known because of his contributions to the Revolution of 1917 and to the victory in the civil wars. He was a profound believer in the Marxist doctrine that Communist revolution, to succeed, must be world-wide. Stalin had been a relatively unimportant Bolshevik, but because he had been responsible for the details of party organization, he had been able to put his supporters in key party positions. He did not share Trotsky's international outlook, but wanted instead to develop what he called "socialism in one country"—that is, in Russia. He used his power in the party to defeat Trotsky and, after five years, to expel him from the country. By 1928 Stalin dominated Russia. He became a thorough dictator, monopolizing the power of government as few men have been able to do in any time or place.

THE FIVE-YEAR PLANS

In 1928 Stalin instituted the first "Five-Year Plan." This was the most important step since the Communist Revolution of 1917; in fact, it amounted to a second revolution. The plan was a design for the whole economic life of the country, which was to be altogether subordinated to the control of the state as a step in the direction of complete Marxian Communism. The plan had been developed over a two-year period. In a thousand pages it took into account every aspect of Russian economic life. For example, it specified how much steel should be produced in a particular plant, how much power the plant would require, and what forms of transportation would be used. Specific goals were established for industry, transportation, power, and agriculture.

A number of reasons are thought to explain Stalin's adoption of the plan. His tight control of Russia made such a step possible. Like any other dictator, he felt the need to strengthen his hold on those elements in the country least loyal to his rule—in Russia, the peasants. Because he feared foreign enemies as well as those that might appear at home, he wanted to build a military machine that only heavy industry (coal, iron, oil, electricity) could produce, and to this end he had to force the Russian people to do without manufactured consumer goods—shoes, washing machines, furniture. Finally, he began to sense that the richer peasants and the small businessmen were developing what the Communists called a "bourgeois attitude," well suited to capitalism but not to Communism.

In industry the plan, and two subsequent Five-Year Plans put into operation before 1939, had marked effect. Although not all the goals were reached, mines were opened, great cities built, and production of steel, electricity, cement, coal, and oil increased several times. For the first time, Russia became an industrialized country. Fearing that the concentration of industry in the Donets Basin was too dangerous in wartime, the government opened a whole new industrial area in the Ural Mountains region. Although the standards of living for factory workers remained low, there was enough enthusiasm among them so that the plans could be carried out without serious opposition.

In agriculture the story was different. There the purpose was to organize the many little farms of individual peasant families into fewer large "collective farms," to be cultivated co-operatively by the peasants under the direction of government managers. The government would set up machine tractor stations, from which the collectives could rent farm machinery. In consequence fewer farm hands would be needed, and surplus population could be moved to the cities to supply labor for the factories.

The peasants bitterly opposed this program. The more prosperous peasants ("kulaks") refused to surrender their lands, and often they burned their crops and killed their animals rather than give them to the government. For its part, the government showed no mercy. It sent the secret police and troops into the villages to burn houses, shoot into crowds of angry peasants, and send thousands of people to Siberia. By 1933 only half as many houses remained standing in Russian lands as there had been in 1928. Livestock was also reduced by half. In the years 1932 and 1933 large areas suffered famines and millions of people died.

In the end all but an insignificant part of the farm land was collectivized. With the smaller number of units to watch, the government was able to secure surplus grain to feed city populations and for export. But the collectives, not the government, owned the land. Individual peasants still owned their own houses, garden plots, and a few animals. Agriculture did not become as productive as expected, but there was some improvement in return for the terrible human misery and loss of life that collectivization had caused.

⌒   COMMUNIST SOCIETY IN RUSSIA

By 1939 Russian society had taken on the characteristics that today most sharply differentiate it from the western world. It was deeply influenced by the theories of Karl Marx, but it was far from being the communist society Marx had envisioned. It was in accordance with Marxian theory that the Communists had put an end to private ownership of "the means of production" (factories, transportation facilities, banks, and the like) and had collectivized the farms. But Marx had expected the communist revolution to occur in an already industrialized country, whereas, before 1917, Russia was relatively little industrialized. But thereafter an astonishingly rapid growth of heavy industry took place. Although in 1939 more than half the people still lived on the land, Russian mines and factories could produce all that was needed to equip the army for modern warfare. Marx had expected the revolution to occur in several well-defined stages. First the workers would take over industry and establish a "dictatorship of the proletariat." Gradually all persons would become workers or would leave the country. After that would come true communism, with every citizen working to his full capacity for the common good. In such a society no government would be needed, and the state could wither away. But by 1939 the Russian state was more powerful than any government previously known in modern times. It was the first of the modern "totalitarian" states; that is, there were no limits to its interference in the work, the lives, and the very thoughts of its citizens. Soviet Russia was not yet the communist state of Marx's dream.

THE GOVERNMENT OF THE
UNION OF SOVIET SOCIALIST REPUBLICS

Communist Russia adopted the name "Union of Soviet Socialist Republics" (often shortened to "U.S.S.R." or "Soviet Union") to indicate that it comprised a number of republics (eleven in 1939, including the Ukraine, recovered in 1923). Of these the Russian Socialist Federated Soviet Republic was the largest and the dominant one. Although there were separate governments in each republic, the Soviet Union as a whole controlled all foreign and many domestic affairs.

In 1939 the government of the Soviet Union was based on Stalin's constitution of 1936, an outgrowth of the two earlier constitutions of 1918 and 1924. But even more than other governments, the Soviet government must be understood not through its written law but through its actual practices. In Soviet Russia it was the Communist party that dominated the state, and in the 1930's it was Stalin who ruled the party.

In the 1930's Lenin's principle was still accepted, that in a revolutionary party, leadership should be in the hands of a small, trained, dedicated group with autocratic power. (See page 263.) Under Stalin, party policy—the "party line," as it was called—was determined by a small central organ of the party, the "Politburo" (Political Bureau). The administrative branch of the party, the "Secretariat," decided to what positions in party or government specific party members or others friendly to the party might be appointed. The powers of these two bodies were theoretically derived from

Joseph Stalin as he looked in the 1920's, when he was eliminating his rivals for control of the Soviet Union.

a general party congress of elected members. Actually, however, the Politburo and the Secretariat controlled the party congress. More important, they also controlled the hundreds of thousands of party "cells" (groups) throughout the U.S.S.R., and these cells in turn controlled the government at the local level. Of this party structure, Stalin became the undisputed master. As secretary general he controlled the Secretariat, and he was the most influential member of the Politburo. His decisions became party policy.

Stalin's program was put into effect not only through the party organization but also through the official organs of government established under the Constitution of 1936. The constitution provided for a two-house "Supreme Soviet" (parliament), consisting of a "Soviet of the Union," with a representative for each 300,000 persons in the Soviet Union, and a "Soviet of the Nationalities," with representatives from each republic or region of the Soviet Union. Between sessions, the business of the Supreme Soviet was in the hands of a group of its members called the "Presidium." The Supreme Soviet elected a "Council of People's Commissars" to act as a kind of cabinet.

But these official organs of government were altogether controlled by the Communist party. The party offered a single official list of candidates for office who were invariably elected; its leading members sat in the Council of People's Commissars; and its party line was the policy of the government.

Only a small percentage of the Soviet people were eligible for membership in the Communist party. Membership was secured only by a long and difficult process, usually beginning with training in one of the Communist youth organizations. Members were expelled if they did not obey orders or did not adhere strictly to the party line of the moment.

An essential feature of Communist government was the secret police. This agency had officers everywhere, it could never be combated, and its very existence spread fear among all classes of people. In the late 1930's there was a virtual reign of terror. Prominent Communist leaders were brought to trial on charges of having conspired against the government. Many of these "confessed" to treasonable actions they could not possibly have committed. Many were executed. Often lesser party members simply disappeared without trial, many of them to slave-labor camps. Army officers and factory and railway officials were also among the victims of the purge, as were many of the police officials and judges who had helped carry out this reign of terror.

Only later, after his death, did the full ruthlessness of Stalin's policy come to light. He removed his most dangerous opponents as described above. The secret police were under pressure to make as many arrests as possible. Those arrested and sent to slave-labor camps furnished workers for particularly distasteful occupations or for jobs that had to be carried on in unpleasant climates that people would otherwise avoid. These may have been some of the reasons for the purges, but that such policy could be continued for years was proof both of Stalin's unchallenged dictatorship and of his suspicious and ruthless nature.

SOCIAL CLASSES

The organization of Russian society reflected both Communist theory and the totalitarian nature of the government. In theory all Russians were workers; but not all workers were treated alike. Factory managers and directors were better paid and enjoyed better opportunities for housing, vacations, and education for their children than did ordinary workers. Government officials were also privileged. For ordinary workers there was little freedom. Town workers could not easily change employment. Peasants might be sent against their wishes to work in factories.

RELIGION, EDUCATION, AND THE ARTS

No aspect of life remained outside the control of the Communist government. The Communists were opposed to religion. They took active measures against all religious groups, especially against the Orthodox Church, many of whose buildings were turned into clubrooms, schools, or museums. Church services were held only with difficulty and on a limited scale.

Education, on the other hand, was of special interest to the Communists. By establishing free public schools they began to wipe out illiteracy. On the higher level they were especially successful with scientific and engineering education. The social sciences, history, literature, and philosophy were usually taught with a narrowly propaganda purpose.

The press was strictly censored and used for propaganda purposes. Music, painting, and the dance were influenced by the state, and composers and painters were expected to glorify the working-class state and to oppose what the Communists called the "bourgeois culture" of the West. Although music, ballet, and literary works of a high order were produced, those particular achievements often failed to win full government approval.

☊ ☊ ☊

In a short time the Communists had established themselves in power, greatly changed Russian society, and so expanded the economy of the country that the Soviet Union could take its place among the great military powers. The achievements of the Soviet regime were remarkable, but they were brought about at bitter cost to the Soviet people.

Persons, Places, and Terms

Grigori Rasputin	Red Army	Union of Soviet
Alexander Kerenski	White armies	Socialist Republics
Leon Trotsky	socialism in one	party line
Joseph Stalin	country	Politburo
	five-year plan	Secretariat
Petrograd	collective farm	party cells
Ural Mountains	kulak	Supreme Soviet
	dictatorship of the	Presidium
Treaty of	proletariat	Council of People's
Brest-Litovsk	totalitarian state	Commissars

To Master the Text

1. What conditions in pre-1914 Russia indicated that the government might have difficulty keeping order? In what ways did the war increase the dissatisfaction of the Russian people with their government? What part had Rasputin in bringing revolution nearer?

2. How did the Kerenski government come into power? What policies did it adopt? Why? What policies would the peasants and workingmen have preferred? Trace the events that led to the overthrow of the Kerenski government.

3. What personal qualities of Lenin and Trotsky explain the Bolshevik success? At what cost did the Bolsheviks withdraw Russia from the war? What opposition did they meet within Russia? Abroad?

4. What kind of army did Trotsky organize? How effective was it? What happened to opponents of the Bolsheviks? Why did the Bolsheviks immediately introduce some Communism into Russia? What specific Communist measures? How did they treat the peasants? Why?

5. By 1921 what disasters had befallen Russia? To what extent were the Bolsheviks responsible? What words and what policies do the initials "N.E.P." represent?

6. How did Stalin and Trotsky differ? Who won their conflict? How?

7. What was the First Five-year Plan? Why did Stalin adopt it? How did it affect the Russian people?

8. What was the collectivization of agriculture? How much land could the individual peasant own after collectivization? What control did he have over his own plot? How did the kulaks react to collectivization?

9. How was the Communist party organized in Russia? In what ways did Stalin control the party? What were the chief organs of government? How did the party control them? How could individuals become members of the party? Did the secret police strengthen the party?

10. What kind of social classes came to exist in the Soviet Union? Why?

11. To what extent did the Communist government seek to influence religion, education, and the arts? Why? With what success?

To Interpret the Facts

1. What hardships or suffering did the Russian people have to endure while the country was becoming Communist? Could the Bolsheviks have forced Communism on the people in any less painful way? How?

2. Was Stalin's decision to develop mining, steel manufacturing, and other heavy industry good for the world power of the Soviet Union? Was it good for the individual Russian?

To Put This Chapter into a Larger Setting

1. Support or attack the following statement: The Communist revolution and Soviet Communism under Lenin and Stalin were as closely in accord with the teachings of Marx as possible in a nonindustrialized country.

2. One reason for the dislike of Communism in the United States is the belief that any Communist regime will inevitably lead to dictatorship and loss of individual liberties. To what extent does the history of Communism in Russia furnish a basis for that belief?

28

The
Democratic
Nations
of Europe

1919-1929

Western Europe did not follow the revolutionary path that postwar Russia took. Most western leaders decried and feared Communism. They still hoped to "make the world safe for democracy." With the fall from power of the emperors of Germany and Austria-Hungary, the tsar of Russia, and the Turkish sultan, the realization of that hope seemed possible. But there were many obstacles to genuine and widespread democracy.

∩ ADJUSTMENT TO PEACE

Peace itself, so long hoped for, soon proved almost as full of problems as war. All countries suffered a period of economic readjustment. Factories had to close down to change from wartime to peacetime machinery. Commerce had to be re-established across new national boundaries. Many people were unemployed; and soldiers returning home, even those who managed to find work, sometimes adjusted with difficulty to the routine of workaday existence.

International relations were equally difficult. In the first few postwar years a number of small-scale wars took place. The Poles, for example, extended their boundary eastward by making a short war on Russia. For another example, Mustafa Kemal (later known as Kemal Atatürk), a Turkish patriot, prevented the treaty between the wartime Allies and the Ottoman Empire from coming into effect at all by leading an uprising that drove Allied forces from Anatolia. He deposed the sultan and set up a republic that included all of Anatolia, both shores of the Straits, and Thrace in Europe. The Turkish capital was moved from Constantinople (now called Istanbul) to Ankara (formerly Angora) in Anatolia. With these and other military operations in progress, it was clear that it would take a long time to re-establish the kind of stability that the world had known before 1914.

THE READMISSION OF GERMANY TO THE FAMILY OF NATIONS

The situation of a defeated, embittered Germany in the middle of Europe, bound by a treaty most Germans thought harsh and unjust, was certain to create trouble. France and Britain differed as to the proper treatment of their recent enemy. Germany was by geographical position and population stronger than France. After 1919 French policy toward Germany was naturally watchful and suspicious. Had it not been for British and American opposition at the peace conference, the French would have balanced the strength of the two countries by taking the Rhineland away from Germany. The British, for their part, saw the German people as potential purchasers of British manufactures and therefore favored a quick German economic recovery. They also regarded German revival as essential to the maintenance of their cherished "balance of power" in Europe.

The most serious problem relating to Germany concerned reparations. In 1921 the final sum was set at something like $32,000,000,000. The French, spending millions on the reconstruction of the battlefield areas, were eager to press for payment from the Germans. But such payments could be made only in gold or in French currency. By the end of the war the Germans had no gold. They could secure French francs only by selling German goods in France. French industry would soon be ruined by a flood of German imports. These economic facts were not, however, generally understood, either by French officials or by the public. Perceiving only that a revived Germany posed a danger to France, the French government pressed the Germans to meet their treaty obligations to the full.

For their part, the German people believed themselves seriously wronged by the huge reparations bill. They resented the "War Guilt Clause" of the

EUROPE
1924

TERRITORY LOST BY

Germany	
Austria-Hungary	
Russia	
Bulgaria	
Ottoman Empire	

UNITED KINGDOM OF GREAT BRITAIN AND NORTHERN IRELAND

IRISH FREE STATE

NORWAY
Oslo •

SWEDEN
• Stockholm

FINLAND
Helsinki •

Leningrad •

Russian Soviet Federated Socialist Republic

Moscow •

UNION OF SOVIET SOCIALIST REPUBLICS

Byelorussian S.S.R.

Kiev •

Ukrainian S.S.R.

Transcaucasian S.S.R.

Armenia

DENMARK
Copenhagen •

Schleswig

ESTONIA

LATVIA

LITHUANIA

DANZIG
E. Prussia (Ger.)
Polish Corridor

POLAND
Warsaw •

Bessarabia

Black Sea

Ankara •

TURKEY

Istanbul •

Aegean Sea

GREECE
Athens •

Syria (Fr.)

Lebanon (Fr.)
Palestine (Br.)
Damascus •
Trans-Jordan (Br.)
Mesopotamia (Br.)

Dublin •
London •

NETHERLANDS
Amsterdam •

Berlin •

GERMANY
Weimar •

Prague •
Bohemia
CZECHOSLOVAKIA
Moravia
Slovakia

Upper Silesia

Budapest •

HUNGARY

Vienna •
AUSTRIA

Slovenia
Croatia

Bucharest •

ROMANIA

Danube

Belgrade •
Serbia

YUGOSLAVIA

BULGARIA
Sofia •

Montenegro

ALBANIA

BELGIUM
Brussels •

LUX.
Saar
Lorraine
Alsace

Paris •
Versailles •

FRANCE

SWITZERLAND

Danube R.

Rome •

ITALY

Adriatic Sea

North Sea

Baltic Sea

ATLANTIC OCEAN

SPAIN
Madrid •

PORTUGAL

Mediterranean Sea

Algiers •
Algeria (Fr.)

Tunis •
Tunisia (Fr.)

Morocco (Fr.)
Sp. Morocco

Treaty of Versailles (see page 379), which declared that Germany alone had provoked the war. Their own wartime propaganda had put all responsibility for the war on the shoulders of the Allies. Besides, business life in Germany had been so disrupted by the loss of the Lorraine and Silesian industrial areas and of all the German colonies that the Germans believed they were quite unable to pay so huge a sum.

In 1923 the reparations question grew into a dangerous international crisis. According to French calculations, the Germans had by that time already defaulted in part of their payments. To teach the Germans a lesson and to make sure of the payments, the French government sent troops to occupy and operate the mines and factories in the rich German steel-making area of the Ruhr valley. (See map, page 184.) The German government advised passive resistance, telling German laborers not to work as long as the French remained. Finally in 1925 the French withdrew without having achieved their goal.

In Germany the Ruhr episode had dangerous consequences. Inflation (the sharp drop in value of the mark, the German currency unit) had already become a serious problem, partly as an inevitable result of war and partly because of the way in which the German government had financed the war. When peace came, the big industrialists favored further inflation so that they could pay back more cheaply the money they had borrowed during the war for the expansion of their businesses. When in 1923 the Ruhr workers stayed home at government request, the government felt obliged to pay them—but it could pay only in worthless paper currency. Thereafter inflation became uncontrollable. The mark sank to the value of a trillionth part of a dollar. The whole life savings of a well-to-do person could not purchase a postage stamp. Thus middle-class people, although still regarding themselves as having a dignified place in society, became as poor as the poorest workers. Salaried people and those living on pensions were in dire straits, for the marks once adequate for their expenses now bought practically nothing. Workers were in an equally desperate plight, for the rise in their wages did not keep pace with the falling value of the mark. Only clever or unscrupulous speculators managed to make money during the inflation.

Finally the government decided that it must bring a halt to the inflation, at no matter what cost. It called in the old marks and issued new currency that the people trusted. Although this expedient worked further hardship on many people, it resulted in a sound currency. Realizing the seriousness of the German situation, the Allies also adopted some new policies toward Germany. In 1924 and again in 1929 committees of Allied bankers worked out easier schedules for reparations payments. The American government made large loans to Germany. For a few years reparations were paid. The French and British governments used the money received from the Germans to make payments to the United States on their wartime loans. But the fundamental impossibility of keeping up such enormous international payments was not generally understood. The problems of the reparations and the war debts remained to poison international relations.

The temporary lull in the reparations controversy permitted the growth of better relations between Germany and the rest of the world. In 1926, partly through the wisdom of Gustav Stresemann, the ablest German statesman of the day, the Locarno treaties were made between Germany on the one hand and its recent enemies, Belgium and France, on the other. In these treaties all agreed not to go to war to change the boundaries between Germany and the other two countries. Britain and Italy guaranteed the agreements. Germany was then admitted to the League of Nations. In 1929 the withdrawal of the Allied armies of occupation from German soil was agreed upon. Although the French were still nervous, people the world over believed that dangerous tensions were really being relaxed and that the world could embark upon a period of peace.

Papering a wall with worthless currency in the early 1920's. Most notably in Germany but also in several other European countries, spiraling inflation so lowered the value of currency that it was actually more useful for decorating walls than for making purchases.

THE SEARCH FOR A GUARANTEE OF PEACE

Ever since August, 1914, there had been the hope that the First World War would be "the war to end all wars." The League of Nations was looked upon as the best hope of peace, but during the 1920's other means were also explored.

The League of Nations had been especially planned as an organization to help preserve peace. Its Covenant (charter) provided for an Assembly, where all the member nations were represented; a Council, in which each of the great powers was permanently represented and to which other members were elected in turn; and a Secretariat, which kept records, planned meetings, and carried on routine activities. It was expected that the Assembly would discuss difficult problems, and that whenever the peace was threatened the Council would plan action to settle the question involved. The League might discipline a nation whose policy threatened war, imposing a boycott or even organizing an armed attack by League members against the unruly nation. A World Court was organized to pass upon international disputes submitted to it. An International Labor Organization was set up to study labor conditions the world over and to suggest improvements.

These organs were quickly in order, and the League did some useful work. It supervised the activities of the powers administering as mandates the former German colonies or former parts of the Ottoman Empire. It provided plans for world-wide attacks on such evils as the international narcotics traffic. In a number of boundary disputes it played a helpful part. But the League could not force a great power to follow a policy contrary to its own selfish interests. Hence in matters most dangerous to peace, the League was powerless.

Two other much-advertised but futile steps toward peace were taken during the 1920's. In the Kellogg-Briand treaty of 1928, sponsored by the American secretary of state, Frank Kellogg, and the French premier, Aristide Briand, forty-five nations promised to "renounce war as an instrument of national policy." But a few years later, when war actually threatened, this promise proved to have no effect. Equally ineffective were efforts to reduce the armed forces of the great powers. By the treaties of 1919-1920, the World War Allies had limited the armed forces of the recent enemies, but not their own. Since it was widely believed that large armaments encouraged wars, disarmament was sought as a step toward peace. But four elaborately planned disarmament conferences had no significant results. Peace machinery in the 1930's was no more effective than it had been in 1914.

☾ THE ATTEMPT TO SPREAD DEMOCRACY

As soon as the war was over, people in the western world observed with satisfaction that democracy seemed to be spreading, just as President Wilson had promised it would. The new states springing up like mushrooms were almost all republics with constitutions paying lip service to democracy. In reality, however, it soon appeared that there was to be more dictatorship than democracy. The examples of Germany and Turkey illustrate this point.

THE WEIMAR REPUBLIC IN GERMANY

The Weimar Republic, established in Germany in 1919 (see page 376), borrowed many ideas from Britain, France, and the United States; but it also retained important characteristics of the old Germany. A president replaced the emperor. In ordinary times the powers of the president were much more limited than those of the emperor; but he had the right in emergencies to govern dictatorially by decree—and also the right to declare that the emergency existed. The two-house legislature of Bismarck's constitution remained, but with greatly extended powers for the popularly-elected *Reichstag*, to which the ministers were now to be responsible. Since certain arrangements for making Germany truly democratic had the unfortunate result of bringing into existence many small parties, none of which could hope to control the *Reichstag*, it was soon apparent that all ministries would be weak and inefficient coalitions of several parties. The establishment of a strong democracy was also held back by the fact that many of the same persons who had administered the institutions of the empire still remained at their posts. The old judiciary was largely retained. The judges generally opposed any tendencies toward liberalism and upheld conservative ideas. The new, small army had a needlessly large number of officers, many remaining from the wartime army and all full of the military pride that had marked the old Germany. Schools continued to instill in children admiration for an aristocratic and authoritarian society.

German stability could not be achieved until definite reparation policies had been adopted. During the first years after 1918 there were many revolutionary attempts in Germany, some supported by Communists and left-wing socialists, others by extreme conservatives. These died down after 1924, however, and the German people, led by Gustav Stresemann as foreign minister and helped by American loans, experienced a remarkable economic recovery. By 1929 the income of the average German was 50 per cent higher

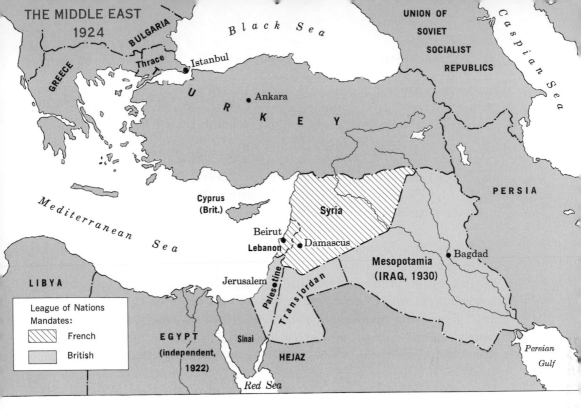

BULGARIA
GREECE
Thrace
Istanbul
Black Sea
UNION OF
SOVIET
SOCIALIST
REPUBLICS
Caspian Sea

Mediterranean Sea

T U R K E Y
Ankara

Cyprus
(Brit.)

PERSIA

Syria
Beirut
Lebanon
Damascus
Bagdad

Mesopotamia
(IRAQ, 1930)

LIBYA

Jerusalem
Palestine
Transjordan

League of Nations
Mandates:

French

British

EGYPT
(independent,
1922)

Sinai

HEJAZ

*Persian
Gulf*

Red Sea

---

than it had been in 1913. Yet there were indications that masses of the German people did not fully trust the new republic. In 1927 they elected as president an aged war hero, Field Marshal Paul von Hindenburg, an extreme conservative with no political skill. Extreme radicals and extreme conservatives played increasingly conspicuous parts in political life.

In 1929 Stresemann died. In the same year a world-wide depression began with the catastrophic collapse of the New York stock market. (Chapter 29.) A moderate chancellor, Heinrich Brüning, labored to preserve the German republic, but in vain. A parliamentary majority failed him as the depression reached Germany, and henceforth he had to depend on "decree government" through the president. This, too, eventually failed him. In 1932 Hindenburg dismissed him and early the next year appointed Adolf Hitler, who immediately set out to destroy German democracy.

THE TURKISH REPUBLIC

Another example of a republic unable to become truly democratic was Turkey. The constitution of the Turkish republic, patterned after those of the western democracies, provided for a parliament elected by all citizens, including women. Much of the real authority of the state was, however, in the hands of Mustafa Kemal, who until his death in 1938 was a benevolent dictator. Kemal had two especially important objectives: to secularize Turkey and to westernize it. He abolished much that was Islamic. For example, he made Sunday instead of Friday the weekly day of rest; he obliged men to replace the fez by the hat and women to come out of the harem; and, most important, replaced the Islamic law of the Koran, previously employed in Turkey as in all Islamic countries, by a new code borrowed from the laws of western nations. To modernize his country he enforced the use of the simpler Latin alphabet in place of the more complicated Arabic and thus made it easier to abolish illiteracy. In the economic sphere he inaugurated many public works: dams, railroads, power plants, irrigation systems. His achievements were truly remarkable, and the advance of his country was both rapid and sound. But even a man of his vigor could not make functioning democratic citizens out of the inexperienced and, at first, largely illiterate Turkish people. Turkey was a developing but not really a democratic state.

ATTEMPTED DEMOCRACY IN EAST-CENTRAL EUROPE

In east-central Europe there were the new republics of Finland, Estonia, Latvia, Lithuania, Poland, Czechoslovakia, and Austria. Their constitutions contained democratic provisions; and in Finland, Czechoslovakia, and Austria, democracy was actually practiced. But in the other new republics and in the older monarchies of east-central Europe, poverty and illiteracy led to the establishment of various kinds of dictatorial and authoritarian regimes. Hungary, for example, claimed still to be ruled by the Habsburgs; but since the new governments of the lands freed from Austria-Hungary would not permit the return of a Habsburg ruler, Hungary had a dictatorial "regent." Until the 1930's these governments battled with the nearly insoluble problems of this region: the need to take land from the great estates and give it to the peasants; the dissatisfactions of national minorities living in most of these countries; the obstruction of trade by the tariffs surrounding the many new countries; the need to readjust the railroads, originally built to center on the capitals of the old Russia or Austria-Hungary and now running in the wrong directions. Before democracy could have any real meaning in these countries, such difficulties had to be alleviated, poverty had to be lessened, and education had to become more widely available. The depression of the 1930's prevented progress toward those goals.

⌒ FRANCE IN THE 1920'S

Although France, where so much fighting had taken place, was severely injured by the war, French recovery was rapid and impressive. In many ways France seemed to grow in strength in the 1920's. It remained a democratic country, although the weaknesses of its political life, such as the too numerous parties and the too frequent change of ministries, still persisted.

FRENCH ECONOMIC RECOVERY

French economic recovery began with the removal of the debris of the battlefields. In a single *département*, 800,000 houses and farm buildings had to be rebuilt, canals and railroads had to be repaired, and millions of acres of farm land had to be restored to cultivation.

The need to clear away and restore great areas had an unexpected advantage, for it helped France compete successfully with the more recently industrialized countries. Since the heaviest World War fighting had been in the parts of France with the most concentrated industry, many important factories had to be entirely rebuilt. Of course the most up-to-date machines and processes were employed. Since the Treaty of Versailles had restored to France the rich iron fields of Lorraine and lent it the Saar coal mines for at least fifteen years (see pages 378-379), France was able to build modern steel mills. The textile industry also flourished, as did other specialties of France like wines and perfumes. In France, agriculture and industry continued to be better balanced than in Britain or Germany. The French economy was strong and sound. France, like Germany, experienced inflation, and for a time the government faced the possibility of bankruptcy. But in 1926 a ministry of the more conservative parties adopted a strong policy, increasing taxes, raising the value of the franc, and bringing about economies in government. Although this policy was hard on the middle class, which lost about four fifths of its savings, it gave France a financially stable government and a basis for general prosperity that lasted throughout the 1920's.

CHANGES IN THE FRENCH EMPIRE

The fact that many colonial troops had fought for France during the war gave a new value in French eyes to the whole empire. A particular effort was made in North Africa to draw the colonies close to the mother country. Ten representatives were sent to the French Chamber of Deputies from the three Algerian *départements;* Algerians were given French citizenship and were allowed to share in their local government. At this time, both Algeria and Tunisia were prosperous and satisfied.

There were, to be sure, colonial disturbances and unrest both in Morocco and in Indochina. In the new French mandate of Syria, where Arab nationalism was strong, there was armed rebellion. Although these troubles were overcome, they were costly, and they indicated dangerous colonial unrest.

◌ GREAT BRITAIN IN THE 1920'S

Victorious Britain experienced many unexpected economic troubles after the war as well as difficulties with its expanded empire. British political life was made more difficult by the failure of various social and economic groups to understand each other's problems or to perceive that new conditions required new policies. But Britain remained staunchly democratic.

ECONOMIC CONDITIONS

On the surface Britain appeared to emerge from the war in a strengthened position. It had an enlarged empire, little war damage to repair, and advantages resulting from the collapse of some of its most energetic commercial rivals. Yet Britain's postwar economic situation proved difficult. During the war years the Americans had taken over many British markets, and the British dominions had learned to make many items that they previously had purchased from Britain. The economic consequences of the peace further injured British business. The ships of the German merchant marine, which Britain had confiscated at the end of the war, made it unnecessary to build new ships in Britain, and two thirds of the British shipbuilders were put out of work. When the French received coal as reparations payment from Germany, they sold it to Britain's old customers, Italy and the Scandinavian countries. Finally, during the war British investors had been forced to sell their overseas stocks and bonds, with the result that the interest payments and dividends no longer enriched Britain. In fact, Britain was no longer a creditor country. New York had become the financial capital of the world, and the Americans were clamoring for the war debt owed them by Britain.

British industrial troubles were, however, older than the war. British machinery was out of date, and the many relatively small British factories and mines could not produce as cheaply as could the great consolidated industries of Germany and the United States. British businessmen were slow to acknowledge these facts. Instead of reorganizing and modernizing their businesses, they looked to the government for subsidies and tried to keep their prices low enough to compete with foreign industry by cutting costs —including wages.

One result of these policies of government and business was the general strike of 1926. The first step was a dispute over wages between miners and mine owners that led to a miner's strike. In sympathy, workers in transportation, metals, chemicals, power, and the building trades also went on strike, until about a sixth of all the working population was idle. The strike was not a success. Many people believed that it had been wrong for the workers to take so drastic an action instead of co-operating with government agencies and Parliament to find a solution to their difficulties. Volunteers kept milk and food deliveries going and operated trains, buses, and the communications systems. In a week the general strike collapsed, although it took longer to settle the coal dispute. The workers learned that in Britain less drastic methods produced more certain results. But industrialists had not learned what they needed to know; British business did not receive a thorough reform.

THE INDEPENDENCE OF IRELAND

The centuries-old problem of English-Irish relations became more difficult during the war. An extremist Irish organization called *Sinn Fein* ("Ourselves Alone") led a violent revolt at Easter time 1916. Although the revolt was suppressed, two years later *Sinn Fein* set up a separate Irish parliament and declared all Ireland an independent republic. When the British government refused to accept the republic, civil war broke out in Ireland. Lloyd George, the prime minister at the time, suggested dividing the Irish island and giving separate parliaments to the larger Catholic southern section and the Protestant northern area of Ulster. In 1921 this solution was finally accepted in both Britain and Ireland, and the southern area became the "Irish Free State." It had a president and parliament of its own; but it still gave allegiance to the king, and it permitted the British navy to use its harbors. Ulster voted to remain with Britain. This arrangement lasted until 1937, when the Irish Free State became the Irish Republic, entirely independent of Britain. Officially it adopted the ancient Irish name "Eire." The six northern counties of Ulster continued outside Eire, attached as a self-governing dominion to Great Britain.

Such was the end of the last important phase of the struggle between England and Ireland. Begun with an English invasion of Ireland in the twelfth century, the conflict was finally brought to a practical solution in the twentieth century with the restored full independence of the greater part of the Irish island.

CHANGES IN THE BRITISH EMPIRE

In many parts of the British Empire there was unrest in the postwar years. In 1922 Egypt was declared independent, although the British kept the right to maintain troops to protect the Suez Canal. In 1930 the British mandate of Mesopotamia was also granted independence as the kingdom of Iraq, and Transjordan received some self-government. Palestine proved an extremely difficult mandate to control because of the hostility between the Arabs and the Jews, who settled in Palestine in increasing numbers in the 1920's and 1930's. In India also there was unrest, for the leaders of the Indian people wanted to move more rapidly toward self-government than the British were willing to permit.

The most significant imperial change was the official recognition of complete equality between Great Britain and the dominions. By the Statute of Westminster of 1931, Britain recognized that the dominions were perfectly free to manage their foreign affairs as well as their domestic concerns; that they were "freely associated as members of the British Commonwealth of Nations"; and therefore they could freely leave the Commonwealth if they wished.

Some of these changes in the empire were steps toward democracy. Within Britain they were matched by one significant change, giving the right to vote to women. But by 1929 it was obvious that British democracy might have a rough road to travel unless economic problems were lessened in the empire at large.

ᴑ ᴑ ᴑ

Any honest observer of the world in 1929 would have been forced to admit that although Britain, the British dominions, France, and a number of the smaller countries of western Europe remained democratic, the hope for the spread of democracy had not been fulfilled. In the other parts of the world, the record was much the same.

Persons, Places, and Terms

Mustafa Kemal	Anatolia	franc
Atatürk	Istanbul	mark
Frank Kellogg	Ankara	Locarno treaties
Aristicle Briand	Ruhr Valley	Kellogg-Briand
Gustav Stresemann	Saar Valley	Treaty
Paul von Hindenburg	Ulster	creditor country
Adolf Hitler	Irish Free State	Sinn Fein
	(Eire)	Statute of
	Iraq	Westminster

To Master the Text

1. What conditions of 1919 made it seem possible that the world was really "safe for democracy"? What conditions just after the war made it difficult for the people of many countries to adjust to peace?

2. In what ways were the treaties of 1919 immediately altered in relation to Poland? To Turkey?

3. How did Great Britain want to treat Germany after the war? Why? How did France want to treat Germany? Why was it difficult for Germany to make reparations payments to France? What arguments did the Germans use to explain their unwillingness to pay? What step did France take to force Germany to pay? What were the results?

4. By 1924 what factors had encouraged inflation in Germany? What was the effect on German society? What action was taken by the German government to halt the inflation? What aid came from abroad? What international peace-keeping agreements did Germany sign?

5. How was the League of Nations organized? What actions could the League take to prevent war? What are some examples of League accomplishments? What was the principal weakness of the League? How were the Kellogg-Briand Treaty and the disarmament conferences expected to help preserve peace? What success did they have?

6. In what ways was the Weimar Republic more democratic than the German Empire had been? In what ways was the authoritarian character of the empire preserved in the republic? What attitude of the people toward the new government was indicated by the election of Hindenburg? By what train of events did Adolf Hitler gain power?

7. List the steps by which Mustafa Kemal strove to make Turkey a western-type state. To what extent did he make it democratic?

8. Was democracy practiced by the new nations of east-central Europe? What prevented a greater degree of democracy?

9. How was France particularly hard hit by the war? Describe the rebuilding of the war-torn areas. How did the French meet the problem of inflation? How did they attempt to strengthen their empire?

CHAPTER 28

10. For what reasons was Britain after the war in a more difficult situation than the other victorious powers? When and for what purpose was there a general strike? With what results?
11. What new disorders occurred in Ireland during the First World War? What kind of government was set up in southern Ireland in 1921? What change was made in it in 1937? How was northern Ireland treated?
12. What changes did the British make in the governments of their Middle Eastern mandates between 1919 and the 1930's? What other changes did they make in their empire?

To Master the Map

1. Compare the maps on pages 42-43 to the territory of Poland on the map on page 400. To what extent was the Poland of the eighteenth century restored after the First World War? What territories that had been Polish before 1772 were not part of the revived Poland?
2. From the location and boundaries of the Turkey that Mustafa Kemal established after the war, what importance in European and world affairs would you expect the country to have?

To Interpret the Facts

1. Does the evidence in this chapter indicate to you that the makers of the treaties of 1919 did their work well? Is there any evidence here that the treaties contained seeds of future war?
2. To what extent was the world of 1929 more nearly "safe for democracy" than it had been in 1919? To what extent was it less so?
3. Compare the problems of Britain, France, and Germany in 1919. Which country made the most complete and rapid economic recovery? Which adjusted its economy most successfully to the demands of the time? Which best adjusted its government to the times?

To Put This Chapter into a Larger Setting

1. In the nineteenth century and up to 1914, in what countries was there the greatest degree of democracy? In what countries between 1919 and 1929? Can the conclusion be drawn that certain economic, social, and educational conditions are required for successful democracy? Support your answer with specific facts.
2. One of the dreams of the peacemakers of 1919 was to make future wars less likely. What steps were taken between 1919 and 1929 to make that hope more realistic? What conditions of the time prevented those steps from being thoroughly successful? How did the success of these steps compare with that of the congress system in use for a few years after the Napoleonic Wars?

29

The World
Outside
Europe

1920-1939

The First World War had as important and sometimes as decisive consequences in the world at large as it had on the European continent. In the
United States, Latin America, and the Far East, important adjustments were
required to meet problems arising out of the war.

☊ THE UNITED STATES

In the United States the sudden end of wartime demands on the
energies and emotions of the people left them with a desire to withdraw
from Europe and from anything related to the war or its consequences. It
took ten years of prosperous isolation, followed by depression at home and
serious threat to their security from abroad, to arouse Americans to the
necessity of participation in world affairs.

ISOLATIONISM

"Isolationism" describes the mood of Americans at the war's end. They
wanted to retire behind their great oceans and leave the world to its own

fate. They demanded that the soldiers be brought home as quickly as possible and that the country be returned to its prewar condition—to "normalcy," to use another word of the time. Soon realizing that the world had not been "made safe for democracy" and that the war had not "ended all wars," they felt tricked and disillusioned. In 1919 the Senate refused to ratify the Versailles Treaty; in 1920 the voters rejected President Wilson's Democratic party and elected Warren G. Harding, first of three successive Republican presidents.

Many United States policies, 1919-1939, reflect the mood of isolationism. The government insisted on full repayment of the wartime loans to the Allies; but at the same time it levied the highest tariffs in American history, so that the debtor countries were hindered in making payments. It limited immigration to such a trickle that the United States suddenly ceased to be a "melting pot." Numbers of Americans became sympathetic to pacifism. It came to be widely believed that if there should be another war, Americans ought to take extreme measures to remain aloof from it. Many people were convinced that if Americans abandoned their principle of freedom of the seas and kept their goods and their fellow citizens off ocean-going ships, the United States would not be dragged into a war. In the mid-1930's Congress passed several "Neutrality Acts," limiting the sale of American goods and the travel of American citizens in a war in which the United States was neutral.

THE BOOM PERIOD OF THE 1920's

Another feature of American life in the decade after the war was rapid industrial expansion, bringing hitherto undreamed-of prosperity to millions of Americans. There were more and cheaper things to buy than ever before. This was the first great age of the automobile, when Henry Ford's mass-production methods, most notably the assembly line, made the Model T Ford inexpensive enough for families of modest means. Moving pictures and the radio became part of everyday life. Electricity powered conveniences to lighten housework, illuminated the night hours, turned the wheels in factories, and sometimes propelled railroad trains. The list could be made a very long one. Demand for luxuries made businesses larger, with greatly increased capital, and provided many new jobs. The Republican party took credit for this prosperity. It sought to remove every hindrance to business by keeping the government out of competing activities (out of the electric power industry, for example) and by relaxing the laws against trusts and

The first moving assembly line, at the Highland Park, Michigan, plant of the Ford Motor Company, May, 1913. A part of the motor of the Model T Ford was put together in less than half the former time as it was pushed from one workman to the next. By applying the same principle to the assembly of the cars themselves, Ford speeded up production until a completed Model T was coming off the assembly line every ten seconds.

monopolies. President Harding was succeeded by the Republicans Calvin Coolidge and Herbert Hoover, who occupied the White House from 1923 to 1933.

The general prosperity did not extend to the farmers. Soon after the war they were plunged into a depression from which they did not emerge. During the war many of them had borrowed money to buy more land in order to take advantage of high wartime prices. Once the wartime agricultural boom was over, interest payments on the borrowed money were hard to meet. Tariffs kept prices high on manufactured goods the farmer must buy, but did not raise prices on the farm products that he sold. Changing dietary habits, in part made possible by better transportation, encouraged the substitution of the truck gardener's vegetables for the great quantities of bread and cake once baked from the farmer's wheat. The government took note of the farmer's plight, but it was unable to offer him much help without abandoning the principle of staying out of business.

THE DEPRESSION, 1929 AND AFTER

The seemingly permanent prosperity of the boom period was abruptly ended by the crash of the New York stock market in October, 1929. This was but the beginning of a downward plunge of the American and world economies. It was followed by the closing of many banks and businesses, the decline of consumer buying, the cancelling of orders to factories, and finally the laying off of millions of employees. Foreign trade almost ceased. It was not long before hungry people in the cities were standing in line—"bread lines"—to receive free meals from charitable organizations. The Republican administration of President Hoover (president 1929-1933) was hindered by its own principles from extensive intervention in the business world. Partly for that reason, in 1932, when there was no end in sight to the depression, a Democrat, Franklin D. Roosevelt, was elected to succeed Hoover.

The Roosevelt administration made a vigorous attack on the depression, offering emergency relief (much of it in the form of employment) to persons without work, and financial assistance to farmers and home owners likely to lose mortgaged property. It tried to raise farm prices by limiting acreage and by buying up surpluses. It encouraged labor unions by limiting the rights of employers to oppose them and by supervising secret elections in plants when there was a dispute among employees as to which union they wished to represent them. It regulated the banks and the stock markets to lessen the possibility of another great crash. Like Bismarck in the 1880's and the Liberals in Britain in 1909, the administration adopted social security laws. The Roosevelt program was known as the "New Deal." Its effectiveness is still a matter of debate. The majority of American people had enough faith in Franklin Roosevelt to elect him to the presidency four times (1932, 1936, 1940, 1944), although businessmen were soon mainly opposed to him. By the end of his second administration the war clouds were appearing again, and the United States, like the rest of the world, was deflected from further economic experiment and reform.

ᴖ LATIN AMERICA

The First World War was not as important a dividing line in Latin-American history as in the histories of Europe and the United States. Although some of the Latin-American countries were allied with the enemies of Germany, their part in the war was too slight to affect them greatly. To understand the Latin America of the 1930's, it is therefore necessary to trace developments from a time earlier than the war—in fact 1825, the time of independence from Spain and Portugal. (See pages 87-91.) It took but a few years after 1825 to prove that the hopes of the Venezuelan patriot Bolívar for a federation of Latin-American states could not be realized. By 1840 there were eighteen separate Latin countries in the Western Hemisphere (twenty after the establishment of Cuban independence in 1902 and the Panama Revolution of 1903). The history of each of these was full of events, for civil and foreign wars, new constitutions and new governments, followed each other with amazing speed. But more important were the great overriding problems facing all the Latin peoples of the Western Hemisphere.

DIVERSITY OF LAND AND PEOPLES

The most important factors in the shaping of Latin-American history were the character of the land itself and the distribution of the peoples in it. From the beginning geography was a decisive influence. Latin America was a vast and varied area, in 1825 stretching from 42° north latitude (the then northern border of Mexico) to 42° south latitude (the then southern border of Chile) and from the Atlantic to the Pacific, including a number of the Caribbean islands. The center of this region lay in the tropics where impenetrable, disease-infested rain forests were so inhospitable to white men that the Amazon basin of Brazil is still today one of the world's least explored areas. Another obstacle to the movements of human beings was furnished by rugged mountains forming the western backbone of the Americas. So high are the Andes that some of their peaks are snow-capped even at the equator. In such a region mule tracks were scarce and roads of any consequence even scarcer. Each of the countries bestriding the Andes had two lowland regions, one along the Pacific and the other east of the mountains, neither of which was in any easy communication with the central, more populous high areas or with each other. The peoples of these three areas were as different from each other and as unacquainted as if they had been citizens of three different countries. As late as 1860 the only route from the interior of Ecuador to the coast was a mule track from Quito, the mountain capital, to the port of Guayaquil. Because of rains, even the mule track was useless for half the year. In 1828 General William Henry Harrison, later President of the United States but then American minister to Colombia, had to make his way to the Colombian capital, Bogota, first by a six-weeks canoe trip up a river and then by horseback over the Andes.

The fact that in many areas the peoples of different races lived apart from each other, often knowing almost nothing of each other, was also a source of division and weakness. This situation was especially found in Mexico, Guatemala, and the Andean countries of Ecuador, Peru, and Bolivia, in each of which more than half of the population was Indian. The Indians, living in their own villages, were almost all impoverished, illiterate, and oftentimes even unable to speak in Spanish. They still clung to many of their age-old traditional beliefs and customs. They had little real communication with the Creoles (families of pure Spanish descent), the owners of the great estates. Between these two groups were the mestizos (mixed Indian-white peoples) better off financially than the Indians, but separated from both Indian and Creole by social custom and economic status. In northeastern Brazil and along the rest of the northern coast of South America, where Negroes or mixed Negro and white peoples were in a majority, there was less division of society according to race. In Chile, Argentina, Uruguay, and southern Brazil, people of European ancestry were in a great majority. During the nineteenth century millions of Germans, Italians, and other Europeans came to settle in these last countries, making them still more solidly European.

SOCIAL AND ECONOMIC PROBLEMS

The greatest problem confronting all the Latin-American countries in the nineteenth century, and still a problem today, grew out of the distribution of farm land. Together the Catholic Church and the Creole owners of great estates controlled a large part of the good land. The few landholders were often very wealthy. Until the middle of the century, Negro slavery was practiced on many estates of the tropical regions. Indian laborers, although legally free, were usually so deeply in debt to their landlords that they were bound to the land they worked by a kind of debt slavery. For these depressed groups there was little hope of escape from their miserable existence. Until late in the nineteenth century there was almost no opportunity for them to secure any sort of education. In Bolivia in 1841 there was not a single school. Nor could poverty-stricken people secure any land of their own. As recently as 1963 a former president of Ecuador could say of Latin America, "In all countries a small upper class enjoys a high standard of living. The lower masses, while making up the great majority of the population, are desperately poor. In between there is a relatively small sector of people of middle class status. The gap from top to bottom is very wide."*

* Galo Plaza Lasso, in Wellesley College, *Symposium on Latin America* (Wellesley, Mass.: Wellesley College, 1963). P. 54.

SOUTH AND CENTRAL
AMERICA
1964

U.S.A.

• Miami

Havana •

CUBA

DOMINICAN
REPUBLIC

JAMAICA

HAITI

Virgin
Islands
(U.S.A.)

Puerto
Rico (U.S.A.)

Caribbean   Sea

ATLANTIC

OCEAN

MEXICO

British
Honduras

GUATEMALA

HONDURAS

EL SALVADOR

NICARAGUA

COSTA
RICA

Canal
Zone (U.S.A.)

PANAMA

TRINIDAD

Caracas •

VENEZUELA

British
Guiana

Surinam
(Neth.)

French
Guiana

• Bogotá

COLOMBIA

Quito •

ECUADOR

Quayaquil •

Amazon   River

B   R   A   Z   I   L

P
A
C
I
F
I
C

P
E
R
U

A
N
D
E
S

Lima •

• La Paz

BOLIVIA

• Brasilia

O
C
E
A
N

M
O
U
N
T
A
I
N
S

PARAGUAY

Asunción •

• Rio de Janeiro

C
H
I
L
E

A
R
G
E
N
T
I
N
A

USPALLATA
PASS

Santiago •

URUGUAY

Buenos
Aires •

• Montevideo

ATLANTIC

OCEAN

Colonies

Another problem was the special position of the Catholic Church. Not only was the church a large landowner, but it controlled most of what education there was. In many places the clergy could be brought to trial only in their own courts. As in France at the time of the revolution, there was a good deal of sentiment for giving many of the secular activities of the church over to the state and for confiscating church property.

LATIN-AMERICAN POLITICAL PROBLEMS

The governments of the Latin-American countries were quite unable to cope effectively with the problems they confronted. Unlike the political leaders in the United States after the American Revolution, Latin-American leaders had almost no experience with the administration of government. (See page 88.) With the exception of Brazil before 1889, all the independent Latin-American countries became republics, but they lacked the solid body of educated, experienced middle-class citizens who had the leisure, the trained understanding, and the education to make a republican government successful. Although most countries had constitutions, few were long-lasting, and none prevented the coming into power of a succession of military leaders who managed to alter the constitutions to suit their own purposes. The most common form of government in nineteenth-century Latin America was the dictatorship of a military man, sometimes a conscientious, hard-working person, devoted to the well-being of his people, sometimes a power-mad man who did not hesitate to employ the most cruel and dishonest methods to keep himself at the head of the state.

Although there was a pretense of democracy in most of the countries— there were elections, not necessarily honest ones—the real problem was not to establish democracy but stability. Lacking a tradition of orderly change, the opponents of existing governments did not hesitate to use armed force. In each country there was likely to be conflict between the conservatives, often called "centralists," and the liberals, sometimes known as "federalists." The conservatives, like the aristocrats at the time of the French Revolution, wanted a strongly centralized government that would preserve the privileges of the Creoles and the church. The liberals wanted power for the local governments, wider suffrage, and less power for the Catholic Church. Disputes over such matters, or between the followers of different leaders, help to explain the frequent occurrence of civil war and revolution. During the nineteenth century Bolivia, the most unstable country, had sixty revolutions, ten constitutions, one disastrous war, and six presidential assassinations.

ECONOMIC AND SOCIAL DEVELOPMENT
AFTER THE FIRST WORLD WAR

Although these many problems still plagued Latin-American countries in the 1920's and 1930's, obvious improvements were being made. Gradually and at enormous expense, railroads were being built inland from the coasts and between cities. One of them crossed the continent from Argentina to Chile. But the railroad mileage was a meager part of what was needed. For example, Brazil, with its people concentrated in a narrow strip along the Atlantic coast, had no continuous north-south line. Although by 1939 the airplane was beginning to supplement the railroad, transportation remained a problem.

Export of products in demand on world markets was also being increased: copper from Chile, petroleum from Mexico and Venezuela, coffee from Brazil, meat from Argentina. But some difficulties attended this growth. Foreign companies, especially from the United States, often owned the mines and oil wells. In time Latin-Americans began to resent this draining of their national wealth to other countries. In the 1930's the Mexican government seized all foreign-owned oil properties, thus creating an international problem that was settled only with difficulty. Another problem was that concentration in many countries on a single export product often resulted in serious depressions when world demand for that product declined.

Although efforts were made to meet the social problems confronting the Latin-American countries—in Mexico the returning of the lands of the great estates to Indian villages, for example—most of the long-term difficulties remained after the First World War. Greater stability of governments, together with more widespread education and more awareness on the part of Latin-American leaders of the basic needs of their peoples, gave promise of improvement for the future.

☯ THE FAR EAST

In the Far East the direct results of the First World War were numerous, even though the fighting in that area had been inconsequential. The fact that the European powers were too preoccupied to take much part in Far Eastern affairs was the real importance of the war for the East, for Japan was thus enabled to have its own way in China, where the new republican government had as yet developed little strength.

THE WAR YEARS AND THE PEACE OF VERSAILLES

When the war began, Japan immediately entered it on the side of its ally, Great Britain, and took over German-controlled areas in China and the German islands in the Pacific. The Japanese government then presented China with "Twenty-One Demands," including a demand for recognition of Japan's special position in southern Manchuria and the Shantung peninsula. China had no choice but to yield. Japan also secured from its wartime allies secret treaties supporting its demands. Even the United States failed to make a clear statement of protest. At the peace conference Japan secured a mandate for the German Pacific islands north of the equator and possession of the former German rights in Shantung, but with the understanding that Shantung would later be returned to China.

At the end of the war Japan enjoyed a new position of strength and dignity among the world powers. It was among the five nations important enough to be awarded a permanent place on the Council of the League of Nations. Its navy was third in size in the world. During the war it had so greatly expanded its manufacturing and had invaded so many new markets that it had been able to become a creditor instead of a debtor nation. The weakness of China and the concessions to Japan in Chinese territory made it seem possible that China would soon become a Japanese protectorate.

JAPANESE-AMERICAN RIVALRY, 1919-1922

It was inevitable that Japan and the United States were soon engaged in intense naval rivalry. Each feared the other in the Pacific. In addition, the United States foresaw that Japanese plans for China would soon destroy the principle of the "open door" (see page 345) and interfere with Chinese American trade. To end Japanese-American tension, the United States invited a great-power conference to be held in Washington, 1921-1922, to discuss both naval disarmament and the relations of all the powers to each other in China and in the Pacific. A ten-year truce in the building of large warships (battleships or "capital ships") was agreed to. The naval powers also promised to scrap as many capital ships as necessary to put the navies of Britain, the United States, and Japan in the ratio of 5:5:3 to each other. By a four-power treaty, the United States, Britain, Japan, and France promised to respect one another's possessions in the Pacific. With this guarantee the Anglo-Japanese alliance was deemed unnecessary and was scrapped—to the relief of the United States, which was thus freed from the danger of finding Britain on the side of Japan in an American-Japanese war. Finally, a nine-power treaty, signed by all the states at the conference, upheld the independence of China, its right to all its territory, and the principle of the Open Door. Japan agreed to restore Shantung to China. All powers agreed not to strengthen their fortifications in the islands of the western Pacific.

The Washington treaties greatly reduced international tensions. The western powers believed that they had made China safe from the aggressive intentions of Japan. Japan was freed from the threat that might have been posed by western fortifications in areas near its shores. All countries enjoyed some lessening of the ruinous cost of naval rivalry. But the treaties did not lead to any other important naval limitation nor to other forms of disarmament, and by the mid-1930's Japan had led the way to scrapping them. In any case, in the 1920's Japan profited most from the lull in the arms race begun in the Washington Conference, for the Japanese soon were able to secure new advantages in China.

JAPAN AND CHINA, 1922-1937

In the 1920's important developments were taking place in both China and Japan. For China the greatest need was for a strong central government, since the republican government that had overthrown the emperor in 1911 (see page 346) had not been able to keep control of the whole country. Rival warlords were maintaining themselves in power in the various regions of China, each trying to defeat all the others. The Kuomintang, or Nationalist group, led at first by Sun Yat-sen and later by Chiang Kai-shek, took the initiative to restore order. Unable to find help elsewhere, the Kuomintang had entered into an alliance with the Russian Communists. Chiang spent four months in Russia, where he learned much about a strongly organized kind of government. By 1927 Chiang, with the help of Chinese Communists, had mastered the region between Canton and the Yangtze valley and set up his capital at Nanking. Immediately thereafter he broke with the Chinese Communists, expelled all Communist members from his government, and tried to destroy the power of the party.

With his control of the rich region of the lower Yangtze River area, Chiang was able to defeat most of the warlords and to establish a fairly well-functioning government. The next years were a period of relative economic prosperity in China. Chiang's popularity made it possible for him to secure the abandoning by the western colonizing powers of most of the "unequal treaties" that had earlier been imposed on China. (See pages 341-342.)

The Chinese Communists, few in number though they were, managed nevertheless to continue a precarious existence in spite of the powerful opposition of Chiang. Mao Tse-tung, their leader, was convinced that Chinese Communism must be based on the enthusiasm of the poor peasantry rather than on the factory proletariat, which was almost nonexistent in China. He established a base in Hunan province in southern China and declared a Soviet Republic. An attack by Chiang Kai-shek's forces was so successful that the Communists had to abandon their base. In a legendary exploit, 100,000 Communists broke out from their stronghold and began what is known as the "Long March," a year-long journey through 6,000 miles of hardship, danger, and constant fighting. About 20,000 of them survived the perilous journey and in 1935 set up a new headquarters at Yenan in northwestern China. There they remained until after the Second World War.

The Japanese used the postwar years in a different way. Their growing nationalism increased the influence of their military men and led to the

Chiang Kai-shek of China and Franklin D. Roosevelt of the United States at a meeting in Cairo, Egypt, in 1943, to discuss the strategy of the war in the Pacific.

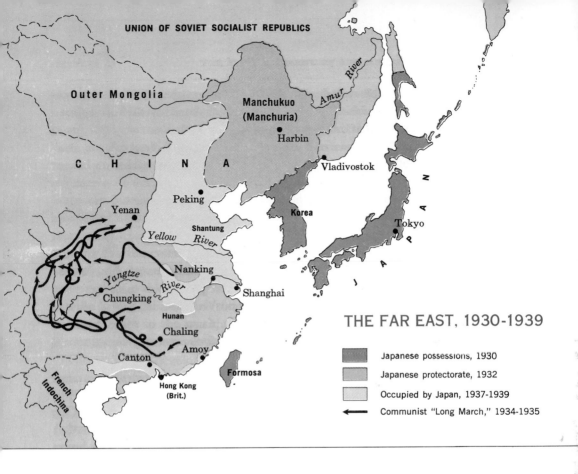

UNION OF SOVIET SOCIALIST REPUBLICS

Outer Mongolia

Manchukuo (Manchuria)

Amur River

Harbin

C H I N A

Vladivostok

Peking

Yenan

Korea

Shantung

Tokyo

Yellow River

Nanking

Yangtze River

Shanghai

Chungking

Hunan

Chaling

Amoy

Canton

Formosa

Hong Kong (Brit.)

French Indochina

N

J A P A N

THE FAR EAST, 1930-1939

Japanese possessions, 1930

Japanese protectorate, 1932

Occupied by Japan, 1937-1939

← Communist "Long March," 1934-1935

strengthening of their army. To improve their economic situation, they sought opportunities for investment in Manchuria, where they had had special advantages since the Russo-Japanese War of 1905. They opened mines and built steel mills to supply their military needs. When the world-wide depression of the early 1930's cut off their other markets, they became so dependent on Manchuria as a place to sell their surplus manufactures that they determined to conquer the region outright.

But to the Chinese, Manchuria was a tributary province of China. Chinese Nationalists noted the intensified interests of the Japanese in the region and attempted to counter them, even going so far as to build railroads paralleling those built by the Japanese. Economic warfare was energetically carried on by both sides. In 1931 actual fighting began between the Japanese and Chinese. Acting apparently without orders from home, Japanese troops began the conquest of Manchuria. Neither The League of Nations nor the United States would go to the aid of China, although both condemned the actions of Japan. In 1932 the Japanese set up a puppet government in Manchuria and named the new state Manchukuo.

In 1937 Japan launched a full-scale attack on China proper, sending its armies southward along the coast, taking most of the port cities, and wherever possible extending its control inland. The Chinese resisted. Chiang's government moved inland to Chungking for safety. This was the situation in the Far East when the world began to slip into the Second World War.

⚲ ⚲ ⚲

The histories of the United States, Latin America, and the Far East reveal the extent of world restlessness and the absence of international co-operation in the 1920's and 1930's. A period of calm prosperity was required if the world were to be able to live in peace. But by 1930 it was evident that world-wide depression was replacing prosperity. Economic troubles were intensified by political developments that soon brought the world for the second time to the brink of global war.

Persons, Places, and Terms

Warren G. Harding	Quito	isolationism
Calvin Coolidge	Bogota	pacifism
Herbert Hoover	Manchuria	bread line
Franklin D. Roosevelt	Yangtze River	Social Security
Chiang Kai-shek	Nanking	New Deal
Mao Tse-tung	Hunan	Twenty-one Demands
	Yenan	Kuomintang
Amazon River	Chungking	Long March

To Master the Text

1. Why did Americans desire to follow a policy of isolationism after the war? How was that policy concerned with war debts? With immigration? With pacificism? How were neutrality laws expected to prevent United States involvement in another great war?

2. How prosperous was the United States after the war? How did the Republican party encourage business? For what reasons were the farmers badly off? Why did the Republican presidents not take measures to aid farmers?

3. How did the depression of 1929 affect the United States? What policies did the administration of Franklin D. Roosevelt adopt to aid the unemployed? To aid farmers? To aid labor? To reform banking?

4. To what extent were divisions among Latin Americans caused by the great size of the area? The jungles and mountains? Racial differences?
5. Who owned most of the land in the Latin-American countries? What special hardships did farm laborers endure? Why did they not take measures to help themselves? How large a middle class was there?
6. What kind of government was most common in Latin America? Were most governments really democratic? Why? Why was it difficult to establish long-lasting governments in Latin America?
7. How and with what effect has Latin-American transportation been improved in recent years? What new products have been developed? With what effect? What part have foreign capitalists played in the economic development of Latin America?
8. What Chinese territories did Japan seize during the First World War? What further concessions were asked in the Twenty-one Demands? What territorial advantages did Japan secure in 1919?
9. Why did the United States fear Japan after 1919? What was the purpose of the Washington Conference? What did it accomplish?
10. By what steps did Chiang Kai-shek secure control of much of China in the 1920's? How did he improve foreign relations? What were his relations with the Chinese Communists? How did Mao Tse-tung manage to keep the Communist party alive?
11. What steps did the Japanese take in the 1920's to improve their economy? How did their efforts lead them to conflict with the Chinese? What military steps did the Japanese take in China in 1931? In 1937? With what results?

To Interpret the Facts

1. What was the greatest single problem of the 1920's in the United States? In Latin America? In Japan? In China? What solutions to any of these problems were beginning to appear in the 1930's?
2. To what extent was geography responsible for economic problems in Latin America? In Japan? To what extent did geography encourage the Japanese attack on China?

To Put This Chapter into a Larger Setting

1. In what other countries and at what other times can you find conditions most nearly resembling those of Latin America in the late nineteenth century? Are there any aspects of Latin-American life for which you can find no parallels elsewhere?
2. Read in other books (see page 523) about the work of Sun Yat-sen, Chiang Kai-shek, and Mao Tse-tung. Report to the class about the particular problems faced by each of these leaders, his way of overcoming the difficulty, and his influence on the course of Chinese history.

30

The Coming
of the
Second
World War

World-wide depression, evidenced by such frightening events as the New York stock market crash of 1929 (see page 416), began a troubled period in world affairs. Economic problems challenged all nations, but all governments did not respond to them in the same way. The western democratic powers, victors in the First World War, tried to preserve their traditional governments and economies by means of somewhat increased but still strictly limited governmental participation in the national economic life. Italy, Germany, and Japan, on the other hand, all eager to alter the world balance of power established by the treaties of 1919-1920, tried to overcome the depression and at the same time to reach their political goals by establishing highly centralized dictatorial governments. The rivalry between these two groups of powers was the prelude to the Second World War.

☊ DEPRESSION, 1929 AND AFTER

The world-wide depression that began in 1929 was the most important world development between the two great wars. Its causes were complex and are still imperfectly understood, but what it meant to the peoples of the world is all too clear.

THE CHARACTER OF THE DEPRESSION

Evidences of economic difficulty appeared in many countries; but to people of the time, it seemed that depression in America was spreading like a contagion over the whole world. After the New York stock market crash, American investors recalled many of their European loans; American purchases from abroad were curtailed; and American tourists could no longer afford to travel in large numbers in Europe. Without American loans, the Germans could no longer pay reparations; and without reparations, the Allies could not meet their debt payments to the United States. Everywhere in the industrial world prices fell, factories were closed down, masses of workers were unemployed. Germany was hardest hit. France was not seriously hurt at first, but by the middle 1930's it also was in trouble. Between 1929 and 1934 world trade shrank by more than two thirds.

METHODS OF MEETING THE DEPRESSION

No government dared let the depression take its course without making every effort to relieve the widespread human misery resulting from it. Officials who, a decade before, had supervised wartime rationing of food and fuel, found it natural to use government funds to care for those now homeless or hungry. All governments expended huge sums in such relief measures. All passed laws intended to stimulate the economies of their own countries, taking little thought of the impact of their programs on other countries. Most governments raised their tariffs to make sure their citizens bought the manufactured goods produced within the country. Even Great Britain, which had a long tradition of free trade, established a tariff to make it easier for the dominions to sell their products in Britain—at the same time, of course, excluding imports that other countries had long been accustomed to selling to Britain. Governments entered into agreements with one another for the exchange of specified amounts of certain commodities. Such economic practices forced all governments to become somewhat more centralized and authoritarian than before. Some became fascist dictatorships.

◌ THE FASCIST DICTATORSHIPS

Strictly speaking, the word "fascist" applies only to Mussolini's government in Italy, but it is often used also for the similar governments established by Hitler in Germany, by Franco in Spain, and by other dictators elsewhere. All were totalitarian in that, like the Communists in the Soviet

Union, they permitted no political parties to exist except their own and attempted to control all aspects of the lives and work of their peoples.

FASCISM IN ITALY

Fascism appeared in Italy within three years of the end of the First World War, and it was well established by the time of the depression. It furnished a model for all later non-Communist totalitarian states.

Postwar conditions in Italy gave the Fascists their opportunity. As elsewhere, economic conditions were bad. Moreover, the peasants believed that during the war the government had promised them land. When it was not forthcoming, they sometimes simply seized it. Factory workers, disappointed in their expectations of improved postwar conditions, staged violent strikes. People began to fear a Communist revolution. Further problems were created by the peace treaties of 1919, which had granted Italians far less territory than they believed was rightfully theirs. Many began to look upon Italian participation in the war as a mistake. Returned army officers found that instead of being heroes, they were regarded as participants in their country's humiliation. But when property owners looked to the government for protection from riotous peasants and workers, and when nationalists demanded of it a strong foreign policy, they found a total lack of leadership. A strong man seemed required to save the state; he appeared in the person of Benito Mussolini.

The Rise of Italian Fascism. Mussolini had not previously been important in Italian politics. He had come of a modest family, his father a blacksmith and his mother a schoolteacher. In his early manhood he had taken up a number of contradictory theories, sometimes going to jail for his beliefs. For a time he lived abroad to escape military service; then he returned home to serve in the army. He edited a socialist newspaper, opposing on pacifist grounds Italian participation in the First World War; then he changed his views and became an ardent supporter of the war, serving as a soldier until he was wounded. After the war he won favor with the disgruntled army officers by arguing in his newspaper that the war, far from having been a mistake, had been Italy's greatest glory.

Neither in these early years nor after he became dictator of Italy did he develop a well-thought-out theory of government or social organization. His qualities of leadership were not so much intellectual as personal. Although he was not a particularly brave man, he gave the impression of tremendous vigor and active energy. As dictator he loved to dash about at great speed on a motorcycle, to address crowds with high-sounding oratory, to play upon the feelings of the Italian people, whose moods he so well understood.

The Fascist party, of which Mussolini was soon the acknowledged leader, began in 1919 as a local organization in Milan, the *Fascio di Combattimento* ("fighting group"). This was an unofficial semi-military body, armed for the protection of its own meetings and to break up those of its rivals. It soon joined with similar groups in a nation-wide Fascist organization. The Fascists used as their symbol the fasces (bundles of sticks) carried before the consuls of ancient Rome as evidence of authority. Their greeting was given in the old Roman way with outstretched arm. Their uniform was the black shirt.

In 1922 came the opportunity for the Fascists to seize power. The socialists called a general strike. This the Fascists strongly opposed, destroying socialist headquarters and newspapers in various cities and finally taking over a number of city governments. Mussolini groomed his Black Shirts for a "March on Rome," where they would seize power by violence unless it was peacefully yielded to them. By rail and automobile many Fascists reached the neighborhood of the capital. Mussolini remained near the Swiss border until his appointment by the king as prime minister was assured. Then he took a night train to Rome.

The Character of Italian Fascism. Once in office, Mussolini replaced officials with his Fascist followers and took other steps to extend his own power or weaken that of his opponents. By 1925 Italy had become a totalitarian state. Other parties were dissolved; the press was closely censored; the Fascist armed groups were transformed into a party militia; a secret police was established. Mussolini was now the dictator of Italy; only lip service was paid to the king. The Fascist party occupied a position similar to that of the Communists in the Soviet Union. Members constituted less than three per cent of the population, but only Fascists could hold public office or secure certain kinds of employment. Membership in the party had to be earned, usually by a period of apprenticeship in the Fascist youth organizations.

Although the Fascists permitted property to remain in private hands, they exercised careful control over it. They also dissolved labor unions and forbade strikes. In place of the unions, they substituted "corporations" of employers, employees, and professional people, whose task it was to establish labor courts where disputes between employers and workers could be settled. Employers welcomed the quieting of labor unrest that followed, but the workers' lot was as unhappy as ever. In 1930 the International Labor Office found that Italian workers were the worst off in Europe.

Two especially successful Fascist policies concerned education and the Catholic Church. By encouraging elementary schools, the Fascists greatly reduced illiteracy. They also settled the long-standing quarrel between the papacy and the kingdom of Italy. (See page 252.) By the Lateran Treaty of 1929, Pope Pius XI recognized the legal right of the kingdom of Italy to the territory of the former Papal States. In return he received a sum of money and recognition by the Fascist government of the independence from Italy of Vatican City and of his sovereignty over it. The church was to have considerable control over education in Italy—an arrangement that soon led to a good deal of friction. The Lateran Treaty had advantages for both sides. It strengthened some of the activities of the church in Italy. On the other hand, it also temporarily freed the Fascist government from the opposition of the papacy.

The Fascist regime was harsh, with its secret police and its unending regulation of every aspect of life and work. The poverty of the mass of the Italian people remained. Nevertheless, Mussolini's government retained its authority until the middle of the Second World War. There was much popular appeal in Fascism, with its uniforms, its parades, its rallies, and its adulation of its *Duce* (leader), Mussolini. On the other hand, the controlled press, the restriction of freedom of meeting, and the impossibility of organizing an opposition party, kept people too ignorant of public affairs and too disorganized to force any important change in the government—much less to overthrow Mussolini.

NAZISM IN GERMANY

In 1923, just a year after Mussolini's "March on Rome," Adolf Hitler attempted a *coup d'état* in Germany. He failed and was imprisoned for several months. During his confinement he dictated a book, *Mein Kampf* ("My Struggle"), which set forth his ideas about Germany's past and what he hoped would be its future. Within a decade he had risen to power and had begun to create a fascist kind of state. His Germany came to be as totalitarian as Mussolini's Italy, and far more powerful.

Hitler and the Rise of the Nazis. Hitler was born in Austria, the son of a minor government employee. Early in life he was left an orphan and thereafter lived a restless existence in Vienna, where he developed many

Benito Mussolini (left) and Adolf Hitler reviewing a military parade during a visit of
Mussolini to Germany, 1937. Mussolini is giving the Fascist salute (also used by the Nazis),
an imitation of the salute of ancient Rome.

hatreds—of nobles and people of wealth, of Marxism, of Austrians of mixed
nationality, and particularly of Jews. He served in the German army during
the war, acquiring the comfortable sense of being a German and of belonging to the German people. When peace came, he settled in Munich, the
capital of Bavaria in southern Germany, where anti-Communism and
extreme conservatism were especially strong and where there were numerous small secret societies, often made up of ex-soldiers. Hitler soon became a
leader in the "National Socialist German Workers' Party," (called by the
nickname "Nazi" from the German pronunciation of the letters "nati").
Although not a man of intellectual gifts, he developed a genius for highly
emotional oratory, inflaming to his audiences. He also exhibited a talent for
party organization and propaganda.

The Nazis, like similar groups elsewhere, maintained a private army of
"Brown Shirts" to protect themselves and to attack rivals—by assassination,

if necessary. When times were prosperous, such semi-military organizations made little headway; but in any moment of national difficulty, they found their opportunity. Hitler's attempted *coup d'état* of 1923 was staged at the time of the Ruhr crisis (see page 401), of which he hoped—in vain, as it turned out—to take advantage. The depression of 1929, so disastrous in Germany, gave him a second opportunity. He had used the intervening years to plan a government and to increase the number of his dedicated followers. He had intensified his propaganda attacks on the Treaty of Versailles, on the government of the Weimar Republic, on the Communists, and especially on the Jews, on whom he blamed the defeat of Germany in the First World War and the ruinous unemployment of the depression years.

Gradually Hitler moved nearer to the moment when he could grasp real power. With each succeeding election his party increased its membership in the *Reichstag*. Big industrialists, great landholders, and army officers—the conservatives of the Nationalist party—came to believe that they could use him for their own purposes if they could place him in high office. In 1933 President von Hindenburg, elderly and almost senile, was persuaded to appoint Hitler chancellor. A few months later, just before the next election, the *Reichstag* building was set afire. Blaming the Communists for the deed, the Nazis stirred up such terror that their party and its ally, the Nationalist party, secured a majority in the *Reichstag*. Hitler then declared a national emergency and secured the dictatorial powers provided by the Weimar constitution for such crises. (See page 404.) At once he began to create what he called the "Third Reich" (the "Third Empire," counting the Holy Roman Empire as the first and Bismarck's Hohenzollern empire as the second).

The Character of the Third Reich. Much of the political and economic organization of the Third Reich, worked out in the space of a few months, resembled that of Fascist Italy, although it was not in any way a copy of the Italian model. The government became a propaganda machine. It made full use of the controlled press and of the radio (which had not been available to Mussolini at the time of the establishment of Fascism). Great mass meetings were skillfully marshaled to work the participants to a high pitch of excitement. By every available means a constant repetition of Nazi arguments was presented to the people, and all opposing arguments were suppressed. The whole German nation was to an extent "brainwashed." The Nazi party flag, the swastika, replaced the flag of the Weimar republic.

Expressions of extravagant devotion to Hitler, the leader or (in German) *Führer*, were encouraged in every imaginable way.

Hitler's reorganization of the government left no practical way for the ordinary people to participate in it. All agencies not under the control of the Nazis were destroyed—the separate German states, for example, whose governments were replaced by Nazi governors; all opposition parties; all labor unions. Although Hitler, like Napoleon I and Napoleon III, held occasional plebiscites (carefully supervised by Nazi authorities) to ratify his actions, there was no real provision for expressions of the popular will by voting or any other means. Only Nazis or persons sympathetic to the Nazis were allowed to hold offices in the civil service, in the universities, or in the courts. In 1934 even the Nazi party itself was purged of those Hitler believed to be disloyal. He had hundreds of members killed by his armed men—simply shot down wherever they happened to be, without even a trial. At all times the secret police, the *Gestapo*, arrested persons suspected of disloyalty and carried them off to concentration camps, from which came dreadful reports of the brutal treatment of prisoners. The Nazis also put great pressure on the churches. They established elaborate secular organizations for bringing up young people to be Nazis.

Hitler's personal anti-Semitism and his belief in the superiority of what he called the "pure German race" resulted in dreadful persecution of the Jews. New laws prevented Jews from holding public office or from engaging in many kinds of business. Jews had no protection against private abuse or beatings or death, and they could leave the country only if they agreed to abandon all their possessions and wealth.

There were many similarities between German and Italian fascism. Both Hitler and Mussolini had been able to rise to power partly because their people were so bitterly disappointed in the outcome of the First World War. In both Germany and Italy fascism was militaristic with its trappings of uniforms, flags, and parades, its private armies, and its nationalist glorification of the state. Hitler, like Mussolini, began to rearm his country—secretly, since in the case of Germany such a course was forbidden by the Treaty of Versailles. Rearmament had a double advantage to Hitler: it not only made him more powerful, but also helped greatly to reduce unemployment in Germany. Both Hitler and Mussolini loudly blamed foreign countries for the troubles in their own lands. In the 1930's both sought opportunities for foreign aggressions in order to justify their own dictatorial ways and to keep the unquestioning support of their peoples.

⌒ THE CRISES OF THE 1930'S

The world situation of the 1930's offered the dictators excellent opportunities for stirring up trouble. The countries of the world had already fallen into two groups. Some could be called "dissatisfied" powers, for they wished to alter the balance of power established by the treaties of 1919-1920, which they believed very unfavorable to themselves. By 1933 all the leading dissatisfied powers—Germany, Japan, Italy, and the U.S.S.R.—had strong dictatorial governments. The "satisfied" countries were led by the democratic victors of the First World War: France, Britain, and the United States. This group also included many smaller or weaker states whose leaders believed that their countries would prosper best if the arrangements made in 1919-1920 were continued. Among this latter group were China and the small nations of east-central Europe created from the former Russian, Austro-Hungarian, and Ottoman empires.

In the 1930's the dictators of the dissatisfied states were willing and able to use armed force. Governments of the time in France and Britain happened to be not particularly imaginative or vigorous, and they lacked understanding of the strength and vigor of the dictatorships. Moreover, they were held back by popular fear of the awful destructiveness of modern war and by the widespread belief that the First World War had been a mistake that should not be repeated.

THE BEGINNING OF A NEW ERA OF AGGRESSION, 1931-1936

A new era of aggression began in the 1930's. One center of conflict was eastern Asia, where Japan established its control of Manchuria and northern China. (See pages 425-426.)

Another center of tension was the Mediterranean and central European region, where the fascist and democratic countries disputed each other. In 1933 Hitler began an attack on the Versailles treaty. His method was to choose a moment when he thought that the western powers probably would not unite against him and to push one of his demands, indicating that Germany would be fully satisfied when this single objective was achieved. In 1933 he demanded that Germany be permitted full rearmament; when he was refused, he withdrew Germany from the League of Nations. In 1934 he indicated that he would unite Austria with Germany; but this time Mussolini mobilized his army in protest, and Hitler gave up the idea for the time being. In 1935 the plebiscite required by the Treaty of Versailles returned the Saar basin to Germany. Gratified by this triumph, Hitler openly built up the armed forces he had already been developing in secret. In 1936 he marched his troops across the Rhine into the western part of Germany, which had been permanently demilitarized by the Versailles treaty. There were protests from Britain and France, but no action.

In 1935 Mussolini, observing the ease of Hitler's successes, embarked upon a career of conquest of his own, attacking Ethiopia, one of the two remaining independent countries of Africa, where Italian arms had met defeat in 1896. (See page 316.) Haile Selassie, emperor of Ethiopia, appealed to the League of Nations to protect his country. The League denounced Mussolini as an aggressor and requested its members to refrain from selling war materials to Italy. But the British, fearing that an embargo on oil sales to Italy or the closing of the Suez Canal to Italian ships would drive Mussolini into alliance with Hitler and possibly touch off a general war, refused to take such steps. By 1936 Italian forces had subjugated Ethiopia.

THE SPANISH CIVIL WAR, 1936-1939

Two months after the collapse of Ethiopia, civil war broke out in Spain. Since 1931, when the Spanish had deposed their king, the country had been a republic. In 1936 a coalition ministry of leftist parties began breaking up landed estates, confiscating church property, suppressing religious teaching in schools, and taking action to curb the army. The conservative elements in the country rushed to protect the landlords, the church, and the army. Civil war ensued. Almost at once planes, men, and money began pouring in from Italy and Germany for the support of the "Nationalists" (the rightists), led by General Francisco Franco. The "Loyalists," as the leftists were called, received aid from the Soviet Union and also from many individual liberals and leftists of various countries. Military men in the dictatorships welcomed this opportunity to try out the new weapons and techniques of fighting they had been developing in their growing armies, for methods of warfare had been going through a behind-the-scenes revolution during the years of peace. In Spain, after terrible loss of life, General Franco was finally victorious over the Loyalists. He promptly set up a fascist government.

THE FINAL CRISES, 1936-1939

Before the end of the Spanish Civil War, events in the Far East and in central Europe led toward a final breach between fascist powers and the democracies. In 1936, shortly after the beginning of the Spanish war, Hitler and Mussolini entered into an alliance called the "Rome-Berlin Axis." In 1937 this was joined by Japan in an agreement called the "Anti-Comintern Pact," directed against the Soviet Union but also useful whenever the three nations wished to work together to put pressure on the divided and uncertain democracies. Thus strengthened, Japan was able to pursue its war against China. In 1938 Hitler was able to march into Austria and annex it to Germany. Only ineffective protests came from France and Britain against so flagrant a violation of the Treaty of Versailles.

In September, 1938, war seemed but a matter of days away. Once in possession of Austria, Hitler determined to take another step toward his dream of uniting all Germans under his dictatorship. The small 1919 country of Czechoslovakia, now almost surrounded by Germany, had a large German minority, the Sudeten Germans, living along the borders of Germany and Austria. Hitler's agents stirred them up to demand annexation to Germany; Hitler prepared to accede to this "request," and Italy and Hungary supported him. The anxious peoples of the world feared that if Hitler annexed the Sudeten region, the western nations would attack him and a new world war would begin. But the British and French decided not to take arms to prevent the annexation. Neville Chamberlain, the British prime minister, believed that if Hitler gained this objective, he would finally be satisfied. After the sharp crisis, Chamberlain, Hitler, Mussolini, and Daladier of France met in the German city of Munich and reached an agreement giving the lands occupied by Sudeten Germans to Germany. A few weeks later Poland and Hungary annexed parts of Czechoslovakia along their borders.

In March, 1939, in clear violation of his Munich promise of six months earlier, Hitler took over what was left of Czechoslovakia. A week later he annexed a part of Lithuania along the German border. Following this pattern, in April, 1939, Italy seized Albania without creating more than a ripple on the surface of international relations.

To ordinary people over the world, the summer of 1939 seemed relatively calm. The Paris edition of the New York *Herald-Tribune* in its July 30 edition carried a headline declaring that danger of war was over and that American tourists were flocking to Europe. Behind the scenes, however, the period between March and August, 1939, was a time of intense diplomatic activity. In March the British and French governments realized that Hitler would not remain satisfied with his Czech success. Perceiving that his next

LITHUANIA

C

GERMANY

GERMANY

POLAND

B

CZECHOSLOVAKIA

Munich

A

HUNGARY

D

E

YUGOSLAVIA

ITALY

ALBANIA

— · — 1937 boundaries

Annexed by Germany

A. Austria, March 1938
B. Sudetenland, Oct. 1938
C. Memel, March 1939

German "Protectorate,"
March 1939

Puppet government
controlled by Germany,
March 1939

Annexed by Poland,
Nov. 1938

Annexed by Hungary

D. Nov. 1938
E. March 1939

Annexed by Italy,
April 1939

objective would be Poland, where the Polish Corridor divided Germany into two parts (see map, above), they promised to aid Poland in the event of a German attack. The great question was now the intention of the Soviet Union. Anglo-French efforts to gain Soviet support were lackadaisical, for Chamberlain distrusted the Russians. Hitler's diplomacy, on the other hand, was vigorous; and to Stalin it seemed to promise many advantages. On August 23 Germany and the Soviet Union announced that they had agreed upon a nonaggression treaty—that is, a treaty not to make war on each other. On September 1, safe from the threat of a Russian move against Germany, Hitler invaded Poland. On September 3 Britain and France honored their promise to Poland by declaring war on Germany.

The Second World War had begun.

Persons, Places, and Terms

Benito Mussolini	Fascism	Third Reich
Pius XI	*Fascio di*	swastika
Haile Selassie	*Combattimento*	*Führer*
Neville Chamberlain	Black Shirts	*Gestapo*
Edouard Daladiér	March on Rome	concentration camp
	Lateran Treaty	Rome-Berlin Axis
Vatican City	*Mein Kampf*	Anti-Comintern Pact
Munich	Nazi party	Munich Crisis
Sudetenland	Brown Shirts	nonaggression treaty

To Master the Text

1. What were the outward evidences of the depression of 1929? Where did the depression first become important? Which country was most affected by it? What laws were passed to counteract it?

2. In postwar Italy, what groups were dissatisfied? Why? By what steps did Mussolini rise to power? By what steps did he transform Italy into a totalitarian state? What popular appeal did Fascism have? What other means did it employ to keep itself in power? How did the Fascists treat private property? Labor unions? Professional people? Businessmen? The papacy? The schools?

3. How did Hitler's early experiences shape his ideas? What was *Mein Kampf?* What methods were used by the early Nazis to destroy their enemies and to increase their own power? What important backing did Hitler secure? What steps led to his becoming dictator?

4. How did the Nazis use propaganda? How did they deal with their opponents? How did they treat the churches? The Jews? How did they use their secret police?

5. In 1930 which were the "satisfied" countries of the world and which the "dissatisfied"? How did the two groups differ in governments? Which was better prepared for war?

6. In what regions of the world could the years 1931-1936 be called an "era of aggression"? How did Hitler plan his aggressive steps in a way to confuse his opponents? List the aggressive steps he took before 1936. List Mussolini's similar steps to 1936. Why did no other government stop them?

7. Explain the outbreak of Spanish Civil War in 1936. What influence did the Spanish Civil War have on international relations?

8. What were the Rome-Berlin Axis and the Anti-Comintern Pact? List the aggressive steps taken by Germany and Japan, 1936-1939, with the support of their allies. Why did the Sudeten crisis not lead to war? What further seizures of territory followed the Munich settlement?

9. Trace the events that led directly to the Second World War.

To Master the Map

Make a small freehand map showing in one color with dates the European territories annexed by Mussolini, 1933-1939, and in another color the areas annexed by Hitler in the same years. What other countries were directly threatened by these seizures? How was the balance of power threatened?

To Interpret the Facts

1. Taking into account (a) the conditions of Italy in 1922, (b) the groups of people who were dissatisfied with their circumstances or whose way of life was being threatened, and (c) the character and early experiences of Benito Mussolini, do you consider it accidental or almost inevitable that Mussolini became dictator of Italy? Why?
2. In what ways were Fascists and Nazis alike in the manner of their rise to power and their methods of keeping power? In what ways different?
3. State the arguments for and against each of the following propositions:
 (a) Fascist and Nazi governments were unnecessarily harsh.
 (b) Fascist and Nazi harshness was justified by the new strength they gave their countries and the improvements they made in the lives of some of their citizens.
 (c) Fascism and Nazism were altogether incompatible with liberty for individuals.
4. Discuss the accuracy of this statement: The Spanish Civil War was an important prelude to the Second World War.

To Put This Chapter into a Larger Setting

1. In how many ways did Fascist Italy and Nazi Germany resemble the Communist Soviet Union? In how many ways differ from it? (Consider such matters as the ownership of land and businesses, the control of citizens by the government, the character and membership of the dominant party, the place of the party in the government, the use of propaganda and of the secret police.)
2. Looking back over the French Revolution of 1789-1795, the Russian Revolution of 1917, and the Fascist and Nazi revolutions, do you accept Lenin's argument that revolutions can most successfully be made by a small, dedicated, and highly trained group? For what historical reasons?
3. Compare the plans and policies by which Hitler tried to strengthen Germany with those of Bismarck for Prussia. How did the purposes of the two men differ? The means and methods they used? What purposes, means, and methods of Hitler were unavailable to Bismarck? Of which would he probably have disapproved? Why?

31

The
Second
World War

The Second World War was in some ways a repetition of the war of 1914-1918. At the start the Germans had the advantage of initiative and surprise, only in the end to be pushed back, slowly and painfully, by a coalition of European powers eventually joined by the Americans. But the larger part played by Japan, Russia, and the United States in the Second World War revealed a shift in the world balance of power. The bombing of cities brought civilians to the front lines of the fighting as never before in civilized times. In terms of demolition of property, lives lost, and great human suffering, the Second World War was the most widely destructive in history; it was mankind's greatest tragedy.

THE TRIUMPHS OF THE AXIS
POWERS, 1939-1940

The period of triumphant German initiative lasted from the invasion of Poland in September, 1939, to the latter part of 1940. The Germans overran Poland and partitioned it with the Soviet Union. They subdued and occupied Denmark, Norway, the Netherlands, Belgium, and France. Meantime in the Far East their allies, the Japanese, made important advances.

THE FATE OF POLAND, 1939

In the invasion of Poland the Germans revealed the effectiveness of their new weapons and new concepts of warfare. A "softening-up" process preceded the ground attack. German bombing planes destroyed centers of communication, aircraft on the ground, and stretches of railroad, interrupting ordinary daily life and thwarting Polish defense plans. Dive-bombers terrified troops and civilians. Then came the *Blitzkrieg* (German for "lightning war"). Tanks rushed over the border from Germany, tearing into the defenses and creating gaps through which came columns of troops riding in trucks, penetrating deeply into the country to surround and destroy concentrations of Polish troops. The Germans seemed to be everywhere; the Poles could not make a stand against them or even lay waste the areas into which the Germans were moving (as the Russians had done in 1812 in the path of Napoleon's invasion; see page 66). Poland's allies, France and Britain, were powerless to send aid to so distant a place. By the third week of September, 1939, western Poland was almost entirely in German control. Obviously this would be a war of movement, little like the trench warfare of 1914.

Meantime, following out the German-Soviet agreement of August, 1939 (see page 439), Soviet troops occupied eastern Poland, and German and Soviet ministers arranged a division of the country—a "Fourth Partition of Poland." Later the Soviets attacked Finland, defeating it by March, 1940, and annexing some Finnish territory. In August, 1940, they also annexed Estonia, Latvia, and Lithuania, all Russian before 1919 and now important defenses against Germany should the unstable German-Soviet alliance collapse.

THE FATE OF WESTERN EUROPE, 1939-1940

While these lightning changes were occurring in eastern Europe, western Europe was strangely quiet. The French and British governments followed an almost do-nothing policy. The French people enjoyed a sense of confident security, for they had long been constructing an elaborate system of fortifications along their eastern border—the "Maginot Line," commonly believed to be proof against all attack. Soldiers stationed along the French-German border in the winter of 1939-1940 found wartime little different from training camp. In the western world this period was called the "Phony War," or, in a play on words with *Blitzkrieg*, the *Sitzkrieg* (sitting war).

But with the arrival of spring in April, 1940, the whole northwestern part of the European continent was suddenly engulfed in a very real war. German troops crossed the border into Denmark. Since it could not resist, the Danish government submitted to German occupation. At the same time German landings were made in Norway. Here there was some effort to resist, but the Norwegians were no match for the Germans. The king fled to Britain, and the Germans established a puppet government under a Norwegian, Vidkun Quisling, whose name has ever since been a synonym for "traitor." The occupation of Denmark and Norway put the Germans into a stronger position to deal with the British both on land and at sea. This unanticipated turn of events shocked the British people into an understanding of the reality of the danger confronting them. The ministry of Neville Chamberlain fell and was replaced by another under the vigorous leadership of the dramatic, intensely patriotic, resourceful Winston Churchill.

On May 10 the Germans began a concentrated assault to drive France from the war. To avoid attacking the Maginot Line they entered France by way of the Netherlands and Belgium. In about three weeks they became the full masters of those two countries by landing parachute troops to seize airfields and bridges, by flattening the center of Rotterdam by bombing, and by using their now all-too-familiar *Blitzkrieg* tactics. The queen of the Netherlands fled to England. The king of Belgium sued for peace—a course of action much criticized by his allies—leaving British and French troops in a desperate plight on the beaches. Between May 29 and June 2, 1940, more than 300,000 British, French, and Belgian troops were carried to England from the French shore at Dunkirk by every kind of big and little boat. This "miracle of Dunkirk," although made possible partly by unwise decisions of the Germans, became one of the thrilling legends of the war.

Two weeks later France collapsed. On June 11, 1940, Mussolini, hoping for a place at the peace conference, declared war on France and Britain. On June 14 German troops occupied Paris and the French government fled. Marshal Pétain, famous general of the First World War battle at Verdun (see page 370), became premier in time to sign the armistice. Hitler arranged for the signing to take place at the same spot in the same railway car (brought from a museum for the purpose) in which the Germans had agreed to the armistice at the end of the First World War. German forces occupied the Atlantic coast of France and all of the northern half of the country. The rest of France was governed by what came to be known as the "Vichy Regime," with its capital at the resort town of Vichy and with Marshal Pétain at its head. It was a totalitarian government with many of the usual fascist features, including anti-Semitism and brutal concentration camps. It attempted to maintain good relations with both Germany and Britain. But many patriotic Frenchmen joined an underground movement, the "Resistance." The Resistance used every method of conspiracy and guerrilla warfare to attack the German occupation forces in France, and it kept in close touch with a "Free French" group in London led by General Charles de Gaulle.

THE FATE OF EASTERN ASIA

French and British involvement in war in Europe enabled Japan to expand in Asia without fear of opposition. With the permission of the Vichy government, the Japanese made use of the ports and airfields of French Indochina. Then in September, 1940, they began the occupation of the whole country. The United States protested the Japanese advances and embargoed iron and scrap steel sales to Japan. The Japanese paid no heed to the warning. They established a new government under more totalitarian lines and entered into a closer alliance with Italy and Germany.

But in spite of their uninterrupted successes, the Axis powers and their Soviet friends could not rest. There could be no peace as long as Britain remained at war with Germany. Nor did it prove possible for the Axis to continue its headlong advance. The two years beginning with the autumn of 1940 were a time of indecision, when neither side could bring the war to a triumphant conclusion.

☿ INDECISIVE YEARS: AUTUMN, 1940, TO AUTUMN, 1942

During the indecisive years, 1940-1942, the war spread to other parts of the world. Important campaigns took place simultaneously in widely separated regions. These included the Battle of Britain, the Axis struggle for the Balkan Peninsula and North Africa, Hitler's war in Russia, and the Japanese-American war in the Pacific—all heroic conflicts, overlapping in time, with the outcome in one area affecting what was happening in others.

THE BATTLE OF BRITAIN, 1940-1941

In August, 1940, Hitler began to prepare for an invasion of Britain. To paralyze British air power in advance, he ordered heavy German bombing of British airfields and manufacturing centers. Daytime bombing soon had to be stopped, however, for the new detective device of radar and the size and skill of the well-equipped British fighter force took too great a toll of German planes. In praise of British airmen Winston Churchill declared that "never in the field of human conflict was so much owed by so many to so few." The Germans next tried night bombing, concentrating on London and on other industrial cities, killing thousands of people and destroying much property. When the warning sirens were heard, people rushed to shelters. Their habits of living were disturbed, their sleep broken; and they never knew when, on returning from the shelters, they might find their homes gone and their relatives dead. Yet in spite of the constant discomfort, danger, and tragedy surrounding city life during the Battle of Britain, the

Winston Churchill greeting British sailors on his return from a wartime visit to the United States in 1942. The enthusiasm of the sailors is an example of the willingness to fight on—against great odds and, when necessary, alone—that Churchill inspired. The ever-present cigar and the "V-for-victory" sign were among Churchill's trade-marks.

people maintained their courage and determination, always inspired by the valiant attitude and eloquent phrases of Churchill. Hitler lost the Battle of Britain and by the spring of 1941 he abandoned his plans for invasion.

British courage and stamina helped stimulate Resistance movements in a number of places, and also made it possible for President Roosevelt to persuade the isolationist Congress to send ever-increasing aid to Britain. In March, 1941, by the Lend-Lease Act, the United States promised to lend war materials to "the government of any country whose defense the President deems vital for the defense of the United States." Lend-Lease aid arrived just in time to save Britain from serious shortages of food and other necessities. Then, in August, 1941, in a spectacular meeting aboard a British warship off Newfoundland, Churchill and Roosevelt signed the "Atlantic Charter," declaring, among other things, that there should be no transfers of territory at the war's end against the wishes of the inhabitants. These steps, and increasing fear of Germany, helped prepare the American people for later participation in the war.

WAR IN THE BALKANS AND THE MEDITERRANEAN AREA, 1940-1941

While the Battle of Britain was in full swing, the Axis powers carried the war into the Balkans and the Mediterranean area. Hitler hoped to secure Romanian oil and a base for further German expansion toward the east, where he believed Germany's future to lie. He was still contemplating an invasion of the Soviet Union, for his alliance with the Soviets was none too stable. Mussolini was looking for glory and for an expansion of Italian territory.

Hitler managed to bring Romania, Bulgaria, and Hungary into alliance with Germany and under his influence. When a Yugoslav *coup d'état* put Yugoslavia under a pro-Soviet regime, he bombed the capital and within a few days subdued the country. But his further progress was delayed by the failure of Mussolini's enterprises. Italian troops attacked the British in Egypt and on the Red Sea coast, and from Albania they invaded Greece. Each expedition was a failure. The situation in Greece became especially difficult, for the British rushed forces there to combat the Italians. Hitler decided to send German troops to aid his ally. At the end of May the combined Axis forces dislodged the British. With the Balkans safe from the Allies, Hitler was in a position to attack the Soviet Union.

HITLER'S INVASION OF THE U.S.S.R., 1941

The wide plains of Russia offered quick success for the *Blitzkrieg* type of warfare. Like Napoleon in 1812 (see page 65), Hitler foresaw an easy summer victory. The Germans would then be relieved of the danger of a Soviet attack at some awkward future moment, and meantime they could secure grain and minerals from the Ukraine and oil from the Caspian Sea region.

In June, 1941, Hitler sent his armies into the Soviet Union. The Finns and Romanians were his allies. The troops advanced along almost the whole western frontier of Russia in what may well have been the most massive military attack ever undertaken. At first the Germans were spectacularly successful, but before the Russian winter set in—three weeks early—they had failed to attain any of their objectives. Like Napoleon's soldiers, the Germans were inadequately equipped for the Russian winter. But Hitler would not pull them back, fearing that if he did so the German front in Russia would collapse altogether. He was now embroiled in that two-front war that all Germans so greatly feared. The Soviets and the British immediately became allies in the struggle against Nazi Germany. Moreover the Americans, anxious to help defeat Germany without having to enter the war, sent great quantities of supplies and equipment to the Soviet Union under Lend-Lease terms. Some shipments went by way of the Arctic Ocean to Murmansk, and some by way of the Persian Gulf (available as a result of a British-Russian invasion of Iran, which established a new government willing to permit the passage of Allied war materiel through the country). Most important was the resolute determination of the Russian people to drive the Germans from their country. Thus the eventual outcome of the German war in Russia was still uncertain in late 1942.

EUROPE UNDER HITLER, 1942

By the summer of 1942, Hitler was in control of more of continental Europe than had been under any single power since Roman times. Only Turkey, Spain, Portugal, Switzerland, and Sweden were free from his influence. Some of the areas nearest Germany had been annexed outright; others were to be treated in the future as colonies; still others were under military occupation. The satellite states (Hungary, Bulgaria, Romania, and Finland) were enlarged. Italy was allowed to occupy some of the conquered territory.

The fate of Europe under the Nazis could not in any case have been a happy one during wartime, but it was made incalculably worse by other factors. The Germans made every possible use of the subjected areas for the advantage of their own war effort, taking great quantities of booty and forcing millions of people to go to Germany to furnish slave labor in German factories. As the war progressed, the demands on the non-German regions became ever greater. Nazi ideas of the superiority of Germans to other peoples also played a part in the treatment of the non-Germans under their control. Some were much more harshly treated than others. The Jews were in the most deplorable situation, for the Nazis were determined to exterminate all the Jewish people. Most of the German Jews had already been exiled, imprisoned, or killed before the war; now came the turn of the Jews in the occupied countries. These hapless people were herded into concentration camps, where mass shootings and death in gas chambers awaited millions of them. This brutality of the Nazi regime had its part in the final defeat of Germany, for it further alienated the people under German control and horrified the other nations of the world.

THE WAR IN THE PACIFIC, 1941-1942

In 1941 war broke out in the Pacific between Japan and the United States, but until mid-1942 it was no more decisive than the war in Europe.

Throughout 1941 tension between Japan and the United States mounted. The Japanese sought to use the period of European preoccupation with war to seize regions from which to secure the essential raw materials increasingly demanded by their growing population and their multiplying factories. They spoke of a doctrine of "Asia for the Asians," which they argued was similar to the Monroe Doctrine. But the United States was determined to maintain the "open door" in China. (See page 345.) After the Japanese began their gradual occupation of China in 1937, American aid was sent to Chiang Kai-shek in Chungking. The Roosevelt government protested Japanese aggression and continued the embargo of war needs to Japan, begun when the Japanese threatened Indochina, the Malay colonies, and the East Indies—possessions of the European countries the United States was supporting. But Roosevelt did not want to take his country into war. He believed the people to be psychologically unready, and he feared that diversion of American war materiel to the Pacific would seriously weaken Allied chances of victory in Europe.

Then suddenly the Japanese turned the tense struggle in the Pacific into a shooting war. On December 7, 1941, they attacked the American naval base at Pearl Harbor in Hawaii with carrier-based aircraft, sinking three battleships, damaging five others, destroying airplanes, and killing more than 2,000 American men. The United States and Great Britain immediately declared war on Japan; Germany and Italy, honoring their treaty with Japan, declared war on the United States. A World War was now truly in progress.

The Japanese acted quickly after the attack on Pearl Harbor, before the United States could recover strength in the Pacific. They captured Guam and Wake islands from the United States and began the conquest of the Philippines. From Britain they took Hong Kong and Singapore. By May, 1942, they completed the conquest of the Philippines and the Malay Peninsula, conquered Burma and closed the Burma Road to Chungking, seized control of the Netherlands East Indies, and were in a position to threaten Australia. But the quick revival of American naval power put the outcome of the war in the Pacific in doubt.

◌ THE TURNING OF THE TIDE, SUMMER, 1942

The early months of 1942 were for both sides a time of mingled hope and discouragement. The Germans had not forced their enemies to accept an imposed peace; the western powers had experienced little but defeat. Then in August for the first time Allied shipbuilding was more extensive than their losses to German submarines. The military picture also changed.

In the Pacific the shift in the balance between Japan and the United States was evidenced by two American achievements. In June the Americans turned back a Japanese expedition making its way toward the United States possession of Midway Island, whence Japanese bombers and transports expected to attack Hawaii. Later the Americans seized and defended the tropical island of Guadalcanal in the Solomons, the first of a series of island conquests leading toward Japan itself. Thereafter it was the Americans who made the advances in the Pacific, slow and costly though they were.

In the Russian theater of the war the year was decisive because of the heroic Russian defense of Stalingrad on the Volga River. The Germans were besieging the city, important to their war effort because it controlled the flow of oil northward from the Caspian oil fields, and of immense psychological importance to both Stalin and Hitler because it bore the name of the Russian dictator. So dogged was the Russian defense and counterattack that in early 1943 the siege was lifted and the German besieging army captured. Thereafter the Russians began to drive the Germans back.

The most spectacular allied victories were in North Africa. In November, 1942, an Anglo-American force landed near the Moroccan and Algerian ports of Casablanca, Oran, and Algiers. The combined use of landing craft to bring up men and equipment needed for land warfare, of guns from naval vessels, and of aircraft—a method of fighting called "amphibious warfare"— was characteristic of the Second World War. At first there was trouble with the representatives of the French Vichy Regime, who still controlled French North Africa; but the Allies were soon able to set up a Free French government under General de Gaulle. German-Italian forces also posed a threat, although at this time they were being driven westward from Egypt by British forces. In May, 1943, the Allies, pressing from east and west, finally defeated the German-Italian armies, and all North Africa fell into Allied hands.

⌒ FINAL ALLIED VICTORY, 1943-1945

By 1943 the Allies were launched on a slow road to victory, although the peoples of the war-torn world had still to live through three more years of labor, hardship, and bloodshed before the fighting was over.

In these latter days of the war the side that could produce an uninterrupted supply of military equipment was at increasing advantage. Until the early months of 1942, German bombers had interrupted and destroyed Soviet and British war plants at such a rate that the success of the whole Allied war effort was in question. By 1943, however, the situation had been reversed. The German air force, weakened by loss of planes on missions abroad and by the ceaseless "round-the-clock" Allied bombings of German factories and cities, was no longer the mighty weapon it had once been. Besides, the Soviet Union had moved much of its heavy industry to safety behind the Ural Mountains. From the United States—safe between its oceans from the relatively short-range planes of that day—vast quantities of war materiel poured into Allied ports. By 1945 more than half of world production for war purposes came from the United States.

The intricate planning required to get the materiel to the right place at the right time went forward with ever-greater efficiency, and also with greater safety as air patrols cut down Allied losses at sea from German submarines. Over-all Allied policy was worked out in meetings among many lesser officials and finally in conferences among Roosevelt, Stalin, and Churchill. The result of all this co-ordinated activity was decisive victory first in Italy, then in Germany, and finally in Japan.

THE DEFEAT OF ITALY

From North Africa it was natural that the Allies should press the war into Italy. In July, 1943, just two months after their victory over the German-Italian forces in Africa, they made an amphibious landing in Sicily, and six weeks later in Italy itself. Two unexpected developments in Italy altered the character of the war in the peninsula. Even before the Allies landed, a *coup d'état* had restored the power of the king. Mussolini was deposed and imprisoned; Fascism was officially abandoned. With the help of the Germans, Mussolini escaped to become the head of a "Fascist Republic" in northern Italy; but in 1945, as the war was nearing its close, he was captured and put to death by the anti-Fascists. The king's government meantime agreed to an unconditional surrender to the Allies in September, 1943. But the war continued in Italy until the collapse of Germany, for German troops in the peninsula refused to honor the Italian surrender terms. They battled the Allied armies with stubborness and skill, falling back to the north only very slowly.

THE DEFEAT OF GERMANY

The final defeat of Germany was achieved by a combination of pressures from east, west, and south, including the Italian campaign. Throughout 1943 the Soviets pushed the Germans relentlessly westward, recovering most of what the Germans had taken from them earlier in the war, and in the next year moving into the Balkans and Poland. It was in France, however, that the Allies achieved their greatest triumph. On June 6, 1944, "D-Day," under the leadership of General Dwight D. Eisenhower, the Supreme Allied Commander, they made a landing on the coast of Normandy. This largest invasion by sea in all history had been in preparation since 1942. Nothing that could add to its success had been thought too great a trouble. Ships and landing craft numbered more than five thousand to transport some 150,000 men, all especially trained for this great venture. Some 1,500 tanks were used and 12,000 planes. Even portable harbors had been constructed. The Germans had no navy to obstruct the Channel crossing and very little air power. On land they opposed the Allied troops with fierce determination but with-

ICELAND

NORWAY

SWEDEN

FINLAND

Murmansk

UNION OF

SOVIET

SOCIALIST

REPUBLICS

Leningrad

ESTONIA

LATVIA

LITHUANIA

Moscow

IRELAND

GREAT
BRITAIN

DENMARK

London

NETHERLANDS

Rotterdam

Berlin

Warsaw

Kiev

Stalingrad

BELGIUM

Dunkirk

GERMANY

POLAND

Normandy

LUX.

Paris

FRANCE

Vienna

HUNGARY

ROMANIA

Yalta

SWITZERLAND

Vichy

YUGOSLAVIA

BULGARIA

CAUCASUS
MTS.

PORTUGAL

SPAIN

ITALY

Corsica

Rome

Albania
(It.)

GREECE

TURKEY

Sardinia

Algiers

Oran

Sicily

Casablanca

Tunis

Crete

Cyprus
(Br.)

Syria
(Fr.)

Morocco
(Fr.)

Algeria
(Fr.)

Tunisia
(Fr.)

Lebanon
(Fr.)

IRA

Palestine
(Br.)

SAUDI
ARABIA

Alexandria

Transjordan (Br.)

Cairo

Libya (It.)

EGYPT

THE SECOND WORLD WAR NOVEMBER, 1942-MAY, 1945

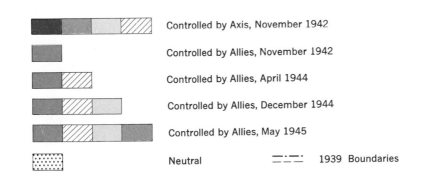

Controlled by Axis, November 1942

Controlled by Allies, November 1942

Controlled by Allies, April 1944

Controlled by Allies, December 1944

Controlled by Allies, May 1945

Neutral   1939 Boundaries

out any real possibility of stopping the invasion. Twenty days after the landing the Allies had more than a million men in France. In August, 1944, still another Allied expedition landed on the Mediterranean coast of France near the mouth of the Rhone. For the rest of 1944 Allied forces in eastern Europe, in Italy, and in France pressed with increasing force upon the Germans, always pushing them back and depleting their supplies and equipment—which, in the battered condition of Germany itself, could not be replaced. By February, 1945, when Churchill, Roosevelt, and Stalin met in conference at Yalta, it was apparent that the Germans could not last much longer. Allied armies entered Germany from east and west, meeting in the middle of the country. On May 2, 1945, Berlin fell to the Russians. Hitler met his death in the ruins of the city. Five days later the Germans surrendered unconditionally, and the war in Europe was over.

THE DEFEAT OF JAPAN

The war against Japan had followed a very different course from that in Europe. President Roosevelt had decided that until the Nazis were defeated,

American soldiers going ashore from their landing craft at Omaha Beach, Normandy, June 6, 1944. The successful landing in France, terribly costly in lives though it was, marked the beginning of the last stage of the Second World War in Europe.

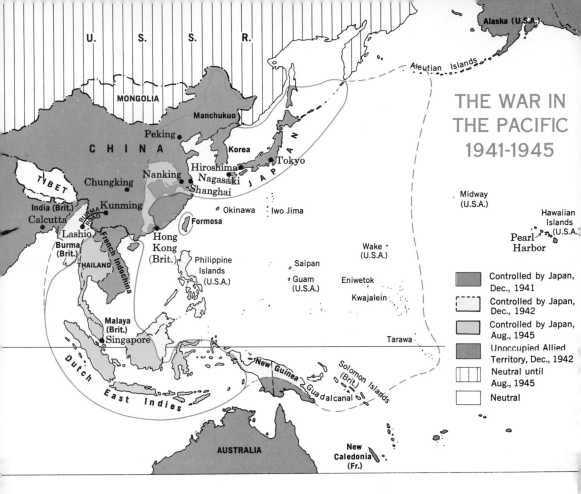

THE WAR IN
THE PACIFIC
1941-1945

Controlled by Japan, Dec., 1941

Controlled by Japan, Dec., 1942

Controlled by Japan, Aug., 1945

Unoccupied Allied Territory, Dec., 1942

Neutral until Aug., 1945

Neutral

the greater part of the American war effort should be applied to Europe. Progress in the Far East was therefore slower than it might otherwise have been, but it was steady. It consisted of "island hopping"; that is, amphibious landings on one tropical island after another, always moving toward Japan. In the larger islands like New Guinea there were long periods of jungle fighting, and always there were hard-fought struggles with the Japanese. The Americans were associated in this part of the war with Australian and other Commonwealth troops. By 1945 the Allied forces were close to Japan itself. At Yalta it had been agreed that after the European war was concluded, the Russians would join the Allies in the war against Japan. They were to be rewarded by recovering rights they had enjoyed in China before the Russo-Japanese War of 1904-1905. Allied military men were much concerned about the problems posed by the difficulties of landing in Japan. At best it was feared that it would cost the lives of half a million Allied soldiers to bring about the final defeat of Japan. To avoid such a costly invasion, it was decided to use the atomic bomb, long secretly in process of construction by American, British, and Canadian scientists. On August 6 and 9, 1945, atomic bombs were dropped on the Japanese cities of Hiroshima and Nagasaki. These two bombs killed 100,000 Japanese people amid the utter ruin of the two cities. The Japanese government then agreed to surrender. On September 2, the Second World War came to an end.

☯ ☯ ☯

For the second time in the century wartime leaders confronted the duty of returning the world to peace. Again, much of Europe lay in ruins. Again, Germany was vanquished. But this time German territory was completely occupied by the victorious armies, and this time Japan was also among the defeated countries. Remembering the failures of the peace of 1919, the statesmen of 1945 were determined to act differently; but it soon became apparent that peace-making in 1945 would be even more difficult than it had been in 1919.

A part of Hiroshima, Japan, after the atomic bomb blast of August 6, 1945. The bomb killed between 75,000 and 80,000 persons; demolished between 62,000 and 90,000 buildings; left most of the buildings that remained too damaged for use; and left thousands of persons crippled, severely burned, or suffering from radiation sickness. After a second bomb was dropped on Nagasaki, Japan surrendered, bringing the Second World War to an end.

Persons, Places, and Terms

Winston Churchill	Pearl Harbor	*Blitzkrieg*
Charles de Gaulle	Midway Island	quisling
Dwight D.	Solomon Islands	Vichy Regime
Eisenhower	Guadalcanal	Resistance
	Volga River	Free French
Maginot Line	Stalingrad	Battle of Britain
Rotterdam	Casablanca	Atlantic Charter
Dunkirk	Oran	"Asia for Asians"
Vichy	Normandy	amphibious warfare
Arctic Ocean	Rhone River	D-Day
Murmansk	Hiroshima	Yalta Conference
Iran	Nagasaki	

To Master the Text

1. Describe *Blitzkrieg*. What part was taken by German forces in the subduing of Poland? By the Soviet Union? What was the fate of Poland? Of Finland? Of the other Baltic states?

2. What happened in western Europe in the winter of 1939-1940? List the countries invaded by the Germans in 1940. Why did Mussolini enter the war when he did? How was France governed after June, 1940? What were the Resistance and Free French movements?

3. What advances did the Japanese make in Asia in 1940?

4. Why can the time from autumn, 1940, to autumn, 1942, be called "indecisive"? What was the purpose and outcome of the Battle of Britain? What influence did it have on the United States?

5. What did Hitler hope to accomplish in the Balkan region in 1940-1941? What did Mussolini hope to accomplish? What Balkan countries was Hitler able to control? Into what areas did Mussolini send troops? With what result?

6. When and why did Hitler attack the Soviet Union? Why did he expect success? What prevented a quick German victory?

7. By the end of 1941 how much of Europe was under Hitler's control? What differences did the Nazis make in their treatment of the various peoples under their control? What was the goal of their policy toward the Jews? In what way did they carry it out?

8. What developments led to the bombing of Pearl Harbor? What were the immediate results of the attack? What conquests did the Japanese make in the months immediately after Pearl Harbor?

9. To what extent did the battles of Midway and Guadalcanal indicate a turning point in the war in the Pacific? To what extent was the battle for Stalingrad a turning point in the war in Europe? How did the American landing in North Africa in 1942 help make the year a turning point for the whole Second World War?

10. What did industries contribute to the outcome of the war?
11. How and when was Italy forced out of the war? What was the fate of Mussolini? What changes were made in the Italian government?
12. Describe the Allied invasion of Normandy in June, 1944. What other invasions of German-held territory were in progress at the same time? Which of the Allies was given the honor of being first in Berlin? Why? When and under what terms did the Germans surrender?
13. Why did war against Japan go more slowly than war in Europe? What was the character of it? When, why, and where was the atomic bomb used? With what immediate and what long-range results?
14. How did the situation in the world at the end of the fighting differ from the situation after the armistice of November, 1918?

To Master the Map

Write the history of the war in maps by showing the following with the use of freehand, traced, or desk outline maps: (1) Soviet and German acquisitions of territory in Poland and the Baltic region, 1939-1940; (2) other lands invaded in 1940 and thereafter controlled by the Germans; (3) Japanese advances in China and French Indochina, 1940; (4) Balkan and North African countries under German or Italian control by spring, 1941; (5) areas in Southeast Asia occupied by Japan by spring, 1942; (6) Russian areas under German control by summer, 1942; (7) areas in Europe, North Africa, and the Pacific conquered by the Allies by April, 1944; (8) areas conquered by the Allies, April-December, 1944; and (9) areas conquered by the Allies from January, 1945, to the German and Japanese surrenders.

To Interpret the Facts

1. To what extent was there a truly co-operative alliance between the Soviet Union and the western Allies? To what extent was there true co-operation among the Axis powers?
2. To what extent was final Allied victory the result of military activity and to what extent the result of such factors as geography, industry, size of population, and quality of leadership? How important were such factors as form of government and organization of society?

To Put This Chapter into a Larger Setting

Compare the three great wars of the past two centuries (the Napoleonic Wars and the First and Second World Wars) by comparing the following aspects of the three struggles: (a) the most widely used weapons and methods of fighting; (b) the adoption during the war of new weapons and new tactics; (c) the contributions of civilians behind the lines to the war effort; and (d) the character and use of seapower.

 32

The
Cold
War

1945 to the 1960's

When Germany collapsed in May, 1945, the victorious powers faced the staggering task of restoring peace and order in Europe. Decisions had to be made about how the defeated nations were to be governed. The assumption of ordinary people in the Allied countries had been that an alliance of the victors would create a new and better world. Just after the war, however, the alliance between the Soviet Union and other Allied countries began to break apart. The immediate postwar concerns of the Soviet Union were rebuilding its battered country and controlling the countries on its eastern border to create a buffer zone against any future attack.

As the Soviet Union consolidated its control over eastern Europe, it tried to ensure that the Soviet definition of Communism would prevail. The United States, the strongest country to emerge from the war, began to see in this spread of Communism a major threat to western capitalism and democracy. Aided by its European allies, the United States developed policies to contain the spread of Communism. To United States policy makers, Communism and the Soviet Union were one and the same. The struggle between the Soviet Union and the United States began shortly after the end of World War II. Since it was fought primarily with words and alliances, although sometimes with bullets, it was called the "Cold War."

⊙ THE DIVISION OF EUROPE: 1945–1947

The combined effects of wartime bombing and invasion, particularly in the industrial areas of Europe, had been devastating. In all of England and Germany, only three major cities—Cambridge, Oxford, and Heidelberg— were untouched by bombs. Warsaw, Vienna, Budapest, and Rotterdam were in ruins. The capital of Germany, Berlin, was so badly damaged that when the Allied leaders met there at the war's end, they decided to move to Potsdam, a smaller city on the outskirts of Berlin. Except for the areas through which the armies had passed, the European countryside was not as badly scarred. Transportation of any kind was difficult, however. The European people also suffered from shortages of all kinds of necessities.

The Soviet Union had been especially damaged by the Nazi invasion and the fighting during the Soviet counterattack. At least 15 million people in the Soviet Union had been killed by the Germans, and 25 million were homeless. The most fertile section of the Soviet Union, from Moscow to the western border, had been laid waste. Almost half of the nation's industry had been destroyed.

All over Europe there were refugees. The Nazis had moved whole populations out of German-occupied zones and scattered them in labor camps across Europe. A large part of Europe's Jewish population had been murdered in concentration camps. The survivors now attempted to return home. Even some Germans were refugees, many having fled in fear of advancing Soviet troops. Yugoslavia and Czechoslovakia celebrated their victory by forcing their German-speaking minorities to leave. When parts of eastern Germany were given to Poland in the postwar settlements, the German population there fled to the west.

Europe lay divided as it had fallen to the victorious Allied troops. With the exception of Germany, there was no attempt to decide which Ally would govern the restablishment of which country. Rather, there was an ad hoc agreement that each would temporarily govern the countries its troops had liberated. Thus, 1945 saw the western European Allies in control of the northern European countries and of Italy and Greece. Yugoslavia, whose resistance forces had successfully beaten back the Nazis, controlled its own borders. The Soviets occupied the remainder of eastern Europe.

THE YALTA CONFERENCE

In 1945, shortly before the war's end, Stalin, Roosevelt, and Churchill met at Yalta to discuss plans for the postwar world. British and American officials had deferred this planning, believing that maximum harmony among the Allies was needed to win the war. Churchill supported de Gaulle and his Free French movement as the rightful government of France, but Roosevelt was hostile to de Gaulle. Roosevelt believed that the British government was overly interested in imperialism, while Churchill resented Roosevelt's expression of anti-imperialism. Churchill was suspicious of Stalin. Roosevelt, on the other hand, believed that he could persuade Stalin in face-to-face meetings to favor the policies of the western Allies.

ESTABLISHING THE UNITED NATIONS

At Yalta the final plans to establish the United Nations took shape. On the American side Roosevelt was convinced that postwar settlements could only be assured if the United States continued to play a part in world affairs. He feared that the United States would withdraw into isolationism as it had after 1919. To help prevent this, he forced through the planning and organizing of the United Nations at Yalta while the war was still in progress.

The major body of the United Nations, the Security Council, was to be in permanent session with a member assigned to it from each of the great powers (the Soviet Union, the United States, China, France, and Great Britain) and from six (later ten) other members among the smaller nations. These smaller countries were to be elected in rotation by the General Assembly, in which every member country would be represented.

At Yalta the Big Three powers agreed to the crucial question of veto power in the Security Council: each of the Big Three would be able to veto a decision of the Security Council. Because the western Allies would dominate the Security Council, and China, a major power, was closely allied to the United States, the veto was a Soviet condition for membership.

Roosevelt's fears that the United States would quickly retire from Europe at the end of the war were well founded. His successor, Harry S. Truman, trusting in part to the American monopoly of the atomic bomb, yielded to popular demand that American troops be brought home as soon as possible. The United States government also scrapped a great deal of war materiel. By 1948 American military forces were at a peacetime strength of one million, while the Soviet Union, which had suffered much greater damage from the Nazis, still kept six million.

POSTWAR SETTLEMENTS

At Yalta, Churchill, Roosevelt, and Stalin agreed to divide Germany into four military zones, to be occupied by the United States, Great Britain, the Soviet Union, and France. The division between the Soviet and western zones was made along the line at which the armies had met in April, 1945, with Soviet troops approaching from the east and the other Allied armies from the west. Berlin, inside the Soviet zone, was divided into sectors, each controlled by one of the four Allied occupation forces. This temporary solution was long-lived; when the Allied foreign ministers met they were unable to agree on any permanent plan.

The question of German reparations for war damage was also decided in a preliminary way at Yalta. The Soviet Union was reeling from its war effort. Stalin still saw his wartime Allies much as he had in the years before the war—as potential enemies of both the Russian revolution and his own power. He feared to reveal the extent of the Soviet Union's losses, but he was determined to get reparation from the Germans.

The Big Three leaders agreed on a total for German payments: $20 billion, with half to go to the Soviet Union. Because the Soviet Union needed to rebuild its industries, it was agreed that reparations could be taken in kind. Germany's industrial plants in excess of its current needs could be dismantled and used for reparations. The Soviet sector of Germany was mainly agricultural; hence an additional agreement allowed the Soviet Union to take some industrial material from the western zones.

At Yalta and later at Potsdam, the Big Three powers agreed unanimously that Germany should be demilitarized and that Nazi leaders should be removed from all posts of influence and brought to justice. Others who had collaborated with the Nazis were to be discovered, punished, and prevented from exerting influence in the future. However, so many Germans had been in some way connected with the Nazi regime that the policy became impractical and soon came to an end. The most spectacular result of the original agreement were the trials of prominent Nazis at the International Military Tribunal at Nuremberg, where a number of them were judged guilty of war crimes and imprisoned or executed.

It was at Yalta, even before the war's end, that the single most important issue of the postwar years first appeared. Stalin's Soviet troops had just driven the Nazis out of eastern Europe. Soviet forces were in occupation of the whole area between the Soviet border and the western line of the Soviet zone in Germany. The disposition of these areas would become a major issue in the approaching Cold War.

To some extent the United States and its western Allies were responsible for the situation. In 1942, with the Germans deep in Soviet territory, Stalin had begged his Allies to attack somewhere on the continent, to draw off part

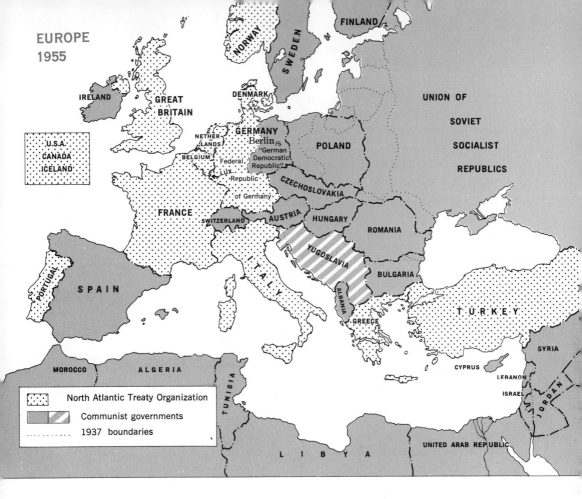

EUROPE
1955

U.S.A.
CANADA
ICELAND

IRELAND   GREAT
           BRITAIN

NORWAY   SWEDEN   FINLAND

DENMARK

NETHER-
LANDS   GERMANY
         Berlin
BELGIUM "German
         Democratic   POLAND
LUX.   Republic"

         Federal.
         Republic
         of Germany

FRANCE   CZECHOSLOVAKIA

         SWITZERLAND AUSTRIA HUNGARY

UNION OF

SOVIET

SOCIALIST

REPUBLICS

ROMANIA

PORTUGAL

SPAIN

ITALY   YUGOSLAVIA

                     BULGARIA

         ALBANIA

         GREECE

MOROCCO   ALGERIA

TUNISIA

TURKEY

SYRIA

CYPRUS

LEBANON

ISRAEL   JORDAN

North Atlantic Treaty Organization
Communist governments
1937 boundaries

LIBYA

UNITED ARAB REPUBLIC

of the German forces from the U.S.S.R. It took two more long years before
the Allies began their major thrust in a landing on Normandy. During that
period the Soviet forces had had to drive the Germans out of Soviet territory and push them westward. Now at Yalta, Roosevelt and Churchill voiced
concern about the fate of the newly liberated countries of eastern Europe.
The Soviet forces, they argued, must establish independent governments in
all Soviet-occupied countries, as had been previously agreed by the Allies in
the Atlantic Charter. (See page 447.) At issue were the governments of
Poland, Romania, Hungary, Bulgaria, and Czechoslovakia.

Stalin's arguments were bitter and passionate. Romania, Hungary, and
Bulgaria, he pointed out, had been Nazi allies and had cooperated with the
Nazis in their invasion of the Soviet Union. He did not intend to give inde-
pendence to these territories only to find them threatening his nation again.
Furthermore, some of the countries of eastern Europe lay across the Soviet

Union's military path into Germany. The Soviet leaders were bitterly determined to make certain that Germany would never be able to threaten them again.

Stalin eventually agreed to the wording of an agreement at Yalta providing that free elections would be held in all liberated countries. But almost immediately it became clear that the Soviet leaders would refuse to give up their hard-won conquests. A minister from the Soviet Union flew into Romania and "convinced" that country's leadership to establish a Communist government from which other parties were excluded. During the same period American diplomats in Poland began to complain that the Soviet forces there were refusing to act on the Yalta agreements.

While the war progressed, Churchill and Roosevelt had chosen to ignore these violations. At Potsdam, however, in July, 1945, the United States and Britain (now represented by President Harry Truman and Prime Minister Clement Atlee) insisted on Soviet compliance. Stalin seemed to agree. As a concession he established coalition governments (National Front governments) in the Soviet-occupied territories. Although firmly under the control of local Communist parties, non-Communist members were allowed to hold posts in these governments.

The Soviets also agreed at Potsdam that ninety days after peace treaties were signed with the occupied countries, Soviet troops would withdraw from these areas. Treaties were signed in 1947 with a number of Germany's former allies: Italy, Bulgaria, Hungary, Romania, and Finland. The western Allies jointly occupied Austria until the conclusion of the Austrian Peace Treaty in 1955. They also occupied Japan after its surrender in 1945: A peace treaty was signed between the Japanese and the western Allies in 1951 and with the Soviet Union in 1952. (See page 501). By the time these treaties were signed, the agreements of earlier wartime conferences had become irrelevant because the Cold War between the Soviet Union and the United States had begun in earnest.

ᔐ THE START OF THE COLD WAR

Although the Soviet leaders' intentions to maintain control over Soviet-occupied areas of eastern Europe had been clear before the end of the war, its western Allies did not react until almost two years after the war's close. The Americans had seen their involvement in the Second World War as an opportunity to open sections of Europe to American influence. While Winston Churchill talked about spheres of influence, giving the Soviet Union eastern Europe and Britain the Mediterranean, the United States had objected that this was merely restoring the old order of things. Postwar Europe was to be open to new influence.

In some ways the events of the postwar period were an extensions of prewar hostilities between a Communist U.S.S.R. and the capitalist West. In the postwar world, however, only two strong powers remained: the United States and the Soviet Union. During the two years after the war, Truman and his advisors began to feel that only the United States could stop the expansion of Soviet power into the vacuum left by the destruction of Nazi power in Europe. Only the wealth of the United States could counter the shortages and suffering that Europeans faced and keep the continent's dissatisfied and desperate people from embracing Communism as the solution to their economic difficulties.

Truman had met Stalin at Potsdam in July, 1945, just after the Americans had successfully tested the atom bomb. American diplomats had believed then that the bomb would give them considerable power in world affairs, but their hopes had been frustrated. The Soviet Union had refused to participate in an American plan to control the spread of atomic weapons. (In Soviet eyes the plan was little more than an American attempt to monopolize control over atomic power.)

To the United States it began to seem that there was a conspiracy by the Soviet Union to take over the world. National Front governments in the eastern European countries had left the Communists firmly in control of that region. In France and Italy strong Communist parties were building up their memberships. Communist ministers were in both governments. The United States believed that Communist guerrilla movements in Greece and Turkey were supported by the Soviet Union. The western Allies began to fear that the Soviet Union intended to expand into western Europe.

THE TRUMAN DOCTRINE

In 1947 the Labor government of Britain declared that it could no longer afford to give economic aid to Greece and Turkey. President Truman asked the United States Congress for the authority to send military and civilian personnel to Greece. He also requested $400 million for Greece and Turkey. It was, he said, only the beginning. Truman declared that the United States would aid all peoples struggling to maintain their freedom against armed minorities or outside forces. This policy soon became known as the "Truman

Doctrine." It was the start of a deliberate American effort to contain Soviet expansion by political, economic, and military means, including drawing a military ring around the Soviet Union and its satellites.

In the same year Truman's Secretary of State, George C. Marshall, announced that the United States was considering a program of economic aid to European countries. The Marshall Plan totaled $5.3 billion. European countries that agreed to stabilize their currencies and work for economic recovery would qualify for aid. Ultimately some $17 billion in aid was given to Europe through this program. In European countries where all resources were being used for food and other necessities, the Marshall Plan was welcomed. It enabled Europeans to rebuild industrial plants destroyed by the war. In that same period Communist ministers in France and Italy were removed from office after United States officials hinted that this would facilitate the granting of economic aid.

In 1949 the creation of the North Atlantic Treaty Organization (NATO) formalized the military alliance of the western European countries against the Soviet Union. In order to retard any attack on western Europe until American forces could arrive, twelve non-Communist countries joined together. The original members were Belgium, the Netherlands, Luxembourg, Italy, Portugal, Denmark, Iceland, Norway, Canada, France, Great Britain, and the United States. NATO was headquartered in Paris. In 1952 Greece and Turkey joined the alliance, and in 1955 West Germany joined. The NATO treaty declared that "an armed attack against one or more" of its members "shall be considered an attack against them all." General Dwight D. Eisenhower was the first Supreme Allied Commander of NATO, and his successors were also Americans.

The Truman Doctrine, the Marshall Plan, and the establishment of NATO were to be the bulwarks of the United States' new policy. As the American attitude toward the Soviet Union shifted from friendship to hostility, the United States' view of Germany underwent an equal but opposite change. German industry, the Americans argued, was the base of Europe's economy. The rejuvenation of Europe rested on the reconstruction of the German economy. A strong Germany also seemed to offer a good means of checking the Soviet Union's expansionism. With this in mind the United States arranged the merging of the Allied zones in western Germany into one economic unit. German industries were allowed to produce goods at a faster rate than had been planned in the earlier postwar agreements. By 1948 the United States was even considering giving Germany political independence.

Most of America's European allies, who had suffered much at the hands of a powerful German nation, were unenthusiastic about this new commitment to a restored, stronger German economy. Britain's Labor government stated that only government ownership of German industry would be sufficient to check the growth of a new militant Germany. France's objections were particularly strong, and French fears managed to delay German rearmament until 1955. The United States, however, insisted on a strengthened Germany, and its European allies, relying deeply on Marshall Plan aid, were forced to accept the American viewpoint.

THE SOVIET SATELLITE COUNTRIES

The Soviet Union responded to the Truman Doctrine and other American economic and political efforts by intensifying its control over eastern Europe and by developing its own brand of containment. National Front governments were dissolved, and the Communist parties in eastern Europe purged their non-Communist members. Soviet leaders ceased to pretend that the eastern European countries were independent nations. They drew, in Winston Churchill's phrase, an "iron curtain" around the Soviet Union and the eastern satellite countries, cutting off most contacts with the nations of the West. After the initiation of the Truman Doctrine, pro-Soviet speakers charged that Americans were interested primarily in expanding their influence throughout the world. The Soviet Union and its allies, they said, were trying to check the spread of American "imperialism."

In Czechoslovakia the Soviet Union's policy change was most abrupt. A 1948 Communist-inspired coup overturned the established Czech government. Czech President Eduard Beneš resigned, and the Foreign Minister, the son of the founder of the Czech nation, was found dead in mysterious circumstances. The country's ties to the West were severed, and parliamentary democracy was abandoned.

The Soviet Union's efforts to take over Yugoslavia, however, ended in failure. The Yugoslavs had a Communist government headed by Marshall Tito, a resistance leader whose forces had successfully liberated the country in 1945. Tito threatened to call out his entire army and then, cut his ties with the Soviet Union. In the postwar years Yugoslavia was one of the few Communist countries to accept economic aid from the West.

To Soviet leaders the new American decision to rebuild Germany may well have been the most disturbing aspect of American policy. The specter of a strong, revived German state deeply alarmed the Soviet Union. Russia had twice been invaded by the Germans in the twentieth century. Thus, the Soviet Union sought to keep Germany divided and weak. As the United States increased its efforts to rebuild the German economy, Soviet leaders renewed their claims to German reparations. By 1947 German industrial production had increased to much higher levels than the Allies had considered desirable in 1945. The Soviet Union demanded that reparations be paid from current German production. The United States countered with the accusation that this was a deliberate effort to permanently damage German industry and force the German people to suffer for an even longer period. The Americans used the new demands by the Soviet Union as an excuse to end reparations entirely.

As part of the effort to counter the Truman Doctrine, Soviet leaders decided that Communist policy in the U.S.S.R. and its satellite countries should be coordinated. The earlier Communist International, an organization dedicated to spreading Communism in the world, had been disbanded by Stalin as a gesture of good will toward his western Allies. Now the Soviet leaders established the Cominform—an organization that was to act as an information link among the various countries of the Soviet bloc. The first action of the Soviet bloc as a group was its refusal to participate in the Marshall Plan.

In the postwar years as the Cold War deepened, Soviet concern about its control over other Communist parties increased. The Soviet Union wanted only one style of Communism in the world, Soviet Communism. Its failure to control Tito in Yugoslavia did not stop the Soviet Union from attempting to define Communist ideology and policy in its satellite countries and in Communist parties throughout the world. In the 1950's the internal economic and political policies of the Soviet satellites were less important to the Soviet Union than their participation in the Soviet defense scheme and their adherence to Soviet ideology. During the Cold War American leaders saw the strong arm of the Soviet Union behind Communist movements throughout the world. This interpretation was not always correct, but it was an accurate reading of the Soviet desires that the U.S.S.R. be the center of a worldwide Communist movement defined and controlled in Moscow.

♋ THE COLD WAR HEATS UP

The Cold War lasted from 1947 to 1962. For over 15 years both the United States and the Soviet Union struggled to dominate and contain the other. The struggle became more equal in 1949 when the Soviet Union tested an atomic bomb, and the United States seemed to have lost a substantial advantage in the world's military balance of power. Throughout the Cold War the United States saw itself as the protector of freedom and democracy. The Soviet Union saw itself, in turn, as the defender and preserver of world Communism. During the 15 years in which the Cold War was fought, the weapons were mainly ideological, political, and economic, although on several occasions fighting was done with bullets.

BERLIN AND GERMANY

The United States' commitment to rebuild Germany was a major irritant to the Soviet Union during the early years of the Cold War. With America's encouragement Germany's industrial production was increasing, its economy was recovering, and by 1948 there was talk among the western Allies of establishing an independent German nation. The western Allies, who feared a Germany that could dominate Europe, wanted a reunification of the nation only if it could be based on free elections. The Soviet Union, which wanted a weak Germany and feared a defeat at the polls in its zone, refused such elections. They could not stop the rebuilding within the larger western zone, but they could keep the country divided.

Meanwhile, the city of Berlin, well inside the Soviet zone, also remained divided. In July, 1948, Soviet-controlled forces blockaded the western sector of Berlin, stopping the passage of food and goods into the city. The reasons for this blockade remain unclear. Some observers suggested that Soviet leaders wished to force the western Allies to abandon the city, thus consolidating the Soviet hold over the eastern zone of Germany. Others pointed out that the United States had only recently stopped the payment of German reparations to the Soviet Union. This, combined with the new talk of a politically independent Germany, may have been more than Soviet leaders would tolerate.

The Berlin blockade may have been a Soviet effort to force the West to negotiate. For whatever reasons, however, the blockade failed. The Allied forces airlifted food and necessities into isolated Berlin for almost a year. In May, 1949, Soviet controlled forces abandoned their effort, lifted the blockade, and allowed goods to move freely into Berlin again. In that same year the three western zones of Germany became an independent country, the "Federal Republic of Germany" (West Germany). Almost immediately the Soviet Union turned the eastern zone into the "German Democratic Republic" (East Germany).

Twelve years later Berlin was again the scene of a Soviet expression of displeasure with events in West Germany. As plans for German rearmament had proceeded in the 1950's, the Soviets had grown increasingly distressed. Stalin's successor, Nikita Khrushchev, met twice with the Americans, in 1955 and 1961, to explain the Soviet Union's concerns. Soviet leaders were also irritated by the existence of a western sector in Berlin, within East Germany. Refugees moved constantly through the poorer eastern sector of Berlin into the more prosperous western sector, which offered access to all of the free world. In 1961 the Soviet Union attempted to solve the refugee problem and expressed its displeasure at German rearmament in a single act: it constructed a wall around the western sector of Berlin, cutting off easy access and most contact between East and West Berlin. For many in the West, the Berlin Wall was a tangible symbol of the division of Eurpoe and the world between East and West.

Events in Germany led to greater tensions between the two sides of the Cold War and threatened to escalate into armed conflict. (During the Berlin blockade one American general suggested that the American army fight its way into East Germany.) War actually broke out, however, in Korea, in eastern Asia, in 1950.

THE KOREAN WAR

In the years that preceded World War II, Korea had been under Japanese control. After the defeat of Japan, Korea was divided into two zones. Soviet troops occupied the North down to the 38th parallel; the United States held the territory to the South. In 1948 both sides withdrew their troops, leaving behind a Communist government in the North and a western-allied government in the South. Then suddenly in 1950, North Korean troops swept down past the 38th parallel, invading South Korea with such force that they threatened to overrun the country.

To the United States this invasion was clearly part of a world-wide Communist conspiracy. Truman believed that the Soviet Union was behind the invasion, and the fact that North Korea used Soviet weapons did nothing to ease American fears. American influence in the Far East had recently been damaged by the establishment of a Communist government on mainland China. Now, Truman believed, a further test of America's power was at hand.

The United States protested the invasion of South Korea to the Security Council of the United Nations. The United States' protest found the Soviet

Union boycotting the Security Council and unable to use its veto power, which suggested that the Soviets may not have been informed of the invasion plans. The council voted to send a peace-keeping mission to South Korea. Although 16 other countries sent representatives, most of the troops were American.

After early reversals, the troops, commanded by General Douglas MacArthur, drove the North Koreans out of the South, then crossed the 38th parallel and invaded North Korea, apparently heading for Manchuria, the nearest border of Communist China. The Chinese, who may have feared that American intentions went beyond the reestablishment of the South Korean government, entered the war on the side of the North Koreans. The combined armies drove MacArthur's troops back to the south, but MacArthur regained the offensive and again pressed north.

Meanwhile, within the United States government the limits of American action in Korea were being hotly debated. Truman and his advisors feared

The Berlin Wall, built by order of the Soviet Union to prevent escape from the Soviet-controlled eastern sector of the city (at the left in the picture) to free West Berlin. No picture can convey the atmosphere of a prison felt by those who stand before the wall itself, which is patrolled day and night by police carrying submachine guns.

THE COLD WAR

	WESTERN HEMISPHERE	WESTERN EUROPE	SOVIET BLOC	AFRICA AND THE MIDDLE EAST	ASIA
1945	Feb.: The Yalta Conference — May: End of the war in Europe — Sept.: End of the Pacific war Oct.: The United Nations established			France withdraws from Syria and Lebanon	Aug.: Americans drop atomic bomb; Sept.: End of war
1946		Republic in Italy; Fourth Republic in France		Jordan independent	
1947		Peace treaties with Italy, Bulgaria, Hungary, Romania, Finland Truman Doctrine — Marshall Plan	Cominform established		India and Pakistan independent
1948	OAS created	Benelux Customs Union established	Berlin blockade and air lift Soviet control over East-Central Europe completed Soviet-Yugoslav rift	Israel independent Arab-Israeli war	
1949		NATO established Federal Republic of Germany (West Germany) established	Soviets explode an atomic bomb German Democratic Republic (East Germany) established	Arab-Israeli truce	Communist victory in mainland China; Chiang in Taiwan Indonesia independent
1950					Korean War begins
1951		European Coal-Steel Community established			Peace between Western allies and Japan
1953			Death of Stalin		Korean truce
1954	U.S. Supreme Court decision on school desegregation	Geneva conference on Southeast Asia		Nasser dictator in Egypt	French Indochina independent
1955		West Germany fully independent	Austrian peace treaty Warsaw Pact created		
1956			Khrushchev's denunciation of Stalin Gomulka in power in Poland Hungarian revolt suppressed	Morocco and Tunisia independent Suez crisis	
1957				Ghana independent	
1958		Fifth French Republic established Common Market established			"Great Leap Forward" in China
1959	Castro dictator in Cuba				
1961		Soviets build the Berlin Wall			
1962	Cuban missile crisis	Algeria independent Second Vatican Council called			

that further actions might precipitate a third world war and began to look for an end to the fighting. When MacArthur publicly objected to Washington's policy, Truman relieved him of his command.

Truce talks began in 1951, but there was no permanent cease-fire until 1953. In the end Korea was left a divided country, with North and South Korea separated by a buffer zone two and one half miles wide.

THE CUBAN MISSILE CRISIS, 1962

As early as 1956 Nikita Khrushchev began hinting that the Soviet Union might be interested in an end to the Cold War. The United States, however, dismissed these overtures as propaganda, and its policy toward the Soviet Union hardened. Then, in 1962, the Cold War invaded the Western Hemisphere.

On the small island of Cuba, about ninety miles south of the United States, guerrilla fighters led by Fidel Castro overthrew the island's dictator in 1954 and established a Communist government. The Cuban revolution had local origins, and initially Cuba was linked neither to the United States nor to the Soviet Union. Economic considerations and the need for political protection soon moved the Cubans closer to the Soviet Union. The United States then organized an economic boycott of Cuba by non-Communist countries and cut off sugar purchases from that country.

In 1962 the United States supported the Bay of Pigs invasion, an unsuccessful effort by American-trained Cuban refugees to overrun the island. The failure of the refugees' invasion made Castro the hero of the Communist world and raised the hopes of Communist revolutionaries throughout Latin America.

That same year the Soviet Union sent missiles to Cuba, armed with atomic warheads that could be launched against the cities of the United States. President John F. Kennedy demanded that the Soviet missiles be removed from Cuba and threatened to take action if they were not. Several increasingly tense days followed. Then an agreement was made between the United States and the Soviet Union by which the missiles were to be withdrawn. The world moved back from the brink of nuclear war.

⌒ ⌒ ⌒

The Cuban Missile Crisis marked the end of the Cold War, at least in its original form. By the 1960's the world had become a more complex place. The countries of the West did not immediately abandon their idea of a monolithic (single) Communist bloc directing a world Communist conspiracy. However, the reality was that both the Communist world and the capitalist-democratic world were now split into many different fragments. The political and economic simplicity of Cold War alliances that had dominated events in the fifteen years after World War II was rapidly disappearing.

Persons, Places, and Terms

Harry S. Truman	German Democratic	National Front
Clement Atlee	Republic	Truman Doctrine
George C. Marshall	North Korea	Marshall Plan
Eduard Beneš	South Korea	North Atlantic
Marshall Tito	38th parallel	Treaty
Nikita Khrushchev	Bay of Pigs	Organization
Douglas MacArthur		(NATO)
Fidel Castro		containment
John F. Kennedy	Security Council	iron curtain
	General Assembly	Cominform
Potsdam	reparations	Berlin blockade
Federal Republic	International Military	Cuban Missile
of Germany	Tribunal	Crisis

To Master the Text

1. What arrangements were made for the temporary government of Germany after the war? How did changes come about in Germany's boundaries? What efforts were made to punish former Nazis? On what grounds? What action was taken to collect reparations from Germany?
2. How was defeated Japan treated immediately after the war? How was defeated Austria treated?
3. Why did President Roosevelt favor the creation of the United Nations?
4. How did western and Soviet aims for the future of Germany differ? Why? Up to 1947, what steps did the Soviets take to realize their aims for all of eastern Europe? Did the western powers realize any of their aims during the same period? Why?
5. Why could Yugoslavia not be considered a Soviet satellite after 1948?

6. Why, beginning in 1947, did the United States adopt a new policy toward the Soviet Union? How were events in Greece and Turkey related to the new policy? Define the Truman Doctrine, the Marshall Plan, and NATO. What is meant by the words "Cold War"?
7. What events marked the Cold War in Germany (including Berlin)? In Korea? In Cuba?
8. What new world conditions were affecting the course of the Cold War by the early 1960's? What new conditions were affecting the western alliance? The Communist bloc?

To Master the Map

1. On the map on page 463, count the countries whose territories were unchanged by the war. Also count those whose boundaries were changed in important ways. In what part of the continent were the changes most numerous?
2. Draw or trace a map of Poland, using different colors for (a) territory that was Polish both before and after the Second World War; (b) former Polish territory annexed by the Soviet Union; and (c) former German territory annexed by Poland.

To Interpret the Facts

1. If you had been an adviser to President Roosevelt or to President Truman later, knowing only what you could have known at the time, what dangers might you have pointed out in the decisions they made? What reasons do you know of or can you imagine for the failure to make adequate provisions against those dangers?
2. Suppose that you were a well-informed official of the American state department returning in October 1945, from a tour of inspection in Europe. In your report to the secretary of state, what problems would you mention as being of particular concern?
3. What policies of the Soviet Union helped bring about the Cold War? How did Stalin justify those policies?

To Put This Chapter into a Larger Setting

1. Make a list of dates and events, 1789-1939, that show the steady expansion of Russia westward, eastward, and southward. To what extent have the Cold War policies of the Soviet Union been a continuation of traditional Russian foreign policy?

 33

The Collapse
of the
European
Empires

1945 to the 1960's

An outgrowth of the Second World War equaling or even surpassing the Cold War in importance was the breakup of the European overseas empires. By the end of World War II, unrest in the colonial world had become so universal and deep-seated that most possessions of the once great empires were able to win their freedom within two decades. In that period the total number of independent states in the world more than doubled.

The restiveness of the colonial peoples had many causes, often reaching far back into the past. For years glamorized images of European life reached Africa and Asia through movies, radio, and picture magazines, sharpening the dissatisfaction of colonials with their own circumstances. During the war colonial soldiers had served with the forces of their mother countries and had used the complicated devices of modern warfare as ably as Europeans. They could no longer accept the idea that they were inferior to Europeans. Enterprising young colonials who had managed to acquire European or American educations were ready to argue for independence and were able to take the lead in bringing it about. They believed that the mother countries, by draining off much colonial wealth, were increasing poverty in the colonies. They pointed to the United States, a one-time British colony that had profited from independence, and to the Soviet

Union, an economically backward country that in a single generation had become one of the world's great industrial nations. American and Soviet leaders tended to encourage this line of argument by speaking out publicly against all imperialism.

Circumstances arising directly from the war aroused anti-colonial feeling still further. Colonists whose lands had been fought over during the war or who had experienced one or more changes of masters were particularly restive by the war's end. Moreover, the imperial powers were too poor and too exhausted to maintain the military forces necessary to keep unwilling colonies in subjection. The mother countries could only choose the manner and sometimes the moment in which to let their colonies go free.

Ω   THE INDEPENDENCE OF INDIA AND PAKISTAN

India, the most prized part of Great Britain's empire, was among the first of the new independent nations. The unrest that long ago had led the British to admit Indians to limited participation in their own government (see page 303) continued between the wars and during the Second World War. Indians were still excluded from British social clubs and from the more spacious compartments on railroad trains. British investors still possessed important businesses like power plants and other utilities. Indian leaders had become convinced that such injustices could only be removed by full independence. In 1945, India was ripe for revolt.

GANDHI AND THE INDEPENDENCE MOVEMENT

Indian independence owed more to Mohandas K. Gandhi (1869-1948) than to any other individual. The son of a comfortably situated Hindu family, Gandhi was educated as a lawyer in London. He was a deeply religious person and, moved by the poverty of the Indian people, he decided to devote his life and talent for leadership to improving their lot. Gandhi lived and dressed in the manner of the poor. His extraordinary moral power was such that he was called the "mahatma" (holy man). He became the leader of the Congress party, the major organization of Indians working for self-government.

Gandhi accepted the belief that the British must leave India. Since he opposed violence and war, he promoted his cause by "civil disobedience," advocating the boycott of British schools, courts, and councils, and urging his followers to do their own spinning so that they could avoid buying British-made cloth. Once he led a twenty-four day march to the sea to enable the participants to make their own salt instead of paying the British salt tax. Often he was imprisoned by British authorities. When his supporters resorted to violence in spite of his stern discipline, he fasted for many days on end as a way of restraining them and of attaining self-purification.

British authorities brought India into the Second World War without Indian assent. Gandhi wanted India to refuse to fight even in order to repel Japanese invasion. But other leaders insisted on supporting the British and India was used as a supply base and her men served as volunteers. Winston Churchill, then prime minister, promised that India would have dominion status like Canada (see pages 299-300) at the end of the war; but Indian leaders demanded independence.

When the Labor party came to power in Great Britain in 1945, India had its opportunity. The Laborites were opposed to employing the armed force which alone could keep India within the Commonwealth; and they were willing, as Churchill's Conservatives had not been, to grant Indian independence immediately. This step was taken in August, 1947.

The new India was not a single state. The Muslim one-fourth of the population were unwilling to live under Hindu rule. Mobs of Hindus and Muslims had already attacked each other, killing perhaps a half million people. To prevent further violence it was decided to make the predominantly Muslim northeastern and northwestern parts of the peninsula into the country of Pakistan, with the larger Hindu state of India in between. (See map, page 500.) In both Pakistan and India, there were minorities who did not share the official religion. Immediately, many Pakistan Hindus fled to India and Indian Muslims to Pakistan. Some 10,000,000 in all changed territories. In 1948, in this period of fear and disorder, Gandhi himself perished by violence. A Hindu religious fanatic shot him while he was holding a prayer meeting.

INDEPENDENT INDIA AND PAKISTAN

Although India and Pakistan faced such overwhelming difficulties as poverty, lack of a common language, and underdeveloped agriculture and industry, both survived, both established republican governments and enjoyed some advantages of independence.

India had two initial assets: the well-developed Congress party and its

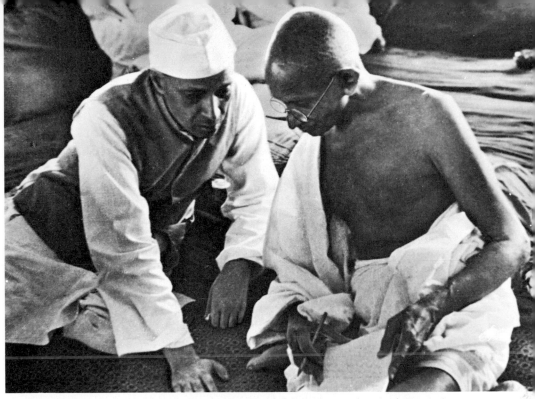

Jawaharlal Nehru (left) and Mohandas K. Gandhi, friends and co-workers in the struggle to free India from British rule. Each contributed greatly not only to winning independence but also to shaping India after independence—Gandhi by his principles and the example of his life, Nehru as leader of the Indian government for seventeen years.

able leader, Jawaharlal Nehru (prime minister 1947-1964), the English-educated friend and co-worker of Gandhi. Democratic practices were followed, although there was no common language except English, and few people could read in any language. In elections symbolic pictures were used to identify parties and candidates.

To combat poverty the government adopted a number of socialistic policies. It regulated prices and took over ownership of most utilities and means of transportation. The government also built irrigation projects, opened mines, and built factories. Consecutive five-year plans sometimes emphasized heavy industry and sometimes agriculture. At first, Indian production grew more rapidly than under British rule and kept ahead of the population growth. Then in 1965-1967 came two ruinous years of drought when Indians avoided mass famine only by importing grain, largely from the United States but also from the Soviet Union. This disaster was a great setback. Population threatened to outstrip the production of food again.

Pakistan not only shared the problems faced by India but had the added great disadvantage of being a country divided by the thousand-mile width of northern India. Weaker than India, Pakistan was more dependent on foreign aid, especially from the United States. But, in 1966, Pakistan turned to the Communist bloc and made an alliance with Communist China. The Pakistani people were not ready for the demands of their first constitution, which was suspended. A second in 1962, providing a strong president and elected legislature, maintained stability. The government abolished old feudal relations and, like India, encouraged education and economic growth.

After independence, India and Pakistan quarreled over the possession of Kashmir. (See map, page 482.) This province was inhabited by Muslims, but its prince was a Hindu who chose to join his land to India. Fighting between India and Pakistan over Kashmir was twice halted by intervention from the United Nations, but no final settlement was achieved. India also engaged in war with the Communist Chinese over the Himalayan border of the two countries.

Nehru was a man of peace who tried to follow a policy he called "neutralism" in dealing with the United States and the Soviet Union. He borrowed ideas and received aid from both, but he tried to keep India free from real dependence on either. To an extent he managed to hold a position of unofficial leadership among nations that wished not to take sides in the Cold War. His death in 1964 was a great loss to India, for there was no one of his stature to succeed him. His daughter, Mrs. Indira Gandhi, became prime minister in 1966.

EUROPEAN WITHDRAWAL
FROM SOUTHEAST ASIA

Unlike India, Southeast Asia had been directly involved in the military aspects of the Second World War. In that area the imperial powers tried for a considerable time after the war to restore their authority, only in the end to lose their colonies.

SOUTHEAST ASIA IN 1945

Before the Second World War all Southeast Asia except Thailand was divided among the European imperial powers. (See page 346.) During the war the Japanese overran the Philippines, Burma, Thailand, Indochina, the Malay Peninsula, and the Netherlands East Indies. (See map, page 455.) The Japanese armies often were welcomed as liberators, and Japanese officials

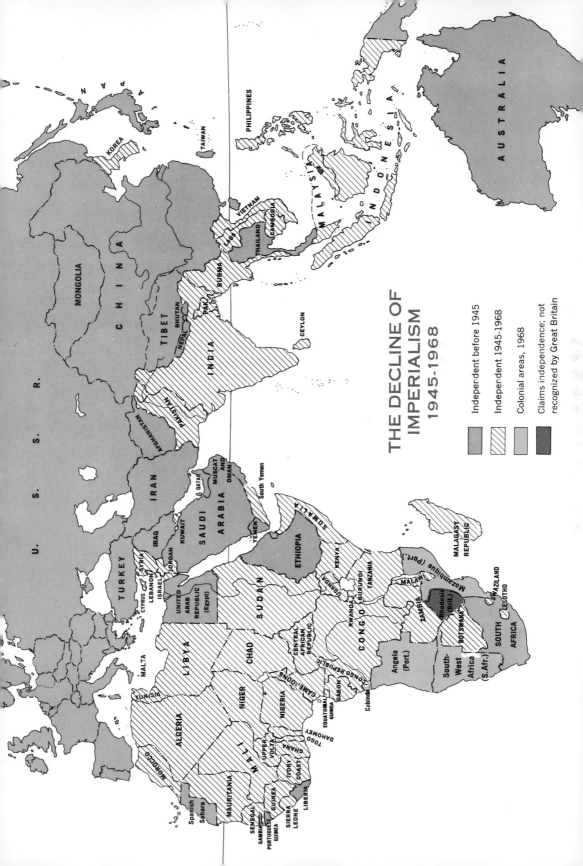

THE DECLINE OF
IMPERIALISM
1945–1968

Independent before 1945

Independent 1945–1968

Colonial areas, 1968

Claims independence; not
recognized by Great Britain

U. S. S. R.

JAPAN

KOREA

MONGOLIA

CHINA

TAIWAN

PHILIPPINES

TIBET

NEPAL

BHUTAN

PAKISTAN

BURMA

VIETNAM

LAOS

CAMBODIA

THAILAND

INDIA

AFGHANISTAN

CEYLON

M A L A Y S I A

I N D O N E S I A

AUSTRALIA

IRAN

TURKEY

IRAQ

SYRIA

LEBANON

ISRAEL

JORDAN

CYPRUS

KUWAIT

QATAR

MUSCAT
AND
OMAN

SAUDI
ARABIA

YEMEN

South Yemen

SOMALIA

ETHIOPIA

MALTA

UNITED
ARAB
REPUBLIC
(Egypt)

LIBYA

SUDAN

CHAD

KENYA

UGANDA

RWANDA

BURUNDI

TANZANIA

C O N G O

MALAWI

ZAMBIA

Rhodesia
(Brit.)

Mozambique (Port.)

MALAGASY
REPUBLIC

TUNISIA

NIGER

CENTRAL
AFRICAN
REPUBLIC

CAMEROONS

NIGERIA

ALGERIA

MOROCCO

Spanish
Sahara

MAURITANIA

M A L I

SENEGAL

GAMBIA

PORTUGUESE
GUINEA

GUINEA

SIERRA
LEONE

LIBERIA

IVORY
COAST

UPPER
VOLTA

GHANA

TOGO

DAHOMEY

EQUATORIAL
GUINEA

GABON

CONGO REPUBLIC

Cabinda

Angola
(Port.)

South-
West
Africa
(S.Afr.)

BOTSWANA

SWAZILAND

LESOTHO

SOUTH
AFRICA

were able to build up native pro-Japanese parties. Soon, however, the Japanese seemed more oppressive than the Europeans. The mother countries expected to be welcomed back after the expulsion of the Japanese at the end of the war. Except for the United States, which gave long-promised independence to the Philippines in 1946, all moved to recover their colonies.

THE ESTABLISHMENT OF INDONESIA

The Netherlands East Indies had already declared independence before the departure of the Japanese. With Japanese approval, Dr. Achmed Sukarno had assumed leadership of the new state. But the Dutch, aided by British troops using American military equipment, tried in vain to suppress the Indonesian rebellion. Finally, the United Nations intervened. Since it became clear that the Indonesians would not permit Dutch settlers to reopen their businesses or even live in safety in their homes, the Dutch government was forced to grant independence to the colony, which in 1949 became the Republic of Indonesia. (See map, page 482.)

But independence did not bring democracy or even peace and prosperity to the islands. Technically trained and experienced Dutch businessmen and administrators had been forced to leave before the Indonesians were ready to take their places. A strong Communist party and the army struggled with each other for political power. Sukarno finally assumed dictatorial authority for life. He was able to win the loyalty of the outlying islanders and to greatly reduce illiteracy, but he wasted too much effort on unsuccessful foreign ventures. In 1965, for example, after Great Britain had granted independence to the states of the Malay Peninsula, he attacked the new Malaysia on the grounds that it was a threat to Indonesia. Although he had support and sympathy from the Soviet Union and Communist China, he could not win the war. In 1967 the Indonesian army seized power and brought about the fall of Sukarno. He left his people scarcely more prosperous than he had found them and facing a serious growth of population.

THE DEFEAT OF THE FRENCH IN INDOCHINA

In Indochina the French after the war were involved in a struggle that proved more complicated, costly, and prolonged than the Dutch war in Indonesia. Indochina had remained loyal to the French Vichy regime (see page 444), which permitted the Japanese to use Indochinese ports and airfields. Toward the end of the war, however, the Japanese completely took over Indochina. The French expected no difficulty in recovering the area; but they were soon confronted by a Communist leader, Ho Chi Minh, who had spent years during the 1930's in exile, mostly in Moscow. The center of Ho Chi Minh's authority was in Hanoi, later the capital of North Vietnam. The French government soon had full-scale war on its hands, so costly that only financial aid from the United States kept it going and so unpopular in France that draftees could not be used to fight it. The struggle continued until 1954, when the French experienced a spectacular defeat at Dien Bien Phu.

An international conference was already in progress in Geneva, Switzerland and it turned its attention to Indochina. France had already given independence to Laos and Cambodia, which had not been involved in the fighting. At Geneva, plans were made for dividing Vietnam into two parts until unity could be restored: A government under Ho Chi Minh's control was established in the north and a pro-western government was organized in the south. Failure of this arrangement, however, led to the Vietnam War between the United States and North Vietnamese-led forces. (Its history is discussed in Chapter 35.)

◠   THE ARAB WORLD AND ISRAEL

The independence movement in the Arab world of North Africa and the Middle East had flourished since the First World War, when the British and French, trying to secure Arab aid against the Ottoman Empire, promised the Arabs independence from Turkish rule. But in 1917 the British government also issued the Balfour Declaration, which favored "the establishment in Palestine of a national home for the Jewish people." Leading Arabs claimed that the policy implied in the Balfour Declaration was contradictory to British promises to the Arabs, and Arab hostility to the Jews increased accordingly.

The situation in the Arab world of North Africa and the Middle East was changing rapidly in 1945. Egypt and Iraq had long been independent, although British troops still guarded the Suez Canal. During the war the Allies had taken Libya from Italy and, not knowing what else to do with it, soon made it independent. The former French mandates of Syria and Lebanon became independent at the end of the war, and Jordan (the former Transjordan) was freed by Great Britain. But France still claimed Morocco,

Algeria, and Tunisia as belonging to its empire; and Great Britain still held the mandate for Palestine. (See pages 407-408, and 410.) The history of independence movements in those areas was soon complicated by the establishment of the Jewish state of Israel in 1948 and by the appearance in 1952 of a military strong man who made himself head of the Egyptian government.

THE MAKING OF ISRAEL

Israel came into existence as an independent state in 1948. It was the outgrowth of nineteenth-century Zionism, a world-wide movement of Jews working for a national Jewish home in Palestine. Jewish immigration into the area became appreciable in the 1930's and greatly increased after the Second World War with an influx of uprooted, homeless Jews, mostly from Germany and eastern Europe. Arab hostility mounted steadily, for the Arabs began to fear that Jews would soon outnumber them in the eastern Mediterranean. In spite of many efforts, the British government was unable to curb either Jewish immigration or violence between Arabs and Jews. In 1947 Britain turned the problem over to the United Nations, which recommended partition of Palestine into Arab and Jewish states. In 1948, the British withdrew and the Jews proclaimed the new state of Israel.

Immediately there came an attack from the Arab League, a loose confederation of Arab states. Israeli forces were well prepared. They soon drove the Arabs not only from the region assigned by the United Nations to Israel but also from some of the land reserved for the Arabs. In 1949 the United Nations secured an armistice, but no real peace, for Israel's Arab neighbors refused to recognize its existence and harassed it in every possible way.

THE INDEPENDENCE MOVEMENT IN NORTH AFRICA

Meanwhile the independence movement gained momentum among the Arabs in French North Africa. The French people quite naturally wanted to keep their African empire, especially because Frenchmen had lived along the Mediterranean coast of Africa since the nineteenth century and also because that area contributed to French prosperity. But there were rebellious movements in each of the French protectorates, none of which could be suppressed without the costly use of force. Finally, in 1956, the French government granted independence to Morocco and Tunisia.

Algeria posed a more serious problem. There a strong native independence movement was opposed by more than a million European settlers. Algeria had long been treated as an actual part of France. Having lived in Algeria as French citizens for generations, the settlers considered the land theirs. A bloody and very costly war broke out between the Muslim Algerians and the French, taking some 250,000 lives. In despair the French people recalled General de Gaulle. Under his leadership the Fourth Republic was replaced with a new Fifth Republic, and a constitution was dictated by de Gaulle. But even this more centralized government did not enable France to subdue the Algerians. De Gaulle had to convince the French people that Algeria must be granted its independence. It became free in 1962.

Adding complication to the Arab independence movement was revolution in Egypt. In 1952 a group of young army officers, eager for reform, angered by the establishment of Israel, and frustrated by Egypt's defeat at the hands of Israel's armed forces in 1948, overthrew the king and established a republic. By 1954 one of the rebels, Colonel Gamal Abdel Nasser, was able to assume dictatorial power. He dreamed of expelling Britain from the Suez Canal and the Anglo-Egyptian Sudan, leading the Arab world to unity, and driving Israel from the eastern Mediterranean. In none of these plans was he fully successful. The British left the Anglo-Egyptian Sudan, but instead of remaining a part of Egypt as Nasser had hoped, it became independent. Briefly, in 1958, the movement toward Arab unity seemed to make progress, for Syria joined Egypt and the new state was called the United Arab Republic. In 1961 Syria withdrew, but Egypt continued to call itself the United Arab Republic, a symbol of Nasser's yet unrealized hopes. As for the expulsion of Israel, the history of the Arab effort to achieve that goal created one of the most serious points of tension in the post-1945 world.

THE ARAB-ISRAELI CONFLICT

The Arab-Israeli conflict passed through a number of stages. To achieve its ends, each side seized upon any opportunity that arose: the Arabs to expel Israel and the Israelis to force the Arabs to recognize the rightful existence of Israel. In 1956 the problem of building a new Egyptian high irrigation dam on the Nile River at Aswan led to the Suez crisis. In accordance with his neutrality policy, Nasser had accepted promises of financial aid from both the United States and the Soviet Union. But American officials, believing that Nasser was overly friendly to the Soviets, suddenly canceled their promised loan. In reply, Nasser seized the Suez Canal. Great Britain and France, to whom the canal was an essential route for oil from the east, landed troops in the canal zone. The Israeli government, fearing any extension of Nasser's power, also invaded Egypt. American and Soviet protests soon caused the withdrawal of all three invading forces. Nasser kept control of the canal while the Soviet Union continued its aid for the Aswan high dam, hoping thus to increase the U.S.S.R.'s already growing strength in the eastern Mediterranean.

In June 1967, war again erupted between Israel and the United Arab Republic, a culmination of sporadic border fighting between Israel on the one side and Syria and Jordan backed by Egypt, on the other. In six days Israeli troops occupied the Sinai Peninsula (see map, page 405), Jordanian land to the west of the Jordan River, and the Jordanian half of previously divided Jerusalem. Because negotiations would imply formal recognition, the Arab states refused to negotiate peace until Israel had abandoned its conquests; Israel refused to withdraw. The Soviet Union, more openly than before, took the side of the Arabs, supplying arms and diplomatic support. After months of stalling, there were no real steps toward permanent peace. Arab-Israeli relations remained an international crisis issue.

◌ INDEPENDENCE FOR SUB-SAHARAN AFRICA

The drive for independence began later in sub-Saharan Africa than elsewhere, but once it began it spread like an epidemic through the French, British, and Belgian empires. Only Portugal managed to keep its African colonies, in spite of criticism abroad and revolts in Africa. By the late 1960's there were more than twenty newly independent states in Africa south of the Sahara.

THE MOVEMENT FOR LIBERATION

The independence movement received its impetus both from Europe and from Africa. In their difficult economic situations after the war, the imperialist countries had to use their resources for their own recovery. The African colonies had contributed less to the mother countries than colonies elsewhere, either in strategic military areas or in economic advantage. The mother countries could not afford to retain them at great cost.

In Africa the war years had encouraged long-developing native dissatisfaction with the colonial status. From the beginning of European settlement in Africa, Africans had protested against interference with their traditional ways. They resented the limitation of the authority of tribal chiefs, the occupation of the best African lands by white settlers, and the restriction of Africans to areas known as "native reserves." Once Africans managed to secure western university educations, they were disappointed to find that they were allowed little or no part in the governments of their own colonies, and that European, not African, technicians and administrators were taking leading roles in colonial economic development. To keep the loyalty of the colonials during the war, the mother countries had made promises of increased self-government and better opportunities for the people of the colonies. However, such promises could not be put into effect immediately, if at all; and they only served to increase colonial dissatisfaction.

The colony that set the pattern of independence for all others in this region was the Gold Coast, a British colony. The British government had plans for a leisurely progress toward self-government for this and all its African colonies. The Gold Coast was a good place in which to start, for it was prosperous and had almost no white settlers. It also had a dynamic native leader, Kwame Nkrumah. He managed to acquire enough political power and demonstrated such capacity for leadership that the British thought it wise to withdraw completely from the colony in 1957. It became an independent country, Ghana. Thereafter Belgium, France, and Great Britain all hastened to let go of their African colonies, in many cases long before proper preparation had been made.

THE PROBLEMS OF INDEPENDENCE

The newly independent states soon found that their troubles were often increased rather than removed by their new status.

One difficulty was political instability, which was often coupled with violence. This problem was in part due to the inexperience of the new leaders and their peoples, even in the colonies where there had been previous beginnings of self-government. The native peoples lacked both the training and the education to take part wisely in republican governments, the type usually set up. Their high expectations of a better life after independence brought widespread disappointment when the actual results were meager or nonexistent. In consequence there was a long series of military uprisings throughout Africa, resulting in the replacement of elected officials with army officers as heads of state.

Another problem grew out of the internal divisions within many of the

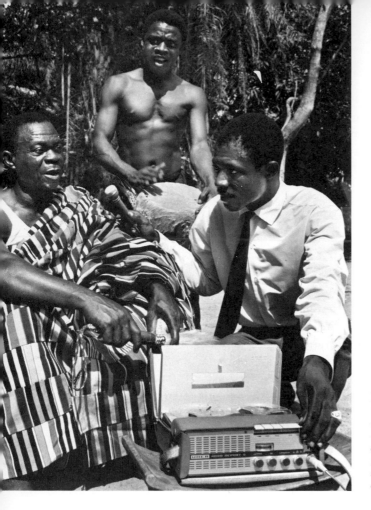

A young Ivory Coast historian is preserving on tapes the legends of his country's history, here being recited to him by an old tribal chief. In such ways, records of the African past are being recovered and evaluated, partly to give citizens of the new African states an appreciation of their own heritage.

new countries. This situation came in part from the manner in which the colonies had originally been carved out in the nineteenth century. Boundaries had often been arranged in Europe simply by drawing lines on maps without consideration or awareness of the fact that the lines cut through tribal groups or put together, under the same colonial government, tribes differing from each other in culture, language, or historical background. The old tribal relationships usually still existed at the time of independence, but since the colonies received independence at different times, there were overwhelming pressures to leave the boundaries as the Europeans had drawn them. It was not surprising under this circumstance that there were many attempts at union between two or more colonies and the breakup of other colonies into two or more separate parts. In both the Republic of the Congo (the former Belgian Congo) and in Nigeria, civil war developed because of the desire of one part of the new state to break away from the rest.

The departure, often enforced, of European technical and administrative experts before Africans could acquire the skills needed to replace them was another difficulty. In the Republic of the Congo the Belgians tried to keep their hold over the rich mining province of Katanga, which the Congolese were not prepared to operate alone. Katanga seceded, and a good deal of bloodshed resulted, only partly relieved by United Nations' peace-keeping forces. There were frequent changes in government before the country was again united.

In places where there were a significant number of European settlers but also a majority of Africans, trouble sometimes developed because the white minority was determined to keep control. The pattern was set by the Republic of South Africa, the former British dominion, known as the Union of South Africa. The white majority followed the policy of "apartheid." This policy was intended to keep black and white peoples totally separated but with the white minority in control. For economic reasons, however, black workers would work for white employers.

A somewhat similar situation arose in 1965 in Rhodesia, which was still a British colony. The British government would not give independence to this colony until its leaders made clear their intention of eventually granting the vote to all native Africans. Since Africans were the great majority of the population, they would thus ultimately control the government. In order not to allow anything so distasteful to the white minority, Ian Smith, prime minister, with the support of the white citizens, declared Rhodesia independent without British consent. The British government would not accept the declaration of independence and, with the support of most of the United Nations, imposed an economic boycott on the country. In spite of the inconvenience caused by the boycott, Rhodesia continued to act as an independent nation.

ᢙ ᢙ ᢙ

The collapse of the European empires was undoubtedly one of the great developments of the twentieth century. It terminated Europe's three hundred years of world domination and helped to make the European powers less wealthy and less mighty. By more than doubling the number of independent countries it made international relations more complicated and more unpredictable. It gave new self-confidence to the poorer peoples of the world. It was a great and confusing movement that could be counted on to produce diverse and important consequences for decades to come.

Persons, Places, and Terms

Mohandas K. Gandhi
Jawaharlal Nehru
Achmed Sukarno
Ho Chi Minh
Gamal Abdel Nasser
Kwame Nkrumah
Ian Smith

Pakistan
Kashmir
Himalayan
   Mountains
Indonesia

Malaysia
Hanoi
Laos
Cambodia
Jordan
Israel
United Arab
   Republic
Sinai Peninsula
sub-Saharan Africa
Ghana
Republic of
   the Congo

Nigeria
Rhodesia
Republic of
   South Africa

mahatma
Congress party
civil disobedience
neutralism
Balfour Declaration
Arab League
Zionism
native reserves
apartheid

To Master the Text

1. List and explain all the reasons (a) why the European nations found it difficult to control their colonies after the Second World War and (b) why the colonial peoples desired independence and believed they might secure it. Why did the very different examples of both the United States and the Soviet Union inspire colonial leaders?

2. For what reasons were the people of India especially eager for independence? What were the important facts of Gandhi's background and experience? In actual practice what did his civil-disobedience program mean? How was it intended to force the British to yield to Indian demands?

3. During the Second World War, what policy did Gandhi want India to follow? What promises did Churchill make? When and how did India become independent? Why and how was it divided?

4. What kind of governments did India and Pakistan set up? How successful were they? What difficulties did they encounter? How did Kashmir affect their relations? What foreign policies did each follow?

5. What were the experiences of Southeast Asia during the Second World War? In the years immediately following? What problems did Indonesia face as a new state? Through what train of events did France lose its Indochinese colonies?

6. What conditions and events helped make Algeria independent?

7. How did Gamal Abdel Nasser come to power? What hopes did he have for Egypt? Which of these did he realize? What prevented his having greater success?

8. What promises did the British and French governments make to the Arabs and Jews during the First World War? Why? How and why did bitterness develop between the Jews of Palestine and the neighboring Arabs in the 1930's and 1940's? Why did the British decide to give up their mandate for Palestine? What events brought the new state of Israel into being?

9. Through what crises did the Israelis pass in their relations with the Arab world?

10. What forces, in Africa and in Europe, led to the rapid independence movement in sub-Saharan Africa? What problems confronted the new African states? In what ways did the new states seem to benefit by independence? In what ways did independence harm them?

To Interpret the Facts

1. To what extent did the colonial powers increase their colonies' desire for independence by bringing them in touch with the ideas, skills, and learning of the modern industrialized world?

2. What evidence is there that independence has been generally beneficial to the former colonies? What evidence can you find to the contrary?

To Put This Chapter into a Larger Setting

1. How important was the Second World War in breaking up the colonial empires? What indications can you find that other factors were as important as or more important than the war?

2. Prepare a report on one of the few African or Asian territories still under European control, pointing out any special problems within the colony, the reasons why the colonial power has been either unable or unwilling to grant independence, and the prospects of the colony for independence at some time in the future.

3. Prepare a report on the background, personality, beliefs, and program of one of the leaders of an African country.

4. In what ways did the United Nations participate in the problems raised by the freeing of the European empires?

5. How was the Cold War involved in the dissolution of the European empires?

34

Reconstruction
and
Revolution

1945 to the 1960's

All parts of the world were profoundly affected by the Second World War, even countries that had not experienced active fighting. The postwar period was a period of reconstruction in many different parts of the world. In western Europe and Japan, the first years of peace saw great efforts directed toward rebuilding destroyed cities and restoring civilian life and international commerce. In the Western Hemisphere the United States attempted to organize the nations of Latin America to secure its political leadership and combat the spread of Communism. In China the great internal struggles that had ended the Manchu Dynasty in 1911 and shaken the country in the following years had been briefly laid aside during the Second World War in order to fight the Japanese. The postwar world saw an almost immediate resumption of the Chinese civil war. This civil war ended in 1949 with the establishment of a Communist regime on the mainland of China. By the 1960's, Europe, much of North America, and Japan were enjoying a period of rapidly increasing prosperity.

☊ WESTERN EUROPE'S RECOVERY AND PROSPERITY

As we have seen, the countries of Europe, with few exceptions, had experienced massive physical damage in the war years, and all had been economically disrupted. Still, at the end of the war, there existed a spirit of hope and a demand for reform growing out of the wartime Resistance movements. The Resistance had attracted people eager for social change: Socialists, Communists, and, in Catholic countries, members of newly formed, Catholic-based Christian Democratic parties.

Resistance leaders demanded, first of all, punishment for those who had collaborated with the Germans. At the moment of liberation, they often put local collaborators to death, sometimes without trial. They also hoped to replace old-line conservative politicians with people of greater competence, more devotion to the public interest, and a zeal for reform. But the association of Communist parties with the Resistance movements alarmed many people both within and outside those countries.

In 1947 pressure from the United States resulted in the removal of Communist ministers from the governments of France and Italy. One year later when the newly established Italian republic held its first election, outside pressure, some of it again from the United States, helped prevent an anticipated Communist victory. Soon old-line conservative politicians were back in power in most countries.

There was no great revolutionary movement after the Second World War to parallel the Russian Revolution of 1917. Eastern Europe became Communist after 1945 only as a result of pressures from the Soviet Union. Elsewhere, any hint of revolution was held back by armies of occupation in the defeated countries and by Marshall Plan aid (see page 466), which helped make possible the amazingly rapid restoration of western Europe. Within a decade most major western European countries were producing more goods than before the war and were able to provide a higher standard of living than their peoples had ever enjoyed before. Cities had largely been rebuilt, and most of the wartime destruction had disappeared.

FRANCE UNDER THE FOURTH AND FIFTH REPUBLICS

Liberated France had to establish a new government, for the Third Republic had disappeared with the German occupation of 1940. After a period of provisional government under General Charles de Gaulle, a Fourth Republic was established in 1946. This Fourth Republic had all the faults of the Third Republic: a weak executive and so many parties that no one of them could ever secure a majority in the National Assembly. De Gaulle, who believed in a strong executive, left public life in disgust. Then in 1958 the Algerian war brought him back into the government with the power to write a new constitution for France. The Fifth Republic, with de Gaulle as

President, was more highly centralized and authoritarian than any French government since the Second Empire (1852–1871).

After the war, as often happens, inflation appeared; and in France it wiped out the savings of many people. Even so, welfare legislation was passed that made life more secure for the least fortunate part of the French population. The government took over the nation's coal mines, banking, insurance companies, and power plants. It instituted a system of social security that included a good half of the population and gave family allowances to workers with children. These measures, added to increased economic progress and political stability under the Fifth Republic, gave France the greatest prosperity in its history.

Once the Fifth Republic was established under de Gaulle, the imposing, uncompromising military man at the head of the nation, it was inevitable that France should seek to reestablish its former leadership on the continent of Europe. De Gaulle rejected the "Cold War" ideology, and he insisted that France, as a great power, must have its own nuclear weapons. Thus, he refused to sign the test ban treaty negotiated by the United States and the Soviet Union. When de Gaulle observed increasing Soviet influence in the eastern Mediterranean, he countered it by trying to win Arab friendship. His main goal in foreign affairs, however, was to reduce British and American influence on the continent of Europe.

GREAT BRITAIN IN ECONOMIC DIFFICULTY

Soon after the end of the war in Europe, an election turned Churchill's Conservative party out of office and replaced it with the first real Labor party majority in British history. Socialistic in policy, the Labor government nationalized the nation's coal mines, the iron and steel industry, communications, transportation, electrical power, and the Bank of England. The Laborites also set up a National Health Service, which employed most of Britain's doctors and paid most medical fees by means of a system of government insurance. These programs, especially the National Health Service, proved so popular that, with the exception of the nationalization of road transportation and the steel industry, they were continued when the Conservative party returned to power in 1951. And a complete system of nationally supported compulsory education had been set up during the war. Thus, Great Britain became more of a welfare state than ever before, using a larger portion of tax money to benefit people with lower incomes.

The cost of these welfare-state programs, coupled with the expense of rebuilding the areas destroyed by German bombing during the war, greatly increased Britain's financial problems. But the country's basic financial troubles were simply a continuation of the downward movement of the British economy since before the First World War. There were too many people living in Great Britain to feed and clothe themselves using their own resources, and so they had to import food and raw materials. To pay for these, the British exported manufactures and derived interest from investments abroad. But a large part of Britain's merchant marine had been lost in the Second World War, and all of Britain's foreign investments, totaling $40 billion, had been sold to pay for the war. In addition, the British government had had to borrow great sums on which interest had to be paid. Loss of Britain's overseas colonies limited still further the national income.

At first the government tried to cope with these problems by retaining its wartime "austerity" program of rationing and other controls and by using Marshall Plan money and loans from the British dominions, as well as by curtailing military and colonial expenses. In the 1950's Britain enjoyed a modest prosperity, and most wartime restrictions were removed. But the government was unable to solve the basic problem of increasing exports sufficiently to pay for all the needed imports. Britain's outdated industrial equipment was in competition with the newly rebuilt plants of Germany and Japan. Great Britain had ceased to be a first-rate world power.

DEMOCRATIC WEST GERMANY

West Germany, the larger, more populous, and more industrialized part of old Germany, was created from the zones occupied by British, French,

General Charles de Gaulle, leader of the Free French in World War II, architect of the Fifth French Republic and its president to 1969, at one of his rare press conferences.

and American troops after the war. (See map, page 463.) The decision of the United States that Germany would be a useful ally against the Soviet Union had led to America's fostering of a strong German government.

In form, West Germany was a democratic republic. It was better organized than the Weimar Republic, and it had more support from the German people, who were now eager to make democracy work in their country. The new nation had a skilled and popular leader in Konrad Adenauer (Chancellor, 1949–1963), head of the German Christian Democratic Party.

So rapid was the recovery of West Germany under its new government that it was said to have experienced an "economic miracle." Money from the Marshall Plan gave West German industries needed funds for rebuilding. Refugees from eastern European countries provided the needed new labor. The payment of reparations to the western Allies and the Soviet Union had been halted. All of this helped speed West Germany's recovery. By 1950 German factories were producing as much as they had in 1936. By 1958 Germany had become the leading industrial country in western Europe. The German government did not nationalize its nation's industries as did the British and the French. Instead, it encouraged private ownership, although economic policies and investments were guided by government controls.

In one area the West Germans failed. Their government was not able to bring about reunification with East Germany. The Soviet Union would not allow the free elections that would have resulted in a reunification. The western Allies refused to sanction reunification unless it was achieved by free elections.

STEPS TOWARD EUROPEAN UNITY

Although western Europe remained after the war, as before, an area of many independent countries, a number of influences encouraged more cooperative activity among its group of nations. The Marshall Plan required a certain amount of cooperation among the countries receiving aid, and NATO gave member countries the experience of military cooperation. It was obvious to thoughtful leaders from the relatively small countries of Europe that a large country like the United States owed part of its affluence to extensive domestic markets unhampered by tariffs. New western European multinational organizations tried to secure the same advantages for small nations there.

In 1948 the "Benelux" countries (Belgium, the Netherlands, and Luxembourg) agreed to gradually reduce tariffs among themselves. In 1951 a more ambitious project, the European Coal and Steel Community, was organized by France, West Germany, Italy, and the Benelux countries. Under this plan the coal and steel industries of the six countries were to be administered as a unit, almost as if they constituted a nation within a nation. At the beginning of 1958, the same countries put into operation the European Economic Community (the Common Market), hoping ultimately to eliminate tariffs among themselves and otherwise to integrate their economic activities. The same six countries also established an organization called Euratom to promote the use of atomic power.

These organizations were successful, and business in all member countries prospered as a direct result of the lessening of barriers to international trade. Great Britain initially refused to join the Common Market because it needed the low-priced agricultural imports that came to it from its former colonies. Friction among other Common Market members also threatened the prospects of European unity. Any policy was sure to harm some business in one or more of the member countries, and members were frequently tempted to protect their own economies against the others.

☊ RECOVERY AND CHANGE IN EASTERN EUROPE

Eastern Europe, like the western Allies, faced the problems of recovery and restoration; but circumstances there were different. The war had taken a frightful toll of life and property in the Soviet Union. Half of Russia's industrial capacity was destroyed, and more than half of the farm animals in the eastern section of the country were killed. In the satellite nations, similar destruction had taken place.

THE SOVIET UNION UNDER STALIN

Stalin remained at the head of the Soviet Union until his death in 1953. There was no relaxation of his personal dictatorship nor of his fearfulness for the safety of the Soviet Union. Because he believed that a western coalition of powers might at any time attack the Soviet Union (see page 462), Stalin based the Soviet postwar five-year plans on the growth of heavy industry and the needs of the military forces. His greatest objective, nuclear power, was achieved in 1949.

By 1950 the Soviet Union was second only to the United States in industrial production. The Soviet Union's recovery from the war, unaided by

Marshall Plan funds that Stalin had refused, proceeded with success comparable to that of the West. The satellite nations of the Soviet Union contributed to this economic and technological advance. They were forced to sell what the Soviet Union needed and to buy what the Soviet Union had in surplus; they could trade only with the Soviet Union. In 1955 the military alliance between the satellite countries and the Soviet Union was strengthened by the signing of the Warsaw Pact.

THE SOVIET UNION AFTER STALIN

The death of Stalin in 1953 was followed by a power struggle among leading members of the Communist party. In the midst of this power struggle, and because of it, the repressive policies begun under Stalin were relaxed. The head of the secret police, one of the rivals for power, was dismissed from office and executed at the instigation of his opponents. Never again did the Soviet secret police recover its unrestrained freedom of action; ordinary citizens were seldom tried in police courts thereafter. Fear ceased to be the chief weapon of the Soviet government. Moreover, a serious effort was made to provide more consumer goods for ordinary people and to build enough houses to take care of the growing population. By 1956 Nikita Khrushchev was winning the power struggle and was on his way to being the undisputed head of the Soviet Union.

In 1956 Khrushchev made an astounding speech to the meeting of the congress of the Communist party of the Soviet Union. What he said was supposedly not for publication, but it was soon known all over the world that he had denounced Stalin for cruelty and listed in detail the "crimes of the Stalin era." Khrushchev even indicated that there were other ways to achieve socialism besides those practiced by the Soviet leaders.

All over the Communist world the speech had startling consequences. In the Soviet Union, writers and artists began to express their own ideas with a new freedom. Many of the slave-labor camps were closed, and in those remaining there was less cruelty. Communist parties in non-satellite countries began to experiment with independence from Moscow. But the greatest consequence of Khrushchev's disclosures came in the satellite countries.

As early as 1953 the relaxation of Stalinist controls had led to an uprising of workers in East Germany. New economic policies had been adopted by the Soviet Union that offered satellite peoples more consumer goods and lower work loads. By 1956 Khrushchev had appeared willing to allow these countries to follow their own national policies in limited ways rather than to keep precisely to the Moscow party line. However, events in Poland and Hungary soon illustrated the limits of this new freedom.

In Poland factory workers rioted in June 1956, and in the resulting confusion a new leader, Wladislaw Gomulka, gained control of the Polish Communist party. The Polish rebellion provoked Soviet leaders to consider a military invasion of that country. Gomulka, however, managed to convince Khrushchev that internal controls could be lightened in Poland without challenging either the Soviet's definition of Communism or endangering Soviet security. Gomulka cooperated more fully with the Soviet Union than did Tito of Yugoslavia, but he gave the Polish people more freedom than they had enjoyed since the Second World War.

In Hungary events took a bloodier course. Workers and students rose in armed rebellion in Budapest in that same year, 1956. They killed party officials and members of the secret police and attacked Soviet tanks. The rebellion spread throughout the country. Imre Nagy, a Hungarian Communist, came to power. Again Khrushchev seemed willing to allow the populist movement to survive since its supporters were Communists and even to tolerate the liberalization of internal laws. But when Nagy announced that he was withdrawing Hungary from the Warsaw Pact, Soviet troops were sent into Hungary. After two days of fighting, the rebellion ended. Many Hungarians were arrested, and some 200,000 persons were deported or fled.

The Polish and Hungarian rebellions tested the limits of the new Soviet policy of liberalization. Economic and even political policies of satellite nations might deviate from Soviet plans, but the satellites must not wander too far from the Soviet Union's definition of Communism. More important, the satellites were not to take any action threatening Soviet security. The Soviet Union's major postwar priorities—to protect its own borders and to defend its brand of Communism—remained in effect.

The Soviet Union's industrial growth was its principal economic feature in the postwar period. Only agriculture was in trouble. Basically the policies of the Soviet Union encouraged industry at the expense of agriculture, and none of the efforts to improve it had been successful.

As economic conditions improved, Soviet policy changed. Society in the Soviet Union became more affluent. Khrushchev himself began to talk about Soviet rivalry with the West as being economic rivalry. He said that "peaceful co-existence" with the West was possible in a political way, and he predicted that the Soviet Union would, in a foreseeable time, outstrip the United States in production.

ᕋ RECOVERY IN JAPAN

While European countries were rebuilding their war-damaged countries, in the Far East another former Axis power, Japan, faced similar problems. The Allies had accepted Japan's surrender in 1945, and American forces under the command of General Douglas MacArthur had occupied the country. Theoretically the occupation was a joint Allied endeavor, but, in fact, it was mainly an American affair.

The Japanese had suffered greatly from the Second World War. Two atomic bombs had levelled the cities of Hiroshima and Nagasaki. Conventional bombing had burned out large sections of other major cities, where most of the buildings were made of wood. In addition the Japanese people faced great economic hardship. A small country of four main islands, with limited natural resources to support a large population, Japan (like Britain) had relied on overseas trade for supplies of food and fuel and for markets for its products. Now the war had stripped Japan of that trade. Japan's Asian empire had been lost, and much of Japan's industry had been destroyed. Food was scarce and, in the immediate postwar years, was available to city dwellers mostly through black-market trading.

American policy in the first years of the occupation had two major aims. First, General MacArthur was to demilitarize Japan, to make certain that nation could never again become a military threat. Second, Japanese society was to be rebuilt in the image of western democracy. The first priority was not too difficult. By the end of the war, the military leaders of Japan had largely been discredited by their failures.

The second goal, the democratization and westernization of Japan, might have proved impossible. Although Japan was neither a western nation nor a democracy in 1945, its many traditional strengths helped to make the reorganization of the country successful. Japan had a highly literate population. It had traditions of discipline, energy, and ingenuity in both political and economic life. And it had a talent for adapting foreign elements to Japanese needs. These qualities contributed to the successful regeneration of postwar Japan.

In the first three years after surrender, MacArthur put into effect the most revolutionary of the occupation policies. Elder Japanese leaders in business, politics, and the military were purged from power. Twenty-five Japanese leaders were tried for their parts in the war. Seven were executed, and most of the remainder were sent to prison for life.

The Japanese constitution was rewritten. The Emperor became only a symbol of the state. The Japanese "Diet" (named in the 19th century after the German government body on which it was modeled) became a parliamentary body. All representatives in the Diet were to be elected by the people. The judiciary was remodeled on the pattern of the United States, with powers separate from the legislature. Under new Japanese law, women were given the same legal rights as men.

The economic reforms of the early postwar period were by far the most revolutionary. American policy makers argued that unless wealth was more evenly distributed in Japan, parliamentary democracy would not succeed. On their orders MacArthur forced the sale of the large landed estates and resold the land to its actual tenants. In addition, he attempted to divide large business conglomerates, the *zaibatsu*, into smaller, more competitive organizations, and he encouraged the formation of labor unions among Japanese workers.

By 1948 the American occupation forces had helped solve the most desperate of the food and housing problems facing Japan. American business leaders began to complain that the attacks on the large zaibatsu firms would weaken the Japanese economy. MacArthur's earlier policies were abandoned. Large Japanese firms were allowed greater freedom, and efforts were made to restrict the growing activities of the newly formed labor unions. After 1948 both American and Japanese leaders focused on the development of Japan's industrial economy to enable it to support Japan's large population.

In 1951 a treaty of peace was made between Japan, the United States, and forty-eight other nations. In 1952 Japan and the Soviet Union signed a separate peace treaty. Throughout the 1950's Japan was a major ally of the United States and continued to receive economic aid. By the 1960's Japan's economic advance was so rapid that between 1960 and 1966 its industrial output more than doubled. Like defeated Germany, defeated Japan was once again an important industrial nation.

☉ THE WESTERN HEMISPHERE

The countries of North and South America escaped physical destruction from the military operations of the Second World War. Even so, all experienced inflation and other economic consequences of the war. The United States emerged from the war as the richest and most powerful nation on earth. Most of Latin America remained an area of developing nations, where the population explosion continued to outdistance economic growth.

The basic difference in development colored all relationships between the United States and the countries to the south. Latin Americans still looked upon the United States as the "Colossus of the North," ready to send troops into any Latin American country to enforce its will. But the United States was also a market for Latin American agricultural and mineral products, and United States' investments were an important source of capital for Latin American economic growth.

After the war the United States called for economic aid for Latin America to reduce the lure of Communism among the poor. The United States also backed the formation of a hemispheric organization to encourage Latin American governments to work together against outside attack or Communist infiltration. To achieve greater Pan American unity in relation to the outside world, in 1948 the United States took the lead in transforming the Pan-American Union into the Organization of American States (OAS).

To combat the poverty so widespread in Latin America, President Kennedy in 1961 established the Alliance for Progress, a program of financial aid for Latin American countries. This project enjoyed little of the success of the Marshall Plan, for it was intended to attack difficult continuing problems rather than to remedy an emergency situation as in war-torn Europe. It proved nearly impossible for even the United States to bring about reforms within independent countries.

Within the affluent United States, the postwar period brought new levels of prosperity. Americans had achieved the highest standard of living in the world. A greater proportion of its people could be counted in the middle class than ever before, enjoying better education, more leisure, and greater comfort. But these very advantages began to highlight the fact that many minority groups, especially black Americans, were denied the opportunity to share fully in the riches of American society. In 1954 the United States Supreme Court declared that enforced separation of black children from others in public schools was unconstitutional. This decision marked the start of the civil rights movement in the United States. In the 1960s the demand for equal rights would lead to public demonstrations, civil disobedience, and to basic changes in American society.

◌ REVOLUTION IN CHINA

The most important new development in the Far East after the Second World War was the establishment of a Communist nation in China. Imme-

During this period of the Communist revolution in China, teams such as this group of young women, sought to inspire loyalty and devotion to the nation. The Mao Tse-tung Thought Propaganda Team put on this performance on the docks during the Shanghai Festival of Workers, Peasants, and Soldiers. Mao's photo is being held aloft.

diately after the end of the war, the truce that had existed between Chiang Kai-shek's Nationalist forces and the Communists led by Mao Tse-tung ended. China's civil war broke out again. The leader of the Communists, Mao Tse-tung, was one of the most dynamic personalities of the twentieth century. As the son of a rich peasant family, Mao understood the concerns and problems faced by the peasants, by far the vast majority of China's population. As a leader he was able to maintain an almost puritanical discipline among his followers.

During the renewed Civil War Mao announced the beginning of land reform in the areas under Communist control. The property of landlords was confiscated and redivided among the landless peasants in their area. Mao knew how important landownership was to China's peasants, many of whom were in the fighting armies. It was the promise of land reform as much as the discipline and excellent leadership that brought the Communist armies victory.

Between 1945 and 1949 the power of the Nationalists steadily eroded. Inflation hurt their cause, but equally destructive was the dishonesty of officials and their lack of interest in real reform. In 1949 the Communists captured Peking and surrounded the Nationalists in several parts of China, including their capital city of Nanking. The Nationalist leader General Chiang Kai-shek and his government officials fled to the island of Taiwan (Formosa).

Although the Communists now took control of the entire mainland of China, the United States refused to recognize the new regime. Through United States' influence, Chiang's government remained the official representative of China in the United Nations.

On the mainland Mao Tse-tung proclaimed the "People's Republic of China." As in the Soviet Union, only one party, the Communist party, was allowed to exist, and it was the real power in the nation. Unlike Soviet leaders, however, Chinese Communists believed that the peasants, not the industrial workers, were the key to Communism and to China's future. Mao argued that only land reform and the increased productivity of the land would lead China to progress and prosperity. Only when agriculture produced enough food would the nation have the necessary surplus of labor and money to invest in large-scale industrialization.

In 1950 the first of three stages of land reform was begun. It was the same land reform that the Communist had tried before the Second World War, but now it was applied to the entire country. The property of landlords was taken, and many of them fled or were put to death. In 1953 the second stage in agricultural reform started with the effort to form peasant cooperatives in the countryside. Because farming small individual peasant plots was inefficient and made the use of large modern machinery difficult, Communist leaders urged villages to farm collectively. Peasants still could own land individually, however.

In 1958 Mao announced a new program: the Great Leap Forward. Peasants would live in communes. Land would be owned collectively. Small-scale industries would be started in villages throughout China. The resulting productivity would lead to China's industrialization. Later, Communist leaders would admit that much of this effort ended in failure. Peasants hated giving up their land, and families hated living in large communal units. The opposition to the program was enormous, and most of the communes had to be abandoned.

As the Chinese leaders struggled to revolutionize Chinese society, China's relations with the Soviet Union worsened. The Soviet leaders had not aided Mao's revolution while it was in progress. But in 1950 Stalin, who had no allies other than the Soviet satellites, was glad to make an alliance with the Chinese Communists, promising them a limited amount of aid. As time went on and Mao's regime was more firmly established in China, Mao began to show more independence toward the Soviet Union. Concerned with preserving revolutionary fervor within China, Mao reacted harshly when Khrushchev began to talk of "peaceful co-existence" with the Western world. He criticized Soviet leaders for abandoning the principles of revolution. The two great Communist powers grew more openly hostile toward each other. Each was suspicious of the other's actions along their long common borders, and each attempted to spread its own version of Communism through the rest of the world. Along its own western border, China followed an expansionist policy by taking over Tibet, which had been independent in practice. China also seized a small portion of mountainous territory claimed by India.

⌒ ⌒ ⌒

By the 1960's citizens in many parts of the world could look back with satisfaction on the events of the past fifteen years. The Cold War had abated. In Europe and Japan the destruction of war had yielded to rebuilt cities and to the beginnings of a new affluence. Most of the colonies of the European powers had become independent. Underprivileged people in many countries were enjoying new opportunities. But there still remained the race between population growth and food production. In the 1960's the expectations of many new and old nations would begin to be given voice. Ironically, the world's new affluence would prove a double-edged sword. It would produce discontent in those nations that had attained it and envy in those that had not.

Persons, Places, and Terms

Konrad Adenauer	Fifth Republic	Diet
Wladislaw Gomulka	National Health	*zaibatsu*
Imre Nagy	Service	Organization of
	Benelux	American
Taiwan (Formosa)	European Economic	States (OAS)
People's Republic	Community	Alliance for
of China	(Common	Progress
Tibet	Market)	Nationalists
	Euratom	Great Leap
Christian Democratic	Warsaw Pact	Forward
Fourth Republic	coexistence	communes

To Master the Text

1. How extensive was World War II destruction? What factors helped speed reconstruction?
2. What governments were set up in France between 1945 and the 1960's? Why were there so many changes? How was France changed economically and socially in the decades after the war?
3. What basic economic difficulties did Great Britain experience after the war? What social and economic changes took place in Great Britain after the war?
4. What factors encouraged rapid postwar reconstruction in West Germany?
5. What steps were taken after the war to bring about co-operative activity between several European countries? Have they succeeded?
6. How did destruction and rebuilding in the Soviet Union differ from the same factors in the west? How did Khrushchev's policies differ from those of Stalin? How did Soviet relations with the satellites and with the outside world change after the death of Stalin?
7. Trace the struggle in China during the 1940's between the Nationalists and the Chinese Communists. What was the final outcome? How did Mao Tse-tung attempt to remake China? What characterized relations between Mao's China and Khrushchev's Soviet Union?
8. In what ways was Japan treated as a defeated country after the war?
9. What were the particular problems of the United States in the postwar years from 1945 to the mid-1960's?

To Interpret the Facts

1. During the postwar period from 1945 to the mid-1960's, in how many ways did the independent countries co-operate with each other financially? Militarily? Against Communism?
2. What specific facts are evidence that the peoples of the world were living in greater comfort in the mid-1960's than in 1939?

To Put This Chapter into a Larger Setting

1. Do you believe that people in the Soviet Union and the satellites were better off under Khrushchev's dictatorship than they were under Stalin's?
2. With another student study the lives and personalities of Chiang Kai-shek and Mao Tse-tung. Report your findings to the class, trying to show what hopes each man had for China and what each did that made possible the victory of Communism in China.

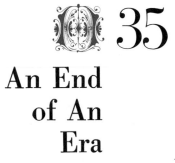 **35**

An End
of An
Era

1960 to 1973

In the 1960's the nations of the world turned away from the concerns that had preoccupied them in the Cold War years to face the problems of a more complex present. The Communist bloc was breaking up. Both China and the Communist parties of France and Italy openly challenged Soviet leadership. Even the eastern European satellites argued that they should be free to define their own paths to socialism. In the West the United States was losing interest in the Cold War. At the same time that the United States was fighting a brutal Asian war in Vietnam to "contain" Communism, its leaders were arranging new alliances with both the U.S.S.R. and the People's Republic of China. In western Europe newly prosperous nations, particularly France, resenting the power of both the Soviet Union and the United States, began to concentrate on their own internal affairs.

The newest figures in the world power equation were the newly independent developing nations. In 1966 China, the most powerful new nation, plunged itself into a political and social upheaval, the "Cultural Revolution." Which goal would shape China's future, China's Chairman Mao Tse-tung asked, revolution or productivity? For other developing countries, such as India, the 1960's brought no dramatic confrontations. Instead, problems of poverty and overpopulation continued, defying all efforts at solution.

⌒ THE GROWING COMPLEXITY OF THE COMMUNIST WORLD

Two issues obsessed Stalin in the years after World War II: the protection of the borders of the Soviet Union and the need to rebuild its economy. By the 1960's the Soviet Union had solved both problems, although not, perhaps, as Stalin had originally intended.

Stalin had seized eastern Europe to provide the Soviets with a buffer zone against attack from capitalist enemies to the west. In 1949 the Soviet Union had developed the atomic bomb to match the weapons of the United States. Within some fifteen years the Soviet Union had a formidable arsenal of nuclear weapons. By then both the Soviet Union and the United States possessed enough military power to destroy each other and much of the rest of the world. Journalists spoke of the "balance of terror" that kept the world at peace. The first step toward controlling these new weapons came in 1963 when Soviet, American, and British leaders signed the Nuclear Test Ban Treaty, a treaty banning above-ground testing of nuclear weapons. All three countries hailed the treaty as a sign of more mature leadership in both West and East. The treaty also indicated that the world's two superpowers were approximately equal in their military technology.

ECONOMIC REVIVAL OF THE SOVIET UNION

By the 1960's the Soviet Union and its satellites had accomplished Stalin's second goal, economic revival. The U.S.S.R. had rebuilt its industries and developed internal supplies of oil for industrial production. Only food production lagged. Peasants often grew more on their privately owned plots than on the large state-owned farms. An American farm worker grew enough food to feed forty-six people; a Soviet farmer grew enough to feed only seven others. Harsh weather added to the agricultural woes of the Soviet Union and often threatened its harvests. In comparison with the West, Soviet standards of living were low, for the U.S.S.R. alloted most of its resources to industry and weapons. By the 1960's, however, the Soviet leadership began to emphasize the production of consumer goods to offer Soviet citizens a better standard of living.

After World War II the original Soviet plan had been to turn eastern Europe into a producer of raw materials for Soviet industry. But in the 1960's, because the Soviet Union no longer desperately needed goods from the satellite nations, it abandoned this idea. Instead, the eastern European satellites assumed greater control over their own economies. By the 1960's East Germany had become the world's tenth-ranking industrial nation. Because both East Germany and Hungary emphasized consumer production, their standards of living were higher than that of the Soviet Union.

The Soviet Union and its satellites began to do business with the West. The "iron curtain" was lifted high enough to encourage foreign investment, trade, and even tourism. Between 1960 and 1965 the U.S.S.R. doubled its trade with the West. In 1966 the Italian automobile company Fiat built a plant in the Soviet Union and tripled that nation's car production within five years. At the same time, the Soviet Union, with its large oil and natural gas resources, began to explore possible Western markets for these products. In the 1960's the increase in trade and foreign investment between the Soviet bloc and the West blurred the economic distinctions between Communist and non-Communist countries.

CZECHOSLOVAKIA SEEKS MORE INDEPENDENCE

In 1968 Czechoslovakia challenged the Soviet Union's political dominance and demonstrated that there were limits to Soviet policies toward the satellites. Alexander Dubcek had become the head of the Czech government. Dubcek was a committed Communist, but he wanted to liberalize politics within his country and to increase individual freedom. Czechoslovakia had always been more oriented toward the West than the other satellite nations, and Dubcek's ideas reflected this older nationalist orientation. As one sign of this orientation, Dubcek withdrew Czechoslovakia from the Warsaw Pact, the military alliance of the Soviet bloc.

As the Czech liberalization movement flowered during the "spring of Prague," Soviet leadership hesitated. The flamboyant Khrushchev had been forced to retire in 1964, and his successors were more cautious men. Alexei Kosygin was now the Soviet Premier. More dominant than Kosygin was Leonid Brezhnev, the Communist party Secretary. Neither wanted to repeat the disasters of the bloody Hungarian rebellion in 1956. Dubcek had also hoped to avoid military intervention and had kept in touch with Soviet leaders by telephone. But developments in Czechoslovakia, released by the new liberalized government policies, were rapidly moving beyond Dubcek's control. Convinced that the Soviet Union had to act if Czechoslovakia was to remain within the Soviet bloc, Kosygin and Brezhnev ordered an invasion of Czechoslovakia by 200,000 Soviet troops. Within a few days Czech freedom was suppressed.

Bitter criticism greeted the Soviet Union's move not only from the countries of the West but also from Communist parties in western Europe. However, Soviet leaders had not been the only ones alarmed by Dubcek's policy changes. Hungary, Poland, and East Germany had agreed to the invasion and had sent token forces to join the invading Soviet troops. Soviet bloc members were worried that their own security would be in danger if Czechoslovakia were allowed to loosen its ties with them. After 23 years of Soviet domination, a Czechoslovakian national identity had remained alive and ready to assert itself. But an equally long period of economic and military alliances, as well as common interests, now held the Soviet bloc together and would act to prevent the defection of any member.

By the 1960's, although economic and political alliances within the Soviet bloc were stronger, the Communist movement as a whole was breaking into a number of splinter groups. When the Soviet Union signed the Nuclear Test Ban Treaty in 1963, Communist China (which wished to develop its own nuclear weaponry) condemned Soviet leaders for abandoning the goal of world revolution. Other Communist countries were also now claiming their independence from Moscow. Yugoslavia, of course, had long maintained its independence. After 1956 the Romanians had taken every opportunity to assert their freedom from Soviet control. Now Albania, a small Balkan country, openly sided with China. After 1968, partly because of the invasion of Czechoslovakia, the western European Communist parties publicly declared their ideological separation from Moscow. Throughout the world Soviet-oriented Communist parties now found they had to compete with Chinese "Maoists" or other independent organizations for leadership.

○ THE VIETNAM WAR

Throughout the 1960's and until 1973, the United States was fighting an undeclared war in Vietnam, a small Southeast Asian country. American involvement in Vietnam dated to the days of the French war in Indochina. After the French defeat an international conference in 1954 divided Vietnam into North and South Vietnam. Elections were to reunite the country, but the government of South Vietnam refused to hold them, fearing it would lose. Soon Communist guerrillas—the Vietcong—were fighting within South Vietnam itself to try to take control of that nation.

American leaders argued that it was necessary to protect South Vietnam against the Communists of the North, just as it had been necessary to contain Communism in Korea. American leaders were worried about the spread of Chinese, not Soviet, influence in Asia. President Eisenhower accepted the "domino" theory, the idea that just as the first of a row of falling dominoes can knock down all the others, so, too, if one more Asian country fell to Communism, the others would follow. Eisenhower and President Kennedy after him sent American military aid to the South Vietnamese. In 1964 it seemed that South Vietnam would fall. In April, 1965, President Lyndon B. Johnson sent the first large force of ground troops to Vietnam, beginning the fateful buildup of American military forces in that country. By 1966 there were 200,000 American soldiers in Vietnam, and American bombing raids occurred almost daily. By 1969 over 500,000 Americans had been sent to Southeast Asia. In turn, North Vietnam sent aid and army units to the Vietcong in the South. Neither the Soviet Union nor China fought in the war, but both sent or sold equipment to help North Vietnam.

ℚ THE MOVEMENT TOWARD DÉTENTE

Détente, a French word meaning "a relaxation," was the name given to the policy of relaxation of tension between the United States and the Soviet Union. By the 1960's American leaders, like those in Moscow, began to find the goals of the Cold War outdated. A decade of steady growth in economic, cultural, and diplomatic ties between the two nations made the policy of détente that emerged in 1969 seem a natural conclusion, although every friendly gesture seemed matched by an equally ugly confrontation.

Progress toward what Khrushchev called "peaceful coexistence" was anything but steady. Even as the superpowers negotiated the Nuclear Test Ban Treaty, Soviet leaders abruptly cancelled a 1961 summit conference because of the flight of American spy planes over their territory. A year later the Cuban Missile Crisis precipitated another dangerous confrontation. Later, observers marked this event as the last in the Cold War. But in 1962, as the world drew back from the brink of nuclear war, the possibility of coexistence between the Soviet Union and the United States seemed a long way away.

In the early 1960's American officials had argued that the Vietnam War was a fight against Communism itself. By the end of the decade, this argument was still used, but it was mostly rhetorical. Even while the Vietnam

Mao Tse-tung, the leader of the People's Republic of China, and President Richard Nixon held historic discussions during Nixon's visit to the mainland of China in 1972. Nixon's trip represented a major shift in American policy.

War continued, President Nixon and his Secretary of State, Henry Kissinger, made plans to open diplomatic relations with the two major Communist countries of the world, the Soviet Union and China. In 1969 as tensions eased under détente, the two countries began talks on the limitation of military weapons. In 1972 a preliminary agreement on arms limitation was signed in Moscow. Détente gave the U.S.S.R. access to the purchase of American grain when in 1972 and 1975 Soviet grain harvests failed.

The year 1972 also included President Nixon's historic trip to the mainland of China. After 23 years the United States had finally acknowledged the existence of the Communist government of China. Plans began for cultural, diplomatic, and economic exchanges between the two countries. In 1975 the Peoples' Republic of China replaced the Taiwanese government (the "Republic of China") as China's representative in the Security Council of the United Nations. Although the United States was still fighting a war against Communism in Southeast Asia, peaceful coexistence with the Communist regimes of the Soviet Union and China had begun.

☊ PEACE IN VIETNAM

Peace negotiations between the United States and North Vietnam had started in 1969, and some American soldiers had returned home during that year. Negotiations stalled, however, and for several years the war dragged on. The war escalated in 1970 when President Nixon ordered an invasion of the nearby country of Cambodia, which, although previously "neutral," was serving as a sanctuary for some North Vietnamese forces. It escalated again during Christmas of 1973 when the President ordered saturation bombing of North Vietnam. Throughout these years the United States Secretary of State, Henry Kissinger, negotiated privately with the North Vietnamese. Finally, in 1973 an agreement was reached that ended American fighting in the war. One year later, following the withdrawal of most American forces, South Vietnam fell to the North Vietnamese army. In 1976 the North Vietnamese government arranged for the unification of the country as the People's Democratic Republic of Vietnam.

THE CONSEQUENCES OF THE VIETNAM WAR

From the American point of view, the war had been a disaster. Over 55,000 men had died and 300,000 had been wounded. More than $140 billion had been spent. From 1961 to 1968 Americans had dropped more bombs on Vietnam than on all the Axis countries in World War II. The war's critics said that the conflict had no purpose. Cold war rhetoric about the need to stop Communism sounded strange in the world of 1973. By the time America withdrew from Vietnam, the United States and Communist countries were trading openly and had signed new diplomatic agreements.

The Vietnam War was the longest and the least popular war in American history. The years of protest against this war had led some Americans to question both their government and the values that had led to the fighting. Over 40,000 young men had fled the United States to avoid military service. (Only in 1977 were some draft evaders able to return home under a limited amnesty offered by President Jimmy Carter.) People in many foreign countries, including America's European allies, had also objected to the United States' conduct in Vietnam. Protests against American policy, particularly by student groups, had been common around the world.

Protest against the war in Vietnam sparked a series of protest movements in the late 1960's in America and in other nations of the world. As people questioned America's right to decide the destiny of Vietnam, they began to question their own society's right to limit their own development. Women, blacks, and other minority groups in America began to question their position within society. In Britain people in both Scotland and Wales began to renew their agitation for separation from the southern English portion of the United Kingdom. In Northern Ireland the conflict over unification with the Irish Republic intensified.

Different circumstances made each protest movement unique. The demand for civil rights among American blacks had begun almost twenty years earlier, and the Scottish cry for independence was over three hundred years old. The Vietnam War brought world-wide protest movements together and gave them a common vocabulary, "self-determination," and a common form, the protest march. In the postwar years the Cold War had shaped people's ideas and values in both East and West. From the late 1960's through the early years of the 1970's, demonstrations and the style of protests helped shape behavior all over the world.

Demonstrations against the Vietnam War, this one in San Francisco, involved people of all ages, although the young predominated. Most of the demonstrations were peaceful, but strikes and sit-ins on college campuses and the burning of draft cards were sometimes met with arrests or other action by the police.

๑   WESTERN EUROPE: INCREASING
PROSPERITY

The Vietnam War was one factor that made it obvious in the 1960's that Europe was no longer at the center of world events. During the Cold War, conflicts between the two superpowers had held center stage. Then world attention had shifted to Asia.

The countries of Europe, no longer needing American financial aid, could express their displeasure with American policies despite their dependence on American military strength for protection. The Common Market was flourishing; lifting tariff and passport boundaries between member countries had been hugely successful. By 1973, when Britain, Denmark, and Ireland were admitted, the Common Market included nine nations. In the years from 1960 to 1973, Europeans turned from the preocccupations of the postwar period to a consideration of the consequences of their rebuilt and generally prosperous economies.

WEST GERMANY

The most successful of the postwar industrial economies was that of West Germany. Wartime destruction of large sections of German industry had necessitated building new equipment. (Both defeated Axis powers, Germany and Japan, emerged from postwar reconstruction with the most modern industries and factories in the world.) After the war the Allies had kept Germany from rearming. All German resources could therefore be used for industrial development. By 1960 German industries were producing twice as much as in the years before the war. By 1975 West Germany had the strongest economy in western Europe.

By the 1960's the West Germans were free to chart their country's future unhampered by the restrictions and controls of other countries. By 1966 West Germany had rearmed and become a full member of NATO. The Christian Democratic party, under Konrad Adenauer, had ruled since the war. In 1963 Adenauer was replaced by Ludwig Erhardt, the former Minister of Economics. In that same year the opposition Social Democratic party won one third of the votes. Its leader, Willy Brandt, was the former mayor of West Berlin, an energetic and popular figure. In 1969 the Social Democrats won the election, and Brandt became the first Social Democratic Chancellor of Germany since the war. Brandt had left Germany during the Nazi period and fought in the Norwegian Resistance movement during World War II. Because he, too, had fought the Nazis, he understood the fear with which the people of the U.S.S.R. and its satellites looked on the revived German nation.

Immediately after World War II, German policy had been to refuse diplomatic contacts with any country that recognized East Germany. As a foreign minister under the Christian Democrats, Brandt had deliberately abandoned that policy. Now as Chancellor, he expanded his earlier contacts and negotiated treaties with the Soviet Union and Poland that acknowledged the postwar borders between these countries. Brandt's policies led to an easing of travel restrictions between East and West Germany. More important, his tacit acceptance of the division of Germany into two countries allowed West Germany to end its preoccupation with postwar conflicts and to face the realities of the world of the 1960's.

FRANCE

The accession of Charles de Gaulle to leadership in the French government in 1958 had led to the freeing of France's colonies and the founding of the Fifth Republic. In the elections of 1962 de Gaulle's position was firmly established, and by 1965 he was wielding nearly absolute power and was the undisputed maker of French foreign policy. De Gaulle's opposition to British and American influence on the continent was legendary. Only in 1973, after his death, was Britain able to join the Common Market. Convinced that France needed its own nuclear arsenal, he rejected the Nuclear Arms Pact in 1963. By 1966, in pursuit of French independence, de Gaulle had withdrawn France completely from NATO. The headquarters of NATO were moved from Paris to Belgium.

In his relations with other European countries, de Gaulle was a French nationalist. He urged the expansion of the Common Market, pleased by the vision of France at the head of a revived Europe. But he undercut Common Market policies whenever they threatened to damage French national interests. That the Common Market failed to unify Europe politically in the 1960's may be attributed partly to de Gaulle's influence and activities.

By the 1960's French business was booming. New urban centers sprang up on the outskirts of older French cities. But the new French economy developed unevenly. There was a sharp contrast between the newness of modern areas and the outdated living and working conditions in older parts of France.

This unevenness may have been partially to blame for France's crisis in the late 1960's. In 1968 university students outside Paris began to protest the dilapidated buildings and the overcrowded conditions in their schools. Their complaint spread rapidly to other sections of society. Parisian students joined their strike, and actual battles between protestors and French police broke out in the University Quarter of Paris. French workers, who were negotiating for higher pay, declared themselves in sympathy with the students. Suddenly, in May some ten million people were on strike against the government of France.

Student leaders believed it was the start of a new French Revolution, but they were wrong. De Gaulle offered the workers substantial wage increases and convinced them to end the strike. At the same time, many students were more interested in the ideological theory of revolution than the economic realities at the heart of the strike. Their revolutionary rhetoric antagonized both workers and the more conservative French middle class. De Gaulle survived the crisis and even won a vote of confidence in the following elections. But this victory only temporarily obscured the real economic grievances of many French people and his own loss of popularity. The next year he insisted that a referendum vote be held on his leadership. He lost and resigned from the government. De Gaulle's successor, Georges Pompidou, kept the Gaullist party in power until 1974.

BRITAIN

Like Japan, Britain is an island nation with a large population. It needs to import food and to export industrial goods. Unlike Japan, however, Britain's outdated industries were never fully modernized during the postwar period. Britain's labor unions were much more powerful than their Japanese counterparts and could ensure British workers a relatively high wage. The far-reaching social programs passed after the war were popular but costly. Britain's coal mines had provided an excellent source of industrial fuel, but after World War II much of the industrial world switched to the use of oil. Britain's coal resources no longer gave it an advantage. Britain's postwar recovery was the most limited in all of Europe.

Psychologically, the British had the largest adjustment to make to the realities of the 1960's. In the nineteenth and twentieth centuries "Britannia" had "ruled the waves," as the old song said, and a good part of the land as well. Industry and empire had made Britain the most powerful country in the world. By the 1960's most of Britain's colonies were freed, and its exports had become too expensive to sell well in competitive world markets. Britain's unfavorable balance of payments grew worse throughout the

1960's. The voters searched for a government that would restore prosperity.

Britain's government changed three times between 1960 and 1973, from Conservative to Labor in 1964 and back to Conservative in 1970. Conservatives believed that Britain's expensive social programs and the high wages paid to its trade union workers caused its problems. But the social programs were popular with voters, and the trade unions were very well organized in elections. Although ideologically opposed to them, the Conservatives made no real attempt either to dismantle the social programs or to limit wages. The steel industry was the one exception. It was nationalized by Labor after the war, denationalized by the Conservatives after 1951, then nationalized again when Labor came back to power in 1964.

From 1964 to 1970 Labor was in power under Harold Wilson as prime minister. The Labor government agreed that the social programs were expensive and that high wages made industrial goods expensive, but Labor was ideologically committed to both. Wilson tried without much success to find some other solution to Britain's economic situation. In 1970 the Conservatives returned to power, and de Gaulle's death in 1973 allowed Britain to enter the Common Market. The solution to Britain's economic problems, however, seemed as far away as ever.

ᕋ   CHANGING CHINA

As leaders in the Soviet Union, the United States, and Europe reassessed their nations' positions in the world of the 1960's, Mao Tse-tung, the Chairman of the People's Republic of China, was doing the same. Mao Tse-tung's programs were not always successful in the years after 1949, but the Chinese claimed they had made major advances. Although population was growing at about 2 percent a year, increased agricultural production helped provide needed food. Education and health care were available to more Chinese than ever before. The generation of children born during the 1940's had never known the chronic insecurity that had been a common feature of peasant life in pre-revolutionary days.

By the late 1960's, however, Mao was in his seventies. His close associate, Chou En-lai, was only a few years younger. In fact, all of China's leaders, the men who had fought together since the 1930's, were now old men. Who, Mao wondered, would rule China after his death? What would become of China's revolution when children who had never known the suffering of earlier times came to power?

Mao was the most powerful of China's leaders. His programs had been dramatic and inspiring. His devotion to China's Communist revolution was unquestioned. But by the 1960's some leaders, among them Liu Shao ch'i, Mao's main opponent, were arguing that the chairman's enthusiastic campaigns had also been chaotic and disruptive. Orderly and systematic planning, these leaders argued, would bring China more prosperity than the disruptive fervor of a "Great Leap Forward."

Mao was the only major Communist leader to have come from peasant stock. In his eyes the revolution had brought a measure of economic equality to China's peasants and had been the means of guaranteeing them the necessities of life. In contrast, Liu Shao ch'i was a "capitalist roader." By this Mao meant that Liu favored encouraging progress through the use of the profit motive employed in the capitalist West. Slowly but surely, Mao believed, this approach would turn China back to the economic inequalities and cruelties of its pre-revolutionary days.

THE CULTURAL REVOLUTION

In 1966 Mao faced a series of problems: the future of China's revolution, the need to find a successor, and a challenge to his authority from within the Communist party. The Cultural Revolution was Mao's solution to all of them. The revolution would rekindle the revolutionary spirit in China's increasingly conservative intellectual elite and awaken its youth to a taste of their elders' revolutionary commitment. The revolution was also a political maneuver, meant to dislodge Mao's opposition from their positions of power.

The Cultural Revolution began with a series of wall posters (Mao himself wrote one) criticizing various Communist elders for abandoning the principles of the revolution. All over China young people called the "Red Guards" were encouraged to challenge those in power. In the factory, the university, the village, in party meetings—wherever the Red Guards saw a lack of commitment to China's revolution—they were to speak out. Intellectual elitism was to be challenged. Ideology was more important than productivity; practical skill was more valuable than theoretical knowledge.

The revolution penetrated all levels of society. For three years almost all aspects of society were disrupted. Agricultural production fell less than factory output, but both lost ground. Schools were closed for three years, and travel between parts of China was difficult. Many highly placed people lost their positions. Some went to jail. Others were demoted to lower-level

A Ballet of the Red Detachment of Women, as performed by children in a factory day care center. In China, indoctrination into Communism extends to all levels.

jobs and urged to rethink their revolutionary commitment. Even after the campaign ended, the goals of the revolution echoed through Chinese society for several years. Students applying to the universities had to demonstrate revolutionary zeal as well as talent. Teachers could be criticized for emphasizing subject matter over ideology. Throughout the revolution, Mao maintained power. He controlled the communications networks and through his ally, Lin Piao, the Red Army. His political opponents were temporarily eclipsed.

After Mao's death Chinese leaders criticized the Cultural Revolution as excessive, wasteful, and unnecessary. For Mao, however, it was his last great campaign, his final effort to save and preserve the revolution to which he had given his life.

ᴕ ECONOMIC STAGNATION IN INDIA

For India, the question of the 1960's was not how fast progress would occcur, as in China, but whether it would be possible at all. India had begun its new life as an independent country in 1947 with great optimism. India was a new democratic society, with leaders educated in Western democratic traditions. Indians believed that their former rulers, the British, had caused much of their poverty. Prime Minister Jawaharlal Nehru, a Cambridge-educated lawyer, and his colleagues were attached to the ideals of democracy and socialism. In the Indian context socialism meant centrally planned government and the general belief that the huge gap between rich and poor should be narrowed. Nehru governed until his death in 1964. In that time India remained "nonaligned," accepting economic aid from both the Soviets and the Americans. Nehru's successors continued this policy.

In 1966 Nehru's daughter, Indira Gandhi, became the head of India's government. Mrs. Gandhi was as capable a politician as her father, and she needed all her skill. Twenty years after its independence in 1947, India's poverty had not greatly altered, and the Indian people's optimism about the possibility of progress was rapidly fading.

India's population had "exploded." In 1900 there had been less than 200 million Indians. In 1969 there were well over 600 million. The rapidly increasing population had literally consumed whatever increases in industrial output and food production had occurred. Per capita income in 1967 to 1968 was $76 a year. The real situation was probably worse than this average figure indicates. One estimate suggested that in the countryside over 160 million people lived on less than $24 a year and that half of India's city dwellers were in the same situation. People began to compare India with China, citing the latter as an example of an Asian country that had solved many of its problems through an emphasis on land reform. Over 80 percent of India's population was in rural areas. The rural poor desperately needed land to farm. But many of India's political leaders represented large landowners, and the Indian parliament had never passed an effective land redistribution law.

In 1969 Indira Gandhi won reelection in a campaign with the slogan "abolish poverty." It seemed an appropriate goal, and there were some signs of improvement. Since 1965 food production had increased in northwestern India through the use of petroleum-based fertilizers. Three good crop years put India slightly in the black in food production. But agriculture in India had always depended on the yearly rains, the monsoons. Good rains brought slight surpluses; bad rains, disaster. The slight economic improvement of the late 1960's only underscored the precariousness of India's economy.

During the 1950's and 1960's India had been called the Asian "experiment" with democracy. Could democracy survive in an Asian environment? In the 1960's many Indians wondered if this was the right question. Perhaps, some Indians suggested, an authoritarian government would have more success in solving India's overwhelming problems.

ᴑ ᴑ ᴑ

By 1973 the Cold War was long over, and the simple political alignments it had created were gone. A more complex world had emerged. Industrial nations competed for markets throughout the world. Developing countries looked for the strategies that would most quickly improve the lives of their peoples. In 1973 many leaders believed that they understood their countries' basic problems. But none of them were fully prepared for the events at the end of the year—an energy crisis brought on by the Arab oil embargo that would symbolize a restructuring of the world balance of power.

Persons, Places, and Terms

Alexander Dubcek	Liu Shao-ch'i	Cultural Revolution
Alexei Kosygin	Lin Pao	Nuclear Test Ban
Leonid Brezhnev	Indira Gandhi	Treaty
Jimmy Carter		Maoist
Ludwig Erhardt	Prague	Vietcong
Willy Brandt	Albania	domino theory
Georges Pompidou	Indochina	détente
Harold Wilson	Democratic Republic	Gaullist
Chou En-lai	of Vietnam	Red Guards

To Master the Text

1. What were Stalin's main concerns in terms of relations with other nations after World War II?
2. What was the major weakness in the economy of the Soviet Union? What physical factors added to this weakness?

3. What was happening to the standard of living in the Soviet Union between 1960 and 1973? In the satellite countries of eastern Europe?
4. Which of the nations of eastern Europe raised major challenges to Soviet domination of their country? What was the outcome in each case? What happened to demonstrate that the Soviet bloc was held together by strong forces within the satellite nations?
5. How and when did American involvement in Vietnam first begin? What were the major arguments for protecting South Vietnam from a takeover by Communist-led forces?
6. When did the large-scale buildup of American forces in Vietnam begin? What was the outcome of the war in terms of victory? Of dead and wounded? In terms of popular feeling in the United States?
7. What term used by Khrushchev was later replaced by "détente"? What was the policy of détente? What were some of the signs of détente?
8. Give some examples of protest movements in the 1960's and early 1970's. Which ones were very old in their origin?
9. Which industrial nation in western Europe had the most succesesful economy?
10. What was the main thrust, or intent, of French policy under de Gaulle's leadership?
11. What were the causes of Britain's economic decline after World War II? How did opinions in Britain differ on the ways to deal with the decline?
12. What were Mao's main concerns in his later years? How did he seek to solve Communist China's problems as he saw them?
13. What were India's main problems in this period? How were Indira Ghandi's successes and failures in politics linked to these problems?

To Interpret the Facts

1. The differences in the amount of apparent progress in India and China led to many comparisons of the value of democracy versus authoritarianism, particularly in the developing nations. How would you interpret and defend each point of view?
2. What was the general trend in economic development in most of the world during the 1960's and early 1970's?

To Put This Chapter in a Larger Setting

1. How would you compare the well-being of the people of mainland China under Communism with their state, or condition, before the revolution?
2. Study the issues involved during Indira Gandhi's period of stern "emergency" rule and report your findings to the class.

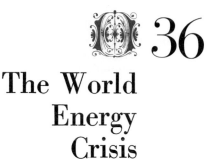

36

The World
Energy
Crisis

1973 to the 1980's

A new era in world history began with the Arab oil embargo of 1973 to 1974. In a short time the oil prices set by the Organization of Petroleum Exporting Countries (OPEC) rose enormously, eventually reaching nine times their pre-embargo levels. The recession that followed the rise in world oil prices was the worst in forty years. The industrialized nations suddenly realized how dependent on cheap energy they had become. The developing countries, although less dependent on machinery, were not immune to the energy crisis. All oil-importing countries faced soaring rates of inflation that reflected the higher cost of fuel. As a result, economic problems preoccupied the leaders of many nations in the mid- and late-1970's.

☾ CHANGE IN THE OIL INDUSTRY

The oil crisis emerged initially as part of the conflict between Israel and the Arab world. Egypt and Syria, still bitter over Egypt's defeat in 1967, attacked Israel again in October, 1973, on the Jewish holy day of Yom Kippur. Although stunned by the attack, the Israelis rallied, quickly neutralized the Syrian attack from the northeast, and crossed the Suez Canal to trap a portion of the Egyptian army that had invaded the Sinai Peninsula, on the Israeli-held side of the canal. By 1974 the fighting had stopped.

THE ARAB OIL EMBARGO

Two days after the Arab-Israeli war began, OPEC, representing the oil-exporting countries, announced the first in a series of sharp oil price increases. OPEC's Arab members, angered by Israel's quick recovery, declared that they would produce less oil and would refuse to sell oil to nations that sided with Israel. Their main targets were Israel's allies in western Europe and the United States. Meanwhile, the OPEC nations made plans to take full control of their countries' oil, control that had previously been in the hands of the privately owned international oil companies. What had begun as an episode in Middle Eastern history ended as a revolution in the world oil industry.

THE EXPANSION OF THE OIL INDUSTRY

In 1973 the industrialized nations of the world suddenly realized that oil had become their single most important source of energy. Throughout the 1950's and 1960's many nations had come increasingly to prefer oil and had closed down their coal operations. In Europe, with the exception of Great Britain, oil had replaced coal as the most important source of energy by 1966. In 1973, 64 percent of Europe's energy came from oil, and 70 percent of that oil came from the Middle East. In Japan, as in Europe, the postwar period saw a conversion from coal to oil, and by 1973 Japan was almost completely dependent on oil imports for its energy needs.

The United States in 1973 had more diversified energy sources, including large domestic sources of oil. To protect American producers, the United States government had imposed quotas on the international oil companies, limiting imports of foreign oil. American industries and private consumers had turned to coal and natural gas where possible because these fuels were cheaper than domestic oil. Nevertheless, over the years the overall effect of

The oil embargo of 1973-1974 led to closed gasoline stations in the United States. Another common sight was huge lines of cars where gasoline was available.

the import quotas was to gradually reduce the amount of oil available from reserves found up to that time.

In 1973 the oil business was largely an American enterprise. The major companies, the technology, and most of the personnel in the oil industry were American. At the beginning of the twentieth century, European countries had controlled most sources of foreign oil through their overseas empires, but the decline of imperial power had allowed American corporations to enter the international oil business. By 1973 there were seven major international oil companies: Exxon, Mobil, Standard Oil of California (Chevron), Gulf Oil, Texaco, Royal Dutch/Shell, and British Petroleum. Only Royal Dutch/Shell and British Petroleum were not based in the United States. These companies had found and developed most of the world's oil resources from the 1920's until 1973.

In general, the companies operated under a concession from each foreign country. In return for the right to locate and develop a foreign country's oil resources, an oil company would agree to pay the country a share of its profits.

The greatest difficulty in the oil business is the need to limit the amount of oil taken out of the ground at any one time. Oil is bulky and difficult to store. Once produced, it has to be sold as quickly as possible. The oil companies always feared that if too much oil were brought to the market at one time, the price would fall sharply. For this reason the international oil companies had always operated as an informal cartel. There was a general agreement among the seven major companies concerning each company's share of the oil market. None of the oil companies tried to put the others out of business by producing a great deal of oil and selling it very cheaply.

The problem of limiting supply became more difficult as oil companies discovered huge oil reserves throughout the Middle East. There was a basic conflict of interest between the oil companies' wish to keep the price of oil high and the oil-rich countries' wish to produce and sell as much of their oil as possible. In addition, the growing spirit of nationalism led many oil-rich countries to ask why a foreign company should exploit their country's oil resources.

The issue was not this simple. Most of the oil-exporting countries were developing nations. Countries like Iran and Iraq had little industry or advanced technology. The rulers of these countries believed they needed the international oil companies to find and produce their oil. They also feared the power of the oil companies, which owned and controlled the refineries and the distribution networks to sell oil on the world market.

In 1951 the government of Iran attempted to nationalize its British-run oil industry. The British Company (Anglo-Iranian) claimed it owned the Iranian oil, organized a boycott, and threatened to sue any other company that used Iran's oil. Two years after nationalization, Iran's oil exports had fallen from $400 million a year to less than $2 million a year. Only after the Shah of Iran was reinstated on his throne with the covert support of the American Central Intelligence Agency did Iran find markets for its oil. Earlier in the century the oil companies had met Mexico's attempt to nationalize its oil industry with a similar boycott.

THE EMERGENCE OF OPEC

If oil-producing countries could not nationalize their oil resources, they could demand an increase in their share of the oil profits. Their confidence grew during the postwar period, as the importance of oil increased in the industrial world. In 1959 when the major oil companies announced a reduction in the price of oil, OPEC was born: the oil-producing countries joined together and forced the companies to retract their decision.

Twelve years later, OPEC was still active. Among its members were the sixteen major oil exporters of the world: Ecuador, Venezuela, Trinidad, Nigeria, Gabon, Algeria, Libya, Iraq, Saudi Arabia, Kuwait, Bahrein, Qatar, Abu Dhabi, Dubai, Oman, and Iran. Many important OPEC countries were Arab. The international companies had for years managed to limit oil production. OPEC's members, however, have not been able to agree on similar limitations. Middle Eastern countries with vast oil supplies were especially reluctant to restrict production and limit their own profits. In 1970 OPEC members finally decided to take control of the production and pricing of their own oil in the near future. Three years later the anger of its Arab members toward Israel pushed OPEC to act on its earlier decision: OPEC raised oil prices, set production limits, and left the oil companies to become managers of the oil operations they had once owned. The most dramatic event of the 1973 to 1974 oil crisis was the Arab oil embargo, but the most significant was the oil-producing countries' declaration of independence.

ᴖ WORLD-WIDE RECESSION

When the Arabs announced their oil embargo, the reactions of the industrialized nations showed which countries were most dependent on Middle Eastern oil. Japan, which relied almost entirely on Arab oil, quickly realigned itself with Arab countries. In Europe, the Netherlands, a Common Market member, was a prime target of Arab wrath. Both Britain and France tacitly accepted the embargo and negotiated private agreements with the Arabs for oil suppplies. The United States, on the other hand, with its own energy supplies, remained unmoved by Arab threats. But Americans suffered from fuel oil and gasoline shortages through the winter of 1973 to 1974, and the prices of these commodities rose dramatically.

Later in 1974, when the Arabs ended the embargo, there was no shortage of oil, but its price was four times higher. An economic recession spread throughout the industrial world as fuel prices increased. By 1975 industrial production had declined in many countries. World steel production dropped by one third. In the industrialized countries millions of people were out of work. Annual inflation rates reached "double digit" (10 percent or more) levels. Labor union benefits and unemployment insurance cushioned the shock for working people in many nations, but the recession was the worst in forty years.

Previously, economists had believed that industrial stagnation and inflation were opposite economic conditions. Now both appeared at the same time. "Stagflation" was the popular term. Although fewer industrial goods were manufactured, their prices rose higher and higer. Few economists were sure how to solve the problem. Economic conditions preocccupied the governments of most European nations in the late 1970's as they struggled to adjust to the oil crisis and to solve their own staggering economic problems. In Germany recovery was relatively quick. In Britain and France, however, the severe economic recession threatened the governments in power.

GREAT BRITAIN'S ECONOMY

In Britain the 1973 oil embargo coincided with a confrontation between the government and the trade unions that had been brewing since the Second World War. In 1973 Britain also entered the Common Market, but Edward Heath, the new Conservative Prime Minister, believed Britain's economy could not improve until its industrial goods became less expensive. Heath decided that wage increases must be limited.

Heath's policy met bitter opposition, especially from Britain's coal miners whose standard of living was well below that of most British citizens. The miners went on strike at the same time as the Arabs declared their oil embargo. Severe shortages of coal and oil crippled life in Britain throughout the cold, dark Christmas season of 1973. Heath abandoned his attempt to freeze wages, but his long delay in doing so cost the Conservatives the next election. In 1974 Labor was back in power. The Labor ministers, who had good relations with the unions, were able to negotiate essentially the same agreement the Conservatives had wanted. The trade unions agreed to accept a limited wage increase to help restore Britain's shaky economy.

By 1978 Britain's economy had dramatically improved. Oil wells discovered in the North Sea had begun to produce. Not only were the British freer of dependence on Arab oil, but they were also able to sell oil abroad. By May, 1978, the inflation rate was the lowest in years, but Labor's freeze on wages had left union members behind in the general economic revival. In 1978 the trade unions refused to agree to Prime Minister James Callaghan's call for a ceiling on wage increases, and soon strike after strike paralyzed the economy. Some settlements gave workers an increase of more than 20 percent. By 1979 the inflation rate was again at 10 percent. The British people were worried about the economy and angered by the strikes. In the 1979 general election they voted for the Conservatives.

Margaret Thatcher, Europe's first woman Prime Minister, headed the new Conservative government. Mrs. Thatcher's government took steps to return government-owned companies to private hands, reduce income taxes, and sharply cut government spending and popular social programs. Britain's balance of trade remained positive but inflation soared. By 1980 over 2 million Britons were unemployed.

In 1981 a new Social Democratic Party was formed largely from moderates opposed to the left in the Labor Party. Later the new party allied itself with the Liberals. The new alliance pointed to a possible basic shift in British politics.

FRANCE: THE COMMUNIST CHALLENGE

The severe mid-1970's recession almost brought a coalition of French Socialist and Communist parties into power in France. In 1975, as prices and unemployment rose, French voters joined the Communist Party in record numbers. Georges Marchais, the French Communist leader, took steps to broaden his party's appeal. In the 1976 party meeting, Marchais denounced Moscow's acts of repression against Soviet citizens and called for "Communism under French colors." Convinced that a coalition might win the election, the Communists joined with France's other major left party, the Socialists, in supporting Socialist leader François Mitterand for the 1978 general elections.

This growing power of the left alarmed France's ruling party, the Independent Republicans. Led by the aristocratic Valéry Giscard D'Estaing, the Independents had taken power away from the Gaullist party after 1974. From 1976 to 1978 Giscard repeatedly offered plans for France's economic revival, emphasizing that external events had caused France's difficulties. Giscard's party warned that the left, if victorious, would nationalize many French businesses. In the same year the Independent Republicans changed their name to the "Republican Party." The Republicans won the elections, but the Communist and Socialist coalition had demonstrated the dissatisfaction of many French voters. The Republicans were overthrown when François Mitterand led the Socialists to victory in 1981.

GERMANY: RECOVERY AND TERRORISM

Germany, in comparison with France and Great Britain, recovered quickly from the 1974 recession. Chancellor Helmut Schmidt refused to stimulate the economy because he feared that this would cause inflation to get out of control. As a result the German economy grew slowly, and unemployment remained at 5 percent, a high figure for Germany. But the inflation rate remained low, less than 5 percent in 1980.

Germany's successful economic recovery was helped by the good relations between labor and management. Since the 1950's Germany had experimented with "codetermination," that is, having trade union representation on companies' boards of directors. In 1974 the Social Democrats and the trade unions urged the expansion of union representation to one half the board membership in each large company.

The former Chancellor and head of the Social Democrats, Willy Brandt, had negotiated the mutual diplomatic recognition between East Germany and West Germany in 1973. Brandt had received the Nobel Peace Prize for this effort. But a year later an East German spy was discovered within Brandt's official circle, and he resigned. His successor, Helmut Schmidt, continued Brandt's policies toward the Soviet Union and its eastern European satellites. The Soviet Union wanted western markets for its oil, and the Germans saw the Soviet Union as a valuable outlet for their industrial products. In 1978 Schmidt and Leonid Brezhnev signed a 25-year agreement pledging economic cooperation between West Germany and the Soviet Union.

Germany escaped the deep economic recession that affected much of Europe in the 1970's, but it was not immune to the world-wide wave of terrorist activities. In Germany in 1976 eleven members of the Bader-Meinhoff terrorist gang were in jail awaiting trial. In September 1977 the gang launched a series of attacks to win their imprisoned members' freedom.

Gang members machine-gunned the head of the government's prosecuting team, kidnapped a prominent German industrialist, and hijacked a Lufthansa plane. West German commandos stormed the plane with its 87 passenger hostages. Hours after this rescue, three of the terrorists were found dead in their cells. German authorities claimed the three had committed suicide: The terrorists accused the authorities of murder.

๑ THE UNITED STATES IN THE 1970'S

Because oil supplies were vital to the United States, it was often argued that government policies should ensure the prosperity and viability of the American oil industry. In 1949, for example, when Saudi Arabia demanded an increased share of oil-company profits from the sale of Saudi oil, the United States government agreed to allow the companies to deduct these increased payments from their American taxes. This tax benefit was soon extended to all international oil companies and was still in effect in 1978.

The quotas on the import of foreign oil, which had protected the domestic American oil producers since 1959, ended only in 1973 when foreign oil prices rose above those for the domestic product. In the late 1970's the nation's oil industry was deregulated. Domestic oil prices were to rise gradually until they were equal to OPEC oil prices. An "excess profits" tax, passed at the same time, aimed at encouraging the oil companies to use their increased profits for the exploration and development of additional oil resources in the United States.

THE WATERGATE SCANDAL

In 1973 and 1974 a dramatic government scandal preoccupied the American nation, despite the oil crisis. During the 1972 election campaign, an alert guard stopped an attempted burglary of the Democratic party headquarters in the Watergate hotel complex in Washington, D.C. Evidence soon began to acccumulate implicating President Richard Nixon and his highest aides in an elaborate scheme to cover up the Nixon administration's part in the burglary. As the scandal mounted, the House of Representatives discussed impeaching the President. In August, 1974, President Nixon resigned to avoid almost certain impeachment. His successor, Gerald Ford, almost immediately after taking office granted Nixon a pardon for any illegal activities he might have committed. Nixon's resignation removed the central figure of the Watergate scandal. But the trials of his aides dragged on for several more years.

This demonstration by Iranian militants in November 1979 was in support of student militants who had seized the American Embassy and still held Americans as hostages. The demonstrators also demanded the return of the Shah, who had fled, and commemorated an attack by his forces on the people in the street a year before.

IRAN

The United States supported Shah Muhammed Riza Pahlevi, the ruler of Iran from 1953 to 1979, with economic and military aid. In return, Iran became a major supplier of oil to the United States. The Shah attempted to modernize his country in the face of ancient Islamic traditions while his secret police repressed his opponents. In 1979 forces dominated by an extremely conservative Muslim leader, Ayatollah Ruhollah Khomeini, created riots and brought about a revolution against the Shah, who fled. He was later allowed to enter the United States for medical treatment. Iranian anger soared, and on November 5, 1979, militant Iranian students stormed the American embassy in Teheran and seized the Americans there as hostages. The Iranians demanded the return of the Shah (who died in 1980) and the return of his wealth. After a long, frustrating period of waiting and negotiations, the hostages were finally freed on January 20, 1981, the same day that Ronald Reagan was inaugurated as President.

THE 1980 ELECTION

The American nation's attention focused almost completely on its declining economy by the late 1970's. Stagflation seemed incurable. Many Americans blamed their declining standard of living on elected officials. In 1976 the American voters turned Republican Gerald Ford out of office in favor of Democrat Jimmy Carter. Four years later Carter lost overwhelmingly to Ronald Reagan, a conservative Republican. Reagan's campaign had promised to "get the government off the backs of the people." Reagan believed that tax reductions, reduced government spending, and freeing business from government regulations would improve the American economy.

◠ JAPAN: SCANDALS AND ECONOMIC GROWTH

In 1976 an American Senate investigating committee heard officials of the American-owned Lockheed Aircraft Corporation admit that they had paid over $7 million in bribes to Japanese officials to win contracts there. Among those indicted in the investigation in Japan was the former Prime Minister, Kauei Tanaka. The scandal cost the ruling Liberal Democratic Party the next election.

Japan's industry declined in the mid-1970's as a result of OPEC's oil price increases. By 1979 Japan had recovered, and not even the doubling of OPEC oil prices in that year lowered Japan's huge sales overseas. Electronic equipment and automobiles were among Japan's leading exports. Japan's large foreign-trade surplus was the envy of its western industrial competitors.

◠ INDIA: RECESSION AND REPRESSION

Although most Indians did not own cars, imported oil fueled India's industrial plants, provided much of its electricity, and produced the petroleum-based fertilizers needed for increased agricultural production. By 1975 the slight prosperity India had enjoyed in the early 1970s had vanished. Oil imports used up India's limited foreign exchange. Food production and the industrial output fell. By 1980 India's annual inflation rate was reported at 27 percent.

Protest against Indira Gandhi's government began to be widespread. Many Indians blamed their reduced standard of living on corrupt government officials. In 1975 a defeated opponent brought suit against Mrs. Gandhi, charging her with election fraud. The Prime Minister herself became the focus of public condemnation. A high court found her guilty of a technical illegality and ordered her to resign. Instead the Prime Minister declared a state of emergency in India. She ordered the arrest of her political opponents and suspended civil rights.

Corruption, the black market, city slums, and rapid population growth had been serious problems in India before and after its independence. Mrs. Gandhi and her younger son, Sanjay, took a series of drastic steps aimed at these chronic problems. Corrupt officials and black-market traders faced immediate imprisonment. Poor slum dwellers in many cities had their homes torn down and were moved to tracts of land outside the cities' centers. Family-planning programs were sometimes forced on the Indian people.

Two years after the emergency began, Mrs. Gandhi called for new elections. Her only opposition was the Janata Party (the People's Party), a hastily formed coalition of both the left and the right. To the surprise of most Indians, Janata won the elections. Neither Mrs. Gandhi nor her son Sanjay won a seat in the government. A new party controlled India's central government for the first time in thirty years. Janata's Prime Minister, Morarji Desai, declared that the "emergency" was over.

Middle-class Indians rejoiced that voters had chosen democracy over authoritarianism, but two years later, in 1979, new elections returned Mrs. Gandhi to power. India's economic conditions had worsened. The Janata coalition had been made up of too many factions to act decisively. Many Indians had approved of Mrs. Gandhi's stern measures against corruption and black marketeering. Memories of authoritarian rule had faded in the face of rapidly rising food prices and black-market prices for fuel oil.

◌ THE SOVIET UNION IN THE 1970'S

Two postwar traditions—economic self-sufficiency and the fear of foreign enemies—protected the Soviet Union and its eastern European satellites from OPEC oil increases and their impact on world prices. Since World War II the Soviet Union had steadily developed its own oil and gas resources. The Soviet Union had also demanded that its satellites use oil from the Soviet Union, even though these supplies were more expensive than Middle Eastern fuels. After 1973 both the Soviet Union and its satellites reaped their rewards as the oil-price situation was reversed.

Food supply was a continuing problem for the Soviet Union. During the 1970's the Soviet Union produced record grain supplies, but an average Soviet citizen ate six times as much bread as an American counterpart. In both 1972 and 1975 the Soviet harvest was a failure. The Soviet Union was forced to buy huge supplies of grain, largely from American farmers. But in 1980 President Carter suspended American grain sales to the Soviet Union to protest the Soviet invasion of adjacent Afghanistan.

In 1980 the Soviets increased the amount of food that it required Poland to send to the Soviet Union. The resulting food shortage in Poland set off a massive general strike there. A growing wave of unrest led by a union movement, Solidarity, developed, leading to more strikes and greater demands for political rights. The Soviet Union countered with veiled and then later, bolder, more ominous threats of intervention in Poland.

☉ CHINA'S NEW POLICIES

China had been protected from OPEC price increases by its policy of isolation from international trade. China had its own oil supplies and was slowly developing them to meet internal needs. As a result China escaped a major economic crisis.

In 1976 the country was plunged into a major political power struggle following the death of both Mao Tse-tung and Chou En-lai. At issue was the future of China's Communist revolution. Mao, the son of wealthy peasants, wanted to ensure China's revolutionary ideals and secure for the peasants an equal place in postrevolutionary China. Chou, a person of urbane charm and elegance, was more concerned with China's place in the world. As hostilities between the Soviet Union and China mounted, Chou had argued that China needed a powerful ally to check Soviet aggression. It was Chou who had favored stronger ties with the United States and who arranged President Nixon's trip to China in 1972. Chou, and his protégé Teng Hsiao-ping, looked forward to the day when the People's Republic of China would become a major world power.

Chou's protégé, Teng Hsiao-ping had been purged during the Cultural Revolution and reinstated only in 1973. Teng believed that China needed rapid economic development, which could be reached only by adopting modified capitalist economic strategies.

The struggle for power began after Chou's death in January, 1976. Mao, old and ill, managed to install an obscure Deputy Prime Minister, Hua Kuo-feng as Acting Prime Minister. Meanwhile, the party newspapers, under control of Mao and his wife, published lengthy attacks on "capitalist roader" Teng. Teng was once more out of favor.

In September Mao died. His only political heir was his third wife, Chiang Ching. Her dedication to the principles of the Cultural Revolution and her hatred of "capitalist roaders" was more extreme than Mao's. Shortly after Mao's death, however, the political situation reversed itself. Chiang Ching and three associates (later called "the Gang of four") were arrested, charged

THE MODERN WORLD

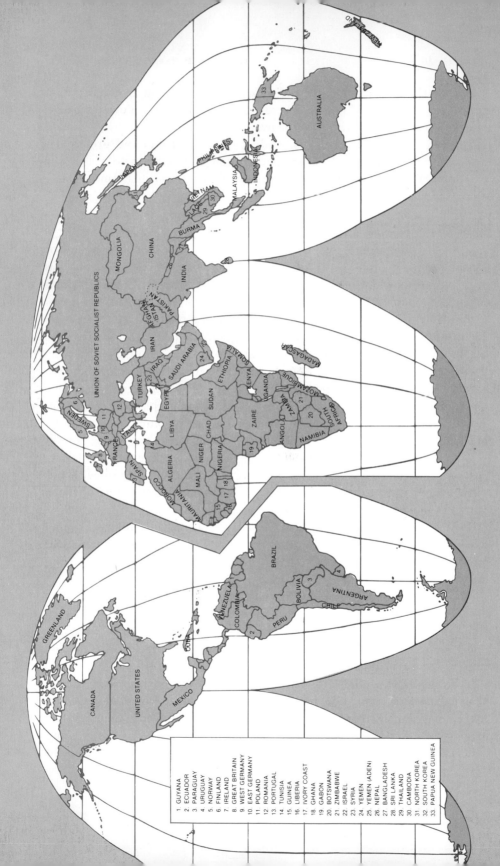

1 GUYANA
2 ECUADOR
3 PARAGUAY
4 URUGUAY
5 NORWAY
6 FINLAND
7 IRELAND
8 GREAT BRITAIN
9 WEST GERMANY
10 EAST GERMANY
11 POLAND
12 ROMANIA
13 PORTUGAL
14 TUNISIA
15 GUINEA
16 LIBERIA
17 IVORY COAST
18 GHANA
19 GABON
20 BOTSWANA
21 ZIMBABWE
22 ISRAEL
23 SYRIA
24 YEMEN
25 YEMEN (ADEN)
26 NEPAL
27 BANGLADESH
28 SRI LANKA
29 THAILAND
30 CAMBODIA
31 NORTH KOREA
32 SOUTH KOREA
33 PAPUA NEW GUINEA

with plotting a coup and altering Mao's will. While western diplomats reported rumors of armed fighting in China's provinces, Teng slowly worked his way back to power and became Deputy Prime Minister. The Gang of Four were held in prison and later put on trial.

In 1978 Teng announced a new 'open door" policy. China wanted trade with western Europe and the United States. By reorganizing rural farms, and using foreign investments to build industries and develop oil resources, China would be a modern nation by 1985. Teng's government declared that the Cultural Revolution had been a mistake. Trade between China and the United States began to grow. Teng himself visited the United States.

During 1979 China invaded North Vietnam in a move aimed also at Vietnam's ally, the Soviet Union. Soviet and Chinese troops skirmished along their common border. As the Chinese government assured the United States it would soon withdraw from Vietnam, wall posters appeared in Peking declaring China's interest in American democracy. Teng himself spoke well of American political freedoms.

Some months later the Chinese had withdrawn from Vietnam and were reassessing both their economic and political programs. Prime Minister Hua publicly announced that China's economic plans had been overly ambitious. "Democracy Wall," where the posters had been displayed, disappeared, and Teng warned publicly of the dangers of "bourgeois democracy." But if Teng and his associates intended to slow the pace of change in China, they remained committed to the concept of change. 'Pragmatism," a dedication to the practical, and rapid modernization were to be China's new priorities.

⟡ ⟡ ⟡

In November, 1979, Iranian students attacked the American embassy in Teheran and took more than 50 Americans hostage. Neither negotiations, threats, nor military maneuvers, including a rescue attempt by the United States, secured their release for a total of 444 days. Americans deplored their fallen international prestige, and some blamed the situation on President Jimmy Carter.

The Iranian actions illustrated a deeper shift in international relations and world power. In 1951 the international oil companies had closed world markets to Iranian oil when a new government had attempted to nationalize Iran's oil. Twenty-nine years later neither the oil companies nor the major industrial nations were in a position to control Iranian actions. It was clear that the new attitude of the oil exporters and their actions had changed the world's economy and power structure.

Persons, Places, and Terms

Shah of Iran (Muhammed Riza Pahlevi)	Gerald Ford	Dubai
	Jimmy Carter	Oman
	Kauei Tanaka	Teheran
Edward Heath	Morarji Desai	OPEC
James Callaghan	Teng Hsiao-ping	Yom Kippur
Margaret Thatcher	Hua Kuo-feng	Central Intelligence Agency
Georges Marchais	Chaing Ching	
François Mitterand		"double digit"
Valéry Giscard D'Estaing	Iraq	stagflation
	Kuwait	embargo
Helmut Schmidt	Bahrein	Social Democrats
Ayatollah Khomeini	Qatar	Lockheed
Ronald Reagan	Abu Dhabi	Janata Party

To Master the Text

1. Explain how the United States' relations with Iran, particularly before the fall of the Shah, were a reflection of the past history of the Middle East and American policy there.

To Interpret the Facts

1. Explain why oil price rises helped lead to a recession and stagflation.
2. Explain why and how the world's centers of political and economic power were affected by the growing power of OPEC's members.

To Put This Chapter into a Larger Setting

1. What led to the Arab oil embargo of 1973? What were the effects in western Europe and in the United States? What had happened after World War II to increase the world-wide demand for oil?
2. What was the United States' policy toward domestic oil producers?
3. Why did the international oil companies act as an informal cartel?
4. When did OPEC really become effective? What measures did it take?
5. Describe the main events in Britain's economic struggles after 1973. The main events in the French and German economies.
6. What were some major events in the United States after 1973?
7. Why were India and the other developing nations so significantly affected by the huge increases in oil prices?
8. Why were the Soviet bloc nations and China almost unaffected by the rise in oil prices?
9. Outline the major events that followed the Cultural Revolution in China.

 **37**

The Twentieth-Century Age of Science

While the world's attention was focused on world wars, depression, and the collapse of empires, other developments were taking place that were no less spectacular in their implications for the future of humanity. There were notable findings in science, brilliant achievements in art and literature, and new steps in the field of religion.

Equally important were the ways twentieth-century scientific and technological discoveries changed people's ways of living and working. Until the 1970's the twentieth century seemed a time of potentially limitless technological progress. New discoveries altered people's productive abilities as well as their daily environment. It was the "Age of Science." The industrial nations set the standard of modern life for the whole world. Developing nations hoped to transform their own traditional lifestyles enough to enable their own entry into this scientific age.

As early as the 1960's, some scientists had begun to caution that massive industrialization could drastically damage the world's natural environment. However, it was not until the 1970's, with the advent of OPEC and spiraling energy prices, that the full cost of an industrial life style could be assessed. By the 1980's many of the inventions that had made the future seem so bright earlier in the century now threatened to blight future prosperity if they remained unchanged.

☊ SCIENTIFIC DEVELOPMENTS

To ordinary people, invention and increased medical knowledge seemed the basis of change in the modern world. But behind the inventors and the medical researchers were the scientists. Although the activities of modern scientists and their findings could only be fully understood by those already highly trained in the field, certain types of scientific research nevertheless captured the public imagination as never before. Scientific discoveries were often reported on the front pages of newspapers. Scientific research was changing, with researchers in each field more dependent than ever on findings made in every other field.

CHEMISTRY

Advances in the field of chemical research were especially concerned with the chemistry of the molecule. Molecular chemistry made it possible to produce new substances with especially desired characteristics: synthetic rubber, plastics, missile and motor fuels, and new drugs are some examples.

BIOLOGY

Biologists used information gained from chemists in their detailed studies of the processes inside the cell. Using an electron microscope and radioactive substances, they gained increased knowledge of processes in living plant cells and were able to produce new types of plants to help feed the growing world population. Studies of DNA, the molecule that controls the activities in every human cell, opened up new fields of research in heredity and genetic engineering.

ASTRONOMY

Until the 1950's all astronomical experiments and measurements had to be performed on the earth, and the chief instrument was the optical telescope. Now radio astronomy, earth satellites, and both manned and unmanned space voyages have revolutionized exploration of the universe.

PHYSICS

The advances in physics moved science beyond the comprehension of the informed nonprofessional. Discoveries in physics made possible the science of electronics and gave us atomic power and nuclear weapons. The basic theory behind the use of the electron microscope, the study of molecules, the study of the interior of the sun, and nuclear power is quantum mechanics. Developed out of the work of Planck, Einstein, Bohr, and others (see page 225), quantum theory consists of the following: (1) a set of postulates in mathematical form, (2) a set of rules for performing mathematical operations on these postulates, and (3) a set of prescriptions telling how to interpret the final mathematical expressions in terms of things that can be measured in the laboratory. Unlike classical physics (see pages 132–134), no accurate model of the theory can be constructed in terms of familiar things like particles or waves. An understanding of the theory demands a knowledge of the advanced mathematics used in the theory.

THE SOCIAL SCIENCES

Along with the advances in the biological and physical sciences came an effort to study society itself and human relationships. Scholars in the social sciences—economics, political science, geography, anthropology, sociology, and psychology—attempted to make their studies more exact in the hope of arriving at the kind of reliable generalizations achieved by other sciences. Economists were the most committed to the use of scientific methods. Statistics helped them reach conclusions (although often contradictory) on matters such as the causes of inflation.

⍵ ART AND LITERATURE

Art and literature reflected not only the scientific atmosphere of the time but also the uncertainties in the minds of people who had lived through the great wars and the great depression.

PAINTING AND SCULPTURE

In painting there was much experimentation with new forms and new ways of looking at the world. "Cubism," for example, was developed by the Spanish painter Pablo Picasso (1881–1973) and by French artist Georges Braque (1881–1963). They looked at nature in terms of cubes, cylinders, and other geometrical forms. They experimented with a way of representing an object "abstractly," not as an observer might see it at a glance but as they knew it to be from their many previous associations with it. One of Picasso's paintings, called simply *Still Life*, is a picture of a violin. Each part of the instrument is seen from its most characteristic angle. The parts are not put together as in a real violin but are placed here and there on the canvas, as they might be in the artist's mind in thinking of the instrument.

"Duke Ladder Not Alone," a painting by Paul Klee (1879-1940). Klee, a Swiss, combined patterns and unrecognizable forms with familiar objects in a highly original manner. Although his style was like no other, in his abandoning of realistic subject matter he was in a mainstream of twentieth-century art.

Picasso painted in many styles, but his cubist style had a wide influence on other abstract painters who tried to emphasize shapes and angles rather than color or subject matter.

Other experimental painters like the Russian Vasili Kandinski (1866–1944), arguing that painting has no more need of subject matter than music, made paintings simply out of color, line, and geometric forms, as did Spanish artist Joan Miró. "Surrealist" painters like French artist Henri Rousseau, on the other hand, gave their pictures the sharp realism of photographs, but they used the subject matter of dreams to express their ideas. Surrealists were trying to explore the subconscious mind revealed in the studies of psychologists like Sigmund Freud. (See page 226). There was much traditional painting, too, but no painter was altogether free of the influences that created these more experimental styles.

Many sculptors shared the painters' interest in distortions and abstractions. Some avoided subject matter and merely put together pieces of material—stone, metal, plastics—to express various moods. Still others imitated the work of wood carvers of Africa and the Pacific islands.

ARCHITECTURE

In architecture the most important development was the "modern" or "functional" style, which had become important before 1914. (see page 228.) Three European architects are important in connection with this style: Walter Gropius (1883–1969) and Ludwig Mies van der Rohe (1886–1969), both Germans, and Le Corbusier (1887–1965), a Swiss. All were trained in the same architectural center in Germany. Gropius and Mies later came to the United States. All three erected buildings designed along functional lines, with little ornamentation. The metal and cement structural parts of the building were exposed and used to emphasize the lines and planes of the design. All used glass extensively and, especially in the lower floors of their buildings, arranged unobstructed, wide openings. Even skyscrapers

The Hyatt Regency Hotel in downtown Los Angeles typifies the growing use of rounded structures in modern architecture, as well as the slightly older trend to vast glass-covered surfaces.

so built seemed airy and open to people who entered them. The United Nations building in New York was partly designed by Le Corbusier. Frank Lloyd Wright (1869–1959) was the most famous American practitioner of this functional modern architecture. Like his European contemporaries, he used a cantilever construction (a steel beam anchored at one end and extending out into space) to give a more open effect to ground floors, with upper floors overhanging. He sought to make his houses seem a part of their landscapes, using local materials and fitting the buildings to the contours of the land. The destruction of European cities during the wars and urban renewal in America gave special opportunity to the practitioners of this functional architecture.

MUSIC

Music also had its experimenters, who tried new scales, the use of dissonances to create impressionistic effects, and new forms in place of the more set sonata form so long employed by composers of symphonies. American jazz was popular the world over, and it influenced the writing of serious music, introducing new rhythms and new uses of instruments. Ballet music introduced startling new effects and a greater intensity of emotion than existed in the older, more restrictive forms. Russian composer Igor Stravinsky (1882–1971) was a notable composer of ballet music. Serious concerts still based most of their programs on older works, but newer ones were also performed by the world's great orchestras. The improvement of broadcasting and of recording had an effect on music similar to that of the invention of printing on the wider dissemination of literature. Such popular singing groups as the "Beatles" in the 1960's became known all over the world.

LITERATURE

Although challenged by movies and television, the novel remained popular and was probably the most influential kind of writing. Novels ranged from the realistic to the psychological to attempts to reproduce a "stream of consciousness" (the disconnected flow of thought constantly running through the human mind). The Irish writer James Joyce (1882–1941), for example, in his novel *Ulysses* described the events of a single day in Dublin as seen through the stream of consciousness of one individual.

Poetry was as experimental as music and painting, and as difficult for the untrained reader to understand. Much symbolism was used, sometimes so closely related to the reading and experience of the poet that it had to be interpreted individually by each reader. Perhaps the most influential poet writing in English was T. S. Eliot (1888–1965), American-born but thoroughly English from long residence. He wrote about the problems of modern people in a society with no generally accepted religious or cultural focus to give them direction.

◌ DEVELOPMENTS IN RELIGION

The twentieth century did not encourage organized religion. Secular interests distracted people from things religious, and a habit of indifference to religion became generally acceptable, especially in cities. The wartime murder of millions of Jews greatly reduced the number of persons practicing Judaism. Any practice of religion was difficult in fascist and Communist countries. Yet, in 1979 there were estimated to be in the world 580,000,000 Catholics, 338,000,000 Protestants, 79,000,000 Orthodox, 14,000,000 Jews, 587,000,000 Muslims, 475,000,000 Hindus, and perhaps 254,000,000 Buddhists.

In the Catholic world the most important mid-century event was the Second Vatican Council called in 1962 by Pope John XXIII (pope, 1958–1963). Its purpose was to promote Christian reunion and to study the relationship of the church to the modern world. The council directed that the liturgy be simplified and that in each country the language of the region be used in the mass. For Protestants the ecumenical movement tended to lessen the emphasis on differences in doctrine among the sects and to encourage greater understanding and co-operation. In general, Protestant churches centered less attention on doctrine and, especially in cities, more on organized efforts to put Christianity into practice through social service activities.

◌ LIFE AND WORK IN THE
TWENTIETH CENTURY

By the middle of the twentieth century, scientific and technological changes had widely altered the lives of hundreds of millions of the world's peoples. At first these changes seemed unquestionably for the better. Only by the 1980's were people beginning to see the full implications of the new life styles they had embraced.

RAPID TRANSPORTATION AND COMMUNICATION

In the field of transportation and travel the most important fact of the half century after the First World War was the greatly expanded use of the internal combustion engine to power autos, trucks, buses, tractors, and airplanes. Cities switched from electric trolleys to buses. Trucks took short hauls away from the steam railroads. Tractors became common on European farms and replaced horses in the United States. By the 1930's air travel was common. In 1958 jet service was inaugurated between the United States and Europe.

In the field of communications the most startling developments were the appearance first of radio networks and then, in the 1940's, of television. People began to speak of the "mass media," for a radio or television program could reach all the people in a country simultaneously. In 1962 the first communications satellite instantly relayed sights and sounds to television viewers on the other side of the Atlantic.

Inventions in the field of communications touched the lives of ordinary people in myriad ways. Governments in developing countries encouraged villages to build radio stations. Radio listeners in remote areas learned about the comforts enjoyed by people in affluent countries or in the cities of their own land. As a result, they often became dissatisfied with their lives. New modes of travel enabled national leaders to journey anywhere. Television cameras reported their words and facial expressions to the people of the host country, and often to the voters back home. It became difficult for anyone to get elected to high office who did not appear to advantage on television. By the 1980's some American educators blamed the visual media for a decline in reading skills among their students.

DEVELOPMENTS IN THE FIELD OF INDUSTRY

New products of industry and new methods of manufacturing brought changes in ordinary living. Clothing became cheaper, more durable, and easier to care for with the use of synthetic fibers like nylon and polyester. Housekeeping chores were lightened by labor-saving appliances, frozen foods, and easy-to-care-for building and decorating materials. Plastics were developed for innumerable uses where cheap or suitable materials were previously unavailable. New metals and alloys of old metals, such as aluminum and stainless steel, came into use.

Factories were revolutionized to employ human labor more effectively. On the assembly line, a system first developed in the United States, each worker performed just one operation as the product passed by on a moving belt. The efficiency of the system soon proved to be so great that products (Model-T Fords in the United States beginning in 1908, for a famous example) manufactured in this way could be sold at greatly reduced prices. Machines were invented to perform various kinds of work previously requiring human labor. In the 1920's many workers lost their jobs as a result, and "technological unemployment" became a major complaint of labor.

Later in the twentieth century the invention and development of computers made possible highly sophisticated automated factories. Computers existed by the 1950's. Originally large and cumbersome machines, these "electronic brains" directed various stages of manufacturing, sorted data, and filed. The development of the "computer chip"—a miniaturization of the computer's basic components—revolutionized computer technology in the 1970's. These tiny chips greatly reduced both the size and cost of computers, while increasing their capacity to "think" (store information). Computers now could run whole factories. By the 1980's it was clear that the labor-saving potential of computers was enormous. The cost in available jobs for a highly computerized society was not fully known.

THE GROWTH OF CITIES

Each of these developments contributed something to what was perhaps the most characteristic factor of twentieth-century life: the muliplication and expansion of cities the world over. In 1900 some 5.5 percent of the world population lived in cities; in 1950, 13 percent; and in 1980, 39 percent. The population explosion brought people to the cities, the growing factories employed them, and improved transportation took them to work and brought food from the countryside to nourish them. Farm machinery, new fertilizers, weed killers, and pesticides enabled fewer and fewer farmers to feed an increasing number of city dwellers.

City living also created some of the greatest problems of the twentieth century: noise, polluted air, crowding, crime, and slums. As early as 1910 in some parts of America, and after World War II in both Europe and the United States, new suburbs appeared. Connected to the cities by rail and highway, these "bedroom" communities allowed city workers to commute to jobs in the city while escaping in the evenings to a less crowded environment. In the 1950's a house in the suburbs was the American dream. As a result many cities lost their wealthier citizens, adding to the urban problems of the post-World War II years.

THE POPULATION EXPLOSION

Another major feature of the twentieth century was a rapidly increasing population growth. In 1980 there were 4.4 billion people in the world, and world population was growing at the rate of 1.7 percent. Medical research that enabled people to survive infancy and childhood and to live longer was largely responsible for this development. By the year 1963 the world death rate was exactly one half of what it had been in the late eighteenth century. Population increases were greatest in the less developed countries, countries least able to support larger numbers of people.

The new weapons in the war against disease were the "miracle" sulfa drugs and other antibiotics and new vaccines. World-wide health campaigns attempted to eradicate many diseases and successfully eliminated smallpox, the first disease to be deliberately wiped off the face of the earth. Better nutrition became possible when vitamins were discovered and their value became known. X-rays and electronic scanning machines aided in the diagnosis of many illnesses. Surgery advanced to the point where bypass operations could be performed on impaired hearts.

REDISTRIBUTION OF WORLD WEALTH

The world in 1973, economically speaking, was divided in two: a few rich industrial countries and many more poor developing nations. The industrial nations of Europe, Japan, and the United States had more than two thirds of the world's wealth, trade, and production. The poorer countries of the world, with more than half the total world population, had less than one third of the world's riches. According to some estimates, as many as two thirds of the world's peoples lived on inadequate rations. Comparing income levels in the mid-1970's, the 24 richest countries produced a gross national product (GNP) averaging $4,550 for each citizen, whereas in the 25 poorest countries, GNP averaged only $116 per citizen.

The gap between rich and poor countries was wide in the early 1970's. In the years following the 1973 oil crisis, a major redistribution of wealth occurred, cutting into the prosperity of industrial nations and leaving some previously poor countries such as Trinidad, an oil producer, much wealthier. However, the oil crisis worsened the economic condition of many already poor countries that needed to import oil. On the other hand, the oil crisis contained a hidden and unforeseen benefit: it made people in industrial nations suddenly conscious of the value of the world's natural resources and of their distribution, and, most importantly, their conservation.

THE ECOLOGY OF ENERGY

Abuse of the world's natural resources had for many years worried those who studied ecology. Ecology is the study of the total relationship between people and their physical environment. During the 1960's ecologists began to examine different aspects of industrial life and warned that any change in a given feature of the earth's environment caused other changes in the environment. As industrial and governmental enterprises stripped coal out of hillsides and laid them bare, and as they dammed rivers, dug tunnels, and built new highways through the countryside, ecologists began to warn that all these activities would have high ecological costs. For example, mercury in industrial waste products dumped into a river would ultimately contaminate the river's fish and affect people who might later eat the fish. Thus, by the late 1960's Americans discovered that after years of industrial pollution, many of their lakes and rivers could no longer support marine life. Atomic testing in the western United States has been found to cause increased cases of cancer among the people present at the time—but only many years after the tests ended.

During the 1970's it became clear that ecological principles applied to the whole of industrial society. Modern industry had prospered on a consumer-oriented economy, emphasizing, especially in America, newness and "throwaway" products at the expense of conservation. This life style used the world resources extravagantly. Thus, the few richest industrial nations consumed well over half the world's natural resources. Such a life style had thrived in a economy where natural resources were cheap. Only in the years following the 1973 energy crisis did people in the industrial nations begin to realize the ecological problems that might affect their way of life.

In the late 1970's many earlier and wasteful energy decisions returned to plague the industrial countries of the world. Trolleys and trains were less convenient than buses and cars, but they had run on less energy. Single-family suburban living was pleasanter than crowded urban life, but each suburban family needed at least one and often two cars, and their individual houses, separated from other houses, were expensive to heat in the winter and cool in the summer. Labor-saving appliances saved labor, but again used costly energy. And while polyester clothing and plastics were convenient and easy to clean, both were petroleum-based products.

❧ ❧ ❧

By the 1980's most of the ecological problems of industrial energy use were recognized. Citizens of industrial countries were more aware than ever before of their use of energy and of its implications for their life styles. Industry had begun to consider and produce a wide range of"energy efficient" machines, from compact cars to microwave ovens. Conservation did not become instantly popular; it caused inconveniences and work. But the increasing cost of energy forced many more peoples to rethink their priorities in life, to practice conservation, and to respect the world's ecology.

Persons, Places, and Terms

Pablo Picasso	Igor Stravinsky	antibiotics
Georges Braque	James Joyce	cubism
Vasili Kandinski	T.S. Eliot	abstract painting
Joan Miró	John XXIII	cantilever
Henri Rousseau		construction
Walter Gropius	assembly line	ecumenical movement
Ludwig Mies van	technological	World Council
der Rohe	unemployment	of Churches
Frank Lloyd Wright	computer chip	ecology

To Master the Text

1. How have recent discoveries in chemistry, biology, and physics benefited the world's peoples? How have findings in each field influenced work in other sciences?
2. What new schools of painting have developed in the twentieth century? How is each of these related to other aspects of twentieth-century life and thought? What sources of ideas have twentieth-century sculptors used?
3. What are the special characteristics of modern architecture?
4. What are some characteristics of the music being composed at the present time? Of modern literature? On what grounds can it be argued that present-day poetry, music, and painting are experimental?
5. What factors in the modern world discourage people from practicing religion? What has the ecumenical movement generally meant?
6. What inventions, now basic to our whole way of life, came into use only after the First World War? Which of these seems to you most revolutionary? Why? Which are the most recent? Which give evidence of

being most likely to change the lives of people in the future? What is technological unemployment?

7. Why is world population increasing so rapidly? In what way is the population growth frightening?

To Interpret the Facts

1. Make a list of inventions that have come into use since 1919, classifying them according to purpose by putting each under one of these headings: (a) for transportation, (b) for communication, (c) for convenience in living, (d) for comfort in living, (e) for more rapid production of goods. Consider the advantages and also the disadvantages of the inventions in each field. To what extent can it be argued that the Industrial Revolution has benefited the human race? Can it also be argued that it has had serious disadvantages?

2. Can you find characteristics that are present in many—or even all—of the arts mentioned in this chapter? Do these characteristics seem especially suited to the present-day world? Why?

3. In how many different ways have the arts, science, and religion influenced each other in recent times?

To Put This Chapter into a Larger Setting

1. To gain some understanding of the relations between the rapid development of science and industry and the expanding use of natural resources, try to answer the following questions:
   (a) How much scientific knowledge do government officials and members of Congress need if they are to make wise decisions?
   (b) Do scientists have any responsibilities for adverse effects of their discoveries?
   (c) What are some major ecological problems that may arise from increased use of coal to replace oil?

2. Prepare a report on one of the modern literary or artistic developments or on a specific writer, painter, sculptor, architect, or composer. Supplement your report with excerpts from written works, reproductions of paintings, photographs of statues or buildings, or recordings of music.

3. Compare the present scientific age to an earlier period when great scientific advances were being made, such as ancient Greece, the Renaissance, or the seventeenth, eighteenth, or nineteenth centuries.

4. To what extent are the special advantages of the modern world more available to all classes of people than was the case under the Old Regime in eighteenth-century France?

Epilogue

Revolutionary change in the last two centuries, seen in a backward glance from the 1980's, appears incredibly rapid and far-reaching. Technological developments alone are fantastic. In 1789 the fastest travel was by galloping horse. In the 1980's supersonic jets spanned the Atlantic in three hours. In those two centuries the industrialized world has passed through an age of iron and an age of steel into an age of computer technology; from water power to steam power to electrical power to nuclear power.

Equally startling are the changed opportunties for learning and knowing. The average person of the eighteenth century was illiterate. In the twentieth century the average person of the western world has skills and a store of knowledge acquired through years of schooling. Further, this education can be continued throughout life by reading, by radio and television, and by travelling. The degree of education each person achieves helps determine that person's chances for advancement in the industrial world.

The despotic monarchies of the eighteenth century have given way to popularly controlled governments or to dictatorships claiming to be democratic and to serve the needs of their people. All governments, whatever their type, take an interest in the welfare of the individual citizen, in his problems of education, sanitation, housing, and social security—matters that would have seemed altogether outside the province of the most despotic eighteenth century ruler.

In other ways, too, the strength and unity of the state have increased in two centuries, not only under the totalitarian governments but in the democracies as well. Wars and the growing military might of neighboring countries have deepened the national feeling of all peoples. Since to exist at all, governments require the loyalty of their peoples, they have used every means at their command to strengthen nationalism. Although the peoples of the world have been drawn together by the ease of travel and by world trade, they have also been driven apart by the strength of rival nationalisms.

The position of Europe in the world has also changed radically. In the late eighteenth century, the seafaring countries of Europe possessed overseas colonies, they controlled the seaborne trade of the world, they had armies without peer. The rapidity of industrialization in western Europe still further increased their military superiority. By 1900 they had divided all the not-yet-Europeanized parts of the world among themselves. Then came the two world wars in which the European nations fought and nearly destroyed each other. Their weakness after the wars left the United States and the Soviet Union the dominant powers of the earth. The overseas colonies, already in some ways strengthened by their European contacts, seized the opportunity to secure their independence.

Revolutionary changes have by no means come to an end. The last years of the twentieth century do not as yet give promise of furnishing a turning point in history. The future cannot, of course, be foreseen, but it can be said that the pace of change is likely to be even greater in the years ahead than it has ever been before.

Some Questions to Answer

1. The wars that have dominated the years since 1914 have witnessed revolutionary changes in weapons and tactics. Discuss the use in the First and Second World Wars and in other warfare since 1914 of (a) the airplane, (b) radar, (c) the truck, (d) the tank, (e) guided missiles, (f) the submarine, (g) amphibious tactics, and (h) the atomic bomb. Make your discussion illustrate the history of warfare.

2. The great wars and the many smaller ones since 1914, together with the rise of powerful and ruthless governments, have resulted in untold misery for millions of people. To gain some insight into the sufferings of masses of people, list the many instances mentioned in this book of (a) large-scale death of civilians as a result of military operations, (b) large-scale permanent removal of people from their homes, and (c) intentional killing of masses of people without a military purpose.

3. One of the problems arising from the great wars has been the difficulty of making peace at the end of each of them. What problems arising from the treaties of 1919 helped bring about the Second World War? How do you explain the fact that, after Germany was defeated in two world wars fought in part to limit German power and aggressiveness, West Germany is today a valued member of NATO?

4. The great wars have been in part responsible for greater than normal ups and downs of economic life. To make this fact clear to yourself, study the case of Great Britain. For each of the following dates, show

whether British economic life was at a high or low level: early 1914, late 1918, 1921, 1928, 1930, 1938, 1945, 1955, and 1964. Do the same thing for the Soviet Union and for Germany.

5. In earlier centuries great wars resulted in many gains of territory, often overseas, by the victor. What European territories are today in the hands of countries that did not control them in 1914? What colonial territories have been gained by any country?

6. Wars are often responsible for the loss of the liberties of the people and for the centralizing of the powers of government. Take in turn each of the major countries of the present world, and for each discover if there has been any permanent loss of liberties by the people or any remarkable strengthening of the powers of government.

7. Has the world become more or less of a unit in the last half-century? To answer this question, list all the ways you can think of in which the peoples of the earth have been kept apart from each other or caused to distrust each other. Then list all the ways in which the peoples of the world have become more interdependent.

8. Wars tend to break down barriers between classes. They also tend to make generals into political leaders. To what extent have the wars of the twentieth century had either of these results?

9. In what ways have the scientific, artistic, and religious aspects of the life of the world's peoples been related to the great wars?

10. In the last half century which countries have ceased to be great world powers? Which countries have risen to be world powers?

11. Reread the Prologue (pages 1-4) of this book. Does it seem to you to describe accurately the past two centuries? Should it be altered in any way?

Using Documents as Evidence

Plans for the United Nations were made during World War II, and the Charter of the United Nations took effect in October, 1945. The Preamble and part of Chapter I of the Charter are printed here.

═══════PREAMBLE TO CHARTER OF THE UNITED NATIONS═══════

We the Peoples of the United Nations, Determined

TO SAVE succeeding generations from the scourge of war, which twice in our lifetime has brought untold sorrow to mankind, and

TO REAFFIRM faith in fundamental human rights, in the dignity and worth of the human person, in the equal rights of men and women and of nations large and small, and

TO ESTABLISH conditions under which justice and respect for the obligations arising from treaties and other sources of international law can be maintained, and
TO PROMOTE social progress and better standards of life in larger freedom,
And for these ends
TO PRACTICE tolerance and live together in peace with one another as good neighbors, and
TO UNITE our strength to maintain international peace and security, and
TO ENSURE . . . that armed force shall not be used, save in the common interest, and
TO EMPLOY international machinery for the promotion of the economic and social advancement of all peoples,
HAVE RESOLVED TO COMBINE OUR EFFORTS TO ACCOMPLISH THESE AIMS.
Accordingly, our respective Governments, through representatives assembled in the city of San Francisco . . . do hereby establish an international organization to be known as the United Nations.

========== Chapter 1 PURPOSES AND PRINCIPLES Article 2 ==========

The organization and its Members . . . shall act in accordance with the following Principles.

1. The Organization is based on the principle of the sovereign equality of all its Members.

2. All Members . . . shall fulfill in good faith the obligations assumed by them in accordance with the present Charter.

3. All Members shall settle their international disputes by peaceful means. . . .

4. All Members shall refrain . . . from the threat or use of force against the territorial integrity or political independence of any state. . . .

5. All Members shall give the United Nations every assistance in any action it takes in accordance with the present Charter. . . .

6. The Organization shall ensure that states which are not Members of the United Nations act in accordance with these Principles. . . .

7. Nothing contained in the present Charter shall authorize the United Nations to intervene in matters which are essentially within the domestic jurisdiction of any state or shall require the Members to submit such matters to settlement under the present Charter. . . .

Compare the Preamble and Article 2 of Chapter 1 of the Charter. Which part is really a statement of purposes or intentions, and which part really spells out the duties and responsibilities of member nations? Item 1 in Article 2 refers to the "sovereign equality of all its [the United Nations'] members." However, only certain members of the United Nations have a veto in the Security Council, and only certain nations are permanent members of the Security Council. What problems might arise from these provisions?

On December 18, 1979, the General Assembly of the United Nations adopted a convention on discrimination against women. This "convention," or proposed agreement, was the result of many years of work, and the ratification of the convention is expected to take many more years. The beginning of the Convention is given below.

THE CONVENTION ON THE ELIMINATION OF ALL FORMS OF DISCRIMINATION AGAINST WOMEN

The States Parties to the present Convention,

Noting that the Charter of the United Nations reaffirms faith in fundamental human rights, in the dignity and worth of the human person, and in the equal rights of men and women,

Noting that the Universal Declaration of Human Rights . . . proclaims that all human beings are born free and equal in dignity and rights and that everyone is entitled to all the rights and freedom set forth therein, without distinction of any kind including distinction based on sex,

Noting that States Parties to the International Covenant on Human Rights have the obligation to secure the equal rights of men and women to enjoy all economic, social, civil, and political rights . . .

Recalling that discrimination . . . is an obstacle to the participation of women, on equal terms with men, in the political, social, economic, and cultural life of their countries, hampers the growth of the prosperity of society and the family, and makes more difficult the full development of the potentialities of women in the service of their countries and of humanity,

Concerned that in situations of poverty, women have the least access to food, health, education, training, and opportunities for employment and other needs . . .

Convinced that the full and complete development of a country, the welfare of the world, and the cause of peace require the maximum participation of women on equal terms with men in all fields. . . .

Compare this document with the Preamble to the Charter of the United Nations and especially with the Charter's first few sentences. Do you agree or disagree that the Convention is basically an extension of the United Nations' original purposes? The Preamble spoke of "mankind" but also referred to "equal rights for men and women." What specific equal rights would women everywhere be granted in this Convention?

Glossary

AGRARIAN, having to do with farming; agricultural.

ARISTOCRACY, (1) the privileged class of nobles; the nobility; (2) government by the nobility.

ABSOLUTISM, government by a ruler, usually a hereditary monarch, whose power is not limited by any other person or group of persons.

BLOC, an informal group, either of persons or of countries, who act together in support of a common cause.

BOURGEOISIE, the middle class; (1) in the eighteenth century, those who lived in comfort or wealth but were not aristocrats or churchmen; (2) in the language of Karl Marx, the factory owners who reaped the profits without working.

BUREAUCRACY, the body of appointed officials who carry out the instructions of an autocrat or of an elected government.

CABINET, (1) in Great Britain and other countries, the leaders of the majority party in Parliament, who head the various government departments and introduce all important bills to Parliament; (2) in the United States, appointed officials who head the most important departments of government and meet with and advise the President; differs from the British cabinet in that its members are not members of Congress.

CAPITAL, (1) property that is used to produce wealth; (2) all businessmen taken together (as distinguished from their workmen).

CAPITALISM, an economic system based on privately owned property, the desire for profits, hired labor, and consumer demand.

CAPITALIST, a person, often a man of wealth, who has invested his money in business in order to secure profits.

CIVIL LIBERTIES OR CIVIL RIGHTS, freedom of speech and religion, the right to vote, and similar rights.

CIVIL MARRIAGE, marriage performed by a government official without the participation of a clergyman.

COMMUNISM, (1) originally, any social and economic system based on the ownership of property by the community as a whole rather than by private individuals; (2) today, usually refers to the beliefs and activities of the Soviet, Chinese, and related Communist parties; (3) as used by Communists, refers to the ideal society predicted by Karl Marx.

CONSERVATISM, an outlook that favors preserving well-tried ways until change is clearly necessary. In the early nineteenth century, conservatives wished to preserve aspects of the Old Regime.

CONSTITUTION, a written document (or, as in Great Britain, a body of traditions and ordinary laws) that sets forth the manner of choosing government officials and the nature of their powers.

DEMOCRACY, a system of government in which all adult citizens (or, at the very least, the great majority of adult males) have a voice, usually by voting periodically for members of lawmaking bodies and for other government officials.

DESPOTISM, government by one person whose power is not limited by anyone else; autocracy.

ECONOMY, the total of all activities by which people earn their livings, including farming, manufacturing, banking, transportation, and the like. The adjective *economic* refers to any aspect of the economy.

ESTATES, the social classes represented in medieval parliaments, usually including the clergy (first estate), nobility (second estate), and well-to-do commoners (third estate).

ETHNIC, having to do with differences among groups of people in such matters as language, customs, a common history, or the like.

FASCISM, (1) Originally, the one-party system of government established in Italy in 1922, characterized by suppression of all other parties, by violent nationalism, and by strict government control of the lives of the people and of the economy; (2) any similar system of government.

FRANCHISE, the vote. To *enfranchise* people is to give them the vote.

FREE TRADE, absence of tariffs.

GUERRILLA WARFARE, warfare carried on by small groups, usually volunteers, who make surprise attacks on the enemy.

IDEOLOGY, a body of thought about some usually controversial topic, as about communism or democracy.

IMPERIALISM, the policy of putting together and maintaining an empire. In the late nineteenth century, imperialism led to the great powers of Europe taking control of most of the rest of the world.

INSTITUTION, something that has been set up *(instituted)* as (1) an established custom or way of doing something (the *institution* of marriage) or (2) an organization for getting something done (a parliament for making laws).

LAISSEZ FAIRE, "let alone," the idea held by early nineteenth-century liberals that government should not in any way regulate business—should not, for example, levy tariffs to influence the course of trade, nor regulate hours or wages.

LEFT, an informal term referring to those persons and groups that desire rapid change.

LEGISLATURE, a group of persons who make laws; usually elected.

LIBERALISM, an outlook that favors change, but not extreme change. Nineteenth-century liberalism, popular among the middle class, favored freedom of the individual from government interference and advocated a certain amount of control of government by the people, particularly the wealthier people.

MERCANTILISM, an economic theory, popular in the eighteenth century, which held that a nation should achieve self-sufficiency—provide as many as possible of its needs itself, and acquire others from colonies—by strict government regulation of commerce.

MINISTRY, the high officials of a government.

MONARCH, a lifelong hereditary ruler, as a king, queen, or emperor.

NATIONALISM, intense pride in one's own country and jealousy or distrust of other countries.

NATIONALIZATION, the taking over by a government of property owned by individuals or companies.

PARLIAMENT, a lawmaking body; a legislature.

PEASANTRY, the European agricultural workers, considered as a group or social class.

POLITICS, the activities of government. The adjective *political* refers to any aspect of government.

POWERS (or GREAT POWERS), those countries, always few in number, that are strong enough to control international affairs.

PROLETARIAT, industrial workers considered as a social class; a favorite Marxist term.

RADICALISM, an outlook that favors rapid and extreme change.

REACTIONARY, so conservative as to stand in the way of all progress.

REPUBLIC, a government headed by an elected official rather than by a monarch.

REVISIONISM, socialism that accepts many of the ideas of Karl Marx but rejects Marx's belief in the necessity of violent revolution.

RESPONSIBLE MINISTRY, a government in which the ministry or cabinet stays in office only so long as it pleases the legislature.

REVOLUTION, (1) any thorough change; especially (2) the overthrow of an established government.

RIGHT, an informal term referring to conservatives.

SECULAR, having to do with worldly as opposed to religious matters.

SOCIALISM, the theory that land, factories, and all other capital should belong to society as a whole and not to individuals.

SPHERE OF INFLUENCE, an area not controlled as a colony but open to economic development by a single imperialist nation.

SUFFRAGE, the right to vote.

TOTALITARIANISM, a system of government in which the state claims unlimited control over the lives and work of its citizens.

Index

Figures in *italics* are references to maps, charts, or pictures.

Key to Pronunciation (based on pronunciation key in *Webster's New World Dictionary of the American Language, College Edition,* © 1959 by The World Publishing Company): **a** = f*a*t; **ā** = *a*pe; **â** = b*a*re; **ä** = c*a*r; **e** = t*e*n; **ē** = *e*ven; **ê** = h*e*re; **ẽ** = *o*ver; **i** = *i*s; **ī** = b*i*te; **o** = l*o*t; **ō** = g*o*; **ô** = h*o*rn; **ōō** = t*oo*l; **oo** = l*oo*k; **oi** = *oi*l; **ou** = *ou*t; **u** = *u*p; **ū** = *u*se; **ŭ** = f*u*r; **g** = *g*et; **j** = *j*oy; **y** = *y*et; **ch** = *ch*in; **sh** = *sh*e; **th** = *th*in; **t̷h** = *th*en; **zh** = lei*s*ure; **ŋ** = ri*ng*; **ə** = *a*go, c*o*mply; **'** = able (ā'b'l); **a** = French b*a*l (intermediate between [a] and [ä]); **ë** = French c*oeu*r (round the lips for [ô] and say [e]); **ö** = French f*eu*, German K*ö*nig (round the lips for [ō] and say [ä]); **n** = French mo*n* (vowel just before *is* pronounced through the nose); **ô** = French c*o*q, German do*ch* (between [ō] and [ô]); **ü** = French d*u*c, German gr*ü*n (round the lips for [ōō] and say [ē]; **kh** = *German* do*ch*, Scottish lo*ch* (a guttural sound produced by arranging the speech organs as for [k] and allowing the breath to escape in a continuous stream, as in [h]).

Adenauer (ä'də-nou'ĕr), Konrad, 496, 515
Afghanistan, 279, 310, 319, *344*, 534
Africa, early European colonies, 323– 324, *331*; exploration, 324–325; independence movements, 476–477, 486–489; geography, 322–323; nineteenth-century imperialism, 310–316, 326–333, *331*; *see also* North Africa
Agadir Crisis (ä'gə-dir'), 361, 362
Agriculture, eighteenth century, 12–13; nineteenth century, 121–122; in Russia, 261–262, 392; in United States, 415
Alaska, 91, 304, *307*
Albania, 266, 362–363, *363*, 438, *439*, 510
Alexander I (Russia), 60, 61, 64, 65, 72, 73, 76, 77, 98, 204, *205*
Alexander II (Russia), 165, 206–209, 257, 271
Alexander III (Russia), 209, 258, 260
Algeciras Conference (al'ji-sir'əs), 278, 279, 315, 361
Algeria, 527; and France, 99, 161, 304, 310, 315, 329, *331*, 408, 484, 493; independence, *481*, 484–485; Second World War, 451, *453*
Alliance for Progress, 502
Alsace-Lorraine, 195, *196*, 271, 377, 378, *400*
Ampère (än'pâr'), André, 133
Angola, *85*, 298, 323, 324, 326, *331*
Anti-Comintern Pact, 438
Anti-Semitism, 241; Hitler's, 433, 434, 435
Apartheid (ə-pärt'hīt), 489
Arab–Israeli War (1973), 524
Arab League, 484
Arab oil embargo (1973–1974), 524–525, 527–528
Architecture, Gothic revival, 130, 131; late nineteenth century, 228; twentieth century, 543–544, *543*
Argentina, 89, 418, *419*, 421
Assembly line, 546–547
Astronomy, 132–133, 540
Aswan dam, 314, *318*, 485–486
Atlantic Charter, 447, 463
Atomic bomb, 456, *456*, 461, 465, 469, 494, 497, 500, 508, 510, 512, 516, 549
Atomic theory, 133, 225
Australia, *14*, 86, 300, 340, 450, 455, *455*
Austria, Concert of Europe, 76–79; Congress of Vienna, 73–76, *74*; Crimean War, 163–165; French Revolution, 41, 42, 44, 50–51; and Germany, 144, 152, 436, 438, *439*; and Italy, 176–178; under Metternich, 71–72; and Napoleon, 60–64, *65*, 66; nationalities, 147, *147*; Old Regime, 11, *18*, 19, 20–21; Partitions of Poland, 41, *42–43*, 50; and Prussia, 183, 187–190; republic, 380, 406; Revolts of 1848, 146–151, *148*, 172; after Second World War, 464; *see also* Austria-Hungary

Austria-Hungary, *191*, and Balkan Wars, 362–363, *363*, Bosnian Crisis, 359–361, 364; collapse, 376, 380; established, 191; First World War, 364–365, 369, 371–373, *372*, 375; and Germany, 271–276; government of, 252–253; nationalities, 253–254; Triple Alliance, 274, *279*, 356–357; *see also* Austria, Hungary
Austrian Peace Treaty, 464
Bahrein (bä-rān'), 527
Balfour Declaration, 483
Balkan League, 362
Balkan Peninsula, Crisis of 1875–1878, 271–274, *275*; in nineteenth century, 265–267
Balkan Wars, 362–363, *363*
Bastille, storming of, 31–32
Bay of Pigs, 473
Beethoven (bā'tō-vən), Ludwig van, 130
Belgium, and Benelux, 496; and Congo, 306, 326–327, *331*, 488–489; Congress of Vienna, 75; First World War, 366, 370, *372*, 374, 377; French Revolution, 49, 51; Industrial Revolution, 115, 118–119, 121–123; Revolution of 1830, 101–102; Second World War, 442, 444, *453*; *see also* Netherlands, Austrian
Benelux, 496, 497
Beneš (ben'esh), Eduard, 467
Berlin, and Cold War, 469–470; Revolution of 1848, 146; after Second World War, 460, 462
Berlin Conference, 326–327
Berlin, Congress of, 273–274, *275*, 305, 312, 359
Berlin-to-Bagdad Railroad, 316–318, *318*, 355
Berlioz (ber'li-ōz'), Hector, 130
Bessarabia, *74*, 76, 400
Bill of Rights (England), 16
Biology, nineteenth century, 134–135, 226; twentieth century, 540
Bismarck, Otto von, 185–187, *186*, *195*, *250*; "Age of," 269–276; diplomacy, 271–276, 279; German colonies, 250, 317, 326, 329; German Empire, formation of, 183, 185, 187–190, 192–195; German Empire, chancellor of, 246–249
Black Hand, 362, 364
Blacks, in Latin America, 418; in United States, 502, 514
Blanc, Louis, 106, 140, 141
Blitzkrieg (blits'krēg'), 443, 444, 448
Bloody Sunday, 264
Boers, 330–333
Bohemia, 380; and Austria, 147, *147*, 149–150, 190, 253–254; Uprising of 1848, 149, 150; *see also* Czechoslovakia
Bohr, Niels, 225, 541
Bolívar (bô-lē'vär), Simón, 89–91, *91*, 417
Bolsheviks, 263, 385–389, *386*
Bonaparte, Joseph, 62

ILLUSTRATION SOURCES

THE ART INSTITUTE OF CHICAGO: 219 (Mr. & Mrs. Martin A. Ryerson Collection), 542 (Cyrus H. McCormick Fund). *BETTMANN ARCHIVE:* 45, 59, 91, 100, 101, 105, 148, 261, 294, 325. *BLACK STAR:* 514 (Peter Lake), 532 (Sippa Press). *BROWN BROTHERS:* 394. *COLLECTION VIOLLET:* 9. *CULVER SERVICE:* 123, 195, 207, 235, 250, 253, 301, 365. *FORD MOTOR COMPANY:* 415. *GAMMA:* 520 (Hugh Vassal). *INFORMATION SERVICE OF INDIA:* 479. *KEYSTONE PRESS AGENCY, INC.:* 512. *METROPOLITAN MUSEUM OF ART:* 10 (Dick Fund, 1935), 131 (Bequest of Mary Stillman Harkness, 1950). *NATIONAL ARCHIVES:* 454. *THE NEW YORK PUBLIC LIBRARY:* 118, 165, 175, 177, 205, 287, 303, 341, 343. *PHOTO RESEARCHERS, INC.:* 532 (Myron Wood). *PUN-PAC PHOTO:* 503. *RADIO TIMES, HULTON PICTURE LIBRARY:* 313. *RAPHO-GUILLUMETTE:* 488 (Marc & Evelyne Bernheim). *A. L. DE SAINTRAT:* 386, 387. *UNITED PRESS INTERNATIONAL:* 402, 424, 446, 456, 471. *U. S. SIGNAL CORPS:* 371. *WIDEWORLD:* 433, 495.

MAPS: Christie McFall